Readings in Canadian Real Estate

FIFTH EDITION

Edited by

GAVIN ARBUCKLE
Ottawa

HENRY BARTEL
York University

Captus University Publications

Readings in Canadian Real Estate, fifth edition

The publisher and the editors gratefully acknowledge the authors,
publishers and organizations for their permission to reproduce their
work in this book. Care has been taken to trace ownership of
copyright material contained in this book. The publisher will gladly
take any information that will enable the rectification of any
reference or credit in subsequent editions and apologizes for any
errors or omissions.

Library and Archives Canada Cataloguing in Publication

Readings in Canadian real estate / edited by Gavin Arbuckle, Henry
Bartel. — 5th ed.

Includes bibliographical references.
ISBN 978-1-55322-258-3

1. Real estate business — Canada. 2. Real property — Canada.
I. Arbuckle, Gavin, 1953– II. Bartel, Henry

HD316.R42 2012   333.330971   C2011-908354-X

Captus Press Inc.
Mail: Units 14 & 15, 1600 Steeles Avenue West
          Concord, Ontario
          Canada   L4K 4M2
Telephone: (416) 736–5537
Fax: (416) 736–5793
Email: info@captus.com
Internet: www.captus.com

Canada ▐◆▌ *We acknowledge the financial support of the
Government of Canada through the Canada
Book Fund for our publishing activities.*

0 9 8 7 6 5 4 3 2 1
Printed in Canada

Contents

6
Canadian Mortgages

7
Valuation and Appraisal

8
The Real Estate Profession

9
Ethics

Preface

This book is designed to be used as a supplementary textbook in introductory undergraduate business school courses in real estate and in urban economics. Such courses tend to attract students of different academic backgrounds and experiences. Accordingly, the articles have been chosen to provide both simple and brief introductions to topics in real estate for complete beginners, and some exposure to more advanced and specialized material.

The articles selected for inclusion in this fifth edition of the book update much of the material in the earlier editions. We have replaced many of the older articles on public policy and research in Canadian real estate markets with recent articles published in leading academic journals. Many of the articles relating to practical issues in Canadian real estate markets, property valuation, and real estate practice have been updated by their authors.

Most of the real estate textbooks suitable for use in an introductory course are published in the United States. In many areas, such as the mathematics of investment analysis or the common law of real property, this causes no difficulty. In others, however, such as the economics and history of housing policy and changes in property tax assessment, the Canadian situation is significantly different from that described in American texts. In addition, many American real estate books devote relatively little space to the role of direct government intervention in housing markets, or to the indirect relationship between government tax and macroeconomic policy and conditions in real estate markets. In Canada, it is impossible to consider the business of real estate separately from the pervasive impact of government economic policies at the local, provincial, and federal levels. Accordingly, this book includes a selection of readings dealing with the economics of government housing and taxation policies in Canada.

Several of the articles included here may use somewhat more advanced statistical and econometric techniques than beginning students can be expected to master. They have been selected for two reasons. First, they should be useful and interesting to students who have taken previous courses in statistics and economics. Second, they serve to make students aware of some of the more important areas of research and controversy in the field of real estate. These articles will serve as a useful introduction to important material even if some of their technical and methodological detail is not easily assimilable by less well prepared students.

The first section, on housing policy, begins with an overview and analysis of Canadian housing policy by J. David Hulchanski. The second article, by Roberto Leone and Barbara W. Carroll, focuses on the Canadian policies towards social housing.

The second section, Macroeconomics, begins with a review of the demographic determinants of housing consumption by Henry Bartel, William L. Marr and Douglas J. McCready. The next article, by John Glen, considers whether the mortgage market problems in the United States are likely to spill over into Canada. The article by William Lim considers some of the sources of real estate price volatility. The fourth article, by Konstantin A. Kholodilin, Jan-Oliver Menz, and Boris Siliverstovs, considers international evidence on the determinants of changes in housing prices.

The third section, Urban Economics, begins with a paper on residential property values in Montreal, Toronto and Vancouver, by Andrejs Skaburskis and Markus Moos. This is followed by a study of price and volume correlations in housing markets by Jim Clayton, Norman Miller, and Liang Peng.

The fourth section, Real Estate Taxation and Policy, begins with a paper by Enid Slack on property tax reform in Ontario. This is followed by an article by Douglas J. McCready that considers the possibilities of charging user fees for some municipal services.

The fifth section, on real estate law, begins with a brief outline of the law by Gavin Arbuckle and Henry Bartel. The remaining three articles address three special aspects of real estate law. Walter H. Posner discusses the transfer of limited interests in real estate. John Zeiler discusses the law governing condominiums. Joanne E. Magee discusses the impact of taxes and tax planning on real estate transactions.

The sixth section, Canadian Mortgages, begins with a consideration of the economics of graduated payment mortgages by Henry Bartel and Alan Marshall. This is followed by a brief description of real estate investment trusts by Gavin Arbuckle and Henry Bartel.

The final article, by Henry Bartel, Michael Daly, discusses the economics of reverse mortgages.

The seventh section, Valuation and Appraisal, begins with an article on commercial real estate valuation by Jim Clayton, David Ling, and Andy Naranjo. This is followed by two articles by John Glen, one on the effects of environmental factors on real estate valuation, and the other on alternative approaches to valuation.

The eighth section, The Real Estate Profession, begins with an article by Walter H. Posner on real estate brokerage. In the second article, Michael Rochon discusses real estate marketing. The third article is a discussion of the impact of information technology on the real estate profession by Michael Rochon.

The final section, on Ethics, contains articles on business and concludes with professional ethics by H.A. Bassford and by Mark S. Schwartz.

We wish to acknowledge the valuable contributions of the various people who have acted as referees for successive editions of this book. Any residual errors are, of course, our own.

We would also like to thank Ms. Pauline Lai and her able editorial staff. Of course, our main obligation is to the authors and publishers who so graciously permitted us to reprint their material.

Finally, we would like to express our appreciation to the Real Estate Centre of Expertise at York University for its financial assistance to the five editions of this book.

GAVIN ARBUCKLE
HENRY BARTEL
Toronto, Ontario
September, 2011

Housing Policy

1

Canada's Dual Housing Policy: Assisting Owners, Neglecting Renters

——————————————————————— J. DAVID HULCHANSKI

1. HOUSING POLICY AND THE HOUSING SYSTEM IN CANADA

For some Canadians, the term "housing policy" evokes images of public housing, government subsidies for low-income households, and programs aimed at helping Canada's unhoused individuals and families. It is easy, though inaccurate, to view housing policy as having this limited scope. After all, 95 percent of Canadian households obtain their housing from the private market. Two-thirds of all households own the house in which they live. About one-third of all renters at any time are on their way to buying a house and are merely passing through the rental market. Only 5 percent of Canada's households live in non-market social housing (defined here as including government-owned public housing, non-profit housing, and non-profit housing cooperatives) — the smallest social housing sector of any Western nation except for the United States.

Canada's housing system, unlike that of most Western nations, relies almost exclusively on the market mechanism for the provision, allocation, and maintenance of housing. This is a problem for house-

Condensed from "What Factors Shape Canadian Housing Policy? The Intergovernmental Role in Canada's Housing System," Chapter 10 in *Canada, State of the Federation 2004: Municipal-Federal-Provincial Relations*, R. Young and C. Leuprecht, eds., Kingston: McGill-Queen's University Press, 2006, pages 221–247.

J. David Hulchanski, PhD (urban planning), is the associate director for research of the Cities Centre and the Dr. Chow Yee Ching Professor of Housing in the Factor-Inwentash Faculty of Social Work at the University of Toronto. <david.hulchanski@utoronto.ca>

holds too poor to pay market rents for appropriate housing. These households generate a "social need" for housing rather than a "market demand" for it. A housing system based on the market mechanism cannot respond to social need. Given the role played by market dynamics, it is easy to assume that government housing policy plays a very small role in Canada. But this is not the case. If it were not for federal government housing policies and programs, past and present, Canada's ownership rate would be much lower and its housing system very different from what it is today.

2. A CONSISTENT HISTORICAL PATTERN

Mortgage lending and insurance institutions were created by federal and provincial government statutes, regulations, and subsidies in the decade following the Second World War. Municipal governments provided the serviced land and zoning regulations that permitted the construction of relatively cheap housing in postwar subdivisions. Since the early 1970s, a steady stream of house purchase assistance programs has helped maintain Canada's ownership rate at about two-thirds.

It was not until 1963 that the federal government, in a program requiring joint provincial funding, began to provide subsidized rental housing for low-income households directly. Specially created provincial housing corporations (such as the Ontario Housing Corporation or the Alberta Housing Corporation) were established to own and manage the housing, under agreements with the federal government. By the mid-1970s, when this program was replaced with a more decentralized and community-based non-profit program, about 200,000 public housing units had been built (about 2 percent of Canada's current housing stock). This was a modest program, because the broader policy objective was to leave as much of the housing system in the market sector as possible.

The Canada Mortgage and Housing Corporation (CMHC), established in 1946, focused public funds almost exclusively on the ownership sector. Although federal legislation in 1949 permitted federal and provincial subsidies for public housing, only 12,000 units had been built by the early 1960s. The CMHC focused mainly on making the amortized mortgage market work for house buyers and for private investors in rental housing. The federal Mortgage Insurance Fund was introduced in 1954 to encourage banks to enter the then risky mortgage lending market. Managing this fund remains one of the major functions of the CMHC, a federal crown corporation. Between the mid-1940s and the mid-1960s, most households obtained at least part of their mortgage loan directly from the federal government.

Most of the history of the role of Canadian government housing policy and programs is therefore a history of efforts targeted at the ownership sector. There was never a policy of tenure neutrality — assisting owners and renters equally. The policy focus on ownership means that over the years, Canadian homeowners have been able to take advantage of various federal subsidy programs, such as the Assisted Home Ownership Program, the Canadian Homeownership Stimulation Plan, the Registered Homeownership Savings Plan, and the Mortgage Rate Protection Program.

Owning a house is a long-term investment that helps maintain a certain standard of living over the course of one's life. The 50 percent of Canadian owners who have paid off their mortgages spend on average only 11 percent of their income on housing and therefore have more funds available for other activities. Moreover, a large, expensive house can be traded for a smaller, less expensive one to free up money, or a reverse mortgage can be negotiated, providing regular annuity payments to the owner. Lifelong renters who cannot afford to purchase a house do not have anything similar to draw on as they age.

Canada's current housing system is the way it is thanks to a long history of government activity and to the ongoing role of all levels of government in supporting Canada's market oriented approach to supplying, allocating, and maintaining the nation's housing stock. The ownership sector of Canada's housing system has always benefited from a well-financed lobby, sympathetic politicians and bureaucrats, and the support of enough voters in our "first past the post" voting system. Canada is one of the few Western democracies that does not have a proportional representation electoral system — which means a broad range of groups and interests cannot win their fair share of seats in our legislatures.

The lack of tenure neutrality has worsened over time. Homeowners have, on average, about double the income of renter households. Not only does it seem counter-intuitive that the bulk of government support would flow to wealthier homeowners rather than poorer tenants, but the numbers that demonstrate this imbalance are rarely reported by the government — politicians or public servants. But occasionally, an official report makes a passing reference to this inequality.

For example, buried in a complicated table in its most recent annual report, the Canada Mortgage and Housing Corporation notes that more individual homeowners (746,157) were helped through mortgage insurance in 2005 than all the social housing units

FIGURE 1
A Litmus Test

"Housing policies provide a remarkable litmus test for the values of politicians at every level of office and of the varied communities that influence them. Often this test measures simply the warmth or coldness of heart of the more affluent and secure towards families of a lower socioeconomic status."

John Bacher, 1993

(633,300) funded in the past 35 years. Furthermore, the CMHC reported that about 7,000 new subsidized housing units were funded in 2005 compared with the almost 653,000 owners who were supported through the public mortgage insurance system — one-tenth the number of new owners who were helped that year. The federal government also reports the $76 million that it will spend on the Affordable Housing Initiative in 2008 (for new subsidized housing), but it does not mention the approximately $6 billion in annual tax revenue that is not collected from owners who sell their houses, due to the decision many years ago not to tax capital gains on the primary residence of homeowners. There is no tax system subsidy for Canadians who rent.

3. THE GROWING GAP

There is nothing wrong with owner occupancy and government house-ownership policies; I merely want to highlight the extent to which this characteristic of Canada's housing system is generally ignored in policy discussions and in intergovernmental considerations of who should do what to improve the housing system.

In recent decades the growing gap between rich and poor Canadian households has increasingly manifested itself in the housing system. The social need for housing exists mainly among renters — tenants whose income (and lack of wealth) cannot generate effective market demand. Meanwhile, public policy decisions since the mid-1980s have further privileged the ownership sector and helped exacerbate problems in the rental-housing sector, problems that include widespread homelessness.

It is important to understand that homelessness is not a "natural" phenomenon. It is the outcome of "normal" —that is, socially sanctioned — practices and activities that are intended to achieve government goals, maintain well-established institutions, or allow certain enterprises to flourish. In other words, it is a by-product of Canada's housing system.

Another feature of Canada's housing system is that 8 percent of Canadians live in dwellings that require major repairs and 5 percent live in overcrowded housing. When we disaggregate this information, we find that almost 20 percent of renters, compared with 10 percent of owners, live in housing that needs major repairs or is overcrowded. Moreover, although the average household spends 21 percent of its total income on housing, owners spend 18 percent, compared with 28 percent for tenants.

It is clear that Canadians are divided into two very different groups according to housing tenure. Owners have roughly twice the income of renters. In terms of wealth, owners have about a quarter of a million dollars in assets (mainly the paid-for portion of their mortgage), while the average renter has about a thousand dollars in savings. Although there is only one housing market, Canada's housing system has two pools of housing consumers with dramatically different incomes and assets.

The income and wealth gap inequity is not static. The problem has become much worse over recent decades. In the late 1960s, the income gap between owners and renters was about 20 percent. By 1999 the gap had increased to 208 percent. Also, the wealth of owners (which, for most people, is mainly the mortgage-free portion of their house) increased from being 29 times that of renters in 1984 to 70 times that of renters in 1999. Poverty and housing tenure are now much more closely connected.

Meanwhile, the feasibility of building rental housing in Canada has declined because of changes to municipal zoning for rental housing. Before the early 1970s and the introduction of condominium forms of ownership, all areas zoned for medium and high residential densities were, by definition, rental districts. Low density zoning tended to be associated with owner occupied housing (although some houses were rented and some had second suites). Since passage of the provincial legislation creating the condominium form of ownership in the early 1970s, rental housing providers have had to compete with condominium providers for zoned building sites. Since renters have about half the income of homeowners, condo developers can always outbid rental developers for residential sites. This is another example of the lack of tenure neutrality in Canada's housing system. The loss of "rental-only" zoning makes it difficult, if not impossible, for investors to build for renters. A condo developer can always outbid a potential rental housing developer because of the higher income and wealth of owners.

Canada's housing system is seriously out of balance; it is discriminatory in the way it treats owners and renters; and it is a system in which the market mechanism of supply and demand works for the ownership sector but not for the rental sector. It has become an increasingly exclusive system, in the sense that some households are excluded from access to housing.

4. JURISDICTIONAL SQUABBLES

Governments at all three levels are always making choices when it comes to decisions that affect the housing system. One important element of the policy debate over housing in Canada — especially the effort to create a more inclusive system (the demands from civil society to help low-income households and end homelessness, for example) — is the jurisdictional issue: Which level of government is or ought to be responsible for what part of the housing system?

The short answer to the above question is that all levels of government have responsibility. They are all continually making decisions that affect housing. Yet disputes over jurisdiction continue. For example, when the federal government tabled proposals for constitutional change in September 1991, housing and "municipal/urban affairs" were two of six sectors offered up as exclusive provincial domains, because they were "more properly the responsibility of the provinces." The federal government, according to the proposal, was prepared "to recognize the exclusive jurisdiction of the provinces ... and to withdraw from these fields in a manner appropriate to each sector." No explanation was offered for why these two, along with tourism, forestry, mining, and recreation, were considered to be "more properly" the responsibility of the provinces. Although this constitutional proposal was rejected by Canada's voters in a national referendum on the Charlottetown Accord, the efforts of the federal government (with its huge annual deficits at the time) to extricate itself from social housing subsidies continued.

In the March 1996 federal budget, the government announced that it would transfer administration of federal social-housing programs to provinces and territories, ending 50 years of direct federal involvement in the administration of social-housing programs. This was a unilateral policy decision, not the settlement of a legal or constitutional dispute over jurisdiction. It was also a financial decision — a means of saving money at the federal level. This policy decision handed responsibility to the provinces, and some provinces passed it on to municipalities. The federal government would no longer be responsible for the stream of subsidies once the initial funding packages for the approximately 500,000 social-housing units expired.

Most provincial and territorial policies and program changes also represent a withdrawal from helping those most in need. It is important, however, to place provincial and territorial budget cuts in housing, social spending, and urban affairs in the context of the federal government's downloading of the deficit onto provincial taxpayers. Federal cash transfers to the provinces and territories have been falling since the early 1980s. Huge amounts of money that were once transferred to provinces and territories were unilaterally withdrawn. The money had previously been used for health, education, and welfare programs (some federal funding, particularly for health care, has since been restored).

This reduction in transfer payments has made it more difficult for provinces and territories to replace federal cuts in social-housing spending should they wish to do so. Most provinces have avoided social-housing spending, except for Quebec and, until recently, British Columbia, although from time to time, some provinces have played an active role in housing. Between 1985 and 1995, for example, Ontario played a significant role in adding to the social-housing stock of the province.

The federal government during the 1990s not only cut the transfer payments to provinces, but also reduced its direct spending on housing, thereby saving the Treasury about $1.5 billion a year. The current $2 billion of federal money spent annually on housing (1 percent of total federal spending) pays for subsidies on about 550,000 social-housing units that were built before the 1993 termination of the federal role in subsidizing new social housing units. Dismantling the social-housing supply program also meant that provinces and municipalities had to bear the indirect costs of inadequate hous-

---

FIGURE 2
A Political Artefact

It is politics — policy decisions by the government of the day, under the specific realities of the times — and not any legal or constitutional constraints that define the federal and provincial roles in housing.

ing and homelessness. These include the costs of physical and mental health care, emergency shelters and services, and policing.

It is politics — policy decisions by the government of the day, under the specific realities of the times — and not any legal or constitutional constraints that define the federal and provincial roles in housing. Furthermore, decisions are made in the context of a historical continuity that privileges housing interventions in the ownership sector and interventions that conform with and are supportive of the market. And the provision of social-housing and programs to help impoverished and homeless households are very expensive.

There is no legal or constitutional impediment to federal or provincial governments engaging in any variety of housing policies and programs. The federal and provincial governments have historically engaged in many different programs, both unilateral and joint. The jurisdictional issue appears to be significant only because politicians raise it when they do not want their level of government to be responsible for addressing a particular housing problem.

5. THE MUNICIPAL GOVERNMENT ROLE

Municipalities themselves vary widely in their efforts to ensure that residents are appropriately housed. Voter turnout at municipal elections tends to be very low, with owners voting in greater numbers than renters and demanding attention from city council on zoning matters. The "not in my back yard" (NIMBY) pressures on municipal politicians make it difficult to locate housing or housing-related services for low-income people in certain areas. City councils rarely vote on a consistent basis in favour of programs or initiatives that target the very poor in their communities.

Strictly speaking, there is a constitutional barrier when it comes to a direct federal-municipal relationship in a policy area. Municipalities can do only what their provinces allow them to do. In practice, however, if federal money is made available to municipalities, it is politically difficult for a provincial government to deny municipal government access to that money. There is a long history of federal government programs that assist municipalities on key housing and neighbourhood issues. For example, the federal government supplied "slum clearance" funding to municipalities under the 1944 National Housing Act (NHA), "urban redevelopment" funding under the 1954 NHA, "urban renewal" funding under the 1964 NHA, and "neighbourhood improvement" funding under the 1973 NHA. After 1973 the federal government directly funded new social-housing projects built by non-profit societies as well as non-profit housing corporations established by municipalities for that purpose.

From that point on, until very recently, the federal government showed no interest in formulating a national urban strategy, in understanding urban trends and the impact of federal policies on cities, or in providing resources in a coordinated fashion.

By the end of the 1990s, it became increasingly difficult for the federal government to do nothing — or at least appear to be doing nothing — about urban social problems. With pressures building from civil society organizations and from municipalities themselves for federal assistance, the prime minister established a Caucus Task Force on Urban Issues. The task force's interim report opens with a now widely accepted assertion that Canadian cities are in crisis. After much talk and many promises, the 2004 and 2005 federal budgets allocated some new funds for housing and municipal infrastructure. As in the past, the federal government is launching housing and urban affairs initiatives in the face of strong political pressures (and during a minority government) — without the jurisdictional debate getting in the way.

6. THE DUALISM IN CANADA'S POSTWAR SOCIAL POLICIES

The history of Canada's housing system provokes many questions. Why did the federal Liberal Party fund so many housing and urban programs when it was in office during most of the 1960s, 1970s, and early 1980s, but not during the 1990s? Why did it seemingly reengaged in these issues by allocating funds for social housing and municipal infrastructure in the 2004 and 2005 budgets? Claiming that the government at certain times "lacks a political will" to take action and at other times "has the political will" to take action is a descriptive statement, not an explanation.

The answers must be set in the context of the differential treatment of owners and renters. There is no evidence that governments have ever intended to make progress towards a more inclusive and just housing system. This was not a policy objective, though it appears in political rhetoric around election time.

The term "welfare state" refers to the set of social practices and strategic accommodations designed to address specific problems of the day relating to both the production of goods and services and their distribution. Since the early 1990s, and in view of the large package of dynamics subsumed under the term "globalization," the welfare state has been undergoing a historic shift that we have yet to fully analyse and understand.

Canada has (or had) what is usually described as a liberal welfare state, in which means-tested assistance, modest universal transfers, and modest social insurance plans predominate, and in which interference with the commodification of goods and services is minimized, the granting of social rights minimized, and dualism maintained between market and state allocation. This dualism explains why there is political will to help one part of the housing system and not the other. It also explains why there was at least some effort to help households most in need of housing assistance during the 1960s and 1970s and why even this minimal government role was cut back in the 1980s and then eliminated in the 1990s.

Until the development of the postwar welfare state, government provision of help to those in need was based on a social assistance model, in which welfare assistance for certain categories of "worthy" poor was designed to allow individuals and families to subsist. After the 1940s the social security welfare state emerged alongside this social assistance welfare state. The social security welfare state was never an anti-poverty welfare state. It was designed to provide wage stabilization for the emerging middle class, not to engage in redistribution to assist the poor.

In contrast to the means-testing of the welfare state, there are two principles of distribution in the social security welfare state: universality and wage replacement. Universality means payments become entitlements, rights of citizenship, or earned benefits. Wage replacement benefits were linked to past earnings and were at levels high enough to maintain a continuity of living standard when the wage earner left the labour market due to illness, unemployment, or disability.

The problem which the social security welfare state sought to address is the maintenance of high and stable levels of mass consumption. The challenge during the postwar years was not how to produce enough, but how to *stabilize* product markets. Since the end of the Second World War, the federal government's housing activities helped focus on achieving high and relatively stable levels of housing starts. This contributed to overall economic growth and provided many well-paying jobs.

The federal government successfully carried out this housing activity in a fashion that is compatible with and assists (rather than replaces) housing, land, mortgage lending, and real estate markets. This aspect of housing policy, part of the social security welfare state, has nothing directly to do with assisting impoverished households obtain adequate housing — which is a function of the social assistance part of the welfare state.

The most relevant feature of Canada's welfare state for assessing the dynamics of housing policy (who gets what, of what quality, and with what state assistance) is the dualism in the provision of benefits. The social assistance welfare state has continued to develop since the last century, but in addition there is now a social security welfare state alongside it. There is some overlap where benefits are universal — although most universal programs have been abolished. In general, however, a dualism existed and continues to exist in many policy areas, including housing.

This dualism means that there are two separate parts to Canada's housing system, a primary and a secondary one, each with its own distinct and unequal range of government activities and subsidies — and each, therefore, with separate policy trajectories. These two mirror the dualism in Canada's welfare state. The primary part of the housing system is a component of the social security welfare state, whereas the secondary part is a component of the social assistance welfare state.

The primary part consists of about 80 percent of households, including most owners and those tenants who live in the higher end of the private rental market. It also includes households in the co-operative housing sector and a few who live in non-profit and public housing. These households have secure tenure in good quality housing appropriate to their needs and at a price they can afford.

The secondary part consists of everyone else, including tenants in the lower half of the rental market (where housing quality is low), residents of poor-quality and poorly managed subsidized housing, and rural and impoverished owners. The division is in large part, though not completely, based on housing tenure (owning and renting).

All three levels of government favour the ownership sector and provide good-quality social housing to a minority of those in need of adequate and affordable housing. They tend to ignore the needs of most low-income renter households.

The dualism in the distribution of state benefits is the key factor shaping Canada's housing policy and programs. The primary part of the housing system receives benefits mainly in the form of entitlements (universal rather than selective) as "natural" parts of the

FIGURE 3
Blinkered Vision

All three levels of government favour the ownership sector and provide good-quality social housing to a minority of those in need of adequate and affordable housing. They tend to ignore the needs of most low-income renter households.

way the housing system operates. These include the government-created and managed mortgage lending system, the government mortgage insurance program, the special tax treatment of capital gains on owner-occupied housing, programs to assist with an initial down payment, and generally superior community services and amenities in districts with higher-cost owner and tenant-occupied housing.

Low-income households, if they receive any benefits at all, generally do so on a selective means-tested basis aimed at meeting minimum needs. Households in the secondary part of the housing system have little or no political clout. Thus, Canada's housing system, for purposes of analysing government activities, consists of two substantially separate and distinct housing subsystems. Government reacts differently to housing problems based on which subsystem the problem is in.

7. POLICY FOR THE PRIMARY PART OF THE HOUSING SYSTEM

For the primary part of the housing system, the federal and provincial governments will continue to play an interventionist role during difficult economic times. The house-building sector is a key part of the economy and, with the support of middle-class owners, is able to mount an effective lobby. Federal government housing activity relating to the primary sector, whether direct (budgetary spending programs) or indirect (tax expenditures), is rarely considered to be a subsidy or a drain on the economy or on the federal budget. Rather, these actions are viewed as the proper responsibility of government in difficult times, and the subsidies are considered incentives and entitlements — as rights associated with investing in and owning housing.

For example, consider the federal government's decision, announced in the 1992 budget, to introduce the Home Buyers' Plan, which allows house buyers to use up to $20,000 in tax-sheltered retirement savings as part of their down payment. This move was resisted by federal officials because it put retirement savings at risk and introduced a windfall benefit for some house buyers, and because there was no evidence that such incentives do anything more than move demand for new houses forward (that is, there is no long-term net gain for the economy). But the pressure "to do something" during a severe construction slump had become so great that the federal government granted the demands of the house-building and real estate lobbies. In the same budget, however, social housing was cut from the expected 12,400 units to about 8,000, and the co-op housing program (about 3,500 units) was terminated. All social-housing supply programs were terminated in the next budget.

Housing plays such an important role in the economy that, during recessions in particular, both the federal and provincial governments have a consistent record of introducing short-term programs that most often are focused on assisting ownership and tenants in the high end of the rental market (the primary part of the housing system), particularly those who are able to buy a house. This type of federal housing program activity results from economic and housing market conditions and the stronger political clout of actors in the primary part of the housing system.

8. POLICY FOR THE SECONDARY PART OF THE HOUSING SYSTEM

Trends in the federal role in the secondary part of the housing system depend on the particular nature of the federal-provincial relations and disputes of the day, the constitutional and social policy philosophy of the federal political party in power, and the effectiveness of national housing and social welfare organizations in mobilizing popular support for specific housing and urban policies and programs.

The federal government can unilaterally do whatever it wants to do in the area of housing. Jurisdictional issues are not in the way. But jurisdictional issues suddenly become a problem if the federal government does *not* want to engage in a housing program. The inbetween measure is the joint-funding formula — an offer of federal money that must be matched by provincial governments. This is a good delaying (or avoidance) tactic, and it allows the federal government to point the finger at the provinces when citizens complain that something should be done. The recent federal funding for some "affordable housing" (not necessarily social housing or housing targeted at the greatest need) is an example. After two years, very few units have been subsidized and very little money has been spent. Since the subsidy levels are relatively shallow, the money may not assist many people currently in the secondary part of the housing system.

The trend in federal housing and urban affairs in relation to the secondary part of the housing system is difficult to predict. For the immediate future, current policies will likely continue, exacerbating the division between the quality of the housing for those fortunate enough to be in the primary part of the housing system and those stuck in the secondary part. Despite growing homelessness in the 1990s, governments did nothing that has resulted in fewer homeless people. The problem is larger today than five years ago when the federal government started its Supporting Communities Partnership Program, which has sprinkled the country with many press releases and some money for services for homeless people. It will take a very serious deterioration in the quality of the existing aging rental stock (which has already begun to occur) and widespread discontent and effective organization by grassroots organizations for positive and effective federal action to be taken.

An emerging reality that has [helped] explain the current federal government's decision to ignore the secondary part of the housing system relates to changes in the broader economic situation. Global economic trends and domestic corporate investment strategies (economic globalization) mean that there is no institutional or structural imperative to do much about the people in the secondary part of the housing system, other than to forestall embarrassment (too many homeless on the streets). A large unskilled pool of labour is no longer required as it once was.

Such a trajectory for federal housing policy also means growing regional disparities between the larger and economically stronger provinces and the rest of the country. Regional housing market situations combined with changes in provincial governments can result in provincial activism in social housing and urban affairs in the wealthier provinces, which only makes regional disparities even greater. Between 1985 and 1995, for example, Ontario produced about 50,000 housing units with its own funds, thereby removing that many Ontario households from the secondary part of the housing system. In addition, up to 1995, Ontario used its own funds to supplement the federal-provincial social-housing program to eliminate what it considered to be the more regressive regulations imposed by the Conservative government in the 1980s and early 1990s.

In the end, the debate over whether and how to address housing needs and homelessness is a political problem, and there is no scientific or objective way to arrive at an answer to a political problem. The nature of the problem is well understood, and potential programs are not complicated or even very expensive for a country with Canada's wealth. The question about serious and effective government action on current housing and urban problems is a question about political will. What pressure is there for government to address homelessness? Why worry about poor-quality housing for poor people, urban and rural? There seems to be no economic or significant political pressure to address problems in the secondary part of the housing system. It is, by definition, secondary — not primary. "All three levels of government will continue to worry about problems as they arise among households in the primary part of the housing system. The major change affecting the "welfare state" and the sense of nationhood since the early 1990s may mean that the secondary part of the housing system does not matter at all.

Decentralisation and Devolution in Canadian Social Housing Policy

—— ROBERTO LEONE & BARBARA W. CARROLL

1 INTRODUCTION

Federalism has a variable effect on public policy. The degree of success of federalism as an organising institution of government largely depends on the policy field that is being discussed. While federalism may assist the creation of some public policies, it might also be an impediment to the creation of other social policies (Obinger et al, 2005). Much of the international coverage of the implications of federalism on public policy has focused on the evolution of decentralisation (Rodríguez-Pose and Gill, 2003; Rodríguez-Pose and Sandall, 2008) and the impact of empowered subnational governance structures to become major actors in public policy development and implementation (Harguindéguy and Bray, 2009; Pearce and Ayres, 2006).

In many ways, applying some of the dominant international literature to Canadian federalism gleans some important insights (Banting, 2005). Since Canada's federal experiment dates back to the country's founding in 1867, it provides a useful laboratory to discuss some of the themes touched on above. For example, federalism has been cited as a reason for the creation of a universal health care system due in part to the policy experimentation aspects afforded by having ten provinces creating social policies (Maioni and Smith, 2003). This argument suggests that, because one province succeeded in creating a universal health care system, the model was adopted by

"Decentralization and devolution in Canadian Social Housing Policy" Roberto Leone and Barbara W. Carroll, *Environment and Planning C: Government and Policy* 28(3), June 2010, 389–404. ISSN 0263-774X (print) 1472–3425 (electronic). Reprinted with permission of Pion Ltd.

the federal government and transplanted to all the provinces. Policy experimentation in federal countries is not merely a Canadian theme (Greer, 2004). However, while this might explain health care policy development in a variety of countries, it does not explain other areas of social policy development. In Canada, for example, the Province of Quebec has an innovative subsidised child care program which has not been adopted by the other provinces or the federal government. Federalism, then, is not a panacea for public policy development; it can at times be a powerful tool and at other times be a barrier to progress.

We will begin by exploring some of the international literature and apply it to Canada. Through the examination some consistencies and deviations will appear in terms of how federalism has evolved over time. Canada has been described as a flexible federation (Dion, 2003). It has at times been seen as a centralised federation and at other times decentralised. In order to obtain a clearer picture of the implications of decentralisation on public policy in Canada, we will explore how it has affected Canadian housing policy from 1945 to the present. The federal government had a leadership role in housing policy in Canada until the mid-1980s and the downward spiral continued until 2001 when the fragmented policy environment needed serious attention. In 2001 the federal government was once again interested in creating and implementing social policies. Our first argument follows from this perspective. We will argue that, once a policy is devolved, the likelihood that it becomes recentralised is remote. Essentially, we contest the idea that Canada has very much flexibility in the degree of decentralisation any more. This is largely due to the province-building thesis. Even with the central government's renewed interest in housing policy, it cannot have full control over the policy area which it enjoyed in the years that immediately followed World War II.

Following the discussion on decentralisation's effect on housing policy, we will explore in greater detail a contemporary housing program, which is known as the Affordable Housing Initiative (AHI). Our evaluation of the AHI will focus on whether the goals and objectives are being met by the policy. The conclusion that we draw from this analysis is that the goals of the AHI are being only partially met. At the same time no government appears to be focused on the horizontal policy outcomes that are also part of housing policy such as homelessness. This leads to our second argument which is that decentralisation is an impediment to the achievement of both program and horizontal policy goals. This conclusion should make enthusiasts of decentralisation cautious about what they aspire to achieve.

2 DECENTRALISATION AND CANADIAN FEDERALISM

As Rodríguez-Pose and Gill (2003, page 334) state, "devolution is a complex and heterogeneous process." While many countries have seen decentralisation as a result of globalisation and its downward pressure from national to subnational units (Rodríguez-Pose and Gill, 2003), decentralisation in Canada started much earlier and was a result of two principal features. The first is a fiscal argument. The constitution enumerates powers for the central government and the provinces, particularly in sections 91 and 92, but these are not rigid delineations. Much of the ebb and flow of Canadian federalism has to do with which level of government has the most money at its disposal (Brown, 2008; Kershaw, 2006). When the central government has money at its disposal, the provinces often would allow centralisation to occur. Likewise, when the provinces had more money vis-a-vis the federal government, they asserted their power. At one point during the mid-1990s, neither level of government had any money, which meant that the provinces were left to pay all of the bills because the constitution granted them the responsibility to provide many of the country's social programs.

In addition to the fiscal federalism rationale for decentralisation, another cause can be attributed to the 'province-building' thesis (Black and Cairns, 1966). The province-building thesis became popular during the 1960s and 1970s because the provinces prior to this time had very little expertise or sophistication in public policy development and implementation. Provincial bureaucracies were small and immature relative to their federal government counterparts. The significance of this idea for public policy is that the federal government simply knew more about the social problems, and the social conditions that underlie these problems, which then meant they could take the lead in solving them. Provincial governments, in contrast, simply could not compete and so they passed social policy development to the federal government. Province building was an attempt to develop a level of policy expertise and sophistication that was at least comparable, if not better, than the federal government. It meant a bigger and better trained bureaucracy, the presence of which will not likely disappear.

Rodríguez-Pose and Sandall (2008, pages 55–59) outline three categories of discourse from which decentralists draw their inspiration. The first of these is the discourse on minorities. This pressure for decentralisation emerges because there is an ethnic, racial, linguistic, or religious basis for identity. People who identify with others accordingly have a desire for self-determination (Rodríguez-Pose and Sandall, 2008, page 55).

In the Canadian context this is one of the reasons Canada became a federal country to begin with. French-speaking people in the Province of Quebec have a shared identity based on ancestry and religion. By becoming a federal country, Canada granted certain cultural protections to the French-speaking people who formed a majority within a defined territory. These were predominantly in the domains of cultural policy and social policy. One of the reasons Canada has a province-building movement was due to the fact that French-Canadian nationalists wanted to see a larger provincial state (McRoberts, 2001).

The second category is a democratic discourse. Decentralists in this category link decentralisation with good governance. They are likely to use words and terminology that are hard to disagree with (Paddison, 1999, page 118), such as openness, access to information, togetherness, and active citizenship (Rodríguez-Pose and Sandall, 2008, page 55). This level of discourse is not as readily visible across Canada. It may be truer in smaller provinces where the bureaucracies are correspondingly smaller, but the large provinces also have large governments and these do not engender a sense of greater openness and other democratic aspects.

The third category of discourse is categorised as an economic one. This discourse is predominantly interested in creating an environment where regions and subnational governments are better positioned to adapt to changing economic circumstances brought about by globalisation (Keating, 1997; Rodríguez-Pose et al, 2009). In a similar vein Courchene and Telmer (1998) stress that much of the force of decentralisation and devolution in North American is due to globalisation. They claim that globalisation is forcing a relationship between major cities in North America whereby the economic lifeline of the hinterland is tied to the success of the global cities it services. In this light, global cities have more in common with other global cities than they do with other cities that fall within arbitrary jurisdictional lines. In fact, the economic pull of these global cities means that their hinterland spans subnational and even national lines making the traditional nation-state design less meaningful (Rodríguez-Pose and Gill, 2003). Because of the presence of this trend, there is pressure for countries to decentralise and devolve power and authority to smaller groups.

Of the three discourses found in countries that are devolving power, only two are seen in the Canadian context. The process for devolution was encouraged by what was called the Quiet Revolution in Quebec during the 1960s, which essentially sought to provide the French-speaking province's state with greater expertise in matters of public policy. It was one way in which the French-speaking province could retain its identity in the face of English North America. We also see the economic discourse in Canada. This one started in the late 1970s, but it has affected the desire for increased decentralisation in Canada. Certainly, as the case will be made in this paper, the economic argument has meant that the federal government has lost the authority and legitimacy it once had in social policy development in Canada, and this change may now be permanent.

Like the UK, Canada can be described as being highly permissive of policy variation (Greer, 2004; Jeffery, 2007; Shaw et al, 2009). Of the three institutional features that contribute to this reality in the UK (Shaw et al, 2009, page 547), only one is really present in Canada with another one written but not followed in spirit. The first institutional feature is a separation of powers between the UK Parliament and the devolved assemblies. This is the feature that is written but is no longer followed in Canada. As stated above, the Canadian Constitution Act, 1867 stipulates what is in the sphere of jurisdiction for the central government, the provincial governments, and concurrent jurisdiction between the two. Over the course of time, governments at national and subnational levels were able to negotiate the other level's involvement in areas where it did not have jurisdiction. Today, Canadian federalism can be described as one of entanglement. There is a significant degree of overlap between the jurisdictional delineations outlined in the Canadian constitution. It has meant that the only check against divergence and devolution is negotiation and consensus among all the actors and this is a difficult feat to achieve.

The second institutional feature (Shaw et al, 2009, page 547) is that intergovernmental relations are largely informal and ad hoc. This is not the case in Canada. Province building had some corresponding implications for Canadian federalism (Chandler and Chandler, 1979). One of these is the emergence of executive federalism. Because the provinces became more knowledgeable about public policy issues, the governments in the provinces were better positioned to enter bilateral negotiations with the central government. This form of interstate federalism began to symbolise the politics and gvernment of Canada. The provinces were no longer novices; they became as strong, if not stronger, than the central government. Today, every provincial government and the national government have a department of intergovernmental affairs for which a minister is responsible. In addition to this, intergovernmental meetings at both the departmental and first ministers' level are regular occurrences in Canada. This runs contrary to what Shaw and his colleagues say about mechanisms that ensure coordination. Canada has such mechanisms, yet coordination is difficult. The presence of strong provincial governments means that their major interest is in maximum federal investment in social policy with minimal interference in terms of how that money is spent.

This leads to the third institutional feature (Shaw et al, 2009, page 547), which is the nature of fiscal relations among national and subnational units. One of the reasons why there is devolution in the UK is due to the use of block grants that attach few strings to how the money is spent. The nature of Canadian federalism has moved from an era where conditional grants were used to one where block grants are used (Brown, 2008). Many of the social programs in Canada started out on a shared-cost basis where 50% of the costs would come from the federal government and 50% of the costs would come from the provincial governments. As one can imagine, if each of the ten provincial governments increased their social spending by one dollar, the federal government would have to contribute ten dollars. For the federal government who funded health care through this model, as well as social assistance spending through the Canada Assistance Plan, the sustainability of shared-cost funding through conditional grants became limited (Leslie et al, 2004). Thus, Canada also went the route of block grant funding, and, as a result, provinces have been free to spend the money more or less how they pleased. The only stipulation for following national standards was essentially the outcome of negotiation and achieving consensus.

There is an alternative method for setting national standards. The central government can establish broad legislative parameters for how money ought to be spent, while giving a block grant to allow the subnational governments the opportunity to spend as they please so long as they do not violate the letter and spirit of the law. This is what has happened in Canadian health policy where national standards are spelled out in the Canada Health Act, 1984. However, the legislative method of establishing national standards is clearly an exception to the rule. The reason why it works in health care is that there is broad consensus on the universality of the Canadian public health insurance scheme. Universal health care, in some ways, has become part of the Canadian identity. There is not a public policy area in Canada that has the same degree of consensus, which means that the federal government cannot unilaterally pass legislation that compels the provinces to comply with the standards it sets. Such an action would certainly provoke provincial governments to seek a judicial remedy to the situation in the absence of a willingness on the part of the central government to negotiate.

The lack of a national consensus in other policy areas means that divergence within a policy area is more likely to occur. There are many measures that determine how important a policy area is to a government. It could be through the measurement of public opinion where governments capture the pulse of the public and create policies that essentially satisfy voters. Importance in Westminster systems can also be measured by who the prime minister places at the head of certain departments (eg senior or junior ministers). Divergence in a policy area is certain to occur when there is a lack of a strong ministerial leadership at the central government level because the portfolio has been given to a minister who may be tested for his or her suitability for a bigger portfolio.

The history of housing at the federal cabinet level has been mixed to say the least. Housing policy and responsibility for the Canada and Mortgage Housing Corporation (CMHC), a Crown corporation that serves as a vehicle for housing policy development, has not always been a high priority for Canadian governments. There has not been a stand-alone housing ministry in Canada. Because of a lack of jurisdiction, housing policy has largely been defined as part of the responsibility for financial policy with the major federal presence being in financing and insuring mortgages (Carroll, 1989). Only during the late 1960s and early 1970s were there ministers dedicated to housing (Carroll, 1989; Streich, 1985). This interest had grown out of the Hellyer Task Force and the urban movement of the 1960s (Carroll, 1989). However, by the late 1970s budget cuts to the departments quickly ended the enthusiasm for ministers and we have only recently had a string of cabinet ministers whose responsibility for housing is stated in their job titles.

As the above discussion suggests, Canada has been consistent with other countries with respect to how decentralisation has occurred over the last number of years. However, what ought to be emphasised is the fact that Canada has a flexible federal framework (Dion, 2003). The history of Canada supports the idea that there is an ebb and flow to federalism. At some points in history it is the federal government that has more power and authority, and at other times it is the provinces that have more power and authority over public policy matters. However, what the case of housing policy in Canada will demonstrate is that, once decentralisation and devolution become entrenched features of a policy area, the possibility of recentralisation is remote. The flexibility of the political system may be overstated because decentralised provinces develop institutional mechanisms that make centralisation more and more impossible.

3 STAGES OF CANADIAN HOUSING POLICY SINCE 1945

Housing policy in Canada is explored because it provides a useful example of the difficulties of recentralisation and the problems associated with fixing a policy area that has been neglected as a result of absent central government leadership. National leadership in Canadian housing policy began with the establishment of the Central Mortgage and Housing Corporation in 1946, which was renamed to its current title of the CMHC. The initial goal of the CMHC was to help returning war veterans find shelter after their overseas missions. This is important to note because it allowed the federal government, which had responsibility for military and veterans affairs, to become involved in local housing markets, assigned to the provincial level of government in the Canadian constitution. The goal of the CMHC was to create a housing community with its main focus on the private housing market. This, however, changed over time as the CMHC was also tasked as a key vehicle to develop and implement public housing programs.

The creation of CMHC is the beginning of the first phase of housing that lasted until 1968 (see table 1). The goal in this stage was to move middle-income earners into single-detached homes so that lower-income groups would be able to have a supply of affordable housing to meet their needs. This process has been called 'filtering' (Carroll and Jones, 2000). This was thought to create a trickle-down effect because middle-income earners would move to suburbs and the cheaper urban homes would be left to the poor. Because this was the stated goal for the housing program in this first stage, the federal government proceeded to implement the national policy with little regard for local or provincial needs. This was part of the Anglo-American trend toward suburban development and new towns which, while developing in the 1930s in Great Britain, came to dominate policy in the postwar years (Carver, 1975; Rose, 1980). The second phase began in 1968 and this was a time of mass social development in Canada. Housing policy development was not too different from what was happening in other social policies (Mishra, 1990). The goal of this stage was comprehensive planning because it was thought that it could solve policy problems through rational problem-solving techniques. It is considered rational because policy makers had a general idea of what a prototypical urban area should look like, and they implemented policies that moved toward their vision. In addition to this, the federal government wanted to gain credit for assisting 'baby boomers' just entering the housing market and their parents who were contemplating their retirement years (Miron, 1988; Rose, 1980). As a result the federal government created the short-lived Ministry of State for Urban Affairs whose goals included cooperation among other levels of government. This has been known more broadly as cooperative federalism which was largely credited for social policy expansion beginning in the early 1960s (Dupré, 1987; Robinson and Simeon, 2004).

TABLE 1
Canadian housing policy stages

Characteristics	Economic development	Social development	Financial restraint	Disentanglement	Disengagement and privatisation	Reengagement
Time	1945–68	1968–78	1978–86	1986–94	1994–2001	2001–present
Intergovernmental	federal leadership	trilevel consultation, 'province building'	provincial leadership	solely provincial	solely provincial	trilevel consultation
Delivery instruments	direct federal loans and grants	cost sharing and direct subsidies and loans	loan guarantees and mortgage insurance	coproduction, private sector partnership	volunteers, local government	cost sharing between governments and the private sector
Housing goals	industrial development, suburban development, physical planning	community development, income integration, demand support	supply support	deconstruction, 'fix up, patch up'	not defined	build projects throughout the country and wide variety of in-place rental subsidy programs
Economic conditions	reconstruction and prosperity	prosperity and inflation	recession and recovery	high government deficits	economic growth and widening social gap	economic growth and high government surpluses
Major demographic force	pent-up demand and returning veterans	'baby boom'	aging population and single families	40 and 50 somethings	smaller nontraditional family unit	seniors requiring affordable housing and highly visible homelessness
Outcomes	large projects, 'corporate city'	widespread uncontrolled subsidies	administrative overlap	nonpolicy small-scale intervention	few new affordable housing spaces created	widespread uncontrolled subsidies

Note: Modified and adapted from Carroll (2002). The reengagement portion of the table has been added to update the table.

Part of the reason why the federal government could no longer act unilaterally pertains to the emergence of province building. Nationalists in Quebec led the intellectual charge for the use of the state for nationalist purposes much like the federal government was doing in the postwar era (McRoberts, 2004). The intellectuals felt that provincial governments could no longer be less skilled than their federal counterpart. The provincial governments needed greater sophistication and expertise to manage their own affairs. With regard to housing policy, this era saw provincial initiatives in many of the provinces — most notably, British Columbia, Ontario, and Quebec — and the provincial governments developed and funded their own initiatives for home ownership and social housing to meet their immediate local needs. The most visible example of province building in housing could have been the introduction of rent control in most provinces as a mirror of federally initiated wage and price controls. Further to this, federal, provincial, and municipal governments aligned their tax policies which saw an increase in construction of rental housing through to the early 1970s. The implementation of rent control programs and the restructuring of the tax incentives to build rental apartments effectively halted the building of purpose-built rental housing by the early 1970s.

While the second phase emphasised building and cooperation, the effect of province building was felt mostly in the third phase. The phase, which began in 1978, saw the first in a series of government measures that concerned fiscal management and restraint. Budget deficits were ballooning and the federal government was finding it difficult to fund its prior commitments in a variety of social policies and programs. The focus had thus shifted to the budget, and this brought a reduction in programs and reduced government spending. While the short-term problem was the budget, the net effect of the decision was that programs and services that were previously delivered by the federal government were passed onto provincial and municipal governments (Hulchanski and Drover, 1986). Because of the patchwork of policies being implemented, it was not uncommon to see nonprofit municipal housing authorities in competition with the private sector. When this occurred less attention was paid to affordable housing projects. The third phase can largely be characterised as a transition between strong federal control to weak or nonexistent federal control.

As the provinces grew stronger and began to take more of a policy lead in housing, a fourth phase emerged which can be described as an era of disentanglement. Disentanglement is a term used to describe how governments limit the amount of overlap between federal and provincial jurisdictions. It was traditionally a term used to describe Canada over the first seventy or so years when federal transfers to the provinces were limited (Simeon, 1979). The same process occurred in many areas of social policies, including housing. Disentanglement essentially ended in 1994 when the federal government announced it was unilaterally ending federal funding for housing projects.

There are many facets to disentanglement. There are revenue and expenditure considerations and program delivery considerations. In terms of the expenditure side of the equation, many of the measures that affected housing policy were contained in the federal budget of that year, which restricted the government's obligations by placing a Can$2.13 billion cap on housing expenditures. In 1995/96 the amount was further reduced to Can$2.03 billion, and in 1996/97 to Can$1.94 billion (Carroll and Jones, 2000, page 280). In terms of program delivery, the federal government agreed to embark upon a consultative process with the subnational governments, which were designed to understand housing policy priorities. Yet by the end of this stage in 1994, no tangible results emerged from the consultative planning process. Thus, both the expenditure and the program delivery considerations essentially saw a severing of the ties between the federal and the provincial governments in housing policy.

The fifth stage is categorised as one of divestment and disengagement. Beginning in 1995, this phase reflects a trend toward devolution and the government pulling out of housing. Not only did governments lack the desire to invest money in housing due to budgetary constraints, but also public perception of government-funded housing was declining (Klodawsky and Spector, 1998). The public was not supportive of government plans to engage in housing, and this resulted in disengagement. Policy decisions related to housing lacked a cohesive national plan, and the provinces seemed to make their policies in isolation. The economic conditions by the late 1990s had significantly improved, which may support the fact that more people were employed and fewer were in need of affordable housing. In housing, much like in other areas of social policy, the total need for the program is the sum of the structural need and frictional need. We can define structural need by grouping people who require long-term housing. Such people will present a host of social problems and will always need a place to stay. Frictional need can be defined as those who require housing on a temporary basis. Such people may be in transition from their location, jobs, or relationships.

In social policy areas like unemployment, there will always be frictional unemployment, even under full employment. To reach full employment a country must address the structural or chronic issues of need (Layton, 2000). This is also the case in housing policy. The problem in Canada during the late 1990s is that the country was experiencing unparalleled economic growth and thus felt that housing was not a priority. However, a perfect storm was brewing insofar as those who have core housing need were finding themselves on the street despite the wealth that was being created. This set the condition for a crisis in housing to emerge where growth in demand was far outstripping growth in supply. The crisis occurred when the federal government was most absent from the policy area, which supports the [perception] that housing policy could not move forward without strong federal leadership. The creation of housing policy had shifted first to the provinces, and then moved to municipalities, the private sector, and various forms of community partnership through nongovernmental organisations or other civil society groups, which left the policy area in an uncoordinated morass.

Understanding this momentum is key to explaining the significance of the final phase of development. We call this phase 'reengagement'. It began in 2001 with the AHI which was introduced that year. The initiative was based on a multilateral agreement with the federal, provincial, and municipal governments on a cost-matching basis of the federal grant (CMHC, 2007). The costs can be matched by any level of government or the private sector. The federal grant can be matched in a number of ways including a grant, an ongoing stream of subsidies, or the value of in-kind donations such as land. The AHI was rolled out in two phases. The first phase began in 2001 with a federal contribution of Can\$680 million. The goal of the first phase was to create new rental housing, renovations to existing housing stock, and conversion projects that create more affordable housing. One of the major stipulations to receiving a grant under the program is that rent prices must be set at or below the median market rents in the location where they are built.

The second phase of the AHI was announced in 2003 with a federal government commitment of Can\$320 million to provide additional funding for housing targeted to low-income households in communities where there is a significant need for affordable housing. Effectively, what this meant was that affordable housing projects were not destined to be the domain of large urban municipalities. Smaller communities who could demonstrate housing need through the creation of a social housing waiting list were in line to receive a federal contribution from that sum of money. Among the priorities set out in the federal funding program was money for Aboriginals, people with disabilities, recent immigrants, and fixed-income seniors. In order to encourage the construction of these housing projects, the federal government paid for 50% of the capital costs of a housing unit up to a maximum of Can$75 000 with the goal of reducing rents to affordable levels for low-income households.

The major difference with this last stage of housing from the earlier phases where the federal government took a leadership role in housing was that the decision making as to where federal money was to be spent was largely decentralised to the provinces, municipalities, and even the private sector. In the earlier phases, in particular, the federal government wanted to control where the funding was going and concentrated it in larger urban centers. Because the central government had better policy expertise in the federal bureaucracy, the provinces simply took the view that the federal government knew what it was doing. However, in this reengagement phase the federal government had to compete with a provincial bureaucracy that was well versed in housing policy itself. The process of province building ensured that the provinces could generate their own plans about affordable housing, which has meant that the federal government may never again enjoy near complete control over the housing agenda as it did in the immediate postwar period.

The reengagement phase is consistent with developments in Canadian federalism in the late 1990s. The presence of successive federal budgetary surpluses and the accord by the federal government and the provinces on the Social Union Framework Agreement (SUFA) led to greater cooperation on social policy initiatives. Cameron and Simeon (2002) call this an era of cooperative federalism where the federal and provincial governments codetermine national policies and priorities. While national policies and priorities may have been jointly agreed to in the area of housing policy, the result was that the federal government simply offered a block grant to the provinces and let them spend the money however they pleased. The provinces used this money to support the objectives they had from the previous era, whether it was local government, nonprofit organisations, or the private sector. This meant that Canadian housing policy had a new funding partner, but the result was still a very fragmented policy implementation.

The fact that housing policy is still as fragmented as it was in the mid-1990s largely supports the idea of 'open federalism' advocated by Prime Minister Stephen Harper. Open federalism was the prime minister's way of telling the provinces, Quebec in particular, that it was going to respect jurisdictions and attach fewer strings to federal dollars so that the provinces could spend as they pleased. However, when we look at the progress made by the federal government leading up to the end of this period, we see that the number of families in need has changed very little in the last forty years (CMHC, 2008a). The federal government has taken a laissez-faire and noninterventionist approach to housing policy, trusting that the provinces and other funding partners will be able to create policies that meet their local needs. The stages of federalism explained above outline the change from centralisation to decentralisation in Canadian housing policy since 1945. They correspond to the idea that Canada has a flexible framework, one that is able to adjust to changing economic and social circumstances. However, this flexibility now appears to be limited by the very nature of the provincial governments gaining control of, and obtaining more policy sophistication in, housing as a result of province building. As we look into the AHI in more detail, the conclusion that recentralisation is difficult once subnational units gain institutional strength and policy capacity will become even more apparent, and that decentralisation will continue to mean that the major policy goals and objectives will not be met.

4 EVALUATING THE REENGAGEMENT STAGE

The AHI has led to a fragmented housing policy implementation across Canada. There is a significant degree of divergence in the kind of housing being built and for which target audiences the affordable housing is meant. Evaluation of the federal initiative after 2001 must be firstly measured against the goals established in each of the phases. The federal government has launched an evaluation of the AHI which was to be completed by the end of 2008. Despite our attempts to access the document, or to obtain information about its contents through contact with the CMHC, we are unable to analyse what the official evaluation has to say about the success and failure of the federal initiative. In the absence of that official evaluation, we have conducted our own evaluation of the AHI on the basis of the information that is available to us. In addition to whether the program is meeting its own objectives, we will also evaluate the extent to which the reengagement phase has met horizontal policy objectives. Our main interest here is to what extent has decentralisation either helped or inhibited meeting such targets.

Table 2 tabulates the number of housing projects according to urban/rural classification. Using Canadian Census data we classify communities as large urban centers when their population is greater than 700 000 inhabitants. Medium urban centers are those cities with populations of between 250 000 and 700 000 inhabitants. Small urban centers are major provincial cities and those with populations generally between 75 000 and 250 000 inhabitants. Communities with 25 000 to 75 000 residents are classified as large rural communities and those communities under 25 000 are considered small rural communities. We also classify suburban communities, which seeks to account for proximity to urban centers. We are not concerned with the population of these suburban communities because we are trying to measure the shift of emphasis in housing policy from urban cores to nontraditional areas of affordable housing construction.

The results of our analysis show that the emphasis on housing projects has shifted away from traditional urban settings. Approximately one third of housing projects are located in small, medium, and large urban centers. This trend is opposite to what occurred a half century ago. In the earlier phases of housing projects the concentration of building affordable housing units was in urban areas. This was mainly due to the federal government's insistence that housing be built in urban cores where it was most needed. Housing tends to be built where there is incentive to do so. In the absence of a centralised authority telling developers where housing should be built, the tendency is for housing projects to be located in areas where it is most cost-effective to do so. To its credit, the second phase of the AHI was designed to allocate funds to high-rent markets; however, it appears that the decentralised nature of the initiative has led to continued growth in the number of housing projects developed in smaller communities.

Another policy outcome has been the number of housing projects that have emerged in suburban cities rather than the urban core itself. Roughly 10% of AHI projects have been devoted to suburban areas. Again, the decentralised nature of housing policy is pushing projects further from urban core areas. One of the major problems with this idea is that large urban centers tend to have more of the services required by low-income individuals. A lack of social infrastructure means that people on tight budgets have to travel further to access these services or they simply do without them (Carroll, 1989). Thus, while people are able to access affordable housing in smaller communities and suburban areas, social services may not be available, particularly for seniors, which affects their quality of life.

Table 3 evaluates the target demographic for affordable housing. As mentioned above, phase two of the AHI was directed toward helping specific groups with housing such as seniors, people with disabilities, and new immigrants. The single category includes people who require hostels or accommodation for one person. Such people may be affected by mental illness or they may be youth at risk. This is distinguished from families which require housing that will accommodate two or more people. Such dwellings are targeted to low-income families, single-parent homes, and immigrant families in need of affordable housing. This table is an aggregate listing of projects assigned to each demographic category. It includes many projects

TABLE 2
Housing projects according to size of municipality

Classification	Number of projects/ classification	Percentage of total projects
Large urban	26	10.3
Medium urban	22	8.7
Small urban	38	15.1
Suburban	26	10.3
Large rural	18	7.1
Small rural	122	48.4
Total	252	100.0

that have received AHI funding which has built dwellings for more than one target demographic. This is why the total number of projects is higher than the number of projects built with AHI money.

In terms of targeting these specific groups, it appears that the AHI is disproportionately helping seniors with 126 projects devoted to them. In addition to this, many seniors' projects were located in small rural communities. Some provinces dedicated most of their housing projects to seniors and ignored other demographics. Conversely, eighty-six housing projects were built to help families who required below the local median cost of housing. Unlike seniors' projects, many projects built to help poorer families had mixed purposes as they often included space for disabled people, which had the smallest number of projects at forty five. These projects were spread between all types of urban and rural settings across the country.

While the number of projects that have been built since 2004 is a positive development, it is questionable whether other objectives in social housing have received any attention. For example, the rise of homelessness has been linked to the declining supply of mental health facilities (CIHI, 2007), yet there has not been much emphasis on boosting the supply of supportive housing. The problem here again is the horizontal nature of policies which also cross jurisdictional lines. The 'support' in supportive housing requires funding from either provincial ministries other than housing or non-governmental organisations (NGOs). The coordination and funding necessary for these did not appear to exist. Additionally, another growing segment of the homeless demographic is youth at risk. However, few projects are targeted specifically at this group. If one were exclusively evaluating the success of the AHI, the conclusion would be that the program is successful since it has built a significant number

TABLE 3
Housing projects according to target demographic

Target Demographic	Number of projects	Percentage of projects
Single (hostel)	26	24.0
Seniors	22	37.3
People with disabilities	38	13.3
Low-income families	26	25.4
Total	252	100.0

Note: Projects that had more than one target were counted more than once.

of social housing projects. Yet, a closer inspection of the projects has certainly revealed a gap in terms of supporting wider housing goals such as the reduction of homelessness. There is little evidence in the analysis of the housing projects that have been built with AHI money, which suggests an overall reduction in the number of homeless people or a core need as a result of this intergovernmental initiative. We expect that the AHI evaluation will have more to say in terms of the impact this initiative is having on the growing number of people who find themselves without a home, so this brief evaluation is by no means definitive.

In addition to the low levels of support for youth at risk, we find very little evidence which suggests that governments are helping to increase the stock of housing for new immigrants. This is something that the funding criteria were interested in promoting, but the kinds of housing built are not directed to immigrants exclusively (CMHC, 2008b). For one, the vast majority of Canadian immigration is occurring in the three largest Canadian cities of Toronto, Vancouver, and Montreal. Part of the issue is that the number of housing projects being built is spread across the country with no direct link to population and where immigrants are going. Where housing projects are being built in suburban areas of these major cities, they are more likely to be built for seniors rather than low-income households. This tends to suggest that housing for new immigrants who require some form of assistance has not been produced to the degree that the initiative desired.

On balance, what can be said about the AHI is that it is working in terms of building affordable and supportive housing for some, but not all, of its target populations. On the face of that news, the

AHI must be deemed a success even if it has not accomplished all that it hoped. What should be deemed an even greater success is that housing policy has reemerged as a field for governments to contribute money, particularly in light of the fact that the phases leading up to reengagement meant that housing policy had been vacated by the federal and provincial governments.

What this new phase of housing has also shown is that social housing is no longer considered to be a policy problem for large urban centers. This is in stark contrast to the previous phases of housing development. The number of projects that are being built in communities with fewer than 25 000 people is high, particularly when many of the visible signs of housing problems are found in larger urban areas. We sought to understand why this might be occurring across the country. One reason may be that seniors and their families are an important voting constituency. In short, it looks good to be helping seniors. Unlike other demographic groups who require social housing, seniors vote in large numbers and helping them is seen as good public relations. Furthermore, the not-in-my-backyard factor is not present for building seniors' housing. People are unlikely to oppose what is seen to be helping seniors. This same sentiment is not as present with other target groups, such as those with mental health issues or immigrants. Senior housing exists throughout the country and is not concentrated in urban areas. This has been a key motivating factor at dispersing housing projects across the country.

The second reason is that there appears to be a high degree of visibility and press received by politicians in smaller communities. In a confidential interview with a Conservative Member of Parliament (MP) from Ontario, he alluded to the fact that many funds for housing projects are easy items for which to take credit. The MP told us that he commissioned a survey in 2005 and among the questions he asked his constituents was what they thought was the MP's most important work in the riding. The result of that survey was that working on affordable housing was the most frequently cited response. This tends to suggest that local politicians are pushing affordable housing projects, and part of the reason for this is that it attracts positive press coverage. During the period of the AHI, few other big ticket public works projects were available for local politicians to take credit.

5 CONCLUSION

As a whole, the AHI demonstrates the potential of a [reemerging] federal presence in Canadian housing policy. In short, without the central government providing large sums of money to build housing, it simply would not be built. However, it also demonstrates the difficulty of producing a housing policy that meets its own objectives in terms of the goals that are set by the program and even the wider policy goals for which housing is associated. The inability of meeting all the policy goals to the same degree, such as building sufficient housing stock for all its target groups, as well as not meeting the wider policy goals of housing, can be attributed to the federal government now needing to negotiate with funding partners. In the case of the AHI, it is not even exclusively the provincial governments in Canada for which an agreement needs to be made. It is also municipalities and/or NGOs that are required to build a housing project. Logic dictates that the more parties that are involved in making a decision, consensus will become a less likely result.

Because the federal government vacated housing policy during the 1980s and 1990s, the provinces were left alone to do the job. They essentially built a bureaucracy that could manage the portfolio and compete with the federal government's expertise. Once such a bureaucratic structure is in place, it becomes too difficult to tear down. As a result, the possibility of federal government control in housing reemerging is not likely. Indeed, they will now have to compete with the provincial governments for policy space and the setting of priorities. As we have seen with the AHI, even though the federal government's program set the priorities, it was up to the individual provinces and communities that directed the money to specific target groups to meet them. The results show that, of the target groups, the number of projects devoted to seniors have disproportionately been met at the expense of building housing for other target groups.

Seniors are a key constituency for government and they are not a divisive group for which to provide funding. In many ways it is an easy decision to build affordable housing for seniors. Governments are effectively taking a path of least resistance. In addition to this, developers are also taking a path of least resistance in the sense that it is far cheaper to build in nonurban cores. As both the state and the private sector coalesce in terms of taking the easy route to building housing projects, the question of whether broader housing goals are being met lingers. It is the claim of this study that the reason why some of the broader housing goals is a result of a lack of coordination that is brought about by decentralisation.

The central government in Canada has long lost its ability to coordinate and influence housing policy. Even though it has set the goals of the program, it has left the provinces to do as they please. This means that the goals will be met only if they are shared by each of the ten provinces in Canada, which are supposed to be treated equally given the SUFA discussed in section 3. In addition to this, the SUFA contains provisions on the use of the federal spending power which constrains unilateral federal action going forward. The SUFA is not a constitutional document which could foreseeably be broken, but there are significant political costs to doing so which likely means that any future attempt to centralise social policy in Canada will face ten provincial and three territorial governments that will oppose the action.

In an area like housing, however, some of the problems require asymmetrical solutions. Not every province in Canada has a major metropolis with a population of over 1 million people. Many provinces themselves do not have populations exceeding 1 million people. It thus becomes hard to craft a federal program that focuses on housing when the need is disproportional. The underlying lesson for other countries who are debating whether or not to embark on centralisation or decentralisation is that some of the decisions that lead down a particular path are hard to undo. Province building has essentially led to provincial government growth, and this growth has effectively erected institutional barriers that make recentralisation difficult to envision. When these decisions block the ability to reach certain policy objectives on a national scale, the conclusion of this study is that one should be cautious of wholesale decentralisation.

ACKNOWLEDGEMENTS

We are grateful to Patricia Streich for providing comments on an earlier draft of this paper.We would also like to thank the journal's anonymous reviewers for their constructive comments.

REFERENCES

Banting K, 2005, "Canada — nation-building in a federal welfare state", in *Federalism and the Welfare State* Eds H Obinger, S Leibfried, and FG Castles (Cambridge University Press, Cambridge) pp 89–138

Black E, Cairns A, 1966, "A different perspective on Canadian federalism" *Canadian Public Administration* 9 27–44

Brown D, 2008, "Fiscal federalism: searching for balance", in *Canadian Federalism: Performance, Effectiveness and Legitimacy* Eds H Bakvis and G Skogstad (Oxford University Press,Toronto, ON) pp 63–88

Cameron D, Simeon R, 2002, "Intergovernmental relations in Canada: the emergence of collaborative federalism." *Publius: The Journal of Federalism* 32 49–72

Canada Health Act, 1984, C.6, s.1

Carroll B, 1989, "Postwar trends in Canadian housing policy" *Urban History Review* 64–74

Carroll B, 2002, "Housing policy in the new millennium: the uncompassionate landscape", in *Urban Policy Issues: Canadian Perspectives* Eds E Fowler, D Siegel (Oxford University Press, Toronto, ON) pp 69–89

Carroll B, Jones, R, 2000, "The road to innovation, convergence or inertia: devolution in provincial housing policy in Canada" *Canadian Public Policy* 26 277–293

Carver H, 1975 *The Compassionate Landscape* (University of Toronto Press, Toronto, ON)

Chandler M, Chandler W, 1979 *Public Policy and Provincial Politics* (McGraw-Hill Ryerson, Toronto, ON)

CIHI, 2007 *Improving the Mental Health of Canadians: Mental Health and Homelessness Canadian Institute for Health Information*, Ottawa, ON

CMHC, Canada Mortgage and Housing Corporation, Ottawa, ON
    2007 *Affordable Housing Initiative Evaluation Plan*
    2008a *Housing Affordability Trends 1981–2001: An Analysis of Selected Metropolitan Areas in Canada*
    2008b *Settling in: Newcomers in the Canadian Housing Market*, 2001–2005

Constitution Act, 1867 (UK), 30 & 31 Victoria, c.3

Courchene T, Telmer C, 1998, "From heartland to North American region states: an interpretative essay on the fiscal, social and federal evolution of Ontario", Centre for Public Management, University of Toronto, Toronto, ON

Dion S, 2003, "The interdependence of governments in Canada", in *Reforming Parliamentary Democracy* Eds D Docherty, L Seidle (McGill–Queen's University Press, Montreal–Kingston, Canada) pp 173–179

Dupré S, 1987, "The workability of executive federalism in Canada", in *Federalism and the Role of the State* Eds H Bakvis, W Chandler (University of Toronto Press, Toronto, ON) pp 236–258

Greer S, 2004 Territorial Politics and Health Policy (Manchester University Press, Manchester)

Harguindéguy J-B, Bray Z, 2009, "Does cross-border cooperation empower European regions? The case of INTERREG III-A France–Spain" *Environment and Planning C: Government and Policy* 27 747–760

Hulchanski J, Drover G, 1986, "Housing subsidies in a period of restraint: the Canadian experience, 1973–1984", Institute of Urban Studies, University of Winnipeg, ON

Jeffery C, 2007, "The unfinished business of devolution: seven open questions" *Public Policy and Administration* 22 92–108

Keating M, 1997, "The invention of regions: political restructuring and territorial government in Western Europe" *Environment and Planning C: Government and Policy* 15 383–398

Kershaw P, 2006, "Weather-vane federalism: reconsidering federal social policy leadership" Canadian Public Administration 49 196–219

Klodawsky F, Spector A, 1998, "Renovation or abandonment? Canadian social housing at a crossroads", in How Ottawa Spends 1997–98: Seeing Red Ed. G Swimmer (Carleton University Press, Ottawa, ON) pp 259–280

Layton J, 2000 *Homelessness: The Making and Unmaking of Canada's Housing Crisis* (Penguin Group, Toronto, ON)

Leslie P, Neumann R, Robinson R, 2004, "Managing Canadian fiscal federalism", in *Canada: The State of the Federation 2002: Reconsidering the Institutions of Canadian Federalism* Eds P Meekinson, H Telford, H Lazar (McGill–Queen's University Press, Montreal–Kingston, Canada) pp 214–229

McRoberts K, 2001, "Canada and the multinational state" *Canadian Journal of Political Science* 34 683–713

McRoberts K, 2004, "The future of the nation-state and Quebec-Canada retentions", in *The Fate of the Nation State* Ed. M Seymour (McGill-Queen's University Press, Montreal, QC) pp 390–402

Maioni A, Smith M, 2003, "Health care and Canadian federalism", in *New Trends in Canadian Federalism* Eds F Rocher, M Smith (Broadview Press, Peterborough, ON) pp 295–312

Miron J, 1988 *Housing in Postwar Canada: Demographic Change, Household Formation, and Housing Demand* (McGill–Queen's University Press, Montreal–Kingston, Canada)

Mishra R, 1990 *The Welfare State in Capitalist Society: Policies of Retrenchment and Maintenance in Europe, North America, and Australia* (University of Toronto Press, Toronto, ON)

Obinger H, Leibfried S, Castles F G, 2005, "Introduction: federalism and the welfare state", in *Federalism and the Welfare State* Eds H Obinger, S Leibfried, and FG Castles (Cambridge University Press, Cambridge) pp 1–50

Paddison R, 1999, "Decoding decentralisation: the marketing of urban local power" *Urban Studies* 36 107–119

Pearce G, Ayres S, 2006, "New patterns of governance in the English region: assessing their implications for spatial planning" *Environment and Planning C: Government and Policy* 24 909–927

Rodríguez-Pose A, Gill N, 2003, "The global trend towards devolution and its implications" *Environment and Planning C: Government and Policy* 21 333–351

Rodríguez-Pose A, Sandall R, 2008, "From identity to the economy: analysing the evolution of the decentralisation discourse" *Environment and Planning C: Government and Policy* 26 54–72

Rodríguez-Pose A, Tijmstra S A R, Bwire A, 2009, "Fiscal decentralisation, efficiency, and growth" *Environment and Planning A* 41 2041–2062

Robinson I, Simeon R, 2004, "The dynamics of Canadian federalism", in *Canadian Politics* Eds J Bickerton, A Gagnon (Broadview Press, Peterborough, ON) pp 101–125

Rose A, 1980 *Canadian Housing Policy 1935–1980* (Butterwork, Toronto, ON)

Shaw J, Mackinnon D, Docherty I, 2009, "Divergence or convergence? Devolution and transport policy in the United Kingdom" *Environment and Planning C: Government and Policy* 27 546–567

Simeon R, 1979, "Intergovernmental relations in Canada today: summary of discussion", in *Confrontation and Collaboration: Intergovernmental Relations in Canada Today* Ed. R Simeon (Institute of Public Administration of Canada, Toronto, ON) pp 1–12

Streich P, 1985 *Canadian Housing Affordability Policies in the 1970s: An Analysis of Federal and Provincial Government Roles* PhD Dissertation, Department of Political Studies, Queen's University, Kingston, ON

Macroeconomics

2

Demographics and Housing in Canada, 1978–1986

———————— HENRY BARTEL, WILLIAM L. MARR
& DOUGLAS J. McCREADY

Several changes in demographic structure have been underway throughout the 1980s: the aging of the population, a decline in fertility rates, smaller families, more single-parent households, more women working outside the home, changes in the source country of Canada's immigrants, and perhaps the tendency for the proportion of the population that is foreign — born to rise and a policy designed to make it rise further. These changes have been documented by other researchers (see Beaujot and McQuillan; Foot; Denton and Spencer; Dumas; Romaniac; McDaniel; Miron, 1988). Since households and individuals with different demographic characteristics are hypothesized to allocate different proportions of their total expenditure on goods and services to shelter expenditure (Marr and McCready, 1989), it is likely that the demographic changes already have and will in the future affect total shelter expenditure.

This study examines the relationship between a household's demographic characteristics and its expenditure on shelter. Assuming that differences among demographic characteristics are found, what factors or influences cause these differences? There are two possible general causes: (1) the demographic differences themselves (e.g., older heads of households have different relative shelter expenditure patterns just because they are older, all else the same), and (2) common non-demographic factors that affect spending patterns such as income, education, household's location, etc. This paper, based on a much larger study, uses micro analysis followed by regression anal-

The authors acknowledge the assistance of Canada Mortgage and Housing Corporation in doing the analysis. For those interested in the data, the complete report "Housing Expenditures: A Look at How Demographic Factors Influence Them" is available from the CMHC or by writing to Dr. McCready, Department of Economics, Wilfrid Laurier University, Waterloo, Ontario, N2L 3C5.

ysis in an attempt to separate the demographic from the non-demographic influences. It is also interesting to look at how responsive expenditures on shelter are to changes in income for different demographic groups. Hypotheses for these income elasticities with respect to permanent income will be put forth and then tested using Canadian data.

All of the data in this study come from the 1978, 1982, 1984 and 1986 Surveys of Family Expenditure by Statistics Canada. In each survey, a sample of Canadian families was asked how they allocated total consumer expenditure among a large group of household items, as well as other questions related to the household's demographic structure. For each survey, it is possible to relate various demographic variables to each household's tenure and type of living quarters as well as to the total dollar expenditure spent on shelter. The household's income before taxes is also provided so expenditure on shelter can be related to its income as well as to total spending on all goods and services. Since the 1984 Survey includes only households in cities of 100,000 or larger, for the regression analysis, the observations used from the other three surveys are also for households in cities of that size. Therefore, these Surveys are a rich source of information and enable us to link demographic characteristics to Canadian household shelter expenditure patterns at four points in time.

Marion Steele (1979) examines both the ratio of housing value or rent to income and the elasticity of housing value to household income with data from the 1971 Canadian Census. She finds that the ratio of housing value or rent to income (there are two separate ratios) rise with the degree of urbanization or the size of the city in which the household resides. Her study also indicates that these ratios rise significantly if the head of the household is 65 years or older. With respect to income elasticity, she finds that it is less than .5 in all areas and is higher in less urbanized areas; there is no clear relationship between the household head's age and the size of the income elasticities, although heads 65 or older seem to have greater elasticities than younger heads of households. The elasticities for owners are higher than for renters, and elasticities increase when permanent income replaces measured income.

John Miron (1984) employs the 1978 Survey of Family Expenditure to examine if shelter expenditure varies by household characteristics, by the size and quality of the dwelling occupied, and by location of the household. He finds little systematic variation in shelter expenditure net of owner's mortgage interest payments across different demographic groups or in different geographic locations although there is some variation in average shelter expenditure when households are disaggregated by income. Shelter costs are influenced by the quality of the dwelling and by the size of the city in which the dwelling is located.

In a later study, Miron (1988) reports some income elasticities from his 1984 study. In short, he finds low income elasticities for shelter expenditure, and concludes that there are only slight differences across demographic groups. The numerical values of income elasticity are about 0.3, although lone-parent households have significantly lower elasticities (about 0.15 or 0.16).

William Marr and Douglas McCready (1989) use the Surveys of Family Expenditure for 1978, 1982 and 1984 to study the allocations of total household expenditure among thirteen broad consumption categories for various demographic characteristics of the household; one of the 13 categories is shelter expenditure. Those in age groups 45 to 54 and 55 to 64 allocate significantly less of their total expenditure to shelter than does the group aged 35 to 44. The proportion increases again for those 65 years and older. For foreign-born heads, generally the longer they live in Canada the higher is their allocation to shelter expenditure. Households headed by females allocate a greater amount of total expenditure to shelter, while households where the spouse works outside of the household allocate less to shelter than other households. Since Marr and McCready deal with proportions, either an increase in the numerator or a decrease in the denominator contribute to this result. Unattached individuals and single parent families allocate proportionally more to shelter expenditure, and married couples with young children allocate proportionally more than couples without children or couples with older children. In a multivariate setting, using regression analysis, certain non-demographic variables are held constant, there still being differences among households in the allocation to shelter expenditure by demographic characteristics such as age, year of arrival for the foreign-born, marital status, gender of household head, and family composition.

All of these studies point to the potential benefit of studying the relationship between expenditures on shelter at the household level and the household's demographic characteristics. If these differences persist and the demographic structure of Canada continues to change, then there would be an impact on total and relative shelter expenditure, which may affect the demand for various types of living quarters.

A complex interaction of demographic and non-demographic variables influence aggregate consumption. If economic growth slows, demographic effects might become more important and, thus, greater awareness of the relationship between consumption and demographic effects is required.

One can estimate demand and consumption relationships at the household level and then form an aggregate by using demographic weights.

This study studies the consumption patterns of individual households using micro data. The micro analysis addresses the issue of different consumption allocations for different birthplace, age, family structure groups as well as for different geographic factors. These micro data can be aggregated to study the overall total consumption propensities for the same variables.

DEMOGRAPHIC CHARACTERISTICS

Shelter refers to total expenditures on principal accommodation as well as expenditures on all other accommodation. Where the Survey Unit (SU) is a combination of more than one SU at the start of the year, the expenditures are combined and consequently the same unit could have both rental and ownership expenses. The latter would also be the case where the unit moved during the year or where the unit owned a vacation property and rented its principal accommodation.

Principal accommodation refers to all expenditures made by the SU on rented living quarters and owned living quarters as well as expenditures on water, fuel, and electricity. Rented Living Quarters refers to expenditures on Rent, Tenants' Maintenance, Repairs, and Alterations, as well as Tenants' Insurance Premiums. Expenditures on Owned Living Quarters refers to the aggregate of expenditures on Maintenance, Repairs, and Replacements, Condominium Charges, Property Taxes, Homeowners' Insurance Premiums, Mortgage Interest, and Other Expenditures. Maintenance, Repairs, and Replacements includes Contract and Labour Costs as well as Materials.

Taking the absolute expenditures and dividing those dollar figures by before-tax income gives some insight into the ability of a household to pay for shelter. Housing expenditures do not exceed 30 per cent on average for any age group in any year.

The literature on income-related expenditures suggests that total spending is a proxy for permanent income which refers to an individual family's expectations of income over the long term and is really a better measure of capacity to spend since it will tend to smooth the income function somewhat. [For a discussion of this see W.L. Marr and D.J. McCready 1989a p. 24. Also, refer to Ketkar and Cho 1982; Ketkar and Ketkar 1987.]

Age

The peak expenditure on shelter costs occurs for those units in which the head of household is 30–39, except in 1986 when the 40–49 year-old household heads have a slightly higher absolute level of expenditures.

When the data are disaggregated, the dominant factor in causing higher expenditures would appear to be the costs of owned living quarters (includes expenditures on maintenance, condominium charges, property taxes, homeowners insurance premiums, and mortgage interest) for which mortgage interest makes up a significant portion.

Expenditures on shelter as a proportion of total spending were higher than the 30 per cent level for those families headed by someone over the age of 70. Institutional care costs are not included in this household expenditure survey as those in jails, hospitals, and senior citizen's homes were not surveyed.

Spending on shelter as a proportion of total spending follows a U shape as the household head ages. Here, rented living quarters follow that pattern while owned living quarters do not, to the same extent. Probably the largest single reason is the low incomes of those under 29 and over 70 relative to the other age groups.

Family Composition

Shelter expenditures are highest in proportion to total spending in aggregate for those who are unattached or who head single-parent families. For both groups, it is rented living quarters which constitute most of the spending.

When a couple has young children in the household, the proportion of spending or income allocated to shelter rises noticeably, which probably reflects moving into a house with its mortgage payments, property taxes, maintenance, etc. But as the youngest child ages, both proportions decline until, when the youngest child is 16 years old or older, both proportions are well below even the married only allocation.

Country of Birth

As a percentage of total expenditures, amongst those for whom the country of birth is known, those who were born in Britain, USA, or Northern and Western Europe spend the most on housing. Most are now middle-aged or older with the pattern of expenditures of those in the older age bracket.

For rented living quarters, it is clear that those born in Canada have a greater expenditure of this type, while for owned living quarters, those from Southern and Eastern Europe tend to have the highest expenditures. Those from Other Asia have the highest percentage of expenditures going to mortgage interest whereas those from Southern and Eastern Europe have the highest percentage of total spending going to property taxes, homeowner's insurance premiums and water, fuel, and electricity.

Year of Immigrant Arrival

There is a correlation between period of immigration and age. Those who came from Northern and Western Europe tended to come around the time of the second world war and immediately following when they were still relatively young. That was followed by a wave of immigration from Southern and Eastern Europe and more recently by Asians. The age pattern probably dominates over their country of origin.

Gender of Household Head

Except for rental quarters and rent, male-headed households spend more on housing but this is not reflected in the ratio of spending to total expenditures. The affordability problem for female-headed households appears to lie in low income, not in the amount being spent on shelter.

Region

Quebec is significantly higher than any other region when rent is compared, particularly in 1984 and 1986. On the other hand, owned living quarters take a larger proportion of total expenditures in British Columbia than is true in any of the other regions.

Atlantic Canada has consistently the lowest proportion of total spending allocated to shelter expenditure. No doubt there will be further changes when the next family expenditure survey is released, given the inflation in housing prices in the Toronto market.

Size of Municipality

There is a direct relationship between the proportion allocated to shelter and the size of the **urban** area. Households, in rural areas allocate an even lower proportion of total spending to shelter.

Income Quintiles

Income quintile does have a significant effect on the proportion of total expenditures being allocated to shelter and this is most pronounced for those family units spending on rented living quarters. For all quintiles, the proportion of total spending being allocated to housing rose after 1978, reaching a peak in 1984 (except for the highest quintile that peaked in 1982) and then declined in 1986. For the highest income quintile, the reduction by 1986 was to below the proportion spent in 1978.

Level of Education
Shelter expenditures on the whole are highest, as a proportion of spending, for those with the lowest levels of education, suggesting that the problem is not housing prices but income level.

Tenure
Those renting their housing spend considerably more as a percentage of their total spending than do those who own their own homes. Consistently, the amount spent as a proportion of total spending for those who have a mortgage is higher than for those who have no mortgage.

In absolute expenditures, the highest expenditures tend to be on housing that is owned with a mortgage. Regular tenants pay more in absolute dollars than those who own homes without a mortgage.

Those who are regular tenants spend more than other tenures in their senior years, whereas those with mortgages spend more than other tenures in their younger years (i.e. under age 29).

Those in the lowest income quintile spend a higher proportion of total spending on housing, regardless of tenure. There is a striking 43.7 percent of total spending devoted to housing by those in the lowest income quintile with mortgages.

Living Quarters
Apartment dwelling costs more as a percentage of total expenditures than does living in single family housing and that is consistent. Of course, it may not be that living in an apartment costs so much as the fact that those who live in apartments may have lower total expenditures, thus increasing the ratio.

At age 30–39, the proportion spent on shelter in 1984 was 19.6 percent if the shelter was single detached but 20.3 percent if an apartment — a difference of 0.7 percent. At 50–59 the difference is 11.6 percent and at over age 69 it is at 11.3 percent.

Living Quarters and Tenure
For those in single detached housing, regular tenants spent the highest proportion of their total spending dollar on shelter. Similarly, those who owned an apartment, whether with or without a mortgage

spent less as a proportion of total expenditures than did those who were regular tenants.

These figures are of interest since the costs associated with the housing would be similar if not lower for renters (it could be argued that condominiums cost more than most rented apartments). The ratio turns out to be higher for the regular tenants than for owners, suggesting that the problem is in the denominator — that is, people with lower permanent incomes (lower total expenditures) tend towards being regular tenants.

Other Variables

As a proportion of total spending, units with a fewer number of bedrooms cost more than those with a large number of bedrooms. This was particularly true for rented living quarters. Spending on owned living quarters increased as a proportion of total spending as the number of bedrooms increased, as did property taxes and mortgage interest.

The highest proportion of total spending was on units with one bathroom. Property taxes do rise as a proportion of total spending, the more bathrooms there are in the dwelling place.

The greatest amount as a proportion of total expenditures appears to be spent on units with two or three rooms. These would likely be rather small apartments occupied by young singles or the elderly. For owned living quarters, spending on shelter represented a larger percentage of total expenditures when the size of the units increased, although the pattern varied depending on the survey year.

Almost invariably, the buildings which were most recently constructed represented a larger proportion of total spending, but the oldest units also represented high levels of spending as a proportion of total expenditures.

ANALYSIS

The analysis is carried out for four dependent variables:

1. weighted ordinary least squares regressions to explain the variance of the proportion of total consumption allocated to shelter,

2. weighted ordinary least squares regressions to explain the variance of the proportion of total household income before taxes allocated to shelter,

3. probit regressions to explain the probability of being a homeowner versus a tenant, and

4. weighted ordinary least squares regressions to calculate the elasticity of shelter expenditure with respect to household income before taxes for all households as well as for sub-groups of the sample.

Each of the binary independent variables has to have an omitted attribute in the econometric analysis, and they are: Geographic Location — Ontario; Education — Nine or Less Years of Education; Mother Tongue — English; Sex of Head — Male; Birthplace and Arrival Time — Canadian-Born; Head's Marital Status — Single or Married; Family Composition — Married Couple Only; Head's Age — 40 to 49; Living Quarters — Single House; Working Status of Spouse — Not Working; Homeowner with Mortgage — All Other Tenure Attributes.

The theory of consumer behaviour argues that a major determinant of the proportion of total consumption allocated to shelter is some measure of the household's income. Milton Friedman (1957) argues that consumption is more closely related to the household's permanent or long-term income level than to its actual income in any particular year; this should be especially true of the proportion allocated to shelter. In a study of household-level consumer spending in the United States, Houthakker and Taylor (1970) found that total household expenditure was a better proxy of permanent income than was actual income. Recent U.S. and Canadian studies of family expenditures, which attempt to relate consumption to demographic factors, use total current expenditure rather than income as the explanatory variable (Ketker and Cho, 1982; Ketker and Ketker, 1987; Marr and McCready, 1989). Therefore, the independent variable used here as a proxy for permanent income is the household's total current expenditure.

PROPORTION OF TOTAL CONSUMPTION
ALLOCATED TO SHELTER EXPENDITURE

We want to explain variations in the proportion of this total consumption devoted to shelter expenditures in terms of the four groups of independent variables.

There are some consistencies in the regression results across the four surveys.[1] Some independent variables consistently influenced the proportion of total consumption allocated to shelter expenditure. The

---

[1] Regression results are available from Dr. McCready, Department of Economics, Wilfrid Laurier University, Waterloo, Ontario N2L 3C5.

consistencies are listed according to the four groups of explanatory variables:

Demographic Characteristics of the Household or Its Head

1. larger sized households (Household Size) allocate significantly less than smaller households to shelter expenditure; in the jargon of economists, there are economies of scale in housing since a married couple can often live in the same accommodation as a single person, and children can double up in bedrooms that were previously occupied by a single individual;

2. households headed by females (Female Head) allocate significantly more to shelter expenditure than male-headed households; female-headed households have on average lower income and total consumption levels, but require a certain level of accommodation with a certain minimum expenditure on shelter; female-headed households must reallocate their total consumption away from other consumer goods and services and towards shelter expenditure;

3. the foreign-born generally allocate more of their total consumption to shelter than the Canadian-born, although the statistical significance varies from survey to survey; in particular, households whose head was born in the "Rest of the World" allocate significantly more to shelter expenditure;

4. in two of the surveys, the most recent arrivals (for foreign-born heads) allocate less to shelter expenditure than households headed by Canadian-born or other foreign-born who came to Canada earlier; this is unexpected since the recent foreign-born require accommodation upon arrival; but two factors are at work: first they occupy relatively cheaper living quarters upon arrival, and second the birthplace variable is picking up some of this effect;

5. households headed by a person who is divorced, separated, or widowed allocate more of total consumption to shelter expenditure than other marital statuses; when this is combined with the fact that many in this group are female and older, the divorced-separated-widowed group who are also female and older allocate relatively high proportions of total consumption to shelter and of course less to other goods and services;

6. as the ratio of children to adults rises (adults are defined in the surveys as persons 16 years and older), the allocation to shelter expenditure also rises;

7. although in the two most recent surveys married couples only and unattached individuals allocate the same proportion of total consumption to shelter, unattached individuals devoted a significantly higher proportion to shelter in the two earliest surveys; married couples with young children allocate more to shelter expenditure than married couples only, but the opposite is the case for couples with older children; households headed by a lone-parent allocate less of total consumption to shelter expenditure than any other family composition category;

8. the relationship between the head's age and the allocation to shelter expenditure is cubic: households with heads in their 20s allocate less to shelter than households with heads in their 30s or 40s, the allocation is lower again for households with heads in their 50s and 60s, and finally rises significantly for households with heads 70 years or older; this points out the fact that there are important reallocations of total consumption as the household ages.

Non-Demographic Characteristics of the Household or Its Head

1. there is a significant inverse relationship between the household's total expenditure (one measure of permanent income) and the allocation of total consumption to shelter expenditure;

2. households headed by a person with a French mother tongue allocate significantly less of total consumption to shelter expenditure than those with an English mother tongue.

Housing Characteristics

1. in most cases, households living in semi-detached, row, duplex, and apartment accommodation allocate more to shelter expenditure than households in single houses, the control group; this is interesting in view of the fact that most Canadian households still aspire to live in a single house;

2. as expected, having a mortgage significantly raises the proportion of total consumption allocated to shelter expenditure.

Given that these are four cross-sectional sets of data, this large number of regularities or consistencies is remarkable since there is always a high probability that random occurrences will influence a household's characteristics at the time of any one survey.

Although lone-parent families have relatively high proportions of total consumption allocated to shelter, the lone-parent characteristic, holding all else the same, actually lowers this proportion. Clearly lone-parents have other characteristics that tend to raise the proportion of total consumption allocated to shelter. In terms of the regression results, small households, households headed by females, households headed by someone who is divorced/separated/widowed, households with high ratios of children to adults, and households with low levels of total expenditure (i.e. low permanent incomes) tend to allocate higher proportions of total consumption to shelter; these are all characteristics of lone-parent families and influenced the single-variable analysis.

Another situation that is similar arises in the case of unattached individuals and married couples only. Unattached individuals tend to have characteristics that are positively related to the proportion of total consumption allocated to shelter, which, when controlled, eliminate the family composition effect in some regressions.

When the other independent variables are held constant or controlled, geographical location does not generally matter. Second, with respect to head's educational level, only one effect appears consistently: households in which the head has a university degree allocate more of total consumption to shelter expenditure than do all other educational groups.

There are some changes across the four years as one moves from 1978 to 1986:

1. the influence of geographic location seems to decline, and especially the differences between Quebec and the Prairies, and Ontario; this implies that (a) the other explanatory variables account for more of the differences over the years and (b) differences in the proportion of total consumption allocated to shelter expenditure that are due just to location become less important in the 1980s; these may reflect a more uniform pattern across Canada both with respect to the other explanatory variables and the housing market;

2. the influence of the head's level of education declines over time (with the possible exception of heads with university degrees, but even here the size of the regression coefficient falls);

3. the effect that household size has on lowering the allocation to shelter expenditure is about the same in 1978 and 1986, but lower in 1982 and 1984;

4. the same but opposite is true for the head's sex: greater influence on raising the allocation in the middle two years and a lower effect at the extreme years;

5. households with heads born in the rest of the world (mainly from so-called third world countries) are increasing their allocations to shelter expenditure over time when compared to the Canadian-born headed households;

6. recent arrivals to Canada allocate less and less to shelter expenditure, which could reflect the rising price of shelter;

7. for the last three surveys, the influence of being a lone-parent family is declining, although the influence on the allocation of total consumption to shelter expenditure is about the same in 1986 as in 1978;

8. still with family composition, the difference between unattached individuals and married couples only (the control group) disappears; this may reflect changes in life styles and in the composition of these two categories with people living longer and having fewer children;

9. the difference between households whose head's age is in the 20s and whose head's age is in the 40s widens, while the difference between those in their 30s and those in their 40s disappears;

10. although households with heads in their 70s or above always allocate significantly more of total consumption to shelter expenditure than other ages, the difference narrows as indicated by the general decline in the size of the coefficients;

11. a rise in total expenditure (one proxy for permanent income) of, say, $1 has a greater digressing influence on the proportion of total consumption allocated to shelter expenditure in 1984 and 1986 than in the two earliest years; if we can speak of an allocation gap between the poor and the rich as income rises, then this gap is widening.

THE ELASTICITY OF SHELTER EXPENDITURE WITH RESPECT TO TOTAL EXPENDITURE

How responsive is a household's shelter expenditure to changes in total expenditure? For a one percent change in income (as measured by a household's total expenditure), what is the percentage change in shelter expenditure, all else the same? To calculate this elasticity, regressions are run with the log of shelter expenditure as the dependent variable and the log of total expenditure as one of the explanatory variables. The coefficient on the log of total expenditure is the estimate of the elasticity; the same set of other independent variables are used in this regression as in the previous analyses. Only the absolute value of this coefficient is used, and it can take three generic values:

1. **Greater than One:** Elastic: percentage change in shelter expenditure exceeds the percentage change in total expenditure,

2. Less than One but Greater than Zero: Inelastic: percentage change in shelter expenditure is less than the percentage change in total expenditure,

3. **Equal to One:** Unit Elastic: percentage change in shelter expenditure equals the percentage change in total expenditure.

Ordinary least squares regressions are calculated for only the 1986 data set. Separate regressions are run for each of the groups examined the coefficients on the log of total expenditure are recorded in Table 1, and all are significant at the .05 level or better.

TABLE 1
Elasticities for some sub-groups, 1986

Income Group		Geographical Location	
15,600	1.207	Atlantic	.490
15,600–27,309	.389	Quebec	.485
27,310–40,122	.444	Ontario	.641
40,123–56,005	.478	Prairies	.531
56,005	.668	British Columbia	.540

Family Composition		Age Groups	
Unattached Individuals	.579	30	.441
Married Couples Only	.491	30–39	.565
Married Couple with Children	.689	40–49	.597
Lone-Parent Families	.751	50–59	.413
		60–69	.662
		69	.669

Birthplace and Arrival Year		Head's Sex	
Canadian-Born	.542	Females	.719
Foreign-Born	.649	Males	.480
Recent Foreign-Born	.520		

All the hypotheses are supported by the results:

1. the income elasticity of the foreign-born (.649) is higher than for the Canadian-born (.542),
2. the income elasticity for recent foreign-born (.520) is lower than for all foreign-born (.649),
3. the income elasticity is higher for the two oldest age groups (.662 and .669) than for younger age groups,
4. the income elasticity for female headed households (.719) is higher than for male headed households (.480),
5. the income elasticity for lone-parents (.751) is higher than for all other family composition groups,
6. the income elasticity for married couples with children (.689) is higher than for married couples only (.491),
7. the income elasticity for unattached individuals (.579) is higher than for married couples only (.491),
8. the income elasticity for the lowest income quintile (1.207) is higher than for any other income quintile, and
9. the income elasticity rises from the second income quintile to the fifth income quintile.

Of course all of these elasticities are the net result of several influences. However, the hypotheses are generally supported.

The 30 Percent Figure

Note that there are very few instances when families are devoting more than 30 percent of their total spending to shelter (broadly defined). To list them, we would have to include those who fit into the following categories:

(i)   over 70 years of age in 1982, 1984, and 1986.
(ii) lowest quintile at every age in 1984.
(iii) lowest quintile, 30–39 and over 70 in 1986.
(iv) lowest quintile, over 70 in 1982.
(v)   unattached individuals in 1982 and 1984.
(vi) families in which neither spouse was working in 1984.
(vii) immigrants who arrived in 1971–75 in 1984 and 1983–86 in 1986.

Is there a problem or are there some general ameliorating factors involved?

Those who are over age 70 may, for example, often have wealth but not current income, which may make their spending less of a problem then might at first be thought. Also, in some other work which the authors have done, it was this group which saved the most, indicating that their other spending was lower. Since it is hard to reduce shelter expenditures, the proportion devoted to shelter is higher.

On the other hand, the evidence that female-headed households experienced spending of greater than 30 percent of before-tax income may be of much greater concern. Since spending on housing is not 30 percent of total spending, this group spends in total less than 100 percent of income. The proportion of households that are female-headed is increasing over time, and the fact that many of these individuals have children in the home and have very little in the way of traditional support systems means that social policy must look further at this group of households. There is some suggestion that wage equity will reduce the problem, but it may take more than that since included in these households are elderly widows, and those without job skills, and those who choose not to be connected to the labour market because of age or children. Thus, pensions for spouses (including the Canada Pension Plan) and job training may be an indirect part of housing policy in that one can either deal with the denominator, i.e., the income level of the household head, or one can deal with the numerator, i.e., the amount spent on housing.

Some of the same considerations may also be present for unattached individuals. In fact, elderly widows would be in both groups. However, amongst unattached individuals, we also have some single young people who are on their first job or attending school/college/university. For them, some housing (perhaps too little) has been provided at universities but not a great deal has been done at community colleges. In any case, the policy choice may be to provide more institutional housing in connection with educational institutions.

The other group that spends more than 30 percent of total spending on housing are the lowest income quintile households in Canada. This became more or a problem in the 1980s than it had been in 1978, reaching a peak in 1984. It remains a problem for two different age groups in 1986. It would appear that the problem is again not as serious for the older age group although single widowed females may have a place in policy setting. The real problem is when there are households (such as the 30–39 year olds in 1986) who cannot afford adequate housing. By the time the household head is 30, the family ought to be past its period of lowest income and be able to afford to spend on housing. The fact that this group spent more than 30 percent on shelter in 1986 suggests that they were heavily mortgaged and down to one income (in the case where families have one spouse stay home in order to raise children when the children are young) or it may indicate a problem with having enough affordable housing. More research is needed on this group of families to see if there are clear indications as to the reasons for their high spending on shelter, relative to total spending.

Shifts in Expenditures on Shelter as Demographics Change

Thomas Espanshade (1978) concluded that a fall in the United States population that was under the age of 15 would increase per capita expenditure on durables. Espanshade finds that a transition to an older population with fewer persons per household decreases average housing expenditures per capita by about 2 percent. Richard Parks and Anton Barten (1973), using data from 14 O.E.C.D. countries, found the same quantitative changes in durable spending if the age shifts from the 0–9 age group towards the 20–64 age group or if the 1–19 age group shifts towards the 65+ age group. Parks and Barten found in their study that a shift to an older population leads to a decline in per capita shelter cost. Marr and McCready (1989) found that a one percent shift out of ages 0–14 or 15–24 towards ages 65+ would reduce real per capita expenditure on shelter by $24.57 and $33.39 respectively. Also, if there were a one percent shift in the population aged 25–64 to ages 65+, there would be a real per capita drop in spending on shelter of $30.04.

In other words, as the population grows older, there can be an expectation that per capita expenditure on shelter will decrease but that as a proportion of total spending, it will become a more significant item in the budget. It will be many years before Canada experiences a shift from the 24–64 age group towards the 65+ age group. While the number of people aged 65+ continues to increase at an increasing rate, it will not be until sometime after 2011 that the proportion of the population aged 25–64 decreases while the proportion over 65 increases. In the meantime, the shift is from the younger age groups to both the 25–64 and 65+ age groups.

Shifts in Shelter Expenditures as Incomes Change

We can see that for the lowest income quintile, the income elasticity of shelter expenditures is greater than one indicating that a one percent rise in income leads to more than a one percent rise in housing expenditure. For all other income quintiles, the income elasticity is positive, but less than one, suggesting a rise in income leads to a rise in housing expenditure but a smaller percentage than the rise in income.

The groups which are spending large amounts on housing already as a proportion of total spending, the one-parent families, female-headed families, and those aged 70+ all have relatively high income elasticities of demand which suggests that they would spend heavily on more housing if they had higher incomes. Similarly, married couples with children would also put an increase in income into more housing expenditure if given the opportunity.

THE SIGNIFICANT FACTORS IN THE REGRESSIONS

Tables 2 and 3 rank the most important explanatory variables for the proportion of total consumption allocated to shelter and for the proportion of total household income before taxes devoted to shelter. Total expenditure of the household, and the presence of mortgage payments are the two most important determinants. But for the purpose of the present study, it is interesting that several of the demographic variables appear consistently in these lists. This attests again to the study's central finding: demographic structure had and will have an important influence on households' allocations of total spending or of income to shelter expenditures.

A few of the demographic variables demonstrate noticeable patterns across the four years as to their ranking for the proportion of household income before taxes allocated to shelter expenditure. The child to adult ratio and a divorced/separated head of household decline in the rankings, while living in an apartment and female headship rise in the rankings. The latter group is a vulnerable popu-

TABLE 2

Most important determinants of the proportion of household income allocated to shelter expenditure

1978	1982	1984	1986
Total Expenditure	Total Expenditure	Total Expenditure	Total Expenditure
Mortgage Payment	Mortgage Payment	Mortgage Payment	Mortgage Payment
Child/Adult Ratio	Child/Adult Ratio	Apartment	Apartment
Divorced/Separated	Divorced/Separated	Child/Adult Ratio	Female Head
Household Size	Age $\leq$ 29	Female Head	Household Size
Age $\leq$ 9	Other Living	Divorced/Separated	Other Living
Apartment	Female Head	Post-Sec Certificate	Child/Adult Ratio
Other Living	Apartment	Duplex	Divorced/Separated
Age $\leq$ 0	B.C.	B.C.	Row House

TABLE 3
Most important determinants of total consumption allocated to shelter expenditure

1978	1982	1984	1986
Total Expenditure	Total Expenditure	Total Expenditure	Total Expenditure
Mortgage Payment	Mortgage Payment	Mortgage Payment	Mortgage Payment
Household Size	University Degree	Apartment	Household Size
Child/Adult Ratio	Other Living	Household Size	Apartment
Other Living	Household Size	Other Living	Child/Adult Ratio
University Degree	Age $\geq$ 70	University Degree	Other Living
Age $\geq$ 70	Child-Adult Ratio	Child/Adult Ratio	University Degree
Unattached Indiv.	Female Head	Female Head	Age $\geq$ 70
Post-Sec. Certificate	Lone-Parent	Divorced/Separated	Divorced/Separated
Some Post-Sec.	B.C.	Duplex	Row House

lation that is having to allocate increasingly greater proportions of household income to shelter over time, an income that in many instances is relatively low.

CONCLUSION

In this study, there are many possibilities for developing tables since the data set is extremely rich. Our purpose has been to examine the relationship between demographic factors and housing expenditures. We conclude by reiterating that the Canadian population is expected to age, more immigration is likely, and more single-parent families are likely to exist. Smaller families, more families with a female head, and more families in which both spouses work are also expected.

As we have seen, the elderly spend a greater portion of income (current or permanent) on housing and the change towards more in this age group will mean a larger portion of societal income going towards housing. Also, female-headed households spend more on housing as do families in which both spouses work.

Smaller families, with a lower child/adult ratio, imply lower spending. Immigration does not lead to significant variance in spending on housing although in the first years in Canada, there is a significant increase in spending as a proportion of income, although this does appear to be significant in our regression results.

BIBLIOGRAPHY

Beaujot, R. and K. McQuillan. *Growth and Dualism*. Toronto: Gage, 1982.

Denton, F.T. and B.G. Spencer. "Population Change and the Canadian Economy: A Survey of the Issues." Ottawa: The Institute for Research on Public Policy, 1987.

Dumas, J. *Report on the Demographic Situation in Canada 1986*. Ottawa: Statistics Canada, 1987.

Espanshade, T.L. "How a Trend Toward a Stationary Population Affects Consumer Demand." *Population Studies* (1978), 147–158.

Foot, D.K. *Canada's Population Outlook*. Toronto: James Lorimer, 1982.

Friedman, M. *A Theory of the Consumption Function*. Princeton: Princeton University Press, 1957.

Ketker, K.W. and S.L. Ketkar. "Socio-Demographic Dynamics and Household Demand." *Eastern Economic Journal* (1987), 55–62.

Ketkar, S.L. and W. Cho. "Demographic Factors and the Pattern of Household Expenditures in the United States." *Atlantic Economic Journal* (1982), 16–27.

Houthakker, H.S. and C.D. Taylor. *Consumer Demand in the United States: Analyses and Projections*. Cambridge: Harvard University Press, 1970.

MacMillar, A. and B. Pazderka. *Microeconomics: The Canadian Context* (3rd edition). Scarborough: Prentice-Hall, 1989.

Marr, W.L. and D.J. McCready. *The Effects of Demographic Structure on Expenditure Patterns in Canada*. Ottawa: Institute for Research on Public Policy, Discussion Paper, 1989a.

Marr, W.L. and D.J. McCready. "Aging of the Population and Spending Patterns in Canada: 1984 and 1986." Paper presented at the Meeting of the Southern Economics Association, 1989b.

McDaniel, S. *Canada's Aging Population*. Toronto: Butterworth's, 1986.

Miron, J. *Housing Affordability and Willingness to Pay*. University of Toronto, Toronto: Centre for Urban and Community Studies, 1984.

Miron, J. *Housing in Postwar Canada*. Montreal, McGill-Queen's University Press, 1988.

Parks, R.W. and A.P. Barten. "A Cross-Country Comparison of the Effects of Prices, Income and Population Composition on Consumption Patterns." *Economic Journal* (1973), 834–852.

Romaniac, A. *Fertility in Canada: From Baby-boom to Baby-bust*. Ottawa: Statistics Canada, 1984.

Steele, M. *The Demand for Housing in Canada*. Ottawa: Statistics Canada, 1979.

APPENDIX

The Variables

Since the Survey of Family Expenditure for 1984 only contains observations for households living in cities of 100,000 people or more, the data used in this section utilizes only observations from these largest cities. The explanatory variables are classified into four groups, and their names and corresponding attributes are as follows:

1. Geographic Location:
    (a) Region of Residence: Atlantic Provinces
        Quebec
        Ontario
        Prairie Provinces
        British Columbia

2. Demographic Characteristics of the Household or its Head:
    (a) Number of Persons in the Household (a continuous variable)
    (b) Sex of the Head: Male
        Female
    (c) Head's Birthplace: Canada
        U.S.
        Southern or Eastern Europe
        Rest of the World
    (d) Head's Time of Arrival in Canada if Foreign-Born
        Within Six Years of Arrival (Recent)
        Between Six and Eighteen Years of Arrival (Mid)
        Prior to Eighteen Years (Distant)
    (e) Head's Marital Status: Married (or living common-law)
        Single (Never Married)
        Other
    (f) Ratio of Children to Adults in the Household (a continuous variable)
    (g) Family Composition:
        Unattached Individuals
        Married Couple Only
        Married Couple Only with Youngest Child under 5
        Married Couple Only with Youngest Child 5–15
        Married Couple Only with Youngest Child 16 or Over
        Married Couple with Other Relatives Only or
            with Unrelated Persons
        Lone-Parent Family Only
        Other Spending Unit

   (h) Head's Age: Less than 30
                           30–39
                           40–49
                           50–59
                           60–69
                           Greater than 69

   (i) Spouse Working, if Present: Yes
                                          NO

3. Non-Demographic Characteristics of the Household or its Head:
   (a) Head's Educational Level:
   Less than 9 Years of Elementary Education
   Some or Completed Secondary Education
   Some Post-Secondary Education
   Post-Secondary Certificate or Diploma
   University Degree
   Not Stated
   (b) Head's Mother Tongue: English
                                      French
                                      Other
   (c) Household's Total Expenditure on Consumer Goods and Services (a continuous variable)

4. Housing Characteristics:
   (a) Type of Living Quarters: Single House
                                      Semi-Detached or
                                           Double House
                                      Row House
                                      Duplex
                                      Apartment
                                      Other (including rooms)
   (b) Class of Tenure: Homeowner without Mortgage
                                 Homeowner with Mortgage
                                 Tenants — Regular
                                 Tenants — Roomers and Rent-Free
                                 Mixed Tenure

Will the US Sub-prime Crisis Head North?

————————————————————————————— JOHN T. GLEN

INTRODUCTION

I believe that there will be a spill over of the US sub-prime crisis into Canada in terms of a reduction of real estate transactions, prices and building activity. To support this forecast, this article compares residential and investment property markets in both countries. After a brief overview of the history of sub-prime lending in the US and the key reasons for the current lending crisis, US and Canadian residential lending practices are compared to see whether the conditions which lead to the US sub-prime crisis also exist in Canada, and then, through the vehicle of debt securitization, it is demonstrated how mortgage backed securities have spread the problem to other parts of the credit markets.

SUB-PRIME GLOSSARY

Definitions

Prime, non-prime and sub-prime are terms relating to a borrower's credit rating. FICO[1] credit rating scores can vary from 300 to 850. TransUnion credit scores vary from 300 to 900.[2]

Prime borrower

A borrower with a very good credit rating and one capable of providing at least a 20%–25% down payment.

"Will the U.S. sub-prime crisis head north?" *Canadian Property Valuation*, John T. Glenn, 52(4), 2008, 18-24, F1-F6. Reprinted with permission of author and Appraisal Institute of Canada.

Sub-prime borrower

This term has come to describe borrowers with fair to poor credit ratings who would not normally qualify for a conventional mortgage requiring a 20% down payment and a credit rating. Some lenders required no documentation of a borrower's income.

Sub-prime borrowers are generally defined as individuals with limited income or having FICO credit scores below 620 on a scale that ranges from 300 to 850.

Sub-prime mortgages

Sub-prime mortgage loans are riskier loans in that they are made to borrowers unable to qualify under traditional, more stringent criteria due to a limited or blemished credit history. Sub-prime mortgage loans have a much higher rate of default than prime mortgage loans and are priced based on the risk assumed by the lender.

SUB-PRIME CRISIS

Beginning in late 2006, the US sub-prime mortgage industry entered what many observers have begun to refer to as a meltdown. A steep rise in the rate of sub-prime mortgage foreclosures has caused more than two dozen sub-prime mortgage lenders to fail or file for bankruptcy. The failure of these companies has caused prices in the $6.5 trillion mortgage-backed securities market to collapse, threatening broader impacts on the US housing market and economy as a whole. The crisis is ongoing and has received considerable attention from the US media and from lawmakers during 2007 and 2008.

Sub-prime statistics[3]

Canada
• Only 5% of borrowers are sub-prime.

United States
• Over 20% of borrowers are sub-prime.

Default rates

Canada[4]
• Overall default rates are less then 0.5%

United States
Early indications from the Mortgage Brokers Association show that US default rates vary based on whether the mortgage has a fixed or variable rate.

In July 2008, the Commercial Mortgage Securities Association compared delinquencies for US prime residential, sub-prime residential and commercial mortgage bonds to July 2008. (See Figure 1)

RESIDENTIAL MARKETS

One measure of the performance of the residential market is housing starts. The second measure is prices of new house and resale homes.

Housing starts

For 2008, Canada Mortgage and Housing Corporation (CMHC) forecast single-family housing starts to decline in all provinces except Newfoundland, Manitoba and Saskatchewan. For 2009, only Newfoundland, Quebec and Manitoba will be exempted from forecast single-family housing start declines.

Meanwhile, for multi-family housing starts for 2008, CMHC forecast multi-family housing (mostly condominiums) starts to decline in all provinces except Quebec, Ontario and Saskatchewan. For 2009, only PEI and Manitoba will be exempted from forecast declines in multi-family housing starts.

Housing prices

According to CMHC forecasts of provincial residential resale activity and prices, total residential resale activity is expected to decline in all provinces except Saskatchewan, while average residential resale price increases will moderate. Only in Newfoundland and Manitoba are prices expected to increase from 2007 to 2008. Alberta's average house prices are expected to increase from 3.6% in 2008 to 5.1% in 2009.

CMHC's publication *Housing Outlook Canada Edition Second Quarter 2008* details housing price forecasts for individual local markets as well.

Housing starts

Five cities stand out in terms of defying the overall trend to fewer housing starts in 2008 compared to 2007 — Regina, Toronto, Ottawa, Montreal and St John's. In Regina, the increase in housing starts is attributable to expected increases in starts of single-family detached homes. In the other four cities, multi-family starts will offset declines in single-family detached homes starts.

FIGURE 1
Securitized Mortgages: Residential vs Commercial Default Rates

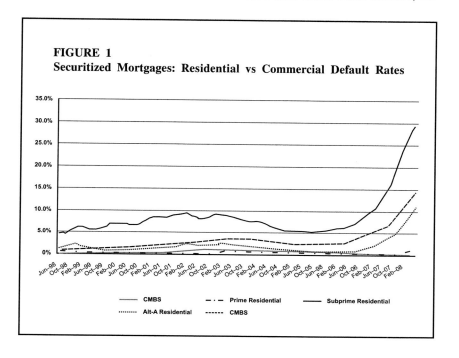

House prices

Prices will increase in all markets from 2007 to 2008 and 2008 to 2009, except for Calgary, which is expected to experience price stability.

Residential mortgage markets

On July 9, 2008, the federal government announced that CMHC would no longer insure 40-year mortgages with zero down payments. Quoting the July 11, 2008 *Toronto Star* article 'Ottawa tightens mortgage rules:'[5]

> Concerned about the "risk of a U.S.-style housing bubble developing in Canada," the federal government has tightened rules on government-backed mortgages, including limiting the use of popular, but controversial 40-year amortizations.
>
> Longer-term rates of up to 35 years will still be allowed under new rules released yesterday, which are seen as a pre-emptive move to quell the kind of housing implosion in the United States not seen since the Great Depression.
>
> "They are obviously quite concerned about what is happening in the United States, and the spillover into Canada," said Jim Murphy, CEO of the Canadian Association of Accredited Mortgage Professionals. "The government is looking at their risk tolerance and the impact on Canadians."

Murphy said 37% of all new Canadian mortgages taken from the one-year period ending in the fall of 2007 were longer than the standard 25-year amortization period.

"Longer-term mortgages have been extremely popular with Canadians," said Murphy.

The new rules, which take effect October 15, would also require a minimum down payment of 5% on new government-backed mortgages and also call for 'consistent' minimum credit-score requirements and loan-documentation standards. Under current rules, it is possible to take out a 40-year mortgage, which has been available on the market for less than two years, with zero down payment.

The regulations will apply to federal agencies such as the Canada Mortgage and Housing Corp., which has an estimated 60% share of the mortgage insurance market.

However, private-sector mortgage insurance rivals such as Genworth Financial, PMI Mortgage Insurance Co. Canada and AIG United Guaranty are free to offer the product.

One difference is that the federal government will no longer provide insurance that protects lenders in the event of a default by the insurers.

The new regulations mean potentially higher sales and prices in the near-term as "buyers jump into the market before they are enforced," said TD Bank deputy chief economist Craig Alexander. "Then, the new rules will likely contribute to the cooling of the housing market."

Interestingly, the Government of Canada action coincides with continuing instability in US Residential Secondary Mortgage Bond (RMBS) markets, with two government backed agencies Fannie Mae and Freddie Mac, which securitize the bulk of US residential mortgage loans through residential mortgage bond securities (RMBSs). In the US, banks are making fewer loans, and on tighter terms, while the securitization market is gone that formerly funded large loans, sub-prime loans and others.

Fannie and Freddie now fund eight out of every 10 loans in the US below the $417,000 level, according to regulatory data. By March 2008, Fannie and Freddie accounted for 97.6% of the mortgage bond market, compared with less than 50% in the first quarter of 2007, according to UBS.[6]

On July 13, 2008, the US Treasury and Federal Reserve took wide-ranging steps to boost Fannie Mae and Freddie Mac. Steps included a line of credit of $2.5 billion US and the Federal Reserve authorized borrowing from the discount window as necessary.[7]

The secondary mortgage market[8] is the arena in which previously originated mortgage loans are bought and sold. It is critically important to the real estate industry as we know it today; not only do mortgage loan resales provide liquidity, but the requirements for marketability also strongly influence the types of loans lenders choose to originate.

In his July 12, 2008 article, 'Good timing: Feds avoid Fannie-style mortgage freefall,' Boyd Erman of the *Globe and Mail* stated that "the changes unveiled by Ottawa this week should help to avoid any danger of a similar, costly debacle in this country.

"The proof is in the performance of bonds issued by Canada Housing Trust, which plays the same role in this country as Fannie and Freddie do down south. Canada Housing Trust is the biggest issuer (besides governments) of bonds in the country and the backbone of Canada's mortgage market.

"The trust's Canada mortgage bonds are holding up fine. The spread between the interest rate on a CMB and a similar Canadian government bond has widened over the past year, thanks to the credit crunch. Yet, in the past month, as the outlook has become dire for Freddie and Fannie, the Canadian situation has been boring. Boring is good. Boring means Canada Housing Trust is able to continue selling bonds and buying mortgages.

"The mortgages behind RMBS in Canada are generally pretty good, i.e., they are insured and have bigger down payments and shorter amortizations than in the US. Also, because mortgage interest is not tax deductible in Canada, we tend to pay down home loans faster, adding to equity and credit quality.

"Until this week, the government was in danger of letting the Canada Mortgage Trust walk into the same trap as Fannie and Freddie, by allowing banks to dilute the quality of Canadian RMBS with more and more dodgy home loans."[9]

By October 2008, further uncertainty led to a decision by the Government of Canada to try to unfreeze credit, by arranging for a program to buy residential mortgages from lending institutions.

CMHC plans to buy up to $7-billion of mortgages from Canadian lenders on October 23. That will be the second wave of purchases under the government's new $25-billion program, designed to help banks and other lenders with financing that will make it easier to lend to consumers. The first $5-billion purchase was at a price that suggests Ottawa could earn roughly $250-million from the $25-billion program. Banks have welcomed the new measure, and many are calling for it to be increased. The government is using its ability to borrow cheaply to provide the banks with cheaper financing for their mortgage portfolios than they could raise themselves.[10]

INVESTMENT PROPERTY MARKETS

Non-residential building permits

In reviewing the value of both residential and non-residential building permits by province for May 2007 and May 2008, statistics indicate that declines in non-residential building permits have out-stripped those in residential. Exceptions to the decline in non-residential are Newfoundland, PEI, New Brunswick, Ontario, Saskatchewan and BC.

As for the value of both residential and non-residential building permits by CMA for May 2007 and May 2008, the pattern is much more complex, with some cities showing ongoing expansion, while other locations (e.g., Ontario) have shown dramatic declines. This type of bifurcation in the market is caused by local factors, such as layoffs in manufacturing.

Non-residential construction declined in all centres in Atlantic Canada, except Moncton. In Quebec, Sherbrooke saw a decline, while certain centres in Ontario were hit with declines, especially Ottawa, Oshawa, St. Catharines–Niagara, Brantford, Guelph, London, Windsor and Thunder Bay. In the prairie provinces, Winnipeg suffered from decreases, while in BC, only Kelowna was exempted from a decline.

OFFICE AND INDUSTRIAL MARKETS

CB Richard Ellis *2008 Canada Market Outlook* summarized its expectations for the major Canadian markets for 2008 as follows:

Office markets

For downtown office markets, the expectations are buoyant, with most markets except Toronto and Ottawa indicating decreases in vacancy and increasing rents.

For suburban office markets, the expectations are less optimistic, with Vancouver, Winnipeg, Toronto, Ottawa and Montreal indicating decreases in vacancy, while Calgary, Edmonton and Halifax should see increasing vacancy.

Rents are expected to increase in Vancouver, Calgary, Edmonton, Toronto, Montreal and Halifax, while remaining stable in Winnipeg.

Industrial markets

For industrial markets, availability is expected to decrease in Vancouver, Calgary and Halifax, remain stable in Edmonton and Winnipeg, and increase in Toronto, Ottawa and Montreal. Rents and prices are likely to rise in Vancouver, Calgary, Edmonton, Winnipeg, Toronto, Ottawa and Halifax. In Montreal, rents and prices are expected to remain stable.

COMMERCIAL AND INDUSTRIAL VALUATION PARAMETERS

The Altus-Insite Investment Survey Overall Capitalization Rates (OCRs) summarize the effect of the sub-prime crisis dramatically. Generally, OCRs have risen 1–4 basis points in most categories including office, retail, industrial and multi-residential markets surveyed across Canada.

Interestingly, the Altus-Insite Investment Survey of Prices per Square Foot/Unit illustrates that the upward trending OCRs have not necessarily affected prices in all locations. If rents have trended upwards, this may have offset the change in OCRs.

As well, Altus-Insite Investment Survey Implied Rents Psf/Unit shows that dramatic increases in rents in Vancouver, Edmonton and Calgary have more than offset the upward trending OCRs for both downtown class AA and class B offices. This upward trending rental effect is limited to downtown class AA in Montreal and Halifax, whereas downtown class B rents decreased. This demonstrates the important interaction of rents and capitalization rates in different types of real estate and locations.

COMMERCIAL MORTGAGE MARKETS

Commercial mortgage-backed securities (CMBS) are bonds created by pooling a group of commercial mortgages and issuing bonds against the security of the underlying properties. The security of the bond is comprised of income producing properties such as commercial and industrial buildings, multi-family units, retail and office spaces. Specific properties are secured against overall debt and subordination of the various tranches can change a tranche's credit rating from AAA to BBB. This is referred to as the waterfall concept. CMBSs are structured to pay investors monthly income consisting of principal and interest for the first tranche rate AAA, and interest only for subsequent tranches. Principal on a CMBS issue's tranches is paid subsequently in order of class. The class A tranche pays principal out fully before the class B tranche receives any principal payments and class C will receive principal payments only after class B is fully paid out.[11]

In Canada, the success of the residential secondary mortgage market has led to the development of a commercial secondary mortgage market. The pioneers in this market were CIBC and Merrill Lynch, but other firms such as TD Bank, Royal Bank and Scotia McLeod (Bank of Nova Scotia) followed.

One notable effect of the sub-prime crisis was the effect on commercial mortgage bond securities (CMBS). In Canada, the effects included the meltdown in the asset-backed commercial paper (ABCP) market as well. At the Real Capital Forum, held in February 2008, David Miller, President of Canadian Mortgage Rating Service Ltd., addressed the question: 'CMBS and mortgage loan securitization in Canada: will they survive?' In Canada 2007 vs 2008 Commercial Mortgage Lending Volumes,[12] indications are that commercial lending volumes will decrease dramatically in 2008.

This would have a damping effect on commercial property transactions. An article entitled *CMBS Market Correction and Commercial Property Valuations*[13] suggests property value decreases by 2.2% for a generic property and 3.1% for a premium property. Moderating income growth forecasts by half could further lower valuations by 5.8% for a generic property and 14.5% for a premium property.

According to Mr. Plessl of RBC Dominion, "Canada's $15-billion a year commercial mortgage lending industry has gone from a period of excess supply into a relative drought — one that could leave the market $3-billion to $4-billion short of what borrowers are seeking in 2008.

"Borrowers who do manage to find a loan that suits their purposes should grab it as quickly and as early in the year as possible, as there is a good chance banks will run out of funds allocated for commercial mortgages around August.

"The primary issue is fallout from the global credit crisis, which has put a halt to one of the industry's key sources of financing, commercial mortgage-backed securities (CMBS). A form of bond comprised of commercial mortgage loans that are packaged and sold to investors, CMBS issuance went from $200-million in 1998 to $4.8-billion in 2006.

"That came to an abrupt halt late last year, when defaults on subprime mortgages in the US spilled over to cause a deep freeze on investor demand for asset-backed debt products."[14] CMBS spreads to swaps have increased significantly from February 2007 to March 2008.

COMMERCIAL REAL ESTATE INVESTMENT MARKET

On August 27, 2008, CBRE forecast that commercial real estate in Canada would fall by as much as 40% in 2008.[15] CBRE compared commercial investment transactions the second quarter of 2008 to the second quarter of 2007. Only Vancouver experienced an increase in market activity. All other major Canadian cities experienced declines. The overall decline in commercial real estate investment in Canada was 24%.

SPECIFIC TRANSACTIONS

One transaction exemplifies the more difficult market brought about by financing issues. The acquisition by Calloway REIT was originally announced on December 2007 and was to consist of 10 properties with a capitalization rate of 6.42%, totaling 2,049,006 sq. ft. for completed projects and a further component for 909,634 sq. ft. of projects under development at a 6.55% capitalization rate, for an overall rate of 6.47%.

A revised press release in April 2008 reduced the number of properties to six, with a capitalization rate of 6.78% for developed properties totaling 1,409,369 and a further component for 358,045 sq. ft. of projects under development at a 7.14% capitalization rate for an overall rate of 6.88%. Both the price and the financing arrangements had changed. Properties in Hamilton, Pembroke, Laval and Winnipeg were excluded.

CONCLUSIONS

Overview

Canada's real estate markets have been affected by the US sub-prime crisis, both directly thorough the tightening of credit and lending and indirectly through the resultant economic slowdown in the housing markets. Industries such as lumber have been affected. Indeed, it could be said that the decline in the US dollar and resultant exchange rates are due in large part to the sub-prime fiasco. The effects are by no means completed, because the political and economic consequences will reverberate throughout the US until the results of the November 2008 presidential and congressional elections are known.

In the meantime, the full effect of the sub-prime crisis on Canada is still undetermined as we approach the end of 2008. The effects will continue through 2009 at a minimum.

Residential markets

In 2008, residential market activity will slow down in all provinces except Saskatchewan. Price increases will moderate in all provinces except Newfoundland and Manitoba. In terms of local markets, price increases will continue to increase, but at a more moderate level than in 2007. In terms of residential mortgage financing, the federal government decision to discontinue CMHC insurance for 40-year amortization mortgages and zero financing will contribute to cooling the housing market.

By August 2008, Canada's housing market showed fresh signs it has exited the boom phase. A Canadian Real Estate Association report showed sales activity slumped 13.1% in the first half of the year.[16] Resale home prices decreased by 2.4% between July 2007 and July 2008.

Western Canada led the year-on-year decline in prices, with Vancouver, Edmonton and Calgary affected. In contrast, Saskatoon and Regina have continued to benefit from significant price increases.

Eastern Canadian cities, especially Toronto and Hamilton, have experienced more moderate increases from prior years. Ottawa, a notable exception, is still benefiting from government-induced local growth.

Investment property markets

The decline in availability of commercial mortgage funds and upward trending capitalization rates will contribute to moderating of prices in most major markets. This will be offset by increasing rents especially for downtown class AA office space. Downtown class B office and suburban office space demand will moderate in most locations.

Industrial availability will generally remain low and rent increases will be moderate, except in high demand locations such as Vancouver, Edmonton and Calgary.

In conclusion, Canadian markets are bifurcated by a combination of local real estate market conditions and economic factors. That said, most markets will experience some moderating trends due to the sub-prime crisis and related factors in 2008 and 2009.

According to CB Richard Ellis Ltd, commercial real estate investment in Canada is forecast to fall by as much as 40% or more this year, the biggest drop since the start of the decade.[17]

Economic uncertainty and hesitation by investors, a reduction in availability of financing and a smaller pool of properties mean a challenging market for commercial sales in 2008.

While residential real estate nationally has suffered a decline in sales, the commercial world has been taking an even worse hit, reflecting the global slump in property markets.

Kim Mercado, manager of national research for CB Richard Ellis, said some buyers are taking a "wait and see approach" to determine where the market is going for commercial deals, which include all office, apartment, industrial and retail properties.

Mercado is quick to point out that 2007 was a record year, with three significant real estate investment trust transactions, including the sale of Legacy REIT, the largest hotel and lodging trust, for $2.5 billion, helping to push sales 33% higher than the previous year.

That is not happening this year. In the first six months of the year, investment in commercial real estate by both foreign and domestic buyers was already showing a steep decline, falling 24% to $10 billion from the same period in 2007.

Of the nine major markets covered in the study, only Vancouver had a slight increase, rising from $1.5 billion last year to $1.6 billion in the first half of this year for a 6.6% increase.

Already, other indications from analysts at the Urban Land Institute and PricewaterhouseCoopers LLP[18] indicate that "the Canadian commercial real estate market will be hit by shockwaves emanating from the economic crisis in the US next year, according to a report by the Urban Land Institute and PricewaterhouseCoopers LLP.

However, in 2009, the Canadian market is more likely to be in for a tough slog rather than the full-blown disaster unfolding in the US, according to the report, which included feedback from more than 700 industry members.

"Overall, Canada may get sideswiped, but should avoid the more serious problems suffered south of its border," the report said.

Upward pressure on capitalization rates may be expected in the next 12 months. The credit crisis is affecting the value of commercial real estate, according to Desjardins Securities analyst Jeff Roberts. Mr. Roberts has raised the capitalization rates he uses to value real estate investment trusts and real estate operating companies.

"The financial crisis over the last month has and will cause real estate cap rates to increase significantly, we believe, despite the scarcity of transaction activity," said Mr. Roberts, adding pricing from deals that closed even as late September do not reflect the current marketplace. He estimates cap rates have risen 50 to 100 basis points since early October.[19]

US developments and expected effect on Canada

Henry Paulson, the US Treasury Secretary, turned to Canada and other Group of Seven industrialized countries on September 21, 2008 to back a sweeping financial relief package to alleviate stresses in the banking system that carries a fast-rising price tag of well over US $700-billion to buy up the bad debt associated with the sub-prime crisis.[20]

Given that the US Federal Reserve and US Treasury had already committed $380 billion in previous attempts to calm the troubled financial markets for a cumulative investment of over $1 trillion US dollars to date, some commentators were calling the latest effort,

"Resolution Trust Two," reminiscent of the process used to overcome the problems caused by the US Savings and Loan crisis in the 1980s.

The ongoing effects of the sub-prime debt led to US government takeovers of Fannie Mae and Freddie Mac, the main holders of troubled RMBS paper, and AIG Insurance, an insurer of collateralized debt securities. In addition, the investment banks Lehman Brothers declared bankruptcy and Merrill Lynch was taken over by the Bank of America.

By September 22, 2008, the last two standalone investment banks on Wall Street surrendered their independence, as Goldman Sachs and Morgan Stanley agreed to transform themselves into holding companies and accept much tighter regulation in a deal that limits their ability to take risks and reshapes international finance.

The decision to fundamentally transform Wall Street to look more like Canada's Bay Street, where investment banks operate under the wing of commercial banks, reflects the growing acceptance by regulators that the independent model has created too much risk in the financial system.

The move will be welcomed by Canadian banks that sought greater clarity from US regulators over the way the industry would be governed in the future, after investment banks were forced to break the rules and seek emergency funds from the Federal Reserve to survive amid the credit crisis.

The decision to place the institutions under Fed supervision and reduce the amount of leverage they can risk for every dollar they hold creates a more level playing field for Canadian and other commercial banks.[21]

END NOTES

1   FICO is a credit score developed by Fair Isaac & Co. It is used by many mortgage lenders that use a risk-based system to determine the possibility that the borrower may default on financial obligations to the mortgage lender. Equifax and Fair Isaac use this system. TransUnion and Experian, also sell their scores to consumers. TransUnion's credit score ranges from 300 to 900. Experian calls its credit score product PLUS Score. The PLUS Score ranges from 330 to 830.

2   Financial Consumer Agency of Canada (2007), 'Understanding Your Credit Report and Credit Score'

3   Canadian Association of Accredited Mortgage Brokers

4   Canaian Association of Accredited Mortgage Brokers, March 2007

5   Wong, Tony, Trichur, Rita and Daw, James (2008), 'Ottawa tightens mortgage rules,' *Toronto Star,* July 10, 2008

6   Saft, James (2008), 'The indispensability of Fannie and Freddie,' *Reuters*, July 11, 2008

7   Murray, Brendan and Kopecki, Dawn (2008), 'Mortgage giants shored up,' *Toronto Star,* July 14, 2008

8   These are known as collateral loans versus equity loans. Collateral lending was heavily promoted in the US as a means of financing new cars, furniture, home renovation, and vacations. The key in collateral lending is the ability of the loan recipient to make payments. We have not had the same traditional of collateral lending in Canada, again because our lenders are more cautious.

9   Erman, Bart (2008), 'Good timing: Feds avoid Fannie-style mortgage freefall,' *Globe and Mail*, July 12, 2008

10 Perkons, Tara, October 2008, 'CMHC to buy $7-billion of mortgages,' *Globe and Mail*, October 21, 2008

11 Cira, Mary Associate Director CIBC Portfolio Advisory Group (Summer 2002), Fixed Income Product Focus — commercial mortgage-backed securities (CMBS)

12 Miller, David (February 2008), Real Capital Forum — Toronto, 'CMBS and mortgage loan securitization in Canada: will they survive?'

13 Barve, N, Bryson, A and Jin, Wei (2008), CMBS World, 'CMBS Market Correction and Commercial Property Valuations.'

14 McLeod, Lori (2008), 'Commercial mortgage market faces shortfall,' *Globe and Mail*, January 30, 2008.

15 Wong, Tony (2008), 'Commercial property sales in steep drop,' *Toronto Star*, August 27, 2008

16 Grant, Tavia, (2008), 'Housing slump stalks Western Canada,' *Globe and Mail*, August 8, 2008

17 Wong, Tony, (2008), 'Commercial real estate projected to tumble,' *Toronto Star*, August 8, 2008

18 Mcleod, Lori (2008), 'Commercial real estate faces pinch,' *Globe and Mail*, October 21, 2008

19 Ratner, Jonathan, (2008), 'Higher cap rates bad news for REITs,' *Financial Post*, October 21, 2008

20 Callan, Eoin, 'Fed allows Goldman, Morgan to become bank holding companies,' National Post, September 22, 2008

21 Ibid

REFERENCES

Altus-Insite, (Q2 2007 and Q2 2008), *Altus-Insite Investment Survey*

Barve, N., Bryson, A., and Jin, Wei (2008), *CMBS World*, 'CMBS Market Correction and Commercial Property Valuations'

Bisson, Chris (2008), 'Mortgage Meltdown - Should we be worried?' *Housing Finance*, University of Guelph Mortgage Centre

Callan, Eoin, 'Fed allows Goldman, Morgan to become bank holding companies,' *National Post*, September 22, 2008.

Calloway REIT (2007), Press Release, December 2007

Calloway REIT (2008), Press Release, April 2007

Canadian Association of Accredited Mortgage Brokers, (March 2007)

Canadian Real Estate Association (2008), 'Average Local House Prices'

CB Richard Ellis (2008), *Canada Market Outlook 2008*

CMHC (2008), *Housing Outlook Canada Edition Second Quarter 2008*

Cira, Mary Associate Director CIBC Portfolio Advisory Group (Summer 2002), 'Fixed Income Product Focus — Commercial Mortgage Backed Securities (CMBS)'

Erman, Bart (2008), 'Good timing: Feds avoid Fannie-style mortgage freefall,' *Globe and Mail*, July 12, 2008

Financial Consumer Agency of Canada (2007), 'Understanding Your Credit Report and Credit Score'

Grant, Tavia, (2008), 'Housing slump stalks Western Canada,' *Globe and Mail,* August 8, 2008

McLeod, Lori (2008), 'Commercial mortgage market faces shortfall,' *Globe and Mail*, January 30, 2008

McLeod, Lori and Carmichael, Kevin (2008), 'Ottawa tightens mortgage rules to avoid 'bubble," *Globe and Mail*, July 9, 2008.

Mcleod, Lori (2008), 'Commercial real estate faces pinch,' *Globe and Mail*, Oct. 21, 2008

Murray, Brendan and Kopecki, Dawn (2008), 'Mortgage giants shored up,' *Toronto Star*, July 14, 2008.

Miller, David (February 2008), Real Capital Forum – Toronto, 'CMBS and Mortgage Loan Securitization in Canada: Will they survive?'

Perkons, Tara, (2008), 'CMHC to buy $7-billion of mortgages,' *Globe and Mail*, October 21, 2008

Ratner, Jonathan, (2008), 'Higher cap rates bad news for REITs,' *Financial Post*, October 21, 2008

Saft, James (2008), 'The indispensability of Fannie and Freddie,' Reuters, July 11, 2008

Statistics Canada (2008), *Non-Residential Building Permits (Monthly)*, May 2008.

Wong, Tony, Trichur, Rita and Daw, James (2008), 'Ottawa tightens mortgage rules,' *Toronto Star*, July 10, 2008.

Wong, Tony, (2008), 'Commercial real estate projected to tumble,' *Toronto Star*, August 8, 2008

Real Estate Volatility and Sunspots

WILLIAM LIM ——————————————————————————

INTRODUCTION

Subprime mortgages and home equity lines of credit (HELOCs), intended to increase homeownership and consumption levels, have been broadly blamed for the "housing bubble" in the United States in the early- to mid-2000s and the subsequent crash. Other explanations, as investigated by Vandell (2008), include: (1) subprime lending largely was displacing other loans that would have been made; (2) the problem with prices was primarily in the supply of new housing, not with the availability and cost of mortgage credit; (3) the problem was not subprime lending per se, but the Fed's dramatic reductions, then increases in interest rates during the early- to mid- 2000s; (4) the housing "boom" was concentrated in markets with significant supply-side restrictions, which tend to be more price-volatile; and (5) the problem was primarily one of fraud and/or misrepresentation on the part of aggressive mortgage underwriters or borrowers, not in the presence of subprime lending per se. In this paper, I suggest a theoretical *demand-side* explanation for the "housing bubble" and the subsequent crash. Shiller (Sep 2007) has looked at a broad array of evidence, and has found that it does not appear possible to explain the housing boom in terms of fundamentals such as rents or construction costs.

This purpose of this paper is to introduce the reader to economic sunspots and how these generate excess volatility in home prices. It is a condensed version of "more academic" papers exploring how economic sunspots increase housing price volatility and appropriate government policies to mitigate the effect of sunspots (Lim 1997, 2009, 2010). These "more academic" papers provide technical analysis, mathematical proofs and detailed discussion omitted in this paper, and also provide extra footnotes and references.

Glaeser, Gottlieb and Gyourko (2010) have concluded that lower interest rates could explain only one-fifth of the rise in U.S. housing prices from 1996 to 2006, and have found no convincing evidence that changes in approval rates or loan-to-market levels could explain the bulk of changes in house prices. They suggest that better corrections for the endogeneity of borrowers' decisions to apply for mortgages need to be made. Therefore, a psychological theory, that represents the boom as taking place because of a feedback mechanism or social epidemic that encourages a view of housing as an important investment opportunity, fits the evidence better.

A housing bubble blog (http://www.doctorhousingbubble.com, January 6th, 2008) considers the demand-driven housing bubble as follows: "Countless people that I know and you may know had a psychological desire to own a home that they bought homes in the last few years disregarding all evidence that a bubble was imminent. Many felt that if the housing payment became too much, they would simply sell. Others had dreams of making a hefty sum when home appreciation hit 20+ percent on a year over year basis … Surreal. Something was not right about that. And the fact that housing has steadily been declining … shows how we were in fact in a bubble fueled by easy financing and to a larger extent, greed." This blog also mentioned widely-held, but mistaken, beliefs like "leasing is equivalent to flushing money down the toilet" which led many to buy homes at inflated bubble prices. Shiller (Sep 2007, p.7) argued that "a significant factor in this boom was a widespread perception that houses are a great investment, and the boom psychology that helped spread such thinking." These beliefs were compounded by a "burgeoning of real estate advertisements" (Shiller, Jun 2007, p.20). Most people also mistakenly cited low interest rates, instead of expected rates of house price appreciation, as the main motivator of a good time to buy a house (*ibid*, p.21). "Money illusion" also appeared to be an important factor (Shiller, Oct 2007).

Lim (1997) introduced a simple general equilibrium model of housing demand to explain short-run booms and busts in the housing market. It is suggested that speculation could cause cyclical movements around the fundamental long-run price, and such speculation arose from the existence of stationary sunspot equilibria. Lim (2009) extends the model by incorporating home equity lending (or mortgage borrowing) which was missing in the earlier work. In economic theory, stationary sunspot equilibria are multiple equilibrium paths around a steady state where the actual path, undetermined by fundamentals, is determined by nonfundamentals or sunspots. Although sunspot prices are stochastic and reflect all publicly available information, they also reflect extraneous information and are excessively volatile.

Shell (2008) elaborates as follows: "'Sunspots' is short-hand for 'the extrinsic random variable' upon which agents coordinate their decisions, that is, one that does not affect economic fundamentals, but can affect economic outcomes. Sunspots are said to matter when the allocation of resources depends in a non-trivial way on the realization of the sunspot variable. Sunspot equilibria are instances of 'excess volatility'. They arise even when expectations are fully rational ... The market economy is a social system. In attempting to optimize her own actions, each agent must attempt to predict the actions of the other agents ... An entrepreneur is uncertain about the moves of her customers and her rivals, and they of her moves. It is not surprising that this process may generate uncertainty in outcomes even in the extreme case in which the fundamentals are non-stochastic. The uncertainty generated by the economy is market uncertainty. It is either created by the economy or adopted from outside the economy as a means of coordinating plans of individual agents. Market uncertainty is not transmitted through the fundamentals. It can be driven by extrinsic uncertainty ... Sunspot models are complete general equilibrium models that offer an explanation of excess volatility. It was by no means a new idea that economies can and do generate excess volatility, but the sunspots model is the first general-equilibrium model to exhibit excess volatility even when agents are fully rational."

Woodford (1984) suggests that preventing sunspot equilibria is a worthy object of policy intervention. Most importantly therefore, Lim (1997, 2009) suggests how tax policy could be used to eliminate sunspots in housing markets and possibly avert future housing crises. If this tax policy is not followed, housing price volatility could increase. An examination of the Case-Shiller home price indexes and U.S. Federal Housing Finance Agency (formerly OFHEO) house price (HPI) and purchase only (POI) indexes suggests that housing price volatility in the U.S. increased after the Taxpayer Relief Act of 1997 which exempted a significant amount of short-term housing capital gains. The increase in housing price volatility in the U.S. and Japan (more than a decade earlier) caused by misguided tax policies could be useful lessons for other countries facing renewed property price speculation.

RELATED LITERATURE

Shilling (2003) found that *ex ante* expected risk premiums on real estate were quite large for their risk, too large to be explained by standard economic models. Furthermore, the results suggested that *ex ante* expected returns were higher than average realized returns from

1988–2002, indicating that real estate experienced unexpected capital losses. As Shilling (2003, p.502) found that "investors appear to price all property types in the same way", for simplicity, this paper would only consider residential housing and ignore commercial real estate in order to focus on how investors form their expectations. The indeterminacy of equilibria led to "the fact that real estate investors appear to be no more uncertain about expected future returns after a decrease in price and fall in return than after an increase in price and return" (Shilling, 2003, p.502). This indeterminacy might also explain Shiller's (Jun 2007) finding that the causes of turning points in real estate remain fuzzy.

Shell (2008) noted that sunspots could also arise from *buyer* search and associated nonconvexities. One of the earliest stopping-rule search models was developed by MacQueen and Miller Jr. (1960). Turnbull and Sirmans (1993) applied this model to *buyer* search behavior as follows: "because the selling price of each seller p is not known until the buyer initiates contact, the buyer's problem is to act as a price taker, searching from seller to seller, sampling repeatedly from the selling price distribution $f(p)$ until one price is found to maximize the net gain from the entire search-purchase activity. Each sampling cycle is conducted at a cost c. The buyer's problem is to find the optimal search stopping rule or reservation price $p*$ which requires the buyer to continue searching until $p*$ is found." Housing prices thus entered the utility function either through the net value of the house (which depended on p) or through leisure (which was reduced with longer search depending on $f(p)$).

Lim (1997) postulated other reasons for having housing prices in the utility function from the extant literature: (1) Generalized wealth effects in expected utility (Dusansky and Wilson, 1993); (2) Endogenous consumption risks (Turnbull, 1994); (3) Scitovsky effects (Scitovsky, 1945); (4) Neighborhood effects or "location, location, location" (Veblen, 1899; Samuelson, 1972; Goodman, 1989). The next section describes Lim's (1997, 2009) general equilibrium model which utilizes housing prices in utility functions to generate sunspots and is intended for the honors or graduate student interested in economic theory. Other readers could proceed to the following section on the model's implications without any loss of continuity.

SUNSPOT MODEL OF HOUSING DEMAND

As is common in the extant literature, housing is assumed to be the only real asset and each agent is constrained to consume the same amount of housing that she has in her investment portfolio. For ease of exposition and without loss of generality, the general equilibrium model used in Lim (1997, 2009) is *deterministic* or *nonstochastic*. There are many identical infinitely-lived agents who enter any given period holding last period's housing stocks (which could be zero) and possibly having to repay their home equity loan or mortgage. An amount of the consumption good is endowed to each agent each period, and to close the general equilibrium model, each agent owns shares of the exogenous mortgage or lending institution from which each agent receives a dividend of the consumption good each period. Each agent has the opportunity of taking out a home equity loan or mortgage. Agents must then decide how to allocate their consumption good endowment, dividend, housing wealth and new loan or mortgage between current consumption, new housing and loan or mortgage repayment.

Agents receive utility from the consumption good and housing as explained in Lim (1997). Housing consumed this period becomes part of an agent's wealth next period, and thus housing is both a consumption and an investment good. More importantly, housing prices p_t are also modeled in the utility function. The overall utility of consumption over all periods is given by discounting the stream of utilities subject to each period's budget constraint (and loan constraint in Lim, 2009). The loan constraint simply states that agents could not borrow more than the value of their homes. Given this setup, the optimality conditions for the agent's problem could be found by setting up the Lagrangean and finding the partial derivative with respect to the consumption good and housing, and noting the Kuhn-Tucker conditions. Proposition 3.1 in Lim (1997, 2009) shows that there exists a steady state housing price **p** and steady state values of all other variables could be derived from this steady state price. The Implicit Function Theorem used in the proof of Proposition 3.1 only implies that there is a unique steady state value of **p**. It does not imply that the equilibrium path of p_t is unique.

Proposition 3.2 in Lim (1997, 2009) then shows that $p_{t+1} = g(p_t)$ and that g is forward stable for a nonempty, open set of economies where it is possible to construct an equilibrium path around the steady state such that $p_t = p + = å_t$, $p_{t+1} = p + = å_{t+1}$, ... for sufficiently small $\{å_t\}$, where the $\{å_t\}$ are independently and identically distributed random variables with mean zero. This means the equilibrium path of $\{p_t\}$ is locally nonunique or indeterminate. The indeterminacy leading to sunspot equilibria is due to multiple equilibria where coordination failures or misperceptions could result in a time path that appears (nonfundamentally) stochastic even though the economy is (fundamentally) deterministic or nonstochastic.

That g is forward stable is sufficient for sunspots to matter in the equilibrium path of housing prices $\{p_t\}$. Utilizing the bootstrapping technique, Lim (1997, 2009) constructs a large family of equilibria by replacing p with $p + \{\mathring{a}_t\}$ such that $p_{t+1} = g(p_t, \mathring{a}_t)$ is the forecast function used by agents. Proposition 3.3 shows there exists an invariant measure for this forecast function. Hence by Rosenblatt's theorem, there exists an invariant distribution for the price formation process $(p_t, \mathring{a}_{t-1})$. This distribution, together with the forecast function g, constitutes a stationary rational expectations equilibrium. Since the random variable $\mathring{a}_t$ is nondegenerate, the equilibrium is stochastic. In short, there exists a nonempty, open set of economies exhibiting nontrivial stationary sunspot equilibria. The volatility in housing prices would lead to volatility in all the other variables, even if the fundamental economy is deterministic or nonstochastic.

Even though our economy was fundamentally deterministic or nonstochastic, sunspots were found to matter, and nonfundamental or excess volatility ensued. If this model had fundamental uncertainty, then with multiplicity of equilibria, coordination failures in expectations formation could result in nonfundamental price paths with higher volatility than what would have been generated by fundamentals alone. That the deviation of house prices from fundamentals is due to price dynamics rather than a reaction to fundamentals is consistent with the empirical evidence of Fraser *et al.* (2008) who studied actual (real) house prices relative to fundamentals in New Zealand and found disparities between actual and fundamental real house prices, that is, the existence of real house price bubbles.

IMPLICATIONS OF THE SUNSPOT MODEL

Financial Contagion

The United States was not the only country that experienced a housing boom in the early- to mid-2000s and subsequent crash and mortgage crisis. Shiller (Sep 2007) mentioned that this boom is unique in its pervasiveness. Dramatic home price booms since the late 1990s have been in evidence in Australia, Canada, China, France, India, Ireland, Italy, South Korea, Russia, Spain and the United Kingdom. The United Kingdom also suffered a crash and mortgage crisis around the same period as the United States. Northern Rock was Britain's biggest casualty of the credit crunch and had borrowed about 26 billion pounds from the Bank of England since it requested emergency funds in September 2007. There were also expectations that Northern Rock would be nationalized.[1] Amongst emerging markets, it was reported that the Mexican housing market was in the midst of a boom which has attracted investment from United States pension funds like CALPERS.[2] There appeared to be no prior example of such dramatic booms (and busts) occurring in so many places at the same time as from the late 1990s to more a decade later.

Spear (1989) showed how financial contagion resulting in an international credit crunch could result from stationary sunspots generating excess volatility. First construct a pair of identical first-order sunspot equilibria on each country under the constraint that no trade occurs between them. Then use the pair of rational expectations equilibrium (REE) forecast functions (the g's) obtained to solve for the sunspot variable (the ε's) in terms of the prices on each country. When the sunspot variable is substituted in terms of one country's price in the other country's forecast function, the sunspot variable is eliminated from the equilibrium pricing. This yields new forecast functions for each country that depend on each country's own prices and prices for the other country. Spear (1989) proved that this construction would show that these forecasts are, in fact, stationary rational expectations equilibrium (REE) forecasts, and proved the existence of endogenously stochastic price processes defined by the new forecast functions. When trade between countries is allowed, define an exchange rate as the ratio of housing prices in both countries. Under this exchange rate regime, no trade between countries is an equilibrium outcome. Therefore, the rational expectations equilibrium (REE) constructed under the assumption that there is no trade across countries would, in fact, be an equilibrium for the model in which trade is not constrained (Spear, 1989). For this equilibrium, the other country's housing prices play the role of sunspot variables, so the uncertainty in the two-country model and resulting contagion are endogenous. Spear's (1989) construction of correlated sunspot equilibria could also be used to explain contagion within a country. Shiller (Jun 2007, Sep 2007) mentioned that the housing boom in the early- to mid-2000s in the United States was a national event due to contagion within the country from an intense national media frenzy over booms in specific regions of the country.

---

[1] "Northern Rock nationalization looms", *Reuters*, Monday, January 14, 2008.

[2] http://www.forbes.com/afxnewslimited/feeds/afx/2007/10/29/afx4271338.html

Monetary Policy

The mortgage interest rate was endogenously determined in the Sunspot Model. If, instead, the mortgage interest rate is exogenously determined, say by a central bank, then a sufficient condition to rule out sunspot equilibria, found by Lim (2009), is for the central bank to set the interest rate equal to the rate of time preference which ensures determinacy of equilibria. If not, housing prices would be (fundamentally) volatile. However, without an "anchor" for the interest rate, sunspots would matter, and there would be nonfundamental or excess volatility as well. This suggests that the Fed's dramatic reductions, then increases in interest rates during the early- to mid-2000s could have played a role in increasing housing price volatility. Meltzer (1995) reported that M1 growth in Japan rose from 3.5% for 1982–1985 to 8.1% in 1985-1988. Meltzer also pointed out that since land is the most durable asset, the increase in M1 growth would increase the price of land. The evidence, however, is mixed. Taylor (2007) found that monetary policy deviations during 2002 to 2005 might have been the cause of the boom and subsequent bust in housing starts and inflation. But Shiller (Sep 2007) pointed out that Taylor did not present an analysis of the model's success in the period before 2000 and disputed Taylor's findings. In Japan, Noguchi (1994) examined the "bubbles vs. fundamentals" argument and concluded that "the land price appreciation during the 1980s cannot be explained unless the bubble element is introduced" (p.11). Monetary policy therefore only acted as a catalyst and not a cause for the Japanese housing price bubble in the late 1980s and the United States housing price bubble in the early- to mid-2000s. The real cause, instead, is misguided tax policy.

Tax Policy

Woodford (1984) suggested that preventing sunspot equilibria is a worthy object of policy intervention. In a general equilibrium model with no lending/borrowing (e.g., no mortgages), Lim (1997) found that there exists a tax policy which would make the steady state determinate; that is, for the housing price evolution function, $p_{t+1} = g(p_t)$, g is no longer forward stable. The tax policy is as follows: if housing and other consumption are complements (substitutes), then housing should be taxed (subsidized). If housing and other consumption are complements and housing is subsidized, then sunspots are more likely to occur since the set of economies (that is, agent preferences) would be larger where g is forward stable. Lim (1997) studied Japanese data and found that housing and other consumption were complements in 1986–1991, yet there was a net subsidy to housing in Japan at that time. This resulted in the Japanese real estate bubble of the late 1980s to early 1990s and the increase in volatility that ensued.

Lim (2009) added lending/borrowing (e.g., mortgages) to Lim's (1997) model and found that in a model with home equity lending, the optimal tax policy for most economies would be a net tax to housing (which differs from the 1997 result). Even if housing and the other consumption good are substitutes, housing should be taxed unless the substitution effect is sufficiently strong. That is, with home equity lending, a housing tax would generally curb nonfundamental or excess volatility in housing prices. The reason is that with home equity lending, there is a propensity for agents to speculate with borrowed funds as they are no longer constrained by their own wealth. This speculation should be discouraged with a tax. Now if a different tax policy is followed — for example, if housing is not taxed and the substitution effect is not sufficiently strong — then sunspots would be more likely to occur. The increased speculation would decrease social welfare for risk averse agents by Jensen's inequality (Shell, 2008). The next section presents some empirical evidence from the U.S. for this result.

THE EFFECT OF THE U.S. TAXPAYER RELIEF ACT OF 1997

The U.S. Taxpayer Relief Act of 1997 exempted the first $500,000 in capital gains from any home sale when the home is held for only two years. It was a very significant reduction (in most cases, an elimination) of the capital gains tax for short-term housing investment (e.g., flipping). Lim (2010) examined housing price volatility (measured by standard deviation) before and after 1997 utilizing U.S. Federal Housing Finance Agency (formerly OFHEO) HPI (house price index) and POI (purchase only index), and Case-Shiller quarterly national home price index and several results are presented as follows: Table 1 (below) shows that the volatility of HPI and POI returns increased significantly from the period 1991-1997 to the period after 1997, suggesting that the reduction or elimination of short-

TABLE 1 Volatility of HPI and POI Returns Before and After 1997				
	HPI % Δ Qtr	HPI % Δ Yr	POI % Δ Qtr	POI % Δ Yr
σ (1991–1997)	0.5%	1.12%	0.36%	0.56%
σ (1998–2009)	1.38%	4.57%	1.32%	4.97%

TABLE 2
Case-Shiller National Index Returns and Risk Premiums (Excess Returns) Volatility (Composite U.S. Seasonally Adjusted), Quarterly, Before and After 1997

	Quarterly Returns	Quarterly Risk Premiums
σ (1987–1997)	0.817156%	0.802664%
σ (1998–2009)	2.687065%	2.674364%

term capital gains tax on housing did increase house price volatility as measured by these two indexes.

The other commonly used index of house prices is the Case-Shiller quarterly national home price index. Table 2 (above) shows that the volatility of returns as measured by the Case-Shiller National Index increased significantly from the period 1991-1997 to the period after 1997, suggesting that the reduction or elimination of short-term capital gains tax on housing did increase house price volatility as measured by the Case-Shiller National Index as well. Lim (2010) also examined regional volatility using the Case-Shiller MSA Index Returns and found that house price volatility increased after 1997 *in every MSA or region of the USA!*

Now sunspot equilibria is a nonfundamental phenomenon. The empirical analysis thus far examined total volatility; in order to examine nonfundamental volatility, we need to control for fundamentals. Table 3 (below) shows that the volatility of fundamentals increased after 1997. However, the volatility of the S&P 500 index increased by only about 10%, while the volatility of quarterly GDP growth increased by 40%. By comparison, HPI return volatility almost tripled (increased 200%) and POI return volatility almost quadrupled (increased 300%) after 1997. The volatility of Case-Shiller quarterly returns and risk premiums (excess returns) more than tripled (increased more than 200%) after 1997. In short, the increase in volatility of fundamentals could explain only a small portion of the increase in volatility of house prices after 1997, suggesting that

TABLE 3
Volatility of Several Fundamentals, Quarterly, Before and After 1997

	S&P500 Qtr Excess Returns	Qtr GDP Growth
σ (1987–1997)	6.8486%	0.5152%
σ (1998–2009)	7.5941%	0.7071%

most of the house price volatility increase after 1997 was nonfundamental or sunspot phenomena!

More formally, a multiple regression which controls for fundamental variables is run. The results are presented in Table 4 (below). The dependent variable is the Case-Shiller U.S. Quarterly Risk Premium or Excess Return, which is the Case-Shiller national index quarterly return less the risk-free rate (measured by the 3-month t-bill rate). We control for the above fundamental variables, the S&P 500 Quarterly Excess Return, which is the S&P 500 quarterly return less the risk-free rate (measured by the 3-month t-bill rate), and the Quarterly GDP Growth rate. The multiple regression first shows that Quarterly GDP Growth is significant in explaining house price changes, consistent with the notion that aggregate house prices are fundamentally driven by aggregate income. What we are interested in, however, are the residuals from the multiple regression, that is, what is not explained by the independent fundamental variables. Table 4 (below) shows that the volatility or standard deviation of these residuals, otherwise known as the standard error of the regression, almost quadrupled (increased almost 300%) from 1987-1997 to 1998-2009. The increase in standard error resulted in a lower R-square and F-statistic after 1997. In short, the multiple regression results show that nonfundamental house price volatility increased significantly after 1997, that is, after the reduction or elimination of short-term capital gains tax on housing.

The empirical evidence presented suggests that national housing price volatility increased after the U.S. Taxpayer Relief Act of 1997.

TABLE 4
Multiple Regression with Case-Shiller U.S. Quarterly Risk Premium (Excess Return) as Dependent Variable and S&P 500 Quarterly Return and Quarterly GDP Growth as Independent Variables, 1987–1997 and 1998-2009 (*:significant at 5%)

	1987–1997		1998–2009	
	Coefficient	T-statistic	Coefficient	T-statistic
Intercept	–0.014112849*	–8.124006067	–0.007746448	–1.66771377
S&P500 Qtr Excess Return	–0.001882663	–0.12897186	0.048163436	0.96227976
Qtr GDP Growth	0.989383928*	5.402817885	1.787437208*	3.407518864
Change in 30 yr Mortgage Rate	0.29752069	1.199894286	–0.151149698	–0.12288264
Std Error (Var Residuals)	0.0061358	(0.00003496)	0.0234622	(0.00051534)
R-Square (Adjusted R-square)	0.4573897	(0.4156505)	0.2794704	(0.2303434)
F-statistic (Significance F)	10.95826	(0.0000235)	5.68873	(0.0022134)
Number of Observations	43			48

Now this tax change reduced the holding period to two years for a $500,000 capital gain exemption for real estate, which represents a reduction or, in most cases, an elimination of the capital gains tax on short-term housing investment (e.g., flipping). The evidence suggests that the housing price bubble in the United States in the early- to mid-2000s was caused by this 1997 Act. The reduction (or in most cases, elimination) of the short-term capital gains tax generated nonfundamental or excess volatility in housing prices, and subsequent home equity lending losses which precipitated a mortgage crisis. By placing housing in a special privileged category for capital gains tax purposes, excess volatility in housing prices ensued. To reduce housing price volatility, it is suggested that the holding period for the capital gain exemption for housing be increased to at least 5 years, perhaps even as long as 10 years (with certain allowances for job relocation)

CONCLUSION

In this paper, economic sunspots and how these generate excess volatility in home prices have been discussed. The "sunspot model" used in Lim (1997, 2009) is a simple infinitely-lived agent model of housing and home equity lending, where housing is both a consumption and an investment good. Housing prices are also found in the utility function due to buyer search behavior (Shell, 2008; MacQueen and Miller Jr., 1960; Turnbull and Sirmans, 1993) and other reasons found in Lim (1997). This model suggests that speculation could cause cyclical movements around the long-run trend (which is fundamentally determined) and could result in excess volatility, housing bubbles/crashes, home equity lending losses and a mortgage crisis.

Such speculation arises from the existence of stationary sunspot equilibria, which has been proven by Lim (1997. 2009) in a series of propositions. Proposition 3.1 shows that there exists a steady state housing price and steady state values of all other variables could be derived from this steady state price. Even though the steady state housing price is unique, Proposition 3.2 shows that it is possible to construct locally nonunique or indeterminate equilibrium paths around this steady state housing price. The difference between a unique steady-state value and a unique equilibrium time path is worth emphasizing. The indeterminacy leading to sunspot equilibria is due to multiple equilibria where coordination failures or misperceptions could result in a time path that appears (nonfundamentally) stochastic even though the economy is (fundamentally) deterministic or nonstochastic. Finally, Proposition 3.3 shows that there exists a stationary rational expectations equilibrium where sunspots matter. The volatility in housing prices would lead to volatility in all the other variables, even if the fundamental economy is deterministic or nonstochastic. If this model had fundamental uncertainty, then with multiplicity of equilibria, coordination failures in expectations formation could result in nonfundamental price paths with higher volatility than what would have been generated by fundamentals alone.

Spear (1989) showed how stationary sunspot equilibria could spill over from one country to another, as one country's price could serve as the sunspot for the other country. Thus nonfundamental or excess volatility in one country's housing prices could lead to financial contagion resulting in an international credit crunch. However, sunspots are not ubiquitous and could often be mitigated by appropriate government policies. It is suggested that the central bank keep monetary policy steady. Dramatic changes in monetary policy could generate extrinsic uncertainty or sunspots, which lead to nonfundamental or excess volatility in housing prices. Meltzer pointed out that the dramatic increase in money supply in Japan in the late 1980s fueled the housing price bubble. However, Noguchi (1994) examined the "bubbles vs. fundamentals" argument in Japan and concluded that "the land price appreciation during the 1980s cannot be explained unless the bubble element is introduced" (p.11). Shiller (Sep 2007) also found that monetary policy did not come out as central in his case studies of housing booms and busts. Glaeser, Gottlieb and Gyourko (2010) have concluded that lower interest rates could explain only one-fifth of the rise in U.S. housing prices from 1996 to 2006. Monetary policy acted only as a catalyst and not a cause for housing price bubbles worldwide.

The underlying cause of the Japanese housing price bubble during the 1980s was extrinsic, exacerbated by misguided tax policies. The major cultural factor was that the Japanese regarded a house as an asset that produced capital gains. It was said that they would buy a house to own rather than to live. Hulme (1996) called this a "land myth" — the pernicious notion that real estate prices could never go down. Compounding the belief that prices could only go up was a sense of limited supply. The "land myth" was a liquidity catalyst, a means to borrow money based on speculation. Between 1984 and 1989, total bank lending grew an average of 9.2% a year, while lending related to real estate grew at a rate of 20% a year. The Japanese housing price bubble was thus amplified by careless lending in the banking sector as financial institutions began "selling money" (Yamamuro, 1996). This resulted in home equity lending losses. The late 1980s housing bubble in Japan is certainly similar to the housing price bubbles in the United States and other countries (like the United Kingdom) in the 2000s.

Lim (1997) derived a tax policy whereby there should be a net tax (subsidy) to housing if housing and other consumption are complements (substitutes). With home equity lending, Lim (2009) found that unless housing and other consumption were strong substitutes, there should be a net tax on housing to mitigate nonfundamental or excess volatility in housing prices.[3] Lim (1997) estimated from Japanese data that housing is likely to be complementary to consumption, and he suggested that the complementary effect of housing is likely to hold in most countries. Therefore, he suggested that a heavier burden on housing and real estate taxes would decrease speculation. This could be implemented by raising the assessments for property taxes (which Ito (1994) says is what "all economists in Japan recommend"), a cautious increase in capital gains taxes for real estate transactions, and a landholding tax to raise the cost of holding land for speculative interests. The last suggestion was actually implemented by the Japanese Government in 1992 to curb short-term property price speculation.

The U.S. Taxpayer Relief Act of 1997 exempted the first $500,000 in capital gains from any home sale when the home is held for only two years. Lim (2010) examined housing price volatility before and after 1997 utilizing the Case-Shiller quarterly national and regional (MSA) home price indexes and U.S. Federal Housing Finance Agency (formerly OFHEO) quarterly HPI (house price index) and POI (purchase only index). The empirical results suggest that national and regional housing price volatility, especially nonfundamental price volatility, increased after the U.S. Taxpayer Relief Act of 1997.[4] Now this tax change reduced the holding period to two years for a $500,000 capital gain exemption, which represents a tax reduction (and in most cases, a tax elimination) to housing, in particular short-term housing price speculation (e.g., flipping). It is therefore suggested that the housing price bubble in the United States in the early- to mid-2000s was caused by this Act of 1997. It generated nonfundamental or excess volatility in housing prices, and subsequent home equity lending losses which precipitated a mortgage crisis. By placing housing in a special privileged category for capital gains tax purposes, excess volatility in housing prices ensued. To re-

---

[3] Lim (2009) abstracts from possible positive externalities to owner-occupied housing which might justify a government subsidy.

[4] Several commentators have also conjectured that the U.S. Taxpayer Relief Act of 1997 may have helped cause the housing bubble. See Bajaj and Leonhardt (2008).

duce housing price volatility, it is suggested that the holding period for the capital gain exemption for housing be increased to at least 5 years, perhaps even as long as 10 years (with certain allowances for job relocation).

In conclusion, I have suggested a theoretical *demand-side* explanation for the "housing bubble" in the United States in the early- to mid-2000s, and the subsequent crash and mortgage crisis. The major contribution of this paper could be in its tax policy recommendation: to mitigate nonfundamental or excess volatility in housing prices, there should generally be a net tax on housing speculation (similar to a "Tobin tax" on currency speculation). This tax would increase welfare by reducing housing price volatility for current and future homeowners. In particular, taxes on short-term housing capital gains should increase. The increase in housing price volatility in the U.S. and Japan (more than a decade earlier) caused by misguided tax policies could be useful lessons for other countries facing renewed property price speculation.

REFERENCES

Bajaj, V., and Leonhardt, D. (2008). "Tax Break May Have Helped Cause Housing Bubble," *New York Times*, December 18, 2008.

Dusansky, R., and Wilson, P.W. (1993). "The Demand for Housing: Theoretical Considerations," *J. Econ. Theory.* **61**, 120-138.

Fraser, P., Hoesli, M., and McAlevey, L. (2008). "House Prices and Bubbles in New Zealand," *J. Real Estate Finance and Econ.* 37(1), 71-79.

Glaeser, E.L., Gottlieb, J.D., and Gyourko, J. (2010). "Can Cheap Credit Explain the Housing Boom?" *NBER Working Paper No. w16230*, National Bureau of Economic Research, Cambridge, MA, USA.

Goodman, A.C. (1989). "Topics in Empirical Urban Housing Research," in *The Economics of Housing Markets* (R.F. Muth and A.C. Goodman, Eds.), Reading, UK: Harwood Academic.

Hulme, D. (1996). "Explosion of Japan's 'Land Myth'," *Asian Business.* 32(7), 53-54.

Ito, T. (1994). "Public Policy and Housing in Japan," in *Housing Markets in the United States and Japan* (Y. Noguchi and J.M. Poterba, Eds.), pp. 215-256. Chicago, IL, USA: University of Chicago Press.

Lim, W. (1997). "Observing Sunspots at Home," *J. Housing Econ.* **6**, 203-222.

Lim, W. (2009). "Contagion And Sunspots Surrounding Speculative Home Equity Lending Losses," *Conference Paper, Financial Management Association 2009 International Meeting*, Reno, NV, USA

Lim, W. (2010). "The U.S. Taxpayer Relief Act of 1997 and the Subsequent Housing Bubble," *Working Paper, York University*, Toronto, ON, Canada

MacQueen, J., and Miller, R.G. (1960). "Optimal Persistence Policies," *Operations Res.* **8**, 362-380.

Meltzer, A.H. (1995). "Monetary, Credit and (Other) Transmission Processes: A Monetarist Perspective," *J. Econ. Perspect.* **9**, 49-72.

Noguchi, Y. (1994). "Land Prices and House Prices in Japan," in *Housing Markets in the United States and Japan* (Y. Noguchi and J.M. Poterba, Eds.), pp. 11-28. Chicago, IL, USA: University of Chicago Press.

Samuelson, P.A. (1972). *Foundations of Economic Analysis*. New York, NY, USA: Atheneum.

Scitovsky, T. (1945). "Some Consequences of the Habit of Judging Quality by Price," *Rev. Econ. Stud.* **2**, 100-105.

Shell, K. (2008). "Sunspot Equilibrium," in *The New Palgrave Dictionary of Economics, 2nd Edition* (L. Blume and S. Durlauf, Eds.). Basingstoke, UK: Palgrave Macmillan (forthcoming).

Shiller, R.J. (Jun 2007). "Historic Turning Points in Real Estate," *Cowles Foundation Discussion Paper No. 1610*, Yale University, New Haven, Connecticut, USA

Shiller, R.J. (Sep 2007). "Understanding Recent Trends in House Prices and Home Ownership," *Cowles Foundation Discussion Paper No. 1630*, Yale University, New Haven, Connecticut, USA.

Shiller, R.J. (Oct 2007). "Low Interest Rates and High Asset Prices: An Interpretation in Terms of Changing Popular Models," *Cowles Foundation Discussion Paper No. 1632*, Yale University, New Haven, Connecticut, USA

Shilling, J.D. (2003). "Is There a Risk Premium Puzzle in Real Estate?" *Real Estate Econ.* **31**(4), 501-525.

Spear, S.E. (1989). "Are Sunspots Necessary?" *J. Polit. Econ.* **97**(4), 965-973.

Taylor, J. (2007). "Housing and Monetary Policy," *NBER Working Paper No. W13682*, National Bureau of Economic Research, Cambridge, MA, USA.

Turnbull, G.K. (1994). "Location and Housing Demand with Endogenous Consumption Risk," *Reg. Sci. and Urban Econ.* **24**, 543-563.

Turnbull, G.K., and Sirmans, C.F. (1993). "Information, Search and Housing Prices," *Reg. Sci. Urban Econ.* **23**, 545-557.

Vandell, K.D. (2008). "Subprime Lending and the Housing Bubble: Tail Wags Dog?" *The American Real Estate and Urban Economics Association 2008 Annual Conference*, New Orleans, LA, USA.

Veblen, T. (1899). *The Theory of the Leisure Class: A Study in the Evolution of Institution*, London, UK/New York, USA: Macmillan.

Woodford, M. (1984). "Indeterminacy of Equilibrium in Overlapping Generations Models: A Survey," *Working Paper, Columbia University*, New York, NY, USA

Yamamuro, H. (1996). "Bubble, then Double Toil and Trouble," *The Daily Yomiuri*. July 31, 6.

What Drives Housing Prices Down? Evidence from an International Panel

KONSTANTIN A. KHOLODILIN,
JAN-OLIVER MENZ & BORIS SILIVERSTOVS ———

SUMMARY

In this study, we suggest an explanation for the low growth rates of real housing prices in Canada and Germany in comparison to other OECD countries over the period 1975–2005. We show that the long-run development of housing markets is determined by real disposable per-capita income, the real long-term interest rate, population growth, and urbanization. The differential development of real housing prices in Canada and Germany is attributed to the fundamentals in these two countries. Canada and Germany are characterized by relatively low average growth rates of real disposable income and relatively high interest rates, resulting in depressed housing prices over a long period of time. Institutional structure accentuates these tendencies. Given the importance of housing wealth for private consumption, our paper aims at drawing the attention of policymakers to the necessity of preventing not only overheating but also overcooling of the housing market that entails lower economic growth rate.

The authors thank Alfred Steinherr, Stefan Kooths, and Oreste Napolitano for helpful comments on this paper and M. H. Pesaran and J. G. MacKinnon for providing us with their code.

"What Drives Housing Prices Down? Evidence from an International Panel" Konstantin Arkadievich Kholodilin, Jan-Oliver Menz, and Boris Siliverstovs. *Journal of Economics and Statistics* 230 (1), February 2010, 59–76. Reprinted with permission of authors and Lucius & Lucius Verlagsgesellschaft mbH.

INTRODUCTION

The last few years have seen a very fast increase in housing prices in many countries. In countries such as Ireland, Spain, the UK, and the USA, the growth rates of housing prices were so high that it raised fears about emerging speculative bubbles. The worries were reinforced by the recent US sub-prime mortgage crisis, which has led to plunging property prices and a slowdown in the US economy. It is feared that the "US scenario" may repeat itself in other countries with booming housing prices. However, these discussions neglect another group of countries, where real house prices have been stagnating and even decreasing over the last decades.

The diverging house price[1] development among OECD countries is illustrated in Figure 1, which shows real house price (nominal house prices net of consumer price inflation) dynamics in 14 OECD countries in 1975–2004. The countries are classified in four groups: a) countries with falling house prices (Germany and Canada — upper left panel); b) countries with stagnating house prices (Japan and Switzerland — upper right panel); c) countries with medium house price growth rates (Belgium, Finland, France, Italy, Sweden, and the USA — lower left panel), and d) countries with extremely high house price growth rates (Ireland, the Netherlands, Spain, and the UK — lower right panel). As can be seen, over the last 30 years, real house prices in Germany and Canada experienced almost uninterrupted decline. Japanese and Swiss house prices grew up to the late 1980s or early 1990s and then started to decrease. In Switzerland a decade later, this decline turned into an upswing, whereas in Japan real house prices continued to fall. In contrast, real house prices of other countries in our sample followed an upward trend, sometimes interrupted for short periods of time.

Until now little attention has been paid to the adverse effects of stagnating or falling house prices. Virtually all discussions have been concentrated upon the dangerous consequences of bursting speculative bubbles in the housing market. Nevertheless, we believe that it is imperative to consider also the dire consequences of prolonged periods of stagnating or even falling housing prices. We will argue below that the economic development in countries with stagnating or falling house prices may have been set on a lower equilibrium growth path. In doing so, our paper aims at drawing the attention of policy-makers and academics to the necessity of preventing not only overheating but also over-cooling of the housing market.

---

[1] See Table 1 for sources of the data.

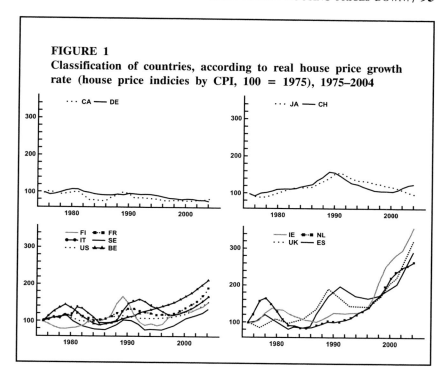

FIGURE 1

Classification of countries, according to real house price growth rate (house price indicies by CPI, 100 = 1975), 1975–2004

The negative consequences of overcooling of the housing market on economic activity are to a large extent the opposite of the consequences of overheating of the housing market. On the one hand, an excessive growth in property values typically leads to excessive private spending — fuelled by the wealth effect (Campbell/Cocco 2007, Carrol et al. 2006, Slacálek 2006, Case et al. 2005) — which is also accompanied by excessive borrowing due to the increased value of collateral. Therefore, decreasing housing prices tend to induce consumers to lower their current spending due to consumption smoothing, since their life-cycle income is negatively affected (Muellbauer 2008). In addition, consumers' demand for loans is negatively affected by falling housing market wealth, thus further depressing consumption. See Iacoviello (2004) for a theoretical model relating changes in housing prices to consumption fluctuations via their amplifying effects on borrowing capacity. On the other hand, similarly to the situation when firms tend to overinvest during a booming housing market, decreasing house prices lead to declining profitability of property relative to construction costs, and hence to lowering firms' Tobin's q of residential investment. Moreover, via the reduced value of collateral, decreasing house prices also depress aggregate business investment (Goodhart/

Hofmann 2008). Taken together, both effects can be strengthened by the effect of house prices on banks' balance sheets, leading to a decrease in credit supply and a negative accelerator effect (Chen 2001). An additional concern about the downward adjustment of house prices comes from historical record, indicating that when it happens the associated drop (in real terms) might be large and it generally takes a protracted period of time before a reversion of the trend takes place (Girouard et al. 2006). This would have implications for the conduct of monetary policy (see, e.g., Iacoviello/Minetti 2008). For example, Bernanke and Gertler (1995) argue that in the aftermath of a monetary tightening, housing investment accounts for a large part of the decline in aggregate demand.

We point out that the magnitude of the effects of positive and negative changes in housing wealth needs not to be the same. This can be traced to mounting empirical evidence on the asymmetric response of households to positive and negative property price changes. For example, (Engelhardt 1996), using the Panel Study of Income Dynamics (PSID) reports that households, which experienced house price depreciation, tend to reduce their consumption, whereas those experiencing real gains do not change their spending and saving habits. Genesove and Mayer (2001) report an asymmetry in behavioral response of home sellers to rises and falls of house prices. Case et al. (2005), based on macroeconomic data for US states, report that increases in housing market wealth tend to positively influence consumption, whereas no significant effect on consumption is detected from declines in housing market wealth.

Our paper contributes to a small body of literature, which analyzes determinants of housing prices based on a panel of countries or regions. The following studies investigate determinants of housing prices using international data: Almeida et al. (2006), Annett (2005), Égert and Mihaljek (2007), Terrones and Otrok (2004), whereas determinants of housing prices in US states have been addressed in Malpezzi (1999), Gallin (2006), Mikhed and Zemcik (2007, 2009) and Holly et al. (2007). Terrones and Otrok (2004), Almeida et al. (2006), and Annett (2005) estimate pooled panel-data models, in which all slope parameters are restricted to be the same across countries. Égert and Mihaljek (2007) and Holly et al. (2007) employ mean group estimators based on the averages of the individual estimates for each country. However, the mean group estimators applied by Égert and Mihaljek (2007) and Holly et al. (2007) do not take into account the fact that some parameters may be identical across countries or regions. There is also a number of studies such as Malpezzi (1999), Gallin (2006), Holly et al. (2007), and Mikhed and Zemcik (2007, 2009), applying panel co-integration tests to housing markets in the USA. It is, however, interesting to observe that these studies arrive at somewhat controversial conclusions regarding the existence of a stationary relationship between house price and a set of fundametals. The conclusion of the existence of a stationary house-price-to-income ratio reached in Malpezzi (1999) was subsequently reverted by Gallin (2006), who uses panel co-integration tests suggested in Pedroni (1999, 2004) and Maddala and Wu (1999). Gallin (2006) finds no evidence of co-integration between house prices, income, and population in a similar panel. However, Holly et al. (2007) further reverse the negative conclusion of Gallin (2006), applying a different approach to testing for co-integration based on the mean group and pooled regressions allowing for unobserved common factors. Mikhed and Zemcik (2007, 2009), who also apply panel co-integration tests of Pedroni (1999, 2004), report no evidence of co-integration between house prices in the USA and set of fundamentals (rents, consumer price index, personal income, and wealth).

In this paper, we apply the pooled mean group (PMG) estimator of Pesaran et al. (1999) to a panel of 14 OECD countries. To the best of our knowledge, this is the first time the pooled mean group estimator is used to analyze the determinants of housing prices. This estimator imposes equal long-run parameters and allows for country-specific intercepts and different short-run parameters as well as error term variances. It can thus be considered as an intermediate case between the pooled and mean group estimators, since it involves both pooling and averaging. The PMG estimator is also different from that of Pedroni (1999, 2004), which only allows for heterogenous long-run parameters. The assumption of common long-run parameters can be considered as a rather restrictive one. However, it seems warranted, given that our analysis includes a relatively homogeneous group of industrialized countries and that allowing for country-specific fixed effects and short-run parameters captures all the relevant heterogeneity across countries.

The paper is structured as follows. In section 2, we describe the standard housing price determinants suggested in the literature as well as the data, which we use in this study. In section 3 our methodology is presented and estimation and specification tests' results are discussed. Section 4 provides an interpretation of our econometric results. Section 5 concludes.

2. DATA

House price dynamics are determined by the interaction of demand and supply for housing (HM Treasury 2003). On the one hand, the demand for housing is typically determined by a mixture of economic (the expected change in house prices, household income, the interest rate, financial wealth, and availability of credit), demographic (population growth, urbanization, household size), and institutional factors (financial and taxation system). One would expect that all above mentioned economic factors but the interest rate positively affect house prices. The same applies to the demographic factors, as they tend to put pressure on the existing housing stock and hence drive the price up. Clearly, institutional factors that facilitate and/or encourage acquiring real estate would also typically be associated with house price increases. On the other hand, the supply of housing depends on the profitability of the construction industry, which is determined by the existing housing stock, house prices and construction costs (the price of land, wages, and material costs). See Girouard et al. (2006) for an excellent survey of the current literature on the determinants of house prices.

Based on theoretical considerations as well as the brief literature review above, we select the following explanatory variables for modeling house prices. They include real disposable income per capita and the real long-term interest rate, which are singled out in Girouard et al. (2006) as being the most important factors for house price development. The latter variable deserves special attention. In our study, the nominal long-term interest rate is deflated using the housing price index and not the consumer price index (CPI) as in Annett (2005), for example. In doing so, we implicitly assume that the expected rate of house price appreciation is equal to the current one. Furthermore, our definition of the real interest rate is based on the considerations of a household, which makes a decision about buying a housing asset. It compares the income it can earn on a bank deposit with "capital gains" stemming from changes in housing prices. The long-term interest rate is chosen because buying a house or an apartment is a long-term investment. We also include demographic variables: population growth and urbanization degree. Finally, institutional factors such as taxation policies, financial systems, etc, are important. However, institional factors are very difficult to measure and, if we are not considering economies in transition (see Égert/Mihaljek 2007), they tend to change only slowly. We approximate the influence of institutional factors by country-specific fixed effects in our empirical model.

Data on housing prices were obtained from the macroeconomic model of the National Institute of Economic and Social Research (NIGEM),[2] which is based on a data set collected by the Bank for

---

[2] http://www.niesr.ac.uk/

TABLE 1
DataSources

Variable	Notes	Source	Code
Nominal house price index	1995 = 100	NIGEM, based on BIS Ireland and Switzerland taken directly from BIS	HP
Consumer price index	all components, 2000 = 100	OECD, Main Economic Indicator	CPI
Real house price index		ln(HP = CPI)	RHP
Real disposable income	national currencies	AMECO	RDI_TOT
Real disposable income per capita		ln(RDI_TOT/POPUL)	RDI
Nominal long-term interest rate		OECD Economic Outlook, No. 80 For Ireland, money market rate, International Monetary Fund (IMF)	LIR
Real long-term interest rate		LIR – Δln(HP)	RLIR
Population	millions of persons	AMECO, for Germany, Federal Statistical Office	POPUL
Population growth		ln(POPUL$_t$ = POPUL$_{t-1}$)	POP
Urbanization degree	log of share of urban population	World Bank, World Market Indicator	URB

International Settlements (BIS). BIS collects price indices not only from national central banks and statistical offices, but also from commercial sources. The house price indices differ in terms of assessment bases and types of dwellings. National indices are mostly calculated based on regional data, which include purchase prices from newly built houses as well as from secondary market transactions. For a detailed description of the BIS data set on house prices, see Englund und Ioannides (1997).

Our data set constitutes an unbalanced panel of 14 OECD countries[3] (Belgium (BE), Canada (CA), Finland (FI), France (FR), Germany (DE), Ireland (IE), Italy (IT), Japan (JA), the Netherlands (NL), Spain (ES), Sweden (SE), Switzerland (CH), the United Kingdom (UK), and the United States of America (US)) and covers the period 1974–2005. The data sources and transformations of the variables used in this study are described in Table 1.

Descriptive statistics of the variables are presented in Table 2. As noted above, the countries in our sample display a heterogeneous pattern of house price dynamics. On the one hand, we have countries like Canada and Germany, where the average growth rate of real house prices was negative, and, on the other hand, we have

---

[3] The choice of countries is determined by the availability of the data.

TABLE 2
Descriptive statistics, 1975–2004

	RHP		RDI		RLIR		Population		Urbanization degree		
	average growth[a]	st.dev.[b]	average growth[a]	st.dev.[b]	mean	st.dev.[c]	average growth[a]	st.dev.[b]	average growth[a]	st.dev.[b]	level in 1975
BE	2.63	6.14	1.98	1.45	1.88	7.08	0.21	0.14	0.10	0.05	94.48
CA	−0.62	4.89	1.81	2.07	4.74	5.54	1.12	0.21	0.23	0.16	75.61
FI	1.41	9.99	2.21	2.82	2.70	10.60	0.36	0.12	0.15	0.28	58.26
FR	2.23	4.65	1.85	1.16	1.98	5.57	0.48	0.10	0.16	0.07	72.93
DE	−0.87	2.34	1.82	1.47	5.47	3.52	0.19[d]	0.48	0.29	0.05	81.17
IE	4.46	7.33	4.39	3.04	−0.86	8.01	0.84	0.63	0.40	0.12	53.63
IT	1.77	8.24	2.09	1.65	1.90	8.98	0.17	0.22	0.09	0.10	65.64
JA	−0.08	4.49	2.21	1.82	3.34	4.06	0.45	0.26	0.49	0.30	56.83
NL	3.38	9.45	1.80	1.49	0.63	10.16	0.60	0.13	0.53	0.19	56.93
ES	3.77	9.38	2.08	1.67	−0.63	9.97	0.62	0.45	0.33	0.28	69.57
SE	0.99	7.43	1.63	1.87	2.85	7.78	0.32	0.22	0.03	0.03	82.73
CH	0.82	4.48	1.00	1.63	1.39	4.79	0.53	0.38	0.66	0.87	55.75
UK	4.09	8.13	2.17	1.66	0.17	7.92	0.22	0.14	0.26	0.45	82.67
US	1.36	3.10	2.09	1.88	2.16	4.00	1.07	0.14	0.30	0.18	73.65

[a] The column reports the average growth rate of the variables during the period from 1975 until 2004
[b] The column reports the standard deviations of the yearly growth rates of the variables.
[c] The column reports the standard deviations of the real long-term interest rates.
[d] The effect of unification on the population growth rates has been accounted for.

countries like Ireland, the United Kingdom, Spain, and the Netherlands which display an average growth rate of more than 3 % per year. Countries with higher growth rate of real house prices tend to be associated with higher volatility. A simple comparison of growth rates of real house prices and real per-capita disposable income reveals a positive statistical association between these two variables, as implied by the economic theory, yielding a correlation of about 0.5. One also observes heterogeneous developments of the real long-term interest rate. Its importance for explaining developments in house prices is revealed by a very high correlation of about −0.94 between the average growth rate of real house prices and the average real long-term interest rate observed during the investigation period. The two demographic variables — population growth and the degree of urbanization — are evolving much slower and are much less volatile variables, which justifies the use of a cross-sectional dimension in evaluating the effects of those variables on house prices. The most rapid average population growth was observed in Canada, the USA, and Ireland. At the same time, countries like Belgium, Germany, Italy, and the UK experienced low average growth rates of population.

Also with respect to the urbanization degree, the countries differ a lot. Countries like Belgium, Finland, France, Italy, and Sweden experienced comparatively lower average growth rates in urbanization, which undoubtedly due to already high proportions of urban population in 1975. Higher growth rates in urbanization are witnessed by the countries like Ireland, Japan, the Netherlands, and Switzerland, i.e., countries that are characterized by a comparatively lower share of urban population in 1975.

3. ESTIMATION AND TESTING

3.1 Model specification

We employ the pooled mean group (PMG) estimator suggested in Pesaran et al. (1999) to our data. The model specification in the error-correction form is as follows:

$$\Delta RPH_{it} = \phi\left(RHP_{i,t-1} - \theta_{i0} - \theta_1 RDI_{it} - \theta_2 RLIR_{i,t-1} - \theta_3 POP_{it} - \theta_4 URB_{it}\right) +$$
$$+ \sum_{h=1}^{p-1} \gamma_{ih} \Delta RHP_{i,t-h} + \sum_{j=0}^{q-1} \psi_{ij}^1 \Delta RDI_{i,t-j} + \sum_{j=1}^{q} \psi_{ij}^2 \Delta RLIR_{i,t-j} +$$
$$+ \sum_{j=0}^{q-1} \psi_{ij}^3 \Delta POP_{i,t-j} + \sum_{j=0}^{q-1} \psi_{ij}^4 \Delta URB_{i,t-j} + \varepsilon_{it}$$

$$(1)$$

where common values are imposed on the long-run coefficients $\theta1$; $\theta2$; $\theta3$, and $\theta4$. At the same time short-run coefficients γ_{ih}, ψ_{ij}^1, ψ_{ij}^2, and ψ_{ij}^3, the error-correction coefficients ϕ_i, as well as the intercepts θ_{i0} are allowed to be group-specific. The zero-mean disturbances ε_{it} are independently and identically distributed across i and t, with the group-specific variance $\sigma_i^2 > 0$. The following variables appear in the equation above: RHP_{it} is the real house price (nominal house price net of consumer price inflation); RDI_{it} is the real disposable income per capita; $RLIR_{it}$ is the real long-term interest rate (nominal interest rate minus growth rate of house prices); POP_{it} is the population growth rate, and URB_{it} is the urbanization degree. The error-correction model above can be derived from the following Autoregressive Distributed Lag model, $ARDL(p; q; q; q; q)$:

$$\Delta RPH_{it} = \sum_{h=1}^{p} \gamma_{ih} RHP_{i,t-j} + \sum_{j=1}^{q} \delta_{ij}^1 \Delta RDI_{i,t-j} + \sum_{j=1}^{q+1} \delta_{ij}^2 \Delta RLIR_{i,t-j} +$$
$$+ \sum_{j=0}^{q} \delta_{ij}^3 \Delta POP_{i,t-j} + \sum_{j=0}^{q} \delta_{ij}^4 \Delta URB_{i,t-j} + \mu_i + \varepsilon_{it}$$

$$(2)$$

Notice that in order to avoid the simultaneity problem, the real long-term interest rate in equation (2) is taken with a lag. This is done in order to evade the appearance of the contemporaneous values of the variable $ln(HP)$ on both sides of the estimated equation. To see this, recall that the dependent variable on the left-hand side is defined as $RHP_{it} = ln(HP_{it}) - ln(CPI_{it})$, whereas the real long-term interest rate is defined as $RLIR_{it} = LIR_{it} - \Delta ln(HP_{it})$, see Table 1 for data definitions.

3.2 Non-stationarity and co-integration

In this subsection, we address important issues when dealing with persistent time series. First, we discuss testing the order of integration of the variables in panel data, while allowing for cross-sectional dependence. Second, we will test for co-integration in our model.

In the panel data literature, a number of panel unit-root tests have been suggested: Maddala and Wu (1999), Hadri (2000), Levin et al. (2002), Im et al. (2003) inter alia. However, as pointed out by Strauss and Yigit (2003) and Jönsson (2005), these tests are based on the rather restrictive assumption of cross-sectional independence, which in reality is very likely to be violated, given economic, political, cultural, and other linkages between different economies. As a consequence, these panel unit-root tests have poor size properties and low power in the presence of cross-sectional dependence.

In our paper, in order to circumvent the problem of cross-sectional dependence when testing for unit roots, we proceed in two steps. First, we apply a cross-sectional dependence (CD) test suggested in Pesaran (2004), where the null hypothesis is that cross-sectional dependence is absent in the data. This test is simple to implement, since it is based on the average of the pairwise correlations of the OLS residuals obtained from the individual regressions in the panel. The CD test statistic has a standard normal limiting distribution. In the second step, depending on the outcome of the CD test, we employ either tests that are based on the assumption of no cross-sectional dependence or the tests suggested in Moon and Perron (2004) and Pesaran (2007) that are robust to the presence of cross-sectional dependence.

Table 3 presents the results of the CD test of Pesaran (2004). The entries in the table are the corresponding test statistics computed using the residuals of the Augmented Dickey-Fuller (ADF) unit-root test regressions with maximum lag length augmentation order k = 0; 1; 2; 3; 4. The ADF test was applied to every cross-sectional unit i = 1; 2; ...; 14 of every variable. The CD test decisively rejects the null hypothesis of no cross-sectional dependence in the

TABLE 3
ADF(p) residuals cross-section dependence test, 1975–2004

Variable	Lag order				
	0	*1*	*2*	*3*	*4*
Real house prices	13.95	9.37	8.36	7.52	7.1
Real disposable income per capita	22.78	19.2	17.89	17.33	15.6
Real long-term interest rate	11.7	8.9	7.61	6.56	6.63
Population growth	4.52	1.66	1.71	1.74	1.37
Urbanization	4.92	4.58	4.21	3.98	4.04

Notes: Table entries are the CD test statistic of Pesaran (2004) applied to the residuals of the individual ADF(p) test regressions computed for each panel variable. nder the null of no cross-sectional dependence it has a standard normal limiting distribution.

residuals from the individual ADF regressions, implying that panel unit-root tests that do not account for cross-sectional dependence are inappropriate.

In the sequel, we apply the panel unit-root tests of Pesaran (2007) and Moon and Perron (2004) that are designed to tackle cross-sectional dependence in the time series. The former test is based on the individual ADF regressions augmented with cross-section averages (henceforth, CADF) in order to filter out cross-sectional dependence in the regression residuals. Since this test is a direct generalization of the panel unit-root test of Im et al. (2003), the corresponding test statistics is referred to as a cross section IPS (CIPS) and is based on the simple average of the individual CADF t-ratios, $\tilde{t}_i$:

$$CIPS = \frac{1}{N} \sum_{i=1}^{N} \tilde{t}_i \qquad (3)$$

The latter test explicitly models the cross-sectional dependence in the data by allowing for up to m common factors in the panel, which are estimated using the principal component analysis. The test statistic t_b^* has a limiting standard normal distribution as both $N \to \infty$ and $T \to \infty$, and $N/T \to 0$.

Tables 4 and 5 present the results of Pesaran (2007) and Moon and Perron (2004) panel unit-root tests allowing for cross-sectional dependence. We apply these tests both to the levels and to the first differences of the time series. It is seen that the test outcomes are

TABLE 4
CIPS panel unit-root test, 1975–2004

Variable	CADF(0)	CADF(1)	CADF(2)	CADF(3)	CADF(4)
	Levels: with intercept and trend				
RHP_{it}	1.85	2.08	1.38	1.26	0.88
RDI_{it}	1.63	1.77	1.53	1.56	1.68
$RLIR_{it}$	3.40***	3.49***	2.91**	2.97***	2.26
POP_{it}	1.95	2.49	1.68	1.40	1.13
URB_{it}	4.00***	3.99***	4.86***	6.25***	9.67***
	First differences: with intercept				
ΔRHP_{it}	2.56***	2.52***	1.95	1.95	1.60
ΔRDI_{it}	3.48***	2.77***	2.22*	1.79	1.51
$\Delta RLIR_{it}$	4.56***	3.97***	2.91***	2.87***	2.12
ΔPOP_{it}	3.81***	3.67***	2.87***	2.35**	1.80
ΔURB_{it}	2.33**	2.20*	2.15*	1.97	3.34***

TABLE 5
Moon and Perron t_b^* panel unit-root test, 1975–2004

	Number of factors			
Variable	1	2	3	4
	Levels: with intercept and trend			
RHP_{it}	0.06	0.11	0.22	0.35
RDI_{it}	0.68	1.00	4.22***	3.31***
$RLIR_{it}$	4.21***	4.64***	8.08***	7.00***
POP_{it}	0.51	0.18	0.04	1.59*
URB_{it}	4.07***	0.45	1.30	0.88
	First differences: with intercept			
ΔRHP_{it}	8.69***	7.96***	8.82***	8.45***
ΔRDI_{it}	8.90***	10.37***	9.97***	10.85***
$\Delta RLIR_{it}$	14.96***	18.07***	17.09***	17.99***
ΔPOP_{it}	12.11***	10.81***	9.38***	9.21***
ΔURB_{it}	7.47***	2.59***	2.13**	4.36***

Notes: Table entries are the t_b^* statistic of Moon and Perron (2004) computed for a given number of factors m = 1; 2; 3; 4. Under the null, the t_b^* statistic tends to a standard normal distribution as T,N → ∞ and N/T → 0. The one-sided 10%, 5%, and 1% critical values are 1.282, 1.645, and 2.327, respectively. '*', '**', and '***' denote statistical significance at the 10 %, 5%, and 1% levels, respectively.

TABLE 6
Pedroni panel co-integration test, 1975–2004

	No time trend		Time trend	
	statistic	p-value	statistic	p-value
Group ADF test	–2.099	0.044	–4.683	0.000

Notes: The panel co-integration test statistic corresponds to the null hypothesis of no cointegration between real house price RHP_{it} and real per-capita disposable income, RDI_{it}. Time dummies were included in the test regression.

somewhat sensitive to the specified lag augmentation p of the individual CADF tests in the case of the Pesaran (2007) test and to the number of factors m in the case of the Moon and Perron (2004) test. Testing the order of integration of the first differences of the variables uniformly leads to the conclusion that they are stationary according to the Moon and Perron (2004) test, whereas the conclusion based on the test of Pesaran (2007) varies with the length of lag augmentation p in the auxilliary unit-root test regressions. Testing the order of integration of the levels of the variables largely leads to the conclusion that real house price RHPit and real per-capita disposable income RDIit are I(1) variables, whereas the real interest rate RLIRit and the degree of urbanization URBit are I(0).

surprisingly, the panel unit root tests indicate that the population growth POPit is an I(1) variable. This, however, would imply that the growth rate of population could increase without an upper boundary — a feature generally characterizing unit root processes — which seems to be at odds with the common perception of a slowly evolving population, especially in our sample of 14 industrialized countries. The likely reason for such an outcome is unmodelled in our univariate analysis structural break in the population growth rate variable. Indeed, as noted in OECD (2007: 12), in the second half of our sample period, i.e., "[b]etween 1990 and 2005, population growth rates for all OECD countries averaged a little over 0.6% per year, half the rate observed in the 1960s and 1970s". Therefore, in the following we will treat the population growth rate variable as an I(0) variable that underwent a structural break during the period under scrutiny (for spurious non-rejection of the unit root hypothesis in time series that undergo structural breaks, see Perron, 1989).

Provided that some of our variables appear to be non-stationary, it is necessary to address the issue of the existence of co-integration in order to rule out the possibility of spurious regression. Unfortunately, to the best of our knowledge, there is no direct test for cointegration that can be applied to the PMG model (1). Instead we test for panel co-integration among the following I(1) variables: real house prices RHP_{it} and real per-capita disposable income RDI_{it}, using the test suggested in Pedroni (1999, 2004). Testing for co-integration between these two variables is similar to the exercise carried out in Holly et al. (2007) for house prices in US states. Holly et al. (2007) also provide a theoretical model justifying the existence of co-integration between these two variables. Pedroni (1999) suggests seven residual-based statistics for testing the null hypothesis of no co-integration. However, based on the evidence from Monte Carlo experiments, Pedroni (2004) suggests the use of the group ADF t-statistic, which displays superior finite sample properties compared to the remaining six statistics. In addition, Wagner and Hlouskova (2009) show that the group ADF t-statistic is least affected by deviations from the model assumption, typically encountered in panel data studies, such as the presence of an I(2) component, short-run cross-sectional correlation or cross-unit co-integration.

The panel co-integration test results are reported in Table 6. In the bivariate model, we are able to reject the null hypothesis of no co-integration at the 5% significance level in the model without a linear deterministic trend and at the 1% with a linear deterministic trend. Observe that in order to account for the influence of common shocks we included time dummies in the test regression. In the next section, we proceed with the estimation of the model parameters, maintaining the assumption of the existence of co-integration between real house prices RHP_{it} and real per-capita disposable income RDI_{it} in the sample of 14 OECD countries.

3.3 Estimation results

Given the fact that we have annual time series with a maximum length of 32 observations, we impose the maximum lag lengths $p = q = 2$ in our benchmark ARDL model. The estimation results reported below are based on the group-specific optimal lag lengths selected by minimizing the Akaike information criterion for every cross section. Our subsequent analysis of the residuals shows that such a lag augmentation structure is sufficient to remove autocorrelation from the residuals of the model. The estimation results are presented in Table 7. Here we focus only on the long-run parameters, the adjustment coefficients of the error correction term, the half-life of shocks, which measures the time necessary for a deviation from

TABLE 7
Pooled mean group estimates of the adjustment coefficients and long-run parameters, 1975–2005

Country	ϕ_i	RDI	RLIR	POP	URB	R^2_{adj}	Half-life, years
BE	−0.079 (0.045)	1.052 (0.129)	0.028 (0.004)	0.484 (0.103)	3.223 (1.022)	0.596	8.4
CA	−0.197 (0.035)	1.052 (0.129)	0.028 (0.004)	0.484 (0.103)	3.223 (1.022)	0.766	3.2
FI	−0.116 (0.041)	1.052 (0.129)	0.028 (0.004)	0.484 (0.103)	3.223 (1.022)	0.564	5.6
FR	−0.276 (0.048)	1.052 (0.129)	0.028 (0.004)	0.484 (0.103)	3.223 (1.022)	0.792	2.1
DE	−0.031 (0.010)	1.052 (0.129)	0.028 (0.004)	0.484 (0.103)	3.223 (1.022)	0.720	22.0
IE	−0.043 (0.014)	1.052 (0.129)	0.028 (0.004)	0.484 (0.103)	3.223 (1.022)	0.758	15.8
IT	−0.175 (0.050)	1.052 (0.129)	0.028 (0.004)	0.484 (0.103)	3.223 (1.022)	0.255	3.6
JA	−0.012 (0.053)	1.052 (0.129)	0.028 (0.004)	0.484 (0.103)	3.223 (1.022)	0.365	57.4
NL	−0.204 (0.047)	1.052 (0.129)	0.028 (0.004)	0.484 (0.103)	3.223 (1.022)	0.619	3.0
ES	−0.108 (0.037)	1.052 (0.129)	−0.028 (0.004)	0.484 (0.103)	3.223 (1.022)	0.567	6.1
SE	−0.091 (0.039)	1.052 (0.129)	0.028 (0.004)	0.484 (0.103)	3.223 (1.022)	0.704	7.3
CH	−0.005 (0.016)	1.052 (0.129)	0.028 (0.004)	0.484 (0.103)	3.223 (1.022)	0.410	138.3
UK	−0.158 (0.036)	1.052 (0.129)	0.028 (0.004)	0.484 (0.103)	3.223 (1.022)	0.839	4.0
US	−0.026 (0.017)	1.052 (0.129)	0.028 (0.004)	0.484 (0.103)	3.223 (1.022)	0.671	26.3

Note: Figures in parentheses are standard errors.

long-run equilibrium to be halved (half-life = $\dfrac{ln(0.5)}{ln(1+\varphi_i)}$), and measures of goodness of fit of our empirical regressions. First, notice that the point estimate of long-run elasticity of real house prices with respect to income is very close to unity and, according to the reported standard error, is also insignificantly different from that value. This finding is consistent with the theoretical considerations in Holly et al. (2007). The effect of the real long-term interest rate on real house prices is found to be significantly negative, as it measures foregone returns on alternative assets compared to returns on housing. Furthermore, the other two explanatory variables population growth and the degree of urbanization, as expected, positively influence real house prices. Second, the heterogeneous estimates of the adjustment coefficient f_i are negative for all countries and are significantly different from zero at the 5% level in 11 and at the 1% level in 9 out of 14 cases. This finding strongly supports the results of the panel co-integration tests presented above on the existence of a co-integration relationship (augmented with the I(0) variables) that forms our error-correction mechanism. The reported negative signs of the adjustment coefficients suggest that correction of disequilibria indeed takes place, albeit its adjustment speed varies from country to country. As seen, for most countries the disequilibrium is half-corrected in less than ten years. However, there are exceptions like Japan and Switzerland, where reported adjustment coefficients are very close to zero and statistically insignificant from zero. This has to be traced to the burst of house price bubbles observed in both countries around 1990.

Third, our model is able to explain up to 80% of the variation in the real house prices. The adjusted R^2 values vary from 0.255 for Italy to 0.839 for the UK.

3.4 Robustness check

All in all, the estimation results presented above point out that our long-run parameter estimates are sensible and, moreover, adjustment towards long-run equilibrium takes place in every country. In this subsection, we check the robustness of our results by estimating the parameters of the dynamic panel data model using the same specification as above, but omitting one country at a time. The results of this exercise are displayed in Figures 2 and 3, where the boxplot of the adjustment coefficient values is presented as well as of the long-run parameter estimates.

In Figure 2 we observe that the adjustment coefficients do not vary much regardless of which country is omitted from our sample, with the exception of perhaps France, for which the interquartile range seems somewhat smaller and more skewed towards zero than for the rest of the countries. Nevertheless, the robustness of our results is supported by the fact that all estimated adjustment coefficients calculated for all combinations of countries have a negative sign with the median fluctuating around –0.1.

The results of a similar exercise concerning the long-run parameter estimates are reported in Figure 3. Also there we observe a remarkable stability of estimates, with one exception. In the panel that excludes France, the estimated coefficient on the real interest rate is almost twice as large as those reported when any other country is omitted. At the same time, omission of France results in a somewhat

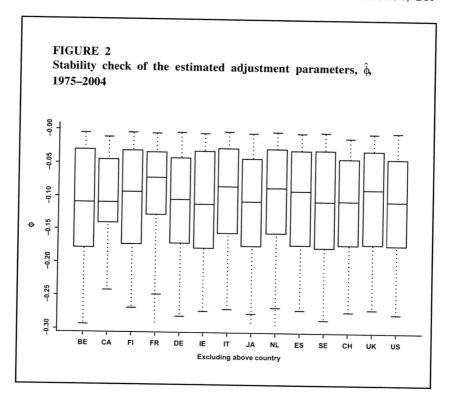

FIGURE 2
Stability check of the estimated adjustment parameters, $\hat{\phi}$, 1975–2004

lower estimate of the real income effect. However, it is still statistically insignificantly different from unity, based on the reported 95% confidence interval. As regarding the other two variables — population growth and urbanization — omitting France from the panel has little impact. Thus, the overall picture is that both the adjustment coefficients and the long-run coefficients display robustness with respect to omitting a single country and the outcome with France omitted could be safely seen as a separate incident. This implies that our main estimation results reported in Table 7 are not due to some outlying observations associated with a particular country.

INTERPRETATION OF THE EMPIRICAL RESULTS

In this section, we address the main question of this paper: What drives real housing prices down? In particular, we concentrate on two countries (Canada and Germany) with falling real housing prices, which are in a sharp contrast to most countries in our sample.

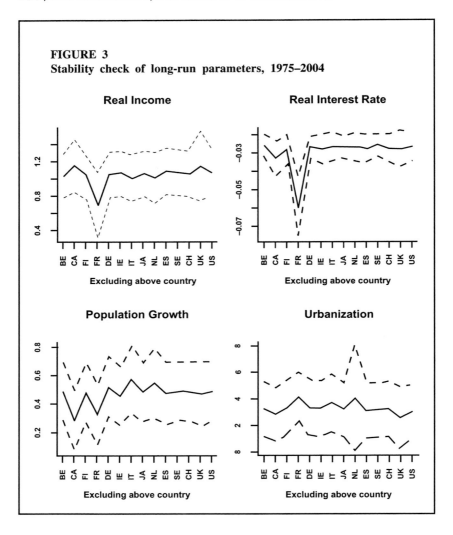

FIGURE 3
Stability check of long-run parameters, 1975–2004

As our estimation results in section 3 show, the following economic and demographic factors determine the long-run development of real housing prices: real disposable income, the real long-term interest rate, population growth, and urbanization. While real disposable income, population growth, and urbanization exert a positive impact on housing price dynamics, the real long-term interest rate dampens the growth of real housing prices. In addition, the long-run coefficient on real disposable income is close to unity, which implies that in the long run real housing prices move in line with real income. Our results are thus in agreement with the implications of the theory (see Holly et al. 2007). In this respect our study differs from those of Annett (2005) and Egert and Mihaljek (2007), who report estimates of the long-run income elasticity considerably lower than unity. At the same time, our results are close to those obtained by Almeida et al. (2006) and Holly et al. (2007).

Furthermore, our model implies that the long-run influence of fundamentals on real housing prices is very similar across different countries. Therefore, the question arises why in some countries real housing prices continue to fall for a protracted period of time, whereas in other countries the housing market is booming. A deeper analysis of fundamentals is necessary to answer this question.

Figure 4 reports the average values of the explanatory variables in our model over the period 1975–2004 for individual countries. We sort these average values in ascending order. A closer look at the figure reveals that Canada and Germany are similar in many respects. These countries show low growth rates of real disposable income per capita and the highest real long-run interest rates. Both countries are characterized by relatively low growth rates of urbanization. The only respect in which Canada and Germany differ is in population growth: Canada is the country with the fastest population growth, whereas Germany ranks near the bottom of the country list. One can safely conclude that it is the fundamentals that curb Canadian and German housing markets and make them different from housing markets of other countries.

The main limitation of the current study is that it exclusively addressed the influence of economic and demographic factors on housing markets. Influence of institutional factors, the importance of which cannot be overstated, was not taken directly into account due to the fact that institutional arrangements are difficult to measure and they tend to change slowly over time. Following standard practice in the panel data literature, their influence was indirectly captured by fixed effects as well as via country-specific short-run coefficients, which are allowed to in our modeling approach. ECB (2003) provides a comprehensive analysis of the institutional characteristics of major European housing markets. The study shows that in general Germany is characterized by relatively stricter taxation policy, discouraging speculation with real estate, less controlled rental markets and less subsidized home-ownership, such that the share of rented dwellings stayed well above 50%, while it dropped considerably in most other European countries over the period 1980–2000 (see ECB 2003: 26). In addition, Germany remains one of the countries with the highest degree of housing market regulation, according to SVR (2006).

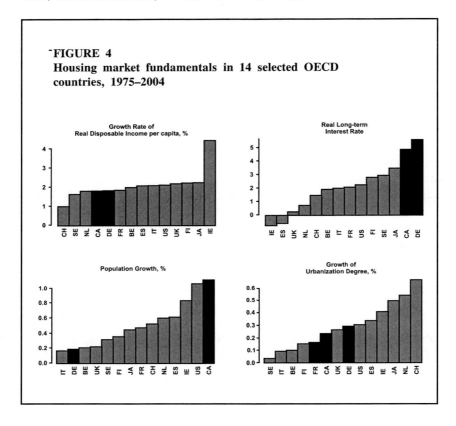

¯FIGURE 4
Housing market fundamentals in 14 selected OECD countries, 1975–2004

Similarly, one can conclude that particular conditions in the Canadian financial system have also contributed to stagnating housing prices over most of the period examined in this study, except for the last few years when the Canadian housing market began its modest recovery. Even if certain restrictions on banks with respect to their mortgage financing were abolished in 1967 (Girouard/Bloendal 2001), the lending behavior of banks remained conservative: "The mortgage credit culture in Canada is rather conservative, with a large majority of mortgages at fixed interest rates and a preference for mortgage terms of five years. Interest bearing term instruments sold to savers remain the primary source of funding for mortgage loans, which subsequently remain largely on the balance sheet of lenders" (see Traclet 2005: 1).

CONCLUSION

In this study, we suggest the following explanation for the weak development in Canadian and German real housing prices in comparison to other industrialized countries. Our econometric analysis shows that the general long-run development of the housing markets in these countries is determined by such factors as real disposable income per capita, and the real long-term interest rate as well as by population growth and urbanization.

The differential development of real housing prices in Canada and Germany can be attributed to the specific values of the fundamentals in these two countries. Canada and Germany are characterized by relatively low average growth rates of real disposable income and relatively high interest rates, resulting in depressed housing prices over a long period of time. Institutional structure accentuates these tendencies. Given the importance of housing wealth for private consumption, our paper aims at drawing the attention of policymakers to the necessity of preventing not only overheating but also overcooling of the housing market, which entails lower economic growth rate.

REFERENCES

Almeida, H., M. Campello, C. Liu (2006), The financial accelerator: Evidence from the international housing markets. Review of Finance 10 (3): 321–352.

Annett, A. (2005), House prices and monetary policy in the Euro area. Pp. 62–86 in: Euro Area Policies. Selected Issues. IMF Country Report No. 05/266, IMF.

Bernanke, B.S., M. Gertler (1995), Inside the black box: The credit channel of monetary policy transmission. Journal of Economic Perspectives 9 (4): 27–48.

Campbell, J.Y., J.F. Cocco (2007), How do house prices affect consumption? Evidence from micro data. Journal of Monetary Economics 54 (3): 591–621.

Carroll, C.D., M. Otsuka, J. Slacálek (2006), How large is the housing wealth effect? A new approach. Economics Working Paper Archive 535, The Johns Hopkins University, Department of Economics.

Case, K., J. Quigley, R. Shiller (2005), Comparing wealth effects: The stock market versus the housing market. Advances in Macroeconomics 5 (1): 1235–1235.

Chen, N.-K. (2001), Bank net worth, asset prices and economic activity. Journal of Monetary Economics 48 (2): 415–436.

ECB (2003), Structural factors in the EU housing markets. European Central Bank.

Égert, B., D. Mihaljek (2007), Determinants of house prices in Central and Eastern Europe. Comparative economic studies 49 (236): 367–388.

Engelhardt, G.V. (1996), House prices and home owner saving behavior. Regional Science and Urban Economics 26 (3–4): 313–336.

Englund, P., Y.M. Ioannides (1997), House price dynamics: An international empirical perspective. Journal of Housing Economics 6 (2): 119–136.

Gallin, J. (2006), The long-run relationship between house prices and incomes: Evidence from local housing markets. The Quarterly Journal of Economics 34: 417–438

Genesove, D., C. Mayer (2001), Loss aversion and seller behavior: Evidence from the housing market. The Quarterly Journal of Economics 116 (4): 1233–1260.

Girouard, N., S. Blöndal (2001), House prices and economic activity. OECD Economics Department Working Papers 279, OECD Economics Department.

Girouard, N., M. Kennedy, P. Van den Noord, C. André (2006), Recent house price developments: The role of fundamentals. OECD working paper No. 475.

Goodhart, C., B. Hofmann (2008), House prices, money, credit, and the macroeconomy. Oxford Review of Economic Policy 24 (1): 180–205.

Hadri, K. (2000), Testing for stationarity in heterogeneous panel data. Econometrics Journal 3 (2): 148–161. HM Treasury (2003), Housing, consumption and EMU. London: HM Treasury.

Holly, S., M. Pesaran, T. Yamagata (2007), A spatio-temporal model of house prices in the US. University of Cambridge.

Iacoviello, M. (2004), Consumption, house prices, and collateral constraints: a structural econometric analysis. Journal of Housing Economics 13 (4): 304–320.

Iacoviello, M., R. Minetti (2008), The credit channel of monetary policy: Evidence from the housing market. Journal of Macroeconomics 30 (1): 69–96.

Im, K.S., M.H. Pesaran, Y. Shin (2003), Testing for unit roots in heterogeneous panels. Journal of Econometrics 115 (1): 53–74.

Jönsson, K. (2005), Cross-sectional dependency and size distortion in a small-sample homogeneous panel data unit root test. Oxford Bulletin of Economics and Statistics 67 (3): 369–392.

Levin, A., C.-F. Lin, C.-S. James Chu (2002), Unit root tests in panel data: Asymptotic and finite-sample properties. Journal of Econometrics 108 (1): 1–24.

Maddala, G.S., S. Wu (1999), A comparative study of unit root tests with panel data and a new simple test. Oxford Bulletin of Economics and Statistics 61: 631–52.

Malpezzi, S. (1999), A simple error correction model of house prices. Journal of Housing Economics 8 (1): 27–62.

Mikhed, V., P. Zemcik (2007), Do house prices reflect fundamentals? Aggregate and panel data evidence. CERGE-EI Working Papers wp337, The Center for Economic Research and Graduate Education — Economic Institute, Prague.

Mikhed, V., P. Zemcik (2009), Testing for bubbles in housing markets: A panel data approach. Journal of Housing Economics 38 (4): 366–386.

Moon, H.R., B. Perron (2004), Testing for a unit root in panels with dynamic factors. Journal of Econometrics 122 (1): 81–126.

Muellbauer, J. (2008), Housing, credit and consumer expenditure. CEPR Discussion Papers 6782.

OECD (2007), Health at a Glance 2007 OECD Indicators. Paris: OECD.

Pedroni, P. (1999), Critical values for cointegration tests in heterogeneous panels with multiple regressors. Oxford Bulletin of Economics and Statistics 61: 653–670.

Pedroni, P. (2004), Panel cointegration: Asymptotic and finite sample properties of pooled time series tests with an application to the PPP hypothesis. Econometric theory 20: 597–625.

Perron, P. (1989), The Great Crash, the Oil Price Shock, and the unit root hypothesis. Econometrica 57 (6): 1361–1401.

Pesaran, M., Y. Shin, R. Smith (1999), Pooled mean group estimation of dynamic heterogeneous panels. Journal of the American Statistical Association 94: 621–634.

Pesaran, M.H. (2004), General diagnostic tests for cross section dependence in panels. IZA Discussion Papers 1240, Institute for the Study of Labor (IZA). Pesaran, M.H. (2007), A simple panel unit root test in the presence of cross-section dependence. Journal of Applied Econometrics 22 (2): 265–312.

Slacálek, J. (2006), What drives personal consumption? The role of housing and financial wealth. Discussion Papers of DIW Berlin 647.

Strauss, J., T. Yigit (2003), Shortfalls of panel unit root testing. Economics Letters 81 (3): 309–313.

SVR (2006), Zur Gefahr von Immobilienpreisblasen. Jahresgutachten des Sachverständigenrates zur Begutachtung der gesamtwirtschaftlichen Lage.

Terrones, M., C. Otrok (2004), The global house price boom. IMF World Economic Outlook, 71–136.

Traclet, V. (2005), Structure of the Canadian housing market and finance system. Bank of Canada. Department of Monetary and Financial Analysis, mimeo.

Wagner, M., J. Hlouskova (2009), The performance of panel cointegration methods. Results from a large scale simulation study. Econometric Reviews, forthcoming.

Urban Economics

The Redistribution of Residential Property Values in Montreal, Toronto and Vancouver

─────── ANDEJS SKABURSKIS & MARKUS MOOS

INTRODUCTION

This study examines the transfers in residential real estate value within Canada's three largest metropolitan areas. Changes in the value of the stock reflect movements in the factors guiding the formation and organisation of cities. Property values adjust over time to shifts in housing demand brought about by changes in the demographic composition of the population, in income levels, in the structure of occupations, in tastes, and in migration and immigration patterns. Property values are modified or preserved by city officials responding to markets and community interests, by developers, and by the corporate elite. The capital stock is changed by investors, by the way their expectations of future opportunities are formed and by the extent to which the changing conditions had been anticipated (Arnott, 1980). Investors, by reacting to the consequences of their own past decisions, may cycle investment between the inner city and the suburbs. Cities may also be shaped by changes in the profitability of investments in other sectors of the economy and by the 'crisis' brought by the overaccumulation in the "primary circuit of capital" (Harvey, 1985, page 6).

Tracking changes in property value can help to place the 'sprawl' issue that has become the main focus of Canadian city planners in a broader context. Attempts to achieve 'sustainability' by re-

─────────────

"The redistribution of residential property values in Montreal, Toronto, and Vancouver: examining neoclassical and Marxist views on changing investment patterns" Andrejs Skaburskis and Markus Moos. *Environment and Planning* A 40(4), April 2008, 905–927. Reprinted with permission of Pion Ltd.

FIGURE 1
Residential Property Value per km2 1971 to 2001:
(a) Montreal, (b) Toronto, (c) Vancouver

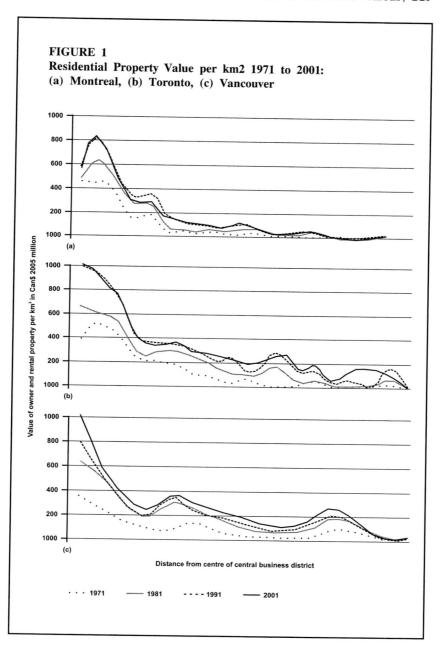

directing investment toward inner cities can be compromised when the policies force low-income transit users to move to places where they have to commute by car. Rising land values brought by regional growth management strategies can displace less affluent households in the neighbourhoods that accept growth (Wiewel et al, 1999). Knowledge of the extent to which real estate values are transferred within the metropolitan area can point to the locations with a growing need of social services and to the emerging housing problems brought about by the market's hidden hand (Downs, 1999). Changing property markets can have broad consequences.

Our interest in this subject was stimulated by Badcock's (1992a, 1992b; Badcock and Browett, 1992) insightful study of the "heart transplant" in Adelaide. He builds on Harvey's (1972; 1978) work by looking at "specific changes" and by showing "the genuine interdependence of changing market conditions and shifts in public policy" (Badcock, 1992a, page 221, emphasis in original). Some of the transfers toward the inner city are brought about by municipal councils trying to attract global capital and by the effect of globalisation on the workforce. Studies of gentrifying neighbourhoods have suggested that cities are undergoing major structural changes that redistribute property value toward the inner city (Hackworth and Rekers, 2005; Hamnett, 2003; Ley, 1988; 1993; Meligrana and Skaburskis, 2005; Smith and Williams, 1986). Hackworth and Smith (2001) show how state intervention has changed the face of gentrification and allowed it to become more widespread. Filion (1991) suggests that the politically astute elites may lock in the character of their gentrified neighbourhoods to restrict the market's ability to adjust to changing demand. Work on filtering shows that the older Canadian stock has been increasing in value at a higher rate than the newer housing, suggesting that property values in the inner city are increasing faster than in the suburbs (Skaburskis, 2006).

A casual look at the 1971 to 2001 profiles supports the restructuring hypothesis as inner-city property values in the three regions increased the most in absolute terms (figure 1). The undulations in the suburbs, however, show higher proportional increases in some sections. Moreover, figure 1 does not distinguish between the value added by new development from the redistributions within the existing stock, and this study's focus is on the redistributions. This paper illustrates the shifts in property value during the three decades since 1971 by using shift-share analysis combined with regressions to account for housing stock additions. Our aim is to augment the two main strands of arguments that explain the movements in the spatial structure of cities. This work tries to put a face on the theoretical arguments.

THE THEORY

The hypothesis suggests that investor interest has been returning to the inner city since the end of the postwar suburban development boom. A neoclassical economist may explain the changes by reference to the commute-cost/lot-size trade-offs made by households, while some geographers and political economists may point to class interests and the conditions maintaining the capitalist order. The neoclassical economists tend to focus on the demand factors and assume that housing supply adjusts toward a new welfare-maximising equilibrium (Alonso, 1964; Mills, 1972; Muth, 1969; Wingo, 1961). The structuralists examine the supply-side forces and their political and social basis (Harvey, 1972; Smith, 1986). Both views are reviewed briefly before we discuss the method and present the findings.

The neoclassical explanations

As cities expand, the periphery moves outward, making all locations within the city relatively more attractive, and this raises land and housing prices throughout the urban area. The price increase reduces the quantity of housing services that households are willing to buy and this change lets them reduce the sum of their housing plus commute costs by moving closer to the centre. This move increases the curl in the price/distance gradient and raises most [of] the value of inner-city property (Muth, 1969).

The traditional neoclassical models assume that the housing stock is malleable, that people have perfect information, that they can make costless transactions, that they commute to the downtown, and that there are no third-party effects — meaning no neighbourhood differences, no pollution, no congestion, and no status or power associations with residential location. The models develop smooth exponentially declining price and density gradients. Simulation models that introduce rigidities and the need to demolish valued structures before rebuilding at higher densities have depicted more complex, even sawtooth, profiles (Brueckner, 1980; 1981; Wheaton, 1982). City growth increases the relative attractiveness of central locations and raises the value of existing property and the potential residual value of the land should the site be converted to a higher density use.[1] With continuing growth and with the aging of the stock, the potential for redevelopment increases but the older buildings closest to the centre may be of a density high enough to maintain a

---

[1] Access improvements can also reduce the value of existing property while increasing land value (Schall, 1971; Skaburskis, 1982). The differential effects of price increases across owners and renters can also induce discontinuities (Skaburskis, 1989).

total property value that exceeds the potential land value that could be gained through redevelopment. Density decreases with distance from the city centre and at some point redevelopment at much higher densities may become profitable. The new buildings form a stark contrast with the older buildings closer to the centre. The redevelopment spreads outward but as these buildings age and land value increases they too are subject to replacement and as the process continues to cycle back from the periphery sawtooth density and property value profiles emerge. Without the need to identify particular changes in the structure of housing demand or in the interests of capitalist, the fixity of buildings and their depreciation within a growing city can explain redevelopment processes that cycle back from the periphery.

Neoclassical explanations of inner-city renewal can also point to the changing nature of the housing demand that motivates investment and construction activity. The increase in the proportion of dual worker households and the reduction in the length of time people expect to stay in a job make central locations more valuable than peripheral ones even when employment is dispersed from the centre. Decreasing household size increases the demand for smaller dwellings and the existing inner-city housing. Improving employment prospects for women increases household formation rates and the demand for inner-city locations (Rose and Villeneuve, 1998; Skaburskis, 1997). The declining average age of household maintainers, the drop in fertility rates, and the growth in incomes are increasing demand for downtown services and amenities and for interesting housing in nearby neighbourhoods. Immigrants also help fuel urban real estate markets (Ley, 1996; Ley et al, 2002). The emerging leisure-oriented character of modern downtowns reflects and reinforces inner-city gentrification (Bunting and Filion, 1988).

The Alonso (1964), Muth (1969) and Mills (1969; 1972) models unrealistically assume that everyone commutes to the city centre, and this is somewhat problematic for an empirical analysis that attempts to illustrate the basic theory. However, most of the neoclassical conclusions apply when jobs are more centralised than residences but dispersed in a circular symmetrical manner (Anas et al, 1998, page 1435). While suburban employment is growing, the central business district (CBD) still has the largest concentration of jobs in most Canadian census metropolitan areas (CMAs) (Heisz and Larochelle-Cote, 2005). The 2001 relative centralisation indices for Montreal, Toronto, and Vancouver are negative (–0.151, –0.111m and –0.096) showing that jobs are more centralised than residences.[2] However, because employment around the three CMAs' airports is approaching that of their CBDs, the analysis recognises both centres.

The structuralist views

Harvey (1972; 1978) articulated a theory of urban development based on the circulation of capital and the crisis created by overaccumulation in any one sector. His analysis takes place within a Marxist framework where wealth transfers across city areas are caused by shifting investments that reinforce class structures. Harvey (1985) argued that investment in the built environment is countercyclical with other sectors of the economy. However, much of Harvey's work has triggered a debate regarding the theory's empirical validity (Beauregard, 1994).

Smith (1979; 1986; 2002) established a direct link between the process of capital switching elaborated by Harvey and the changing of inner cities due to gentrification. Smith argues that suburban expansion during the postwar years resulted in overinvestment and the emergence of a rent gap as inner-city land values decreased. Industrial production became scarce in downtown areas, and the focus of economic activity shifted away from traditional manufacturing to the information and service sectors. In the post-Fordist City, the move of capital away from the downtown resulted in inner-city decline which, in turn, created the potential for inner-city regeneration. Redeveloping the districts and renovating the buildings in inner-city neighbourhoods could restore the land values lost due to the flight of capital.

According to Smith (1986), white-collar professionals and nonfamily households have renewed their interest in the inner city. He sees gentrification as the final manifestation of a larger movement of capital within the economy. He contends that the demographic factors and consumption patterns discussed by neoclassical economists can change urban form, but cannot explain why there was sudden investment in the inner city. The explanation for inner-city revitalisation is found in the falling rate of profits in the suburbs due to overinvestment creating a rent gap in the inner city. Conceptually, the term 'rent gap' denotes the difference between capitalised land rent and potential land rent, and the empirical estimation of these

---

[2]   The relative measure of centralisation lies between -1 and 1 and is defined as $\Sigma E_{i-1} P_{i-1} - \Sigma E_i P_{i-1}$ where census tracts are ordered by increasing distance from the CBD and P_i and E_i are the cumulative proportions of the residential population and employment through census tract i.

terms has been the subject of some debate (Badcock, 1990; Bourassa, 1993; Clark, 1995; Ley, 1987).

It is within the work of Badcock (1992a; 1992b; 1997; 2000; 2002; Badcock and Browett, 1992), and others (Brenner and Theodore, 2002; Maher, 1994; Marcuse and van Kempen, 2000; Wyly et al, 2004), that capital switching and urban inner-city revitalisation are linked to shifts in the class structure related to larger forces of global economic restructuring and changes in governance. Global economic restructuring — often coined as a transition from Fordist to post-Fordist regimes of accumulation — has polarised employment at two opposite extremes of the pay scale: white-collar professionals and low-level service workers. The two-tiered employment structure and the diminishing role of the welfare state have resulted in a declining middle class, creating an ever-growing gap in income between those at the top and those at the bottom of the pay scale (Brenner, 2004; Castells, 2002; Esping-Anderson et al, 1993; Filion, 2001; Lipietz, 2001; Sklair, 1991). The 'social polarisation' that is thought to follow from the new employment structure has been well documented, as have criticisms surrounding the universality of the theory (Baum, 1997; Dorling and Woodward, 1996; Hamnett and Cross, 1998; Musterd and Ostendorf, 1998; Sassen, 1990; 1991). Social and economic bifurcation can be expected to change the structure of cities, especially through segregation and income inequality (Bourne, 2002; Marcuse and van Kempen, 2000; Townshend and Walker, 2002; Walks, 2001).

THE MOVE FORWARD

Regardless of theoretical dispositions, there is mounting evidence of inner-city property value appreciation more generally than of that initially observed in gentrifying neighbourhoods (Badcock, 1992a; 1992b; 1993; Beauregard, 2005; Hackworth, 2005; Ley et al, 2002; Meligrana and Skaburskis, 2005; 2006). This paper adds further empirical evidence to the growing literature that has been developing along the structuralist and neoclassical veins. Similar predictions emerge from both frameworks, and both theories can explain cyclical changes in land values. We have stated earlier how the fixity of buildings and depreciation in a growing city can explain the rent-gap notion underlying cyclical development patterns in the neoclassical framework. Others have already pointed out how Smith's (1986) conceptualization of the rent gap has its roots in the writings of Engels and Marshall, and that Smith's idea, although presented from a Marxian point of view, is also contained within neoclassical models of property dynamics (Badcock, 1990; Clark, 1987; Evans, 1973).

Harvey (1973) accepts that neoclassical theories may explain land-use patterns, but stresses that political economy approaches look for underlying interpretations of these patterns and reveal class structure and uneven development. Neoclassical and political economy theorists have fought pitched battles in trying to explain urban development patterns (Badcock, 1990; Bourassa, 1990; 1993; Clark, 1995). Our work does not attempt to resolve these theoretical debates but, rather, illuminates where empirical trends can be explained by neoclassical descriptions and structural interpretations, and concludes by showing that both grand theories need to make room for more local contingencies.

METHOD

The hypothesis guiding this exploration suggests that inner-city property values increased more than suburban values after accounting for differences due to the addition of new dwellings. Our aim is to reveal and describe the order underlying an aspect of change in the urban spatial structure. Kloosterman and Musterd (2001, page 623) describe "cities as rich, multifaceted and historically contextualized spatial phenomena [that] encompass almost every aspect of social life." Both theoretical models are broad brush and the research design has to cut through the complexity of place to avoid getting lost in "almost every aspect of social life." We ask, in general, how did property value profiles change since 1971? The profiles show the the cross-section of values with distance from the city centre. We recognise that distance is not perfectly correlated with the commute time specified in the neoclassical models. Distance is not always equal to accessibility. But the measure is constant over time and not changed by the addition of highways or transit systems and is unaffected by changes in congestion levels. It is a simple measure.

At least two methodological issues are raised by the research questions: one concerns the definition of the 'centre' within a polynucleated metropolitan area and the other seeks an adjustment for the ease of adding buildings on undeveloped peripheral land.

Defining the centre

The centre of the metropolitan region is traditionally defined as the CBD and more than a half (52%) of Montreal jobs compared with 44% of Montreal's population were within a 10 km radius of this centre in 2001. The corresponding numbers for Toronto are 33% of jobs and 23% of the population. Vancouver had 55% of its employment within the 10 km ring and 41% of its residents. While employment is more centralized than residences, adding support for the neoclassical models, the main airports in each region are forming employment centres to rival the CBD. In Toronto 16.9% of the region's 2001 employment was in the CBD compared with 14.3% in the vicinity of the airport. In Vancouver the proportions were 20.3% and 10.4% and in Montreal 15.8% and 11.5% (Heisz and Larochelle-Côté, 2005). The other employment nodes in each of the metropolitan areas are smaller. The Pearson's correlation between the two distance variables is 0.42, 0.40, and 0.81 for Montreal, Toronto, and Vancouver, suggesting that there are enough differences, at least in Montreal and Toronto, to avoid collinearity problems. The regions will be modelled as having two centres, but this does not offer a rich enough description of the geography in which the changes take place.

The metropolitan areas will also be described by the characteristics of their 1971 housing stock. The age and density of housing in a census tract reflects the evolution of a city and its growth outward from its old centre. The regressions will include variables describing the proportion of the 1971 census tract's housing stock that was built before 1946 and the proportion built in the postwar era, 1946 to 1960.[3] The 1971 dwelling density is also included to offer another measure of centrality. The correlations between the distance to the centre and the pre-1946 proportion and the density variables are between –0.50 and –0.56 for Montreal and Toronto but a little weaker for Vancouver. The correlation for the proportion of 1946 and 1960 stock variables with distance is in the 0.14 to 0.21 range for the three regions. The correlations of the three variables with the distance to the airports are very much weaker in all metropolitan areas. The estimated regression models will be used to construct profiles that show the order within the field of highly dispersed property values. The dispersion itself will be illustrated to place the conclusions developed by both theories in a humbling context.

Accounting for net additions
The change in the value of residential property in each part of the city will be the greatest in the census tracts with the most developable land. We adjust for the value of new additions by using shift-share analysis on both unit counts and property value and subtracting the estimated value of the shifts in the number of dwelling

---

[3] The 1971 Canadian census used enumerators trained in assessing the age of buildings and sought consistency in assigning periods of construction across the dwellings in a neighbourhood with similar buildings (source: author's key informant interviews in 1979). The self-reporting in later censuses makes the period of construction statistics less accurate.

units. Regressions are also used to account for the effect of differences in the number of additions across the census tracts. The change in the value of owner-occupied dwellings and of rental dwellings will be regressed against the five variables describing location (the two distances, the density, and two age of stock variables) and variables describing the number of net owner-occupied and net rental additions. Since an additive functional form is used in the regressions, the coefficients for the net change variables describe the effect on total tract real estate value of increasing the stock by one dwelling unit.

Other studies have shown that for each four or five new additions one older unit is lost in the inner city and practically none are lost in the suburbs (Skaburskis, 1981). The coefficient for the inner city could at best reflect the value of a new dwelling less about one quarter or a fifth of the value of the older dwellings that were demolished. The effect of demolitions may be reduced by the conversion of existing units to multiples, or exaggerated by the deconversion of previously converted houses. The additive functional form of the regression means that the effect of including the net-units-added variables is constant across the region. In a sense, the inclusion of these variables takes away the same amount of investment per net dwelling unit regardless of its location and is insensitive to the fact that demolitions and conversions are mostly in the inner city. The distortion would be exaggerated should the value of the new dwellings vary systematically with distance from the centre. We examine the possible bias by using the combined 1991 and 1996 public use microdata files on households to develop ratios of the average value of dwellings in the central municipalities, which are identified in the microdata files and roughly correspond to our definition of the inner city, compared with the average value of suburban dwellings. Table 1 shows that the average value of owner-occupied units built in the City of Montreal in the 1990s was 0.978 of the average value of the dwellings built in the suburban municipalities. Since the average price of the units does not vary with distance from the centre measured in this crude way, we expect that the inclusion of the variables in the regression model will adequately control for differences due to additions. The rental ratio for Montreal (0.809) suggests that the model will understate the shifts toward the inner city by as much as 20% of the value of the new stock.

The third column for each CMA presents the average weighted by the number of dwellings in each tenure category. The statistics show a little higher value for owner-occupied dwellings in the inner city but not enough higher to compensate for the effect of losing one quarter or a fifth of an older dwelling to create the new unit

TABLE 1
Ratio of central city to suburban dwelling values: 1991 and 1996
(source: Statistics Canada public use microdata files on households,
1991 and 1996 combined).

	Montreal			Toronto			Vancouver		
	owners	renters	average[a]	owners	renters	average	owners	renters	average
pre-1946	1.019	0.911	0.945	1.112	0.910	1.029	1.151	0.922	1.033
1946–60	1.233	0.862	0.973	0.937	0.912	0.921	1.200	0.879	0.972
1970s	1.227	0.809	0.979	1.145	0.740	0.947	1.195	1.059	1.131
1980s	1.057	0.862	0.953	0.939	0.912	0.929	1.239	0.879	1.128
1990s	0.978	0.809	0.908	1.039	0.740	0.892	1.110	1.059	1.094

[a] Average of the two ratios weighted by the number of units in each tenure by period of construction.

depicted in table 1. The statistics point to tenure differences and show that the bias in controlling for differences in stock additions is reduced by integrating the two tenures. The Montreal and Toronto statistics show that the regression models will understate the shift in value toward the inner city. The inner-city average housing prices and rents in Vancouver are higher than in the suburban municipalities but the prevalence of the multiple converted dwellings that were demolished in the inner city to make way for new buildings will reduce or eliminate the overstatement. The differences in the ratios of demolitions to conversions and deconversions within the inner city will skew the comparisons of changes taking place in the gentrifying neighbourhoods as opposed to the declining inner-city areas in ways that we cannot assess here.

The data and the shift-share analysis

The analysis uses census tract data for 1971, 1981, 1991, and 2001 for the Montreal, Toronto, and Vancouver metropolitan areas. Census tracts are small statistical subdivisions delineated by Statistics Canada to have between 2500 and 8000 people and to be somewhat homogeneous with respect to population characteristics, economic status, and living conditions (Statistics Canada, 2005). The tracts' areas vary depending on population density. Their boundaries remained mostly unchanged in the parts of the metropolitan areas that were built up in 1971, but tracts were added and split as the suburbs grew. To allow comparisons across time, the 1991 and 2001 tracts were adjusted to correspond with the 1981 census boundaries and a small number of 1971 tracts were split using weighted averages.

Statistics at the tract level are available on a large number of variables including the average value of dwellings, as assessed by the homeowner, and on average rents. The average rents were capitalised using ratios that were estimated with the public use microdata files. The value of the rental buildings was calculated by multiplying the annual average rent by 18.49, 19.49, and 21.13 for Montreal, Toronto, and Vancouver. These rates were estimated by using the 1991 and 1996 public use microdata, files on households to regress the logs of value and rent against the number of rooms bedrooms, building types, and state of repair of each dwelling. To help account for differences in dwelling quality, the logs of household income, major source of income, and household size were included. The coefficients estimated with the owner's data were then used with the rental data to predict the price of the dwelling. The coefficients estimated with the rental regression were used to predict the rents that would be charged in the owner-occupied dwellings. The ratio of predicted value to rents in each equation was calculated. The average of the two census years and two sets of predictions were used to construct the capitalisation factor. The total value of residential real estate in each tract was calculated by multiplying the average value of the rental and the owner-occupied dwellings by the number of rental and owner-occupied units. All dollar values were adjusted to 2005 levels using the Bank of Canada's consumer price index.

Changes in property value were examined at both the census-tract and city-sector levels. Each of the three CMAs was divided into four areas: inner city, old suburbs, new suburbs, and exurbs. The definition of inner city, suburbs, and new suburbs roughly follows the approach adopted by Bunting and Filion (1996) and Walks (2001) that uses the predominant age of buildings as the key distinguishing factor. We define the 'inner city' as being formed by the census tracts that had in 1971 twice the average CMA proportion of houses built before 1946. The inner city forms a 10 to 11 km ring about the CBD in each of the three metropolitan areas. The 'new suburbs' are the tracts with more than two thirds of their housing stock built between 1971 and 2001. The 'old suburbs' are the remaining census tracts and identify the neighbourhood developed during the rapid postwar suburban expansion of the cities. 'Exurbs' are the rural or low population density tracts. While there are no hard and fast rules on how to define the different parts of the city (Brown and Burke, 1979; Filion, 1987; Ley, 1988), this method was used by others because it is easily duplicated for most North American cities (Walks, 2001) and it defines city areas according to when its capital stock was developed. This particular attribute best suits the purpose of this study.

The shift-share analysis was carried out in four steps. First, CMA real estate growth rates were calculated for each census year. Second, real estate values are predicted for each tract by multiplying its state-of-period value by the rate at which values increased across the whole metropolitan area. Third, the difference between the actual end-of-period and the predicted value is calculated to yield the 'value shift' statistic. Fourth, the shift in the number of dwelling units — calculated in the same manner as the shift in value — is multiplied by the average value of the units at the beginning of the period and this number is subtracted from the 'value shift' to yield an 'adjusted shift' statistic that offers a rough estimate of the changes in the tract's property value after accounting for changes in its number of units.

TABLE 2
Distribution of real estate value within the three metropolitan areas (source: Statistics Canada P-Census 1971, 1981, 1991, 2001)

	1971	1981	1991	2001
Montreal (n = 641)				
Inner city	0.269	0.231	0.215	0.213
Inner suburbs	0.634	0.611	0.555	0.525
New suburbs	0.094	0.153	0.224	0.255
Exurbs	0.003	0.005	0.005	0.006
CMA[a] (Can $ million 2005)	92,100	144,600	201,690	194,110
Toronto (n = 589)				
Inner city	0.335	0.282	0.243	0.231
Inner suburbs	0.567	0.528	0.428	0.396
New suburbs	0.085	0.178	0.309	0.359
Exurbs	0.013	0.012	0.020	0.014
CMA (Can $ million 2005)	145,760	227,440	371,800	406,700
Vancouver (n = 230)				
Inner city	0.331	0.280	0.283	0.268
Inner suburbs	0.477	0.460	0.409	0.381
New suburbs	0.165	0.241	0.289	0.328
Exurbs	0.027	0.019	0.019	0.023
CMA (Can $ million 2005)	61,070	139,890	156,930	198,600

Note: Total value of real estate is calculated as sum of total owned dwelling values plus sum of annual gross rent multiplied by a capitalisation rate. CMA[a] — census metropolitan area.

CHANGES IN RESIDENTIAL PROPERTY VALUE BETWEEN 1971 AND 2001

Table 2 shows the changes since 1971 in the distribution of residential property values across the inner city, the older suburbs, the new suburbs, and the exurbs as defined in the last section. In all three metropolitan areas, the share of property value in the inner city de-

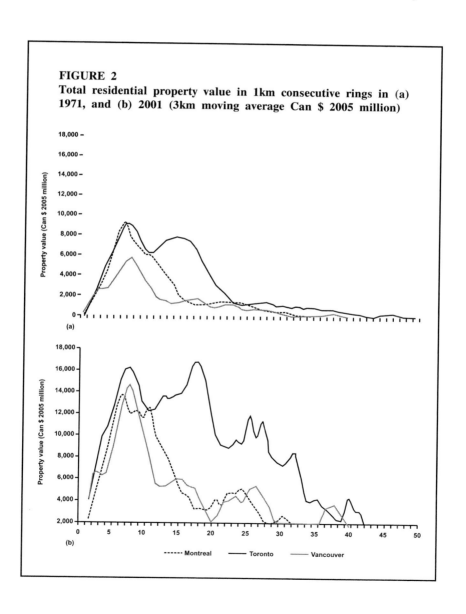

FIGURE 2

Total residential property value in 1km consecutive rings in (a) 1971, and (b) 2001 (3km moving average Can $ 2005 million)

creased but the rate of decrease has declined. In Toronto and Montreal, the decrease in the inner city's share over the three decades is from one third to approximately one quarter of their region's total real estate value. Montreal, known for its strong inner-city residential concentration, had the lowest share of property value in the inner city and experienced the smallest decline in shares. Table 2 understates the changes taking place in Vancouver during the 1980s due to the speculative housing price bubble doubling prices just before the 1981 Census and then halving them in the following six months (Skaburskis, 1989). Cycles are also created by the irrational exuberance of households, which has little to do with shifts in consumer preferences or readjustments within the capitalist order.

The residential property value in each 1 km ring around the centre of the CBD was computed to compare the changes occurring in the inner city with those further out. The census tracts increase in size with distance from the centre due to their lower density and some of the outlying rings contain no census tract centres and, therefore, no data. Figure 2 shows the 1971 and 2001 distributions of property value in each ring. A 3 km moving average is used to smooth the profiles. All three metropolitan areas had peaks 5 to

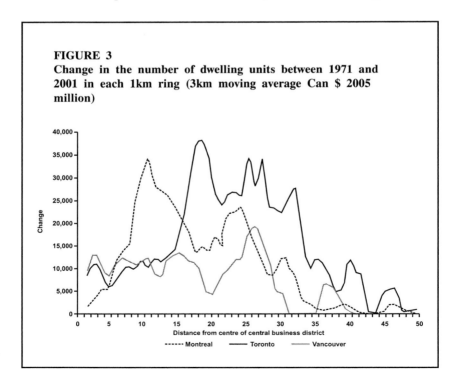

FIGURE 3
Change in the number of dwelling units between 1971 and 2001 in each 1km ring (3km moving average Can $ 2005 million)

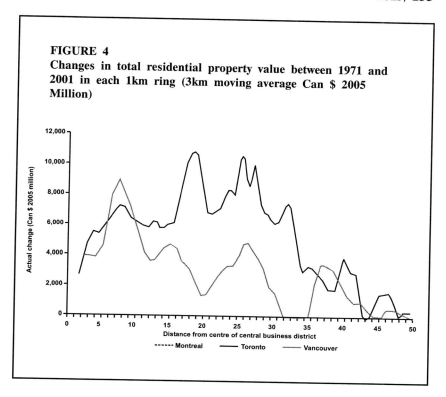

FIGURE 4
Changes in total residential property value between 1971 and 2001 in each 1km ring (3km moving average Can $ 2005 Million)

8 km from their centres in 1971 with only Toronto showing a burgeoning suburban ring in the 10 to 20 km radius. Even before the separatist-induced out-migration from Montreal, Toronto had more extensive suburbs than the other cities. The bulk of Toronto's property value in 2001 extends to 30 km from the centre while in Montreal and Vancouver housing investment is highly concentrated in a 2 to 10 km ring.

The changes in the size and total value of the ownership and rental housing stock are illustrated in figures 3 and 4. During the three decades, the value of ownership and units increased proportionally more than the number of dwelling units. These statistics add support to the redistribution hypothesis: inner-city values have increased more than their number of dwelling units. Figure 4 shows the 1971 to 2001 net increase in the number of occupied dwelling units in each 1 km ring. While the suburbs grew in each of the three metropolitan areas, the greatest increase was in suburban Toronto, the region with the most suburban development in 1971. Mon-

TABLE 3
Means and standard deviations (SD) of variables used in the regressions, illustrating the changes in the census tracts between 1971 and 2001.

	Montreal mean	SD	Toronto mean	SD	Vancouver mean	SD
Change in value renters (Can $ 2005 million)	54.4	72.8	108.2	157.0	169.5	161.3
Change in value owners (Can $ 2005 million)	104.5	158.5	331.9	716.6	426.8	391.0
Distance from central business district	10.4	7.7	15.2	9.9	13.4	9.4
Distance from airport	15.4	6.9	18.0	9.7	16.2	8.3
Rental units added	262.7	530.1	387.9	669.7	614.4	759.5
Owner units added	586.5	1055.2	905.3	2407.4	964.5	1365.7
Dwellings per km^2 in 1971	2,815.3	3,131.2	1,458.2	1,886.9	1,158.3	2,251.0
Percentage pre-1946 stock in 1971	27.6	29.2	22.8	28.9	19.4	19.6
Percentage 1946–60 in 1971	32.6	22.8	34.5	26.1	36.8	16.4
Number of census tracts	641		592		231	

treal shows the largest increase in dwelling units at the edge of the inner city in the 18 to 12 km ring. Vancouver's growth is more even across the first 30 km but the largest peak is 27 km from the centre, in part due to the way census tract centres fall across the defined rings. The change in the value of real estate (figure 4) closely follows the changes in the number of units in the three suburbs but not in the inner cities where they increased much more than unit counts. Vancouver's inner-city property values spike points to the re-valuation of the location as well as to the new high-priced development on the reclaimed industrial land near the edge of the downtown.

Table 3 presents the means and standard deviations for the variables used in the regressions, and the estimated coefficients are in table 4. The variable on the left side of the regression equation is the difference in the 2001 and 1971 value of property in each census tract expressed in Can $ 2005 million. The coefficients for the two tenures have the same sign in most cases. The negative coefficients for the distance variables show that the largest increases in property values are in the tracts closest to the two centres but the variance in the estimates is too high in most cases to support statistical conclusions. Higher density areas have slightly lower price increases but have higher rent increases compared with lower density tracts. In all cases, the tracts with the higher percentage of dwellings built before 1946 increased in value the most compared with tracts with newer

TABLE 4
1971 to 2001 change in residential real estate value of owner-occupied and rental units in census tracts as a function of distance, additions, density, and age of stock.

	Montreal		Toronto		Vancouver	
	owners	renters	owners	renters	owners	renters
Distance from central business district	−0.812	−0.212	−2.955*	−0.423	−4.013	−1.698*
Distance from airport	−2.148**	0.196	−0.369	−0.069	0.198	−0.336
Rental units added	−0.007	0.140**	−0.104**	0.217**	−0.155**	0.171**
Owner units added	0.412**	0.003*	0.308*	0.007**	0.301	0.028**
Dwellings per km^2	−0.004**	0.001*	−0.007	0.004**	−0.025**	0.007**
Percent pre-1946	0.052	0.474**	1.724**	0.239**	4.947**	0.370
Percent 1946–60	−0.093	0.131*	1.475**	0.060	2.307*	−0.238
Constant	77.877**	−5.390	64.502*	12.251	130.487*	58.363**
R^2	0.843	0.909	0.947	0.938	0.764	0.897
n cases	640		592		231	

** p-value <0.001; * p-value <0.05.

stock. Very good (law variance) estimates were developed for the net additions variables, and their magnitudes are in line with expectations. In Vancouver the regression shows that one net homeowner addition during the 1971 to 2001 period added $301 000 (in 2005 $) to the property wealth of a census tract. In 1991, after the 1980s increase in property values, the average value of an owner-occupied dwelling as reported in the public use microdata files was $374 000 in 2005 $. The size of the estimated coefficients for the net additions variables ring true. They are also the most important determinants of change in the property value of the census tracts. Regressing the two distance, the density, and the two age variables on the change in the value of the homeowner's stock yields R^2 of 0.244, 0.095, and 0.117 for Montreal, Toronto, and Vancouver.

Regressing the two net additions variables by themselves yields R^2 of 0.831, 0.940, and 0.688 for the three regions. The main changes in property value are due to the construction of new buildings and not due to investors changing their views as to the relative value of the inner city as opposed to the suburbs.

Figure 5 shows the change in the predicted total value of real estate within each ring, and figure 6 presents the change in predicted value within each ring divided by the land area of the tracts in each ring. The graphs are constructed by using the regressions described in table 4 but run on the pooled ownership and rental data. The estimated regressions are used to predict the change in value in each

FIGURE 5
Predicted increase in total residential property value between 1971 and 2001 after accounting for the change in the number of dwellings

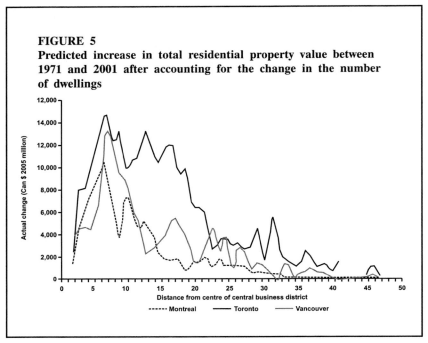

FIGURE 6
Predicted 1971 to 2001 increase in total residential property value in each 1 km ring divided by the land area in each ring after adjusting for differences in unit change (3km moving average)

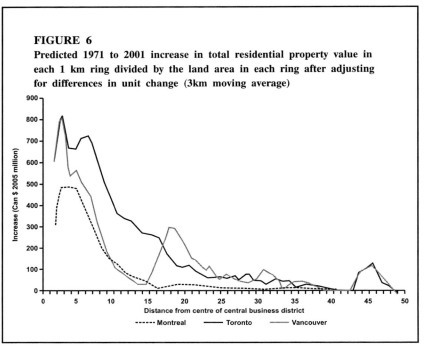

census tract considering its distances from the two centres and its housing density and age profiles.

The additions per tract are kept at the mean level for the CMA. The wiggle in the predicted profiles is due to differences in the age and density of the tracts as well as to differences in the size of the land mass brought about by natural features and the presence of unincorporated land. Dividing by the land area of the census tracts within the rings yields the much smoother but steeper profiles of figure 6. The graphs show a marked increase in the growth of property value with proximity to the city centre. The redistributions of property values, after controlling for the effect of net additions to the housing stock, are clearly in favour of the inner city. The predicted changes are large enough to overcome reasonable scepticism regarding the controls for the effect of net additions.

THE SHIFTS IN REAL ESTATE VALUES BY DECADE BETWEEN 1971 AND 2001

Table 5 presents the shifts in the number of dwelling units and in the total value of residential real estate between 1971 and 2001 across the four city sectors in each region. As expected, the inner cities and the old built-up suburbs show a relative loss of the region's share in the number of dwelling units and in total property value. In Toronto and Vancouver, the exurbs also had a declining share of dwelling units but only in Vancouver did the exurbs lose some of their share of property value. These statistics suggest that Toronto's exurban growth is, on average, in the form of expensive developments. The patterns of exurban growth suggest that the 'sprawl' issue is aggravated most by the growth of the new suburbs and not by exurban development.

The last four rows of table 5 present the 'adjusted shift'. The 1971 average value of the housing in each census tract was multiplied by the shift in units and subtracted from the shift statistics in the middle four rows. The adjustment accounts for the differences in shift in property value that are due to net additions. The initial, as opposed to the final, value of units is used because it provides a base value. Any value above and beyond can be considered a value increase during the period. More importantly, since most tracts grew below CMA growth rates it is intuitive to subtract out the value of the 'lost stock' using the base year value. The added stock in some tracts, especially in the new suburbs where most of the CMA growth occurred, is also valued at base year levels because this allows for higher valuation due to quality differences to be retained as part of the shift in value. Table 5 shows that the inner city, new suburbs,

TABLE 5
Shifts in the number of units and in residential real estate value between 1971 and 2001[a]

	Montreal	Toronto	Vancouver
Dwelling units			
Inner city	−143,223	−209,808	−60,388
Inner suburbs	−86,892	−194,621	−59,344
New suburbs	226,783	409,008	129,936
Exurbs	3,332	−4,579	−10,204
Shift in real estate value (Can $ 2005 million)			
Inner city	−10,825	−42,415	−12,415
Inner suburbs	−21,102	−69,838	−18,866
New suburbs	31,243	111,917	32,103
Exurbs	684	336	−822
Adjusted shift in real estate value[b] (Can $ 2005 million)			
Inner city	6949	2245	1,070
Inner suburbs	−10,722	−32,637	−8,933
New suburbs	3,494	29,488	7,020
Exurbs	279		904
Number of tracts	641		589

[a] Shift estimated as difference between predicted and actual values.
[b] Shift in real estate value adjusted by 1971 value of unit change.

and exurbs gain value and that the losses are in the postwar suburban ring. The outward shift is not just from the investors developing the suburbs as suggested in the structuralists' arguments; transfers both outward and inward are also taking place within the built-up city.

Figure 7 illustrates the decennial shifts across the tracts in each of the metropolitan areas. The maximum shifts are in the $6000 million range and the few outliers are truncated at $1000 million to help illustrate the main changes in values. The ordinary least squares fitted values that show a flattening of the gradient in Montreal and Toronto were calculated before truncating the shift variable. The dispersion of values is surprisingly uniform. While there are more positive shifts in the suburban regions than in the inner city, both city areas have tracts that gained and lost their share of the value of the metropolitan housing stock. The distribution of the 1990s shifts favours the inner city at the expense of the older suburbs located some 10 to 20 km from the centre. The shifts toward the Toronto suburbs were the greatest in the 1970s and reversed direction in the

FIGURE 7
**1981–2001 shift in residential property values by tract: (a)
Montreal, (b) Toronto, (c) Vancouver**

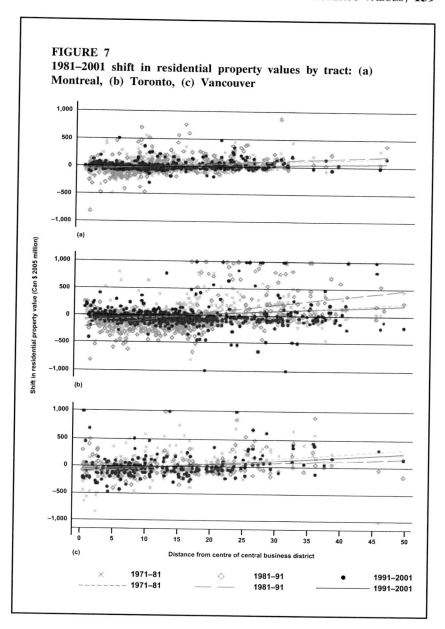

1990s. Again, with the help of imagination, one might see a cyclic movement between suburb and inner city but the overall dispersion of the shifts suggests that local factors are the most important.

TABLE 6
The shift in the value of owner-occupied and rental units per census tract by decade for Montreal, Toronto, Vancouver between 1971 to 2001 as a function of previous decade's shift, dwelling additions, housing stock density, and age.

	Montreal		Toronto		Vancouver	
	owners	renters	owners	renters	owners	renters
1971–81						
Distance from CBD[a]	−1.420**	0.664*	−1.517*	1.259**	−0.418	1.700*
Distance from airport	0.285	0.941**	0.830	−0.423*	1.201	0.199
Rental units added	0.009	0.151**	−0.001	0.179**	−0.028	0.213**
Owner units added	0.125**	0.002	0.250*	0.013**	0.362**	0.018
Dwelling density	−0.001	−0.003**	−0.004	−0.015**	0.003	−0.022**
Percentage pre–1946	0.299**	0.474**	0.454*	0.815**	1.163**	1.186**
Percentage 1946–60	−0.178	−0.002	0.082	0.288**	−0.525	1.331**
Constant	−21.167*	−47.869**	−71.535**	−58.746**	−120.900**	−134.160**
	0.466	0.739	0.6	0.794	0.779	0.697
1981–91						
Distance from CBD	−1.460**	0.837**	2.061**	1.286**	−0.401	2.331*
Distance from airport	1.257**	0.550*	−0.735	0.040	−0.519	−2.174*
Previous decade's shift	−0.156**	−0.189**	−0.254**	−0.216**	−0.040	−0.121**
Rental units added	0.022	0.178**	−0.078**	0.256**	−0.019	0.191**
Owner units added	0.161**	−0.006	0.375**	0.009**	0.254**	0.013
Dwelling density	0.002**	−0.002**	0.004	−0.017**	0.004**	−0.016**
Percentage pre–1946	0.364**	0.477**	0.926**	0.729**	1.404**	−0.279
Percentage 1946–60	0.022	−0.052	0.233	0.016	0.353	0.716**
Constant	−57.620*	−38.026**	−138.883**	−54.658**	−89.249**	−37.118
R^2	0.706	0.663	0.939	0.781	0.816	0.733
1991–2001						
Distance from CBD	−0.852**	0.167	0.090	0.077	−3.397*	0.863
Distance from airport	−0.530	−0.015	−0.718	−0.258	5.005**	−0.236
Previous decade's shift	−0.188**	−0.038**	−0.366**	−0.133**	−0.407**	−0.207**
Rental units added	−0.059**	0.134**	0.070**	0.205**	0.015	0.229
Owner units added	0.142**	0.004	0.286**	0.003*	0.259**	0.007
Dwelling density	0.002**	0.000	0.011**	0.001	0.006*	−0.009**
Percentage pre–1946	0.244**	0.115**	0.381	−0.175*	−0.278	0.339
Percentage 1946–60	−0.176*	−0.090*	0.226	0.106	0.258	0.763
Constant	−9.192	−7.441*	−132.608**	−5.696	−161.496**	−48.946**
R^2	0.558	0.652	0.933	0.789	0.749	0.815
n–cases	640		592		231	

** p-value <0.001; *p-value <0.05.
[a] CBD — central business district.

The table 6 regression coefficients for the three decades were estimated simultaneously for each metropolitan area and tenure using Stata's seemingly unrelated regression procedure to take advantage of the intercorrelated error terms. The spatial variables show the degree to which the shifts have favoured the neighbourhoods

FIGURE 8
Shift in total value of property in each 1km ring after controlling for changes in number of dwelling units: (a) Montreal, (b) Toronto, (c) Vancouver

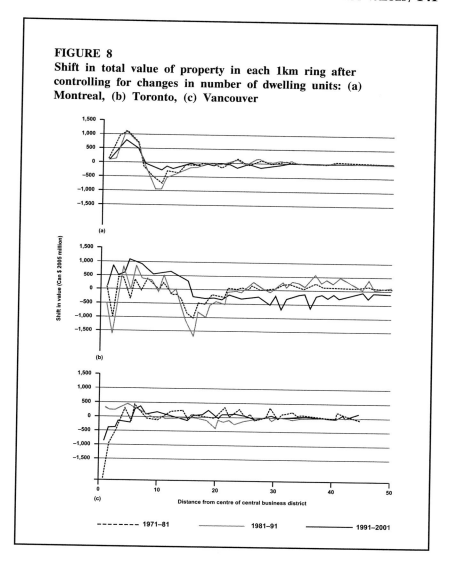

with the older stock as well as some of the postwar suburbs. The higher density tracts had negative shifts in the 1970s but had positive or no effect in the 1990s. Vancouver rental value shifts were negative in each of the three decades for the rental sector.

The Montreal and Toronto tracts with the highest proportion of the pre-1946 stock increased the most in each decade, and in the first two decades in Vancouver. The property values in the tracts with the highest proportion of dwellings built during the postwar

FIGURE 9
1971–2001 shift in residential property values per km2: (a)
Montreal, (b) Toronto, (c) Vancouver

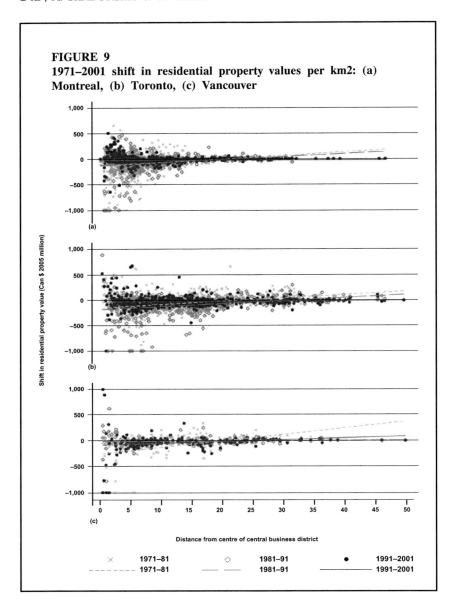

suburban boom from 1946 to 1960 increased somewhat in the Toronto and Vancouver markets. The main differences across tenures
are in the changes for the distance from the centre variable. The
shifts in the ownership stock decrease in magnitude or stay the same

with distance while the opposite is true for the rental stock. The value of the rental stock tended to increase the most with distance from the city centre.

The lagged shift variable consistently shows that the tracts experiencing the most growth in value during one decade — rental or ownership — if the other variables are held constant, have less growth in the following decade. In Montreal, a $1 million increase in the total property value of a census tract during the 1970s is associated with an average decrease in the next decade's shift by $0.164 million. A $1 million shift in the 1981 to 1991 decade was met by a $0.335 and a $0.383 million decrease in the 1990s shift in Toronto and Vancouver. Property value appears to increase up to a point in a neighbourhood before investor interest moves to the places that were left behind in the previous decade. The distance variables either yield estimates that are not distinguishable from zero or yield positive coefficients. In the 1970s and 1990s, the overall shift in property value was outward in Vancouver after controlling for the effects of the other variables. Figure 8 illustrates the predicted shifts by showing the total change in the value of the tracts in each consecutive 1 km ring after keeping the unit changes constant at each metropolitan area's mean tract value.

Montreal has a clear and consistent shift toward the inner city at the expense of the neighbourhoods 8 to 12 km from the centre. The differences in the shifts have evened out over time. The 1990s are characterised by transfers to the inner city from the older suburbs. Vancouver's shift is toward the inner city in the 1970s but the direction reversed during the next two decades. Consistent with the table 5 statistics, Vancouver's growth in property values is even across distance with only a small increase in the centre. Toronto's property values in the 12 to 20 km rings declined in the 1970s and 1980s relative to the inner city and the new suburbs. The 1990s brought the value transfer to the inner city while residential property values grew at a slightly lower rate in most of the new suburbs.

The variance in the shift variable is not correlated with distance from the centre when using the census tract as the unit of analysis; some tracts in both the inner city and in the suburbs increased their share of the region's property value while others lost value. The variance, however, is heteroskedastic when the shares are expressed in dollars per unit of land area. The large variation in the suburban shares is muted by the large size of their tracts and accentuated by the much smaller inner-city tracts. Figure 9 shows the dispersion of the shifts per unit area of land. While the lines fitted with ordinary least squares do rotate over time to favour the inner city, the largest changes in value per unit area of land are by far within the inner city and if there is a cycle to be observed then it is within the inner-city census tracts. The inner cities of Canada's three largest metropolitan areas had a higher rate of investment than the suburbs during the last decades of the century.

CONCLUSIONS

The differences in the growth of property value within the three metropolitan areas are mostly due to differences in the growth of the housing stock. The redistributions that are discernable favour the inner cities in the three largest Canadian metropolitan regions. The losses are not in the new suburbs even after accounting for the effect of new additions, but in the older suburbs. The study could not find a cycle in property value change, due, in part, to the limited time span, but it shows the difficulty of drawing useful generalisations about the movement of capital from one part of an urban region to another. The neighbourhoods that gain above average levels of investment in one decade tend to have below average levels in the next decade, a cycle of sorts. Ownership and rental markets do appear to move differently within the city, again a suggestion of a possible cycle. Development increases in a part of the city up to some threshold and then moves to areas that received less development in the previous decade. The threshold may be set by cost/technology considerations, by zoning, or by the changes in neighbourhood power as described by Filion (1991). The negative correlation over time is consistent with the seesaw effect of development and redevelopment depicted in the neoclassical simulation models that consider the fixity of real estate and the aging and depreciation of buildings, but can equally be explained within the framework of the structuralists' rent gap.

The shift of investment across broad city sectors predicted by neoclassical location theory and by political economists or geographers appears to be taking place but the variation across tracts in all sectors is so high as to encourage further study of the role of neighbourhood conditions and local factors in the shaping of cities. Postmodern urban theory that questions the universality of theory and emphasises the complexity of urban form adds a theoretical facet to the conclusion that perhaps the study of individual neighbourhoods ought to supersede, or at least complement, broad generalisations (see also Hackworth, 2005; Shearmur and Charron, 2004). The shift of property values from the suburbs to the inner city also corresponds with findings of inner-city gentrification and displacement of lower income households (see, for example, Madden, 2003;

Walks, 2001). In a broader social context rising inner-city property values reveal challenges related to housing affordability and displacement.

ACKNOWLEDGEMENTS

We would like to thank the journal's referees for their insightful comments. We also would like to thank John Meligrana for his advice and assistance in conducting this work. We are grateful for a grant from the Social Sciences and Humanities Research Council of Canada that made this work possible. All errors and opinions are the authors'.

REFERENCES

Alonso W, 1964 *Location and Land Use: Toward a General Theory of Land Rent* (Harvard University Press, Cambridge, MA)

Anas A R, Arnott R, Small K, 1998, "Urban spatial structure" *Journal of Economic Literature* 36 1426–1464

Arnott R, 1980, "A simple urban growth model with durable housing" *Regional Science and Urban Economics* 10 53–76

Badcock B A, 1990, "On the non-existence of the rent-gap, a reply" *Annals of the Association of American Geographers* 80 459–461

Badcock B A, 1992a, "Adelaide's heart transplant, 1970–88: 1. Creation, transfer, and capture of 'value' within the built environment" *Environment and Planning A* 24 215–241

Badcock B A, 1992b, "Adelaide's heart transplant, 1970–88: 2. The 'transfer' of value within the housing market" *Environment and Planning A* 24 323–339

Badcock B A, 1993, "Notwithstanding the exaggerated claims, residential revitalisation really is changing the form of some western cities: a response to Bourne" *Urban Studies* 30 191–195

Badcock B A, 1997, "Restructuring and spatial polarization in cities" *Progress in Human Geography* 21 251–262

Badcock B A, 2000, "The imprint of the post-fordist transition on Australian cities", in *Globalizing Cities: A New Spatial Order?* Eds P Marcuse, R van Kempen (Blackwell, Oxford) pp 211–227

Badcock B A, *2002 Making Sense of Cities: A Geographical Survey* (Arnold, London)

Badcock B, Browett M, 1992, "Adelaide's heart transplant, 1970–88: 3. The deployment of capital in the renovation and redevelopment submarkets" *Environment and Planning A* 24 1167–1190

Baum S, 1997, "Sydney, Australia: a global city? Testing the social polarization thesis" *Urban Studies* 34 1881–1901

Beauregard R A, 1994, "Capital switching and the built environment: United States, 1970–89" *Environment and Planning A* 26 715–732

Beauregard RA, 2005, "The textures of property markets: downtown housing and office conversions in New York City" *Urban Studies* 42 2431–2445

Bourassa S, 1990, "Another Australian view of the rent-gap hypothesis" *Annals of the Association of American Geographers* 80 458–459

Bourassa S, 1993, "The rent-gap debunked" *Urban Studies* 30 1731–1744

Bourne L, 2002, "The changing dimensions of inequality and polarization in Canadian cities", in *The Diversity of Urban Development and Urban Life* Ed. I Kim (National University Press, Seoul) pp 296–309

Brenner N, 2004 *New State Spaces: Urban Governance and the Rescaling of Statehood* (Oxford University Press, Oxford)

Brenner N, Theodore N, 2002, "Cities and geographies of 'actually existing neoliberalism'" *Antipode* 34 350–379

Brown P, Burke P, 1979 *The Canadian Inner-city 1971–1976: A Statistical Handbook Canada Mortgage and Housing Corporation, Ottawa, ON*

Brueckner J, 1980, "Residential succession and land use dynamics in a vintage model of urban housing" *Regional Science and Urban Economics* 10 225–293

Brueckner J, 1981, "Testing a vintage model of urban growth" *Journal of Regional Science* 21 23–35

Bunting T, Filion P, 1988, "Introduction: the movement towards the post-industrial society and the changing role of the inner-city", in *Essays on Canadian Urban Process and Form: The Changing Canadian Inner-city* Eds T Bunting, P Filion (University of Waterloo Department of Geography Publication Series,Waterloo, ON) pp 2–24

Bunting T, Filion P, 1996, "The dynamics of the dispersed city: its spatial and temporal dynamics", in *The Dynamics of the Dispersed City: Geographic and Planning Perspectives on Waterloo Region* Eds P Filion, T Bunting, K Curtis (University of Waterloo Department of Geography Publication Series, Waterloo, ON) pp 9–54

Castells M, 2002 *The Information Age: Economy, Society and Culture, Volume 1: The Rise of the Network Society* (Blackwell, Malden, MA)

Clark E, 1987 The Rent-gap and Urban Change: Case Studies in *Malmo 1860–1985* (Lund University Press, Lund)

Clark E, 1995, "The rent-gap re-examined" Urban Studies 32 1489–1503

Dorling D, Woodward R, 1996, "Social polarisation 1971–1991: a micro-geographical analysis of Britain" *Progress in Planning* 45(2) 63–122

Downs A, 1999 "Some realities about sprawl and urban decline" *Housing Policy Debate* 10 955–974

Esping-Anderson G, Assimakopoulou Z, van Kersbergen K, 1993, "Trends in contemporary class structuration: a six-nation comparison", in *Changing Classes: Stratification and Mobility in Post-industrial Societies* Ed. G Esping-Anderson (Sage, London) pp 32–57

Evans AW, 1973 *The Economics of Residential Location* (Macmillan, London)

Filion P, 1987, "Concepts of the inner-city and recent trends in Canada" *The Canadian Geographer* 31 223–244

Filion P, 1991, "The gentrification–social structural dialectic: a Toronto case study" *International Journal of Urban and Regional Research* 15 553–573

Filion P, 2001, "The urban policy-making and development dimension of fordism and post-fordism: a Toronto case study" *Space and Polity* 5 85–111

Hackworth J, 2005, "Emergent urban forms, or emergent post-modernism? A comparison of large US metropolitan areas" *Urban Geography* 26 484–519

Hackworth J, Rekers J, 2005, "Ethnic packaging and gentrification: the case of four neighbourhoods in Toronto" *Urban Affairs Review* 41 211–236

Hackworth J, Smith N, 2001, "The changing state of gentrification" *Tijdschrift voor Economische en Sociale Geografie* 92 464–477

Hamnett C, 2003, "Gentrification and the middle-class remaking of inner London, 1961–2001" *Urban Studies* 40 2401–2426

Hamnett C, Cross D, 1998, "Social polarisation and inequality in London: the earnings evidence, 1979–95" *Environment and Planning C: Government and Planning* 16 659–680

Harvey D, 1972 *Society, The City and The Space Economy of Urbanism* (Association of American Geographers, Washington, DC)

Harvey D, 1973 *Social Justice and the City* (Arnold, London)

Harvey D, 1978, "The urban process under capitalism: a framework for analysis" *International Journal of Urban and Regional Research* 2 101–131

Harvey D, 1985 *The Urbanization of Capital* (John Hopkins University Press, Baltimore, MD)

Heisz A, Larochelle-Côté S, 2005 *Work and Commuting in Census Metropolitan Areas 1996–2001* (Statistics Canada, Ottawa)

Kloosterman R, Musterd S, 2001, "The polycentric urban region: towards a research agenda" *Urban Studies* 38 623–633

Ley D, 1987, "Reply: the rent-gap revisited" *Annals of the Association of American Geographers* 77 465–468

Ley D, 1988, "Social upgrading in six Canadian inner cities" *The Canadian Geographer* 32 31–45

Ley D, 1993, "Gentrification in recession: social change in six Canadian inner cities, 1981–1986" *Canadian Geographer* 13 230–256

Ley D, 1996, *"The new middle class and the remaking of the central city"* (Oxford University Press, Oxford)

Ley D, Tutchener J, Cunningham G, 2002, "Immigration, polarization, or gentrification? Accounting for changing house prices and dwelling values in gateway cities" *Urban Geography* 23 703–727

Lipietz A, 2001, "The fortunes and misfortunes of post-Fordism", in *Phases of Capitalist Development: Booms, Crises and Globalization* Eds R Albritton, M Itoh, R Westra, A Zuege (Palgrave Macmillan, Basingstoke, Hants) pp 17–36

Madden J, 2003, "Has the concentration of income and poverty among suburbs of large metropolitan areas changed over time?" *Papers in Regional Science* 82 249–275

Maher C, 1994, "Housing prices and geographical scale: Australian cities in the 1980s" *Urban Studies* 31 5–27

Marcuse P, van Kempen R (Eds), 2000 *Globalizing Cities: A New Spatial Order?* (Blackwell, Oxford)

Meligrana J, Skaburskis A, 2005, "Extent, location and profiles of continuing gentrification in Canadian Metropolitan Areas, 1981–2001" *Urban Studies* 4 1569–1592

Mills E, 1969, "The value of urban land", in *The Quality of Urban Environment* Ed. H Perloff (Johns Hopkins University Press, Baltimore, MD) pp 231–253

Mills E, 1972 *Studies in the Structure of the Urban Economy* (Johns Hopkins University Press, Baltimore, MD)

Musterd S, Ostendorf W, 1998, "The changing distribution of incomes in Dutch cities: myth and reality" *GeoJournal* 46 29–39

Muth R, 1969 *Cities and Housing* (University of Chicago Press, Chicago, IL)

Rose D, Villeneuve P, 1998, "Engendering class in the metropolitan city: occupational pairings and income disparities among two-earner couples" *Urban Geography* 19 123–159

Sassen S, 1990, "Economic restructuring and the American city" *Annual Review of Sociology* 16 465–490

Sassen S, 1991 *The Global City: NewYork, London, Tokyo* (Princeton University Press, Princeton, NJ)

Schall L D, 1971, "A note on externalities and property valuation" *Journal of Regional Science* 11 101–105

Shearmur R, Charron M, 2004, "From Chicago to LA and back again: a Chicago-inspired quantitative analysis of income distribution in Montreal" *The Professional Geographer* 56 109–126

Skaburskis A, 1981, "Determinants of housing stock losses" *American Real Estate and Urban Economics Association Journal* 19 181–184

Skaburskis A, 1982, "Externalities and property prices: a test of the Schall hypothesis" *Journal of Regional Science* 22 213–223

Skaburskis A, 1988, "Speculation and housing prices: a study of Vancouver's boom-bust cycle" Urban Affairs Quarterly 23 556–580

Skaburskis A, 1989, "Inversions in urban density gradients: a brief look at the Vancouver metropolitan area's density profile" *Urban Studies* 26 397–401

Skaburskis A, 1990, "The differential impact of a uniform access improvement" *Environment and Planning A* 22 689–693

Skaburskis A, 1997, "Gender differences in housing demand" *Urban Studies* 34 275–320

Skaburskis A, 2006, "Filtering, city change and the supply of low-priced housing in Canada" *Urban Studies* 43 533–558

Sklair L, 1991 *Sociology of the Global System* (Harvester Wheatsheaf, New York)

Smith N, 1979, "Toward a theory of gentrification: a back to the city movement by capital, not people" *Journal of the American Planning Association* 45 538–548

Smith N, 1986, "Gentrification, the frontier, and the restructuring of urban space", in *Gentrification of the City* Eds N Smith, P Williams (Allen and Unwin, Winchester, MA) pp 15–34

Smith N, 2002, "New globalism, new urbanism: gentrification as global urban strategy" *Antipode* 34 427–450

Smith N, Williams P (Eds), 1986 *Gentrification of the City* (Allen and Unwin, Winchester, MA)

Statistics Canada, 2005 *Canadian Census Standard Geography Classification* http://www.statcan.ca/english/Subjects/Standard/sgc/geography.htm

Townshend I, Walker A, 2002, "The structure of income residential segregation in Canadian metropolitan areas" *Canadian Journal of Regional Science* 25 (1) 1–24

Walks A, 2001, "The social ecology of the post-Fordist/global city? Economic restructuring and socio-spatial polarisation in the Toronto urban region" *Urban Studies* 38 407–447

Wheaton W, 1982, "Urban spatial development with durable but replaceable capital" *Journal of Urban Economics* 12 53–67

Wiewel W, Persky J, Sendzik M, 1999, "Private benefits and public costs: policies to address suburban sprawl" *Policy Studies Journal* 27 (1) 96–114

Wingo L Jr, 1961 *Transportation and Urban Land Use* (Johns Hopkins University Press, Baltimore, MD)

Wyly E K, Atia M, Hammel D J, 2004, "Has mortgage capital found an inner-city spatial fix? *Housing Policy Debate* 15 623–685

Price-volume Correlation in the Housing Market: Causality and Co-movements

JIM CLAYTON, NORMAN MILLER &
LIANG PENG

INTRODUCTION

Housing markets play an important role in the economy. For example, Bertaut and Starr-McCluer (2002) show that residential properties accounted for about one quarter of aggregate household wealth in the United States in the late 1990s, and Tracy and Schneider (2001) show that housing wealth accounts for about two-thirds of the wealth of the median U.S. household. Changes in home prices and trading volume seem to have significant economic impacts on builders, brokers, lenders, appraisers, furniture consumption as well as local property tax collections and related local government budgets, in addition to local affordability and wealth. A rapid surge in home prices and trading volume after 2000 has been seen across many areas in the United States, and it is followed by a recent decline in house prices and trading volume. These phenomena generate a lot of discussion regarding whether the US has been in a "housing bubble" (see, e.g., Case and Shiller 2003). Despite the importance of the housing markets and the economic and policy implications of changes in home prices and trading volume, some important aspects of housing markets are not well understood.

A well known pattern in the housing market is that prices and trading volume seem to correlate with each other: trading activity tends to be more intense (i.e., more transactions and less time on the market before sale) when prices are rising compared to falling markets. The positive correlation between prices and trading volume appears to be inconsistent with standard rational expectation asset market models, in which housing prices are present discounted values of the future service streams (see e.g. Poterba 1984). A conventional interpretation of the correlation is that price changes cause changes in trading volume. The causal relation is built on one of three factors: equity constraints,[1] nominal loss aversion (homeowners are less willing to sell their homes in a falling market to avoid realized losses), or the option value of homeowners (homeowners wait to sell when the upside benefits exceed net carrying costs, see Cauley and Pavlov 2002). Stein (1995), Genesove and Mayer (1997), Lamont and Stein (1999), and Chan (2001) provide theoretical and empirical evidence for equity constraints of home sellers. Genesove and Mayer (2001), Cauley and Pavlov (2002), and Engelhardt (2003) provide evidence for nominal loss aversion.

Although research regarding the causal relation between prices and trading volume greatly improves our understanding of the dynamics of the housing market, a few important questions have not been satisfactorily answered. First, is a positive price–volume correlation widely observed across markets? It is striking that there is mixed evidence regarding the relation between prices and trading volume, and the evidence is from either aggregate national level data, or from small panel data (up to 22 metropolitan areas). While a positive price–volume correlation is found by Stein (1995), Berkovec and Goodman (1996), Andrew and Meen (2003), and Ortalo-Magné and Rady (2004), a negative relation is found by Follain and Velz (1995) and Hort (2000), and no significant relation is found in commercial real estate by Leung and Feng (2005).

Second, does the causal relation from prices to trading volume necessarily explain the contemporaneous price–volume correlation? The causal relation, though strongly supported by empirical evidence, more naturally implies a lead–lag relation instead of a positive correlation. While it is possible that a lead–lag relation at high frequency helps generate a contemporaneous correlation at low frequency, or a correlation at the same frequency due to possible positive autocorrelations of prices, to date no empirical study has been conducted to assess the extent to which the causal relation from house prices to trading volume helps explain the price–volume correlation.

---

[1] Falling prices reduce homeowners' home equity values. Therefore, when homeowners want to sell their houses, to ensure that the proceeds from selling would be sufficient to repay their mortgages and provide down payments on new homes, they need to ask for higher prices, which increases the time on the market and reduces the trading volume.

Third, is the price–volume correlation necessarily, or solely, due to the causal relation between prices and trading volume? Houses are not only assets, but also consumption goods. While the supply of many assets such as common stocks may be fixed in the short term, the aggregate demand and supply for housing in a market is often elastic. In fact, Smith (1976), Hanushek and Quigley (1980), DiPasquale and Wheaton (1994), and Malpezzi and Maclennan (2001) among others, provide evidence of negative price elasticity of housing demand and positive price elasticity of housing supply. Therefore, shocks to the housing market may affect both home prices and trading volume, and thus cause co-movements of them, which may lead to a price–volume correlation. Further, there is a solid theoretic foundation for the co-movements of prices and trading volume in housing markets. Wheaton (1990) provides theoretical evidence that exogenous variables such as demand shocks can affect both vacancy and sales time, which usually relate negatively to turnover, and prices in housing markets. More theories along this line are proposed by Krainer (2001), Ortalo-Magné and Rady (2006), and Novy-Marx (2007). While the theories suggest that the price–volume correlation could simply be co-movements, there is no empirical study for such co-movements and the extent to which they help explain the price–volume correlation.[2] Moreover, Wheaton (1990) also predicts that trading volume itself can affect house prices: a higher rate of successful matching between buyers and sellers reduces the supply of for-sale units; therefore, sellers adjust their reservation prices upward.[3] This causal relation from trading volume to prices might also help explain the price–volume correlation in the housing market, although there is no empirical study on this possibility at this moment. This paper aims to shed light on these three questions using an unusually large panel dataset which comprises 114 metropolitan statistic areas (MSAs) in the U.S. and covers a sample period from 1990:2 to 2002:2. First, we fit to the data a bivariate VAR model with both prices and volume (measured with turnover) being endogenous, and estimate how exogenous variables, such as conditions in the labor market, the mortgage market, and the financial market, and lagged endogenous variables affect both prices and vol-

---

[2] While there is a large literature in finance about the determinants of trading volume as well as return-volume relations in the stock market, this paper focuses on the theories that are specifically developed for housing markets and motivated by the fact that houses are both consumption goods and investments.

[3] It is worth noting that many housing analysts presume that volume increases lead price increases. For example, Miller and Sklarz (1986) show that changes in sales volume in Honolulu and Salt Lake lead price changes by one or two years.

ume in housing markets. We test Granger causality from prices to trading volume (Stein 1995 theory) and from trading volume to prices (Wheaton 1990 theory), to compare and contrast the Wheaton (1990) and Stein (1995) theories. In this step, we also estimate three alternative specifications of the VAR model. Specifically, we separate positive changes in house prices from negative changes to test an asymmetric relation between house prices and volume implied by Stein (1995), which is due to that equity constraints are binding in falling markets. Further, housing markets are well known for being heterogeneous, particularly in terms of supply elasticity. Therefore, we break down our sample into two groups of MSAs, with above and below median supply elasticity respectively, and estimate and Granger causality tests for each group.

Second, we empirically analyze determinants of prices and trading volume in housing markets and investigate the existence and magnitude of the co-movements between prices and trading volume, as well as to what extent they help explain the price–volume correlation. For each specification of the VAR model, we decompose the changes in prices and volume respectively into two components: the fitted part (explained by our VAR model) and the residual, and investigate if our model captures the price volume correlation in the data. Further, we decompose the fitted values into three components: a price-caused component (explained by lagged prices), a trading volume-caused component (explained by lagged trading volume), and a co-movement component (explained by exogenous changes in the economy), and study how each component helps explain the fitted price–volume correlation. Finally, we use impulse response functions to describe the responses of prices and trading volume to shocks.

This paper provides original insights into the determinants of prices and trading volume in the housing market. We find that both house prices and trading volume are significantly affected by changes in the labor market, which include changes in total non-agricultural employment, average household income, and the unemployment rate. The housing market is also significantly affected by the level and trend of mortgage rates (we use the national average interest rate for 30 year fixed rate mortgages). When the mortgage rate is high and when it is falling, both home prices and trading volume are low. Interestingly, the stock market performance also has a statistically significant effect on house prices. When the S&P 500 index is high (level) or when it shows a down turn (trend), home prices tend to be low and trading volume tend to be high.

We find strong evidence that home prices Granger cause trading volume. Moreover, it is the decreases in prices, not the increases, that affect future trading volume, which is direct evidence of support for Stein (1995). We also find some evidence that trading volume Granger causes home prices, which, derives mainly from markets with low supply elasticity. This appears to indicate that in markets where supply can easily adjust, trading volume does not seem to affect future prices. The fact that trading volume more significantly affects prices in supply constrained markets seems consistent with Wheaton (1990). Overall, we find supporting evidence for both Stein (1995) and Wheaton (1990).

We find a statistically significant positive price–volume correlation in the housing market, and this correlation seems to be explained by co-movements of house prices and trading volume instead of the causal relations between prices and volume.

Specifically, we find the positive correlation is almost completely explained by the home prices and trading volume fitted by our panel VAR model. In addition, we find that the price-caused components of prices and volume are negatively correlated, which indicates that the Granger causality from prices to trading volume does not appear to help explain the positive price–volume correlation. We also find that the trading volume-caused components of prices and volume are positively correlated in markets with high supply elasticity, but negatively correlated in markets with low supply elasticity. Therefore, the Granger causality from trading volume to prices does not seem to provide a good explanation for the average price–volume correlation that is positive. Finally, the co-movement components of prices and volume are significantly positively correlated for markets with both high and low supply elasticity; therefore exogenous shocks seem to explain the positive price–volume correlation well. Overall, our empirical evidence suggests that home prices and trading volume indeed Granger cause each other, but the causal relations do not appear to be driving the positive price–volume correlation, at least not at quarterly frequency.

This paper is original in four aspects. This is the first study that investigates the contemporaneous price–volume correlation in the housing market using a large panel data set comprising a large number of markets (114 MSAs) that are arguably distinct from each other. Second, this paper is the first to test the Granger causality between house prices and trading volume and compare and contrast Stein's (1995) and Wheaton's (1990) theories. Third, this paper is the first to empirically study the comovements of prices and trading volume caused by exogenous economic/ demographic shocks. Finally, this paper is the first to assess the extent to which the co-movements of prices and volume and causality between them, respectively, help explain the price–volume correlation.

The paper proceeds as follows. The next section presents the econometric model. "Model Specifications and Data" discusses the specification of the model and the data. Empirical evidence is presented in Section "Empirical Evidence". Section "Conclusions" provides conclusions.

ECONOMETRIC MODEL

The Model

We use a bivariate VAR model to analyze the determinants of both house prices and trading volume. This approach has a few important merits. First, it allows us to directly test the Granger causality between prices and trading volume. Wheaton (1990) suggests not only that turnover and house prices are jointly determined, but also that greater market turnover itself can generate higher house prices by reducing sales time and increasing seller reservations, which predicts that turnover Granger causes house price changes. On the other hand, Stein (1995) and others suggest that house price changes should Granger cause turnover, due to equity constraints, loss aversion, or the option value of homeowners. While all the above predictions provide important theoretical insights, they have not been tested using large cross-sectional time series data in the literature.

Second, this approach enables us to better understand the determination of house prices and trading volume, and decompose prices and volume respectively into four components: the component determined by exogenous variables; the component determined by lagged prices; the component determined by lagged trading volume; and the component determined by other unknown variables. This decomposition allows us to calculate the price–volume correlation using each of the four components of the price and volume and assess the direction and magnitude of the correlation due to each of the components.

We now build the bivariate panel VAR model. We assume that both the equilibrium housing price level and turnover are functions of quarterly dummy variables, exogenous variables and lagged endogenous variables.

$$\begin{pmatrix} P_{i,t} \\ q_{i,t} \end{pmatrix} = \begin{pmatrix} a_i \\ b_i \end{pmatrix} t + \sum_{s=1} A_s d_s + \sum_{s=1}^{k} B_s \begin{pmatrix} P_{i,t-s} \\ q_{i,t-s} \end{pmatrix} + CX_{i,t} + \begin{pmatrix} \varepsilon_{i,t}^p \\ \varepsilon_{i,t}^p \end{pmatrix} \quad (1)$$

In Eq. 1, d_s is a dummy variable for the sth quarter, which equals 1 if period t is the $_s$th quarter and 0 otherwise. For the ith MSA in period t, $P_{i,t}$ denotes the log of the equilibrium price, $q_{i,t}$ denotes the log of the turnover (measured with the ratio of existing single family home sales to the units of existing single family homes),

$X_{i,t}$ is a k by 1 vector of exogenous variables that affect either the demand or supply in the market, $\varepsilon_{i,t}^p$ and $\varepsilon_{i,t}^q$ are error terms. Coefficients and are scalars. A_s is a 2 by 1 vector. B_s is 2 by 2 vector. C is a 2 by k vector with k being the number of exogenous variables in $X_{i,t}$. All variables on the right side of the equation can affect either the demand or supply in the housing market, and thus ultimately determine the equilibrium price level and turnover. While the functional forms of the demand and supply curves themselves are interesting, this paper focuses on the aggregate effect of the explanatory variables because it appears sufficient to help us test the two lines of theories regarding the price–volume correlation. It is not this paper's research goal to estimate the demand or supply curve of houses.

Four points are worth noting in Eq. 1. First, the equation includes lagged market prices as explanatory variables, and thus allows them to affect the equilibrium price and trading volume. This accommodates the causal relation from market prices to trading volume as predicted by Stein (1995).

Second, the model allows lagged trading volume to affect both the price and turnover, which essentially allows market participants to update their private valuations based on historical trading volume. This enables us to test the Granger causality from trading volume to prices, which Wheaton (1990) suggests. In addition, this accommodates the feedback effects proposed by Novy-Marx (2007), which suggests that a demand shock may increase the buyer-to-seller ratio in the market, and thus reduce the time on the market and increase the turnover of housing units. Changes in trading volume, consequently, can help sellers update their information set and thus change their asking prices, which shifts the supply curve.

Third, the prices in our model are nominal prices. We chose nominal prices instead of real prices because an important theory that aims to explain that the price–volume correlation relies on nominal loss aversion of homeowners (see, e.g. Genesove and Mayer 2001; Engelhardt 2003). Moreover, existing research suggests that people often make financial decisions in nominal terms. For example, Shafire et al. (1997) argue that money illusion is common in a wide variety of contexts. Particularly, they find that a majority of survey respondents focus on nominal rather than real gains in assessing hypothetical gains/losses when selling a house.

Finally, our model controls for the heterogeneity in the housing market in two ways. First, our model includes MSA-specific dummies, which would capture all unobserved time-invariant MSA characteristics, such as geographic attributes. Second, our model includes economic variables at the MSA level, which help capture local economic conditions that are time-variant. However, our results should be interpreted with caution: the estimated parameters should be treated as averages across the MSAs in our sample or subsamples, and our analysis can be interpreted as analysis of an average MSA. Note that this is not necessarily a problem—the theories we test are general and should apply to all MSAs; therefore, results from an average MSA serve our research purposes.

Since our data include price indices (with the index level normalized to 100 for 1995:1) rather than actual prices, we can not estimate (1) directly. Instead, we estimate the first order difference of (1)

$$
\begin{pmatrix} \Delta p_{i,t} \\ \Delta q_{i,t} \end{pmatrix} = \begin{pmatrix} a_i \\ b_i \end{pmatrix} t + \sum_{s=1,2,4} A_s d_s + \sum_{s=1}^{k} B_s \begin{pmatrix} \Delta p_{i,t-s} \\ \Delta q_{i,t-s} \end{pmatrix} + C \Delta X_{i,t} + \begin{pmatrix} v_{i,t}^p \\ v_{i,t}^p \end{pmatrix} \quad (2)
$$

We assume the error terms have zero means and are orthogonal to all explanatory variables. The quarterly dummies in (2) are first-order differences of the dummies in (1), but we use the same notations to simplify the illustrations. The system in (2) is essentially a fixed-effect panel VAR model. In our estimation, we use the within transformation to eliminate MSA dummies, so variables in (2) become demeaned.

Tests and Analysis

Based on the results of estimating the model in (2), we conduct the following analysis. First, we test the null hypotheses that house prices do not Granger cause trading volume, and trading volume does not Granger cause house prices. The null hypothesis that house prices (trading volume) do not Granger cause trading volume (house prices) essentially imposes the constraint that the coefficients of all lagged prices (trading volume) are 0 in the second (first) equation of (2), which can be easily tested with a F-test. These hypotheses are expected to be rejected if the theories by Stein (1995) and Wheaton (1990) are valid.

Second, we investigate the existence and magnitude of the price–volume correlation. The price–volume correlation is defined as the correlation between changes in home prices, i.e. $\Delta q_{i,t}$, and changes in trading volume, i.e. $\Delta p_{i,t}$ (both are demeaned using the within transformation). We do not use the correlation between $p_{i,t}$ and $q_{i,t}$ because prices have trends and are not stationary, while the trading volume is bounded between 0 and 1; therefore, the correlation between them in a long sample period does not seem to make much economic sense.

Third, we assess how well the fitted prices and volume in our model (explained by both exogenous economic changes and lagged prices and volume) help explain the price–volume correlation. We decompose $\Delta p_{i,t}$, and $\Delta q_{i,t}$, respectively into the fitted values and re-siduals (unexplained by our model), and then calculate the correla-tion between the fitted price and fitted volume and the correlation between the residuals, respectively. We compare the "fitted" correla-tion and the "residual" correlation with the raw price–volume corre-lation. The comparison helps us assess how well our model captures the price–volume correlation overall.

Fourth, we analyze the degree to which the Granger causality between prices and trading volume and the co-movements of the price and volume help explain the price–volume correlation respec-tively. This time, we decompose the fitted values of $\Delta p_{i,t}$, and $\Delta q_{i,t}$, respectively into three parts: the price-caused component (explained by lagged prices), the trading volume-caused component (explained by lagged trading volume) and the co-movement component (ex-plained by other variables). We then assess the significance and mag-nitude of the correlations for different components and investigate how well each component helps explain the fitted price–volume cor-relation.

Finally, we study how shocks in exogenous variables affect the dynamics of the price and trading volume in the housing market. We construct and plot impulse response functions to describe how prices and trading volume react to exogenous shocks respectively. The im-pulse response functions help shed light on the economic sources of the price–volume correlation.

MODEL SPECIFICATIONS AND DATA
Model Specifications

This section discusses our choice of exogenous variables $X_{i,t}$ in the panel VAR model. We categorize variables that may affect the demand and/or supply in the housing market as labor market related, mortgage market related, and financial market related variables. Note that our estimation uses the demeaned first-order differences of the log values of these variables.

Changes in the labor market and local demographic conditions likely affect housing demand and/or supply for several reasons. First, increasing immigrants and the growth of the local economy and/or population may increase demand for dwellings such as single family homes. Therefore, we include the total non-agricultural employment as an exogenous variable. Second, changes in income may increase housing demand. Consequently, we include the average household in-come as another exogenous variable. Thirdly, changes in the unem-ployment rate imply that the number of people who need to search for jobs in and out of a specific area is changing, which likely affects the housing demand and supply in the area. As a result, we include the unemployment rate as the third labor market related variable.

Mortgage market conditions likely affect house prices and turnover as well, for borrowing cost is another ostensible exogenous variable that affects housing demand and supply. We consider two variables that may be relevant. The first one is the mortgage rate per se. It is plausible that home buyers are less financially constrained when mortgage rates are lower. The second one is the trend in mortgage rates. Among other possibilities, potential buyers have the real option to delay their home purchases until mortgage rates are more favorable. Consequently, when mortgage rates seem to be falling, potential buyers may choose to postpone their home purchases, and housing demand may decrease. A measure of the trend in quarter t is the change of mortgage rates from quarter $t - 1$ to quarter t. Since the autocorrelation of the change in mortgage rate is indeed positive and fairly large (0.13), the change from quarter $t - 1$ to quarter t does help capture the trend.

In our estimation, we use the national average interest rate of 30 year fixed rate mortgages and its first order difference to capture the mortgage rate level and trend. Since to our knowledge there is no theory that articulates the specific effects of these two variables, the interpretation of the coefficients demands caution. Fortunately, our tests rely on the aggregate effects for these two variables, not the specific manner in which they affect the housing market.

The stock market may also affect the housing market, even though the effects might be complicated and ambiguous. First, the well known wealth effect suggests that an increase in wealth may increase consumption, including consumption of housing. Therefore, a booming stock market may increase housing demand. Second, a booming stock market may help mitigate the liquidity constraints of moving families, for they have the option to use proceeds from selling stocks to help defray down payments for new homes. This might affect both the demand and the supply in the housing market, given that many families are simultaneously buyers and sellers. Finally, houses may appear to be less attractive assets when investors believe that stocks are better investments. The competing effect may reduce housing demand. While we lack rigorous theories with unambiguous predictions regarding the effects of the stock market, we try to use two variables to capture the effects: the S&P 500 index level, which may proxy for the financial wealth and/or constraints of households, and the gross return of the S&P 500 index, which may proxy for the trend of the stock market. In our estimation, we essentially use the first-order and the second-order differences of the S&P 500 index.

Data

This paper compiles data from five sources. First, the U.S. Bureau of Census (BOC) provides quarterly estimates for single family housing units for 209 MSAs in 1990:2 and for 280 MSAs in 2000:2. The difference in the number of MSAs is mainly due to changes in MSA boundaries and the establishment of new MSAs. Second, the Office of Federal Housing Enterprise Oversight (OFHEO) provides transaction-based quarterly house price indices at the MSA level (using BOC 1999 MSA definitions). Third, Moody's Economy.com provides quarterly measurements for existing single family home sales, total nonagricultural employment, average household income, population, single family home permits, and the unemployment rate at the MSA level (using BOC 1999 MSA definitions). The sources for these variables are respectively the National Association of Realtors (NAR), Bureau of Labor Statistics (BLS), Bureau of Census, and Internal Revenue Service (IRS). IRS records seem to be used to estimate migration between MSAs, which is then used to estimate population. Fourth, NAR provides the time series of the national average interest rate for 30 year fixed rate mortgages. Finally, CRSP provides the time series of the S&P 500 index.

The sample period in our analysis is from 1990:2 to 2002:2, and the time frequency is quarterly. We hope to fit our model to high frequency data, since the causal relation between prices and trading volume is more likely to be identified in high frequency data. The highest frequency we are able to obtain is quarterly.

Our analysis uses MSAs that satisfy the following three requirements. First, a qualifying MSA needs to exist in 1990:2 (1990 Census period) and 2000:2 (2000 Census period), and has single family housing unit data in the two periods. Second, the MSA also needs to have unchanged definitions and boundaries in the sample period. To check whether the boundaries have changed, we first check if the MSA name has changed from 1990:2 to 2000:2. If the name remains the same, we manually check the BOC historical records of boundary changes to verify if the MSA has unchanged boundaries. 114 MSAs satisfy the first two requirements. The third requirement is that MSAs cannot have any of the following variables missing: existing single family home sales, total nonagricultural employment, the unemployment rate, average housing income, single family home permits, and the house price index. Using all three requirements, we end up with 114 MSAs,[4] which are listed in the Appendix.

---

[4] A list of excluded MSAs, PMSAs, and NECMs is available upon request.

In our analysis, trading volume is measured by turnover, which is defined as the ratio of existing single family home sales to the stock of existing single family homes. Since we only observe the number of single family units for the two Census quarters, we estimate the units in other time periods using the following formula.

$$unit_{i,t} = init_{i,t} - 1 + completion_{i,t} - demolish_{i,t} \qquad (3)$$

In (3), for MSA i in period t, unit $_{i,t}$ is the single family units, completion i,t is units completed, and demolish $_{i,t}$ is the units demolished.

We estimate completion i,t using permit information as well as the relation among permits, starts, and completions. According to BOC, actual starts in new home building are on average 2.5% more than permits and the completion rate is 3.5% less than starts. Therefore, we assume that 100 issued permits will lead to $100 \times 1{:}025 \times 0{:}965 = 98{:}9$ new units. It is also worth noting that completion of new units may not be in the same quarter as permit issuances. According to the BOC, almost all (97% to be exact) constructions start in the same quarter when permits are issued. Further, 20% of starts are completed in the same quarter, 49% in the next quarter, 19% in the third quarter, 7% in the 4th quarter, and 6% in the 5th quarter or beyond. The above relations help us estimate completion$_{i,t}$ using the following equation.

$$\begin{aligned} completion_{i,t} = 0.989 \times (\,&0.2\,permit_{i,t} + 0.49\,permit_{i,t-1} \\ &+ 0.19\,permit_{i,t-2} + 0.07\,permit_{i,t-3} \\ &+ 0.06\,permit_{i,t-4}) \end{aligned} \qquad (4)$$

We estimate demolitions after estimating completions. We assume the same number of demolished units per period,[5] and calculate the demolished units per quarter using the following equation.

$$\left(unit_{i,1990:2} + \sum\nolimits_{t=1990:2}^{2002:2} completion_{i,t} - unit_{i,2002:2} \right) \div 40 \qquad (5)$$

After we estimate the completion and demolished units, we use eq. 3 to estimate the units of single family homes in each of the non-census quarters.

As a robustness check, we also estimate the existing single family units using an alternative method based on the relation between

---

[5] We also assume constant demolition rates as a percentage over total units, and our results are robust to this assumption.

FIGURE 1
Home price indicies for the U.S. MSAs

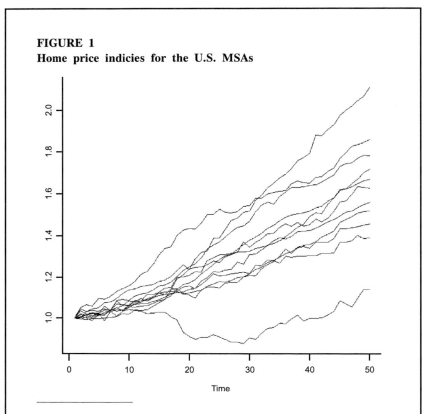

This figure plots the deciles of OFEHO quarterly home price indices (nominal) in the U.S. from 1990:2 to 2002:2 where the deciles are created using the total appreciation of home prices in the sample period. The index levels are normalized to 1 in 1990:2

population and housing units. Our data indicate that single family housing units are almost perfectly correlated with population across MSAs and over time. In fact, two cross-sectional regressions of single family units on population in 1990:2 and 2000:2, respectively, both generate R-squares around 0.99 when accurate housing units and population data are available from the BOC.

Furthermore, a regression of the ratio of housing units to population in 2000:2 against the same ratio in 1990:2 generates an R-square of 0.98, which seems to indicate that the housing unit–population ratio is highly stable across time. Therefore, for each MSA, we

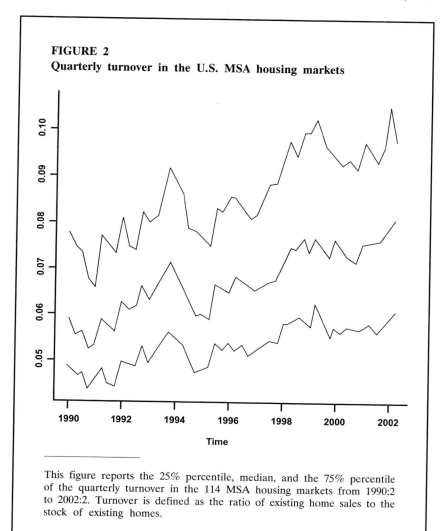

FIGURE 2
Quarterly turnover in the U.S. MSA housing markets

This figure reports the 25% percentile, median, and the 75% percentile of the quarterly turnover in the 114 MSA housing markets from 1990:2 to 2002:2. Turnover is defined as the ratio of existing home sales to the stock of existing homes.

estimate the ratio of single family housing units to population in a given period with a time–distance weighted average of the ratios in 1990:2 and 2000:2. We then estimate the existing housing units in that period with the product of population and the estimated ratio. The turnover estimated with the alternative method is highly corre-lated with the turnover estimated using permits. In a regression of the turnover estimated with permits on the turnover estimated with

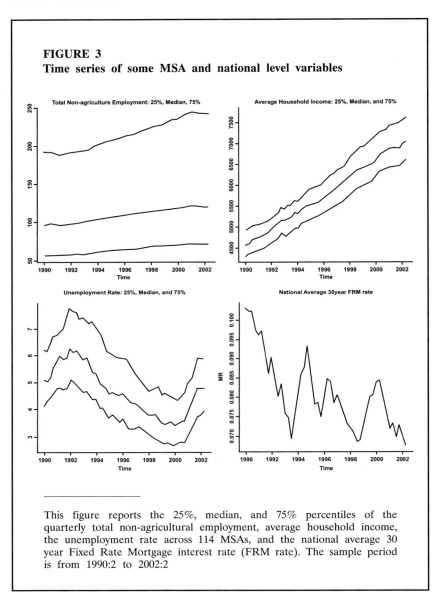

FIGURE 3
Time series of some MSA and national level variables

This figure reports the 25%, median, and 75% percentiles of the quarterly total non-agricultural employment, average household income, the unemployment rate across 114 MSAs, and the national average 30 year Fixed Rate Mortgage interest rate (FRM rate). The sample period is from 1990:2 to 2002:2

population/unit ratio, the coefficient is 1.02, and the R-square is 0.98. In addition, all our empirical findings remain unchanged when we use the turnover estimated from population/unit ratios. Therefore, we only report the results using turnover estimated with permits.

Figure 1 plots the deciles of the 114 home price indices where the deciles are created by the total change from the beginning to the end of the sample period. Figure 2 plots the across-MSA 25% percentile, median, and 75% of the estimated market turnover. Figure 3 plots the across-MSA 25% percentile, median, and 75% of the non-agricultural employment, average household income, unemployment rate, as well as the time series of the 30 year fixed rate mortgage rate. Since we estimate our VAR model using first-order differences of log values of these variables, we provide some statistics for the first order differences in Table 1, including across-MSA averages of their means, medians, variances if applicable, autocorrelations, and correlations, as well as t-statistics if applicable.

EMPIRICAL EVIDENCE

Determinants of Prices and Trading Volume

We first estimate different specifications of the fixed effect panel VAR model in (2). The first specification includes contemporaneous exogenous variables, which is the benchmark specification due to its simplicity.[6] The second separates the positive values from negative values of log differences in house price indices, and thus allows for asymmetric effects of house prices on turnover, which help us directly test Stein's (1995) theory. Malpezzi and Maclennan (2001) and others point out that the determination of house prices varies dramatically across time and markets with different supply elasticity. To understand possible heterogeneity in the determination of house prices and turnover and whether it affects the price–volume correlation, we re-estimate the first specification for MSAs with above and below-median long term supply elasticity. The measure we use for long term supply elasticity is the ratio of the change in population to the change in the house price index over the sample period. Holding constant the increases in population in a market, the greater is the increase in house prices, the "tighter" is the market and the lower the long term supply elasticity. Figure 4 plots the histogram of the long term supply elasticity across MSAs.

We use AIC to choose the optimal lag order for endogenous variables, which is 3 for all specifications. We use only three quarterly dummies to avoid the multicollinearity of the four dummies due to the within transformation. The model is estimated with feasible

---

[6] We conduct robustness checks for this specification by also including squared contemporaneous exogenous variables and lagged exogenous variables. Our estimation results are very similar and our Granger causality test results are intact.

TABLE 1
Data Summary

	Home price	Turnover	Employment	Household income	Unemployment	Mortgage rate	S&P 500 return
Panel A. Means, medians, and standard deviations							
Mean	0.963%^{b} [40.34]	0.450%^{b} [7.98]	0.448%^{b} [21.69]	0.889%^{b} [74.11]	-0.072% [-1.48]	-0.876%	2.181%
Median	0.929%^{b} [35.55]	0.468%^{b} [4.55]	0.475%^{b} [22.33]	0.882%^{b} [70.04]	-0.358%^{b} [-3.65]	-1.196%	2.871%
Std. dev.	1.316%	10.696%	0.712%	0.928%^{b}	7.646%	5.068%	7.701%
Panel B. Autocorrelations							
1 quarter	-0.130^b [-4.48]	-0.321^b [-26.66]	0.225^b [10.20]	-0.083^b [-4.02]	0.253^b [11.12]	0.135	-0.087
2 quarter	0.079^b [4.09]	-0.063^b [-4.84]	0.206^b [11.91]	0.236^b [19.95]	0.110^b [6.44]	0.078	0.103
3 quarter	0.100^b [5.67]	0.052^b [2.72]	0.148^b [9.71]	-0.163^b [-12.52]	0.006 [0.33]	-0.049	0.246
4 quarter	0.069^b [3.57]	-0.007 [-0.35]	0.018 [1.14]	-0.022 [-1.37]	-0.068^b [-3.67]	-0.252	0.027
Panel C. Correlations							
Home price	1	0.056^b [3.79]	0.030 [1.88]	0.023 [1.95]	0.047^b [3.02]	-0.065^b [-4.38]	-0.074^b [-6.01]
Turnover		1	0.029^a [2.19]	0.142^b [9.07]	-0.032^a [2.35]	0.106^b [9.02]	0.001 [0.09]
Employment			1	0.243^b [15.92]	-0.342^b [-20.79]	0.084^b [7.39]	0.113^b [10.25]
Household income				1	-0.136^b [-10.33]	0.237^b [19.63]	-0.065^b [-7.10]
Unemployment					1	-0.064^b [-5.18]	-0.124^b [-9.77]
Mortgage rate						1	0.030
S&P 500 return							1

This table reports across-MSA averages of the means, medians, standard deviations for the first order differences of the log values of the home price index, housing market turnover (the ratio of existing single family home sales to the stock of existing single family homes), total non-agricultural employment, average household income, the unemployment rate, the national average 30-year fixed mortgage rate, and the S&P 500 index, as well as corresponding t-statistics if applicable in Panel A. Panel B reports the 1 to 4 quarter autocorrelations and corresponding t-statistics if applicable. Panel C reports across-MSA average correlations among the variables and the corresponding t-statistics

a denotes significance at the 5% level
b denotes significance at the 1% level

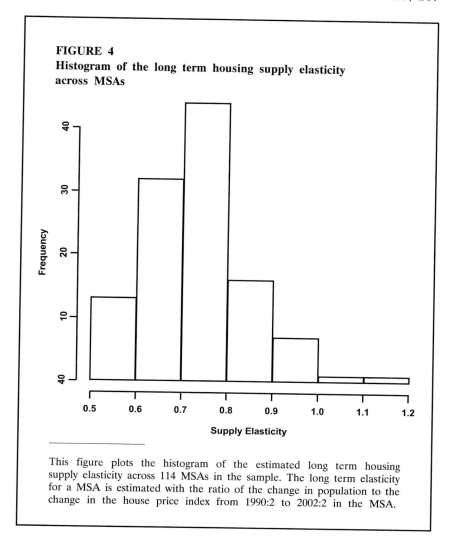

FIGURE 4
Histogram of the long term housing supply elasticity across MSAs

This figure plots the histogram of the estimated long term housing supply elasticity across 114 MSAs in the sample. The long term elasticity for a MSA is estimated with the ratio of the change in population to the change in the house price index from 1990:2 to 2002:2 in the MSA.

GLS that allows for heteroskedasticity across MSAs. We calculate t-statistics using heteroskedasticity-robust standard errors according to Kezdi (2003). Kezdi (2003) shows that the robust standard deviations allow serial correlation and heteroskedasticity of any kind, as well as unit roots and unequal spacing. They also have good small sample properties.

Table 2 reports the estimation results of the first specification. The results indicate that labor market shocks affect both prices and

TABLE 2
Panel VAR estimation

Panels, variables, estimation

Panel A. Regression results

Variables	Eq. 1: Home price		Eq. 2: Turnover	
	Estimate	t-Stat	Estimate	t-Stat
1st quarter dummy	0.001^b	2.73	0.002	0.58
2nd quarter dummy	−0.001	− 1.10	0.003	0.73
4th quarter dummy	-0.004^b	− 6.30	-0.010^a	− 2.20
Total employment	0.094^b	3.81	0.581^b	2.98
Household income	0.043^a	2.27	0.941^b	6.29
Unemployment rate	0.003	1.29	-0.037^a	− 2.04
Mortgage rate level	-0.071^b	− 15.29	-0.294^b	− 8.02
Mortgage rate trend	0.055^b	15.47	0.434^b	15.40
S&P 500 level	-0.028^b	− 7.43	0.047	1.58
S&P 500 trend	0.018^b	6.80	-0.071^b	− 3.38
Home price lag 1	-0.200^b	− 15.11	0.386^b	3.70
Home price lag 2	0.080^b	6.14	−0.015	− 0.14
Home price lag 3	0.121^b	− 9.67	−0.043	− 0.44
Turnover lag 1	−0.000	− 0.14	-0.439^b	−32.37
Turnover lag 2	0.001	0.77	-0.253^b	−17.32
Turnover lag 3	0.005^b	2.63	-0.074^b	− 5.40
R^2	0.12		0.23	

Panel B. Granger causality tests

Hypotheses (alternative)	Prices → turnover	Turnover → prices
F statistics	4.811	2.436
P value (significance)	0.002	0.063

This table reports the estimation for the following two-equation fixed effect panel VAR model

$$\begin{pmatrix} \Delta p_{i,t} \\ \Delta q_{i,t} \end{pmatrix} = \begin{pmatrix} a_i \\ b_i \end{pmatrix} t + \sum_{s=1,2,4} A_s d_s + \sum_{s=1}^{k} B_s \begin{pmatrix} \Delta p_{i,t-s} \\ \Delta q_{i,t-s} \end{pmatrix} + C\Delta X_{i,t} + \begin{pmatrix} v_{i,t}^p \\ v_{i,t}^p \end{pmatrix},$$

where $p_{i,t}$ is the log value of the home price index level, $q_{i,t}$ is the log value of market turnover, d_s is a dummy variable for sth quarter, and $X_{i,t}$ is a vector of exogenous variables (all in log values), which include total non-agricultural employment, average household income, the unemployment rate, the 30 year fixed rate mortgage rate, the trend of the mortgage rate, the S&P 500 index level, and the trend of the S&P 500 index. We use the within transformation to eliminate MSA dummies, and then estimate the model using feasible GLS that allows for heteroskedasticity across MSAs. We calculate t-statistics using heteroskedasticity-robust standard errors
[a] denotes significance at the 5% level
[b] denotes significance at the 1% level

trading volume in housing markets. On the one hand, both the total non-agricultural employment and the average household income positively affect both the prices and trading volume in housing markets, and the effects are statistically significant. On the other hand, the unemployment rate has an interesting impact on housing markets. Increases in the unemployment rate increase (albeit insignificantly) home prices and significantly reduce trading volume. This seems to be consistent with the spatial lock-in phenomenon (see Chan 2001, for example) which states that home sellers who are hurt by the increased unemployment rate are likely to be subjected to financial constraints and thus need to raise their asking prices (so that the proceeds from selling their homes would be large enough to repay their mortgage and provide a down payment on a new home). This behavior shifts the supply curve upwards and thus causes lower trading volume and higher transaction prices.

Table 2 confirms the importance of the mortgage market in the determination of prices and trading volume. When the mortgage rate is high (low), home prices are significantly low (high), and so is trading volume. Furthermore, when the mortgage rate demonstrates a rising (falling) trend, both home prices and trading volume increase (decrease), which is consistent with the potential homebuyers' rational behavior, although other possibilities can not be ruled out. When the mortgage rate is rising, potential homebuyers would be better off purchasing sooner and locking in the mortgage rate. Yet, when the rate is falling, it seems rational for them to wait and postpone their home purchases. The effects of the mortgage level and trend are consistent with shifts of the housing demand.

It is interesting that the stock market has significant effects on the price and turnover in the housing market. First, home prices are significantly lower, and the trading volume is (insignificantly) higher when the S&P 500 index is higher, which appears to indicate a shift of the supply curve to the right side (a decrease in sellers' asking prices). This finding seems consistent with Stein (1995) etc: the more financial wealth a household has (possibly due to higher stock prices), the less likely the household is financially constrained and thus it sets a lower ask price. Second, home prices are significantly higher and trading volume is (insignificantly) lower when the stock market shows an uptrend. It is premature to make any conclusions regarding the economic mechanism; however, we conjecture that private valuations of homeowners may be affected by their expectation of the economy in the future. A booming stock market may create higher housing demand in the future, and homeowners may adjust their private valuation upward accordingly, which may shift the sup-

TABLE 3
Panel VAR estimation: asymmetric effects of house price changes

Panels, estimation, price changes

Panel A. Regression results

Variables	Eq. 1: Home price		Eq. 2: Turnover	
	Estimate	t-Stat	Estimate	t-Stat
1st quarter dummy	0.001^a	2.82	0.002	0.49
2nd quarter dummy	−0.001	− 1.06	0.003	0.69
4th quarter dummy	$−0.003^b$	− 6.17	$−0.010^a$	− 2.37
Total employment	0.093^b	3.78	0.582^b	2.98
Household income	0.042^a	2.24	0.947^b	6.33
Unemployment rate	0.003	1.29	$−0.037^a$	− 2.03
Mortgage rate level	$−0.071^b$	− 15.21	$−0.295^b$	− 7.99
Mortgage rate trend	0.055^b	15.43	0.434^b	15.34
S&P 500 level	$−0.028^b$	− 7.52	0.050	1.69
S&P 500 trend	0.018^b	6.80	$−0.070^b$	− 3.31
Home price lag 1 positive	$−0.170^b$	− 7.42	0.063	0.35
Home price lag 2 positive	0.086^b	3.67	−0.108	− 0.58
Home price lag 3 postive	0.117^b	5.56	−0.115	− 0.69
Home price lag 1 negative	$−0.234^b$	− 10.26	0.731^b	4.05
Home price lag 2 negative	0.073^b	3.08	−0.128	− 0.67
Home price lag 3 negative	0.123^b	5.52	0.045	0.25
Turnover lag 1	−0.000	0.00	$−0.440^b$	−32.44
Turnover lag 2	0.002	0.88	$−0.255^b$	−17.40
Turnover lag 3	0.005^b	2.70	$−0.075^b$	− 5.44
R^2	0.12		0.24	

Panel B. Granger causality tests

Hypotheses (alternative)	Prices → turnover	Turnover → prices
F statistics	4.016	2.516
P value (significance)	0.001	0.056

This table reproduces the estimation of the panel VAR model in Table 2 with positive changes in lagged log house price indices separated from negative changes
[a] denotes significance at the 5% level
[b] denotes significance at the 1% level

ply curve upward. We leave the exploration of this possibility for future research.

Table 2 also suggests that lagged prices and trading volume significantly affect home prices and trading volume. The first-order autoregressive coefficients are significantly negative for both prices and trading volume, therefore, prices and volume tend to reverse in the next quarter, which may indicate the adjustments of the housing market to exogenous shocks. An adjustment of market supply to a demand shock appears consistent with the feedback effects predicted by Novy-Marx (2007). The negative coefficients of lagged prices and trading volume are also consistent with the overshooting of home prices predicted by Ortalo-Magné and Rady (2006).

Table 2 also reports the tests of Granger causality between prices and turnover. We find strong evidence that prices Granger cause turnover, with the F statistic being 4.811, and the P value being 0.002. This directly supports the theory by Stein (1995), and is consistent with empirical evidence provided by Chan (2001), Engelhardt (2003), Genesove and Mayer (1997), Genesove and Mayer (2001), etc. At the same time, we find weak evidence that turnover Granger causes prices, with the F statistic being 2.436, and the P value being 0.063, which provides some evidence for the part of the theory in Wheaton (1990) that suggests turnover might affect prices, particularly in tight markets.

Table 3 reports the results of the second specification, which separates positive values from negative values for lagged log differences of house prices and thus accommodates asymmetric effects of house prices on turnover. While almost all results in Table 2 remain, we find that, in the equation with turnover being the dependant variable, the negative value of one-quarter lag log difference of house prices is significantly positive at the 1% level, while the positive value and all other lagged house prices are insignificant. This indicates that decreases in house prices reduce market turnover, but increases in house prices do not have significant effects. The result is consistent with theories in Stein (1995) etc., which suggest that equity constraints or loss aversion due to decreasing house prices reduce market trading volume.

Tables 4 and 5 report the results for MSAs with high and low supply elasticity respectively. While our early results remain, these tables reveal interesting differences across markets with different supply elasticity. First, turnover Granger causes prices in tight markets (MSAs with low supply elasticity) but not in loose markets (MSAs with high supply elasticity). Relating to Wheaton (1990), this seems to indicate that sellers more likely raise their reservations as a reaction to increasing trading volume in markets with an inelastic supply of housing. Therefore, in tighter markets, due to the lack of new homes, sellers are able to profit more from increasing housing demand. Second, the results seem to suggest that homebuyers in tight markets are less financially constrained. The first piece of evidence for this is that house prices in tight markets are less sensitive to mortgage interest rate levels and trends, possibly due to the fact that homebuyers are less financially constrained. This may have interest-

TABLE 4
Panel VAR estimation: high supply elasticity MSAs

Panels, estimation, supply elasticity

Panel A. Regression results

Variables	Eq. 1: Home price		Eq. 2: Turnover	
	Estimate	t-Stat	Estimate	t-Stat
1st quarter dummy	0.003^b	3.88	0.002	− 0.43
2nd quarter dummy	−0.000	− 0.23	0.005	0.90
4th quarter dummy	−0.002	− 1.91	−0.007	− 0.53
Total employment	0.047	1.35	0.357^b	1.40
Household income	0.057^a	2.24	0.977^b	5.20
Unemployment rate	0.000	0.04	-0.078^b	− 2.97
Mortgage rate level	-0.102^b	-15.41	-0.289^b	− 5.97
Mortgage rate trend	0.080^b	13.74	0.431^b	11.55
S&P 500 level	-0.030^b	− 5.54	0.009	0.24
S&P 500 trend	0.018^b	4.76	-0.081^b	− 2.92
Home price lag 1	-0.155^b	− 8.42	0.511^b	3.77
Home price lag 2	0.128^b	7.11	0.222	1.68
Home price lag 3	0.146^b	8.35	-0.161	− 1.25
Turnover lag 1	−0.003	− 0.99	-0.421^b	−22.45
Turnover lag 2	0.000	0.08	-0.247^b	−12.23
Turnover lag 3	0.003^b	1.13	-0.049^a	− 2.54
R^2	0.16	0.24		

Panel B. Granger causality tests

Hypotheses (alternative)	Prices → turnover	Turnover → prices
F statistics	5.592	0.912
P value (significance)	0.001	0.434

This table reproduces the estimation of the panel VAR model in Table 2 using MSAs with above median long term supply elasticity of housing, which is measured with the ratio of the change in population to the change in the house price index over the sample period. The higher is the ratio, the "looser" is the market and the higher is the supply elasticity
[a] denotes significance at the 5% level
[b] denotes significance at the 1% level

ing implications on the risk of home equity: although houses tend to be more expensive in tight markets, they are less risky in the sense that their prices are less sensitive to mortgage interest rates. The second piece of evidence is that growth in average household income has weaker effects on house prices in tight markets than in loose markets, which seems to suggest that income is less likely a financial constraint for homebuyers in tight markets with high house prices. Third, growth in employment has stronger effects on house prices in tight markets than in loose markets, which is sensible given the low supply elasticity in tight markets.

Overall, we find that, first, exogenous variables, such as employment, household income, the mortgage rate, etc., play significant roles in determining prices and trading volume in the housing market, which supports the theories (e.g. Wheaton 1990) that argue for the effects of exogenous variables as a possible explanation of the price–volume correlation. Second, our results reject the hypothesis that prices do not Granger cause trading volume at the 1% level, and reject the hypothesis that trading volume does not Granger cause prices at the 10% level (at the 5% level for markets with low supply elasticity). The Granger causality tests provide strong evidence for Stein (1995) etc. and some evidence for Wheaton (1990). Third, we find decreases in house prices reduce trading volume while increases in house prices do not affect trading volume, which is a strong evidence supporting Stein (1995) etc. Fourth, we break down the MSAs into two groups with high and low supply elasticity respectively, and find very interesting heterogeneity. We find that trading volume Granger cause prices in tight markets, but not in loose markets. We also find that house prices in tight markets are less sensitive to variables related to financial constraints on homebuyers, including mortgage interest rates and average household income. Moreover, we find growth in employment has stronger effects on house prices in tight markets.

Decomposing the Price–volume Correlation

This section analyzes which relations — the Granger causality between prices and trading volume or the effects of exogenous variables — help explain the price–volume correlation in housing markets. We first calculate the raw price–volume correlation for each MSA using the series of home appreciation rates and changes in trading volume. Then, based on results from estimating the panel VAR model, we decompose the home appreciation rates and trading volume (both demeaned due to the within transformation) into fitted components and residuals.

$$hp_{i,t} + h\hat{p}_{i,t} + u_{i,t}$$

$$tp_{i,t} + t\hat{p}_{i,t} + v_{i,t} \tag{6}$$

We then calculate the correlation between $h\hat{p}_{i,t}$ and $t\hat{o}_{i,t}$, as well as the correlation between $u_{i,t}$ and $v_{i,t}$, which is the component of the price–volume correlation that cannot be explained by our model.

Panel A in Table 6 reports the across-MSA averages of the raw price–volume correlations, the "fitted" correlations, and the correlations between residuals, using Table 5 Panel VAR estimation: low

TABLE 5

Panel VAR estimation: low supply elasticity MSAs

Panels, estimation, supply elasticity

Panel A. Regression results

Variables	Eq. 1: Home price		Eq. 2: Turnover	
	Estimate	t-Stat	Estimate	t-Stat
1st quarter dummy	0.003^b	− 0.36	0.005	0.89
2nd quarter dummy	−0.001	− 1.72	−0.001	− 0.12
4th quarter dummy	-0.005^b	− 6.93	-0.016^a	− 2.42
Total employment	0.156^b	4.52	0.788^b	2.65
Household income	0.020	0.71	0.943^b	3.96
Unemployment rate	0.006	1.91	-0.004^b	− 0.17
Mortgage rate level	-0.034^b	− 5.29	-0.292^b	− 5.24
Mortgage rate trend	0.037^b	7.55	0.434^b	10.20
S&P 500 level	-0.026^b	− 5.09	0.090^a	2.02
S&P 500 trend	0.018^b	5.02	-0.064^a	− 2.04
Home price lag 1	-0.278^b	-14.62	0.230^b	1.41
Home price lag 2	0.002^b	0.12	−0.319	− 1.92
Home price lag 3	0.077^b	4.33	−0.018	0.12
Turnover lag 1	0.002	0.65	-0.451^b	−23.13
Turnover lag 2	0.003	1.19	-0.260^b	−12.32
Turnover lag 3	0.007^b	2.91	-0.093^b	− 4.70
R^2	0.13	0.23		

Panel B. Granger causality tests

Hypotheses (alternative)	Prices → turnover	Turnover → prices
F statistics	2.814	2.827
P value (significance)	0.038	0.037

This table reproduces the estimation of the panel VAR model in Table 2 using MSAs with below median long term supply elasticity of housing, which is measured with the ratio of the change in population to the change in the house price index over the sample period. The lower is the ratio, the "tighter" is the market and the lower is the supply elasticity.
[a] denotes significance at the 5% level
[b] denotes significance at the 1% level

supply elasticity MSAs estimation results in Tables 2, 3, 4 and 5: the benchmark specification in Table 2, the asymmetric specification in Table 3, and subsample estimation for high supply elasticity markets (Table 4) and low supply elasticity markets (Table 5). The table also reports t-statistics of testing two-sided hypotheses that the correlations follow a distribution with 0 mean.

We have a few interesting findings. First, we find evidence of the statistically significant positive price–volume correlation. The raw

TABLE 6
Price–volume correlations

Decomposition, specification and average

Panel A: decomposing raw

Specification	Raw		Fitted		Residual	
Benchmark	0.048^b	[3.26]	0.168^b	[13.19]	0.014	[1.01]
Asymmetric	0.048^b	[3.26]	0.165^b	[12.85]	0.016	[1.19]
High elasticity	0.072^b	[3.45]	0.214^b	[12.17]	0.018	[0.95]
Low elasticity	0.025	[1.20]	0.108^b	[5.97]	0.005	[0.28]

Panel B: decomposing fitted correlations

Specification	Co movements		Price-caused		Turnover-caused	
Benchmark	0.588^b	[134.01]	−0.868^b	[−101.53]	0.076^b	[5.97]
Asymmetric	0.589^b	[133.70]	−0.791^b	[−105.15]	0.021	[1.61]
High elasticity	0.529^b	[76.11]	−0.475^b	[16.63]	0.628^b	[76.40]
Low elasticity	0.548^b	[91.87]	−0.599^b	[−41.46]	−0.229^b	[−12.01]

This table reports the decomposition of the price–volume correlations. The "raw correlation" is the correlation between the raw home appreciation rates (first order differences of log home price index) and the raw market turnover changes (first order differences of log turnover). Using the estimation results of the panel VAR model in Tables 2, 3, 4 and 5, we decompose both home appreciation rates and market turnover changes (both with MSA specific across-time means subtracted). In Panel A, we decompose them respectively into two parts: the one explained by our panel VAR model ("Fitted"), and the regression residual ("Residual"). In Panel B, we decompose the "Fitted" components into three parts: the part explained by lagged home appreciation rates ("Price-caused"), the part explained by lagged turnover ("Turnover-caused"), and the part explained by all other variables ("Co movements"). Correlations between the same components of home appreciation rates and market turnover changes are calculated and reported. All reported values are means across MSAs, and t-statistics are also reported
^{b} denotes significance at the 1% level

correlation is 0.048 (0.072 in markets with high elasticity and 0.025 in markets with low elasticity) and significant at the 1% level (insignificant for markets with low elasticity). Second, we find strong evidence of positive correlations between "fitted" prices and volume. The "fitted" price–volume correlations are much higher than raw price–volume correlations. They are 0.168 and 0.165 for the benchmark and asymmetric specifications, and 0.214 and 0.108 for subsamples of MSAs with high and low supply elasticity. All "fitted" price–volume correlations are significant at the 1% level. Finally, the correlations between residuals are always lower than the raw price–volume correlations, and are insignificant. Panel A seems to indicate that our model captures the price–volume correlation well.

To investigate the extent to which the price–volume correlation is explained by the Granger causality between prices and trading volume and by the exogenous shocks, we further decompose the "fitted" parts of both $hp_{i,t}$ and $to_{i,t}$ into three components — the component explained by lagged prices, the component explained by lagged trading volume, and the component explained by all other variables. We then calculate the correlation between the same component of house prices and trading volume, and thus have three correlations: the correlation between price-caused prices and trading volume ("Price-caused" in the table), the correlation between trading volume-caused prices and trading volume ("Turnover-caused" in the table), and the correlation between prices and trading volume caused by other variables ("Co-movements" in the table).

Panel B of Table 6 reports the three types of price–volume correlations, and the corresponding t-statistics of two-sided tests that the correlations follow distributions with zero means. We have a few interesting findings. First, we find that the "comovement" component of the price–volume correlation is statistically significant at the 1% level under all specifications and for all subsamples. Moreover, the correlation ranges from 0.529 to 0.589 for different specifications or subsamples, which is much higher than the raw correlation and the "fitted" correlation. Second, the "price-caused" component is statistically significant at the 1% level but is negative. The negative "price-caused" component of the price-volume correlation seems to be caused by the positive effect of prices on future turnover and the negative autocorrelation of prices at quarterly frequency. Third, the "turnovercaused" component is significantly positive on average across MSAs, but varies dramatically across markets — it is significantly positive for MSAs with high supply elasticity, but significantly negative for MSAs with low supply elasticity. This seems to be caused by the negative autocorrelation of turnover and different effects of turnover on house prices in different markets: in loose (tight) markets, higher turnover tends to reduce (increase) house prices in the next quarter.

Overall, our results provide strong evidence of the existence of positive price–volume correlations at quarterly frequency. Furthermore, the positive correlation seems to be fully explained by fitted prices and volume in our model. A novel finding is that the positive price–volume correlation appears to be mainly caused by co-movements of prices and volume due to exogenous shocks. Lagged prices seem to lead to negative price–volume correlation for all markets, and lagged trading volume leads to positive price–volume correlation in MSAs with high supply elasticity but negative price–volume correlation in MSAs with low supply elasticity, and thus both lagged prices and trading volume do not seem to explain the positive price–volume correlation well.

Impulse Response Analysis

We use impulse-response functions to provide a more intuitive description of how shocks in exogenous variables generate the co-movements of the price and turnover in housing markets. The impulse-response functions are constructed using estimation results of the first specification (Table 2). We build the analysis on the level model in (1) instead of the first-order difference model since the level model seems more intuitive. As a result, the impulse responses are for the absolute price level and turnover in the market, not their changes. Also, the benchmark case is a market in which all exogenous variables remain unchanged, and thus the price and turnover do not change over time.

Conventionally, the shock introduced equals one standard deviation of the underlying variable, which, however, does not seem to be the most appropriate approach in our study. First, most exogenous variables in our study are not mean-stationary; instead, they have trends and cycles. It is not clear how to define a meaningful standard deviation for these non-stationary variables. Second, most MSAs have experienced fairly smooth growth in the sample period. For these MSAs, standard deviations of the growth rates of economic variables are very small, and do not appear to represent meaningful shocks. As a result, we define a shock as a 5% absolute change in the level of the underlying variable.

We construct a conventional type of impulse response functions that are based on one shock in one variable and no shock in others. It is worth noting that this simple approach is often not suitable to study impulses in endogenous variables. A shock in an endogenous variable often has contemporaneous effects not only on the endogenous variable itself but also on other endogenous variables. Hence, it is inappropriate to assume a shock on one endogenous variable while keeping other endogenous variables fixed. To address this composition effect (defined by Koop et al. 1996), researchers often use either orthogonalized impulse responses or generalized impulse responses. However, since we are interested in how shocks in exogenous variables affect both the price and turnover, it appears reasonable to entertain perturbations in an exogenous variable, while assuming no extra shocks in other exogenous or endogenous variables.

To construct the impulse response functions, we first let all contemporaneous exogenous variables (except the one representing the source of shock), lagged endogenous variables and intercepts be 0, and then introduce a 5% one-time shock in the variable that represents the source of the shock. Since the VAR system is a log linear system, a shock that equals log (1.05) implies that the corresponding variable has an unexpected increase of 5%. The values of the price and trading volume over time are then calculated by repeatedly plugging into the VAR system all estimated coefficients and the lagged endogenous variables.

Figure 5 plots the dynamic responses of both the price and turnover in the housing market to a 5% exogenous increase in the total non-agricultural employment, the average household income, the unemployment rate, and the mortgage rate, respectively. We do not report the standard deviations of the responses since we are interested in the patterns of the expected responses, not the statistical significance. The pre-shock values of both the price and turnover are 1, which means the values are 1 times the values in the benchmark case. Values greater than 1 suggest positive deviations from the benchmark level. For example, 1.02 means the variable is 2% higher than the benchmark level.

Note that the responses to shocks in the mortgage rate should be interpreted with caution. Empirically, changes in the mortgage rate also result in changes in the trend, so the aggregate effects will be more complicated than what the impulse response functions show. However, these two functions can be interpreted as thought experiments. Suppose the effect of the trend is fixed, the impulse response functions show the net effect of a change in the level, which is useful to know.

Note that in Fig. 5, the series that have higher absolute values of deviations from 1 in Period 1 are for turnover, while the other series are for house prices. We observe a few interesting patterns. First, trading volume reacts much more dramatically to exogenous shocks than prices do, which corroborates Andrew and Meen (2003) and Hort (2000). For instance, after a 5% increase in the average household income, trading volume increases by about 5%, while the price increases by less than 1%. This is consistent with the conventional wisdom that, in real estate markets, changes in trading volume more accurately represent changes in market conditions than changes in prices, (see Berkovec and Goodman 1996, for instance).

Second, some shocks appear to generate co-movements of the price and volume, while others seem to cause the price and volume to move in opposite directions. We call the first type of shocks Type I shocks, and the second type of shocks Type II shocks. Since the price–volume correlation is positive in our sample, it is very likely that our sample is exposed to more Type I shocks than Type II shocks. However, one should be cautious that the price–volume correlation in a market can be negative, particularly if Type II shocks dominate Type I shocks. The positive price–volume correlation in our data might be a small sample phenomenon in the sense that we happen to be in an economy where Type I shocks dominate in frequency and/or magnitude.

FIGURE 5

Responses of home prices and market turnover to exogenous shocks

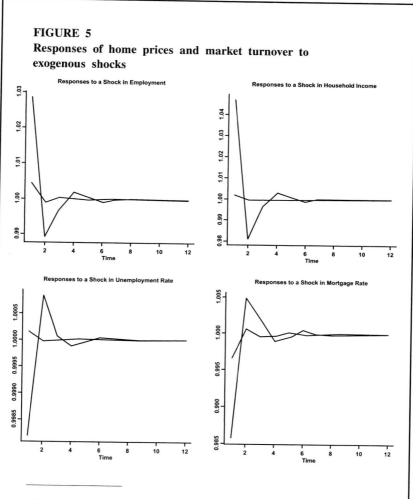

This figure reports the responses of home prices and market turnover (both in level) to a 5% one-period shock in the total non-agricultural employment, average household income, the unemployment rate, and the mortgage rate (in level). To construct the responses, we first let all contemporaneous exogenous variables (except the one representing the source of shock), lagged endogenous variables and intercepts be 0, and then introduced a 5% one-time shock in the variable that represents the economic source of the shock. The values of the price and trading volume over time are then calculated by repeatedly plugging into the VAR system all estimated coefficients and the lagged endogenous variables. In each graph, the series that has a higher absolute value of deviation from 1 in Period 1 is for turnover, while the other is for house prices

The third finding is that overshooting of the price and volume is very common. Particularly, the overshooting of trading volume is observed in all four scenarios. This is consistent with the theories by Novy-Marx (2007) and Ortalo-Magné and Rady (2006), which both imply or predict overshooting, though rely on different mechanisms.

CONCLUSIONS

Using an unusually large panel data set consisting of housing markets in 114 MSAs from 1990 to 2002, we study the determinants of home prices and trading volume in the housing market. We find that the housing market is affected by shocks in the labor market, mortgage market and the stock market. Moreover, house prices Granger cause trading volume, but the effects are asymmetric: decreases in house prices lead to lower trading volume, while increases in house prices have no effect.

We also find that trading volume Granger causes prices, but only in markets with low supply elasticity. Our results also provide insights regarding heterogeneity across markets. In tight markets (low supply elasticity), house prices are less sensitive to mortgage rates and average household income, but more sensitive to growth in employment.

We find a significant and positive price–volume correlation at quarterly frequency. Our model captures the price–volume correlation well: after controlling for the price–volume correlation explained by our model, there is no significant price–volume correlation left. Furthermore, we find that the Granger causality of prices on trading volume appears to lead to a negative price–volume correlation, while the Granger causality of trading volume on prices leads to a positive price–volume correlation in markets with high supply elasticity, but a negative price–volume correlation in markets with low supply elasticity. Therefore, the Granger causality between prices and trading volume does not help explain the price–volume correlation well, while the co-movements of prices and volume, which are caused by shocks in exogenous variables, are significant, substantial, and positive for all markets. Using impulse response functions, we find that trading volume reacts more dramatically to economic shocks than home prices do. We also observe overshooting of trading volume in the adjustment process to shocks.

ACKNOWLEDGEMENTS

We thank Michael LaCour-Little, participants of 2005 AREUEA mid-year conference, seminar participants at Colorado University at Boulder, and two anonymous referees for insightful comments. All errors are ours.

APPENDIX: THE LIST OF THE 114 MSAS IN OUR ANALYSIS

TABLE 7

The list of the 114 MSAs in our analysis

MSAs	
Abilene TX MSA	Albuquerque NM MSA
Alexandria LA MSA	Albany GA MSA
Amarillo TX MSA	Anchorage AK MSA
Asheville NC MSA	Athens GA MSA
Atlanta GA MSA	Bakersfield CA MSA
Baton Rouge LA MSA	Bellingham WA MSA
Benton Harbor MI MSA	Billings MT MSA
Binghamton NY MSA	Birmingham AL MSA
Bloomington IN MSA	Boise City ID MSA
Bismarck ND MSA	Cedar Rapids IA MSA
Cheyenne WY MSA	Charlottesville VA MSA
Columbia MO MSA	Colorado Springs CO MSA
Corpus Christi TX MSA	Columbia SC MSA
Columbus OH MSA	Daytona Beach FL MSA
Decatur IL MSA	Des Moines IA MSA
Decatur AL MSA	Dothan AL MSA
Dubuque IA MSA	Eau Claire WI MSA
El Paso TX MSA	Erie PA MSA
Fayetteville NC MSA	Florence SC MSA
Fort Wayne IN MSA	Fresno CA MSA
Fort Walton Beach FL MSA	Gainesville FL MSA
Green Bay WI MSA	Greensboro-Winston-Salem-High Point NC MSA
Honolulu HI MSA	Huntsville AL MSA
Indianapolis IN MSA	Iowa City IA MSA
Jacksonville FL MSA	Jackson MI MSA
Jackson MS MSA	Joplin MO MSA
Knoxville TN MSA	Kokomo IN MSA
Lafayette LA MSA	Lancaster PA MSA
Lake Charles LA MSA	Lima OH MSA
Lincoln NE MSA	Las Cruces NM MSA
Lubbock TX MSA	Lawrence KS MSA
Lynchburg VA MSA	Madison WI MSA
Mansfield OH MSA	Merced CA MSA
Mobile AL MSA	Modesto CA MSA
Montgomery AL MSA	Monroe LA MSA
Nashville TN MSA	New Orleans LA MSA
Ocala FL MSA	Oklahoma City OK MSA
Orlando FL MSA	Owensboro KY MSA
Panama City FL MSA	Pensacola FL MSA
Pueblo CO MSA	Reading PA MSA
Redding CA MSA	Reno NV MSA
Roanoke VA MSA	Rockford IL MSA
Rochester MN MSA	Rochester NY MSA
San Diego CA MSA	San Angelo TX MSA
Savannah GA MSA	San Antonio TX MSA
Sheboygan WI MSA	Sioux Falls SD MSA
Springfield MO MSA	Spokane WA MSA
Springfield IL MSA	St. Cloud MN MSA
State College PA MSA	St. Joseph MO MSA
Syracuse NY MSA	Tallahassee FL MSA
Toledo OH MSA	Topeka KS MSA
Tucson AZ MSA	Tulsa OK MSA
Tyler TX MSA	Waco TX MSA
Wausau WI MSA	Wichita KS MSA
Wichita Falls TX MSA	Wilmington NC MSA
Yakima WA MSA York PA MSA	Yuba City CA MSA Yuma AZ MSA

REFERENCES

Andrew, M., & Meen, G. (2003). House price appreciation, transactions and structural change in the British housing market: A macroeconomic perspective. Real Estate Economics, 31,99–116.

Berkovec, J. A., & Goodman, J. L. (1996). Turnover as a measure of demand for existing homes. Real Estate Economics, 24, 421–440.

Bertaut, C. C., & Starr-McCluer, M. (2002). Household portfolios in the United States. In L. Guiso, M. Haliassos, & T. Jappelli (Eds.), Household portfolios. Cambridge: MIT.

Case, K. E., & Shiller, R. J. (2003). Is there a bubble in the housing market? Brookings Papers on Economic Activity, 34, 299–362.

Cauley, S. D., & Pavlov, A. D. (2002). Rational delays: the case of real estate. Journal of Real Estate Finance and Economics, 24, 143–165.

Chan, S. (2001). Spatial lock-in: do falling house prices constrain residential mobility? Journal of Urban Economics, 49, 567–586.

DiPasquale, D., & Wheaton, W. C. (1994). Housing market dynamics and the future of housing prices. Journal of Urban Economics, 35,1–27.

Engelhardt, G. V. (2003). Nominal loss aversion, housing equity constraints, and household mobility: evidence from the United States. Journal of Urban Economics, 53, 171–195.

Follain, J. R., & Velz, O. T. (1995). Incorporating the number of existing home sales into a structural model of the market for owner-occupied housing. Journal of Housing Economics, 4,93–117.

Genesove, D., & Mayer, C. J. (1997). Equity and time to sale in the real estate market. American Economic Review, 87, 255–269.

Genesove, D., & Mayer, C. J. (2001). Nominal loss aversion and seller behavior: Evidence from the housing market. Quarterly Journal of Economics, 116, 1233–1260.

Hanushek, E. A., & Quigley, J. M. (1980). What is the price elasticity of housing demand? Review of Economics and Statistics, 62, 449–454.

Hort, K. (2000). Prices and turnover in the market for owner-occupied homes. Regional Science and Urban Economics, 30,99–119.

Kezdi, G. (2003). Robust standard error estimation in fixed-effects panel models. Budapest University Working Paper.

Koop, G., Pesaran, H. M., & Potter, S. M. (1996). Impulse response analysis in nonlinear multivariate models. Journal of Econometrics, 74,119–147.

Krainer, J. (2001). A theory of liquidity in residential real estate markets. Journal of Urban Economics, 49,32–53.

Lamont, O., & Stein, J. C. (1999). Leverage and house-price dynamics in US cities. Rand Journal of Economics, 30, 498–514.

Leung, C. K. Y., & Feng, D. (2005). Testing alternative theories of property price-trading volume with commercial real estate market data. Journal of Real Estate Finance and Economics, 31(2), 241–255.

Malpezzi, S., & Maclennan, D. (2001). The long-run price elasticity of supply of new residential construction in the United States and the United Kingdom. Journal of Housing Economics, 10, 278–306. Miller, N., &

Sklarz, M. (1986). A note on leading indicators of housing market price trends. Journal of Real Estate Research, 1(1), 99–109.

Novy-Marx, R. (2007). Hot and cold markets. Real Estate Economics, forthcoming.

Ortalo-Magné, F., & Rady, S. (2004). Housing transactions and macroeconomic fluctuations: A case study of England and Wales. Journal of Housing Economics, 13, 287–303.

Ortalo-Magné, F., & Rady, S. (2006). Housing market dynamics: On the contribution of income shocks and credit constraints. Review of Economic Studies, 73, 459–485.

Poterba, J. M. (1984). Tax subsidies to owner-occupied housing: An asset-market approach. Quarterly Journal of Economics, 99, 729–752.

Shafir, E., Diamond, P., & Tversky, A. (1997). Money illusion. Quarterly Journal of Economics, 112, 341–374.

Smith, B. A. (1976). The supply of urban housing. Quarterly Journal of Economics, 90, 389–405.

Stein, J. C. (1995). Prices and trading volume in the housing market: A model with down-payment effects.

Quarterly Journal of Economics, 110, 379–406. Tracy, J., & Schneider, H. (2001). Stocks in the household portfolios: A look back at the 1990's. Current Issues in Economics and Finance, 7,1–6. Wheaton, W. C. (1990). Vacancy, search, and prices in a housing market matching model. Journal of Political Economy, 98, 1270–1292.

Real Estate Taxation and Policy

4

Property Tax Reform in Ontario: What Have We Learned?

————————————————————————— ENID SLACK

INTRODUCTION

No tax has been more strongly criticized than the property tax. It has been described as unfair because it is unrelated to ability to pay or to benefits received, unsuitable because it supports services that are not related to property, and inadequate because it does not generate sufficient revenues for municipalities to meet their rising expenditure needs. Its effects on housing investment, land use, and urban development have been castigated, and its political unpopularity has long been acknowledged. Notwithstanding these criticisms, the property tax remains the main source of revenue for municipalities in Canada.[1] Not only is it a valuable mechanism for funding local governments, but it is also essential in sustaining local autonomy. The formulation of property tax policy, at both the provincial and the local levels, thus has important consequences for the overall workings of municipal government.

This paper describes and evaluates the recent property tax reform in Ontario. The first section of the paper describes the unique characteristics of the property tax that make reform particularly challenging. The second section provides a brief history of property tax reform in Ontario. The third section describes the recent property

Reproduced with the permission of the Canadian Tax Foundation from, Enid Slack, "Property Tax Reform in Ontario: What Have We Learned?" (2002) 50:2 *Canadian Tax Journal* 576–85.

Of Enid Slack Consulting Inc., Toronto. This paper relies heavily on an earlier article by the author, "Understanding the Evolution of Property Tax Policy" (2000) vol. 6, no. 11/12 *Focus on Assessment and Taxation* 89–96.

tax changes in Ontario. The fourth section evaluates the property tax reform and sets out some lessons for tax policy.

CHARACTERISTICS OF THE PROPERTY TAX

There are several characteristics of the property tax that differentiate it from other taxes and also make it difficult to reform.

First, the property tax is a very visible tax. Unlike the income tax, for example, the property tax is not withheld from taxpayers' earnings at source. Generally, it must be paid directly by taxpayers in periodic lump-sum amounts. Consequently, taxpayers tend to be much more aware of how much they pay in property taxes.[2] Furthermore, the property tax finances services that are very visible, such as roads, garbage collection, snow removal, and neighbourhood parks. This visibility is desirable from a decision-making perspective because it makes taxpayers aware of the costs of local public services. This awareness enhances the accountability of local governments for their expenditure decisions. The ability to raise property taxes (or to reform the tax), however, is more constrained than is the case for other taxes.

Second, the base of the property tax does not increase automatically over time because property values respond more slowly to annual changes in economic activity than do incomes. Furthermore, few jurisdictions update property values for taxation purposes on an annual basis. This means that, to maintain property tax revenues in real terms (or to increase those revenues), it is necessary to increase the rate of the tax. As with visibility, inelasticity leads to greater accountability because when taxing authorities need to increase tax revenues, they have to justify the increase in the tax rate. However, inelasticity also leads to greater taxpayer resistance.

Third, in most North American jurisdictions, it is common for the property tax to favour single-family residential owner-occupied properties over apartments and commercial and industrial properties. Favourable treatment of single-family residential properties is achieved in three ways:

1. The assessment system deliberately underassesses single-family residential properties as compared with apartments and commercial and industrial properties of comparable value.
2. Many jurisdictions have legislated lower tax rates on single-family residential property.
3. Property tax relief measures are often provided to residential property owners (and, in some cases, tenants) in the form of tax credits, homeowner grants, or tax deferrals. These measures are not generally available to nonresidential properties.

188 / E. SLACK

At the same time, this differential treatment does not necessarily reflect the differential use of services by different property types.[3]

Fourth, some have argued that property taxes are regressive. This means that the burden of the tax is relatively heavier for low-income households than for high-income households. Whether or not property taxes are regressive, this perception has led governments to introduce a number of different tax relief schemes for residential properties.[4] Nevertheless, increases in the property tax are often met with resistance on the grounds that low-income households cannot afford to pay the tax.

HISTORY OF PROPERTY TAX REFORM IN ONTARIO

The modern history of property tax reform in Ontario began with the report of the Ontario Committee on Taxation (the Smith committee) in 1967.[5] This committee, like similar committees in other provinces at that time, condemned the property tax for being regressive and for being inequitably administered (because properties of similar value were not assessed the same amount). The report recommended, among other things, that real property be assessed at "actual" value and that the province play an increased role in assessing real property. At that time, property assessment was a local function.

The province took over the assessment function from municipalities in 1970 and made a commitment to adopt full market value assessment as the base for property taxes throughout the province. The proposed market value assessment was one of the most important tax changes considered in Ontario because it implied tax shifts from some sections of the community to others. Since those on the losing side are most likely to be unhappy, it may be expected that any government that proposes to carry out such a policy change is not going to find it easy and will likely have to compromise and negotiate with the affected groups. Ontario's experience over the subsequent 30 years certainly shows this to be true.

Following several postponements of the scheduled date for the introduction of province-wide market value assessment, the 1976 provincial budget set out a series of reforms to the tax system that were needed before market value assessment could be introduced. In other words, assessment reform could not be implemented without tax policy reform. The proposed reforms included taxing residences on 50 percent of market value and other properties on 100 percent, a uniform business tax, limits to exemptions, phase-ins, and other tax changes.

After the release of the budget, the provincial government appointed the Commission on the Reform of Property Taxation in Ontario (the Blair commission) to consider the property tax proposals in more detail. The Blair commission reported in 1977[6] and supported the main recommendations of the 1976 budget. The government's response to the Blair commission was to issue yet another set of proposals in 1978 known as "the alternative system." This document supported the budget proposals but removed the idea of a uniform business tax. It made some other changes as well.

Yet another committee — the Provincial-Local Government Committee — was established in 1978 to consider the same proposals. The committee's report[7] supported many aspects of the alternative system, with two major changes. First, residential properties were to be taxed on 50 percent of market value, but now multiple residences were to be taxed on 75 percent of market value. Second, Metro Toronto was to be allowed to deviate for up to three years from the general 50 and 75 percent rates proposed for residential and multiresidential properties — for example, by setting rates at 45 and 80 percent, respectively. This change was designed to cushion the impact on Metro Toronto, where apartments were even more overassessed than in other municipalities. In short, the effect of these tax policy recommendations was to reduce substantially the tax shift that would have occurred from full market value assessment, especially for owners of single-family residences.

Notwithstanding all of the efforts to cushion the impact of market value assessment, the treasurer announced in 1978 that property tax reform would not be implemented. In November 1978, the minister of revenue confirmed that none of the changes proposed earlier would be legislated but that municipalities could, at their option, apply to the province under then section 86 of the Assessment Act for reassessment within classes of property (single-family homes, apartments, commercial properties, etc.). Many municipalities across the province exercised this option; Metro Toronto did not.

A new Liberal government in 1985 once again took up the challenge of property tax reform. It commissioned a further study of assessment and property taxation. The resulting report (appropriately titled *Taxing Matters: An Assessment of the Practice of Property Taxation in Ontario*)[8] also recommended market value assessment, but yet again, the government backed away from implementation.

In 1993, the New Democratic Party (NDP) government commissioned another study to review property taxation (as well as other forms of taxation) in Ontario. The Ontario Fair Tax Commission made several recommendations on property taxation and municipal and education funding.[9] Unlike any other study of property tax reform, however, it recommended unit value assessment — a relatively new concept in Ontario. Unit value assessment focuses on the size of the property and not on variables such as location.[10] This recommendation was not implemented either.

The NDP government established the Greater Toronto Area (GTA) Task Force in 1996. Problems with the property tax in Toronto had become urgent by this time: assessment appeals were eroding Metro Toronto's tax base, and there was a feeling that businesses were leaving Metro because of high property taxes. To the extent that appeals are successful, the assessment base is eroded, and all taxpayers then face higher tax rates. These inequities have also created what has been referred to by the Toronto Board of Trade as "the hole in the doughnut"; higher taxes on businesses in Toronto relative to the rest of the GTA provided an incentive for businesses to leave Toronto. Among its recommendations, the GTA task force recommended actual value assessment.[11] The task force completed its work under the new Conservative government.

In response to the task force report, the government established the Who Does What Panel to address issues in property taxation as well as the realignment of provincial and local responsibilities. The panel recommended the implementation of a uniform value-based assessment system province-wide (current value assessment) with variable tax rates.[12] The provincial government implemented the new assessment system in 1998. The tax policy reform that followed, however, was probably more complicated than anyone had ever imagined.

RECENT REFORM OF PROPERTY TAXES IN ONTARIO

Starting in January 1998, a uniform assessment system based on "current value" (similar to market value) was implemented province-wide. Every property was assessed as of the same valuation date, June 30, 1996. The next reassessment has been done for 2001; after 2005, annual updates will be done using a three-year rolling average.

The change to a uniform province-wide assessment system by itself would have resulted in large shifts in tax burdens within and between classes of property. For this reason, tax policy changes were introduced along with assessment reform. Indeed, the provincial government introduced seven pieces of legislation in all.

Before the reform, municipalities were required by legislation to levy differential tax rates on residential and non-residential property. Specifically, the residential rate had to be 85 percent of the non-residential rate. Following the assessment reform, municipalities are allowed to levy variable tax rates for different classes of property:

- residential,
- multiresidential,
- commercial,
- industrial,
- pipelines,
- farms, and
- managed forests.

Subclasses to which rate reductions apply are vacant commercial (35 percent reduction), vacant industrial (30 percent reduction), farmland pending development, and certain theatres in the city of Toronto. Furthermore, the commercial class can be divided into three subclasses according to value, with graduated tax rates applied to each subclass. The tax rate on farms and managed forests is legislated to be 25 percent of the residential tax rate.

As well, optional classes that municipalities can choose include

- new multiresidential,
- shopping centres,
- office towers,
- parking lots and vacant land,
- professional sports facilities, and
- large industrial.

Variable tax rates permit municipalities to shift tax burdens among property classes within provincially determined ranges of fairness. Transition ratios were calculated for each property class to reflect the relative distribution of burden by tax class before reform ("the starting point"). Transition ratios were calculated as the effective tax rate (property taxes relative to market value assessment) for each property class relative to the residential class. The transition ratio for residential properties—the benchmark—was set equal to 1.00.

Ranges of fairness were set by the provincial government as shown in table 1.

Municipalities could set their tax ratios so as to maintain the transition ratios, move toward the range of fairness, or vary tax ratios within ranges of fairness. For example, if the transition ratio on multiresidential properties was 4.1, a municipality could reduce it to 4.0 or below, or it could maintain it at 4.1. It could not increase it to 4.2 or beyond. In short, municipalities are not allowed to worsen the inequities, but they can maintain or reduce them.

Variable tax rates within ranges of fairness were used to allow municipalities to maintain the existing tax burdens between classes and reduce the impact of a reassessment. These provisions raise the question whether these discrepancies between classes of property should be allowed to remain. Two arguments can be made. On the one hand, provincial ranges of fairness could be considered to be inappropriate because the property tax is a local tax. Since municipal politicians are accountable to the electorate, they should be responsible for setting tax rates without provincial restrictions. On the other hand, municipalities are unlikely to eliminate the discrepancies on their own (especially if it means shifting tax burdens onto residential properties), and thus some form of provincial regulation is required to achieve fairness. The compromise (recommended by the Who Does What Panel and implemented by the provincial government) was to establish provincial ranges of fairness and require only that municipalities not move further away from them.

In addition to variable tax rates, the province legislated phase-in provisions and tax deferrals to address the shifts that would occur within classes of property, especially within the residential property class. Municipalities, at their option, can apply a phase-in for up to eight years for assessment-related tax changes. Interclass subsidization is not permitted; for example, tax decreases in the commercial class cannot be used to subsidize tax increases in the residential class. Different schemes can apply to different classes; different phase-in periods can be used for decreases and increases. Municipalities are required to establish a program to mitigate assessment-related tax increases for residential properties owned by low income seniors and the disabled. They can design their own mitigation programs.

The timing of phase-ins is also controversial because of the conflict between moving to a fairer system as quickly as possible and lessening the impact on those whose taxes will increase. One could argue, on the one hand, that the existing inequities should not be allowed to continue; on the other hand, it may not be wise to create undue hardship by not phasing in the tax changes.

Even with all of the tax policy reforms and phase-in mechanisms, however, there were still large shifts in tax burdens. In particular, the tax burden on small retail commercial properties increased relative to large office towers because of the recession in office markets in June 1996 (the valuation date). To reduce the shift onto small commercial properties, the provincial government introduced optional classes for office towers, shopping centres, and parking lots. Also, it introduced optional capping. Municipalities could limit tax increases on commercial, industrial, and multiresidential properties to 2.5 percent a year for three years (1998, 1999, 2000). This meant that the property tax could not increase more than 2.5 percent on any of these properties over what it was before reform. Furthermore,

TABLE 1
Provincial Ranges of Fairness

Property class	Allowable range of fairness
Multiresidential	1.0–1.1
New multiresidential	1.0–1.1
Commercial	0.6–1.1
Office building	0.6–1.1
Shopping centre	0.6–1.1
Parking lots and vacant land	0.6–1.1
Professional sports facility	0.001–1.1
Industrial	0.6–1.1
Large industrial	0.6–1.1
Pipelines	0.6–0.7

any tax increases over the three-year period resulting from increased expenditures, for example, would have to be financed from the residential property class. This measure was designed to move some of the burden away from the non-residential property classes and onto the residential class.

The result of capping was to freeze the assessment roll based on 1997. In other words, the new assessment roll was not used to tax multiresidential, commercial, or industrial properties from 1998 to 2000. Capping also meant that there was no effort to remove or even reduce the inequities in property tax burdens within the commercial, industrial, and multiresidential property classes. Instead of capping of the amount of the tax increase arising from a reassessment, the tax itself was capped.

Only Toronto chose the capping option initially. When it became clear that there were large tax increases on small commercial properties in other municipalities in Ontario, the provincial government introduced another piece of legislation that restricted property tax increases on commercial and industrial properties to 10 percent in 1998, an additional 5 percent in 1999, and an additional 5 percent in 2000. These rate restrictions were not optional, but municipalities could decide how to achieve the 10–5–5 target — through phase-ins, capping, or some other method. This legislation has resulted in freezing the assessment roll for commercial and industrial properties across the province.

For 2001 and subsequent years, municipalities are required to limit the assessment-related property tax increases on commercial, industrial, and multiresidential properties to 5 percent per year. Municipal levy increases (that is, year-over-year municipal tax increases) are not permitted in a property class if a municipality's tax ratio for that class exceeds the prescribed threshold ratio. The following threshold ratios (where thresholds represent provincial averages) have been prescribed: commercial, 1.98; industrial, 2.63; and multi-residential, 2.74. Essentially, this means that, for those municipalities over the threshold levels for all three property classes, any tax increase resulting from budgetary increases has to be borne by residential property taxpayers. A frozen assessment listing is no longer required for the administration of the new 5 percent limit.

EVALUATION OF THE RECENT REFORM

The result of the Ontario property tax reform is a tax system that has not changed much in terms of equity but has changed dramatically in terms of the complexity of administration. Current value assessment is being used for residential properties. This means that residential taxpayers have finally moved to a market value system — in some cases, with a phase-in. The assessment on multiresidential, commercial, and industrial properties, however, has virtually been frozen at pre-reform levels.

A uniform assessment system with variable tax rates provides much more visibility and accountability than the previous system, in which property tax differentials were hidden in the assessment method. Wherever anyone locates in the province, similarly valued residential properties are assessed at a similar value. Tax rates differ by location depending on the level of service and local government decisions about relative tax burdens.

In terms of neutrality, differential property taxes will be distortionary unless they reflect different benefits received. It can be argued, for example, that the benefits from local public services are different for different property classes. In particular, a case can be made on benefit grounds for taxing non-residential properties at a lower rate than residential properties. However, it appears that, under the Ontario property tax reform, differential property tax rates reflect the desire to maintain relative tax burdens and not to achieve fairness based on benefits received from municipal services.

Because of the focus on tax stability for each tax class, the initial goal of the reform — to achieve equity based on ability to pay — as lost completely. The inequities between classes of property have not been eliminated, and the inequities within classes (other than the residential class) have not been reduced. The reform has meant that the assessment function has been downloaded to a corporation comprising mostly municipal officials; the tax-setting process is, to a large extent, controlled by the provincial government. Although municipalities have control over the level of taxes, their control over the distribution of taxes among classes of property has been severely constrained by the province.

Attempts to simplify property tax administration have failed. The system for setting tax rates is so complicated and has changed so many times that some municipalities have been unable to set tax rates correctly. As a result of the capping legislation, property tax bills that were issued in 1998 had to be reissued in some cases in 1999.

Important lessons can be learned from the reform of property taxation in Ontario. The longer you wait to reform a tax, the more difficult it will be. Annual reassessments for property tax purposes will create far fewer shifts in taxes than a reassessment after 40 years.

The ability to reform the property tax is more constrained than is the case for other taxes because of the visibility of the tax. It is particularly difficult to shift tax burdens onto residential property. Favouritism toward residential property is an inherent part of the property tax system. Trying to change the way this tax is levied is politically difficult. At the very least, phase-ins and tax deferrals are an essential part of the tax policy design.

Taxpayers need to have confidence in the assessed values and the process used to derive them. This means taking the time to do the assessment properly. Furthermore, before property tax reform is implemented, it is necessary to undertake an impact assessment to determine the shifts in taxation. This needs to be done in advance so that tax policy can be designed before the reform comes into effect, and not in a piecemeal fashion in response to problems as they occur.

More generally, the lesson from the Ontario experience is that, no matter how economically desirable the long-run outcome of any policy change may be, its transitional effects may be sufficiently undesirable in political terms to kill it. From a public choice perspective, the losers from a change in policy tend to be very vocal (even if they are the minority) because they value their losses more than the gainers (even if they are the majority) value their gains. This problem is not unique to property taxes, but it is particularly significant in this case because of the visibility of this tax.

NOTES

1 As Harry Kitchen notes in his paper at this symposium, in 2000 property taxes accounted for more than 53 percent of municipal revenues in Canada. See

Harry Kitchen, "Canadian Municipalities: Fiscal Trends and Sustainability" (2002) vol. 50, no. 1 *Canadian Tax Journal* 156-80.

2 In some cases, however, mortgage institutions include property tax payments with monthly mortgage payments. This procedure reduces the visibility of the property tax for taxpayers to whom these arrangements apply.

3 It has been suggested that non-residential properties use fewer services than residential properties but pay more in taxes. Users of non-residential property often provide their own garbage collection, security, and fire protection. For example, see Harry Kitchen and Enid Slack, *Business Property Taxation*, Government and Competitiveness Project Discussion Paper no. 93-24 (Kingston, ON: Queen's University, School of Policy Studies, 1993), 23.

4 For a discussion of the incidence of the property tax and property tax relief schemes, see Richard Bird and Enid Slack, *Urban Public Finance in Canada*, 2d ed. (Toronto: Wiley, 1993), 88.

5 Ontario Committee on Taxation, *Report* (Toronto: Queen's Printer, 1967).

6 Ontario, *Report of the Commission on the Reform of Property Taxation in Ontario* (Toronto: Government of Ontario, 1977).

7 Ontario, *Report of the Provincial-Local Government Committee on Property Tax Reform* (Toronto: Government of Ontario, April 1978).

8 Ontario, *Taxing Matters: An Assessment of the Practice of Property Taxation in Ontario* (Toronto: Ministry of Revenue, 1985).

9 Ontario, *Fair Taxation in a Changing World: Report of the Ontario Fair Tax Commission* (Toronto: University of Toronto Press in cooperation with the Ontario Fair Tax Commission, 1993).

10 For a discussion of unit value assessment, see Enid Slack, "Property Taxation," in Mila Friere and Richard Stren, eds., *The Challenge of Urban Government: Policies and Practices* (Washington, DC: World Bank Institute, 2001), 269-79, at 272.

11 Greater Toronto Area Task Force, *Greater Toronto: Report of the GTA Task Force* (Toronto: Queen's Printer, January 1996).

12 Ontario, Who Does What Panel on Local Governance, *Recommendations* (Toronto: Who Does What Panel, 1996).

User Charges or Property Taxes

DOUGLAS J. McCREADY ─────────────────────────

While urban government in Canada is no longer the focus of a federal government department, a great deal of attention has been directed to urban problems in the past two decades. And most of that attention has been at the provincial level where the financial relationships between municipalities and the provincial governments have been of prime importance. Since there are ten provinces and two territories in Canada, each with its own municipal organization, it is difficult to generalize about the relative importance of differing aspects of local government finance in Canada.

THE CURRENT STRUCTURE OF CANADIAN MUNICIPALITIES

The consequence of local government being a creature of the provincial governments, not recognized in any constitutional documents means that the responsibilities (read expenditures) and revenue sources differ greatly, as does the structure of the municipalities (one-tier and two-tier). New Brunswick, for instance, took over most functions that had traditionally been municipal responsibilities during the 1960s. Ontario has established 13 two-tiered regional governments, each with its own Act, but generally water, sewage, arterial roads, health, welfare, and police protection are assigned to the upper tier while street lighting, fire protection, garbage collection, parks and recreation, and libraries remain the responsibility of the lower-tier municipalities.[1] British Columbia also has two-tiered

---

The research was made possible by an Initiatory Research Grant from the University. Reproduced by permission of the author.

[1] Canadian Tax Foundation *Provincial and Municipal Finances*, 1981 (Toronto: Canadian Tax Foundation, 1983) p. 226.

governments at the local level, but the lower tier has generally been left with greater responsibilities than in Ontario.

Table 1 indicates the variation between the provincial/local responsibilities for 1984. Note the heavy reliance on local governments in Manitoba, British Columbia, Nova Scotia and Ontario in contrast to the low reliance on local government revenues in Newfoundland, Prince Edward Island, and New Brunswick.

As for reliance on different revenue sources, there is also a great deal of variation. Property taxes on real estate (land and improvements) have been the chief source of municipal revenue, accounting for 46% of municipal revenues in 1967 and 35% in 1984, while transfers from provincial governments accounted for 40% of municipal revenues in 1967 and 48% in 1980.[2]

Heavy reliance on property taxes and the vilification of that tax has resulted in many studies of assessment methods and the relationship of property tax to provincial responsibility and grants.[34] Generally, most of the task forces or Royal Commissions tackling the problems of urban finance have been urged by both municipal and provincial politicians to consider the role of provincial grants to the municipalities since those are seen as being more equitable than real property taxes.

Furthermore, municipal politicians wanted to be able to increase services at a faster rate than inflation but felt constrained to keep property and other tax increases to "not much more than the rate of inflation." Since the personal income tax revenue elasticity in Canada is greater than one, as long as the provinces were co-operative in sharing their increased revenues the municipal revenues increased through grants.

Not one of the reports mentioned above leaves the impression that other sources of revenue are to be extensively tapped. In most instances, that would appear to be a result of the terms of reference

---

[2] Richard M. Bird and N. Enid Slack *Urban Public Finance in Canada*. (Toronto: Butterworths, 1983) p. 57.

[3] The term vilification was suggested by Bird and Slack, *ibid*, p. 60.

[4] Some of the studies include:

New Brunswick, *Report of the Royal Commission on Finance and Municipal Taxation in New Brunswick* (Fredericton: Queen's Printer, 1963).

Saskatchewan Local Government Finance Commission. *Final Report of the Local Government Finance Commission*. (Regina: Government Printing, 1986).

Manitoba Assessment Review Commission. *A Fair Way to Share*. (Winnipeg: Government Printing, 1982).

Parliamentary Assistant to the Treasurer and the Minister of Revenue *Taxing Matters*. (Toronto: Queen's Printer, 1985.).

TABLE 1

Local government revenues and expenditures (in millions of dollars)

	Property and Related Taxes	Sales of Goods and Services	Transfers	Own Service Revenues
Newfoundland	90.8	25.6	91.6	138.4
Prince Edward Island	10.7	7.1	81.5	20.0
Nova Scotia	269.2	92.3	749.6	421.1
New Brunswick	86.6	51.3	157.8	148.9
Quebec	140.7	731.8	5,010.0	4,189.5
Ontario	6,272.4	1,535.6	6,685.1	8,655.2
Manitoba	514.9	141.6	854.3	785.6
Saskatchewan	583.6	146.7	733.1	870.0
Alberta	1,142.6	771.0	2,696.1	2,698.5
British Columbia	1,340.2	445.2	1,734.3	2,084.4

	Transportation and Communications	Health	Education	Social Services	Gross Expenditures
Newfoundland	64.5	0.0	19.2	0.0	243.1
Prince Edward Island	4.4	0.0	72.1	0.0	99.0
Nova Scotia	56.6	82.2	534.7	142.2	1,144.6
New Brunswick	69.1	2.6	—	—	310.8
Quebec	982.8	5.9	4,445.5	23.8	9,669.1
Ontario	1,450.9	835.8	6,345.9	1,106.6	15,043.8
Manitoba	179.0	113.6	699.8	41.7	1,593.9
Saskatchewan	191.3	226.0	709.8	12.1	1,614.9
Alberta	550.9	938.0	1,747.5	50.2	5,570.0
British Columbia	331.6	105.5	1,660.6	5.7	3,893.9

Source: Canada, Statistics Canada, *Local Government Finance, 1984* (latest issue). Ottawa: Ministry of Supply and Services, 1988. Various tables.

rather than a deliberate decision on the part of commissioners or task forces to recommend against other types of revenue. Indeed, most often, the issue to be investigated was the assessment function in real property tax, and only this one aspect of municipal revenue sources was examined; but even when the total municipal finances were reviewed, property tax and provincial grants to municipalities dominated. Even a study carried out by Bird and Slack for the Ontario Economic Council entitled *Residential Property Tax Relief in Ontario* (which one would think from the title might refer to prices for goods and services) contains nothing on "other" revenues.[5]

Typically, since the major local revenue from their own sources is the property tax, constituting 55.5% of those revenues, and since school boards get approximately half of those revenues (usually a little more), there is an assumption on the part of many that the property tax is itself like a user charge.[6] Many references are made to the fact that police services, for instance, are worth more to the higher-valued property and, consequently, there is a presumption that property taxes are not income redistributive.[7] The property tax being seen as a user charge is accentuated by recent moves on the part of provincial governments to give seniors tax credits on their personal income tax (or grants) to alleviate the amount of the property tax going into schools, from which, it is argued, they receive no direct benefit.[8]

If the property tax is to become a neutral tax insofar as being a factor in mobility of factors of production (i.e., labour and capital), the property tax must not differ extensively from taxes in neighbouring jurisdictions. If own source revenues are to vary as between jurisdictions, they can only do so as benefits vary (i.e., a benefit tax), and thus user charges are most reliable in designing benefit taxes.[9]

---

[5] R.M. Bird and N.E. Slack *Residential Property Tax Relief in Ontario* (Toronto: University of Toronto Press, 1978) p. viii.

[6] The calculation is made from Statistics Canada. *Local Government Finance, 1983*, (Ottawa, 1986), Table 3.

[7] See many general texts on public finance.

[8] What about the reduction in neighbourhood vandalism and noise? What about the productivity advances? These are all of benefit to seniors, along with many other indirect and, perhaps, unmeasurable benefits. While it is granted that the child and, even more, the parent (in these days where schools are viewed as an alternative to child care for working parents) receive a major portion of the private benefits, society itself benefits in no small part, particularly at the junior level.

[9] McCready, D.J., "Is Wealth Taxation a Plausible Reform?" *Canadian Public Administration*, XXXIV, 2 (Summer 1991), pp. 260–71.

One excellent source of material, although now dated, is Richard M. Bird's *Charging for Public Services: A New Look at an Old Idea*.[10] While that document examines in some detail the theoretical issues related to user charges, it also undertakes a rather thorough empirical compilation of user charges (in the municipal field there is more on Ontario user charges than the other provinces). Unfortunately, his more recent *Urban Public Finance* avoids the issue of user charge, which is in line with the emphasis by municipal and provincial politicians on general taxes rather than product pricing.[11]

In Table 2 we note that some functions lend themselves to user charges more readily than others. Certainly, expenditures on Culture and Recreation and Housing; large portions of expenditures on Natural Resources and Transportation and Communication; and small portions of expenditures on Protection of Persons and Property and General Services could be financed by user charges. For Canada, as a whole, over 10% of municipal spending could be fully transferred to user charges.

THE ECONOMIC THEORY OF PROPERTY TAXATION

The property tax is a particular type of wealth tax based on visible and immovable wealth. Thus, it shares with the wealth tax many of the difficulties the wealth tax exhibits.[12]

The property tax, if raised in one jurisdiction as compared to other jurisdictions, will cause immobility of capital invested in the high-rate jurisdiction, in the short run. The tax is capitalized and reduces the value of the property. Thus, the tax reduces the value of the property and is fully borne by the current owner of the property.

To illustrate, if the rate of return on capital were 10%, an asset worth $10,000 would yield $1,000. Now, suppose property tax is imposed (increased) at $50 per $1,000 of property value. Income is reduced to $500, and the property value will now be $5,000. Subsequent owners will do so at the lower price and, consequently, will not bear any burden of the tax.

---

[10] R.M. Bird *Charging for Public Services: A New Look at an Old Idea* (Toronto, Canadian Tax Foundation, 1976).

[11] R.M. Bird and N.E. Slack *Urban Public Finance in Canada* (Toronto, Butterworths, 1983).

[12] See McCready, *op. cit.*

TABLE 2
Municipal funding of government spending by function per capita (in 1981 dollars, 1988)

	NFLD.	P.E.I	N.S.	N.B.	QUE.	ONT.	MAN.	SASK.	ALTA.	B.C.	CANADA
Culture & Recreation	33.35	34.81	30.06	40.45	62.07	87.66	66.28	97.29	97.77	89.07	77.19
Education	35.79	0.02	104.19	0.00	72.12	294.86	195.70	267.91	196.63	117.92	180.51
General Services	41.02	20.70	36.89	25.21	98.67	66.48	64.77	64.09	89.21	44.50	71.64
Health	0.09	0.09	84.24	3.67	0.85	50.16	87.51	203.07	235.87	24.32	57.60
Housing	9.10	1.00	13.40	6.14	0.00	15.62	15.53	11.51	24.50	17.50	11.94
Labour	0.00	0.00	0.00	0.00	0.00	0.00	0.00	0.00	0.00	0.00	0.00
Natural Resources	25.88	14.67	62.14	50.25	65.68	102.05	82.43	93.62	117.73	60.01	83.65
Oil & Gas	0.00	0.00	0.00	0.00	0.00	0.00	0.00	0.00	0.00	0.00	0.00
Other	8.32	14.91	2.86	0.00	117.30	21.37	30.89	0.00	152.40	107.26	65.90
Protection of Persons & Property	26.94	26.08	81.44	80.93	102.08	128.96	102.17	88.15	101.95	113.66	109.15
Research Establishments	0.00	0.00	0.00	0.00	0.00	0.00	0.00	0.00	0.00	0.00	0.00
Social Security	0.01	0.00	60.39	0.00	2.98	34.63	2.86	10.49	10.82	0.90	17.09
Trade & Industry	0.00	0.01	3.20	0.43	0.00	1.41	0.00	0.00	6.86	3.60	1.75
Transportation & Communication	79.33	43.48	44.09	72.91	137.68	74.25	108.03	140.33	204.55	86.60	107.38
TOTAL	259.82	155.76	522.89	280.01	659.44	877.45	756.16	976.46	1,238.28	665.35	783.80

Capital invested in improvements will, in the long run, flee the high-tax jurisdiction since maintenance expenditures on old assets will be reduced, and new investments will be reduced. The extent of mobility may be tied to labour mobility (particularly if the capital is invested in household improvements), but can occur without the mobility of labour. However, as capital flees to the lower-rate jurisdiction, labour productivity and wages will rise in the low-rate jurisdictions to lose population as well.

In Canada, such "voting with your feet" is less common than it is in the United States. First, there are fewer independent jurisdictions (regional and metropolitan governments are more common in Canada). Thus, mobility from Detroit to Wyandotte, Grosse Isle, Grosse Point, Dearborn, or Southfield (all part of metropolitan Detroit) will not have any counterpart in Canada. Indeed, Canadian centres are not even on provincial boundaries (aside from Ottawa-Hull and Lloydminster), and so the property tax differential is rarely accentuated by differences in income and sales taxes (as it would be in Washington D.C., with Maryland and Virginia within easy commuting distance).

A NEW TAX FOR LOCAL GOVERNMENT

Local governments have been able recently to impose "development" or "lot" levies on newly developed residential properties and, in Ontario, that is being spread to commercial properties.

"Lot" levies are not property taxes in the sense that they do not become capitalized in the value of the property. Thus, they do not hamper the mobility of capital in the short or long run, nor do they discourage maintenance.

Development charges thus act like a "benefit" tax in that they make the recipient of the benefit (the property with all services, such as roads, servers, water and other utilities) pay for the benefit rather than having the already existing land holders pay for the improvements through decreasing property values.

The economic effect of lot levies may be to reduce economic growth in high-rate jurisdictions. Alternatively, to generate economic growth there may be tax competition in which "lot" levies are reduced (the logic says competition could drive the levy down to zero), and fewer amenities will be provided (curbs and other costs of services may be decreased).

From the perspective of the current homeowner, development charges provide great advantages over property tax hikes. So also do other user charges or benefit taxes.

CURRENT STATUS OF PRICING SERVICES

Despite the heavy emphasis in official documents and in public discussion on property tax and provincial grants to municipalities, there have been and will continue to be sales revenues for goods and services sold by municipalities. These include remittances from enterprises like Kitchener Gas (the corporation's shareholder being the City of Kitchener) and various public utilities owned by municipalities.[13] The amount, however, remains small relative to other sources of revenue, varying from 15.3% of local government revenues in Alberta and New Brunswick to 6.0% in Prince Edward Island.[14]

The most current information is found in Table 3. Note there that Alberta on a per capita basis pays almost six times more than New Brunswick in user fees, yet the same percentage of local revenues comes from pricing in both provinces. In general, as one moves west, per capita payments for goods and services rise, the lowest being in Newfoundland and the highest being Alberta. While the figures in Table 3 include water, it does not include remittances of profits from own enterprises that may have been established to sell various utility and transportation services.

Note that in Tables 1 and 3, despite some pretty basic differences regarding their reliance on locally raised funds (per capita) and despite differences in the degree to which user charges are relied upon, there are striking similarities across provinces. Almost 50% of all local revenues derives from provincial transfers (Prince Edward Island and Nova Scotia being the only provinces that deviate greatly) and of own revenues, real property taxes constitute the major source of revenues. This homogeneity is surprising when one considers the heterogeneity as between provinces (culture, historical development, ethnic background) and the fact that it is a provincial responsibility to determine the role of local government.

It is almost impossible to ferret out much information on the wide variety of pricing policies for a wide range of activities. There is even less in the way of rational statements of the objectives of municipal user charges. The homogeneity mentioned above is true here as well. No province differs in making the principles clear.

---

[13] In fact, the Province of Alberta accounts for over half of all the profits remitted from municipal corporations, with Quebec, Saskatchewan, and British Columbia being the only other provinces with this form of income.

[14] The explanation lies in the fact that even though New Brunswick has the third lowest per capita sales revenues, it permitted the municipalities only a small amount in real property taxes, paying for most services directly with provincial funds.

TABLE 3
Sales of goods and services, 1983 (in thousands of dollars)

Province	Sales of Goods and Services	Total Revenues	Per Capita Sales of Goods and Services	Percent of Total Revenues
Newfoundland	20,028	185,906	34.77	10.8
Prince Edward Island	5,718	95,511	46.11	6.0
Nova Scotia	78,984	1,113,598	92.06	7.1
New Brunswick	43,053	281,574	61.07	15.3
Province of Quebec	949,294	8,780,207	145.71	10.8
Ontario	1,444,168	14,272,895	164.11	10.1
Manitoba	133,258	1,543,188	127.52	8.6
Saskatchewan	145,003	1,521,954	146.32	9.5
Alberta	810,371	5,302,530	345.57	15.3
British Columbia	493,807	3,714,842	175.23	13.3
N.W. Territories	16,805	85,013	240.07	19.8
TOTAL	3,816,802	36,897,218	153.61	10.3

Source: Statistics Canada, *Local Government Finance, 1983*, (Ottawa, 1986), Table 3.

In many instances, the activities that earn municipalities sales revenues are legally those conducted by special-purpose legislative bodies. Water is a prime example, with Public Utilities Commissions, which are elected at the same time as municipal councils, being responsible for setting the prices. Public library boards and transit commissions are usually appointed, but their decisions are only dealt with in a cursory manner by municipal politicians, as the charges they impose are only a minor part of their total revenues.

In the cases of library boards that this researcher is familiar with, the prices charged for borrowing privileges are viewed as making up the difference between the grant given by the municipality and the costs of salaries, new books, utilities, etc. Pricing borrowing privileges has nothing to do with average or marginal cost and very little to do with the desire to redistribute wealth, except that on occasion there may be an extra fee for non-taxpayers in the municipality.[15]

Yet, there are other examples, perhaps far more numerous (arenas, fair grounds, and theatres come to mind), in which municipal politicians want the board to run the enterprise as a non-profit business but where the board puts little effort into setting prices because they know that any deficit will be covered. In such instances, there is not even an incentive to keep costs under control and, thus, for many people such enterprises epitomize the poor management practices of government.

The special purpose bodies of local government are so numerous that accurate counts by municipal leaders of such bodies in their own municipalities are not likely. As of 1968, the Bureau of Municipal Research had estimated that in Ontario there were more than 3,200 such bodies. In Toronto, 13 of these were essentially self-financing (i.e., Toronto Transit Commission), while many others (of the 101) played some role in controlling their own finances.[16]

SOME CANADIAN EXAMPLES

Urban Transit

In his study of urban transit user charges, Bird notes an attitude on the part of the Executive Co-ordinator of Ontario's Urban Transit Program, in a paper presented to the National Tax Association,

---

[15] The City of Kitchener Public Library, for instance, charges for a computerized library card to residents of Kitchener but $25.00 (per annum) to non-residents, up from $2.00 in the past (the change was made effective July 1986.

[16] Bureau of Municipal Research, *Civic Affairs* (Toronto) 1968.

that he claims is prevalent. The only sources of additional financing seriously discussed by transit authorities are the general revenues of municipal, provincial, or federal government.[17] Ontario, British Columbia, and Alberta each have provincial subsidy programs to defray operating deficits from general tax revenues, which rewards transit authorities for poor management. If there is a profit, no subsidy will be available. Consequently, either fares will be set too low, or costs will be permitted to escalate in order to qualify for the subsidy.

The basic fare structure in most Canadian cities is a flat basic fare, with a discount for volume purchases, senior citizens, students, and children. The argument used against zoned fares and peak load pricing is the difficulty in administering and policing such a fee structure. Further, the cheaper prices for students, in particular, cannot be justified on the basis of marginal cost for, often, they are the very ones who cause peak load problems.

Urban transit authorities argue for greater subsidization from general revenues because they argue that realistic prices would reduce ridership when personal automobiles and taxicabs are not paying full prices. Moreover, they suggest that higher prices hurt those families most dependent on public transit, those who are poorest. These are equity arguments for a lesser reliance on user charges, but have relatively little to do with economic efficiency. In fact, efficiency and equity would be enhanced if user prices were properly set, based on marginal cost for all three modes of transportation.

It can also be argued that non-users benefit from the externality (less congestion on roads and other types of transit services) and, consequently, at least a portion of transit costs ought to be borne out of general taxes.

In 1982, in a survey conducted by Kitchener, in the province of Ontario, less than 40% of costs was derived from fares in municipalities of under 25,000 people. The survey results are found in Table 4. It will be noted that the largest transit systems (those with the greatest external benefits in decreased congestion) recovered the most from user charges. Surprising, it is not! Small systems receive a larger provincial subsidy towards any deficit incurred (25% of operating cost as opposed to 13.75% for those over 1,000,000 population base).

---

[17] R.M. Bird *Charging for Public Services: A New Look at an Old Idea* (Toronto, Canadian Tax Foundation, 1976) p. 68.

TABLE 4
Percent of average cost recovered through transit charges, Ontario, 1982

Population Size	Average	Standard Deviation
0–25,000	39.1	10.3
25,001–50,000	35.5	9.4
50,001–100,000	48.5	9.9
100,001–200,000	48.4	8.8
200,001 and over	60.4	10.2
TOTAL	43.6	12.6

Water

Fully 27.8% of all sales of goods and services are accounted for by water.[18] Even a brief review of water pricing in Canada suggests that sharing costs has been of prime concern amongst public utility managers, with equity and efficiency considerations being almost forgotten.

A typical municipal water rate structure is that of Waterloo in 1986, with a flat rate of 21.5 cents per cubic metre of water used and a monthly service charge that depends on the pipe size entering the property (currently $1.40 for the 15 cm and 25 cm pipe connection, which are the two sizes to residences). While this is a typical structure, variations can be found that include a monthly charge and a decreasing marginal rate as volume increases. Another rate structure does not involve metres, but rather is based on the number of rooms or the number and type of water outlets.

No municipality in Ontario fails to charge at least some price for water. Yet, about 5% of current water revenue derived from the property tax in 1975.[19] Table 5 outlines the basic type of charge in 1983. Almost 40% of the communities have a flat rate, but the majority of those are in smaller municipalities.

Kitchener reports on some larger municipalities in which a decision had to be made as to whether to expand the capital facility. In every case, when they switched from flat rate to metered rate, the

---

[18] Calculated from Statistics Canada, *Local Government Finance, 1983*, (Ottawa, 1986), Table 3.
[19] A conclusion drawn by R.M. Bird *op cit.*, p. 143.

demand for water fell drastically, and what had been a fully utilized system now had excess capacity.[20]

It should be noted that those municipalities that use a declining block rate schedule induce overuse as well. Many users do not consume enough to get above the minimum bill; hence, their demand may be higher at the margin than it would be otherwise. Further consumers with swimming pools, dishwashers, large lawns with sprinkling systems, and multiple vehicles to wash receive a subsidy from those in lower-income categories who do not receive lower water rates. Finally, no municipality tries to charge for the peak load marginal costs experienced in the June to September months, or in the late afternoon and early evening when lawns are watered and, instead, they argue for more capacity — not marginal cost pricing at all!

No locality that this author knows of differentiates rates by distance from the main water source; yet this also would be logical under a system of marginal cost pricing.

Recreation Facilities

Since leisure time is increasing and many of the capital costs for swimming pools, tennis courts, and arenas are borne out of general tax revenues, there is a legitimate question about how to price the facility usage. Recreation authorities tend to set fees to cover operating costs only.[21] They also tend to set fees far below those of private not-for-profit organizations like the Y.M.C.A. As a consequence, there is a clamour for even more of these public facilities.

Kitchener and Waterloo are two cities with a common border, Kitchener having a population of about twice that of Waterloo (110,000 vs. 55,000). Kitchener Parks and Recreation runs three indoor swimming pools and is constructing another; Waterloo has none, but has one in the planning stage. Kitchener has such demand for their swimming lessons that people line up all night to be sure to be able to register their children. In the last 12 months there have been demands that Waterloo residents be charged a significantly higher fee for use of Kitchener facilities, and that Kitchener build at least one more facility. Yet there is a Y.M.C.A. in each city, with room for additional registrations for swimming lessons. The fee for swimming lessons at a Kitchener pool is $15.00 for eight weeks, while at the Y.M.C.A. it is $21.25 for seven weeks. There is an extra

---

[20] H.M. Kitchen *Local Government Enterprise in Canada*, (Ottawa, Economic Council of Canada, 1986), p. 36.
[21] H.M. Kitchen *ibid.*, p. 45.

$5.00 for a child from outside Kitchener, but still the cost per lesson is $2.50 while the Y.M.C.A. cost per lesson is $3.03. For a Kitchener child, that works out to $1.88 per lesson. If the price were set by the market (both the city and the Y.M.C.A. currently subsidize those in financial need), the city pools would raise their fee and, perhaps, then the taxpayers would not have to pay the high capital costs of building new facilities. This example contributes to the discussion of what happens when incorrect prices are charged and also points to the foolishness of having property taxes subsidize facilities that are in competition with private for-profit and non-profit institutions.

There is, again, pressure from recreationists to keep fees low. Typical is the concept that fees must be kept low, otherwise many people can't afford them. Is there a legitimate need, or would they make other choices? If there is legitimate need, couldn't the redistribution take place through general revenues and/or expenditures (a transfer) and "proper" prices be charged, thus keeping the information system in place? If the transfer is through prices to everybody who wants the good, the greater money cost and the information on which allocation decisions are made is lost, too.

No municipality in Canada, so far as this author can determine, charges admission for parks or the playgrounds in those parks. In fact, some homes associations within municipalities have requested, and received, from cities creative playground equipment, swings, slides, and benches for their privately maintained parks areas, and those items are almost exclusively used by the members of the association. Use of park facilities without an admission price may be based on the difficulty of exclusion for, unlike urban parks in London, England, most urban parks in Canada remain unfenced. On the other hand, there appears to be no defence for not charging private organizations such as homes associations for equipment placed for their usage.

Sometimes nominal fees are charged for organized activities held within the parks for children during the summer but, even in these cases, the fees do not begin to cover staff costs, let alone overhead. Again, in many instances these summer programs compete with day camps run by the Y.M.C.A., Y.W.C.A., various churches, and private organizations, but those other organizations cannot compete in terms of price because the municipality price is not equivalent to marginal cost.

As for peak load problems, most pools and skating rinks charge an admission that does not vary except that children often pay less. In the case of ice arenas, there are some municipalities that do differentiate their fees (for non-profit groups, for time-of-day, or for day of the week). Golf courses that are municipally owned also frequently have weekday and weekend rates and, sometimes, fees depending on the tee-off time. Pricing for peak loads is clearly "correct", but little understood.

DOES CANADA CONTRIBUTE TO THE DEBATE ABOUT USER CHARGES?

The use of user charges in Canada is not highly developed. First, there has been no interest on the part of those in positions of responsibility in the underlying rationale of user charges, nor has there been any push in the direction of user charges. Second, Canadian municipalities have little experience with pricing goods and services, and those special-purpose bodies that do have experience do not typically rely on prices for their major revenues. Moreover, these bodies view user charges as a source of supplemental funds or, alternatively, have a backup of being able to tap municipal or provincial general revenues to cover deficits when they do set prices, thus negating any rational effort to set "correct" prices.

"Appropriate" user charges are potentially very powerful in terms of allocating resources efficiently and, if imposed in a rational way to a wide range of services, may increase rather than decrease equity. "Appropriate" in this case involves finding the marginal cost (both private and social) and establishing a price (and tax) that sets the total equal to the total marginal cost. Alcohol sold by the Liquor Control Board of Ontario stores has a price now that is largely tax and profit for the government, but no one (at least in this author's knowledge) has measured whether the price paid by the consumer equals marginal cost (of producing the alcohol and of the vandalism and damage to health caused by alcohol usage).

Bird, in his book on user charges, makes the point that in Canada there needs to be a drastic change in social attitudes to accomplish "appropriate reform in pricing public goods."[22] Specifically, he remarks that so long as people accept the "authoritarian role of the nursery governess, telling us what is good for us on the assumption that we are too stupid, too ignorant, too perverted (by nature or by advertising), or too perverse to do what is in our own interests", there is little hope of greater reliance on prices for products.[23] Further, since egalitarians believe that rationing by price is especially hard on low-income people, it is necessary to educate those people that it is the middle- or upper-income peo-

---

[22] R.M. Bird *op cit.*, chapter 21.

[23] R.M. Bird *ibid.*, p. 235.

ple — who drive large automobiles into the city core, who have large lawns to water, who use golf courses, skating rinks, and higher education — who receive subsidies from taxes paid in large part by lower income people.[24] Only if changes occur in social attitudes and knowledge can Canadians expect a change in the use of prices for public services.

It would be very wrong to argue that there are not circumstances where general tax collections are preferable to user charges. When externalities exist, when public goods (indivisible goods) exist, when marginal cost is virtually zero, and when decreasing costs exist over the relevant quantities, there exists a strong case for public provision with subsidization in whole or in part. Yet, for the many other products provided by local governments, there would be advantages in charging the "correct" marginal cost price. Otherwise, the concept of charging for goods and services is discredited. While there are costs associated with finding the correct charge, those costs can be balanced by the gains in efficiency (including providing goods in the quantities desired and of the type wanted), and where they can't be justified, general tax revenues are the fallback. Yet, given the new technology, information systems that permit marginal cost pricing should have become more reasonable to implement.

Overall, this author would argue that Canada's experience with user charges teaches three things. First, there must be a public acceptance of such charges (and perhaps that needs to be accompanied by greater redistribution in the general tax system). Second, acceptance will come only through the use of properly designed charges and a commitment on the part of administrators to set full marginal cost prices and not rely on deficit subsidies. Moreover, the commitment must be general since pricing public transit, for instance, at full marginal cost while not charging private automobiles, or taxicabs full marginal cost, defeats the purpose of adding to consumer sovereignty and economic efficiency. Third, there needs to be a greater understanding among politicians and civil servants about the operation of a price mechanism. In private business, failure to set "correct" prices is often cause for business failure, but in the public sector there would be little room for error for we would not tolerate public goods being dropped from the basket of available commodities if the monopoly public authority made the wrong pricing decision.

---

[24] R.M. Bird *ibid.*, p. 234.

REFERENCES

Stephen J. Bailey "Paying for Local Government: Charging for Services" *Public Administration*, LXIV (Winter 1986) pp. 403–21.

Richard M. Bird *Charging For Public Services: A New Look at an Old Idea.* Toronto: Canadian Tax Foundation, 1976.

Richard M. Bird and N. Enid Slack *Residential Property Tax Relief in Ontario.* Toronto: Ontario Economic Council, 1978.

——— *Urban Public Finance in Canada.* Toronto: Butterworths, 1983.

Canada. Statistics Canada. *Local Government Finance, 1983.* Ottawa: Department of Supply and Services, 1986.

Canadian Tax Foundation. *Provincial and Municipal Finances, 1983.* Toronto: Canadian Tax Foundation, 1983.

Douglas G. Hartle *Political Economy of Tax Reform: Six Case Studies* Discussion Paper No. 290. Ottawa: Economic Council of Canada, 1985.

Harry M. Kitchen *Local Government Finance in Canada.* Toronto: Canadian Tax Foundation, 1984.

——— *Local Government Enterprise in Canada.* Discussion Paper No. 300. Ottawa: Economic Council of Canada, 1986.

Douglas J. McCready "Is Wealth Tax a Plausible Reform" *Canadian Public Administration* XXXIV, 2 (Summer 1991), pp. 260–71.

Real Estate Law

Outline of Real Estate Law

—————— GAVIN ARBUCKLE & HENRY BARTEL

Real estate law is relevant to the work of real estate professionals in two principal ways. First, it establishes the framework of rights and obligations within which transactions take place. Even the most routine transfer of an interest in property follows forms and procedures rooted in centuries of legal evolution. A working knowledge of this framework is necessary if real estate professionals are to understand the reasons for using particular forms and terms of transactions, and thus to be able to distinguish those that may be selected for mere convenience from those that are critically important to protecting the interests of their principals and clients. Second, real estate law contains elaborate rules for resolving disputes between the parties to transactions. A general knowledge of this law should enable the real estate professional, in close cooperation with the real estate lawyer, to foresee possible sources of dispute before they arise, and take care to arrange the terms and execution of the original transaction so as to minimize the risk of costly renegotiation and litigation.

THE REAL ESTATE AGENT

A real estate agent or real estate broker is, essentially, someone who is legally authorized to represent someone else, the principal, in a real estate transaction. Taking Ontario as an example, the governing

This paper was written in 1986 for the first edition of this book. The authors would like to thank John Zeiler, of the firm Leve and Zeiler, in Toronto, for refereeing this paper. Needless to say, any remaining errors in fact or in interpretation are ours, and not his.

legislation is the *Real Estate and Business Brokers Act*, which defines, among other things, a real estate broker as

> a person who, for another or others, for compensation, gain or reward or hope or promise thereof, either alone or through one or more officials or salesmen, trades in real estate, or a person who holds himself out as such.

A real estate salesman, by contrast,

> means a person employed, appointed or authorized by a broker to trade in real estate.

The distinction is important. A salesman cannot act on his own: that is, without generally having first entered into an employee-employer relationship with a real estate broker. Any business undertaken by the salesman must be done on behalf of, and in the name of, the broker. It is the role of the broker, therefore, that warrants closer attention.

The Canadian Real Estate Association is the national association of real estate agents. It owns the trademark "Realtor," which it licenses to local real estate boards and their members. It has also drafted a code of ethics that has been adopted by member boards. Provincial organizations, such as the Ontario Real Estate Association, are responsible for educating agents as well as representing industry concerns at the provincial level. They also have accepted responsibility for the self-regulation of real estate professionals.

In Ontario, the *Real Estate and Business Brokers Act* prohibits trading in real estate by anyone who is not registered as a broker or salesman with the Registrar of Real Estate and Business Brokers. Only people who have completed the program of courses and requirements established by the Ontario Real Estate Association are eligible to apply for registration. Finally, local real estate boards exist that, among other things, operate multiple listing services available to members, which help achieve quicker sales. Not all real estate agents are members.

The framework within which real estate agents operate, therefore, is not only the legal one suggested above, but also includes the rules and regulations of self-governing professional bodies. Apart from setting requirements for registration as brokers and salesmen, these bodies establish standards of competence and ethical conduct for real estate professionals and set up a disciplinary system to enforce compliance with them. They regulate when and how salesmen/brokers can earn commissions, prohibit misleading statements, and provide penalties for violations that can be as severe as deregistration.

Listings and the Listing Agreement

Prospective sellers or vendors contract with real estate brokers to sell, trade, or lease their property or some right in their property. Such a contract, called a listing agreement, usually specifies what a broker must do to earn his commission, which generally includes showing the property to the ultimate purchaser or introducing the purchaser to the vendor. Apart from the express terms of the vendor-broker agreement, the agreement is also covered by general laws and regulations of brokers.

Real estate brokers list properties for sale or rent in basically one of three ways. In an **open listing**, the agent is not obliged to do anything. The vendor retains the right to sell the property himself and can not only sell independent of the broker's assistance, but also negotiate with any other agent or possible buyer. In an **exclusive listing**, the vendor names one broker with exclusive rights to sell the property. The agent is required to make a conscientious effort to make a sale and, in effect, the vendor can only deal with prospective buyers through that agent. Finally, in a **co-operative listing**, accomplished through a **multiple listing service**, the appointed agent is able to employ the services of other brokers to secure a sale. Details of the listing are circulated to a number of agents, thereby improving the chances of making a sale. In return for this, the vendor would expect to pay a slightly higher rate of commission than for using other listing methods.

The listing agreement sets out the terms on which the vendor is willing to sell, but it is not a legally binding offer to sell in terms of contract law. There is no legal requirement that the vendor accept any offer, even if the offer is in the exact terms set out in the listing agreement.

The relationship between a vendor and a real estate broker is one of principal and agent, and the **law of agency** therefore prevails. The principal pays a commission to the agent for his services. The agent is authorized to bring the person for whom he acts into contractual relations with other persons, who are called third parties. Note that it is the real estate broker who is the agent of the buyer or seller of real estate, and who is authorized to negotiate contracts. The salesman is an employee or authorized representative of the broker.

An agency relationship can be created in several ways. In real estate, there is usually a written agreement between the owner of the property and a registered real estate broker to list the property for sale. The agreement sets a limited time period for the listing.

Duties of the Agent

Once the listing agreement is signed, there are certain duties that an agent has to his principal. For one, he must perform his contract. He must act in good faith, and avoid conflicts of interest — for example, he cannot act for both buyer and seller in a transaction unless both parties are informed of it and agree to it. A broker who participates in a transaction with a principal, or who has an interest in a transaction where he is also acting as an agent, faces strict legal standards for proving that no conflict or interest exist. He may be open to lawsuits by the principal if the broker fails to act properly as an agent.

An agent cannot make secret profits on a transaction; both parties to the transaction must know of, and agree to, any payments. The agent has a duty to inform his principal of all facts that might affect his decision: for example, the credit worthiness of the other party, the economic prospects for the property, possible zoning and legal changes, etc. Furthermore, the agent must be competent — that is, he must exercise a degree of care and skill expected of an average person in that profession.

In addition to the duties of the agent, there are certain remedies that a principal has against an agent who fails to carry out those duties. He may dismiss the agent. He may sue the agent for breach of contract and damages suffered. He can recover property belonging to him from the agent. He may sue to get a full accounting of funds that the agent dealt with on behalf of the principal. He may refuse to pay the agreed upon commission.

Failure to carry out his duties may also result in the local real estate board or regulatory body suspending or revoking the broker's privileges or registration. Criminal prosecution may result from fraudulent actions. Section 383 of the Criminal Code makes it an offence to give or receive a secret commission, and several other sections create offences arising from agents' violations of their duties to their principals. Finally, the broker is responsible for indemnifying people for damages they suffer as a result of wrongful acts by his subordinates. These claims may be brought by the principal for whom the agent was acting or, in some circumstances, by third parties involved in the transaction. A listing agreement sets out not only the terms of the principal-agent relationship but, typically, also the circumstances under which a lawsuit may be brought by the principal against the agent.

The Agreement of Purchase and Sale

The single document most often prepared by real estate practitioners is the agreement of purchase and sale or, simply, the "offer to purchase." Under the *Statute of Frauds*, any contract pertaining to real property must be in writing. While there is no legally prescribed form, some provisions are required by provincial statutes, and real estate brokers and associations have developed standard forms that they recommend for use by their members. Such forms normally provide for:

(a) the names of the vendor (or vendors, if it is a matrimonial home) and the purchaser;

(b) the name of the vendor's real estate agent;

(c) the full legal description of the lands to be conveyed, usually as found in the title documents (urban residential properties can be described by streets bounding the property and its measurements) — note that all buildings and other improvements are assumed to be conveyed along with the land they are on;

(d) the price;

(e) a variety of numbered clauses setting out specific provisions.

These numbered clauses include:

1. the amount of the **deposit** by the purchaser, who holds the deposit, how interest on the deposit is treated, and what happens to it if the transaction is not completed;

2. **financing provisions**, which must precisely outline the type of mortgage and its terms and conditions;

3. a list of any **fixtures and chattels** that are or are not included with the rest of the property — it should be clear what is included and what the vendor can remove to avoid disputes, and it should be clear what the value is of various items, since the purchaser is liable for land transfer taxes on the real property and retail sales taxes on chattels at the time of closing;

4. the **irrevocability** clause states that the offer by the purchaser is valid for a stated time and cannot be withdrawn earlier. Since there is no consideration given for including this clause in the offer to purchase, it can be made binding only by signing under seal. Similarly, if the vendor makes a so-called counter offer, which is really an offer of sale, it should be signed under seal;

5. completion or **closing dates** need to be specified (on the closing day, it is usual for the solicitors for each party to meet at the Land Titles or Registry Office and exchange completed documents, deeds or transfers for registration, and money and keys to the property);

6. the **time for searches** clause provides the necessary time, often up to 30 days, for the purchaser's solicitor to search title, order a survey if none is at hand, get the Surveyor's Certificate, confirm zoning and building regulations, and search for possible encumbrances, at the Sheriff's Office for judgments, the Municipal and Provincial Offices for Statutory Liens, check for work orders, and verify that the building is insurable at a reasonable cost.

The agreement of purchase and sale becomes a binding contract upon acceptance by the vendor. It is critical that the purchaser inspect the property and be aware of its condition. Any required repairs (such as outstanding work orders) become his responsibility if and when the offer is accepted unless the contract provides otherwise or the damage to the property occurs after the offer is made. Should the purchaser require some of this work to be done by the vendor, he must make this a condition in his offer.

Further conditions in the offer to purchase are provisos that make the purchaser's offer conditional on the title being good, free of liens, mortgages and other claims not specified in the agreement. They also require the purchaser's solicitor to make the necessary searches within the required time, and any objections to title to be made within a specified time: otherwise, the purchaser must accept them.

The property and buildings on the property are at the vendor's risk until closing. The purchaser has the right to, and should, inspect the property immediately before closing. In the case of substantial damages having occurred between the time of the offer and the closing date, the purchaser has the option of terminating the agreement and recovering any money paid, or accepting the proceeds of the vendor's insurance and completing the purchase.

There is also an adjustments clause that provides that the purchaser must pay the vendor, on closing, cash equal to any prepayments he has made on insurance premiums, rent, mortgage interest, taxes, local improvements, water and assessment rates, and the cost of fuel, which continue to cover and pertain to the property after the closing. The vendor pays for all expenses up to the closing date, the date as of which the purchaser assumes responsibility for the expenses.

There are certain other clauses that may be very important. The vendor should warrant that he is not a non-resident of Canada under the terms of the *Income Tax Act*. Under Section 116 of the Act, a non-resident vendor of taxable Canadian property is required to pay a withholding tax on capital gains equal to 25% of the estimated gain or provide acceptable security in order to obtain a certificate fixing the estimated proceeds of the transaction. If the vendor is a non-resident and either fails to obtain a certificate or underestimates the proceeds of the transaction, then the purchaser is liable for payment of tax owing on the transaction. The purchaser or his solicitor should ensure the residency status of the vendor.

The purchaser should also assure that his future intended use will comply with any zoning laws, and should make his offer conditional on the property's use and development complying with the *Planning Act*. The transfer of existing fire insurance from the vendor to the purchaser should be assured, or alternate provision made, in order to ensure continuous coverage.

There may be a urea formaldehyde clause wherein the vendor undertakes that it is not present in the house. If the purchaser is very concerned about this, he may instruct his solicitor to replace this clause with a stronger one providing explicit remedies should urea formaldehyde insulation be later discovered.

Finally, once the vendor accepts the purchaser's offer, he will also agree to pay commission to the named agent.

The purchaser accepts responsibility for registering all necessary forms, such as the deed, and pays the costs of such registration. If the vendor is taking back a mortgage, it will be his responsibility to register it. Also, the vendor is responsible for discharging any mortgages that are not being assumed by the purchaser.

The agreement of purchase and sale has been seen as a long, although not necessarily complex, document that has significant legal implications. It is important, therefore, to consult a lawyer before the purchaser makes and transmits the offer since, afterwards, the lawyer's hands tend to be bound to a significant degree, unless fraud or misrepresentation can readily be demonstrated.

INTERESTS IN REAL PROPERTY

A distinction is sometimes made between real estate and real property, in that the former is said to consist of the tangible attributes of land and any improvements, while the latter includes the associated "bundle of rights."

Real estate can be thought of as including three **physical interests**: the measured-off area of the earth's surface (the land) plus any buildings and attachments, crops, trees, shrubs, streams, and so on; subsurface space, extending some distance down towards the centre of the earth; and above-surface air space extending some distance above the earth. **Legal interests** in real estate consist of the rights of possession, control, enjoyment, and disposition.

The term real property can, therefore, be seen to be a combination of the physical interest and the legal interest: that is, the physical real estate with the attendant bundle of rights. All property that is "not real" in this sense is referred to as personal property or chattel property.

These ownership rights can be broken down into three categories: **freehold estates**, which are associated with ownership; **possessory estates**, where possession and use of the estate is separate from the ownership; and **non-possessory interests**, such as easements and security interests, which carry neither ownership nor possession.

Individuals may own property singly or jointly with someone else. **Single ownership** obviously involves no division of rights, and the property is completely owned by a single individual or corporation. Many possible variations of co-ownership exist, but two are most common.

Tenancy in Common and Joint Tenancy

Tenancy in common arises whenever two or more people have an undivided interest in a property. The shares of property held do not have to be equal, but normally rents are received and expenses paid in proportion to these shares. Any of the owners can sell or will his share in the property to others. **Joint tenancy**, by contrast, involves a co-ownership of equal shares or proportions, and includes **the right of survivorship**. This means that if one of the joint tenants dies, the surviving joint tenants automatically receive that person's share in equal proportion. Irrespective of whether the joint tenant bequeaths his share by will, the right of survivorship will override the bequest. A joint tenant can, however, sell his share or give it away during his lifetime, thus automatically changing the joint tenancy to a tenancy in common. A joint tenancy must be specifically created and conform to the so-called "four unities" of title, time, possession, and interest.

COMMUNITY PROPERTY LAWS AND FAMILY LAWS

Every province has some form of community property laws or family laws. In Ontario, for example, the *Family Law Reform Act of 1978* and its revision the *Family Law Act of 1986* define not only net family property in general but a concept known as the matrimonial home. This basically holds that, irrespective of whether the spouses own their principal residence alone or together, they both have an equal share or interest in the home upon separation or divorce. Thus, neither spouse can sell or otherwise dispose of or encumber a **matrimonial home** unless the other spouse consents or it is so allowed by court order or separation agreement. This also extends, for example, to taking out a mortgage, and requires that the other spouse, not just the owner, be notified if some legal action is to be taken that would affect the matrimonial home, such as an impending mortgage foreclosure.

General **community property** laws usually consider the husband and wife co-owners of all property acquired by either spouse during their marriage. Furthermore, the usual presumption is that all property of the two spouses is community property, unless it is explicitly held separately. Clearly, real estate professionals must be aware of basic family law provisions in their province and how these affect the abilities of spouses to transact in real estate. A simple rule of thumb is to require signatures of both husband and wife in selling property in order to ensure a good conveyance.

CONDOMINIUMS

Two special types of ownership are condominiums and co-operatives. The concept of a **condominium** dates back to Roman times, although in Canada it has only recently been recognized in law (for example, the first *Condominium Act* was passed in Ontario in 1967). A condominium is a legal concept that separates ownership rights into certain parts that are owned individually and certain parts that are owned in common. For example, a condominium can be a group of apartments that are individually owned and controlled, whereas the common elements of the building, such as lobbies, corridors, exterior walls, and so on, are jointly owned by all apartment owners.

In a condominium, the owners and developers of the property must file a master deed, called a Declaration and a Description with the Land Registrar. These papers describe the property and define common areas, among other things, and also require approval under the *Planning Act*. They define the rights of individual condominium owners and their responsibilities in terms of the overall operating expenses of the entire property.

Individual owners can sell or mortgage their unit and are directly responsible for the property taxes levied on their unit. Collectively, the unit owners elect a board of directors responsible for day-to-day operations and maintenance. Each unit owner is entitled to a single vote. Provincial legislation sets out the required organization, the funding provisions for maintenance and insurance, etc. The board of directors can also levy special assessments or require contributions by owners to meet expenses voted by the group of owners.

CO-OPERATIVES

In **co-operative housing** the building or land is owned by a single corporation, and individuals purchase shares in the company that carry with it the right to lease a specified area. Each shareholder/ owner pays a monthly assessment to the corporation, which in turn pays all taxes and expenses. Similar to condominiums, the owners elect a board of directors. One significant difference between co-operatives and condominiums is that since individuals get "proprietary leases" on designated units rather than owning them outright, they do not have individual responsibilities to meet the company's debts. If some owners default on their payments, the co-operative corporation must still meet its obligations, such as real estate taxes and mortgage payments. The other co-operative owners must collectively make up for any deficiencies. This can have serious consequences if a series of defaults occurs. In a condominium arrangement, one owner's default does not require others to meet the obligations.

OTHER OWNERSHIP FORMS

There are certain basic legal entities for owning real property beyond those of individual persons. Their purposes may include a pooling of capital, limiting the liability of individual investors, and giving unsophisticated investors access to expertise.

A **general partnership** must be registered under the appropriate provincial act, and does not provide a limitation on individual liabilities. Individual partners are responsible for the payment of taxes and may, therefore, also claim real estate losses for tax purposes. Each partner has an equal vote in directing the partnership, unless the original partnership agreement provides otherwise, and can also bind all other partners in the course of a normal business transaction. The death of a general partner automatically terminates the partnership and forces a reorganization, unless there is an agreement to the contrary.

A **corporation** is a separate legal person or legal entity in the eyes of the law. There are many types of corporations, including: government corporations, such as the Canada Mortgage and Housing Corporation, or Air Canada; municipal corporations; charitable corporations; educational corporations; and business corporations that may be federally or provincially incorporated. The rights and requirements of the corporation will be determined by how and where the corporation is set up. One of the main advantages of a corporation is that it limits the personal liability of investors to the amount they invest, so that they are not liable for the debts of the corporation itself.

Income to the corporation is subject to corporate income tax, and subsequent dividend payments to shareholders are subject to personal income tax. This has the obvious disadvantage of double taxation. Closely held corporations, namely those with few owners and shares that are not publicly traded on stock exchanges, can often reduce the incidence of double taxation by treating shareholders as company officials and paying their salaries and other compensation.

A **trust** can be basically any arrangement wherein real property is transferred to a trustee who holds and administers it for the benefit of someone else, the beneficiary. Trusts are common in wills and estate planning. A trust has the advantage of not being subject to tax on income that it distributes, and the disadvantage that beneficiaries are unable to direct the management of the property on which they rely for their income.

LAWS AFFECTING REAL PROPERTY

There is a mass of provincial and municipal laws and regulations that may apply to individual real estate transactions. It is the role of the real estate lawyer to identify any relevant laws and to ensure that any necessary steps are taken to comply with the requirements. Some provincial real estate associations publish legal handbooks summarizing the most important laws and regulations for their members.

Among the more important laws affecting real estate transactions are those governing the subdivision of large pieces of land into smaller ones for sale. Provincial legislation, such as the *Planning Act* in Ontario, typically requires that subdivisions be formally approved in advance. In Ontario, a purchaser or mortgagee who purports to buy or take security in improperly subdivided land acquires no legal interest in the land. The purchaser must ensure as part of the title search that the vendor has complied with any *Planning Act* requirements that apply.

The sale of a business, part of a business, or part of a business's assets requires that the purchaser be given considerably more information than is necessary in a sale of residential property. For example, in Ontario, the *Real Estate and Business Brokers Act* requires that a purchaser in this sort of transaction be given profit and loss statements and extensive financial records of the business in order to be a valid sale. The *Bulk Sales Act* may require that the selling business present an affidavit from its creditors stating that the proposed sale of part of the business or its assets will not prevent the business from satisfying their claims.

Transactions involving rented residential properties are governed by landlord and tenant laws. These typically limit the ability of the landlord to terminate tenancy, and require notice in advance and reasons for doing so. Other terms of these laws may limit the conditions and amounts by which rents may be increased.

It should be noted that there are a variety of claims against real estate that are not required to be registered under the Registry or Land Titles systems, that are good even against a buyer of property who was not aware of them. These claims may not be discovered by routine title searches. They include some writs of execution issued by courts against a debtor who owns land, claims of unpaid municipal and corporate taxes, and government liens and required property improvements. These can generally be found by requesting a search in the Sheriff's Office in the case of writs of execution. Government liens and work orders may be traced through municipal or provincial offices.

CONTRACT LAW

A contract is a promise or a set of promises that the law will enforce. More broadly stated, a contract is an agreement between two or more parties, involving the transfer of something of value. The parties to the contract must have the legal capacity to enter into a contractual agreement and there must be mutual consent to a genuinely intended act: only then is the agreement a legally binding contract.

Essential to any contract is an offer and its acceptance. An **offer** must give a clear signal that an individual is willing to enter into a legal relationship. It is not a mere "invitation to treat," such as an announcement that a property is for sale, inviting prospective buyers to bid. A listing agreement, signed between a prospective vendor and a real estate broker, is not considered to be an offer to sell, but simply an agreement to list.

An offer usually has a specific time period while it is open and before it expires. It can be revoked or withdrawn at any time before it is accepted, unless it has a specific clause in it making it irrevocable. To make the offer irrevocable, there must be consideration for it, or it must be made under seal. The offer must be complete and definite in its terms, and not merely an indication of negotiations about to start. Finally, all offers made for the purchase of a vendor's property must be presented by the real estate broker to his client.

Acceptance of an offer must be unconditional and cannot be binding if any attempt is made to change the terms specified in the offer, or if the conditional acceptance is subject to further advice or negotiation. The offeree or his agent must communicate the acceptance back to the offeror in order for the agreement to become effective. One interesting point is that an offer accepted by mail is deemed to be effective the moment the acceptance is dropped in the mailbox, irrespective of whether the offeror ever receives the mail. If the offeror specifies the manner in which an acceptance is to be received by him, or he states that it must be made within a specified time period, then the offeree must make his acceptance in the manner required.

CONSIDERATION

A gratuitous promise to do something is not legally binding. The promisor must receive something of value in return, known as **consideration**. This consideration need not be equal in value to what is received; even as trivial a consideration as a "peppercorn" meets the requirement.

A promise without consideration can be made legally binding if it is made under seal. Usually, a red paper seal or sticker is attached to the document or, in the case of corporations the corporate seal, to reflect the fact that the parties knew that they were signing under seal.

Legal capacity to enter into a contract refers to the fact that under common law certain classes of individuals may lack the ability or capacity to enter into a legally binding contract; for example, minors (or infants), lunatics, drunkards, illiterates, and blind persons, among others.

A distinction exists between a **void contract** and a **voidable contract**. In the first case, no contract exists or has ever existed. A voidable contract, by contrast, is an existing contract that is binding unless and until one of the parties decides that he does not wish to be bound by it. Infants, mental incompetents, and intoxicated persons usually make voidable contracts, and they have a later choice as to whether their contracts should remain in effect.

Illiterates and **blind persons** will also not be bound by a contract they signed if either they were not informed of what was in the contract or the contents of the contract were misrepresented to them.

There are other potential parties to a contract that may require special attention. **Executors of estates**, for example, must **all** sign an agreement, since the absence of even one signature may void the contract. Here it is prudent to request a notarized copy of Letters Probate that identifies all executors to ensure that all have signed. If the deceased left no will, Letters of Administration will identify all court appointed administrators, who must sign the agreement of purchase and sale. Finally, the real estate agent should ask the solicitor for the estate to confirm who has the power of sale and authority to sign contracts, including whosoever may have authority to list and sell property if there is any doubt.

When **corporations** enter into contracts, the most important thing to verify is that the person signing the contract on behalf of the company has the authority to do so. It is also common, although not legally required, to ask that the document be fixed with the company seal and, sometimes, to ask to see a certified copy of the resolution of the company's board of directors authorizing the transaction.

The legality of a contract may depend upon when it is signed and dated. Under the *Lord's Day Act of Canada,* there is a clear prohibition against buying or selling real estate on a Sunday. The Act may no longer apply, however, as the result of a recent case involving the *Charter of Rights and Freedoms*.

Contracts pertaining to property interests are affected by the *Statute of Frauds* requiring that such contracts be in writing. A contract to build or repair a house may be outside the Statute, whereas a lease concerning land, or a house, must be in writing to be enforceable. In British Columbia in particular, all contracts concerning interests in land must still be in written form.

The **mutual consent** or "**meeting of minds**" between parties to a contract is essential to creating a valid contract. If it is not present there is no valid contract, even if all other requirements are met. While minor variations to an agreement, such as later filling in a particular detail or minor fact, will not invalidate the contract, major variations would. Similarly, if instead of a minor error a **mistake of fact** is made that is fundamental to the contract, the contract may be avoided, but more usually gives rise to a remedy.

There are several types of mistakes. A **common mistake** is one where each of the contracting parties has made the same mistake about some underlying fact — for example, they may have contracted to buy and sell a house that has been completely burned down. In such cases the impossibility of performance of the contract makes the contract null and void. If the mistake is rectifiable, however, the court will seek to do so.

A **mutual mistake** arises if two parties misunderstand each other; for example, the vendor may think he is selling property *A* while the buyer thinks he is buying property *B*. The court will enforce the contract as a reasonable third party would interpret it, if at all possible.

A **unilateral mistake** arises where one party is mistaken about the fundamental character of the contract and the other party knows it; in this case no contract exists.

Another area affecting the validity of a contract is concerned with **misrepresentation**. A representation is a statement with regard to some existing fact, matter or circumstance affecting the contract, as opposed to a matter of opinion. A misrepresentation is a false statement of fact. Note that a principal is liable for any misrepresentation made by his agent with express or implied authority; for example, the owner of a property listed for sale will be liable for misrepresentations about the property made by the broker or salesman.

There are several types of misrepresentations. Innocent **misrepresentation** arises if a person is induced to enter into a contract on the basis of a material statement made by the other party that, unbeknown to either party, later turns out to have been wrong. In this case, the person can avoid the contract and recover any payments or deliveries made under it if he does so prior to closing.

Fraudulent misrepresentation occurs if a person knows a material representation to be false, but still makes it, with the purpose of inducing the other party to enter into the contract to their detriment. The deceived person who acted on this information and suffered a loss because of it can resist the enforcement of the contract and claim in tort for damages.

Negligent misrepresentation arises from a breach of duty of care, diligence, and skill. A real estate agent who represents certain facts about a given property that turn out to be incorrect, and have thereby misled, say, a perspective buyer, can face a claim in tort for damages. In particular, statements about the financial situations of other parties to the contract, about the extent of the property, about carrying costs of the property, about zoning restrictions, and about the truth of information in a listing can all give rise to a case of negligent misrepresentation. In the real estate profession, not only agents, but salesmen, appraisers, and others holding themselves out as experts can be liable.

One final consideration affecting contracts is where undue influence and duress are applied. **Undue influence** exists where one person so dominates the mind of another person as to deprive the latter of the ability to make an independent decision. Generally, this situation may arise where the two parties stand in a special relationship to each other: for example, a parent and child, a doctor and patient. The contract so formed is voidable at the option of the victim.

Duress involves direct threats of harm or injury or imprisonment either against the person being coerced or against someone close and dear to him. Again, the contract is voidable at the option of the victim.

Contracts can be discharged, that is, brought to an end, in a number of ways. **Discharge by performance** is the obvious way and the one anticipated by the parties to the agreement. All parties have fulfilled all obligations under the contract.

Discharge by agreement arises when the parties themselves mutually agree not to complete the contract. This may occur at any time during the contract. It may arise if there is a clause or term in the contract that states that under specified circumstances, or in the case of non-fulfilment, the contract will automatically terminate. Or it may happen that some material alteration to the terms of the contract is necessary, in which case the effect is to discharge the original contract and replace it with a new one.

Discharge by frustration occurs if it becomes impossible to perform the contract because of some changed or unanticipated circumstances. Interpretation of the Doctrine of Frustration has resulted in some complex cases, since the courts have been quite reluctant to excuse parties for the failure to perform their promises.

Discharge by operation of law can arise by virtue of the bankruptcy of one party, by the application of one of the provincial *Limitation Act*s, or where a contract is superseded by a later contract. For example, the obligations under the agreement for purchase and sale end when they are replaced by the terms of the closing contract involving the actual execution of the deed of conveyance.

Finally, a contract may be terminated by **breach**. If one part breaks the contract, the injured party may no longer have to carry out his obligations under the contract, but he does acquire the right to take legal action.

If a contract is breached, there are certain **remedies** available to the injured party. One can conceive of two types of breaches. If a breach goes to the "root" of the contract — that is, its fundamental terms — the injured party has the option to accept the breach, consider his obligations under the contract at an end and sue for damages. Or he may consider the contract still in force and sue for performance, that is sue to force the other party to carry out his obligations. If the breach does not go to the root of the contract, the injured party can sue for damages, but is still bound by the contract.

In every breach of contract, the injured party can sue for **damages**. These damages will be equal to the loss caused by the breach, and reasonably foreseeable as a consequence of the breach, at the time the contract was made. For example, suppose that a prospective purchaser of a house decides not to go through with the transaction after he has signed and completed an agreement of purchase and sale, but before the actual closing date. He will lose his deposit, and may be sued by the vendor for further damages, especially if the vendor then has to sell to someone else at a less advantageous price.

Specific performance is a remedy that may be ordered by the court. In some situations, damages will not be an adequate remedy, and the court may force the party in breach of contract to carry out his obligations. For example, breach of a land or property transaction may be such that damages are an insufficient compensation, and the court can order the conveyance to be completed.

An **injunction** is a discretionary remedy, like specific performance, that the injured party is not entitled to as a right, but that may be ordered by the court. The purpose of the injunction is to restrain the party in breach of contract from doing something he had contracted not to do.

In conclusion, it is clear that in the area of contract law, the courts will attempt to resolve disputes between contracting parties on the basis of broad and extensive legal principles. The interpretation of a contract is often complex. It is important to identify the key practical issues. Verbal representations, assurances, and changes in contracts are often not legally enforceable and courts will generally only enforce written contracts. In general, and in real estate in particular, it is very important to include everything in the written document on which the parties want to be able to rely.

MORTGAGES

The common law conception of a mortgage is a secured loan made by the mortgagee (the lender) to the mortgagor (the borrower) in return for the conditional conveyance of an interest in land. The interest is usually ownership in fee simple. The condition is that if the debt is repaid on time, the conveyance becomes void and the interest in the land reverts to the mortgagor. If the debt is not repaid as scheduled, the condition expires and the mortgagee can take steps to exercise his right as owner of the interest. Thus, mortgages are conveyances of title under the land registry system (or charges on land under the land titles system) and, thus, must be registered at the registry office or land titles office to secure the rights of the parties against third parties who may be involved in later transactions involving title to the land.

The mortgagee does not obtain immediate and irrevocable title to the mortgaged land as soon as the mortgagor fails to meet a scheduled payment. The mortgagor retains the right to repay his debt at a later date and take back his interest in the land, unless the mortgagee obtains an order of foreclosure from a court. This court order specifies a deadline by which the mortgagor must repay his debt. If he fails to do so in time, the land becomes the mortgagee's absolutely.

The terms on which remedies other than foreclosure are available to mortgagees against defaulting mortgagors vary from province to province. One important remedy is to sue the mortgagor to repay, just as a creditor can sue any defaulting debtor. Another remedy is to request to have the land sold under the supervision of the court. The mortgagee is entitled to recover his principal owing, accrued interest, and costs from the proceeds of the sale, with any remaining funds going to the mortgagor or other encumbrancers. If the debt exceeds the proceeds of the sale, the mortgagee can still sue the mortgagor to recover the balance in some provinces.

The obligations of the mortgagor under the mortgage contract are not limited to making the scheduled payments of the agreed interest and principal. In addition, he contracts to keep the property adequately insured in the name of the mortgagee, to pay the taxes on the property, and to keep the premises in a reasonable state of repair.

CONCLUSION

Unfortunately, no brief outline such as this can do more than identify the main areas of the law with which the real estate practitioner should be familiar. There is really no substitute for extensive reading if one hopes to become conversant with even the most important aspects of the multitude of laws affecting real estate transactions, let alone their technical details. With that in mind it is recommended that the readers refer to some of the following references on real property law and business law in general for further information.

REFERENCES

Falconbridge, J.D. *The Law of Mortgages* (4 ed.) W.B. Rayner and R.H. Mc-Laren, eds. Agincourt, Ont.: Canada Law Book Company, 1977.

Foster, William F. *Canadian Real Estate Agency Law*. Don Mills, Ont.: Canadian Real Estate Association, 1978.

Rhodes, F.W. *Williams' The Canadian Law of Landlord and Tenant*. (4th ed.) Toronto: Carswell Company, 1973.

Sinclair, A.M. *Introduction to Real Property Law*. Toronto: Butterworth & Co. (Canada) Ltd., 1969.

Smyth, J.E., and D.O. Soberman *The Law and Business Administration in Canada* (4th ed.). Scarborough, Ont.: Prentice-Hall of Canada, Ltd., 1983.

Taylor, Frank R. *Leading Court Decisions in Canadian Real Estate*. Vancouver: Butterworth & Co. (Canada) Ltd., 1978.

Additional sources would be the individual Provincial Real Estate Association's text books used in their certification programs. In Ontario, for example, there is the book *Real Property Law*, Ontario Real Estate Association, 1983.

Transfers of Limited Interests in Real Estate

WALTER H. POSNER ⎯⎯⎯⎯⎯⎯⎯⎯⎯⎯⎯⎯⎯⎯⎯⎯⎯⎯⎯

The Fee Simple Estate in a property is termed the "ownership" of the property, although in fact the absolute ownership of all land remains with the State forever. Fee Simple Estates are distinguished by the characteristics that they always are:

- Freehold (i.e., of indefinite duration); and
- of the whole parcel of land; and
- of the complete bundle of property rights, less any expressly excluded from the Crown Grant, or contracted away in terms of a Private Limitation, or taken away in a Public Limitation.

The holder of the Fee Simple Estate in a property (the so-called "owner of the property") can contract the rights in the Estate, either

- collectively ("all the Vendor's right, title and interest"), and permanently, through the medium of the contract of **Purchase and Sale**; or
- individually (or in combinations that are less than the whole Fee Simple Estate), and for a limited period, in a **Limited Interest**, after which the rights revert to their "owner." The individual property rights most commonly contracted in Limited Interests, are

  1. **the right of possession to the exclusion of all others**, which founds a Possessory or Leasehold Estate and is arranged in a contract of **Lease**. A Lease is a contract in which the owner

⎯⎯⎯⎯⎯⎯⎯⎯⎯⎯⎯⎯⎯⎯⎯

Walter Posner, B.Comm., L.L.B., A.L.O., is a specialist in real estate leasing and has developed courses on the subject for the Real Estate Institute of Canada and York University.

of an Estate in Real Property who owns the right to exclusive possession of the property (the Lessor) contracts to another (the Tenant) a part of its rights, including the right to exclusive possession of an identified portion of the property (the Premises) for a limited period (the Term) and for a consideration (the Rent), retaining the Reversion (the right to recover those rights at the end of the Term); and

2. **the right of ongoing, but not exclusive, use** of a portion of the property, which founds a Non-Possessory Estate, and is arranged in a contract of **Easement**, such as a Right-of-Way.

It is fundamental to all Limited Interests that they are confined to

• the Term for which the Interest is granted, which may be lengthy, but must be limited; and
• the Premises that is the subject of the Interest; and
• the Rights actually granted to the tenant by the party who did then have title to those rights.

In contrast to disposals by Purchase and Sale — in which the parties have few choices to address because, by definition, the disposal always is permanent, the subject always is the whole parcel of land, and the rights generally are all those in the vendor's bundle — in disposals of Limited Interests, the parties arrange the Term of the Interest, the portion of the property that is the Premises, the particular property Rights that are transferred to the tenant, and the obligations of each party.

For the purpose of marketing its property, a lessor will choose the rights and other conditions of the Interest it offers, and its asking price for that package. The price should be a reflection of the leasing package of which it is part, and take account of all relevant considerations, including location; the class of the building, and its amenities; the class of its tenants; the amount of the subject space and its condition and improvements; the rights and conditions offered; and any incidental benefit introduced into the package to induce the tenant to agree a larger rent than it otherwise would (the Tenant Inducements). A generous leasing package can be expected to command a higher price than a stingy one.

The Contract is negotiable, and the prospective tenant also has an opportunity to influence the leasing package before closing it by adding rights and conditions or lessening restrictions.

In the final analysis, it is the Lease the parties close that defines each party's rights, undertakings (covenants), and obligations. Rights not addressed in the Lease are not transferred (and remain with the lessor and available for inclusion in a later contract with another lessee); and obligations not covenanted are not owed. When in doubt, first search the Lease for an answer.

Each party to a Lease has many opportunities to affect the package they are attempting to close, and some departures are exceedingly subtle and difficult to recognise and evaluate, without training and experience. This chapter will address some of the subjects that commonly impact on the worth of a Limited Interest and deserve to be addressed in an evaluation thereof, namely:

1. The quality of the Physical Assets.
2. The covenants and conditions of the Contract.
3. The form in which the Price of the Interest is expressed.

THE QUALITY OF THE PHYSICAL ASSETS

The location, the class of the building and its technology, amenities, parking and other facilities, and the quality of its tenants, are relevant factors that are capable of evaluation by the application of the **Comparative Approach to Value**, the method appraisers employ for estimating the market value of assets.

The amount of the occupiable space also is relevant to the evaluation, but is expressed in a variety of forms. All parties need to comprehend the form in which the amount is expressed, and to appreciate that the amount thus expressed is not comparable with the amount of another space that is expressed in a different form, without one first being restated in the same form as the other.

In the determination of the number of units of space in enclosed premises, there will be features — such as whether the structural columns, the outside walls, or other obstructions, like radiant heater-units, are to be excluded — that are the subject of differing views. To express the amount of space as a number of units (e.g., square feet) without prescribing how the number is to be determined is a dangerous practice, for the parties cannot be sure how each contentious feature will be resolved, nor how the amount of space will be quantified.

In order to be able to determine the premises' number of units of space, the parties should agree on the method of doing that: either by spelling out the method agreed, in full detail, or by adopting by reference, a method of measurement that is published by a professional association or institute. But uniformity from one transaction to the next should not be expected to follow, even if the choice of common terminology — Usable Area, Rentable Area, and Leasable Area — may suggest otherwise.

Usable Area, for example, is a term used both

- to identify one of the four methods of measurement defined in the American National Standard Method for Measuring Floor Area in Office Buildings, that is published by the Building Owners and Managers Association International (BOMA), in which it is the amount of *the interior area* (measured from the centre of the walls that separate the premises from an adjoining tenant space, and from the finished surface of the premises' side of all other walls), without excluding columns and projections; and also
- by Space Planners, in analyses of the amount of space that will accommodate the people and property the tenant intends to house in the premises, to describe *the interior area the tenant is able to use because it is unobstructed*; and in this form, Usable Area excludes columns, projections and internal walls.

Rental Area, too, is a multi-definition term, being both

- another of the four methods in BOMA's publications, in which it is the Usable Area of the premises grossed-up with the premises' proportion of the common area on its floor of the building and, since 1996, also with its proportion of common area of the building as a whole (with the result that the Rentable Area of premises *exceeds* its Usable Area, by at least 10% and, conceivably, as much as 40%); and also
- the method in the Standard Method of Establishing Rentable Floor Areas in Industrial Buildings, published by the Society of Industrial and Office Realtors (SIOR), which resembles BOMA's Usable Area method rather than its Rentable Area Method. In the SIOR method, Rentable Area does not include any gross-up, and it differs from BOMA's Usable Area method only in the respect that measurement is from the exterior face of the exterior walls, without deductions for interior walls, columns, transformer rooms and other obstructions the method lists (e.g., all fully enclosed exterior staircases).

Leasable Area is a term that has not been defined in any published method of measurement, which may account for it being the preferred term in methods of measurement that are spelled out in the contract, and which the parties do not want confused with a published method. It is particularly favoured by shopping centre developers, who have not been catered for in a published method, and who rely on imposing a method personally compiled (hence the common term Gross Leasable Area — GLA — for the total occupiable space in a shopping centre).

In truth, parties who spell out the method of measurement in their contract can name their method/s as they wish, even choosing a term that already is associated with a published method that bears little resemblance to their own. It is not the name that is decisive, but the method the name represents, and the method must be analysed in every instance.

Different methods of measurement produce differences in the number of units of space that describes the amount of occupiable space, but the differences are generally moderate, save for BOMA's Rentable Area Method, which is the only method that incorporates a gross-up to bring in an apportionment of common area; not even shopping centre lessors have followed that lead. There is a separate gross-up factor for each floor, and the factor differs from building to building and from floor to floor in the same building, according to the spaciousness of the lobbies, corridors, washrooms, and common facilities on the particular floor. And the gross-up factor can change during the Term, should the occupiable area on the floor change.

The method of measurement the parties adopt needs to be identified clearly and unambiguously, and to be thoroughly understood. Comparisons between premises must be based on each space's amount being expressed in the same form, preferably one with minimum distortion, like "BOMA's Usable Area, 1980 Printing."

The **condition and extent of completion** of the premises is another physical factor that is relevant to an evaluation of the worth of the Limited Interest, and is likely to be considered by the lessor when it compiles its leasing package. The commoner choices are:

- A lessor can offer the premises **"As is"** (i.e., without any work by the lessor before delivery). This form generally imposes on the tenant whatever reconditioning, repairs and improvements the premises need; but the form is not necessarily a negative, for the premises may be in proper condition, and already be improved to market Base Building standards.

- Premises that are not yet substantially constructed may be offered by a lessor on a **"Shell"** basis (i.e., completed to the minimum extent that defines the boundaries of the space that is the subject of the Limited Interest). Shell completion is common in shopping centres developments, but without standardization in the make-up of the Shell package. What the Shell package includes is listed in the Lease's Schedule of Landlord's Work, but construction the lessor does not undertake (commonly one or more of the store-front, the rear wall, floor-covering, ceiling, mechanical and electrical distribution, sprinklers) is left for the tenant's attention, at a sizable cost for which the tenant must make provision in its evaluation of those premises. In a building that offers its premises on a Shell basis, premises previously occupied impose a lesser completion outlay on the tenant than an unused space.

- A lessor may offer its premises "**Turnkey**" (i.e., completed by the lessor in **every** respect that its incoming tenant requires), so that the tenant need not make provision for any construction costs, and can expect to "turn the key" and commence use of the premises (and can also expect to pay a higher rent).
- A lessor may offer its premises "**Partial Turnkey**" (i.e., improved by the lessor only in respects listed in the contract). Partial Turnkey packages vary greatly from transaction to transaction, some barely exceeding the market Base Building completion standard, others only falling short of Turnkey because the contract excluded a single item. But all Partial Turnkey packages offer less improvements than Turnkey Packages, which, by definition, are open-ended.

A distinction needs to be drawn between completion work that is part of what brings the premises up to its market's Base Building standard (and would normally be the lessor's responsibility), and that which is part of the Leasehold Improvements (and would normally be the Tenant's responsibility). Should the Lease contractually redirect either responsibility, it is reasonable to expect that the evaluation of the premises will be affected.

THE COVENANTS AND CONDITIONS OF THE LEASE

The covenants and conditions that the Lease attaches to the property rights it offers on a Limited Interest also have a direct bearing on the evaluation of the whole leasing package, whether subtracting from the rights, or restricting the tenant's freedom to exercise them. It is in the interests of the lessor to retain as much of its Fee Simple as it can for use in future transactions, and the lease it proposes provides an opportunity to constrain the rights it agrees to transfer to the tenant. All leases are different, and need to be analysed and evaluated according to individual content.

The only subjects the parties must agree about in order that their Lease be legally enforceable (termed the Essential Elements) are:

- The identities of the **Parties** to the contract; and
- The boundaries of the **Premises** (the cube space of which the tenant is granted exclusive possession); and
- The **Term Certain** of the grant (not merely the length of the Term, but the particular period of that length); and

- **The Consideration** for the grant (usually, but not necessarily, the monthly rent).

Agreement on these subjects alone, coupled with the parties' reciprocal intent to contract the lease, will create a Leasehold Interest. But a lease confined to those subjects alone is unlikely. On the contrary, leases of commercial premises generally are very lengthy and technical, and non-uniform. Although they are likely to address a predictable set of subjects, they will do so in forms that vary. The only limitation on the subjects addressed, and how they are expressed, is that the contract must not be contrary to the law of the place where the property is. Lease content usually fits into the outline that follows.

1. A description of the Parties;

2. The Demise (the transfer), in which the Real Estate contracted is described: not only the Premises, but also other property (like parking stalls, storerooms, outside signage locations) and real interests (like options to purchase, or to lease);

3. The Term Certain (which requires any two of the commencement date, the period or the termination date), and associated provisions, such as options to renew, rights of first refusal, rights of early termination, overholding without agreement;

4. The rent the tenant covenants to pay monthly *in advance*, which is termed the **Basic** or **Minimum Rent**. It includes the Consideration element, and may be agreed as an unconditional amount or as a formula that is to compute the amount (e.g., a dollar rate per annum per unit of space actually delivered, or an agreed percentage of the revenue the tenant derived from the premises);

5. Any supplement to the Basic Rent that the tenant covenants to pay annually *in arrear*, which is termed **Supplementary Basic Rent** and, generally, is agreed as a formula that aims to preserve the Basic Rent from the effects of inflation: e.g., **Percentage Rent** (each year's supplement is the amount by which an agreed percent of the tenant's revenue from the premises exceeded the Basic Rent paid for that year), or **Indexed Rent** (generally the index adopted is the All-Items Consumer Price Index, and the increase in the index in each year of the Term is applied to the Basic Rent for the same year to compute the year's supplement);

6. The **Additional Rent** the tenant covenants to pay, and when. The term embraces all amounts, other than Basic Rent and

Supplementary Basic Rent, that the tenant covenanted to pay the lessor in terms of their Lease, although its principle component is the tenant's premises' proportion of the lessor's outlay on some or all non-capital operating costs (which includes realty taxes);

[Note: The forms of lease that obligate payment of Additional Rent are the subject of a separate section below.]

7. **The Operating Covenants** undertaken by each party to define what the covenantor undertakes it
   • *will* do; and
   • *will not* do (these being termed Restrictive Covenants).

   Covenants that obligate the tenant to carry on its business in a manner that adds to its costs, or to incur costs to somebody other than the lessor — e.g., for insurance or signage or labour or advertising or utilities (which costs are not part of the rent, because they are not payable to the lessor) — should be expected to affect the evaluation of the premises to the extent the tenant would not have incurred those costs but for the covenant in the Lease;

8. The articles that regulate eventualities that are capable of frustrating the Lease: e.g., destruction, expropriation, default; and procedural and administration regulations.

Forms of Lease that Give Rise to Additional Rent

A tenant's rent obligations are limited to its contractual covenants in its Lease. The form of Lease in which the tenant's only rent covenant in favour of the lessor is its covenant to pay Basic Rent is termed **a Gross Lease**. Because the Basic Rent will be the lessor's gross revenue from the lease, which is to cover the lessor's operating costs *and* the return on its investment, the Basic Rent should be expected to be highest when it is expressed in the context of the Gross Lease format.

Forms of lease that include a tenant covenant to pay the lessor Additional Rent (including operating costs), over and above the Basic Rent, are differently termed, according to the reach of the covenant. For example:

• The form in which the tenant covenants to pay, by way of Additional Rent, its premises' proportion of *all* non-capital operating costs that the lessor outlaid during the Term of the Lease is termed **a Net Lease**. There are lessors who persist in distinguishing their form of Net Lease by calling it a **Triple Net Lease**, which is a term that graced one of the forms used during the transition from Gross Leases to Net Leases, but now is obsolete and obscure. Nowadays Triple Net is used to describe a form of lease that is more net than Net, by virtue of (i) including in its definition of operating costs amounts that, in principle, should not be included (either because they were not outlaid, or were not costs of operation: e.g., capital costs), or (ii) overstating the lessor's actual outlay in a particular operating cost. Such forms do not merely reimburse the lessor's operating cost outlay in full; they also generate an additional profit centre for the lessor.

- In both the Net and the Triple Net forms, the covenant is for payments, and nothing more. There is a form of Net Lease in which, in addition to its covenants to pay Basic Rent and Additional Rent, the tenant also covenants to attend to operations as they arise. This is the form that is appropriate to term **a Net and Carefree Lease** because the Basic Rent is net to the lessor, and the upkeep is carefree to the lessor. However, there are lessors who apply this term to forms of Net Lease in which the tenant has not covenanted to shoulder the operational cares, and the lessor has not been freed of the cares of upkeep, but retains the labour responsibility.

- The form in which the tenant covenants to pay the lessor, by way of Additional Rent over and above the Basic Rent, its premises' proportion of only individual operating costs that are specified in the lease is termed a **Semi-Gross Lease**. The operating costs singled out are likely to be those that, like realty taxes and utilities, can be substantiated by the production of a paid bill, without any need for an audit. A lease can also be Semi-Gross in form, by virtue of listing valid operating costs that are excluded from the covenant.

The term by which a party describes its lease form conveys what is to be expected in the form, but it is the form itself that is to be analysed to determine the true classification of the form. Parties commonly term their leases altogether inappropriately in relation to what is found to be the actual content.

THE FORM IN WHICH THE PRICE OF THE INTEREST IS EXPRESSED

Parties must assume that, in the process of compiling the leasing package on which it offers to lease its premises, a lessor will have calculated the price for which it will contract that particular package of rights and obligations.

At the core of a lessor's price will be its determination of the **Net Effective Rent** (i.e., the lessor's price for only the right to exclusive possession for the Term arranged — which is the lowest common denominator of all leasing packages). The lessor should be expected to have adjusted its Net Effective Rent to take account of the value rights, undertakings and Tenant Inducements it combined with the core right to produce its leasing package, and the Basic Rent component of that package. The Basic Rent may be only a part of the price for the interest (and generally that is the case), with other components of the price being addressed separately, e.g., in the parts of the proposal respecting Supplementary Basic Rent or Additional Rent or a payment to a third person.

But lessors do not reveal to prospective tenants how they determined the Basic Rent for the leasing package they offer. They do not disclose their computation and, actually, add to the atmosphere of mystery by expressing the Basic Rent in formula form rather than as an amount that is certain and final. The usual formula is a dollar rate per annum per designated unit of space (e.g., "$ per annum per square foot of BOMA Usable Area — 1980 printing"), which is termed a **Rent Rate**, and provides the means of computing the amount of the annual Basic Rent (the rate multiplied by the number of units of space *actually delivered* to the tenant), and of the monthly Basic Rent payments (one-twelfth the annual Basic Rent). Expressing the Basic Rent in Rent Rate form opens the door to a new potential for variations, particularly in the choice of the units of space, and how they are to be measured and quantified. A Rent Rate has a different meaning each time it is used, and the dollar rates in different leases cannot be usefully compared until all have been adjusted to a common form and meaning.

Each Rent Rate reflects the leasing package of which it is a part, and will be judged as an expression of the worth of the premises in the context of that leasing package. A generous package can be expected to produce a higher rate; and equally, a lesser package should be reflected in a lower rate. Certainly the Rent Rate (and the Basic Rent that is its product) can only be evaluated relative to its leasing package, and evaluation must stand over until the whole package has been researched, and its worth evaluated. The Basic Rent should be the last price component the parties settle upon.

Many of the variations will impact on the package and its Basic Rent component, as Table 1 will illustrate.

Within the body of any comparison based on rent rates, it is essential that what is compared has been equivalenced in respect of the effect of all features in the package that can be expected to vary from transaction to transaction. The Basic Rent likely is Face Rent

TABLE 1	
Variable	*Impact*
Amount of space offered	More space results in more rent, and more fit-up costs, but not necessarily more benefit.
The space unit selected, and the method of measurement	The unit may be one that inflates the number of units. More units results in more rent.
The period the rate remains fixed	A step-up in the rate during the Term effectively changes the rate throughout the Term.
The length of the Term	An abnormally short Term is, in effect, a disguised step-up.
The Term commencement date	If inadequate time is allowed for fit-up, there will be pre-opening costs that could affect the rent.
The condition of the space	If the condition of the space is below market standards, the tenant's costs increase, and the rent should be less.
Is there to be a covenant for Supplementary Basic Rent?	If not, then the rent has inflation factored into it.
Is there to be a covenant for Additional Rent?	Expressing rent in Net form evades the lessor's operating cost record; its definitions of Operating Costs and Proportionate Share should affect the rent.
The Tenant Inducements (TI)	Whatever the form of the TI, if it is not separately recouped, then its amortization is factored into the rent amount.

(a concoction that aims to put on the Basic Rent the particular "face" the lessor wants to project), and the challenge is to discover all factors that did influence the determination of the Basic Rent to which its parties agreed. That is an especially difficult task in relation to leases of commercial premises, because of differences in the factors the respective parties may have found significant, and in their evaluation of each factor.

It would be better to avoid comparisons solely on the basis of rent rates, or even Basic Rent. Leasehold transactions should be compared according to a less vulnerable standard. The total cash outflow the tenant is obligated to incur in terms of the Lease (the Bottom-line Cost) is a standard that will expose all variables in competing leasing packages, and the effect of each on its price, and will lend itself to be restated in a common context in relevant respects, e.g., time-frame and unit of space.

THE LEGAL FORMALITIES FOR LEASING CONTRACTS

Although the absolute ownership of all land in Canada remains forever with the federal government, land control is a provincial jurisdiction in terms of Canada's constitution, and is not uniform across the country. The formalities required by law in respect of agreements concerning land derive from a common source, England's *Statute of Frauds of 1677*, which remains in force in Alberta, Saskatchewan, Manitoba, Newfoundland, Prince Edward Island, and the Territories, because those legislatures have not re-enacted the original statute. British Columbia, Ontario, New Brunswick and Nova Scotia have replaced the English statute with their own enactments in similar but not identical form.

Ontario's *Statute of Frauds* (Ch. 481) is a representative example, and its Section 1 (2) states:

All leases ... of any ... lands ... are void unless made by deed.

"Deed" means a writing solemnly executed (preferably under seal, or confirmed by a sworn declaration); and "void" means not legally binding. But the unequivocal language of the statute has not proved as insurmountable as one might expect: for the courts have been willing to circumvent invalidity by focusing on the "fraud" element in their application of the statute, and have modified the statute by the Doctrine of Part Performance. The result is that leases that lacked the required formality have been validated because the parties' subsequent conduct showed clearly that the contract was not tainted with fraud.

The statute conditionally excludes from its provisions Leases for a term of three years or less. But all **Leases** not excluded (which includes all leases for more than three years) must be in writing and solemnly executed, or they will be invalid until the formalities have been complied with or the parties have clearly confirmed their contract by an act of Part Performance sufficient to take the contract outside the objectives of the *Statute of Frauds* (e.g., delivering possession for the fit-up).

The *Statute of Frauds* also addressed **Agreements for Lease**, but omitted to define the requirements for a binding Agreement for Lease. Conceptually, Agreements for Lease are interim contracts to serve the period between the date the parties commit to each other and the execution of the Deed of Lease; and when the parties invoke this approach to finalization, they subject themselves to documentation in two stages: an Agreement for Lease that later is replaced by the executed Lease. The question is, what must the interim document address in order to be binding?

It is clear that the Agreement for Lease needs to include reciprocal covenants to solemnly execute the Deed of Lease, when it is presented (because those covenants comprise the "adjustment for the lease"). But it is also clear that the Agreement for Lease need not be comprehensive and address everything the Lease is to contain. How are the parties to pinpoint the matters the interim agreement does need to confront?

The test the courts have applied is that an Agreement for Lease requires that its parties have agreed about all subjects that are "matters of substance." But the courts have not laid down an *objective* test to identify what are "matters of substance," and have applied the test case by case. Apart from the Essential Elements of the Lease which, by definition, are matters of substance, it is the subjects the parties did raise for agreement in the transaction, and did not abandon, that are its matters of substance, the inference being that the subjects they elected not to raise at the interim stage, and left over for the second stage document, were ones they did not consider substantial matters.

By virtue of also being agreements concerning land, Agreements for Lease, too, must be in writing and signed by or on behalf of all its parties, albeit not solemnly (and only Ontario's Statute of Frauds has excluded from those formalities, Agreements for Lease for a term of three years or less). However, the penalty for noncompliance in this respect is that no action can be brought on the agreement until the formalities have been met (the effect of which matches the effect of the court's interpretation of "void" in relation to Leases).

There are circumstances that favour the adoption of Two-stage documentation (e.g., when the lease commitment is reached before the premises have been substantially constructed, and the final data is not yet determinable), but Two-stage documentation is invoked in Canada even when the circumstances do not warrant that format. There are dangers in resorting to the two-stage approach unnecessarily. It opens the way for disputes on the subject of whether every matter of substance was agreed, and to the risk that, despite expectations to the contrary, agreement on the subjects left for second-stage agreement may elude the parties, and the Lease may never be executed, for reasons real or artificial.

In respect of commercial premises, Leasing has become a highly sophisticated enterprise that should never be underestimated, and deserves to be prepared for, by means of training and experience. In Canada, York University's Atkinson College offers a unique credit course on the subject of Commercial Leasing. The Real Estate Institute of Canada (REIC) offers a similar course as a qualifying credit towards its CLO designation.

THE ORGANISATIONAL FRAMEWORK

By virtue of being an agreement concerning land, a Lease falls within the definition of "a trade" in "real estate," in terms of Ontario's Real Estate and Business Brokers Act, and it is an offence for anyone other than a licensed broker or salesman to represent a party to a trade in real estate. However, the statute exempts some categories from licensing, including:

• a full-time salaried employee of a party to the trade; and
• a party's solicitor, in the course of his practice.

There are other exemptions with little relevance to leasing transactions, and a party to a lease who wants to be represented in the dealings effectively is limited to either its full-time salaried employee (for a lessor, its leasing agent and for a tenant, its leasing officer), or its solicitor, or a licensed broker or salesman.

Regulation of trading in real estate also is a provincial jurisdiction, and there is not one law on the subject for the whole country. Each province has its own statute on the subject: for example, *The British Columbia Real Estate Act, The Real Estate Agent's Licensing Act* in Alberta, *The Real Estate Brokers Act in Saskatchewan,* the *Real Estate Brokers Act in Manitoba, The Real Estate Brokerage Act in Quebec, The Real Estate Agents Act in New Brunswick, The Real Estate Trading Act in Prince Edward Island, The Real Estate Brokers Licensing Act* in Nova Scotia and the *Real Estate Trading Act* in Newfoundland. There will be variations in the different provinces' statute.

There are established associations of persons who operate professionally in a common activity. Though membership of these associations is voluntary, it is limited to those who meet qualification standards. Licensed real estate brokers, for example, have an association structure that a broker joins by becoming a member of the Real Estate Board for the district in which he/she practises. The Real Estate Boards in each province are members of the province's Provincial Real Estate Association, which is a member of the national Canadian Real Estate Association. When a licensed broker joins a Real Estate Board, he/she is required to contractually commit to abide by a Code of Ethics that regulates business conduct, and is policed by the association.

Another voluntary association of real estate professionals is the Real Estate Institute of Canada (REIC), which is the only association that has a division for leasing agents and leasing officers, both those who must be licensed, and those exempt from licensing. REIC limits membership to those who hold its designations: FRI (Fellow of the Real Estate Institute, granted to licensed brokers and unlicensed qualified Real Estate professionals), CPM (Certified Property Manager), CRF (Certified in Real Estate Finance), and ALO (Accredited Leasing Officer). Each designation has an education qualification, and REIC offers regular courses in its specialty subjects. It too, requires its members to commit to a Code of Ethics.

Lessors (and presumably their leasing agents) can join BOMA (the Building Owners and Managers Association International), which has offices in Toronto and other major cities. BOMA established BOMA Institute in 1970, to respond to the demand for education in property management, building maintenance and energy conservation, and it now offers a number of Real Estate courses that include a leasing component, although it does not offer a leasing designation. Its members also have to commit to a Code of Ethics.

A voluntary association catering for persons involved in the acquisition, management or disposal of Rights-of-way Easements for public agencies and investor-owned companies is International Rights of Way Association, of 13650 Gramercy Place, Gardena, CA 90249, which offers education courses for its designation SR/WA.

THE GRANTOR'S INTEREST

One cannot grant a greater interest in a property than one has and, accordingly, the acquirer of an interest in real estate should ensure that the person it contracts with for an interest in land does have all the property rights that it offers to convey.

In a contract of lease, the lessor need not be the owner of the property, but must be the person who holds the right to possession of the premises during the whole period of the interests it offers, and the acquirer should establish the limits of the offeror's interest. In a contract of Purchase and Sale, however, the vendor should be the Fee Simple owner of the property.

All ownership now is termed to be Fee Simple, and theoretically complete. In practice, however, it is not realistic for a purchaser to expect the bundle of property rights it acquires to still be complete and intact. The likelihood is that the vendor's bundle of rights has been whittled down in some respects that are determinable by all. Subtractions usually emanate from (1) Public Limitations by government legislation to meet an over-riding public interest; or (2) Private Limitations in the body of past dealings, notified by a means recognised by law.

Public Limitations on Title

A Fee Simple owner's freedom to use its property however it wishes has always been subject to rules of behaviour recognized in common law, like the law of nuisance. And that freedom has been further constrained by local Land Use legislation, in an ongoing process.

Property is a provincial jurisdiction in Canada, and there is not a single code of Land Use controls that applies uniformly throughout the country. Each province has its own separate *Planning Statute* that dictates the planning policy for the province. It is likely to delegate to each municipality and local authority the responsibility for adopting its Official Plan (in which its land is divided into Land Use Districts, like Public/Recreational, Residential, Commercial/Retail, Industrial or Agricultural), and enacting bylaws that implement that policy within its boundaries (detailing each District's definition, for example). The result is that Land Use controls differ from one municipality to the next, and conformity is not to be expected.

Zoning bylaws are regulations that generally control the use of a property, and place limitations upon permitted uses, the erection of structures, the types of construction, the shape, size, height, bulk, spacing, and other matters relating to the structures on the property, and zoning should be separately researched for each property at the planning office of its local authority.

Zoning aims to group together uses that are compatible, and to separate incompatible uses within a municipality and between neighbouring municipalities. That a desired use or structure is not allowed under current zoning is not an insuperable obstacle, however. For zoning is not rigid and unchanging; rather, it is adaptable and provides procedures for bylaw amendments (a lengthy process) and variances, so as to permit development. The *Ontario Planning Act*, for example, provides for Committees of Adjustment to decide minor variances expeditiously.

Building and Electrical Codes and legislation on such subjects as Conservation, Pollution Controls, Toxic Emissions, Hazardous Wastes, and Heritage Preservation are other examples of police limitations on the freedom of owners of real property. Buyers must beware and make the enquiries that are prudent.

Private Limitations on Title

Subtractions from the Fee Simple also occur in person-to-person transactions. Individual rights may have been excluded from the initial grant (e.g., mineral rights), or withheld from a previous transfer (e.g., a height restriction or a use restriction), or dealt away for a limited period that has not expired (e.g., in a lease, or easement, or mortgage). Not all prior subtractions bind subsequent acquirers of an estate in the property, however. Which do depends on the circumstances, and the rules of the land registration system of which the property is part.

Although all land in Canada is still held from the Crown in right of Canada, each province has introduced its own land registration legislation. Two systems of land registration are maintained in Canada today. The older system, Deeds Registration (also known as the Registry System) is still the only system maintained in Nova Scotia and New Brunswick. The later system, the Land Titles System (also known as the Torrens System, after its creator), is the only system maintained in British Columbia, Alberta, Saskatchewan and Northwest Territories. The other provinces maintain both systems for the present. Thus, the register of transactions for a property may be maintained under one system or the other; and which it is is a primary consideration, because each system imposes fundamentally different protections and obligations on those acquiring interests in properties on its registers.

The systems have in common that separate registers are initiated in respect of each land grant by the Crown within the system, and are maintained in respect of later Deeds whereby that land is transferred, subdivided, charged, encumbered or affected in any way. But the systems differ in the respect that in the Land Titles System, the provincial government examines each Deed lodged with it for entry in its register and adjudicates thereon before it admits the claim to the Lot register, whereas in the Registry System it does not, and enters all claims lodged for notation against the Lot.

In the Land Titles System, the Registrar will certify indefeasible title to a property to a named individual, and the interests and charges to which the title is subject, and guarantees the accuracy of the certificate, supported by a compensation fund. By contrast, registration of a claim in the Registry System is not proof that the claim is valid, and enquirers have to make their own judgment in that regard. The register is only a listing of unsubstantiated claims in the chronological order in which each was entered as the claimant's means of giving public notice of the claim.

The guiding principles in the Land Titles System are:

1. **The Mirror Principle**, which conveys that the register is an accurate and reliable reflection of all current facts that have been registered and are material to that title. The system does not allow consideration of facts capable of registration but not registered, even if it can be proved that the person who dealt with the land had actual knowledge of those facts. This is in direct contrast to the Registry System in which the register is notice of claims registered but not validated, and parties dealing on the land are bound by all claims of which they had knowledge, either actual or constructive (e.g., notation on title).
[Note: Despite the above, both systems accord some protection to unregistered interests that are accompanied by actual possession.]

2. **The Curtain Principle**, which refers to the indefeasible aspect. The Registrar's certificate is the conclusive source of the owner's title, and persons dealing with the land need not seek or verify further. This, too, is in direct contrast to the Registry System, in which persons dealing with the land have to make their own judgment on the relevance and validity of each claim noted on the title, and of each claim of which they have actual knowledge from other sources.

3. **The Insurance Principle**, which refers to the compensation feature that also is not part of the Registry System.

Because persons cannot successfully grant land rights that they do not have, and because the land registers provide the means of learning which rights a grantor does not have at the time of a grant, prudent acquirers of interests in or charges on land search title before concluding an acquisition. Whether the land is in a Registry System or a Land Titles System is essential intelligence. If the land is in a Land Titles System, the Certificate of Title is the prudent enquiry. If the land is in a Registry System, however, the Registry provides an Abstract (a listing of all claims noted on the title, going back 40 years), and the acquirer (usually through a lawyer) determines which entries it will accept, and which it will not. It is in respect of Registry System transactions that Title Insurance would be an attractive safeguard; yet despite being an established part of the titles system in the U.S.A. for many years, title insurance was not offered in Canada until recently.

Condominiums

JOHN ZEILER ————————————————————

The concept of the condominium is not a new idea. The term "condominium" originated in Roman law, and in Latin, it meant "joint dominion" or "co-ownership".

Originally, the condominium was conceptualized as part of an array of real property interests that could effectively provide affordable housing. Therefore, the first approaches to condominium in Ontario were geared towards lower priced housing. Over the last several years, the condominium concept has become popularized by appealing to so called "empty nesters," who wish to have luxury accommodation without the responsibility of looking after the upkeep and maintenance of the property. In addition, pressure has built for municipalities to maximize the use of infrastructure and services (roads, subways) and to generate increased realty tax revenue by increasing density. The result is a boom of condominium development. Therefore, the residential market for condominium living has changed and has become an integral part of the total housing industry.

In addition, the use of the concept has been extended into commercial, industrial and recreational/resort type condominiums. The recent major overhaul of regulations for creating condominiums and for their ongoing operation is found in the Ontario *Condominium Act*, S.O. 1998, c. 19. Each province has its own legislation to regulate condominiums. The Ontario legislation provides for four new types of condominium development: namely, vacant land condomini-

John Zeiler, B.A., LL.B., practises law with Swanick & Associates. He is an adjunct professor and part-time instructor of the Faculty of Professional Studies and Liberal Arts, Atkinson College, York University. He has taught courses in real property law and international trade and business.

ums, leasehold condominiums, common element condominiums and phased condominiums.

The opportunity thus arises for residential developments of high rises and townhouses through fee simple ownership or through a leasehold estate ownership on land held under a long-term ground lease of at least 40 years less a day to 99 years by a lessor. The leasehold condominium may be renewed on expiry for periods of at least 10 years. The unit owners in a leasehold condominium will have the flexibility to deal with their respective units and common elements as would occur in a standard condominium project. The existing freehold (fee simple) condominium is referred to as a standard condominium. By allowing for leasehold condominiums, institutions have the ability to retain the reversionary interest in underutilized land while still allowing for housing or other uses during the present time, and providing rental generation under the ground lease for the ultimate owner of the fee simple interest.

Vacant land may be divided into specifically designated units within the condominium. This type of condominium allows unit owners the flexibility to add structures after the condominium's registration. Single-family or mixed-use types of residential development are thus possible.

The phase condominium allows for incrementally creating a multi-building condominium community that is governed through a single condominium corporation. Owners are thus allowed to create several buildings in phases to be governed by a condominium corporation. Because all unit owners may share a specific facility or amenity without the need to divide the land into several developments and condominium corporations, they are able to avoid those lengthy and complicated agreements that are necessary to integrate the different phases.

The common element condominium allows each owner of a fee simple interest to also have an interest in the adjoining common elements, facilities or common parcel of land, and for these owners to be bound by the restrictions set out in the declaration creating the common element condominium. Therefore it is possible to have a community of single-family homes allowing each owner an interest in a common parcel of land that can serve as a park for the home owners community.

These new concepts provide flexibility in planning, development and utilization of land. From golf courses, industrial plazas, and common docks for boats to recreational communities, the uses of the condominium concept appear endless, limited only by the imagination of the developer and the economic feasibility of the project.

PURPOSE AND SCOPE

The condominium is a creature of statute, and the basic purpose of the statute for a non-common element condominium is to:

(i) Divide a property into units that can be individually owned while the common elements are shared by the owners of the units.

(ii) To provide an administrative framework to enable the owners of the individual units to manage the overall property and assets of the condominium. It is the intent of the Act to provide, by statutory means, for the ownership of space and of all the material parts that are within that space. Therefore, one ends up with ownership in fee simple of a portion of air space enclosed by the boundaries of a defined unit.

Condominium, other than a common element condominium, is a very flexible concept because it is a system of property ownership allowing a parcel of land to be divided into individual units and allowing the common areas to be owned by all the individual unit owners jointly as tenants in common. As mentioned previously, the size or use of a condominium development will be limited or defined by the zoning requirements, the imagination of the developer, or the economic feasibility of the project.

PATH TO CREATING A CONDOMINIUM

The path to creating a condominium involves the preparation of several documents. These basic documents are the declaration, description, by-laws, and house rules. Together with the *Condominium Act* itself, these four documents form the constitutional basis for the creation and continuous statutory and contractual authority for the functioning of the condominium. It is important to understand each of these documents and the role that each plays in the condominium process. The documents are as follows:

1. The Declaration

The declaration is the major written document that is prepared by the developer of the project. Under the terms of the *Condominium Act*, certain provisions are mandatory and must be incorporated in the contents of such a document. These include the fact that the lands in question are to be governed by the *Condominium Act*; the proportions of common interest attached to each unit; the proportions in which owners are to contribute to the common expenses; the specification of parts of the common elements that are to be used by the owners of one or more of the units, but not by all of the owners; an address for service; a mailing address for the corporation; a statement of any conditions, such as noise warning provisions, that the approving authority as defined in the *Ontario Planning Act* requires, as well as the consent of persons having a registered mortgage against the land.

In addition, the declaration may contain a number of other matters that would generally incorporate: the list of responsibilities in governing the condominium community through the corporation, consistent with its objectives and duties; the statement as to the division of the functions of repair and maintenance between unit owners and the corporation; the insurance requirements; and any special conditions or restrictions dealing with the occupation and use of the units. There could be any number of provisions incorporated in this document where it is felt that entrenchment is an important integral aspect associated with such an ownership concept.

Because any amendments must be made with the written consent of either 80% or 90% of the unit owners, depending on the nature of the amendment or, in certain circumstances, by court order or by the Director of Titles for an apparent inconsistency or error, the declaration has very limited scope for amendment. A procedure is set out in the Act whereby owner consent must be solicited. Notices of the amendment(s) and meetings to consider it must be sent to all mortgagees as well as owners of the units. If the mortgagee of any unit owner retains the right to exercise a unit owner's vote or consent, the mortgagee can give such notice to the corporation and vote on or consent to the amendment.

The Land Registry officials no longer physically inspect a development to determine if it has been substantially completed as required by the Act and its regulations. Instead, they rely upon a certificate of an engineer or architect confirming that the building has been constructed to the standards prescribed in the legislation. This certificate is a prerequisite for being able to register the project as a condominium.

2. Description

The description is the major document prepared by the surveyor. It involves and contains the architectural and structural plans of the building, a specification of the boundaries of each unit by reference to the building and other monuments, and diagrams showing the shape and dimensions of each unit and its location, vis-a-vis other units and the building. The description also includes the layout of the exclusive common use areas and the units to which they are attached. Therefore, areas such as parking spaces, balconies and lockers could be found in this category. Easements and other interests appurtenant to the condominium property are also included.

The regulations associated with the Act define and detail the requirements that must be met for the visual diagrams (the requirements for the surveys and ability to establish unit boundaries by reference to monuments) in order to ensure that they are specific and definite enough that if the project is destroyed it may be rebuilt exactly as it was, including both location and configuration. The Act provides the specific items to be included for a vacant land condominium. The surveyor provides a certificate verifying that the units are substantially accurate. The architect and, in most cases, the engineer provide certificates that the building has been constructed in accordance with the regulations.

The co-ordination and integration of planning principles and procedures is reflected in treating condominium plans like subdivision plans for approvals under the *Ontario Planning Act*. When both the declaration and description have been reviewed by the appropriate officials and have been approved, then, upon their registration, the condominium will come into being, and the condominium corporation will automatically come into existence.

3. By-Laws

The role of the by-laws is to offer provisions that are reasonable and consistent with and not contrary to the declaration or Act. The by-laws basically set out the rules and procedures with regard to: the administration of the condominium through the qualifications, election, resignation and removal procedures for Directors; the holding of meetings and functions of the Board of Directors; the appointment of officers; and the procedure for the assessment and collection of contributions towards the common expenses. The new Act broadens and clarifies the subject matters, which will be dealt with by the by-laws. These include: raising the quorum at owner's meetings from the owners who own 25% of the units of the corporation to 33-1/3%; remuneration to directors of the corporation; allowing the corporation to object to assessments under the *Ontario Assessment Act*; and the establishment of procedures with respect to the mediation of disputes between the corporation and unit owners.

Most condominiums will pass borrowing by-laws to borrow money for expenditures not listed in the budget for the current fiscal year. A new feature is the ability to pass by-laws setting occupancy standards for units for residential purposes. Assessments can be included in the cost of maintaining the common elements and repairing damage for those who contravene such standards. In order to clarify what features and fixtures are covered by condominium insurance versus unit owner insurance for repairs after damage, the by-laws usually define a standard unit.

By-laws must be passed by a resolution of the directors and at a duly called meeting of the corporation by owners owning not less than 51% of the units. The by-law so created and approved is ineffective until a copy of same has been registered in the Land Registry Offices, together with a certificate certifying that the by-law is a true copy, duly passed at meetings of the Board of Directors and owners.

4. The Rules or House Rules

These deal with matters respecting the use of the common elements and/or the units for the purposes of promoting the safety, security or welfare of the owners and of the property, as well as to prevent unreasonable interference with the use and enjoyment of the common elements and condominium assets and of other units. Therefore, the so called rules regulating the manner of behaviour of people, pets and parking within the condominium development are set out in the rules. The rules must be "reasonable" and consistent with the declaration, by-laws and the Act.

The Board prepares the rules and amendments or repeals thereof, and notifies the owners of the condominium of the rules approved by the Board. Unless a meeting of owners is requisitioned to consider the rules, the rules become effective and binding on all the condominium owners 30 days after the giving of such notice to the owners by the Board of Directors. If a duly constituted meeting is called, the rules will become effective if passed by a majority of the owners of those present, personally or by proxy, at the meeting. If the owners have amended or repealed a rule within the prior two years, the Board cannot pass a similar revision of same without the approval of the owners.

SOME BASIC CONCEPTS

In order to understand the condominium concept, it is necessary to understand the component features of a condominium, as well as how it functions. The property comprising the standard, leased or phased condominium development is divided into units that are individually owned, and the balance of the development is known as the common elements.

The actual definition of the unit of the condominium is a matter that is determined by the developer of the project. In most instances, the unit is described as the underside surface of the unfinished walls, ceilings, and floors surrounding the air space. As well, other aspects of the development can be defined by means of a unit, such as locker area and parking spaces. Again, it is the developer who makes this decision and defines the boundaries of such entities.

The common elements of the development are owned by the individual unit owners as tenants in common, in accordance with the percentage attached to each of the units as set out in the declaration. The percentage figure is also determined by the developer. There is no set criterion for the basis of determining such a percentage figure. Usually, this figure is based on the relationships of square footage and/or initial selling prices.

In the process of creating the documents for the condominium, choices have to be made by the developer with regard to the designation of common element areas. Certain aspects of the development can be determined to be limited common elements, which are for the exclusive use of the owners of the unit to which they attach. The most likely candidates would be the parking area in front of the unit, balconies, patios and, possibly, a small rear yard. This type of designation offers an appropriate balance between providing exclusivity of use to the unit owner and providing a measure of control by the condominium corporation through the by-law and house rules as to how that use can be carried out.

Repair and Maintenance

One of the difficult legal concepts in condominium law centres around the obligations of repair and maintenance. The Act provides that the obligation to repair after damage and the obligation to maintain the units are exclusive of each other. It should be noted that the obligation to repair after damage does not include the repair of improvements made to units after registration of the declaration and description. The inclusion of the definition of a standard unit(s) in the condominium documents is an attempt to clarify what is an improvement and what are standard features for each similar type of unit. Therefore, this would ensure that each unit owner of similar types of units has the same features and fixtures. Generally speaking, the terms and provisions of the declaration vary this obligation. Instead of providing for the mutual exclusivity of repair and maintenance, the developer, through the declaration, separates the obligation of maintenance and repair between the common elements and the units. In other words, the corporation will be responsible for the repairs and maintenance of the common elements, while the unit owner will be responsible for the maintenance and repairs of his/her unit. The very delicate and difficult question of determining what is repair and what is maintenance is thus avoided. As well, since the unit has probably been defined in the manner previously set forth, then the unit owner is restricted, in his/her maintenance and repair obligations, to keeping up an aesthetically pleasing home and to being a good housekeeper. The corporation has the powers to make any repairs an owner was obligated to make and that he/she fails to do. The cost of such repairs will be added to the owner's contribution towards common expenses.

One of the factors favouring the unit description as above and separating repair and maintenance functions centres around the responsibility and accountability for the government of the project by the board of directors. The interdependency involved in a multiple unit community requires responsible control of the maintenance and repair of mechanical, plumbing and electrical facilities by a board of directors rather than individual unit owners, as well as a central source of funds to pay for same.

Termination of a Condominium

The new Act spells out the various ways that the government of all or part of the condominium property may be terminated. The owners may, on consent, terminate the project from being governed by the Act. If the owners of 80% of the units and 80% of those persons who have registered claims against the condominium property, at the date of voting at a specially called meeting, vote to no longer be a condominium, then the property will no longer be a condominium.

The Act provides for the situation where extensive damage has occurred to units or parts of or the whole of the building in which the units are contained. When damage has occurred to the buildings, the Board shall determine, within 30 days of the damage, whether substantial damage has occurred. Within that 30-day period, two qualified persons, not affiliated with the Board, estimate the damage so that the Board can then determine if there has been substantial damage. If the board so determines, the corporation must then repair the damage, within a reasonable time; unless, after making the determination, a duly constituted meeting of owners of the corporation is requisitioned and held within 30 days of receiving notice, and such owners who own 80% of the units vote to terminate the condominium project. If the owners vote for a termination, then a notice to this effect is placed on title, and the project is no longer governed by the *Condominium Act*. The owners become tenants in common of the lands and interests appurtenant to the land in the same proportion as the common interest that each unit owner has in the project.

Provision is made for termination of the project as a condominium upon sale of the project or part thereof, and the consent of owners owning 80% of the units and 80% of those having registered claims against the units. Dissenters to the sale may dispute the fair market value. In such instance, mediation and then arbitration will occur to determine if the sale value was too low. If the fair market value is higher, the dissenter will benefit based on the higher value.

Also, the Ontario Superior Court of Justice may, on an application by the corporation, owner or encumbrancer, terminate the condominium scheme. In each event, the ownership of the property would devolve as above. Termination by expropriation is another way of terminating the government of the project as a condominium.

Insurance

Another difficult aspect of condominium is the matter of insurance coverage. The philosophy associated with such coverage is to have comprehensive coverage and unity of control of funds. This means that the condominium corporation wishes to ensure that the property is fully and properly protected by insurance. To ensure this factor, the obligation is left to the corporation to obtain such insurance coverage, maintain it and pay for it from the contributions toward common expenses. Generally, the coverage is for the full replacement value of the project, without taking into account depreciation. Also, the policy usually covers all risk situations so that there is the widest possible coverage. By centralizing the control of this type of policy in the hands of the corporation, it ensures that there is a unified insurance policy procedure that is comprehensive and extensive and covers all aspects of the physical structure of the condominium. The mortgagee waives its right to claim insurance dollars in order to have the money put towards repair of damage, in the event that damage does occur to a part of the condominium development.

In order to maintain proper insurance coverage, most condominium corporations retain an appraiser every three years to update the replacement cost of the project.

The unity of control of funds is important to ensure that a responsible party will have control of the funds from the insurance company and use same towards the payment of contractors doing the repairs to the damage. As a result, most developments provide for an insurance trust agreement. This is an agreement with a trust company, providing that the trust company will receive any proceeds of insurance monies in the event of damage, and it will oversee the disbursement of such funds to the contractors who are doing the actual repairs as a result of the damage.

Under the Act, the condominium corporation is deemed to be the occupier of the common element for purposes of occupiers' liability. The corporation has the power to sue for damages to the common elements on its own behalf or on behalf of any owner. Therefore, the insurance policy of the corporation usually provides for public liability coverage by the corporation to protect its exposure as a result of the corporation being deemed to be the occupier of the common elements.

Further protection is afforded the individual unit owners because appropriate notice must be given in the event of cancellation of the corporation's policy, and there will be no problems in determining which insurance companies will provide the repair funds if individual unit owners take out separate insurance that provide overlap coverage.

The individual unit owner is advised to obtain appropriate coverage for any improvements made to the interior of the unit, as well as his/her furnishings and chattels against fire, theft and other risks. Also, the owner should insure his/her liability resulting from loss of occupancy as a direct result of damage to his/her unit. It must be understood that if damage occurs to the unit, then the unit owner would still be obligated to make his/her payments for any mortgage, common expenses and realty taxes, even if he/she has to live elsewhere and pay rent in the interim. The unit owner is the occupier of his/her unit and, as such, must protect himself/herself with public liability coverage within his/her unit.

The Corporation will protect itself for boiler and other machinery if it is liable for damage due to the use or ownership of such equipment.

Most Boards will acquire directors' and officers' liability insurance. Since this is a volunteer Board, it is reasonable to provide coverage to a unit owner assuming responsibility as a director/officer for damages arising through the actions, omissions and decisions while performing the functions of officers and directors.

Common Expenses

The common expenses of the corporation comprise the expenses arising from the performance of the duties and objects of the corporation as well as expenses that have been deemed common expenses in the Act or in the declaration. The unit owners of the condominium are obligated to contribute monies monthly to meet the obligations of the corporation. The common expenses comprise a number of elements, including, inter alia, maintenance and repair, the payment for any contracts as part of the upkeep of the property (i.e., elevators, landscaping), payment for any common utilities, legal fees and auditing fees, as well as premiums for the insurance policies.

The developer of the condominium attaches to the unit in the declaration a percentage factor of the obligation for each unit owner to contribute towards the common expenses. The Board, based upon the preparation of the budget, assesses each of the condominium owners in order to obtain, monthly, sufficient dollars to run the corporation. Each owner has an obligation to contribute towards the common expenses in the proportion specified in the declaration for his/her unit.

Usually, each corporation establishes a procedure for the assessment and collection of common expenses. That procedure is often set forth in the by-laws of the corporation, and it usually involves the Board of Directors preparing a budget estimating the common expenses for the next year's operations. Based on this budget forecast, assessment notices are sent to the condominium owners advising them of the monthly contributions that must be made. Many declarations provide for the payment of common expenses by post-dated cheques and the requirement to provide 12 post dated cheques. If the Board determines that its estimate of expenses was not sufficient, then the Board, at any time, can advise the members of the condominium corporation (being the unit owners) of a further assessment in order to meet the ongoing expenses.

In the event that a unit owner fails to contribute towards the common expenses, the corporation has been given the power to register a lien against the unit for the arrears of common expense payments. This lien will also include all reasonable costs, charges and expenses incurred by the corporation in connection with the lien collection. This lien must be registered within three months of the initial default and, once registered, covers subsequent, continuous defaults. Before the lien can be registered, written notice of the lien must be given, at least 10 days prior to registration of the lien, to the defaulting owner. The corporation is protected for the recovery of such lien amount due to the fact that the lien, when registered, has priority over any prior encumbrances, which includes any prior mortgages registered against the title of the unit owner, but not arrears of realty taxes, provided proper notice has been given. The ultimate power given to the corporation is the ability to enforce the lien in the same manner as a mortgage (i.e., power of sale or foreclosure). Also, if an owner is in arrears of common expenses for 30 days or more prior to a meeting of owners, such unit owner forfeits his/her right to vote at such meeting.

If there is a mortgage registered against a unit and the unit owner has defaulted in common expense payments, then the mortgage usually provides that the unit owner is deemed to be in default under the mortgage. The mortgagee, besides making the payments to bring the common expenses into good standing, has the right to declare the mortgage due and payable and to take all actions thereunder. Also, the mortgagee usually preserves the right to vote or consent at owner's meetings in lieu of the unit owner.

Reserve Funds

One of the important additions to the *Condominium Act* was the recognition and enhancement of the importance of planning for long-term repairs and maintenance. There was a need to provide a procedure and mechanism to ensure that the building would continue to be well maintained. Also, it was important that unit owners be able to plan and budget their funds so as to reduce the number of occasions for which they would have to pay thousands of dollars at one time for needed repairs or replacements. This was accomplished by requiring each corporation to maintain reserve funds for major repairs and replacements of the common elements and assets of the corporation, including matters such as roofs, roads, sidewalks, sewers and elevators. The property comprising the condominium development is considered to be a private development, and the interior roads and services and their repair and maintenance are the responsibility of the unit owners.

The Act requires the Corporation to conduct a reserve fund study by a qualified, independent party, inter alia, an accredited appraiser, architect or engineer. The study shall consist of a physical analysis of the site and a financial analysis for a period of 30 years from the date of the study. There are three categories of study: a comprehensive study, an updated study not based on a site inspection and an updated study based on a site inspection. For a newly registered condominium, a comprehensive study should be conducted within the year following its registration. Thereafter, a study must be done every three years.

The professional conducting the study determines the life expectancy of the various portions of the common areas and the expected repair and replacement costs for such items. Based on this calculation, the Board is able to determine the amount that must be collected yearly in order to meet the obligations to deal with the necessary replacements and repairs. At the outset, 10% of the budget amount exclusive of the reserve fund, as a minimum, must be collected with each budget and set aside in the reserve fund. These funds are to be held separate from the operating funds of the corporation.

Once the plan has come into effect, the Board must assess and collect from each unit owner the amount needed to meet the financial targets in the study on a year to year basis. Once the Board receives the study, it has 120 days to devise a funding plan to ensure compliance with the study. Within 15 days of devising the plan, the Board shall notify the auditor and unit owners. Thirty days after notifying the said parties, the Board is obliged to implement the plan. The reserve fund contribution by each unit owner could be less than or exceed 10% of the budget amount and, therefore, provide sufficient funds for the major repairs and replacements based on estimated costs and life expectancy of the common elements and condominium assets.

Financial Controls

Successful financial control of the condominium is usually based upon setting up proper procedures for budgets and monitoring budgetary performances, as well as providing a yearly statement of income and expenses. Also, a balance sheet as part of the financial presentation is provided to the unit owners of the corporation. This material, together with the auditor's report, is forwarded to the unit owners prior to the annual meeting. This exercise allows for an appropriate review of the financial activities of the corporation. In addition to reviewing the financial performance and financial calculations at an annual meeting, the owners must appoint an auditor, who is their representative, or ombudsman, in overseeing and monitoring the financial performance of the corporation. The auditor is appointed by the owners at the annual meeting. An audited financial statement must be prepared each year and approved by the owners at the annual meeting. This report will also comment on the board's adherence to the targets established in the reserve fund study and the current status of actual repairs/replacements and the amount of reserve funds.

Status Certificates

A purchaser or mortgagee of a condominium unit will request a status certificate from the condominium corporation. Besides providing such person with copies of: the last financial statement of the corporation; the corporation's current budget; the declaration; the by-laws; the house rules; the management agreement; and the current insurance certificates, the status certificate confirms whether the unit owner is in arrears of common expense payments. Also, the corporation confirms: whether there is a breach of any of the by-laws or house rules; whether any judgments have been rendered against the corporation; and whether any special assessments and/or substantial additions or alterations to the common elements are being planned. It should be noted that the information contained in the certificate is binding against the corporation in favour of the person requesting the certificate, and the corporation must provide the certificate within 10 days after the receipt of the request and payment for same. If the corporation fails to give such information within the time limit, then the corporation shall be deemed to have given a certificate stating no default and no increase in the common expenses since the budget, and that no assessment to increase the contribution to the reserve fund has been made.

The Developer of a New Condominium

Concern about conveying complete and accurate information and to provide rules for protection of consumers purchasing units is a hallmark of the new Act. This theme begins with the initial purchase of a newly built condominium. A comprehensive disclosure statement describing the development in detail, plus copies of the condominium rules, declaration, by-laws, description, budget and important agreements are given to the purchaser with the executed purchase agreement. From this moment, a 10-day cooling off period begins for the purchaser. During this time, such purchaser may cancel the agreement and receive the return of his or her deposit. After that, the purchaser is bound to the deal unless there is a major change to the disclosure statement. In such event, a 10-day period restarts to allow the purchaser to cancel the deal.

The Builder must be accurate with the budget and figures for the common expenses for the first year of operation. If the actual operational costs are more during the first year, the Builder must pay the condominium corporation the difference.

Sweetheart deals for property management and services can now be set aside by Board resolution on 60-day notice and within one year of the election of a new, independent Board of Directors, respectively.

The Builder, once it no longer owns a majority of the units, must within 21 days call a meeting to elect a new Board. At that time, there is an extensive list of items, agreements, records and documents to be delivered to the new Board. Included is an audited statement of operations from registration until turnover to the new Board.

Enforcement

The remedies available in the arsenal of the unit owners have been greatly expanded under the Act. The Act includes:

(a) the ability to have an inspector appointed to investigate records and documents, and then report to the court with a summary to the Board of Directors and unit owners

(b) the court appointing an administrator to, if necessary, exercise some of the powers of the Board of Directors

(c)   the injection of alternative dispute resolution procedures by the inclusion of mediation and arbitration

(d)   a court order for damages if the declarant (the party registering the condominium) has made a false and misleading statement to unit owners who sustained damages relying on such statements

(e)   a court order for compliance by two or more corporations governed by an agreement for cost sharing of facilities or services

(f)   a court order terminating a residential lease of a unit for a tenant in contravention of a court order

(g)   a court order providing relief to a unit owner, mortgagee, declarant or condominium corporation if there has been conduct that is oppressive or unfairly prejudicial to the applicant requesting the court order

(h)   any other remedy not specifically provided by the Act for failure by a person to perform a duty imposed by the Act.

Fines can be expensive: up to $10,000 for an individual and up to $25,000 for a corporation.

Directors and officers could be subject to fines or other punishment if they permit or acquiesce in the commission by the condominium corporation of an offence under the Act.

If the corporation obtains a judgment, then such judgment is an asset of the corporation. In the same manner, the corporation may be sued as a representative of the owners of the units and can be sued in respect to any matter dealing with the common elements or the assets of the corporation. In the event that a judgment is obtained against the corporation, then such judgment is binding against each owner at the time of the judgment, and each owner will share the judgment in accordance with his/her percentage responsibility of contributions to the common expenses.

Administration

As part of the administration of the condominium, the corporation has the general responsibility and duty to control, manage and administer the common elements and assets of the corporation. In addition, the corporation has the duty to effect compliance by the owners with the Act, the declaration, the by-laws and the rules. This means that it is the corporation's responsibility, through its Board of Directors, to ensure that the unit owners are abiding by the rules of their community. Each owner and each person having a registered mortgage against a unit has the right to the performance of any duties of the corporation set out in the constitutional documents of the corporation. Therefore, if one of the unit owners has breached a term or provision of the constitutional documents, it is imperative that the Board deal with same. Usually, this means that the Board will attempt, in a low-key fashion, to discuss the breach, including correspondence, with the unit owner in question. It is hoped that this will resolve the matter at this stage. If this is not successful, then the corporation will generally engage the services of its solicitor to deal with the recalcitrant unit owner. If these methods fail, the condominium must follow the enforcement remedies available to it. The duties also apply to any lessee of a unit, and the lessee is responsible for following all of the same rules of the community as does an owner, except for the duty of payment of common expenses, which is the responsibility of the owner. In addition, the corporation can provide a lessee with a notice that the unit owner has defaulted in his contributions to the common expenses, in which event the lessee is obligated to make the common expense payments from his/her rent and is deemed, by so doing, to have satisfied his/her rental obligations. If the lessee does not abide by a Court Order, or fails to abide by the notice of the corporation to make the common expense payments, then the Court has the power to terminate the lease. The Court will require the landlord to have notice of such proceedings. Therefore, the powers given the Court under this Act supersede the provisions for termination in the *Landlord and Tenant Act*.

Potpourri

As mentioned earlier for a newly constructed unit, the Act provides a number of safeguards and procedures for the prospective purchaser. Initially, the developer must prepare a disclosure statement that sets out fully and accurately information regarding the project, including the number of units, recreational and other amenities, the significant features of the proposed condominium constitutional documents, a budget statement for the first year and any other relevant matters. The budgetary statement must be accurately prepared, including an accurate assessment of the costs to be met, as well as of reserve funds. In the event that the total amount incurred for the common expenses exceeds the amount set out in the budget statement for the one-year period covered by the budget, then the declarant developer has the liability to pay to the corporation the amount of such excess, except if the excesses occur due to the termination of the management agreement.

Deposit Money

For newly built residential condominiums, the Ontario New Home Warranty Programme (ONHWP) designates persons, usually solicitors, to receive deposit monies. The purchaser is protected for up to $20,000 of deposit monies in the event of bankruptcy or other events that cause the builder to abandon the project. For a builder to use deposit monies in excess of $20,000, insurance coverage with an insurer must be arranged. Because of the ONHWP protection and additional insurance coverage, builders can use the deposit monies to help finance construction of the project.

The Act does impose trust obligations on deposit monies and the requirement to pay interest thereon for the sale of all types and uses of condominium units. All such deposit monies are payable to the solicitor of the condominium developer or a trustee as provided for under the Act.

The purchaser is entitled to interest at the prescribed rate set by the regulations on the deposit monies from the day the money was paid until the date the unit is available for occupancy or possession. The Builder has an obligation to pay the interest on occupancy date. Alternatively, the Builder can pay the interest on the date a deed can be tendered with the payment of additional interest based on the interest amount that should have been paid on interim occupancy until the final closing date.

Builder's Obligations for New Condominium Units

There are implied covenants in purchase agreements of new condominiums: to sell the residential units not being retained for leasing; to take all reasonable steps to deliver to the purchaser a deed to the unit without delay; and to hold in trust monies received from a purchaser on behalf of the condominium corporation. The builder is under a duty to complete the building and to register the project as a condominium.

Leases

In the disclosure statement, the builder must set out the percentage of the units it intends to lease rather than sell.

The owner of a unit must, within 30 days of leasing a unit or renewing a lease, notify the condominium corporation about the lease, provide information about the tenant and provide the tenant with copies of the constitutional documents of the condominium. The condominium must keep a record of such tenancy information.

Management

One of the other usual documents in any condominium corporation is the hiring of a manager whose staff will assist with the day to day administration of the condominium's functioning. Since the Board of Directors is, in essence, a part-time directorship, it is necessary for most condominiums to have someone on a full-time basis to look after the day to day problems and ensure that all monies to be collected are collected and all expenses and bills that have to be paid are paid. To prevent the original developer from establishing a sweet heart deal, the Act provides, with regard to any management agreement that was created prior to the individual owners' taking over the control of the condominium corporation, that the corporation may by Board resolution terminate such agreement upon giving 60 days' notice in writing. Generally, most other agreements created by the developer may be terminated within 12 months of the turnover meeting to the purchasers.

Interim Occupancy

With most new condominiums, it is quite natural for people to move into the project prior to its registration as a condominium. In such circumstances, the purchasers enter into an interim occupancy agreement and pay to the developer a monthly charge based on: the amount of interest the purchaser would be paying on the unpaid balance of the purchase price at the prescribed rate in the regulations; a reasonable estimate of municipal taxes attributable to the unit; and the projected monthly common expense contribution for the unit. Subject to certain modifications under the Act, the person entering into possession must comply with the rights and obligations during interim occupancy set out in such agreement. The Act provides, in most instances, that the *Tenants Protection Act* does not override the provisions of the occupancy agreement.

Path to Registration

The developer will be cognizant of the procedure that must be followed in order to finalize the registration of the condominium. The process would be started by an application to the Ministry of Housing or to the regional level of government that has authority to deal with such applications. The *Condominium Act* ties in the provisions of the *Planning Act* dealing with plans of subdivision to the process for reviewing the proposed condominium plan associated with an application for a condominium. The structural plans are usually exempted from the requirements of the *Planning Act*, but the other documentation making up the condominium plan would be circulated, as would a plan of subdivision, to ensure that it complies with the municipal requirements and other planning input. Therefore, the plan is circulated to a number of government departments, as well as the municipality and regional municipality, if applicable, where the development is situated. Each of these sections and sectors will review the material to determine whether there should be any conditions attaching to the approval or whether there are any objections to such a project. The municipality will thus review the project in detail. The approval will be given by the municipality, including any agreements they require to be entered into, such as a site plan agreement. Assuming that all of the ministry departments and the municipality concerned approve the project without conditions or confirm that the conditions have been complied with, then the approval from the Ministry of Housing or local authority will be given by signing the original plan.

In addition, the declaration (the written, main constitutional document) and description, being a detailed depiction of the structural plans, must comply with the regulations. Certificates of the solicitor, architect or engineer and surveyor are relied upon by the officials in the Land Titles Office to confirm that the project has been built and substantially completed in accordance with the regulations and is in compliance with the Act. The description is reviewed by the Examiner of Surveys at the Land Titles Office to ensure the drawings are thorough and complete, as required by the Act and regulations.

Government of the Project

Once the declaration and description are registered, the project becomes governed by the *Condominium Act*, and the condominium corporation comes into existence. The Act then provides that the developer must turn over the operations of the corporation to the owners of the individual units. Therefore, a turnover meeting of the owners is provided for, at which time the owners elect a Board of Directors and appoint an auditor. The Board, elected at the time when the declarant developer owns a majority of the units, shall, no more than 21 days after the declarant ceases to be the registered owner of the majority of the units, call a meeting of the owners to elect a new board. It is at this turnover meeting that the declarant will hand over all of the records of the corporation, including the constitutional documents, all financial records, the as-built architectural and structural plans, an unaudited financial statement, and information that is the basis for the reserve fund; and, within 60 days after such meeting, an audited financial statement from the time of the creation of the corporation until the turnover meeting must be given to the newly elected Board.

The administrative vehicle that allows for the government of the condominium project is the condominium corporation, which acts through its Board of Directors. It is a special type of corporation that is not subject to the terms and provisions of the *Business Corporations Act* and, in particular, does not bestow limited liability on the owners of the units of the corporation. There is now a requirement that the corporation in Ontario comply with the *Corporation Information Act* and file information about directors and officers for public purposes.

The corporation has the basic responsibility to manage the property and assets of the corporation. The corporation's affairs are handled through a Board of Directors, and the method of electing such directors and the number of directors is usually set out in the by-laws of the corporation. The Board of Directors must act honestly and in good faith and must also ensure that their personal interests do not conflict with the interests of the corporation. It is anticipated that there might not be as strict a performance requirement imposed on the directors of the condominium as on the directors of a corporation under the *Business Corporations Act*. Directors of the condominium must exercise the care, diligence and skill that a reasonably prudent person would exhibit in comparable circumstances. This is a volunteer board, and they meet periodically (usually about once a month). The directors will be elected at duly called meetings of owners, and each unit owner shall be entitled to one vote. If there are more than six directors in the corporation, then the directors may form an Audit Committee to assist in the financial obligations associated with the running of the corporation. Generally speaking, a director is not paid for acting as a director of the corporation unless so specified in a by-law that establishes the remuneration to be paid and the period that it covers, but which is not to exceed three years. If there is such a by-law, there is usually an honorarium type of payment made to each director for acting on the Board of Directors.

The responsibilities of a director are not eliminated by delegation of day to day responsibility. They must make the final decisions based on information provided by the manager or committee chairmen. It is their duty to set up proper procedures and controls. Liability insurance is taken out by the corporation to provide some comfort. Also, insurance protecting against theft or dishonesty is recommended for employees or officers of the corporation. The corporation must indemnify a director for any liability or costs incurred as a result of an actual or proposed claim or for expenses incurred in performing his/her responsibilities. This indemnification is limited if there is a breach of a duty or responsibility to act honestly and in good faith under the Act.

A director who has a direct or indirect material interest in a contract must declare his/her interest and the extent of same. He/she must not be counted as part of the quorum, nor be present during discussion of the matter or vote. Although this restriction applies to material contracts or interests, a director would be prudent to abide by this procedure for any possible conflict of interest. At an owner's meeting, with proper notice of the director's interest in the contract having been set out in such notice, the owners can approve the contract by two-thirds of the votes cast at a meeting for situations where the director or officer has not complied with all the procedures for disclosure and voting as set out in the Act. In either event, the contract would be valid, and the director would not be accountable for any profits. The disclosure shall be recorded in the Board minutes as part of its procedural requirements.

At the meeting of the Board of Directors, the actual officers of the corporation are elected or appointed by the Board of Directors. As a matter of practice, the Board has the ultimate review and responsibility for the overall functioning of the affairs of the condominium, but usually leaves the actual day to day administration to the appointed manager.

CO-OP

One of the other forms of multiple ownership that one sometimes finds in the residential field is the concept of a commercial co-op. The basic example consists of a corporation owning a parcel of land on which is situated the building or development that is to be dealt with by means of the co-operative scheme. The individuals who wish to become owners purchase shares in the corporation and, at the same time, obtain an occupancy right to a particular unit.

Each shareholder of the corporation is an owner whose ownership is proportionately based on the number of shares held in the corporation. As long as the shareholder is in good standing, he/she is entitled to retain the ownership of the shares, as well as occupancy of the unit.

The constitutional documents of such a scheme would include the by-laws that would set out in detail the administrative mechanics for electing the Board of Directors and such other matters as holding owners' meetings and assessment procedures. In addition, there could be an occupancy agreement that each owner agrees to sign, and in which he/she agrees to be bound by the rules and covenants that govern the project. One must remember that positive covenants (i.e., obligations to repair etc.) do not run with the title to the land, and therefore each time there is a change of ownership, the control factor for enforcing these covenants has to be by way of contractual documentation entered into by the new purchaser.

The unit owners would pay a monthly fee, which would incorporate a portion of the mortgage, realty taxes and other general operating expenses that would be similar to living in a condominium development.

The differences between a co-op scheme and a condominium scheme are as follows:

1. In a condominium scheme, one acquires title in fee simple to a specific unit; whereas in a co-op scheme, one is the beneficial owner of shares and only has an occupancy right to a unit.

2. In a condominium scheme, one is able to have individual flexibility as to financing, whereas in the co-op scheme there is a mortgage that covers the whole of the property since the property cannot be fragmented. Therefore, if one co-op unit owner defaults in his/her monthly maintenance payments, which incorporates a portion of the mortgage payments, then all of the members of the co-op would be in default, unless they made up the individual difference. In a condominium scheme, each party has his/her own individual financing and, if one party defaults, it does not affect the other condominium owners.

3. The realty taxes cover the whole of the project in a co-op. They are not fragmented as in a condominium scheme, where there is provision for the breakdown of the assessment of the project among the units and common elements. Therefore, in a condominium, each unit owner gets a separate tax bill and, if the unit owner defaults, the other condominium owners are not affected.

4. The individuals in a condominium scheme deal with familiar entities such as mortgages and deeds; whereas, in the cooperative scheme, the parties are dealing with shares, promissory notes, and pledges and must, initially, abide by the provisions of the *Securities Act*.

5. There is no requirement for establishing a reserve fund in the co-op, and the co-op owners must discipline themselves in establishing good accounting and planning procedures.

One of the advantages to the co-op scheme is the fact that the by-laws can provide that the Board of Directors must approve any transfer of shares to new purchasers. This right would not be applicable in the condominium scheme as it would interfere with the right of alienability: that is, the right to transfer one's fee simple interest in the unit and proportionate share of the common elements. Therefore, in the co-op scheme, you can have some say in who will be your neighbour.

From a functional point of view, there is generally little difference in the government of projects utilizing either the condominium or co-op scheme.

TIME SHARING

The concept of time sharing has had some limited success. Most of the success revolves around recreational or resort properties, wherein an individual purchases a block of time to use a unit at a particular resort. Generally speaking, the project is probably registered as a condominium, and then the developer of the condominium either sells or leases an ownership interest in a particular unit to multiple purchasers. The purchases are based on a weekly time frame, and a buyer generally acquires an undivided one-fiftieth interest in the unit, together with the right to occupy the unit for a particular week in each year. The time-share owner would pay a portion of the operational expenses each year based on the length of time of the time share owned. A similar procedure is involved if it is by way of a leasehold scheme. The leasehold right can be limited for a number of years. Professional management is very critical to the success of a time-sharing project, and most projects work on a basis of a 50-week year, allowing two weeks to be set aside for maintenance, repairs and other ongoing preventative work that must be done to keep the development in first class shape.

One of the newer features has been the concept of pooling or exchange of units. By this mode, an individual who has purchased a time-share unit for a particular week in the year can, in essence, go to a central registry operated for the time-sharing association and choose where he or she would like to go for a holiday. Such an owner can determine if there are any units in such a location by way of a time-sharing scheme available for occupation during the week in question. His/her unit would also be subject to use by another time-sharing owner during that week.

CONCLUSION

As one can see, community life style for recreational purposes or for full-time occupation and ownership is subject to complex legal concepts and limitations, strictures, arrangements and obligations. To fully understand all of the implications, one would be wise to discuss such a purchase in advance with a professional adviser.

Taxes and Tax Planning

A basic knowledge of tax law and tax planning is essential for real estate investors and developers because of the major impact of taxes on real estate cash flows. It is also important knowledge for real estate professionals such as brokers, agents and appraisers.

Taxes are important considerations in determining:

- where to invest;
- how real estate is financed;
- how arrangements with investors are structured;
- what is done with land while it is vacant;
- the timing of various construction costs;
- how leases are structured; and
- how sales of real estate are structured.

Real estate is subject to many forms of taxation by local, provincial and federal governments. Reducing or postponing the payment of these taxes will increase after-tax cash flows to investors.

The taxes that have an impact on real estate cash flows and property values in Canada include:

- Property taxes imposed by provincial and local governments;
- Income taxes, sales taxes, payroll taxes and capital taxes imposed by federal and provincial governments;
- Land transfer taxes imposed by provincial and local governments on the transfer of real estate; and

---

Joanne E. Magee is an associate professor of income tax law at York University.

- Probate fees levied on the value of a deceased taxpayer's estate by provincial governments.[1]

Much has been written on all of these topics over the years but most of it is in such technical language that it is only suitable for a tax lawyer or accountant. The objective of this paper is to provide a clear and concise explanation of the relevant principles of Canadian tax law and tax planning in non-technical language. The paper emphasizes a conceptual approach to the taxation of real estate that looks at the history and objectives of the Canadian tax system and the legislative intent of the rules that have been developed and refined over the years.

OVERVIEW OF THE TAXATION SYSTEM IN CANADA
The Financing of Federal, Provincial and Local Governments

The authority to levy taxes is set out in the Canadian Constitution (the *Constitution Act*), which provides for two levels of government — federal and provincial — and sets out the powers and responsibilities of each level and the relationship between the two. There are actually three levels of government because the Constitution grants the provinces the authority to create local governments. Local governments, in turn, are often structured as two-tier arrangements, with regional (or county) governments and municipal governments.

The taxes collected by the federal, provincial and local governments are used to finance government spending, as are government borrowings. Because local governments are created by provinces and provinces do not want to be responsible for the repayment of local government debt, local borrowings are tightly controlled by provinces. A provincially organized authority exists in each province to centralize this function by issuing bonds or debentures. The funds are then lent to the local governments for capital projects. In some provinces, municipalities can also borrow on their own on a restricted basis. The federal government provides grants (called "cash transfer payments") to the provinces to supplement their tax revenues and

---

[1] All provinces (with the exception of Quebec) levy probate fees on the value of an estate when a will is "probated." Probate is a legal process confirming that a will is valid and is necessary in many circumstances. Whether or not real estate needs to be probated will depend upon whether it is held inside a private corporation, how title is registered (if it is personally owned) and the relevant provincial law. If the real estate does not need to be probated, it is sometimes included in a separate will that is not subject to probate.

borrowings, and provincial governments provide cash transfer payments to local governments to supplement their tax revenues, user fees and borrowings.

The federal government is responsible for the following spending programs:

- Federal social programs (such as Employment Insurance, Old Age Security and the Canada Pension Plan);
- Interest on the national debt;
- The operations of the federal government;
- Transfer payments to the provinces; and
- National defence.

The provincial governments, in turn, pay for the following major items:

- University education;
- Health care;
- Provincial government social programs;
- Provincial government operations; and
- Transfer payments to local governments.

Local governments pay for the following items:

- Public school education;
- Services (roads, public transit, sewers, water, policing, garbage); and
- Social programs and community services.

Objectives of the Tax System

Although the main objective of the tax system is to raise revenues, taxes also play a major role in Canadian social and economic policy. Governments use the tax system to redistribute wealth and to encourage certain economic activities (and discourage other ones) by providing tax concessions to select groups of individuals and businesses. For example, if the government wanted to help Canadians purchase their first homes, it could either grant a tax concession to real estate investors, builders or home buyers (such as the Homebuyer's credit and the RRSP Home Buyer's Plan[2]), or fund

---

[2] The RRSP Home Buyer's Plan was introduced in 1992 by the federal government. Under the current rules a "first-time homebuy" (a taxpayer who has not owned a home for the previous five years or has a disability) can withdraw up to $25,000 from his or her RRSP on a tax-free basis. The withdrawal must be repaid over 15 years according to a formula: any payments that are skipped are included in income. The Homebuyers Tax Credit is a non-refundable tax credit of $750 ($15\% \times \$5,000$) for "first-time homebuyers" who acquire a qualifying home after January 27, 2009.

construction or mortgage financing through some program using direct grants. With the exception of homes for new home buyers and affordable housing for low-income earners, investment in real estate is not normally an economic activity that governments want to encourage, although this is not always the case.[3]

Canada's tax system has also been designed to be fair and equitable, and one way that it meets this objective is by being *progressive*. If a tax is progressive, it is designed so that a higher income individual pays relatively more tax than a lower income individual. (A *regressive* tax, on the other hand, forces a lower income individual to pay a higher percentage of his or her income in taxes. A *proportional* tax makes every taxpayer pay the same amount.)

The graduated rates in the Canadian personal income tax system are designed to make it a progressive system. Property taxes and sales taxes, on the other hand, are regressive because lower income individuals normally spend a higher percentage of their total income on accommodation and on the consumption of goods and services than do higher income individuals.[4] One of the most regressive taxes is a *poll tax* (or head tax), which is charged based on the number of people in a household.[5]

---

[3] Two examples of rules favouring the investment in real estate (but not necessarily homes for new home buyers, or affordable housing for low-income earners) include the following:

1. The federal and provincial income tax exemption for capital gains from the disposition of a principal residence. This exemption has been in place since the taxation of capital gains was introduced in 1972.
2. The Multiple Unit Residential Buildings (MURBs) program that was introduced in the 1970s to increase the supply of rental housing. The owner of a MURB (which was a registered rental property) was granted a tax concession that rental property owners are not normally granted: increased writeoffs for the cost of the building. Under normal rules, a capital cost allowance (tax depreciation) claim on a rental building is limited so that rental losses cannot be created (or increased) by the claim. These special rules for MURBs were repealed a decade later.

[4] The federal and provincial governments counteract this regressivity by exempting basic necessities, such as groceries and prescription drugs, from their sales taxes and by providing refundable sales and property tax credits in their income tax systems for low income individuals and families.

[5] Although there are no poll taxes in Canada at the present time, there have been poll taxes in the past. See Harry Kitchen, *Property Taxation in Canada*, Canadian Tax Paper No. 92 (Toronto: Canadian Tax Foundation, 1992).

Direct versus Indirect Taxes

The Constitution allows both the federal and provincial governments to levy taxes, but restricts the type of taxes levied by the provincial governments to direct taxes. Only the federal government can levy indirect taxes.[6] Definitions and examples of direct and indirect taxes are set out below.

- *Direct taxes* are taxes that are actually borne by the person who pays the tax. The income tax and the retail sales tax are two examples of a direct tax.[7]
- *Indirect taxes* are taxes that are paid by one person but are actually borne by another. The customs and excise tax (which is paid by an importer or manufacturer of goods) and the manufacturer's sales tax (which existed before 1991) are two examples of an indirect tax.[8]

Although the provinces could theoretically extend their constitutionally-granted powers to levy all types of direct taxes to local governments, local taxes have generally been limited to property taxes.[9]

History

Prior to confederation, provincial customs and excise taxes accounted for a substantial proportion of provincial government revenues but, after transferring these indirect taxes to the new federal government in 1867, the provinces began to develop new forms of direct taxation. These direct taxes include property taxes, corporate

---

[6] The predecessor to the current constitution, the *British North America Act*, contained the same restriction.

[7] Although the burden of corporate income taxes is passed on to investors, suppliers, customers and employees, corporate income taxes are direct taxes [according to the decision in *Bank of Toronto v. Lambe* (1887), 12 AC 575]. See also Gerald La Forest, *The Allocation of Taxing Powers under the Canadian Constitution*, Canadian Tax Paper No. 46 (Toronto: Canadian Tax Foundation, 1976).

[8] The provinces levy sales and excise-type taxes on goods such as tobacco and gasoline by imposing them at the retail level so that they are paid directly by the consumer.

[9] There have been municipal income taxes in the past in Canada, and several cities in the United States currently levy income taxes. Many U.S. cities also levy fuel taxes and sales taxes (e.g., a hotel and occupancy taxes), as do some Canadian cities (e.g., Vancouver). See Harry Kitchen, *Municipal Revenue and Expenditure Issues in Canada*, Canadian Tax Paper No. 107 (Toronto: Canadian Tax Foundation, 2002) generally and at pages 13, 40 , 224, 229, 336 and 337. Income taxes, sales taxes and fuel taxes are also important ways that could be used by municipalities to supplement their revenues if allowed to. Some Canadian cities levy a land transfer tax (e.g., Toronto, which also levied a vehicle registration tax for a short time).

capital taxes, inheritance taxes,[10] gasoline and tobacco taxes and sales taxes. Income taxes, which were very unpopular, were the last to be introduced at the provincial level, but have become a major source of provincial tax revenues.

From confederation in 1867 to World War I, the customs and excise taxes taken over from the provinces provided about 80% of federal government revenues. Federal income taxes were first imposed by the *Income Tax War Act of 1917* as a temporary measure to finance World War I, and sales taxes soon followed after the war. After World War II, the tax system was reformed, and the *Income Tax Act* of 1948 was introduced, containing measures designed to finance the Canadian post-war welfare state and to stimulate economic growth. Among the changes introduced with the 1948 Act was the current capital cost allowance system of tax depreciation for writing off the cost of buildings and other depreciable property.

The federal income tax system was reformed a second time after the 1966 Report of the Royal Commission on Taxation and this resulted in the adoption of the present *Income Tax Act*,[11] which came into force in 1972. Among the changes introduced with the 1972 Act was the taxation of capital gains, which had been tax-free up to that time.[12] The system was reformed at third time in 1987.[13] The system is fine-tuned at least once a year at budget time.

A great many of the recent changes in income tax law have had an adverse affect on real estate. Why real estate? Because investors who purchase real estate generally purchase real estate to earn a profit, but sometimes the profit is not earned until the property is resold (at one-half of the regular rate, if it is a capital gain). In the meantime, the property can be highly leveraged (with mortgage financing), and any rental income that is earned can be sheltered with interest expense, capital cost allowance and other deductions; or they may be rental losses that an investor can claim against his or

---

[10] Although inheritance taxes have now been repealed, all provinces (with the exception of Quebec) levy probate fees (discussed at supra note 1), which are a type of inheritance tax.

[11] R.S.C. 1985 (5th Supp.), c. 1. Unless otherwise specified, all references to the Act and to the Regulations are references to the *Income Tax Act* and its Regulations. A reference in the notes to s. 18(2)(c), for example, is a reference to paragraph (c) of subsection (2) of section 18 of the Act (or, more simply, paragraph 18(2)(c)).

[12] One-half of a capital gain is now "taxable" as compared to 100% of most other types of income (s. 38(a)).

[13] Tax reform in 1987 lowered Canada's personal and corporate income tax rates and broadened the base on which personal and corporate income taxes are calculated. The United States, which is Canada's major trading partner, made similar changes around the same time.

her other sources of income. This has made real estate somewhat of a tax shelter which, in turn, has resulted in many restrictions on real estate deductions.

Federal-Provincial Agreements and Harmonization

At the beginning of World War II, income taxes were levied by the federal government and seven of the provinces. In 1941, as a wartime measure, the provinces agreed to vacate the field of income taxation in return for grants from the federal government. This arrangement has continued to the present time with a series of federal-provincial "tax rental" and "tax collection" agreements that are renewed every five years. Under the tax collection agreements first established in 1962, all provinces except Quebec agreed to use the federal income rules to calculate personal taxable income and tax credits, and to levy their personal taxes as a percentage of the basic federal tax. Only Quebec has had its own personal income tax system and has collected its own personal income taxes.

Similarly, since 1962, most provinces have levied their corporate income taxes based on the federal rules. At the present time only Quebec and Alberta have their own rules for corporate taxable income and collect their own corporate income taxes.[14]

In 1997, the tax collection agreement was changed to allow the provinces other than Quebec to also compute personal tax directly on provincial taxable income but still have their taxes collected federally by the Canada Revenue Agency (CRA). This new "tax on income" (or TONI) approach allows the provinces to create their own deductions, tax brackets and tax credits, thus providing the provinces with more flexibility in terms of tax policy and providing taxpayers with a more transparent (albeit a more complex) personal tax system. To date, there are no substantial differences between the federal and provincial systems for individuals, except for Alberta, which has a flat provincial tax rate rather than a graduated rate structure (which is more progressive).

Sales taxes are levied by the federal government and all provincial governments except Alberta. Payroll taxes and capital taxes (on the debt and equity capital of corporations) are levied by both the federal government and some provincial governments.[15]

---

[14] Even so, the provincial corporate income tax rules for these two provinces are, for the most part, very similar to the federal rules.

[15] In recent years, capital taxes have been phased out because they are considered to be unfair. Nova Scotia is the only province which still has a capital tax on ordinary corporations and it is to be eliminated on July 1, 2012. At the federal level, there is only a capital tax on financial institutions.

While it is certainly politically expedient to allow both the federal and provincial governments the flexibility to levy their own taxes, it is not very efficient. Reducing the number of different types of taxes paid by Canadians by reorganizing and harmonizing the federal and provincial income and sales tax systems would not only simplify the tax system for Canadians, it would reduce the cost of collecting taxes for taxpayers and government. One of the ideas discussed during the last series of federal-provincial tax agreement negotiations in the early 1990s was the possibility of allowing provinces more control over their personal tax systems and allowing the federal government exclusive domain over corporate income taxes and sales taxes. (Revenues from all three taxes would still be shared.) One of the advantages of having more federal control over corporate income taxes and sales taxes is that it would allow Canada to better respond to the global economy. This is important because Canada is particularly vulnerable to international pressures because of its large amount of foreign investment.

Although the idea of allowing the federal government exclusive domain over corporate income taxes and sales taxes seems to have died, there is still hope for the harmonization of these taxes. With Ontario harmonizing its corporate tax system effective for 2009 taxation years, only two provinces (Quebec and Alberta) now require corporations to file separate corporate tax returns and have separate corporate tax administrations to deal with this. Several provinces also have harmonized their retail sales taxes with the federal goods and services tax (GST): Newfoundland, Nova Scotia, New Brunswick, Quebec, Ontario and (subject to a referendum in the fall of 2011) British Columbia. These harmonized provincial sales taxes (HST) have generally resulted in lower costs for business (because of input tax credits) and higher costs for the consumer (because of a broader base that includes services). The GST and HST are discussed in greater detail at the end of this chapter.

International Competitiveness and Tax Reform

During recent years, Canada has responded to the increasing globalization of business and the increasing mobility of international labour and capital by reforming its income tax system to keep its rates as low as its major trading partners. This has resulted in a decline in corporate tax revenues and an increasing dependency on other taxes.[16]

---

[16] Because tax deductions and credits are different in each country, international tax comparisons are usually done by comparing taxes as a percentage of GDP in each country. International comparisons show that the overall tax-to-GDP ratio in Canada

The increasing internationalization of business and finance has also caused Canada to take steps to improve its system for taxing income earned on foreign investments and the income earned by foreign entities owned by Canadian taxpayers.[17]

Payroll Taxes

Payroll taxes are used to finance social security, unemployment insurance and health care. There are four major payroll taxes: two federal payroll taxes (unemployment insurance and Canada pension plan premiums), as well as up to two provincial payroll taxes (workers' compensation and provincial health tax premiums[18]).

Payroll taxes are easy to collect but have two distinct disadvantages. First, to the extent that the burden of payroll tax is borne by workers in the form of decreased wages, payroll taxes distribute the tax burden unfairly among Canadians. Second, payroll taxes reduce employment: particularly in the short term, and particularly in the case of small businesses, which tend to be more labour intensive than larger enterprises.

THE PROPERTY TAX SYSTEM IN ONTARIO

Municipal governments provide taxpayers with public school education, services (such as roads, public transit, sewers, water, policing, garbage), social programs (such as welfare, child care and homes for the aged) and community services (such as skating, swimming, and libraries). These services are financed using:

- property taxes,
- provincial grants, and
- user fees.

The term "property tax" generally refers to all property and related taxes, including:

---

in 2007 (33.3%) was lower than the average of 30 OECD countries (35.9%), but higher than the United States (28.3%). See OECD Factbook 2009 at http://puck.sourceoecd.org/vl=4475360/cl=29/nw=1/rpsv/factbook2009/10/04/01/index.htm.

[17] Major changes have also been introduced, which severely restrict the types of income that can now be earned in foreign countries without being subject to tax in Canada. Reporting requirements have also been introduced for individuals and corporations holding foreign investments and for foreign trusts, and Canada has tax information sharing agreements with many foreign countries.

[18] At the present time, only Manitoba, Newfoundland, Ontario and Quebec levy their health tax premiums as payroll taxes.

- residential and non-residential (commercial) property taxes,
- special assessment charges for the cost of local improvements (e.g., hydro, water, sidewalks, sewage systems) and special development charges for other infrastructure requirements (e.g., libraries, roads, parkland, public transit).

Property tax is one of the oldest types of taxes still in existence.[19] Although provincial grants and user fees have been increasing in importance over the years, property taxes are still the primary source of revenue for municipal governments. In many provinces, provincially imposed property taxes are used to help finance public education.

Since there is little uniformity in property tax systems across Canada, this discussion is restricted to Ontario property tax.[20]

In Ontario, the property tax system has worked as follows since 1998:

1. Property tax in Ontario has consisted of a municipal tax and a provincial education tax. The province allows municipalities to set different tax rates for seven different property classes,[21] to divide the "commercial" class into three subclasses and to use up to six other optional classes.[22]

2. The provincial government is responsible for passing legislation, setting assessment policies and determining education tax rates.[23] Individuals who own more than one property (e.g., a home and a cottage) are required to pay education tax on each property.

3. The Municipal Property Assessment Corporation (MPAC), a not-for profit corporation, is responsible for determining current value assessments (CVAs) and classifications.[24] The Assessment Act currently provides for an assessment every four years and for assessment increases to be phased in over four years (see next heading). Assessment decreases are not subject

---

[19] Certain properties are exempt from property taxes. All provinces have exemptions for churches and cemeteries. Ontario also has exemptions for schools, universities, hospitals, museums and certain other uses.

[20] For a fuller discussion of property taxes, see Kitchen, note 10 above; Kitchen, note 17 above, chapter 10; and Karen Treff and David Perry, *Finances of the Nation 2002* (Toronto: Canadian Tax Foundation, 2002), chapter 6.

[21] The seven property classes are residential/farm, multi residential, commercial, industrial, pipelines, farmlands, and managed forests.

[22] The optional classes are new multiresidential, shopping centres, office towers, parking lots, vacant land and large industrial.

[23] Assessment legislation is contained in the Ontario Assessment Act and the education tax rates are set out in Part IV of this Act. The municipalities have no authority to change education tax rates.

[24] Every Ontario municipality is a member of MPAC.

to phase-in. The last CVA valuation date was January 1, 2008 and the next one is January 1, 2012.[25]

4. The municipality is responsible for setting municipal tax rates. Each municipality does this annually for each property class after it sets its budget and examines the amount of tax that can be raised based on the estimated value of all property assessments. The municipality is responsible for collecting both the education and municipal tax portion of property taxes and remitting the education tax to the Ontario government.[26]

5. The Assessment Review Board (ARB), an independent tribunal of the Ministry of the Attorney General, is responsible for hearing assessment appeals.[27]

Current Value Assessment (CVA) method

The current value assessment (CVA) method is a value-based assessment based on the amount that a willing buyer would pay to a willing seller under normal market conditions. The name is a bit of a misnomer because the values used are old "current values".

The Assessment Act currently provides for an assessment every four years and for assessment increases to be phased in over four years. January 1, 2008 valuations are used to determine phased-in CVAs for 2009 to 2012 and January 1, 2012 valuations will be used to determine phased-in CVAs for 2013 to 2016.

For example, if a residential property with a 2008 CVA of $500,000 (based on a January 1, 2005 valuation date) was reassessed at $600,000 (January 1, 2008 valuation date), the $100,000 increase in CVA would be phased each year by 25% of the total CVA change ($25,000), until the final "destination assessment" of $600,000 is reached in 2012 and the assessments would be as follows for 2008 to 2012:

2008	$500,000	(based on January 1, 2005 valuation date)
2009	$525,000	
2010	$550,000	
2011	$575,000	
2012	$600,000	(destination assessment based on January 1, 2008 valuation date)

---

[25] A property owner who disagrees with the CVA must file a Request for Reconsideration with MPAC. For additional information about assessment and the assessment appeal process, see www.mpac.ca.

[26] In some cases there may also be a county or regional tax rate set by the county or regional government. Northern Ontario properties that fall outside of municipal boundaries are subject to a Provincial Land Tax, administered by the Ministry of Finance.

[27] For additional information about the ARB process, see www.arb.gov.on.ca.

In the fall of 2008, MPAC sent notices advising property owners of this information for 2009 to 2012. If a property undergoes a change in CVA during the four-year phase-in period (due, for example, to new construction, renovations or demolition, or revisions to the CVA due to a successful ARB appeal or MPAC Request for Reconsideration), the phased-in CVA and destination assessments will change and MPAC will advise property owners of the revised values.

Assessed Values and Assessment Methods

There are two basic types of assessment:

- *unit-based assessment*, which is based on the size of the property; and
- *value-based assessment*, which is based on an estimate of the property value.

Value-based assessment, such as the CVA method used by the Province of Ontario, is the more popular of the two methods and is used to compute assessed values across Canada and in most developed countries in the world.[28]

The Case for Unit-based Assessment

The main argument for unit-based assessment is that the cost of servicing properties has more to do with the size and location of a property than its actual values. Proponents of unit-based assessment also say that it encourages the purchase of smaller properties and compact development in existing areas. This is important because an existing area (such as Toronto) is cheaper and easier to service than a sprawling suburban development because an existing area already has sewers, roads and other services.[29]

---

[28] For an excellent discussion of additional policy and implementation issues and related research, see Harry Kitchen, Property Taxation: Issues in Implementation, (Working Paper, 2005) at http://www.aucc.ca/_pdf/english/programs/cepra/PropertyTaxation-IssuesinImplementation.pdf

[29] The 1996 Report of the Task Force on the Greater Toronto Area estimated that the savings resulting from a more compact pattern of development would be between $700 million and $1 billion per year (on average) for the next 25 years.

The Case for Value-based Assessment

One of the main arguments for value-based assessment (and against unit-based assessment) is *equity*, and one of the measures of the equity (or fairness) of a tax is its *progressivity*. If owners of properties with high assessment values also have high incomes, property taxes will be progressive and equitable. If the owners have low incomes (e.g., retirees on fixed incomes), property taxes will be *regressive* (and not equitable).

One of the major disadvantages of unit-based assessment is its regressivity: it tends to shift tax burdens from high-income households (which are more likely to live in high-value houses) to low-income households (which are more likely to live in low-value houses). A property tax based on value-based assessment, on the other hand, is more progressive because it often ties in more closely to a taxpayer's ability to pay (i.e., a taxpayer's income and/or wealth). However, the Ontario Fair Tax Commission found that this was not always true — particularly in older, downtown communities, where neighbourhoods are less homogeneous than in the suburbs.

Value-based assessment includes three basic assessment methods:

- market value assessment, which bases assessments on the current values of properties.

- actual value assessment (AVA), which was the method recommended in the 1996 Report of the Task Force on the Greater Toronto Area. Under AVA, residential land and buildings are valued separately (with adjustments for such factors as location, access to public transit and roads), and residential assessments are based on a three-year moving average of these values (which reduces year-to-year fluctuations). Commercial AVA assessments are based on the current in-use rental values of real estate (which is an improvement over using resale values, which may have a speculative element).

- local option assessment, a term that is used here to describe the assessment method, which was used in the past in Ontario where each municipality had the power to assess its properties using the values it chooses.

The CVA method of assessment used in Ontario is a hybrid of market value assessment and AVA. As a value-based assessment method, CVA is probably more equitable than a unit based assessment method, but will not be as effective at containing urban sprawl and reducing infrastructure investment. It is hoped that coordinated planning and development between all levels of government in Ontario will work towards this goal in any case.

THE INCOME TAX SYSTEM

Basic Rules

The Canadian income tax system is based on the residence of its taxpayers (not their citizenship).[30] Residents of Canada are taxed on their world-wide income, and non-residents are taxed only on certain types of Canadian source income, such as the taxable capital gains on the disposition of Canadian real estate.[31]

There are three types of taxpayers in Canada: individuals, corporations and trusts.[32] Individuals and trusts established by a person during his or her lifetime must report their income on a calendar year basis. Corporations and other types of trusts can use any 12-month period to report their income but, once established, this period (called a taxation year) can only be changed with the permission of the CRA.[33]

A taxpayer's taxable income is his net income under Division B of the Act minus special deductions under Division C. Net income under Division B is the sum of a taxpayer's income from:

- employment
- business
- property (such as rental income)
- taxable capital gains net of allowable capital losses
- other income (such as retirement income)

minus

- other deductions (such as child care expenses and contributions to a registered retirement savings plan (RRSP)).

Net income is an important subtotal in the computation of taxable income because it is used as a measure of economic income for the purposes of many credits in the Act that are based on a

---

[30] Corporations are considered to be resident in Canada if their mind and management is in Canada or if they are incorporated in Canada (s. 250(4)).

[31] Canadian domestic law states that a non-resident must file a tax return reporting taxable capital gains from the disposition of Canadian real estate and certain other sources of Canadian income, such as Canadian employment and business income. The law also states that a flat Canadian withholding tax must be withheld from rental, interest and other payments paid to non-residents. These rules can (and are) overruled by the provisions of the various income tax treaties negotiated between Canada and its trading partners.

[32] Partnerships do not file returns and pay tax. Instead, they allocate their income to their partners, who pay the tax. Partnerships meeting certain asset, revenue or expense tests must file a partnership information return reporting the income or loss allocated to each partner.

[33] Interpretation Bulletin IT-179R (1993), para. 2.

EXHIBIT 1
Major Division C deductions

Individuals Only

- $750,000 Lifetime capital gains exemption for shares of qualified small business corporations[a]

Corporations Only

- Dividend income received from taxable Canadian corporations[b]
- Charitable donations[c]

All Taxpayers

- Eligible losses from other years[d]

---

[a] s. 110.6.
[b] s. 112.
[c] s. 110.1.
[d] s. 111.

"means" test. The major Division C items that are deducted from net income in computing taxable income are set out in Exhibit 1.

Rental Income (Loss)

The tax treatment of a taxpayer's rental income or loss is very much determined by whether the income is *business income* or *property income* — i.e., whether the activities relate to the passive activity of owning real estate property or the more active activity of carrying on a rental business. This is important, as it affects a taxpayer's ability to claim certain real estate development costs as deductions[34] and affects how a non-resident of Canada will be taxed.[35]

---

[34] See ss. 20(1)(cc) and 20(1)(dd), which restrict the deduction of expenses of representation (e.g., regarding rezoning) and site investigation, respectively, to those relating to a business. See also s. 18(3.4), which exempts "a corporation whose principal business is throughout the year the leasing, rental or sale, or the development of lease, rental or sale, or any combination thereof, of real property owned by it to or for a person with whom the corporation is dealing at arm's length" from the restrictions in s. 18(3.1) for the deduction of interest and other soft costs incurred during the course of construction.

[35] Income earned from a business in Canada by a non-resident is subject to tax under Part I of the Act: the rules and rates are the same rules for non-residents as for residents. If the rental income is property income, however, Part XIII applies and a tax equal to 25% of the gross rents must be withheld and remitted by the tenant. No deductions are available unless an election is filed under s. 216 of the Act.

Over the years, one of the principles that have evolved in the courts is the presumption that a corporation will be considered to carry on a business.[36] Unfortunately, this rule does not apply to individuals. In the case of an individual, rental income will generally be treated as property income except when services are provided that are not incidental to the ownership and maintenance of the property. For example, the rental of an apartment building by an individual would be rental income, but the running of a hotel (with maid and laundry services) would be a business.[37]

In order to calculate a taxpayer's rental income or loss, the following steps should be followed.

Step 1	Determine a taxpayer's gross rents for each property.
Step 2	Deduct operating expenses for each property to compute the income or loss figure.
Step 3	Compute the overall net rental income or loss for all properties, including any rental income allocated by a partnership.[38]
Step 4	Deduct capital cost allowance on each of the properties owned using the appropriate rates, but do not create or increase an overall loss position.

If the net result is a profit, it is subject to tax. If the net result is a loss, it is then necessary to determine whether any rental operation resulting in a loss contains a personal element. If the rental operation has no personal element and is clearly commercial, the loss will be deductible against other income. If the rental operation has a personal element — because, for example, it results from the rental of a room or apartment in a home or the rental of a vacation property when it is not being used, or the rental of a property to a relative — it will then be necessary to consider, first, whether the activity is undertaken in "pursuit of profit". If an activity with a personal element is found to be in "pursuit of profit" — because it can be established, based on the facts, that the taxpayer carried on the activity in a business-like manner and intended to make a profit outside of an eventual capital gain on the sale of the property — the

---

[36] See Interpretation Bulletin IT-420R3 (1992), para. 13 on this point.

[37] For a complete list of criteria, see Interpretation Bulletin IT-434R (1982), para. 2 to 8.

[38] Partnership rental income allocated to a partner is net of capital cost allowance.

loss will be deductible from other income.[39] If this cannot be established, the loss of a rental activity with a personal element will be denied.

Construction of a Real Estate Project

The Act contains special rules restricting claims for capital cost allowance and interest and other expenses in the case of real estate. The purpose of these rules is to prevent real estate deductions from being used as a tax shelter (to offset other income) while real estate appreciates in value.

Costs Incurred in Connection with the Land Purchase and While It is Vacant

The cost of land for tax purposes includes its purchase price and acquisition costs (such as legal expenses and land transfer tax), as well as interest and property taxes capitalized under the rule in subsection 18(2). Subsection 18(2) requires that all interest and property taxes incurred in respect of vacant land be added to the cost of the land unless one of the following exception tests is met:

1. Interest and property taxes on vacant land can be deducted if the land is *used in a business other than a real estate resale or development business* (e.g., land used as a parking lot by a manufacturing business);[40]

2. Interest and property taxes on vacant land can be deducted if the land is *held primarily for the purpose of gaining/producing income from the land* for the year;[41]

3. Interest and property taxes on vacant land can be deducted to the extent of any *income from the land* (e.g., if the land is rented to a farmer or parking lot operator and earns rental income);[42]

4. Interest and property taxes can be deducted to the extent of a taxpayer's *base-level deduction* if the *principal business* of the corporation of the taxpayer is leasing, rental, development

---

[39] This doctrine was established in the Supreme Court of Canada's decisions in *Stewart v. Canada*, 2002 SCC 46 and applied in *Walls v. Canada*, 2002 SCC 47. The fact situations in these two cases had no personal element, and the losses were allowed.

[40] s. 18(2)(c).

[41] s. 18(2)(d).

[42] s. 18(2)(e).

or resale of real estate.[43] (Such a corporation is often referred to as a *principal business corporation.*[44]) A principal business corporation's base level deduction is $1 million multiplied by the prescribed rate of interest[45] (but this $1 million limit must be shared among associated corporations as defined in section 256).

Costs Incurred While the Building is under Construction (s. 18(3.1) Capitalizes Most Soft Costs)

During construction, not only are the interest and property taxes non-deductible, most of the costs incurred cannot be deducted. (One exception is landscaping.) Instead, they must be added to the cost of the building (not the land), and deducted as capital cost allowance later, when the building is available for use.

There are two basic types of costs incurred during the construction of a real estate project: *hard costs* (which include the cost of bricks, cement, wiring, heating and cooling systems, elevators, and architectural and engineering design fees) and *soft costs* (which include interest, property taxes, and various fees and overhead costs). All hard costs must be capitalized and added to the cost of the building; it doesn't matter when they are incurred.[46] However, soft costs incurred after the building is completed may be deducted according to special rules. (See Exhibit 2 for a list of common soft costs and their tax treatment.)

There are some common exceptions to the capitalization rule in subsection 18(3.1). Landscaping expense paid (which was already mentioned) is one. Another is a post-construction financing fee, because it is incurred during the construction period but is not related to the construction phase. A third exception results from a special rule that says that soft costs can be deducted against any rental profits in the year of construction if the project is completed or partially completed during the year (but you cannot create a loss).[47]

---

[43]   s. 18(2)(f).

[44]   Regulation 1100(12).

[45]   s. 18(2.2).

[46]   s. 18(1)(b).

[47]   s. 20(29).

EXHIBIT 2
Common soft costs and their tax treatment

Item	Tax Treatment
Interest	Capitalize if land is vacant (s. 18(2)) and if building is under construction (s. 18(3.1)). Deduct if building is available for use (s. 20(1)(c))
Property taxes	Capitalize if land is vacant (s. 18(2)) and if building is under 18(3.1)). Deduct if building is available for use (s. 9)
Fees (legal, bank, accounting)	Capitalize if building is under construction and the fee relates to construction (s. 18(3.1). If building is not under construction, amount must be capitalized if it relates to the purchase of an asset (s. 18(1)(b)) or written off on a straight-line basis over five years if it relates to the issue of shares or debt or partnership units.[†] In any other case, deduct 100% (s. 9)
Landscaping	Deduct in the year paid if it relates to business premises (s. 20(1)(aa)).
Maintenance, insurance	Capitalize if building is under construction and the fee relates to construction (s. 18(3.1)). Otherwise deduct 100% (s. 9).
Expenses of representation	Capitalize if building is under construction and the fee relates to construction (s. 18(3.1)). Otherwise deduct 100% (s. 20(1)(cc)).
Site investigation	Capitalize if building is under construction and the fee relates to construction (s. 18(3.1)). Otherwise deduct 100% (s. 20(1)(dd)).
Utilities service connection	Capitalize if building is under construction and the fee relates to construction (s. 18(3.1)). Otherwise deduct 100% (s. 20(1)(ee)).

[†] s. 20(1)(e). If the fees relate to the issue of debt, and the loan is repaid in less than five years, the balance of the fees are written off in the year that the loan is repaid. If the bank fee is annual (e.g., a letter of credit fee), it can be written off 100% each year (s. 20(1)(e.1)).

After Construction Is Completed

Once construction is completed, there is no requirement to capitalize soft costs. As long as the building is available for use, capital cost allowance can be claimed. The general rule is that each rental building costing $500,000 or more must go into a separate capital cost allowance class.[48] The purpose (and effect) of this rule is to recognize immediate recapture of capital cost allowance claimed on the sale of the property. For example, if a building originally costing $1,000,000 has had capital cost allowance claims of $300,000 made over the years, its undepreciated capital cost will be $700,000. If it is sold for $1,200,000, the $500,000 profit will be taxed as $300,000 of recaptured capital cost allowance (which is regular business or property income) and a $200,000 capital gain (which is only one-half taxable).[49]

Most buildings are in Class 1, which has three rates because of a change made in 2007 for previously unused (i.e., new) non-residential buildings acquired after March 18, 2007. The general Class 1 rate is 4%, and this rate still applies to many buildings: all residential buildings and any non-residential building that was not acquired "new" after March 18, 2007. The 4% rate means that capital cost allowance (CCA) may be claimed at the rate of 4% on a declining balance basis (2% in the first year). For previously unused (new) buildings acquired after March 18, 2007, the Class 1 rates are 10% (5% in the first year) if the building is used 90% or more for manufacturing or processing in Canada and 6% (3% in the first year) for any other non-residential use. [50]

Another general rule is that you cannot create a rental loss with capital cost allowance. As a result, in most cases, a real estate property will only create a tax shelter against non-rental income (i.e., deductions that offset other income, such as salary) if it has actual net cash rental losses. If a taxpayer owns more than one rental property, capital cost allowance on one property can be used to offset rental income on other rental properties; *but* capital cost allowance cannot be used to create or increase a rental loss to offset other income, such as salary.[51]

The following properties are exempt from this rental income restriction:

---

[48] (Reg. 1101(1ac)).

[49] Properties other than real estate rental properties are pooled into one CCA class. The effect of this is that you can offset recapture of capital cost allowance by purchasing another asset of the same class. In the example given above, if another asset of the same class costing at least $30,000 had been purchased before the end of the year, the $30,000 of recapture would have been avoided.

[50] Buildings used for farming or fishing that are of frame, log, stucco on frame, galvanized iron or corrugated metal construction may qualify as Class 6 assets and be eligible for capital cost allowance at the rate of 10% (5% in the first year).

[51] (Reg. 1100(11) to (14)).

- buildings that are not used more than 50% for the purpose of gaining or producing rental income;[52] and
- buildings owned by a principal business corporation (as defined earlier).

If the rental income is earned by a Canadian controlled private corporation,[53] it is important to determine whether the income qualifies as Canadian *active business income*, since, if it does:

- the income is eligible for a lower initial tax rate, and
- the shares of the corporation may qualify for the lifetime $500,000 capital gains exemption for shares of qualified small business corporations.

Two types of real estate activities carried on by Canadian controlled private corporations qualify as Canadian active business income. They are:

- income from the development and resale of Canadian real estate (but not capital gains); and
- rental income from a property in Canada if
    (a) it is incidental to an active business (such as the temporary rental of excess warehouse space by a manufacturing business); or
    (b) it results from a rental business that employs more than five full-time employees throughout the year; or
    (c) it results from rentals to an association that deducts the rent payments in computing its Canadian active business.[54]

SALES OF REAL ESTATE

Capital Gains versus Income

When a real estate investment is sold, the profit may be taxed either as business income (which is 100% taxable) or a capital gain (which is only one-half taxable) — it all depends upon the facts of the situation. For example, an investor who buys lots, builds houses and sells them for a living would report the profit on the sale of the houses as business income. A long-term investor, who uses or rents

---

[52] See regulation 1100(14) and the decision in the case of *Canada Trust Co. v. MNR*, 85 DTC 322 (TCC).

[53] A Canadian controlled private corporation is a private corporation (not listed on a Canadian stock exchange) that is incorporated in Canada and not controlled by a non-resident or a public company, or a combination of the two (s. 125(7)).

[54] See definitions of active business income and specified investment income in ss. 125(7) and 129(6).

his or her real estate for several years before selling it, is more likely to report the gain or loss on its sale as a capital gain. (The same logic holds in the case of losses.)

Because determining whether a profit on the sale of real estate on account of capital or income is one of the most commonly litigated areas in tax law, the courts have developed a series of tests that are used to differentiate between the two. The courts look at a taxpayer's whole course of conduct for the period before, during and after the transaction and the factors that motivated the sale to determine whether the taxpayer's intention was to resell the property for a profit. In looking at intention, the courts look at the taxpayer's *primary* intention in purchasing the property (e.g. to rezone it and build a shopping mall), and his or her *secondary* intention (i.e., the profitable alternative that the taxpayer had in mind in case he couldn't get the proper zoning or financing to develop the property). Exhibit 3 sets out some facts that the courts would consider in assessing a taxpayer's primary and secondary intention.

Computation of a Taxable Capital Gain and Allowable Capital Loss

A taxable capital gain is one-half of a capital gain and an allowable capital loss is one-half of a capital loss. A capital gain (or capital loss) is computed as the *proceeds of disposition* received (which is generally the selling price of the property) net of selling costs (such as legal expenses and commissions), minus the *adjusted cost base* of the property. The adjusted cost base of the property is the cost of the property adjusted for certain items. The adjusted cost base of land and/or a building would include:

- the original cost of the land and/or building plus legal fees, real estate commissions, land transfer taxes and other costs relating to its purchase;
- in the case of land, any interest and property taxes incurred when the land was vacant that were not deductible; and
- in the case of a building, any soft costs incurred during the period of construction that were not deductible.

Allocation of Proceeds between Land and Building

When real estate is sold, the proceeds of disposition must be reasonably allocated between land and buildings to determine the tax consequences of the sale.[55] The general rules are as follows.

---

[55] s. 68.

EXHIBIT 3
Determining whether a profit is a capital gains versus income — tests developed by the courts to assess intention

Facts indicating capital gain	Facts indicating income
• Intention is to hold the property a long time	• Intention in buying the property is to resell it
• Property is held a long time	• Property is held a short time
• Sale is unsolicited	• Property is listed or advertised for sale
• Expropriation	
• Primary intention feasible, but sale occurred because primary intention was thwarted	• Primary intention not feasible
• Location and zoned use of the land is suitable	• Location and zoned use of the land not suitable
• Evidence that intention carried out	• No evidence that intention carried out
• Property not highly leveraged	• Property highly leveraged
• Debt is long-term	• Debt is short term
• Taxpayer is not a real estate investor or broker	• Taxpayer is a real estate investor or broker
• Co-investor is not a real estate investor or broker	• Co-investor is a real estate investor or broker
• No history of trading in real estate	• History of trading in real estate

Source: Interpretation Bulletin IT-218R (1986), para. 3.

- If the proceeds received for a building are less than the building's undepreciated capital cost (its original cost less capital cost allowance) the result is a terminal loss that is fully deductible.[56] For example, if a rental building with a cost of $580,000 and a undepreciated capital cost of $365,000 is sold for $300,000, the owner will have a terminal loss of $65,000, which is fully deductible.

---

[56] s. 20(16) of the Act. Special rules apply if a reasonable allocation of the proceeds results in a terminal loss on the building (which is fully deductible) and a capital gain on the land (which is only one-half taxable). In this case, the terminal loss will be denied (to the extent of the capital gain), and the capital gain will be reduced by the same amount (s. 13(21.1)(a)). Similarly, if a building is disposed of but the land is retained, the terminal loss will be reduced to one-half of the loss otherwise deductible (s. 13 (21.1)(b)). These rules were introduced to counteract the decision in *The Queen v. Malloney's Studio Limited*, 78 DTC 6278 (SCC), a case where the taxpayer was able to have no proceeds allocated to a building that was demolished (disposed of for zero proceeds) immediately prior to the sale of the property.

- If the proceeds received for a building are greater than a building's undepreciated capital cost, there will be recapture (which is fully taxable); if the proceeds received are greater than the actual cost of the building, there will also be a capital gain (which is only one-half taxable). Consider the same example of a rental building with a cost of $580,000 and a undepreciated capital cost of $365,000, but assume, in this case, that it is sold for $590,000. The taxpayer, in this case, would have recapture of $215,000 ($580,000 − $365,000) and a taxable capital gain of $5,000 (1/2[$590,000 − $580,000]), and would include both these amounts in income.

- The amount of proceeds allocated to land will determine whether there is a taxable capital gain or an allowable capital loss on the sale of the land.

As a rule of thumb, a vendor will prefer to allocate more proceeds of disposition to land (than a building) because the tax on a capital gain is less than the tax on recapture. At the same time, a purchaser will prefer to allocate more of the amount paid to the cost of the building purchased because this will increase the amount of capital cost allowance that can be claimed in the future.

The allocation that is negotiated should be set out in the agreement of purchase and sale of the property since (according to the CRA) if "the parties to the agreement are dealing at arm's length, the agreement is *prima facie* evidence of the reasonableness of the allocation specified therein. A taxpayer's allocation is further supported where there is evidence of hard bargaining between the parties involved in arriving at that allocation."[57]

The Act provides for a one-sided adjustment if a transaction takes place between non-arm's length parties for proceeds that are not equal to a property's fair market value (unless it is a gift).[58] This one-sided adjustment is a deterrent that is designed to prevent non-arm's length taxpayers from transacting at amounts that are not fair market values; if they do, this one-sided adjustment results in double tax.[59]

---

[57] Interpretation Bulletin IT-220R2 (1990), para. 5 as amended by IT-220R2SR (1994).

[58] A gift (other than to a spouse) is deemed for tax purposes to be a sale at fair market value with a two-sided adjustment. The donor is taxed on the taxable capital gain based on the fair market value deemed proceeds and the donee's cost of the asset is the same fair market value (s. 69).

[59] Section 69. The rules work as follows using, as an example, a property worth $100,000. If the actual proceeds of disposition is greater than fair market value (e.g., $120,000), then the vendor uses the actual proceeds (of $120,000) to determine his or

Non-arm's length is a defined term — some common examples of taxpayers who are deemed by the Act to be non-arm's length because they are related (for tax purposes) are:

- parents and children (including grandchildren and in-laws)
- siblings and siblings-in-law
- spouses
- a taxpayer and a corporation controlled by the taxpayer or a related person.

When non-arm's length parties have made a reasonable attempt at establishing fair market values, and the agreement of purchase and sale contains a price adjustment clause (which serves to adjust the proceeds in light of a CRA assessment), the CRA will generally allow both parties to the transaction to adjust the price at which the transaction took place at fair market value.[60] Price adjustment clauses are, therefore, advisable in all purchase and sale agreements between non-arm's length parties.

FORMS OF OWNERSHIP AND INCOME TAXES
Individual Ownership
If real estate is owned by an individual, any rental income or loss and any profit on the sale of the real estate is included in the individual's taxable income for the calendar year and is subject to personal income tax. The personal income tax system is a graduated system with four federal rates, provincial tax and provincial surtaxes.[61]

Exhibit 4 sets out the four federal tax brackets in 2011.

Exhibit 5 sets out the provincial rates in the Province of Ontario for 2003. The tax payable in each case is reduced by a taxpayer's eligible tax credits.[62]

---

her capital gain, recapture and/or terminal loss; but the purchaser is limited to the fair market value of the property in determining his cost of the property (i.e., $100,000) (s. 69(1)(a)). If the actual proceeds of disposition is less than fair market value (e.g., $95,000), it is the vendor who computes his or her tax consequences based on the property's fair market value (of $100,000), and the purchaser must use the actual proceeds received (of $95,000) as his cost (s. 69(1)(b)).

[60] Interpretation Bulletin IT-169 (1974).

[61] A surtax is a tax on tax.

[62] There are personal credits for various amounts, including a basic credit, a credit for age 65 and over and credits for certain dependants and medical expenses, which are indexed for inflation. There are also credits for other amounts, such as tuition and education expenses and donations, which are not indexed.

EXHIBIT 4
Federal personal income tax rates for 2011

Taxable Income	Tax
First $41,544	15%
$41,544–$83,088	22%
$83,088–$128,800	26%
Over $128,800	29%

EXHIBIT 5
Ontario personal income tax rates for 2011*

Taxable Income	Tax
First $37,774	5.05%
$37,774–$75,550	9.15%
Over $75,550	11.16%

* A provincial surtax of 20% also applies to basic Ontario tax in excess of $4,078 and a provincial surtax of 36% applies to basic Ontario tax in excess of $5,219. There is also an Ontario health premium which is levied on taxable income income in excess of $20,000.
See http://www.rev.gov.on.ca/en/tax/healthpremium/rates.html.

Individuals are also subject to an alternative minimum tax (AMT) calculation, but only pay AMT when it exceeds their regular tax liability. AMT is calculated on adjusted taxable income in excess of $40,000 at the federal rate of 15% (adjusted for certain tax credits) plus surtaxes and provincial taxes. The purpose of the AMT is to calculate a tax at a fairly low rate (15% on income over $40,000) on an alternative tax base that treats all income the same and denies a deduction for special tax deductions. There are several AMT adjustments, but only two are applicable to real estate investments:[63]

---

[63] Other adjustments are listed in Division E.1 of the Act.

- The first adjustment is for capital gains and loses.[64]
- A second adjustment denies a deduction for losses and carrying charges (such as interest expense) relating to an investment made after 1995 in
  - a partnership in which the taxpayer was a passive partner,
  - a limited partnership, or
  - a tax shelter.[65]

Owning real estate personally rather than through a corporation has some advantages and disadvantages. These are summarized in Exhibit 6.

General Partnership

A partnership exists when persons carrying on a business in common with a view to profit arrange to share any resulting profits and losses. With a partnership, the income or loss flows through to the partners and is taxed in their hands. This means that the partnership must first compute its income or loss as if it were a separate taxpayer and then allocate amounts to each partner in accordance with his partnership interest.[66] Because partnership income is taxed on this flow-through basis, any withdrawals of cash from a partnership (called "drawings") are tax-free.[67]

When a partner eventually sells a partnership interest, the profit or loss on the sale is usually considered to be a capital gain or loss and is computed as the difference between the proceeds of disposition received (net of selling costs) minus the adjusted cost base of the partnership interest. To compute the adjusted cost base of his or her partnership interest, a partner must keep track of his original cost, add the income allocated each year and subtract any losses and drawings, including (or deducting) 100%, rather than one-half, of any capital gain (or loss).[68]

A general partnership does not provide any liability protection for its partners: each partner is jointly and severally liable for the

---

[64] 30% of the excess of capital gains over capital losses for the year must be added back for AMT purposes (s. 127.52(1)(d)).

[65] s. 127 (5.2)(c.1) to (c. 3).

[66] s. 96.

[67] If the adjusted cost base of a partnership interest becomes negative, there is no immediate capital gain unless the interest has been sold or the partner is a passive investor or a limited partner (s. 40(3)).

[68] There are other additions and deductions in computing the adjusted cost base of a partnership interest, but these are the major ones.

EXHIBIT 6
Advantages and disadvantages of holding real estate personally rather than in a corporation

Advantages

1. Rental losses can be used to offset other sources of income.
2. Less expensive to set and maintain than a corporation.
3. It is possible to incorporate later on a tax-free basis as long as the property is not inventory.[a]
4. There is no capital tax on the investment because capital tax only applies to corporations.
5. Rental income qualifies as earned income for RRSP purposes.[b]

Disadvantages

1. No limited liability.
2. The income is not eligible for a deferral of tax unless it is Canadian active business income.
3. No anonymity unless the property is owned by a corporation acting as a bare trustee.[c]
4. Capital cost allowance limited to rental income.

---

[a] s. 85(1).

[b] A taxpayer's RRSP contribution limit is the lesser of the money limit for the year (in 2011, $22,450) and 18% of a taxpayer's earned income as defined in s. 146(1).

[c] The term bare trust is used to describe an arrangement in which a bare trustee (usually a corporation) holds a real estate property in trust for the actual owner of the property. Under a bare trust arrangement, the title to the property is registered in the name of the bare trustee, but the beneficial ownership is conveyed to the actual owner by means of a trust agreement. The use of a bare trustee is common in the real estate industry because it allows the actual owner of the property to remain anonymous.

debts of the partnership and for any wrongful acts or omissions of any partners acting in the ordinary course of the partnership's business. This is referred to as joint and several liability and is the major disadvantage of using the partnership form of business organization. It is possible to mitigate this problem by:

• having the partners incorporate companies to hold their partnership interests,[69]

---

[69] To accomplish this, each partner would incorporate a company and sell his partnership interest to the company, electing under s. 85 to have the transaction take place on a tax-free basis.

- structuring the partnership as a limited partnership rather than a general partnership (this is only feasible if the partners are passive investors), or
- incorporating the partnership on a tax-free basis as soon as losses stop and profits begin to be earned.[70]

The advantages and disadvantages of owning real estate in a partnership as compared to a corporation are similar to those set out in Exhibit 6 above.

Joint Venture

As indicated above, a partnership, by definition, must carry on a business with a view to profit. If there is no business being carried on, the co-ownership arrangement will be a joint venture rather than a partnership. This is the major difference between a partnership and a joint venture. Under common law, a joint venture will either be a *joint tenancy* or a *tenancy in common*.

Joint ventures are common in situations where the co-ownership arrangement is limited to a single undertaking or property. Rather than the partnership owning the real estate, the joint venturers themselves are registered on title either as joint tenants or as tenants in common. The difference between a joint tenancy and tenants in common is important, particularly on death:

- *Joint tenants* take title to the property at the same time and must own the same amount. Joint tenants cannot "will" their interests: on death, the interest in the property automatically passes to the surviving joint tenants.
- *Tenants in Common* can take title at different times, can own different amounts and can will their interests.

For tax purposes, the major difference between partnerships and joint ventures is how capital cost allowance (CCA) is calculated. In a partnership, CCA is deducted at the partnership level because the partnership (not the partners) owns the real estate. In a joint venture, each venturer can determine his or her own CCA claim because he or she owns (a proportionate share of) the real estate directly. As a result, a joint venturer can determine his own CCA claim, whereas a partner cannot.

---

[70] Section 85(2), where a s. 85(1) rollover is available. In some jurisdictions, land transfer tax will be payable on the transfer of the land from the partnership to the corporation. As a result, this alternative will not be attractive.

Limited Partnerships, Passive Partnerships and Tax Shelters

Limited partnerships combine the flow-through advantage of general partnerships with the limited liability advantage of corporations. The only caveat is that limited partners must be passive investors: they can have a say in key decisions, but they cannot manage the business.[71] This makes limited partnerships ideal for syndicating rental properties and other investments with large writeoffs to passive investors.

Limited partnerships are set up under provincial limited partnership legislation. They must have one general partner (which is usually a company with no assets) who manages the property. The remaining partners are limited partners. Each limited partner has limited liability — each limited partner's liability is limited to his or her capital account and any debts guaranteed personally.

The Act contains several restrictions for limited partnership losses and deductions, the most important being that limited partnership losses are limited to the investor's at-risk amount, which is essentially the adjusted cost base of his or her partnership interest less any debts owed by him to the partnership.[72]

The terms *tax shelter* and *promoter* are defined terms that are subject to a set of very complicated rules. Essentially, a tax shelter is an investment that can be written off over four years, and a promoter is the person who sells the shelter.[73] The rules provide that a tax shelter must be registered, and that the promoter of a tax shelter must file a special tax shelter information return indicating, among other things, who the investors are, how much was invested by each person and what the annual writeoff is for each investor. The intent of these rules is to enable the CRA to monitor tax shelter investments more closely.

---

[71] If they do, they lose their limited liability status under provincial law.

[72] Two other restrictions were discussed previously. These are:

  (a) the AMT adjustment, denying a deduction for losses and carrying charges (such as interest expense) relating to an investment made after 1995 in
- a partnership in which the taxpayer was a passive partner,
- a limited partnership, or
- a tax shelter

    (see text surrounding note 65).

  (b) the rule giving rise to an immediate capital gain if the adjusted cost base of a limited or passive partnership interest becomes negative (see note 67).

[73] See ss. 162 and 237.1.

Corporations

Corporate tax rates are complicated because there are rate reductions being phased in over the next few years. Corporations that are resident in Canada pay federal tax at a general rate of 28%[74] (plus applicable provincial taxes) on taxable income earned in Canada. Income that is not eligible for any other special tax treatment is eligible for a federal tax rate reduction of 11.5% in 2011 (10% in 2010 and 13% in 2013 and subsequent years).[75] The corporate tax rate including surtax but net of this reduction in 2011 is 16.5% (28% − 11.50%)

The Small Business Deduction

In 2011, the federal corporate rate is reduced to 11% by the 17% "small business deduction" for the first $500,000 of Canadian active business income earned annually by a Canadian controlled private corporation (CCPC).[76] Many provinces also offer similar rate reductions for active business income.[77] Public companies and private companies controlled by non-resident and/or public companies are not CCPCs and are, therefore, not eligible for the small business deduction.[78]

As mentioned earlier, only two types of real estate activities carried on by CCPCS qualify as Canadian active business income:

- income from the development and resale of Canadian real estate (but not capital gains); and

---

[74] The 28% is the net of a 38% statutory rate and a 10% abatement for income earned in a province. The purpose of the 10% abatement leaves room for provinces to tax corporate income. Some provincial corporate rates are higher than 10% and some are lower than 10%.

[75] All rate reductions are prorated for non-calendar taxation years that include January 1st of the year mentioned. These federal tax rate reductions do not apply to income that eligible for the following special tax treatments
- the 17% small business deduction
- the Canadian manufacturing and processing income (discussed later in these notes) and
- the refundable tax provisions for investment income

[76] This $500,000 annual limit is shared by associated corporations (as defined in s. 256). This prevents a taxpayer from multiplying the available annual limit by incorporating more than one company.

[77] In Ontario, for example, the low small business rate for CCPCs is 4.5% on the first $500,000 annually whereas the general corporate rate is 11.75 for calendar years ending December 31, 2011 (because the rate is 12% for income earned to June 30, 2011, reducing to 11.5 effective July 1, 2011, 11% effective July 1, 2012 and 10% effective July 1, 2013). The manufacturing and processing rate is 10%.

[78] See definition of Canadian controlled private corporation in s. 125(7).

- rental income from a property in Canada if:
  (a) it is incidental to an active business (such as the temporary rental of excess warehouse space by a manufacturing business); or
  (b) it results from a rental business that employs more than five full-time employees throughout the year; or
  (c) it results from rentals to an associated corporation that deducts the rent payments in computing its Canadian active business income.[79]

This restricted definition of Canadian active business income prevents most investors from incorporating holding companies to own real estate rental properties to take advantage of the low small business rate on Canadian active business income unless the business employs more than five full-time employees.

Investment Income

Taxable capital gains and rental income not meeting the Canadian active business income test constitute "investment income" when they are earned by private corporations. This investment income is taxed at the regular 28% federal rate plus an additional 6-2/3% tax that applies only to investment income. This combined 34-2/3% initial federal rate ensures that investment income is taxed at approximately the same initial rate whether it is earned directly by an high income individual investor[80] or through his or her private holding company.[81] On the payment of dividends out of investment income, there is a refund of tax (26.67%) that reduces the net federal rate to 8% (34.67% – 26.67%) and the combined federal-Ontario rate in 2011 to 19.75% (8% + 11.25% for December 31 year ends). The general corporate income tax rates and the rates applicable to CCPCs earning Canadian active business income and private corporations earning investment income are set out in Exhibit 7.

The tax systems for CCPCs earning active business income and private corporations earning investment income are somewhat complicated — but there are (at least) three good reasons for this:

---

[79] Note 54 above.

[80] The top personal rate in Ontario is 46.41% in 2011.

[81] The total corporate rate on investment income is 46.42% in 2011, including the 11.75% Ontario tax.

EXHIBIT 7
2011 Corporate income tax rates in Ontario (December 31 year ends)

	General	Canadian Active Business Income (CCPCs)	Investment Income (Private corps.)
Basic federal rate	38.00%	38.00%	38.00%
Federal abatement for provincial tax	(10.00)	(10.00)	(10.00)
	28.00	28.00	28.00
Federal rate reduction	(11.50)	–	–
Small business deduction	–	(17.00)	–
Refundable tax on investment income	–	–	6.67
Federal tax	16.50%	11.00%	34.67%
Ontario tax			
— 4.5% small business rate	–	4.50	–
— 11.75% regular rate	11.75	–	11.75
Total tax	28.25%	15.50%	46.42%
Tax refunded on payment of dividend	–	–	(26.67)
Net tax after dividend	28.25%	15.50%	19.75%

1. One reason is to reduce the net corporate rate (after the payment of dividends) to about 20%. This is necessary because the personal tax system taxes dividends using a method that provides a tax credit for this level of corporate tax.[82]

2. A second reason is to allow CCPCs earning Canadian active business income a tax deferral as long as income is retained and reinvested in the active business. This is because it is often hard for small businesses to obtain financing from other sources, such as banks and outside investors.

3. A third reason is to not allow private companies earning investment income any deferral of tax. As a result, the corporate rate reduction for this income occurs only when the income is paid out as a dividend.

$750,000 Capital Gains Exemption

Another important personal income tax deduction is available to owners of Canadian controlled private corporations earning Canadian active business income: the $750,000 lifetime capital gains exemption for capital gains on the sales of shares of qualified small business

---

[82] The system works as follows. First, the amount reported as taxable income is the dividend received multiplied (or "grossed up") by 1.25% (a formula amount that compensates for a 20% corporate tax rate). Second, a dividend tax credit is provided that is approximately equal to the 25% gross-up. The dividend gross-up and credit system applies only to dividends from Canadian corporations received by shareholders who are Canadian individuals. [Canadian dividends received by corporations are totally tax-free (because of a deduction under s. 112) except for a temporary 33-1/3% Part IV tax levied on private corporations until they pay out such dividends to shareholders (s. 186)]. For example, if a $100 dividend is received by an individual taxed at the top rate, the individual pays federal tax of $36.25 (29%) on $125 of taxable income (s. 2(1)), and subtracts a $16.67 federal dividend tax credit (two-thirds of the $25 gross-up) (s. 121). Provincial taxes are owing as well as the $19.58 of federal tax ($36.25 – $16.67). In Ontario this results in total tax of $31.33 (31.33%) at the top rate, which is far less than the 46.41% that is owing on regular income at the top rate.

Canadian public company dividends have an even higher gross-up and dividend tax credit because they pay a higher rate of corporate tax: 16.5% in 2011, and 15% in 2012 and subsequent years. This enhanced gross-up (41% for 2011 and 38% for 2012 and subsequent years) and tax credit system for eligible dividends provides them with a lower personal tax rate than "non-eligible" having a 25% gross up. For example, whereas the top marginal rate of "non-eligible" dividends is 31.33% (see above), the top marginal rate on eligible dividends is closer to the rate for capital gains (23.21% in Ontario).

Private companies that have a general rate income pool (GRIP) account can also pay eligible dividends but CCPCs that have all their income taxed at lower rates because of the small business deduction for Canadian active business income and the refundable tax treatment for investment income (such as rental income and taxable capital gains) and receive no eligible dividends will not have a GRIP account.

corporations (QSBCs).[83] The $750,000 capital gains exemption is really a misnomer, because the deduction is only $375,000 (1/2 × $750,000), because it is claimed against the taxable (1/2) portion of a $750,000 capital gain.

The $375,000 capital gains deduction is essentially the least of two amounts:

1. A taxpayer's unused lifetime limit: $375,000 *less* any deduction claimed in prior years.[84]

2. A taxpayer's net taxable capital gains[85] to date *less* any capital gains deductions claimed in prior years *less* a taxpayer's cumulative net investment loss (CNIL) account. A CNIL account is the sum of a taxpayer's post-87 investment and rental losses and expenses minus his or her post-87 investment and rental income and expenses.

In order to qualify as shares of a QSBC, the shares must pass the following three tests:

Test #1 — The Company Must Be a Small Business Corporation at the Date of Sale

A *small business corporation* is a CCPC that has all or substantially all (at least 90%) of its assets (at fair market value) either:

- used primarily (50%) in an active business carried on principally (50%) in Canada by itself or a related corporation, or
- invested in shares or debt of another connected SBC, or
- a combination of the two.

For example, a rental business would qualify as a small business corporation if it was large enough to employ more than five full-time employees (including family members) throughout the entire year. If the rental business qualifies, then it is necessary to value all the assets in the company to determine if at least 90% of the assets (at fair market value) are used in that business (or some other active business carried on in Canada). Examples of assets that companies commonly have that would not be considered to be used in an active business are:

---

[83] s. 110.6.

[84] Including the general $75,000 capital gains deduction, which was repealed as of February 22, 1994.

[85] That is, taxable capital gains net of allowable capital losses and net capital loss carried over from other years under s. 111(1)(b).

- cash or investments in securities that are not working capital used in an active business; and
- vacant land held but not used in an active business.

If a CCPC carries on an active business but does not meet the 90% test, it is possible to fix the situation before the shares are sold by disposing of some of the assets that do not qualify. For example, if a company had investments in securities that did not qualify, the investments could be sold and (the after-tax proceeds) used either to invest in the active business, pay off debts or pay a dividend to shareholders.

Test 2 — 24 Month Holding Period Test
To meet this test, the shareholder (or a related person or partnership) must have owned the shares for 24 months prior to the date of sale.

Test 3 — More Than 50% Holding Period Test
To meet this test, the CCPC must have more than 50% of its assets (at fair market value) used primarily (more than 50%) in an active business carried on principally in Canada by itself or a related corporation.

Advantages and Disadvantages
Exhibit 6 compared the advantages and disadvantages of holding real estate personally as compared to holding it in a corporation. Exhibit 8 looks at the advantages and disadvantages of holding real estate through a corporation in a more comprehensive manner.

Real Estate Investment Trusts
Real estate investment trusts (REITs) are pools of funds that are invested in mortgages and commercial real estate that offer investors an easy way to invest in a diversified portfolio of real estate-related investments, with an annual income and potential for capital gains. There are currently several publicly-traded REITs in Canada. All of these REITs are listed on the Toronto Stock Exchange and operate as closed-end trusts. (A closed-end trust does not redeem units when unit holders want to sell, as open-end mutual funds do.)

An investor in a REIT is paid out his or her share of income (after expenses) each year, with some funds making payments monthly or quarterly. An investor in a REIT pays tax on the income allocated; the REIT itself does not pay tax. But because the income allocated for tax purposes is sheltered by capital cost allowance, an investor usually receives a tax-free return each year. The capital cost

EXHIBIT 8
Advantages and disadvantages of holding real estate in a corporation

Advantages

1. Limited liability.

2. If the income is Canadian active business income eligible for the small business deduction, there is a substantial deferral of tax. If the income is investment income, the rate is almost the same as the top personal rate.

3. Remuneration options, if the shareholder can be considered to be an employee of the company (e.g., salary, accrued bonus, pension plans, company cars).[a]

4. Income splitting with family members as shareholders.[b]

5. Estate planning/freezing opportunities.[c]

6. Possible availability of $500,000 QSBC lifetime capital gains exemption (discussed above).

7. No limitation on CCA if the corporation qualifies as a principal business corporation.

8. Anonymity of investors.

Disadvantages

1. Corporate losses are trapped in the company and cannot be used to offset other income of the shareholders. Any overall loss can be carried back or forward against income from the corporation.

2. Costs of setting up and maintaining (incorporation costs and ongoing legal and accounting fees).

3. Capital taxes.

4. Dividend income earned is not earned income for RRSP purposes (but salary is).

---

[a] To be considered an employee, the shareholder or family member must provide services to the company. Any remuneration paid must be reasonable in the circumstances or it will not be deductible (s. 67).

[b] s. 74.1 provides that income earned on property transferred (or loaned) to a spouse or minor child is taxed in the transferor's hands, and s. 74.2 attributes capital gains where property is loaned or transferred to a spouse. If a transaction is properly structured, these attribution rules can be avoided, and family members owning shares can pay tax on the dividends received and any capital gains on the sale of the shares. This type of planning is referred to as income-splitting because it splits income among family members and results in lower taxes.

[c] The purpose of estate planning is to minimize taxes that are paid on the deemed disposition on death. The purpose of estate freezing is to freeze the value of a taxpayer's estate (without giving up control over the asset) so that the tax liability is also "frozen" (unless tax rates increase). This is done by using tax-free rollover provisions (either s. 86 or s. 85(1)) to convert a taxpayer's common shares to fixed value voting preferred shares, and transferring the future value of the corporation (normally) to the children by issuing them new common shares.

allowance claimed reduces the investor's adjusted cost base of the REIT and, as a result, will increase the investor's capital gain on the eventual sale of the unit. This deferral and the fact that only one-half of the eventual capital gain is taxed make REITs advantageous from a tax point of view.

CAPITAL TAXES

Federal and provincial capital taxes are a significant cost for many large real estate corporations. Capital taxes are levied on a corporation's taxable capital, which is generally its debt plus its share capital and its retained earnings.[86] If a company owns a large amount of real estate, it will likely have a large amount of taxable capital and will, therefore, owe a large amount of capital tax. Smaller corporations are either exempt from capital tax or are subject to capital tax at lower rates.

As noted earlier, in recent years, capital taxes have been phased out because they are considered to be unfair. Nova Scotia is the only province which still has a capital tax on ordinary corporations and it is to be eliminated on July 1, 2012. At the federal level, there is only a capital tax on financial institutions.[87] that pay very little income tax. It acts as a minimum tax because it is reduced by any corporate surtax paid by the corporation (which in turn is determined by the amount of income tax paid).[88] As a result, large profitable corporations do not pay the LCT, but large corporations that are not as profitable often do. As noted earlier (in note 16 above), capital taxes are being phased out both provincially and federally because they are considered to be unfair. In its 2003 budget, the federal government announced a plan to reduce its "large corporation" capital tax and eliminate it entirely for companies other than financial institutions by 2009. Five provinces (British Columbia, Nova Scotia, Quebec, Saskatchewan and Ontario) have also announced plans to eliminate or reduce their capital taxes.[89]

---

[86] Only the capital allocated to the particular taxing jurisdiction is taxed. The taxable capital computation also contains a deduction for investments in other companies, which prevents double-counting any capital relating to intercorporate investments.

[87] The first $10 million of taxable capital is exempt from LCT, but related corporations must share this $10 million limit. (In the case of Canadian controlled private corporations, the limit must be shared by associated corporations.)

[88] Any corporate surtax paid in a year in excess of LCT can be carried back three years or carried forward seven years to reduce the LCT liability in the year.

[89] For further details on the various capital tax rates, exemptions and filing deadlines, see Preparing Your Corporation Tax Returns (CCH) (most recent edition).

THE GOODS AND SERVICES TAX (GST)
General Rules

Sales taxes are levied by the federal government and all provincial governments with the exception of Alberta. The federal government levies the GST and the rate is currently 5%. The term harmonized sales tax (HST) is used to signify a provincial retail sales tax that is "harmonized" with the federal GST because it follows most of the same rules. In 2011, several provinces have an HST: Newfoundland, Nova Scotia, New Brunswick, Quebec, Ontario and (subject to a referendum in the fall of 2011) British Columbia. The retail sales taxes in the other provinces (Prince Edward Island, Manitoba, Saskatchewan and Alberta) and territories are not harmonized and do not apply to the sale or rental of real estate.

The GST applies to the sale and rental of real estate unless the transaction is an "exempt supply" listed in Schedule V of the *Excise Tax Act*. Long-term residential rents of one month or more and sales of used residential complexes are the two main types of real estate supplies that are exempt from GST.[90] Sales of commercial and new residential properties and all commercial leases are taxable.

Businesses making taxable supplies in Canada must register for GST purposes. (There is an exemption for small suppliers with annual supplies of $30,000 or less.) GST registrants are also registered for HST purposes and must charge the 5% GST (and the relevant HST) at the time of each sale and can claim a GST (and HST) input credit for any GST (and HST) paid on any related goods or services purchased. The credit is claimed in the first return filed after the date of purchase. Registrants remit the difference between the tax charged on sales and the input tax credits claimed on purchases. If no tax is owing (because no sales have been made or because the tax collected in the period is less than the input tax credits), the tax registrant can claim a refund.[91]

---

[90] Other exempt supplies include health care services (e.g., most services provided by doctors and dentists), child care services (e.g., day care), educational services (e.g., schools, colleges, and universities), financial services (e.g., interest, insurance, dividends and stock broker commissions), and government taxes (e.g., property taxes and land transfer taxes).

[91] Section 245(2) of the *Excise Tax Act* requires GST registrants with annual revenues (from taxable and zero-rated supplies) of $6 million or more to file monthly GST returns, and registrants with annual revenues between $500,000 and $6 million to file quarterly GST returns. Annual GST returns are due for those with annual revenues of $500,000 or less. Quarterly filers may elect to file annually, and annual filers may elect to file quarterly, if they so wish.

Costs Incurred in Real Estate Transactions

Most costs incurred by real estate investors will include GST.[92] The main exceptions to this rule are exempt supplies, such as interest, insurance, property taxes and land transfer taxes. However, if exempt items are initially paid by a GST registrant and then billed to a third party, the items will be subject to GST. This happens, for example, when a landlord bills a commercial tenant for property taxes and when a lawyer bills a client for land transfer taxes paid on the purchase of real estate.

Commercial Leases

Landlords of commercial properties must register for GST purposes and must charge GST to their tenants on payments of rent and any other charges that they bill to them (such as property taxes, common area expenses and management fees). Landlords of commercial properties are also eligible for input tax credits for the GST paid on the purchase of goods and services.

Residential Leases

Because long-term leases of residential real estate (i.e., leases of one month or more) are exempt from GST, residential landlords can neither charge GST nor claim input tax credits for any GST paid on any purchases relating to such leases. Taxpayers making only exempt supplies cannot register, do not charge GST and cannot claim GST input tax credits.

Purchase and Sale of Real Estate

Sales of used residential complexes[93] (including houses and apartments) are exempt from GST — all other sales are taxable. This means that no GST can be charged on the sale of used residential complexes and no GST input tax credits can be claimed on the purchase of related goods and services. Sales of new or *substantially renovated* residential real estate[94] are taxable supplies, as are sales of commercial real estate.

---

[92] Unless the vendor is not a GST registrant because of the $30,000 small supplier test.

[93] The definition of *residential complex* is in s. 123(1) and includes a single dwelling house, a residential condominium or apartment complex, but excludes a hotel or boarding or lodging house that provides all or substantially all accommodation for periods of less than 60 days.

[94] This ensures that a renovator of homes or other residential complexes for resale is treated the same as a residential builder of new properties. Section 123 of the *Excise Tax Act* defines a substantial renovation to be

When real estate is purchased for use in a taxable supply, it is considered to be used in a *commercial activity,*[95] and there is an input tax credit available for the GST paid at the time of purchase.[96]

In some cases, a property may only be partly used in a commercial activity and partly used for some other activity. For example, the first floor of a rental property could be a commercial space, and the second floor could be a residential apartment (either leased or used by the landlord for personal purposes) — in this case, only the first floor of the property would be a taxable supply and used for a commercial activity. Similarly, a doctor or dentist could use the first floor of his property for his medical practice (which is an exempt supply) and lease the second to a commercial tenant (a taxable supply and commercial activity).

In such a case, if the property is used 90% or more for a commercial activity, a full input tax credit is still available for the entire amount of GST paid. If the use is less than 90%, the credit is prorated based on the percentage used for commercial activity.[97] (Use is generally determined based on the percentage of floor space used.)

When real estate (other than used residential real estate) is sold by a GST registrant, the vendor must charge GST on the full purchase price even if the property was only partially used in a commercial activity. However, the vendor can claim a GST input tax credit at the time of sale (according to a formula) for any GST that was initially paid but not previously eligible for credit.[98]

"... the renovation or alteration of a building to such extent that all or substantially all of the building that existed immediately before the renovation or alteration was begun, other than the foundation, external walls, internal supporting walls, floors, roof and staircases, has been removed or replaced..."

The term "all or substantially all" is not defined, but is generally considered to mean 90% or more.

[95] s. 123(1) of the *Excise Tax Act.*

[96] s. 193(1) of the *Excise Tax Act.*

[97] Section 206 of the *Excise Tax Act.* This rule is modified if the owner of the property is an individual: in this case, there is no input tax credit if the personal use of the property exceeds 50% and the property is considered to be a residential complex.

[98] The formula computing the credit multiplies the percentage of non-commercial use (immediately before the date of sale) by the lesser of:
• the GST paid on the purchase of the property and all improvements; and
• the GST charged on the sale.

As a result, a GST registrant who owns property with 80% commercial use will get an input tax credit at the time of purchase for 80% of the GST paid and will get a

Similarly, a taxpayer who is not a GST registrant is also required to collect GST on the sale of commercial real estate[99] and is entitled to a rebate for the GST initially paid on the purchase of the property and on subsequent improvements according to a similar formula.[100] For example, a dentist who has used a building for his dental practice (which is an exempt supply) must charge GST when the building is sold but is eligible to claim a GST rebate for the GST paid previously.

It is possible to avoid charging GST when one GST registrant is selling real estate to another GST registrant even if the sale is a taxable supply subject to GST. To do this, the purchaser and the vendor must make a joint election agreeing that the purchaser of the real estate (rather than the vendor) will pay the GST.[101] Because the purchaser will also be claiming an input tax credit for the GST to be paid on the same return, there will be no amount owing in respect of the transaction. This election avoids the problem of the purchaser having to pay the GST initially before claiming it back as an input tax credit. Of all the rules discussed in this section, this is probably one of the most important for commercial real estate.

LAND TRANSFER TAXES

Land transfer taxes are provincial taxes that are payable on the transfer of the beneficial ownership of real estate located in a province. In Ontario, the rules look through bare trustee[102] and partnership arrangements[103] to determine whether or not there has been a change in beneficial ownership.

---

credit for the remaining 20% of the GST paid when the property is sold (as long as the property does not go down in value).

[99] s. 226 of the *Excise Tax Act*.

[100] s. 257 of the *Excise Tax Act*.

[101] The election must be made in the first return following the date of the transaction. The form for this election is called a GST 60.

[102] Bare trusts are described in Exhibit 7. Prior to July 18, 1989, bare trust arrangements also allowed purchasers to avoid paying Ontario land transfer taxes because the property could be acquired by acquiring the shares of the bare trustee corporation and amending the trust agreement. This is no longer possible.

[103] For example, if two individuals form an equal partnership, with one partner contributing real estate and the other cash, there will be land transfer tax payable on the 50% of the value of the property transferred. Similarly, if an equal partnership is wound up with each partner receiving an undivided 50% interest in the real estate, there would be no land transfer tax payable on the dissolution of the partnership.

The rates, which are applied to the fair market value of the property transferred, vary depending on whether the property is a residential or commercial property. The Ontario rates for commercial properties and residential properties with two or more units are

- 0.5% on the first $55,000, and
- 1% over the excess over $55,000.

The rates for a single unit residential property are the same for the first $250,000. After that, the rates are:

- 1.5% over $250,000 but less than $400,000, and
- 2% over $400,000.

TAX PLANNING VERSUS TAX AVOIDANCE

In non-technical terms, a tax avoidance transaction is a transaction that looks, on the surface, as if it follows the letter of the law but offends one of the several specific anti-avoidance rules in the *Income Tax Act* or the major one — the general anti-avoidance rule (GAAR).

Because GAAR looks at the substance rather than the form of a tax-motivated transaction, the introduction of GAAR has changed the way tax planning is done in Canada. Before GAAR, the predominant authority for tax planning was the dictum from the 1935 Duke of Westminster case that stated that "every man is entitled if he can to order his affairs so that the tax attaching under the appropriate Act is less than it would otherwise be." Now the rule is quite the opposite. The General Anti-avoidance Rule (GAAR) provides that if a transaction results in a *tax benefit* (i.e., a reduction or deferral of tax), and it is reasonable to conclude that it was undertaken *primarily for tax reasons* and it results in a *misuse or abuse* of the rules in the Act, then the tax benefit will be denied (even if the transaction follows the letter of the law).

Since 1993, GAAR has been administered centrally by a GAAR committee in Ottawa, and each CCRA office must refer cases to this committee before GAAR will be applied. Since it takes about 10 years for a tax case to get to court, and the CCRA has been very careful in determining which cases it will attack with GAAR, there have been have very few GAAR decisions to date. But, as the court said in *Jabs Construction*[104] (a GAAR case that the CCRA lost): "Section 245 is an extreme sanction. It should not be used every

---

[104] 99 DTC 279 (TCC). This case was heard in the Tax Court of Canada, which is the lowest level of court that hears tax decisions. Decisions of the Tax Court are

time the Minister gets upset just because a taxpayer structures a transaction in a tax-effective way, or does not structure it in a manner that maximizes the tax."

Information Circular IC-88-2 and its supplement provide a series of examples of when Revenue Canada considers that GAAR will apply.[105] At the time of writing, there have been no GAAR cases at the Supreme Court of Canada, and there is still great uncertainty as to how strong GAAR is and whether it will apply to a particular method of reducing taxes. The most common area of disagreement between Revenue Canada and taxpayers (and their advisors) is whether a transaction constitutes a *misuse or abuse* of the Act. Making a tax-deductible RRSP contribution clearly does not — but there are many much more complicated transactions that are not as clear-cut.

In the meantime, the government is monitoring what it considers to be tax avoidance activities much better than it did in the past. Better monitoring allows it to react faster with specific legislation to "close down" loopholes. A few decades ago, governments would wait until the time of an annual budget to announce changes in the law aimed at closing tax loopholes. Now, we often see such changes announced by press release (between budgets). This "draft legislation by press release" is a mixed blessing. While it can be criticized as changing the rules of the game in the middle of play, it protects taxpayers and their advisors because it eliminates uncertainty for many taxpayers who are not sure whether the deductions in a tax shelter would offend GAAR or some other general rule and want to avoid the potential reassessment of tax and interest in the future.

---

appealed to the Federal Court of Appeal. Decisions of the Federal Court of Appeal are appealed to the Supreme Court of Canada, which is the highest court in Canada.

[105] Examples in IC-88-2 which apply to real estate include:

• the tax-deferred transfer of land inventory first to a partnership and then to corporation (to avoid the restrictions in s.85(1) that would have denied a tax-deferred transfer if the land inventory was transferred directly to the corporation) (para. 22), and

• the tax-deferred transfer of land inventory to a partnership, followed by the withdrawal of partnership capital exceeding the adjusted cost base of the partnership interest (which uses the partnership rollover provisions to effect a sale for cash) (para. 12).

The rules for tax-deferred transfers to corporations and partnerships are discussed in section 3.5 of a subsequent chapter.

CONCLUSION

Tax law is technically complex and always changing. Many of the recent changes affecting real estate have had an adverse affect on real estate investment. This is because investors purchasing real estate generally purchase it to earn a profit, but sometimes the profit is not earned until the property is resold (at half of the regular rate, if it is a capital gain). In the meantime, the property can be highly leveraged (with mortgage financing), and any rental income that is earned can be sheltered with interest expense, capital cost allowance and other deductions; or they may be rental losses that an investor can claim against his or her other sources of income. This has made real estate somewhat of a tax shelter that, in turn, has resulted in many restrictions on real estate deductions for income tax purposes.

Taxpayers who understand the legislative intent of the current tax laws, as well as their shortcomings, will not only find it easier to remember the rules and related planning opportunities; they will also be better able to understand changes in the system as they occur (and, perhaps, predict them).

REFERENCES FOR FURTHER READING

The need to keep current in income tax law is met by a variety of publications. Because tax material quickly becomes obsolete, only references to publishers have been provided.

The most important references are publications of the Canadian Tax Foundation (www.ctf.ca), Carswell (www.carswell.com), CCH (www.cch.ca) and Knotia (www.knotia.ca). These organizations publish a variety of materials electronically and in paper form. Some electronic materials are updated daily.

Some professional associations and universities also offer courses on real estate taxation. The notes for these courses are also a valuable resource.

Canadian
Mortgages

Inflation, Housing Affordability and the Graduated Payment Mortgage

───────── HENRY BARTEL & ALAN MARSHALL

INTRODUCTION

Over the past two decades there have been many changes in the housing and mortgage markets. In particular, high and volatile inflation rates have resulted in a variety of new mortgage instruments being introduced. At the same time, there have been some concerns about the affordability of housing, as the cost of housing has risen at rates in excess of the general inflation rate, particularly in some of the larger urban centres. The purpose of this paper is to examine some of the responses of mortgage lenders to the problems that have resulted from inflation, and to suggest that the graduated payment mortgage could be a practical solution to some of the problems faced by lenders and borrowers alike.

It is useful to begin with an historical perspective in order to consider why the nature of mortgage contracts changed in the first place, which is the subject of the next section. After that is a brief discussion of rollover mortgages, which were a response to the inflationary times in the late 1960s. This is followed by a discussion of the "tilt effect," or the real-payment twist, which demonstrates that rollover mortgages were only a partial response to the problems associated with inflation. The ensuing section examines the graduated payment mortgage and how it addresses some of the problems faced by participants in the mortgage market. A brief section dealing with indexed mortgages, savings fund assisted mortgages and shared appreciation mortgages follows. The final section provides some concluding remarks.

Reproduced from *RESOURCE, The Canadian Journal of Real Estate*, October 1988, pp. 19–25, with permission of Real Estate Institute of Canada.

HISTORICAL BACKGROUND[1]

The type of mortgage most relevant up to the early 1930s was a 5 year, 50 percent loan-to-value ratio mortgage, with interest payments due usually every six months to a year, little or no repayment of the principal, and the interest rate fixed for the term of the loan. At the end of the 5 years the entire mortgage principal became due, eventually leading to the name "balloon" mortgage as it is now called, and had to be refinanced with either the same or some other lender. It was almost an ideal instrument from the lender's perspective since he could issue a 5 year bond to match the term of the mortgage, arrange for his coupon payments to coincide with the mortgage interest received, and count as his profit the spread between the two rates.

Furthermore, with a 50 percent downpayment required, the mortgage loan was considered very secure.

From the consumer/borrower's point of view the mortgage arrangement was also quite satisfactory. Prevailing mortgage rates were close to medium term bond rates, interest and whatever principal payments were generally manageable in relation to income, and refinancing at the end of the 5 year term, could be looked forward to with the not unreasonable expectation that no particular difficulties would be encountered.

All this changed drastically during the depression of the early 1930s. With staggeringly high unemployment rates in the range of 20 to 30 percent, as well as lower incomes in general, more and more borrowers were finding it difficult to meet their periodic interest (and principal) payments. Lenders finding themselves in a liquidity squeeze were often either unwilling or unable to refinance the loan at the end of the 5 year term. Moreover, the security of the 50 percent equity cushion largely disappeared as real estate prices plummeted, resulting in real capital losses to the lenders when they foreclosed.

Largely in response to these conditions, a new type of mortgage came into being that lasted into the early 1970s — the level payment, high ratio, long term, fixed interest, fully amortized mortgage, that we shall also refer to as the standard or traditional mortgage. Level payment of course simply meant that the periodic payment was held constant in nominal terms over the life of the mortgage. High ratio meant that the allowable loan-to-value ratio was increased to 80 percent, which in turn provided greater accessibility to the hous-

---

[1] We are indebted to Dr. E. Sussman of CMHC for originally providing some background material on the history of mortgages in Canada.

ing market by a larger segment of the population. To encourage lenders to provide such high-ratio loans, the federal government under the *Dominion Housing Act*, established in the mid-thirties, undertook direct loans at subsidized rates.

The design of the mortgage was intended to make it attractive to both lenders and borrowers. The long term of the mortgage, initially a 10 year period with a renewal option of another 10 years, was intended to reduce the risk of having to refinance every 5 years. The interest was fixed for the duration of each of the 10 years, reducing the risk of interest changes for a longer period than before. Of course, on renewal, the second 10 year mortgage would be financed at then prevailing interest rates. The full amortization feature ensured that at the end of the 20 year term the house was completely paid off, and a potentially risky "balloon" payment was avoided.

With the balloon payment mortgage, the lenders could finance the mortgage with a balloon payment bond and exactly match the cash flow pattern of the mortgage, working on a spread basis with a minimal level of risk. The fully amortized, blended principal and interest payment mortgage is a simple, ordinary annuity. In order to work on a pure spread basis, the mortgage lender would have to issue an annuity to finance the mortgage. Except for those issued by life insurance companies, securities that are pure annuities are not commonly issued by mortgage lenders. Therefore, for many mortgage lenders, a new element of risk was being introduced.

When an intermediary cannot exactly match the pattern of cash inflows and outflows, they have incurred some interest rate risk. Such risk can be measured by duration, developed by Macauley (1938). For a standard, balloon payment bond, the duration is:

$$D_{Bond} = \frac{1+i}{i} = \frac{1+i+n(c-i)}{c(1+i)^n - (c-i)} \tag{1}$$

where, i = the current market yield rate

c = the coupon rate of the bond

n = the term to maturity of the bond

The duration of an annuity, such as the level payment, fully amortized mortgage is:

$$D_{ANN} = \frac{1+i}{i} = \frac{n}{(1+i)^n - 1} \tag{2}$$

where i and n are as defined above. Therefore, it can be seen that for an intermediary financing fully amortized mortgages with standard balloon payment bonds, the amount of interest rate risk differs on the asset (mortgage) and liability (bond) sides of the balance sheet. For mortgages and bonds of identical maturities and comparable interest rates, the duration of the bond will be longer than the mortgage. This implies that the liabilities have more interest rate risk than the assets.

From the perspective of a life insurance company, the fully amortized blended principal and interest mortgage is less desirable than the balloon payment mortgage, due to duration considerations. Life insurance companies have liabilities of extremely long duration. Thus, they are continually looking for investments that will allow them to lengthen the average duration of their assets.

THE ROLLOVER MORTGAGE

With the fixed rate, level payment mortgage that was predominant until the late 1960s, financial intermediaries were generally unable to operate on a pure spread basis. They were forced to intermediate along the yield curve, that is, lending long term and borrowing relatively short term. They financed the mortgages with funds borrowed at the longest terms they could get, most often for a maximum period of 5 years. As long as interest rates remained stable, the lenders would be able to continue to finance the mortgages at spreads that were profitable. Given the post-depression experience of fairly stable longer term rates, this practice may have been justified. With inflationary pressures increasing by the late sixties, lenders found themselves in the untenable position of holding mortgages at long term and fixed rates, yet having to refinance them at short rates which were rising, and even exceeding the rate they were earning on their mortgage portfolios.[2]

To avoid potential lenders leaving the mortgage market, mortgage terms were reduced to 5 years during which the mortgage rate would remain fixed. After that it would be rolled over for another term of 5 years at then prevailing interest rates, and so on, until the

---

[2] There were examples of firms that were engaged in more extensive intermediation on the yield curve, financing long term mortgages with short term deposits. When interest rates began to climb these firms found themselves squeezed even more.

mortgage was fully amortized. In all other important aspects the roll-over mortgage was the same as the standard mortgage.

The rollover mortgage was in essence the first attempt by lend-ers at coping with accelerating inflation, and as inflation continued to rise during the 1970s, the rollover period was shortened at first to 3 years (in 1978), then 1 year (in 1980), and even 6 months. Clearly, these moves were aimed at reducing the interest rate risk faced by the lenders by attempting to keep their assets and liabilities matched with respect to maturity.

For a lender unable to fix its cost of borrowing for any appre-ciable term, the rollover period can be made virtually continuous. This is what we refer to as the variable rate mortgage (VRM). This mortgage had been available in the U.K. and Australia for some time, and was adopted in the U.S. in the 1970s. Although available in Canada, the VRM has not taken a significant share of the mort-gage market, possibly because of consumer resistance to shouldering all the interest rate risk. The rollover mortgage is still the dominant mortgage instrument in the Canadian market.

The shortened term of the rollover mortgage served to reduce the interest rate risk borne by the lenders by shifting it onto the consumer/borrowers. Benefits to consumers were claimed to be con-tinued mortgage money availability, and slightly reduced interest rates on mortgages in recognition of the new risk-sharing aspects of the shortened roll-over mortgage.

While variable rates and shortened terms helped lenders, they did little for borrowers. Lenders' primary concern was earning a rate of return sufficient to compensate for the loss of purchasing power, plus earning some profit. They were largely unaffected by the impact of inflation on the values of properties. In fact, once a mortgage was in place, the impact of inflation on the property values served to reduce the risk borne by the lender, by reducing the debt ratio on the property.

However, from the borrower's perspective, inflation had a dou-ble impact. First, mortgage payments were rising due to the impact of inflation on interest rates increasing substantially the proportion of disposable income spent on mortgage rates. Inflation also drove up house prices. Therefore mortgage payments for prospective bor-rowers were rising due to the larger principals required to finance increasingly expensive housing. These two factors combined to cause monthly payments to increase at a rate substantially greater than the inflation rate. This, in turn, caused the minimum qualifying incomes to increase proportionately, thereby squeezing many people out of the housing market at the margin.

THE REAL-PAYMENT TWIST

The real-payment twist, also called the "tilt-effect," derives from the fact that during inflationary times the value of the payments on an equal or level-payment mortgage decreases in real terms. In other words while the nominal payment remains constant over the life of the mortgage, the borrower/consumer faces high real payment costs early in the term and progressively lower real payments at the end of the term. For many consumers at or near the margin, they face the prospect of over-extending themselves for several years until their incomes catch up to the demands of their mortgages. As their incomes continue to rise, the fixed payment mortgage becomes less and less burdensome.

We shall illustrate with the following example (see Table 1). Assume that the rate of inflation is known with certainty. Two inflation scenarios are presented: 4 percent, approximately the rate of inflation experienced in the late 1960s; and 12 percent, approximately the rate of inflation a decade later. The real rate of interest is assumed constant at 3 percent, yielding nominal mortgage rates of 7 and 15 percent for the two scenarios respectively.[3] As shown in Table 1, the monthly payments resulting from a conventional 25 year amortization jump from $350 to $623 as inflation jumps from 4 to 12%. In effect, there is almost a doubling of nominal payments to be made every month for the life of the mortgage.

The most obvious effect is that the qualifying income to be able to get such a mortgage rises from $14,000 to almost double at just under $25,000, assuming a loan-to-income ratio of 30 percent, which is a commonly applied debt-service ratio. This implies that fewer people will be able to afford houses and/or may have to settle for a lesser priced house, even though their income may have kept up with inflation. To alleviate some of the pressure on home buyers, lending institutions which in the past used a loan-to-income ratio of 25 percent have gradually increased this ratio to 30 and even 33 $\frac{1}{3}$ percent, have applied the ratio to gross rather than after-tax income, have included spousal income or used family income, and have excluded counting annual taxes, insurance fees, and certain other expenses.

This of course has only mitigated against the negative inflationary effects. By substantially increasing the proportion of total dispos-

---

[3] For expositional simplicity, we are ignoring the cross-product in the expression $i = r + f + rf$, where i is the nominal rate, r is the real rate and f is inflation rate. At low real rates and inflation rates the cross-product term, rf, is not economically significant, but is of greater concern at higher levels of inflation, such as scenario 2.

328 / H. BARTEL & A. MARSHALL

TABLE 1
Illustrative example of nominal and real payment flow of a level-payment mortgage

	Low Inflation Scenario 1	High Inflation Scenario 1	
		Mortgage 1	Mortgage 2
Amount of Mortgage	$50,000	$50,000	$50,000
Length of Mortgage	25 yrs.	25 yrs.	30 yrs.
Rate of Inflation	4%	12%	12%
Annual Mortgage Interest Rate	7%	15%	15%
Monthly Payment	$350	$623	$614
Qualifying Income	$14,000	$24,920	$24,560
Real Value of Monthly Payment			
After 5 Years	$ 288	$ 353	$349
After 10 Years	237	201	198
After 15 Years	194	114	112
After 20 Years	160	65	64
After 25 Years	131	37	36
After 30 Years	—	—	21

Notes:
[1] All figures are rounded to the nearest dollar for presentation, although all calculations were done without rounding.
[2] All assumptions are explained in the text.

Source: Calculations by authors

able income that must be spent on a given unit of housing, fewer dollars are left for spending on other consumer items and discretionary savings are squeezed severely. Moreover, default risk has risen substantially. In periods of high unemployment and a much increased frequency of temporary layoffs, both of which have been coincident with the high inflation rates of the last few years, the inordinately high proportion of housing costs relative to total income have in fact resulted in the much higher incidence of default than previously experienced.

The real-payment twist that results from inflation, and is more pronounced the higher the inflation rate, becomes evident from the schedule of real monthly payments shown for Scenarios 1 and 2. It is

FIGURE 1
The real-payment twist: Real value of monthly mortgage payments

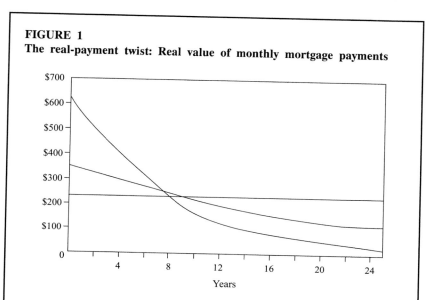

Note: The steeper curve corresponds to the high-inflation scenario 2, while the gently sloped curve describes the real value of the payments under the moderate inflation scenario 1. Of course, without inflation, the real value of the payments remains constant.

also graphically shown in Figure 1. With zero percent inflation and a mortgage interest rate of 3 percent, the level-payment is $237.

As we can see from Figure 1, under Scenario 1, the real value of the monthly mortgage payments exceeds that of the zero-inflation situation until the tenth year. With high levels of inflation and interest rates (Scenario 2) the level payment rises to $623, but exceeds the zero inflation scenario payment in real terms for a little more than 8 years, and ultimately dropping in real terms to only 6% of the original payment amount.

Note that at such a high inflation rate, increasing the amortization period from 25 to 30 years (mortgage 2) has almost no effect (see Table 1). The nominal monthly payment drops from $623 only to $614 and, therefore, the difference in real payments is almost negligible, especially in later years. Thus, lengthening the amortization period, even substantially, does not result in a substantial decrease in monthly payments.

What really does happen, in effect, is that the consumer pays most dearly for that extra amortization. By paying only $614 a

330 / H. BARTEL & A. MARSHALL

TABLE 2
Interest and principal repayment on mortgage 2

	Total Payment	Interest Paid	Principal Paid	Outstanding Principal
1st Year	$7,372	$7,269	$103	$49,897
2nd Year	7,372	7,253	119	49,778
3rd Year	7,372	7,235	137	49,641
4th Year	7,372	7,213	159	49,482
5th Year	7,372	7,189	183	49,299

Notes:
[1] All figures are rounded to the nearest dollar for presentation, although all calculations were done without rounding.
[2] All assumptions are explained in the text.

Source: Calculations by authors

month rather than $623, the consumer pays $9 × 12 × 25 = $2,700 less over the 25 year period. In return for paying this $2,700 less under mortgage 2 than under mortgage 1, he/she has to pay another 5 years of $614 per month, or $36,840 extra. Another way of looking at the cost of an increased amortization period is in Table 2.

During the first five years of the 30 year amortization period, the constant or level payment of $614 only pays off approximately $701 of the outstanding principle. It can be shown, therefore, that by prepaying that $701 and, in effect, taking out a mortgage in the amount of $49,299 instead of the originally suggested $50,000, then taking out the amortization period for 25 years will result in the same $614 monthly payment. In other words, the last 5 years of the proposed 30 year amortization period are "saved" by virtue of the $701 prepayment. In general, this example would suggest that during periods of high inflation the consumer's interests are better served by reducing recommended, or allowable, amortization periods.

From the lender's perspective, the benefits of lengthening the amortization period are minimal. The duration of the 25 year amortization mortgage is 6.48 years. By increasing the period over which the mortgage is amortized by five years, the duration increases by only 0.29 years to 6.77 years. In addition, the risk of the mortgage will increase in another respect because very little of the principal has been paid over the first five years. By way of example, several years ago, there were many situations where consumers were faced with mortgage renewals at very high interest rates. The level of interest rates was contributing to a slump in housing prices such that the value of the homes had fallen to less than the principal balance outstanding on the mortgages. Rather than renew, many consumers simply walked away[4] from their homes, or waited to be evicted.

In general, we have seen that any level-payment mortgage will suffer from a real-payment twist during periods of inflation. This is the case, however, for fully anticipated and constant levels of inflation. If future inflation levels are underestimated at the time the mortgage is written, lenders will suffer and borrowers will gain. In part this is due to the fact that the real interest rate of the mortgage will be lower than intended and in fact may be negative. Furthermore, since lenders have to borrow the funds at short time periods, they may find short-term rates exceed their long-term lending rates. Since the borrower can usually refinance if market rates drop substantially, either by virtue of an open mortgage that allows higher than contracted-for repayments on principal, or by reason of having such a prepayment option albeit with an interest penalty clause or, finally, because the Interest Act of Canada provides for early prepayment after 5 years, the ultimate risk of inflation uncertainty is essentially borne by the lender. It is not surprising, therefore, that lenders sought some means of renegotiating the mortgage interest rate, at least every five or less years, ultimately leading to some sort of variable rate mortgage instruments.

GRADUATED PAYMENT MORTGAGES

The graduated payment mortgage (GPM) can avoid the real-payment twist ex-ante if all inflation is fully anticipated and constant over the relevant time period. In terms of dealing with inflation, the GPM simply provides for lower initial nominal payments and higher nominal payments down the road, with the increases graduated in accordance with the level of expected inflation.

Mathematically expressed, the payment stream can be worked out as follows. Let the initial monthly payment be M_0 which is determined by discounting N future mortgage payments by a discount factor i; then,

---

[4] We shall abstract from the legal implications that such actions might or might not have.

$$M_0 = \frac{P}{\dfrac{1-(1+i)^{-N}}{i}} \tag{3}$$

The discount factor can be approximated by $i = r - g$, where r is the nominal interest rate and g is the growth factor by which the mortgage is graduated.[5] The monthly payment stream is given by,

$$M_n = M_{n-1}(1+g) = M_0(1+g)^n \tag{4}$$

for $n = 1, \ldots, N$

If the growth factor of the mortgage, g is equal to the anticipated inflation, then the expected value of the payments, M, would be constant, in real terms, eliminating the real-payment twist.

When the payments are adjusted monthly, as suggested by equation 4, the mortgage is called a "pure" GPM. In practice, because people tend to receive salary and wage rate adjustments once, or maybe twice per year, most GPMs are written to have the payment graduated annually. Additionally, the type of GPM usually observed grows for a finite time period, after which it is converted into a standard level payment mortgage over the balance of its life. In the ensuing discussion, we will continue to use the "pure" form of the GPM.

To illustrate, let us return to the high inflation scenario (#2) presented in Table 1. The principal amount of the mortgage is $50,000, and inflation is anticipated at 12%, resulting in a nominal rate of 15%. In Table 3, we have produced some of the relevant data for the 25 year amortization mortgage using growth rates of 0%, the standard mortgage, 6%, half the rate of inflation, and 12%, the rate of inflation.

Note the marked effect that the GPM has on income thresholds, i.e., affordability. The qualifying income for the same amount of principal is reduced to $9,480, less than 40 percent of that for the conventional mortgage ($24,920) by graduating at the expected rate of inflation.

However, the reader is cautioned that graduating at the full rate of anticipated inflation, as in the example, is unrealistic in its implementation, and risky. This growth assumption was used to demonstrate that the GPM can eliminate the tilt effect. However, one

---

[5] The exact discount rate is given by $(1 + i) = (1 + r) / (1 + g)$. The approximation $i = r - g$ results in an overestimate of the required discount rate for the specified amortization.

TABLE 3
Illustrative example of nominal and real payment flow of a pure graduated payment mortgage compared to a level-payment mortgage

| | Level Payment | Graduated Payment | |
		at 6%	at 12%
Amount of Mortgage	$50,000	$50,000	$50,000
Length of Mortgage	25 yrs.	25 yrs.	30 yrs.
Rate of Inflation	12%	12%	12%
Annual Mortgage Interest Rate	15%	15%	15%
Initial Payment	$623	$414	$237
Qualifying Income	$24,920	$16,560	$ 9,480
Real Value of Monthly Payment			
After 5 Years	$ 353	$ 314	$ 238
After 10 Years	201	240	242
After 15 Years	114	183	246
After 20 Years	65	139	250
After 25 Years	37	106	254
After 30 Years	—	—	21

Notes:
[1] All figures are rounded to the nearest dollar for presentation, although all calculations were done without rounding. The real value of the payments for GPM graduated at the rate of inflation grow slightly because we used the discount rate approximation, which ignores the cross-product term.
[2] All assumptions are explained in the text.

Source: Calculations by authors

should recognize that if this high rate of inflation were to abate somewhat (as it has in the 1980s) the borrower's income would not rise quickly enough to keep debt service ratios at manageable levels. Second, we have not shown the principal outstanding at each year. For the first 17 years, the payments are less than the interest, and the principal balance is growing until it peaks at about $140,000 at that time. The present value of this balance at its peak (taken at the rate charged on the mortgage) is about $20,000. This may be cause for legitimate concern, as one may be concerned about the real debt ratio. If the value of the house has increased at the rate of inflation, the real debt ratio on the property always declines. From the consumer's perspective, the mortgage burden will always be a constant proportion of income, provided income grows at the rate of inflation.

A more realistic scheme sets the graduation growth rate at a rate below the rate of inflation. For the purposes of illustration, we have chosen to use a growth rate set at half the anticipated inflation rate. This reduces the tilt effect substantially while reducing qualifying income by about a third, to $16,560. At the same time, it is less risky for the consumer than the full inflation rate graduation, leaving some cushion for incomes to *not* keep pace with inflation. If real incomes do remain constant, then the burden of the mortgage will lessen over the years. The principal balance does rise as the interest exceeds the payments for the first 13 years, although it peaks at about $75,000 at that time.

The above formulas, and the concept of the graduated payment mortgage, could be modified to include life-cycle considerations, although this has apparently not been done yet. As is well known, young families starting off usually have to borrow against their future income stream in the earlier years. During their middle years, they traditionally save most of their money, and become dissavers again during their latter and retirement years. The standard level-payment mortgage, therefore, even abstracting from the difficulties wrought by inflation, imposes a heavy real cost on the family in the earlier years when it can least afford to bear it. An additional staggering or graduating of real costs could be undertaken by using some proxy for expected productivity and hence real wage gains.

Of course, the GPM as it presently stands does not accommodate fluctuating and/or unexpected inflationary changes. These are the obvious risks that the lender bears if actual inflation outstrips expected inflation. Similarly, the borrower can suffer significantly if actual inflation is less than expected inflation since the real cost of the monthly payments will rise, unless adequate provisions are made for prepayment of the mortgage without severe penalties attached.

For mortgage lenders such as life insurance companies, the GPM offers an opportunity to lengthen slightly the duration of their mortgage portfolios. For the GPM the duration is:

$$D_{GPM} = \frac{1+i}{1-g} - \frac{n(1+g)^n}{(1+i)^n - (1+g)^n} \tag{5}$$

For the examples in Table 3, the durations are 8.60 years (6% growth) and 11.30 years (12% growth), compared to the duration of 6.48 years for the standard mortgage. These increases are quite large, particularly when compared to that from increasing the amortization to 30 years, which was 6.77.

We have demonstrated that the GPM is a good candidate to deal with many of the problems faced by mortgage market participants. It lowers the income thresholds for entrants into the owner-occupied housing market. While it can be structured to completely eliminate the tilt effect, we suggest that this is too risky. Rather, many of the benefits can be achieved by graduation of the payments at less than the anticipated rate of inflation. By leaving some of the tilt effect, the real debt service ratio declines, which may be desirable to many.

OTHER MORTGAGE INSTRUMENTS

There are other mortgages that have the potential to answer some of the problems faced by mortgage market participants, which we will discuss, albeit briefly, here.

Indexed mortgages, also known as price level adjusted mortgages (PLAM), are a step beyond the graduated payment mortgage by accommodating both expected and unexpected inflationary variations, and thus fully eliminating the real-payment twist, ex post. The indexed mortgage has a number of advantages from the consumer/borrower's perspective. For one, it assures that the real burden of the mortgage payment remains constant. The real burden is denominated in terms of the real interest rate, and as long as the consumer's income keeps pace with the general price level, the mortgage payment will remain a fixed and manageable proportion of overall income. Unlike the GPM, where the growth rate is contractually determined ex ante, allowing the possibility that payments will grow at a rate in excess of inflation, this possibility is eliminated with the PLAM. It does imply, however, that borrowers can no longer over-extend themselves in terms of the payments required relative to their income level in the hopes that future inflation will ease that burden. Thus loan-to-income ratios may have to come down again, and the easing of other restrictions will have to be reversed. Consumers would, however, be assured that their burden remained constant and that the final payment, however large in nominal dollars it might possibly be, completely paid off the mortgage.

From the prospective lender's perspective it might be argued that they would be more willing to provide PLAM, if they were allowed to issue price level adjusted deposits (PLAD) as well. There is some concern, however, that allowing for too many price indexed instruments in the financial markets would institutionalize inflation and thereby make it too restrictive to combat effectively.

The savings fund assisted mortgage (SFAM) is a mortgage instrument that was designed to help consumers cope with mortgage payments in the early years of the contract. While the SFAM does not correct the tilt problem, it does alleviate it somewhat by addressing the initial affordability problem, subsidizing payments with high present values.

There are two problems foreseeable in the implementation of the SFAM. First, the consumer borrows an amount in excess of the amount needed to finance the purchase which is used to subsidize the early mortgage payments. There is a question as to whether this gross amount of the mortgage or the net amount (gross less savings fund) would need to be used for the purposes of maximum allowable debt ratios for mortgage insurance purposes. The second problem is that the Interest Act of Canada requires that the full cost of interest be stated in the mortgage contract, which is the internal rate of return over the term of the contract. For the SFAM this would be higher than market level interest rates, which may cause consumers to reject the scheme.

Shared appreciation mortgages (SAM) contracts are similar to convertible bonds and debentures in that the borrower, in return for paying a lower interest rate, gives up part of their equity at some time in the future. Naturally, the greater the portion of equity growth shared with the lender, the greater the interest rate concession the consumer will get.

While this type of contract does make housing more affordable to buyers at the margin, they do so at the expense of depriving the consumer of some of the benefits of home ownership. One benefit of owning a house is that a home is a good investment that holds its value in the face of inflation. At the end of the contract, the consumer has no debt, but also does not own the full equity of the home. There are many schemes to buy out the equity, the most straight-forward being a straight buy out for cash or in exchange for a conventional mortgage.

SUMMARY

This paper has examined some of the impact of inflation on the housing and mortgage markets and how lenders and borrowers attempted to cope with the problems through mortgage innovation. We have suggested that the graduated payment mortgage offers potential to deal with many of these problems and is a good compromise between the interests of borrowers and lenders. Unfortunately, its availability is not that widespread. Recent concerns about the affordability of housing, particularly in the larger urban areas may cause lenders and consumers to seek alternatives that will allow some easing of the payment burden, particularly in the early years.

We believe that the graduated payment mortgage offers advantages over both the savings fund assisted mortgage and the shared appreciation mortgages, which are alternatives that address the affordability issue. The price level adjusted mortgage will also reduce initial payments and hence improve affordability, but the debt service burden remains constant over the life of the loan, which consumers may not accept. We also see some institutional problems in implementing these plans.

Outline of Real Estate Investment Trusts

───────── GAVIN ARBUCKLE & HENRY BARTEL

INTRODUCTION

The real estate investment trust, or REIT, is an increasingly important form of corporate organization. A REIT owns a portfolio of properties and distributes the income they generate to its owners. In Canada, REITs are the oldest form of income trust, which possess tax advantages over other types of company. The growth of REITs is part of a general trend towards the securitization of asset ownership. Just as mortgages have been bundled into tradeable mortgage securities, so REITs represent the securitization of privately held real estate. While the vast majority of real estate assets are still owned by single individuals or corporations, interests in more properties can now be traded in the form of units of REITS. This provides numerous advantages to both investors and owners of real properties.

A real estate investment trust is defined by a declaration of trust, a legal document. The declaration of trust establishes how the trust will be managed and sets a limit on the amount of debt the REIT will be allowed to issue. The trust acquires and manages real estate properties and distributes the income to the holders of units of the trust. If the REIT is publicly traded, the units can be bought and sold on stock exchanges just like the shares of incorporated companies. Legally a trust is required to pay out a minimum proportion of its current income to the unitholders, usually 90% in Canada. Thus the REIT is a form of ownership most suitable for holding properties generating a fairly predictable income. Since the REIT

This article has been written specifically for this volume.

retains little income for its own use, real estate projects that do not generate current income, such as much development and construction, are not as well suited to REIT ownership. REITs must rely on money raised in the form of debt or from the sale of additional units to finance major property acquisitions. One often observes two real estate firms with linked ownership — a regular corporation that acquires and develops properties, and then sells the completed properties to a related REIT, which manages them and distributes their income.

Although the tax rules are complicated, essentially the income of an income trust avoids double taxation. Income received and distributed by normally incorporated companies is taxed twice. It is subject to the payment of corporate income tax paid by the company, and is also subject to personal income tax paid by the recipients if it is distributed in the form of dividends. In the case of income trusts, income is not subject to corporate income tax. It is taxed only once, as personal income, when it is distributed to the unitholders of the trust.

In Canada there has been a possible legal problem surrounding the liability of unitholders for claims against an income trust. Normal corporations provide limited liability to protect their shareholders from claims against them. For example, in the case of bankruptcy, the shareholders of a company are not liable to pay the debts of the bankrupt company from their individual assets. Their potential losses are limited to the amount they invested in the shares. Income trusts were originally seen as something different from limited corporations, more similar to mutual funds for real estate, so that they did not explicitly provide their unitholders with limited liability. While the issue has not been settled in litigation, there remains the remote possibility that unitholders of a trust might be found personally liable for claims against the trust. This legal risk has deterred large pension and mutual funds from investing in income trusts. The Ontario government is currently considering legal changes to provide limited liability protection to the unitholders of income trusts, who would then be in the same position as the owners of common stocks in incorporated companies. Other provinces are expected to follow suit.

THE ADVANTAGES OF REITS FOR ENTREPRENEURS

REITs enjoy superior access to equity capital compared to taxable corporations and proprietorships. Real estate owners and developers in the past have been highly dependent on debt, particularly loans from banks. In Canada, the willingness and ability of banks to lend to finance real estate projects have tended to vary over the business cycle. Not only has bank debt often been difficult and expensive to obtain, but failure to repay a legal debt could lead to bankruptcy or the seizure of property by the lender. The supply of funds from wealthy individuals and pension funds for direct investment in real estate has tended to be small.

REITs are able to sell ownership units in a diversified portfolio of properties. Ownership units are equity interests, and do not carry the legal obligation to make specific payments like a bond or other debt obligation. The largest REITs have their units traded publicly on stock exchanges, so that they are liquid and easy to value. This makes them attractive and affordable for a mass of small investors and pension funds. Investors of this type are far more willing to buy shares in a diversified portfolio of properties held by a REIT than they would be to invest in a single property, or in the shares of a real estate developer engaged in a limited number of projects. The tax advantage and liquidity of REIT units enable REITs to assemble large diversified portfolios of properties.

ADVANTAGE OF REITs FOR INVESTORS

From the point of view of the investor, REIT units are attractive for a number of reasons. The avoidance of double taxation of income tends to allow REITs to pay an attractive after-tax yield relative to bonds and dividend-paying stocks. Many REITs offer tax deferral on income by including a substantial return on capital in their payouts. The investor pays an increased capital gains tax on sale of the units, but receives the money from the return of capital free of current income tax. Modern portfolio theory suggests that a fully diversified portfolio should include some exposure to real estate assets, and REIT units are a convenient and liquid means of including real estate in a portfolio.[1] In Canada the CIBC World Markets Canadian REIT Index gained 7.5% in 2000, relative to a 14% decline in the S&P/TSX Composite Index. In 2001 the REIT index gained 27.7%, relative to a stock market decline.[2] This has made REIT units attractive for capital appreciation as well as income, at least in recent years.

---

[1] See Mull and Soenen.

[2] Gary Marr, "REITs proved to be safe bet in turbulent 2002," *Financial Post*, January 8, 2003, IN1, IN3.

Finally, in recent years the spread between REIT yields and the yields on bonds, dividend-paying stocks and other income-producing investments has been quite large. This has made REIT ownership very attractive to investors seeking high current income, such as many retirees.

Compared to direct property ownership, REITs provide management, diversification, and liquidity. Most investors have little interest in acting as property managers or landlords, whether they be individuals or pension managers. REITs provide professional management services. Due to the cost of real property, individuals and, even, pension funds could afford to buy outright only a few properties. By owning shares in a variety of REITS, investors can spread their risk over many properties. Most direct real estate ownership is illiquid. The market value of individual properties is difficult to estimate, and it may be difficult and costly to arrange a quick sale. Partnership interests in property are difficult to sell. Publicly traded REIT units are valued continuously by the stock market. The shares of REITs are easily bought and sold.

TYPES OF REIT

There are several types of REIT, which should be distinguished. The largest REITs are publicly traded on stock exchanges. There can also be *private REITs*, which have been formed to take advantage of the tax advantages of REIT organization, but whose units are not publicly traded. In the United States, there are a large number of *mortgage REITs*, which hold portfolios of mortgages rather than owning and managing properties. Private and mortgage REITs are not significant in Canada.

The most common characteristics of REITs have changed over time. REITs have been more common in the United States than in Canada, and there have been several shifts in the way they have tended to operate. In the 1960s and 1970s, many REITs held a wide variety of types of properties — residential, commercial, and industrial. This allowed them to enjoy the tax and money-raising advantages of REIT organization, but made efficient management difficult. More recently REITs have tended to specialize in only one type of property, so as to develop management expertise and to form companies where the risk and return characteristics of the properties could be clearly observed by investors. In Canada, REITs are almost all specialized in the type of property they hold — some hold only large office buildings, others shopping centres, others retirement homes.

Older REITs in the United States were often entirely passive investors — they owned properties, but hired independent firms to manage them. This approach led to difficulties of supervision and conflicts of interest, and most modern REITs actively manage the properties they own.

CHARACTERISTICS OF DIFFERENT TYPES OF PROPERTIES

REITs have different risk and return characteristics which depend on the types of properties they own.

Hotel and motel REITs tend to be high risk in terms of the variability of their returns and unit prices. These properties tend to be very sensitive to overall economic conditions. They tend to have short-term leases, which means there is a chance that lease renewals may yield lower rents. The lodging business tends to have few barriers to entry, so that new, competing properties may be constructed where they will reduce the returns from existing buildings. Lodging revenues may also be reduced due to health or security problems, such as the recent SARS outbreak in Toronto, or increased fears of terrorism.

REITs that specialize in the ownership of self storage facilities are also associated with high risk. Leases tend to be relatively short, and entry into the business by new, competing facilities tends to be relatively easy. The businesses require substantial management staffs, which makes costs difficult to control.

Some REITs own portfolios of shopping centres — often specializing in shopping centres of particular sizes or characteristics. In the United States, one finds REITS holding mainly large regional outlet malls, others with large local malls, and still others holding mainly small strip malls. These also tend to be associated with high risk. Their revenues are derived from highly cyclical retail businesses that face varying consumer demand and intense competition.

Office building REITs tend to be associated with lower risk than many other types of property. They tend to have longer leases, often up to five years, which reduces the uncertainty surrounding lease renewals. Office buildings take a relatively long time to plan and build, so that the risk of new entry into the market is low and predictable compared to other types of smaller and cheaper buildings.

Apartment building REITs face fairly average risks compared to those holding other types of properties. They tend to have high management costs, may face high tenant turnover, and are subject to fluctuations in demand conditions created by cyclical overbuilding. On the other hand the overall level of demand for residential accommodations is determined by fairly predictable demographic factors, and the short term nature of leases offers flexibility in setting rents.

Industrial properties tend to have very long term leases yielding stable returns. Typical industrial leases provide that tenants pay all of the operating costs of the property, so that the management expenses faced by the REIT are limited. These tend to be fairly low risk properties unless the tenants are drawn from high risk or troubled industries.

Medical and retirement care REITs face a different type of risks. On the one hand, the demographics of an ageing population guarantee a predictably increasing demand for these facilities. On the other hand, the involvement of governments in setting prices for some health services or in operating directly competing facilities themselves introduces an element of government risk not found with other types of property.

RISKS AND VALUATION OF REITs

REITs combine the features of real property and marketable securities. The value of a REIT is thus determined by two types of factors — the value of the properties owned by the REIT, and the stock market and economic conditions that influence the valuation of REIT units. Thus, the market value of a REIT is not merely the sum of the values of the properties it owns. REIT units are securities whose value depends, in part, on their relation to alternative financial instruments, such as stocks and bonds.

Valuation of the underlying properties of a REIT involves the same sorts of calculations involved in appraising any real property. For residential properties, the main element in valuation is the market price as revealed by recent sales of comparable properties. For business properties, the main element in valuation is the discounted present value of net cash flows. Estimating cash flows requires forecasting the income generated by current tenants allowing for the risk that they will default on their rent, and forecasting the rents expected to be obtained from future tenants, given expected trends in rents and the supply and demand of that type of property. Future expenses and financing costs must also be estimated.[3]

---

[3] A useful detailed discussion of valuation methodology applied to REITs is found in Louis W. Taylor, "Financial Analysis of REIT Securities", in Richard T. Garrigan and John F.C. Parsons, eds., *Real Estate Investment Trusts: Structure, Analysis and Strategy* (New York: McGraw-Hill, 1998), 339–70.

Estimating the value of REIT units also involves forecasting economic and financial market conditions. The return to REIT units reflects the demand and supply of the types of properties held by the REIT, so that general economic conditions will affect their values in the same way that they affect the values of common stocks. On the other hand, since REITs pay high and fairly stable dividends, they are often seen as bond substitutes by investors seeking yield. Their prices tend to move with bond prices to some extent, falling when interest rates are rising, and rising when interest rates decline.

Apart from the basic elements of valuation — based on the underlying properties and financial market conditions — there are several factors to watch out for in evaluating the management of a REIT. The quality of management of a company is a key component in valuation, yet it is an intangible factor that is difficult to estimate. In the case of REIT management there are a few warning signs that should alert analysts to potential problems. Among these are the level of debt, unrelated acquisitions, and dealings with related companies.

Since REITs must pay out most of their income, acquisitions of new properties must usually be funded by issuing new units or by debt. Issuing new units dilutes the ownership interest of existing unitholders, while issuing debt raises the risk that the REIT might not be able to maintain its current level of dividend payment. Failure to maintain the dividend rate because of a decline in income or an increase in interest expenses usually causes a significant decline in the value of REIT units. Part of the cyclical behaviour of real estate markets is caused by the tendency of investors to buy over-valued properties with borrowed money during a boom, followed by bankruptcies when property returns decline below the level necessary to service the debt. Some American REITs took on excessive debt in the 1970s and 1980s, and suffered financial failure when the real estate market declined. In the current market environment, a debt to equity ratio of around 50% is fairly common for REITs, and a substantially higher debt level could be grounds for concern.

Unrelated acquisitions may also be a sign that management of a REIT may be losing focus. Many of the advantages of a REIT are derived from the supposed predictability of returns, and the professional expertise of the management. REIT returns are supposed to be predictable since they are derived from management of a known portfolio of properties, and increases in those returns are expected to come from fairly predictable rent increases over time, not from capital gains. A high level of acquisitions, particularly in different types of property, may be a sign that management is attempting to speculate in property in the hope of generating capital gains. This may turn out to be successful, but it is a considerably riskier type of business than managing properties for income, which is what most REIT investors expect. If a REIT has specialized in owning one type of property, it may be expected to have developed some expertise in managing that type of property — expertise that may not carry over to other types of property.

A couple of American REITs illustrate the dangers of unrelated acquisitions. In one case, a REIT had a long and profitable history of managing rehabilitation hospitals. It then started acquiring unrelated types of properties using debt and ended up in bankruptcy. Among the various properties that had to be disposed of in bankruptcy proceedings was a racetrack — why would a bunch of hospital administrators imagine that they had any idea of how to run a racetrack? In a similar case, an American REIT with a history of managing retirement homes issued debt to acquire a large and struggling chain of discount motels — leading, almost inevitably, to financial difficulties and the collapse of the price of the units of the REIT. In retrospect, unitholders should have sold their units as soon as these unrelated acquisitions were announced — both because of the increase in debt involved, and the clear sign that managers were reaching beyond their areas of expertise.

A third and more difficult problem in evaluating REITs is the fact that their performance is often tied closely to that of related companies. For example, a REIT may have a large share of its properties rented to a single tenant. The prospects of the REIT cannot be analyzed separately from the prospects of the tenant. Even if the REIT is well managed and well financed, if the tenant runs into financial problems, and cannot continue paying rent, the value of the REIT will be badly affected.

An even more complicated case arises when a REIT is closely tied to a single real estate development company. Often, the REIT will lend money to the developer to build a property and then take ownership of the property when it is completed. Often, the managements of the REIT and the development company are closely related, and there may be a large degree of common ownership in the two companies. There may be conflicts of interest between the unitholders of the REIT and the shareholders of the developer. The financial dealings between the two companies may be so complicated and opaque that it is difficult for an outside analyst to determine whether the prices and interest rates of the various loans and purchases between the two companies are fair to the owners of the REIT or not. In any case, analyzing the financial value of the REIT without considering the risks and returns of the related development company would clearly be inadequate.

FINANCIAL PERFORMANCE OF REITS

There is empirical evidence that REITs are characterized by sub-stantial agency costs — that is, that managers behave in ways that promote their own interests at the expense of the unitholders. Management fees are often linked to the total value of the portfolio managed, rather than to its rate of return. This creates an incentive for managers to make acquisitions even if they end up paying exces-sive amounts for properties. There is evidence that institutions and REITS tend to overpay for real estate, buying properties at prices substantially in excess of market rates.[4] REIT units typically trade at a substantial discount to the underlying asset value of the properties owned.[5] This suggests that investors are aware of the agency costs that create a conflict between managers and unitholders, and dis-count the value of REIT units accordingly. In the context of the books and articles touting the many advantages of REITs, it is worth noting Graff's conclusion: "... it is reasonable to expect that REITs in general, and larger-capitalization REITs in particular, will continue to be a great deal for management, but a risky proposition for out-side investors."[6]

Financial research on the performance of REIT units relative to other financial instruments suggests that they may be riskier than they appear. The mere fact that yields on REITs are persistently much higher than those on corporate bonds signals that financial markets must be attaching a substantial risk premium to them. Su-perficially, REIT units might appear to be close substitutes for bonds. They promise a high, regular payout of income derived from a well known set of real estate properties. Statistical studies generally show, however, that the financial behaviour of REIT unit prices is more closely correlated with that of small common stocks than that of bonds.[7] In part, this may be due to the fact that many REITs are themselves relatively small companies. REIT prices are also much more correlated with small stocks than with indexes of

---

[4] Richard A. Graff, "Economic Analysis Suggests that REIT Investment Characteris-tics are Not as Advertised", *Journal of Real Estate Portfolio Management* 7(2): 99–124, at 109, 110.

[5] Ibid, p. 113.

[6] Ibid, p. 117.

[7] See references cited by Graff, op. cit.; Jim Clayton and Greg MacKinnon, "The Time-varying Nature of the Link Between REIT, Real Estate and Financial Asset Re-turns", *Journal of Real Estate Portfolio Management* 7(1): 43–54; Liang, Youguo and Willard McIntosh, "REIT Style and Performance", *Journal of Real Estate Portfolio Management* 4(1): 69–78.

real property values. That is, they are valued as management companies rather than as mere sums of the values of the properties they own.

REFERENCES

Allen, Marcus T., Jeff Madura and Thomas Springer. 2000. "REIT Characteristics and the Sensitivity of REIT Returns." *Journal of Real Estate Finance and Economics* 21(2): 141–52.

Ambrose, Brent W., Steven R. Ehrlich, William T. Hughes and Susan M. Wachter. 2000. "REIT Economies of Scale: Fact or Fiction." *Journal of Real Estate Finance and Economics* 20(2): 211–24.

Ambrose, Brent W., and Peter Linneman. 2001. "REIT Organizational Structure and Operating Characteristics." *Journal of Real Estate Management* 21(3): 141–62.

Block, Ralph L. 2002. *Investing in REITs: Real Estate Investment Trusts.* Princeton, N.J.: Bloomberg Press.

Clayton, Jim and Greg MacKinnon. 2001. "The Time-Varying Nature of the Link Between REIT, Real Estate and Financial Asset Returns." *Journal of Real Estate Portfolio Management* 7(1): 43–54.

Dagys, Andrew. 1998. *Common Sense Investing in Real Estate Investment Trusts.* Scarborough: Prentice-Hall.

Garrigan, T., and John F.C. Parsons, eds. 1998. *Real Estate Investment Trusts: Structure, Analysis and Strategy.* New York: McGraw-Hill.

Graff, Richard A. 2001. "Economic Analysis Suggests that REIT Investment Characteristics are Not as Advertised." *Journal of Real Estate Portfolio Management* 7(2): 99–124.

Hayward, Paul. 2002. "Income Trusts: A 'Tax Efficient' Product or the Product of Tax Inefficiency?" *Canadian Tax Journal* 50(5), 1529–69.

Liang, Youguo, and Willard McIntosh. 1998. "REIT Style and Performance." *Journal of Real Estate Portfolio Management* 4(1): 69–78.

Mull, S.R., and L.A. Soenen. 1997. "U.S. REITs as an Asset Class in International Investment Portfolios." *Financial Analysts Journal* (March–April): 55–61.

Mullaney, John A. 1998. *REITS: Building Profits with Real Estate Investment Trusts.* New York: John Wiley & Sons.

Reverse Mortgages: Supplementary Retirement Income

———————————HENRY BARTEL, MICHAEL DALY &
PETER WRAGE

Abstract A large proportion of the elderly have very low incomes. Nevertheless, they often have a considerable investment in their houses. A reverse mortgage is a method of dissaving which allows these individuals to convert some of the equity in their homes into a steady income stream while retaining their residence in these homes. Unlike conventional mortgage loans, which require mortgaging future income to acquire a real asset, reverse mortgages involve obtaining a mortgage loan on the house to provide a future steam of income, thereby liquidating wealth already accumulated.
Upon retirement, many elderly homeowners are faced with the following dilemma: If they wish to remain in the house in which they have spent most of their lives and to which they may have an emotional attachment, they must accept what is often an inadequate retirement income while eventually leaving a sizeable bequest to their heirs. Alternatively, they can sell their home, which many are reluctant to do, and move to rented accommodation. In so doing, they generate for themselves a higher retirement income from the proceeds realized upon the sale of their house. However, uncertainly as to their life expectancy tends to deter them from selling. As long as they retain ownership of and continue to live in their house, they are provided with a "rent-free" service. If they sell their house, the capital derived from the sale and the income it generates could be depleted before their death.

From *The Journal of Risk and Insurance*, September 1980, Vol. XLVII, No. 3 at 477–90. Copyright American Risk and Insurance Association. All Rights Reserved. Reproduced with Permission.

The objective of a reverse mortgage is to allow individuals to convert some of the equity they have in their homes into a steady income stream, without giving up residence in them. It is the reverse of a conventional mortgage in the sense that the individual receives a monthly payment rather than making one.

Two methods of arranging for such a scheme are available. One method is the straightforward reverse mortgage (RM) in which the monthly payment received accumulates over time as a lien against the house. The other method is the RAM or reverse annuity mortgage, which involves the explicit purchase of an annuity with the proceeds of the mortgage loan. If the individual puts a low priority on retaining ownership of the house and is interested primarily in a steady income for life with a guaranteed lifetime tenancy, then he/she may elect the "home reversion" scheme, a variant of the basic RAM idea.

HOME REVERSION

The home reversion or "split equity" plan involves the outright sale of the house in return for a lump-sum payment and/or a life annuity from the proceeds. The important consideration here is that this plan requires a deferred sale. Thus, the householder no longer owns the house, although he or she can continue to live in it until death, at a nominal rent fixed at the outset.

This idea was introduced by the Canadian Province of Nova Scotia in March of 1979. Directed at retired homeowners, the plan's intent is for improving pensions by converting the equity in their house into a regular monthly benefit. Upon the death of the pensioner, the house would be sold to recoup the money paid to the pensioner, with a first option given to the deceased's immediate family. The plan would be set up and administered by some government body or agency. The potential underwriting risks are expected to be reasonable enough to make the program marketable.

Such a scheme has already been in operation for a number of years in Britain. Home Reversions Limited, a private company, offers plan whereby it purchases the individual's house outright in return for both a guaranteed fixed annuity for life, and lifetime occupancy. The current market value of the house is discounted by the individual's or couple's life expectancy, and annuity payments continue until the death of the last survivor, at which time the property is released to the company. The annuity is paid monthly in advance, less a fixed nominal rent of one pound per month. The contract requires the annuitant to purchase insurance covering the property and to maintain the property in good condition. A minimum age of 69 years is recommended for entering into this plan because the annual annuity benefit at younger ages does not seem to be worthwhile financially.

Variations on the basic scheme allow the annuitant to retain some equity in the house, with a corresponding reduction in the annuity. This variation would permit the individual to obtain some of the potential appreciation in the value of the house, whether in real or nominal terms by retaining, say, 50 percent of the equity.

A more personalized variation of the home reversion plan has been in operation in France (and to a lesser extent in Belgium and Italy) for decades, and according to that country's Ministry of Finance it remains a popular practice. It is estimated that about 400,000 elderly people in France receive "rentes viageres" income not only on their houses or small farms but also on apartments and even houseboats.

The "vente en viager," as it is called, is a transaction between two parties arranged in a legal manner through a "notaire" who specializes in property matters. It involves a complex negotiation in which the value of the property, the age and health of the owner or owners, and the resources of the would-be buyer come into play. In effect, the elderly person sells his or her property to a buyer and the price, minus a down-payment ("bouquet"), is divided by the seller's life expectancy calculated by the "notaire" with the resulting amount paid by the buyer to the seller as a monthly ("rente viagere") income until the latter dies, whereupon the payment ceases and the house reverts to the buyer. This system not only is enshrined in property law but also is included in French income tax regulations.

Unlike the practice in the United Kingdom, this practice is declining in France for two primary reasons, To begin with, owing to the personalized nature of the arrangement, the buyer takes a considerable gamble, as there is no mortality risk-sharing on the part of buyers. Furthermore, as a result of the absence of an effective secondary market, the buyer must contemplate living in the same community indefinitely. In a mobile society, such a home reversion or split equity arrangement would not be a particularly attractive investment for an individual. The answer to these problems would appear to be the establishment of a more institutionalized and sophisticated market such as that which has developed in the United Kingdom.

REVERSE MORTGAGES

The reverse mortgage is strictly a debt instrument that does not confer any ownership rights to the issuing company. Thus, rather than sell part or all of the house, a loan is arranged with the house as security. Calculated over either a fixed term or for life, the homeowner receives a periodic payment which, in accumulating over time as a mortgage loan secured by the house, is worked out so as not to exceed some proportion (say 75 percent) of the current market value of the house. The mortgage loan falls due for repayment at some prescribed future date.

Recently the Metropolitan Trust Company, the first company in Canada to offer such a scheme, began test-marketing its "Independent Income Mortgage" in Toronto. The program works as follows: every year, for a maximum of ten years, the company pays the individual a mutually agreed-upon fixed sum, discounted at the going interest rate (currently 11 percent). The principal accumulates in the form of a mortgage on the house. An initial fee of $500 is charged, with an annual amount of $100 thereafter, to cover all costs (appraisal, administration, and so on). Thus, for example, to receive an annual net income of about $3,000 the homeowner would incur a mortgage liability of about $60,000 by the end of the ten years.

As the money is a pure loan, no income tax considerations are involved. Furthermore, no problem exists as to the individual's possible qualification for various forms of government aid or income supplements as might accrue to elderly retired persons. Under this particular plan no income requirement or age limit is imposed. In one sense the risk is negligible to the individual, since he or she can cancel the contract at any time. Risks does exist, however, to the extent that the contract has variable interest arrangements, linked to prevailing market mortgage rates.

At the end of the ten years, the individual has a number of options. Renewal for another term is possible if the house has appreciated sufficiently (up to 75 percent of the increased value) or the debt can be converted into a regular first mortgage loan to be repaid by the mortgagee or members of the mortgagee's family. Alternatively, the individual may sell the home at its new value, pay off the debt, and keep the remainder. (Death of the spouse leaves all options open for the survivor.) Note that if the house appreciates at just under 3.5 percent a year, after ten years the increase in equity will more than offset the total accumulated mortgage interest.

The major disadvantage of the reverse mortgage, as currently offered in Canada, is that such a contract is for a fixed term only, as only life insurance companies can offer lifetime contracts under current legislation. This limitation presents the danger of leaving elderly persons with up to 75 percent of their equity depleted exactly at a time when they are most vulnerable to reductions in their income. The spectre of forcing an elderly person out of his or her house at such a time could create such adverse publicity that companies in Britain refuse to engage in fixed-term arrangements. Partly for this reason but also because of certain provisions of that country's Finance Act[11], the reverse annuity mortgage with its lifetime guarantee feature has garnered much appeal, although it is a more complicated financial arrangement.

REVERSE ANNUITY MORTGAGES

Like the reverse mortgage, the RAM is a pure debt instrument. A mortgage loan is taken out which, in turn, is used to purchase a lifetime annuity, and repayment of the principal is deferred until the death of the owner, or prior sale of the property. The periodic annuity payment made to the individual is reduced by the interest on the mortgage loan.

What this transaction amounts to in dollars and cents may be demonstrated using an example from a case in Britain (Illustration I). A 75 year-old woman owning a $50,000 house takes out a $40,000 (80 percent) mortgage loan for which she receives an annuity guaranteed for life. The gross annuity per annum is $4,136. If she is a taxpayer, the minimum tax rate of 33 percent applies to the interest component of the annuity, amounting to $148 per annum. Conversely, she also benefits from a tax deduction on the mortgage interest payable which, at 33 percent, adds $792 to the net annuity. After paying the $2,400 mortgage interest (here fixed at 6 percent), she has a net annual income of $2,380. Note that if she is a nontaxpayer, her annual income is reduced to $1,736.

Thus, under the current British scheme, the attractiveness of a RAM to the homeowner is due largely to the tax refund earned on the mortgage loan interest. If the pensioner has no other taxable income, the amount of the annuity will be substantially less. In such a case the value of the house, in conjunction with the individual's age (and thus life expectancy), will be of crucial importance. The higher the tax rate to which the individual is subject, the larger will be the tax refund on the mortgage interest and, thus, the higher will be the final annuity proceeds. In general, the British schemes advise a minimum age of 70 or 72 years before this package becomes particularly attractive for individuals of any tax bracket.

Variations on the basic RAM scheme include, for example, a lump-sum payment which precedes the basic annuity; a reappraisal of the house after, say, the first five years with the annuity readjusted

---

[1] Under the Finance Act, 1974, mortgage interest payments on such a loan are deductible for income tax purposes provided not less than nine-tenths of the proceeds of the loan are applied to the purchase of a time annuity by the person to whom the loan is made.

ILLUSTRATION I

British example of RAM benefits for a 75 year old woman, owning a $50,000 house

	Annual Income
Gross annuity	$4,136
Less: Income Tax at 33 percent	148
Net Annuity	$3,988
Less: Mortgage Interst at 6 percent	2,400
Actual Annual Income	$1,588
Plus: Tax Deduction on Mortgage Interest	792
Potential Annual Income	$2,380
Non-Taxpayer Income	$1,736

Source: Adapted from an illustration of a Home Income Plan offered by Hambro Provident Assurance Limited, London, England, 1978.

---

accordingly; and a life annuity preceded by a guaranteed fixed-term annuity. It also should be possible to arrange for a variable annuity whereby the annual payment is increased by some constant factor. For example, if higher expenditures are anticipated in later years, such as increased medical expenses, home care services, and so on, the pensioner might like to see the annuity payment increase by 5 or 10 percent each year.

REVERSE MORTGAGES VERSUS REVERSE ANNUITY MORTGAGES

No conceptual difference exists between a Reverse Mortgage and a Reverse Annuity Mortgage, although institutional, legislative, and regulatory factors may make one more desirable than the other. For example, the currently offered, strict RM is available for a fixed term only. Nor is there any reason why that particular scheme could not be offered on a lifetime basis. It may be the case that, as in Canada, only life insurance companies, and not trust companies, can engage in "guaranteed-for-life" business. Still, instead of using an arbitrarily chosen term for the RM, the term could be set for a period equal to the individual's life expectancy. Alternatively, the RM could be made renewable indefinitely, with the annual payments calculated (reduced) to assure that the available home equity would not be exhausted prior to the end of the full life expectancy. Under this arrangement, the individual still suffers the risk of living past his/her life expectancy, the point at which the mortgageable equity is fully liquidated. Whether one could insure separately against this particular contingency only, on a cost-feasible basis, is difficult to assess at the moment, because the program is in its infancy and the demand for such an insurance scheme has yet to be determined[22].

Risk works both ways, however. Under the RM, the individual assumes the risk of outliving the term of the contract. Under the RAM, the individual's heirs assume the risk of his/her not living long enough. These risks arise because the annuity payment is based on the pensioner's life expectancy. The longer the life expectancy, the smaller will be the periodic payment. However, if the individual should die six months after fully paying for a 15-year expected-life annuity, the remaining 14.5 years accrue to the company instead of the heirs[33]. The life insurance company is entitled to the gain because it assumes the risk that an individual will live past his/her life expectancy. The risk to the insurance company is pooled, and thus is significantly lower than the risk to the individual and the heirs.

Another problem with the RAM is that its earned-income component, i.e. the interest portion of the annuity received, is treated as taxable income. This interest income also reduces the dollar amount of government support to pensioners because many of the government retirement income programs are income-tested. Yet, conceptually, the annuity interest component serves only as an offset against the mortgage interest that falls due, the reconciliation of which is accomplished "internally" with a straight reverse mortgage. Unfortunately, income-tested government support programs are unlikely to consider the associated mortgage interest payment in their income support calculations. In Canada such mortgage interest is not tax deductible if incurred expressly to facilitate the earning of annuity income. Thus, while it is true that the mortgage interest deductibility feature makes the RAM particularly attractive for certain age-sex-house equity combinations, as currently operated in Britain, this advantage also extends with equal force to the straight RM. The optimal choice between the RM and the RAM would therefore appear to depend much more on who will bear the mortality risk, and the institutional constraints which are operative at that time.

---

[2] The fact that the market value of the house may appreciate during this time could reduce such a risk considerably.

[3] In the U.K., Hambro Provident has a Capital Protection Plan whereby an individual can ensure that the loan amount repayable on early death will be limited.

WHAT AFFECTS REVERSE ANNUITY MORTGAGE BENEFITS?

The benefits arising under the RAM scheme are sensitive to the individual's sex and age, to whether the person is single, married, or wishes to take out the contract jointly with another person (such as two sisters), to current property values and prevailing interest rates, and to marginal tax rates where applicable. To observe this sensitivity, consider Illustrations II to IV.

First, consider the sex-age-single/marital configuration in Illustration II. The "potential annual income" nearly doubles for a female if she purchases the RAM at age 70 instead of age 65, $1,279 instead of $667. It increases to $2,048 if she postpones purchase until age 75. A male at each age is significantly better off, simply because his life expectancy is approximately five years lower. Thus, a 70-year-old female, for example, will receive benefits equivalent to those of a 65-year-old male. If, however, a married couple acquires a RAM jointly, so that the benefits continue to be paid until the death of the last surviving spouse, the number of expected annuity payments will increase to the point where the periodic payment approaches an unacceptably small amount. Thus, for a 65-year-old female who takes out a RAM with her 70-year-old husband, instead of alone, the annual benefit is reduced from $667 to #371. This illustration demonstrates why, in Britain, there are suggested minimum age requirements, especially for couples.

Illustration II (as well as Illustration III) also focus on three classes of annual income: actual, potential, and non-taxpayer. In all cases the mortgage interest tax deductibility accounts for the highest annual benefit. (This conclusion holds also for straight RMs.) In Canada, for example, where the annuity interest component is taxable, but the mortgage interest is not tax deductible, the relevant benefit is shown as "actual annual income." The higher the marginal tax bracket, the lower the figure will be. If the individual pays no taxes, the applicable benefit is shown as "non-taxpayer income." In Britain, as in the United States, the deductibility of mortgage loan interest payments accounts for the highest benefits from the RAM scheme. The higher the marginal tax bracket, the higher is the "potential annual income," as seen in Illustration III. In fact, with mortgage loan interest payments deductible under a RAM, the higher his/her marginal tax bracket, the lower are the ages at which the individual can receive approximately the same annual benefits.

The sensitivity of the net income from the RAM to different interest rates may be the greatest concern. As seen from Illustration IV, an unambiguous and significant decrease occurs in all types of

ILLUSTRATION II
CALCULATIONS OF ANNUAL RAM BENEFITS BY SEX, MARITAL STATUS, AND AGE*

		Female			Male			Couple (Last Survivor)		
		65 (17.5)	70 (13.8)	75 (10.6)	65 (13.7)	70 (10.9)	75 (8.5)	65 (20.0)	70 (16.5)	75 (13.3)
Gross Annuity	(6%)	$3,694	$4,303	$5,072	$4,303	$5,072	$5,881	$3,400	$3,818	$4,303
Less: Income Tax	(10%)	147	145	144	145	144	144	150	146	145
Net Annuity		$3,547	$4,159	$4,928	$4,159	$4,928	$5,737	$3,251	$3,671	$4,159
Less: Mortgage Interest	(8%)	3,200	3,200	3,200	3,200	3,200	3,200	3,200	3,200	3,200
Actual Annual Income		$ 347	$ 959	$1,728	$ 959	$1,728	$2,537	$ 51	$ 471	$ 959
Plus: Tax Deduction on Mortgage Interest	(10%)	$ 320	$ 320	$ 320	$ 320	$ 320	$ 320	$ 320	$ 320	$ 320
Potential Annual Income		$ 667	$1,279	$2,048	$1,279	$2,048	$2,857	$ 371	$ 791	$1,279
Non-Taxpayer Income		$ 494	$1,103	$1,872	$1,103	$1,872	$2,681	$ 200	$ 618	$1,103

* Notes:

1. The example is calculated for a house valued at $50,000 with an 80 percent ($40,000) mortgage.

2. Figures are: on an annual basis;
   rounded to nearest
   dollar; and
   may not add due to rounding.

3. Life expectancy always is rounded up, to compute the term of the annuity.

4. Column headings XX (YY.Y) represent the case of an individual, or male/female couple, aged XX, with a life expectancy of YY.Y years. For example, for a female 65 (17.5) means that she is 65 years old with a life expectancy of 17.5 years.

5. Last survivor annuities are for male/female couples, with the female aged XX and the male five years older. The life expectancy YY.Y is calculated to the death of the surviving spouse.

Source: Calculations made by authors.

ILLUSTRATION III
ANNUAL RAM BENEFITS TO A 75-YEAR-OLD WOMAN SUBJECT
TO DIFFERENT TAX RATES

		Annual Income with		
		10% Tax	20% Tax	30% Tax
Gross Annuity	(6%)	$5,072	$5,072	$5,072
Less: Income		144	287	431
Net Annuity		$4,928	$4,785	$4,641
Less: Mortgage Interest	(8%)	3,200	3,200	3,200
Actual Annual Income		$1,728	$1,585	$1,441
Plus: Tax Deduction on Mortgage		$ 320	$ 640	$ 960
Potential Annual Income		$2,048	$2,225	$2,401
Non-Taxpayer Income		$1,871	$1,872	$1,872

Notes:
1. The example is calculated for a house valued at $50,000 with an 80 percent ($40,000) mortgage.
2. Figures are: on an annual basis;
        rounded to nearest dollar; and
        may not add due to rounding.

Source: Calculations made by authors.

annual incomes associated with higher interest rates. It follows that with successively higher levels of inflation which drive up nominal interest rates, the houseowner will be worse off in terms of the potential RAM benefit both in nominal and real terms. Moreover, the two-point interest spread assumed between the annuity rate and the mortgage rate may become insufficient to cover rising administrative and other costs. Finally, as a tendency exists during periods of inflation to shorten maturity terms, life insurers may become increasingly reluctant to commit themselves to annuities exceeding 10 years at fixed annuity rates, unless they can offset this liability with an investment of an equal term, such as holding the associated mortgage themselves. Yet if variable-rate RAMs are considered, the uncertain dollar benefit may discourage some elderly homeowners from seriously considering RAMs.

THE EFFECTS OF INFLATION

Inflation not only drives up interest rates and thus reduces the potential RAM benefit, it also drives up house values. The current market price of the house will be higher, therefore offsetting some

---

ILLUSTRATION IV
ANNUAL RAM BENEFITS TO A 75 YEAR OLD WOMAN UNDER
DIFFERENT INTEREST RATE COMBINATIONS

		Annual Income with Annuity/ Mortgage Rates of		
		6/8%	8/10%	10/12%
Gross Annuity		$5,071	$5,603	$6,159
Less: Income Tax	(10%)	144	197	252
Net Annuity		$4,928	$5,406	$5,906
Less: Mortgage		3,200	4,000	4,800
Actual Annual Income		$1,728	$1,406	$1,106
Plus: Tax Deduction on Mortgage Interest	(10%)	$ 320	$ 400	$ 480
Potential Annual Income		$2,048	$1,806	$1,586
Non-Taxpayer Income		$1,871	$1,603	$1,359

Notes:
1. The example is calculated for a house valued at $50,000 with an 80 percent ($40,000) mortgage.
2. Figures are: on an annual basis;
rounded to nearest dollar; and
may not add due to rounding.
3. Successively higher interest rates are assumed on the basis of various expectations about future inflation rates. A constant two-point spread is assumed for administrative and other cost considerations.

Source: Calculations made by authors.

---

of the loss incurred from higher interest rates. More importantly, however, the appreciation in the value of the house can be used by the pensioner to increase the annuity payment.

Consider Illustrations V and VI. Suppose that the average price of a house increases at 8 percent per year due either to a 3 percent real appreciation plus a 5 percent inflationary factor, or due to zero real appreciation and an 8 percent nominal price rise. After five years, the $50,000 house used in this example will have a market value of $73,466. With an 80 percent mortgage, this increase would allow $58,773 to be used for a RAM. But $40,000 was previously committed, leaving $18,773 available for a "new" or additional RAM. Illustration II showed the RAM benefit at the original value of the house. Illustration V shows the additional RAM benefits that accrue from the $18,773, using the same assumptions, but having increased everyone's age by five years. Illustration VI shows the total RAM benefits that would start in the sixth year and last for life.

ILLUSTRATION V
CALCULATION OF INCREMENTAL ANNUAL RAM BENEFITS ARISING AFTER FIVE YEAR APPRECIATION IN HOUSE VALUE BY SEX, MARITAL STATUS, AND AGE*

		Female			Male			Couple (Last Survivor)		
		70	75	80	70	75	80	70	75	80
		(13.8)	(10.6)	(7.9)	(10.9)	(8.5)	(6.4)	(16.5)	(13.3)	(10.6)
Gross Annuity	(6%)	$2,020	$2,300	$3,023	$2,380	$2,760	$3,363	$1,792	$2,020	$2,380
Less: Income Tax	(10%)	68	67	68	67	67	68	69	68	67
Net Annuity		$1,952	$2,313	$2,956	$2,313	$2,693	$3,295	$1,723	$1,952	$2,313
Less: Mortgage Interest	(8%)	1,502	1,502	1,502	1,502	1,502	1,502	1,502	1,502	1,502
Actual Annual Income		$ 450	$ 811	$1,454	$ 811	$1,191	$1,793	$ 221	$ 450	$ 811
Plus: Tax Deduction on Mortgage Interest	(10%)	$ 150	$ 150	$ 150	$ 150	$ 150	$ 150	$ 150	$ 150	$ 150
Potential Annual Income		$ 600	$ 961	$1,604	$ 961	$1,341	$1,943	$ 371	$ 600	$ 961
Non-Taxpayer Income		$ 518	$ 878	$1,521	$ 878	$1,258	$1,861	$ 290	$ 518	$ 878

* Notes:

1. This example is calculated for a house initially valued at $50,000 that appreciates at 8 percent per year for five years to $73,466. With an 80 percent mortgage, this raises the mortgage amount from $40,000 to $58,773, allowing an additional RAM to be raised for $18,773 at the end of the five years. Note that all beneficiaries are now five years older.

2. Figures are: on an annual basis;
    rounded to nearest dollar; and
    may not add due to rounding.

[3] Life expectancy always is rounded up, to compute the term of the annuity.

[4] Column headings XX (YY.Y) represent the case of an individual, or male/female couple, aged XX, with a life expectancy of YY.Y years. For example, for a female 70 (13.8) means that she is 70 years old with a life expectancy of 13.8 years.

[5] Last survivor annuities are for male/female couples, with the female aged XX and the male five years older. The life expectancy YY.Y is calculated to the death of the surviving spouse.

Source: Calculations made by authors.

ILLUSTRATION VI
CALCULATIONS OF COMBINED ANNUAL RAM BENEFITS BY SEX, MARITAL STATUS, AND AGE*

	Female			Male			Couple (Last Survivor)		
	65 (17.5)	70 (13.8)	75 (10.6)	65 (13.7)	70 (10.9)	75 (8.5)	65 (20.0)	70 (16.5)	75 (13.3)
	70 (13.8)	75 (10.6)	80 (7.9)	70 (10.9)	75 (8.5)	80 (6.4)	70 (16.5)	75 (13.3)	80 (10.6)
Gross Annuity (6%)	$5,714	$6,683	$8,095	$6,683	$7,832	$9,244	$5,192	$5,838	$6,683
Less: Income Tax (10%)	215	212	212	212	211	212	219	214	212
Net Annuity	$5,499	$6,472	$7,884	$6,472	$7,621	$9,032	$4,974	$5,623	$6,472
Less: Mortgage Interest (8%)	4,702	4,702	4,702	4,702	4,702	4,702	4,702	4,702	4,702
Actual Annual Income	$797	$1,770	$3,182	$1,770	$2,919	$4,330	$272	$921	$1,770
Plus: Tax Deduction on Mortgage Interest (10%)	$470	$470	$470	$470	$470	$470	$470	$470	$470
Potential Annual Income	$1,267	$2,240	$3,652	$2,240	$3,389	$4,800	$742	$1,391	$2,240
Non-Taxpayer Income	$1,012	$1,981	$3,939	$1,981	$3,130	$4,542	$490	$1,136	$1,981

* Notes:

1. This example is calculated for an individual who takes out a RAM for a house valued at $50,000 with an 80 percent ($40,000) mortgage and then, after five years, takes out another RAM for $18,773, which reflects the increase in the price of the house being appreciated at 8 percent per year. In other words, it adds Illustrations II and V together. Thus these are the total benefits received as of the beginning of the sixth year.

2. Figures are: on an annual basis;
   rounded to nearest dollar; and
   may not add due to rounding.

3. Life expectancy always is rounded up, to compute the term of the annuity.

4. Column headings XX (YY.Y) represent the case of an individual, or male/female couple, aged XX, with a life expectancy of YY.Y years. For example, for a female 65 (17.5) means that she is 65 years old with a life expectancy of 17.5 years.

5. Last survivor annuities are for male/female couples, with the female aged XX and the male five years older. The life expectancy YY.Y is calculated to the death of the surviving spouse.

Source: Calculations made by authors.

Interestingly enough, the increase in benefits is substantial, in many cases a near doubling of benefits. This result underscores the sensitivity of RAM benefits to the age factor, in this case an increase of five years, with the resulting reduction in the life expectancy.

The frequency with which such a readjustment of RAM benefits can be undertaken depends on the rate of price increases, as well as on the cost of house appraisal and associated administrative costs.

In principle, it would be possible to raise the annuity benefits to concur with rises in the price level. The straight RM scheme currently offered in Canada has this built-in possibility, because there is an annual house appraisal with an option to change to payment to the elderly homeowner. Recall that the total cost associated with this illustration was a fixed and guaranteed $100 per year. In the case of the RAM, moreover, it should be possible to increase the annual benefit by more than the inflation rate because of the continuously reduced life expectancy the individual would have remaining. It thus becomes a variable annuity, with periodic benefit increases linked to expected inflation rates.

SUMMARY AND CONCLUSIONS

The implications of a Reverse Annuity Mortgage scheme, and its variants, seem to be generally favorable. First and foremost it would remove an imperfection from the financial market which compels people to make an all-or-nothing choice. Either they retain full ownership of their home and accept a low retirement income, or alternatively they sell their home in order to generate a higher retirement income and move to rented accommodations. This new class of financial instruments would permit elderly homeowners to fine-tune the amount of any bequest (embodied in the value of their home) which they might want to leave to their heirs. In addition, the demand for housing should increase because the house now becomes a more divisible asset. Second, it would address itself particularly to the needs of the low-income groups, as the ratio of home equity to income is higher among the former. Third, it would provide an increased demand for mortgage funds, particularly at a time when the high proportion of aged in the population might suggest a decreased demand for new housing. Fourth, during a prolonged period of inflation, the house could still provide protection against price rises, especially where the RAM is periodically increased to remain in fixed proportion to the value of the house. This advantage does not apply to the Home Reversion Plan, as that plan involves a deferred sale and hence the elderly person no longer has an equity in the house.

These various types of reverse mortgage and home reversion plans have not been immune from criticism. The suggestion has been made that such schemes would result in over-housing of senior citizens. However, one could argue that this kind of situation is no different than that which exists in the case of young couples who buy a house with a conventional mortgage before rearing a family, or, for that matter, other individuals or couples in different circumstances.

It has also been claimed that these schemes would encourage elderly persons to stay in homes which they cannot afford to maintain and as a result, their houses are more likely to fall into disrepair. Hence the implication that they would be better off selling and moving into something more manageable. Yet it is often forgotten that some individuals will opt to remain in their homes regardless of their income. In this case, to the extent that the inadequacy of their income prevents them from maintaining their home, reverse mortgage schemes by increasing their retirement incomes could mean that individuals can afford the maintenance cost. Indeed, it is perhaps somewhat paradoxical that, faced with the rising costs and consequent financial strain of homeownership, the very act of parting with an interest in their home, through a reverse mortgage, may generate the income to enable senior citizens to remain there for the rest of their lives. Needless to say, it is still in a person's own interest to maintain the house if they are to benefit from any future increase in its value. (Under the reversion plan, individuals would presumably have the same responsibilities as any other tenant.)

The optimal choice between home reversion, RMs, and RAMs probably depends on who wishes to retain the security of ownership (equity), who will accept the mortality risk, and what institutional, legislative, and regulatory constraints are in operation. Most likely, all these instruments will find market acceptance, and many variations thereof will spring up, to accommodate the diversity of preferences found in the marketplace.

Valuation and Appraisal

Commercial Real Estate Valuation: Fundamentals Versus Investor Sentiment

——————————— JIM CLAYTON, DAVID C. LING &
ANDY NARANJO

INTRODUCTION

Classical finance theory posits that prices of assets traded in relatively frictionless markets reflect rationally estimated risk-adjusted discount rates and future income streams; there is no role for investor sentiment. If mispricing does occur, it is quickly eliminated by the actions of informed arbitrageurs who compete to capture the abnormal returns. The inability of the standard present value model to explain dramatic run-ups and subsequent crashes in asset prices, such as the internet stock "bubble" in the late 1990s and other price anomalies, has led to the development of the "behavioral" finance approach to asset valuation. In these behavior models, investor sentiment can have a role in the determination of asset prices — independent of market fundamentals.

The behavioral approach explicitly recognizes that some investors are not rational and that systematic biases in these investor's beliefs induce them to trade on non-fundamental information (i.e., sentiment). Baker and Wurgler (2007) define investor sentiment as a misguided belief about the growth in future cash flows or investment risks (or both) based on the current information set. The behavioral approach is also predicated on "limits to arbitrage." Arbitrageurs face non-trivial transaction and implementation costs that prevent them from taking fully offsetting positions to correct mispricing. In addition, rational risk-averse investors are unable to arbitrage away the mispricing because the unpredictability of investor sentiment exposes them to "noise trader risk" (DeLong et al. 1990). Hence, to the extent that sentiment influences valuation, taking a position opposite to prevailing market sentiment can be both expensive and risky. It is therefore important to understand the relative influence of fundamentals versus sentiment in asset valuation.

Private commercial real estate markets are characterized by higher transaction costs and substantially less liquidity than public stock markets. Thus, if relatively small frictions in the stock market can cause sustained periods of overvaluation, it seems plausible to posit that private real estate markets are potentially more susceptible to such episodes. The inability to short sell private real estate restricts the opportunity for sophisticated traders to enter the market and eliminate mispricing, especially if they believe the property market is overvalued. Limits to arbitrage might therefore be expected to lead to larger deviations of prices from fundamental value in the presence of sentiment investors.

Despite the potential importance of investor sentiment in private real estate markets, no previous research directly investigates the relative roles of fundamentals and investor sentiment in the pricing and return generation process.[1] This paper examines the relative influence of fundamentals and investor sentiment in explaining the time-series variation in property-specific national-level capitalization rates.

Our specific innovations are twofold. First, we apply a new dataset to the study of cap rate determinants that includes fundamental variables and both survey (direct) measures of investor sentiment and composite (indirect) measures of investor sentiment constructed from a set of sentiment proxies. Second, the nature of our data allows us to utilize an innovative econometric approach to the analysis of the relation between sentiment and property pricing. More specifically, we derive an equilibrium model of cap rates specified as a function of real estate space and capital market fundamentals that is estimated using error-correction techniques, thereby capturing both short and long-run pricing dynamics. The primary contribution of the paper is the exploration of the impact of time-varying fundamentals and investor sentiment on property pricing. To summarize our findings, we find evidence that investor sentiment significantly impacts pricing, even after controlling for changes in expected rental growth, equity risk premiums, T-bond yields, and lagged adjustments from long run equilibrium.

The remainder of the paper proceeds as follows. "Background and Previous Literature" discusses the relevant literature, including key insights from sentiment-based theories of stock pricing as well as

---

[1] Hendershott and MacGregor (2005a, b) test whether cap rates, and hence property values, reflect rational projections of future rental growth and expected returns, thereby providing an indirect test of the role of sentiment.

previous empirical studies of the determinants of variations in real estate cap rates. In "Modeling Prices and Cap Rates", "The Dynamic Nature of Real Estate Pricing and Cap Rates", and "Empirical Specification" we present our conceptual and empirical models of cap rates. Section "Data" discusses the data. "Results" and "A Vector Error-Correction Model" contain our empirical findings and robustness checks. We conclude with a summary.

BACKGROUND AND PREVIOUS LITERATURE

Both sentiment and limits to arbitrage are necessary conditions for the existence of mispricing. More specifically, in a market characterized by heterogeneous investors, the existence of short sale constraints can generate deviations in asset prices from fundamental values. Optimistic investors take long positions, while pessimistic investors would like to take short positions. Short-sale constraints, however, may inhibit the ability of rational investors to eliminate overpricing, even over sustained time periods. Therefore, rational investors may sit on the sidelines when they believe prices are too high relative to fundamentals, leaving market clearing prices to be determined, at the margin, by overly optimistic investors as in Baker and Stein (2004).

Most behavioral finance research has followed a "bottom up" microeconomic approach that appeals to biases in individual investor psychology to explain how and why investors might overreact or under-react to past returns and information about market fundamentals.[2] Brown and Cliff (2004, 2005) and Baker and Wurgler (2006, 2007) offer a new "top down" macroeconomic approach, the first step of which is to derive measures of aggregate investor sentiment for stocks. Brown and Cliff (2004, 2005) employ both survey measures of investor sentiment as well as sentiment measures derived from a principal component analysis of a set of potential sentiment proxies. They find that investor sentiment is highly correlated with contemporaneous stock returns but has little short-run predictive power (Brown and Cliff 2004). However, taking a longer term perspective (2 to 3 years), periods of high sentiment are followed by low returns as the market mean reverts (Brown and Cliff 2005).

Baker and Wurgler (2006, 2007) also employ principal component analysis to construct a sentiment measure, and they extend the literature by quantifying the differential effect of sentiment on the

---

[2] Hirshleifer (2001) and Barberis and Thaler (2003) provide reviews of the extensive behavioral finance literature.

cross-section of stock returns by identifying which stocks are likely to be more affected by sentiment. Consistent with model predictions, their results suggest that when beginning-of-period proxies for investor sentiment are high (low), subsequent returns are relatively low (high) for stocks that are either more speculative in nature or for which arbitrage tends to be particularly risky.

Real estate investors monitor market sentiment in several ways. First, they may subscribe to data services that provide regular survey-based information about investment sentiment (such as the quarterly RERC Real Estate Report used in this paper). Many investors also monitor variables related to "capital flows" into the real estate sector. For example, they may track data on mortgage flows, the dollar volume and number of properties sold, and capital flowing into real estate investment vehicles (e.g., commingled funds for institutional and high net worth investors) under the belief that there is a common sentiment component embedded in these investor activity variables.[3]

Although regarded as important by practitioners, there has been relatively little academic work aimed at understanding the role of fundamentals versus investor sentiment and capital flows in real estate pricing dynamics. A contemporaneous correlation between capital flows and cap rates does not by itself imply causation. Capital flows and property prices (and hence cap rates) might both respond in a similar fashion to fundamental economic variables and risk factors, such as unexpected inflation, changes in real interest rates, or revisions in risk premiums. For example, if both capital flows and property prices increase when positive economic news is released, then a negative contemporaneous correlation between capital flows and cap rates does not prove that capital flows cause or predict cap rates.

The lack of research examining the role of fundamentals versus sentiment and capital flows in real estate markets is partly due to data limitations. Ling and Naranjo (2003, 2006) examine the dynamics of commercial real estate capital flows and returns. Their work provides evidence that capital flows into public (i.e., securitized) real estate markets do not predict subsequent returns, but that returns do affect subsequent capital flows into these securitized real estate mar-

---

[3] As part of the growing behavioral finance literature, researchers have also begun to carefully explore the impact of "flows" and trading activity on asset prices in public markets. See, for example, Warther (1995), Edelen and Warner (2001), Froot et al. (2001), Brown et al. (2002), Griffin et al. (2007), and Fama and French (2007). Clayton (2003) reviews much of this literature with a focus on the implications for private real estate.

kets. Fisher et al. (2007) extend the work of Ling and Naranjo (2003, 2006) by investigating the short-and long-run dynamics among institutional capital flows and property returns in the largest US metropolitan areas. The authors find some evidence that lagged institutional capital flows influence current returns at the aggregate level, but the evidence is less convincing when disaggregated by metropolitan area and property type. These papers provide useful empirical characterizations of the dynamics of real estate capital flows and pricing, and therefore provide a solid foundation on which additional research can build. However, their results do not directly address the role sentiment plays in real estate markets, as they do not explicitly relate capital flows to investor sentiment within a model of property pricing.

Shilling and Sing (2007) examine the rationality of investors' expected income growth rates and total return forecasts in private commercial real estate markets. Their findings are consistent with models of investor irrationality. Furthermore, Shilling and Sing find evidence that investors act overly optimistic and that they generally anchor their expectations to the previous period. Finally, Ling (2005) provides preliminary univariate evidence consistent with real estate pricing being driven at times by investor sentiment.[4]

MODELING PRICES AND CAP RATES

Archer and Ling (1997) argue that three "markets" play a role in determining commercial real estate prices: space markets, capital markets, and property markets. Local market rents are determined in the space market (i.e., the market for leasable space). Required risk premiums for assets with varying profiles of cash flow risk are determined in the capital market. Finally, property markets are where asset-specific discount rates, property values, and cap rates are determined.

Property-specific discount rates are determined by the interaction of the risk-free rate, investor risk premiums, and the risk profile of the specific property. For a given stream of expected net operating income (NOI), the equilibrium property price at time t, P_t^e, should equal the present value of the NOIs discounted at the assumed constant unlevered risk-adjusted rate, r_t. That is,

---

[4] Gompers and Lerner (2000) study the relationship between flow of funds (commitments) into venture capital funds and the valuation of new investments (firms) financed by the venture capital funds. Their findings are consistent with an uninformed demand/sentiment explanation of the link between fund flows and valuations.

$$P_t^e = \frac{NOI_1}{(1+r_t)} + \frac{NOI_1(1+g_{t=2})}{(1+r_t)^2} + \frac{NOI_3(1+g_{t=3})}{(1+r_t)^3} + \dots$$
$$+ \frac{NOI_{T-1}(1+g_{t=T}) + NSP_T}{(1+r_t)^T} \tag{1}$$

where T is the expected holding period in years and NSPT is the expected net sale proceeds in year T.[5] It is well known (e.g., Geltner et al. 2007, pp. 209–210) that if, at time t, NOI is expected to grow at a constant rate gt, and NSP is expected to remain a constant multiple of NOI, then Eq. 1 simplifies to a valuation formula in which P_t^e is solely a function of the expected growth in NOI and the property specific risk-adjusted discount rate. That is,

$$p_t^e = \frac{NOI_1}{r_t - g_t} = \frac{NOI_1}{R_t^e} \quad or \quad \frac{P_t^e}{NOI_1} = \frac{1}{r_t - g_t} \tag{2}$$

Note that property values can be expressed as a multiple of first-year NOI and the size of the multiple is a function of (1) the property-specific discount rate, and (2) expected changes in NOI.[6] The equilibrium cap rate at time t, Re, is merely the

$$r_t^e = r_t - g_t \tag{3}$$

It is important to note that the level of NOI has no impact on the cap rate. Rather, it is the excepted change in NOI that affects the price investors are willing to pay per dollar of first year NOI. Of course, it is unlikely that NOI growth rates and future discount rates are expected to be constant forever. Nevertheless, Eq. 3 is an approximation that motivates our empirical cap rate specification and is consistent with a more general present value model that allows for time-variation in NOI growth and the discount rate to impact commercial property valuation and hence the cap rate.[7]

---

[5] NOI is assumed to include a reserve for expected capital expenditures and other nonrecurring expenses, such as leasing commissions.

[6] State and federal income tax effects also affect property values and, therefore, price/NOI multiples, as may the amount and cost of mortgage financing.

[7] Geltner and Mei (1995) and Plazzi et al. (2004) both adapt variants of Campbell and Shiller's (1998) log-linearized present value model with time-varying discount and "dividend" growth rates to study the relative contributions of time-variation in expected future returns versus property income in property valuation. Both studies conclude that in the short run, property price fluctuations are driven primarily by changes in expected returns and not expected rents.

The risk-adjusted discount rate has two components: RF_t, the rate of return available on a risk-free. Treasury bond with a maturity equal to the expected holding period of the property; and RF_t, the required risk premium, which is property, market, and time dependent. Clearly, RF_t, is determined outside local space and property markets, as yields on Treasury securities are determined by the bid and ask prices of Treasury market investors from around the world.

What about the determinants of RF_t? In the capital markets, commercial real estate competes with all other assets for a place in investors' portfolios. According to classical portfolio theory, investors will select a mix of investments based on the variances and covariances of the returns among the possible assets. As investors bid for their optimal portfolio mix, their bidding simultaneously determines the required risk premiums for the universe of investments according to their risk (variance and covariance) profiles. Thus, the pricing of risk depends on risk preferences articulated in the broader capital as well as the specific risk profile of the investment, which is determined by current and expected future conditions in the space market in which the property is located.

THE DYNAMIC NATURE OF REAL ESTATE PRICING AND CAP RATES

In highly liquid public securities markets, asset prices are believed to adjust quickly to changes in market fundamentals such as interest rates, inflation expectations, and national and local market conditions. However, in private, commercial real estate markets, observed cap rates may adjust more gradually to the arrival of new information because of numerous property market inefficiencies, such as high transaction costs, lengthy decision making processes and due-diligence periods, and informational inefficiencies. A number of authors have estimated structural models derived from theoretical cap rate models to investigate property price dynamics (Sivitanides et al. 2001; Hendershott and MacGregor 2005a, b; Chen et al. 2004; Plazzi et al. 2004, Chichernea et al. 2008; Sivitanidou and Sivitanides 1999).

To capture both long-run and short-run cap rate dynamics, we employ an error correction model (ECM) similar to Hendershott and MacGregor (2005a). This framework allows us to model cap rates as an adjustment process around equilibrium values. Error correction models are based on the idea that two or more time series exhibit a long-run time-varying equilibrium to which the system tends to converge. The long-run influence in the error correction model is achieved through negative feedback and error correction, and this influence measures the degree to which long-run equilibrium forces drive short-run price dynamics (see, for example, Engle and Granger 1987 and Hamilton 1994).

Following the Engle-Granger two-step method, a long-run cap rate model is specified in levels. The second-stage, short-run, adjustment model is specified in first differences and includes a long-run error correction term from the estimation of the long-run (equilibrium) model. In the first-stage, theory and econometric evidence are used to determine if the various data series contain unit roots and are cointegrated. If the data series are cointegrated, a long-run equilibrium relation (i.e., a cointegrating regression) can be specified in levels as:

$$R_t = \beta_0 + \sum_{i=1}^{n} \beta_i X_{it} + \upsilon_t \tag{4}$$

where R_t is the observed cap rate and X_{it} are theoretically-based explanatory variables at time t. From this regression, we can estimate residuals as the difference between the actual and estimated equilibrium values of the cap rate.[8] If the residuals from Eq. 4 are stationary, they may be used as an error correction term in the short-run cap rate change model as follows:

$$\Delta R_t = \alpha_0 + \sum_{i=1}^{n} \alpha_i \Delta X_{it} - \gamma \upsilon_{t-1} + \varepsilon_t \tag{5}$$

where $\Delta R_t = R_t - R_{t-1}$ is the first difference of the cap rate, ΔX_{it} are first differences of the explanatory variables, and $\hat{\upsilon}_{t-1}$ is the error correction term (the lagged residuals from the long-run regression). Estimation of Eq. 5 provides evidence on short-run cap rate dynamics (the α_i's) and adjustments to the previous disequilibrium in the long-run relation, γ (the speed of adjustment parameter). If $\gamma = 1$, there is full adjustment, while $\gamma = 0$ suggests no adjustment. A more general specification of the short-run model may also include multiple lags of the explanatory and dependent variables.

EMPIRICAL SPECIFICATION

Based on our earlier theoretical discussion of equilibrium factors influencing cap rates, we employ the following empirical model to each of the nine property types (see property type discussion in the next section). In the first-stage, we estimate:

---

[8] The specification in Eq. 4 uses the results of Eq. 3 to specify the equilibrium cap rate as a function of the discount rate, rt, and expected NOI growth, gt, but does not impose the exact relationship, Rt=rt- gt, that holds under the constant growth assumption.

$$R_t = \beta_0 + \beta_1 NOIGRW_t + \beta_2 RP_t + \beta_3 RF_t + \upsilon_t \qquad (6)$$

where $NOIGRW_t$ is the expected growth in NOI, RP_t is the unlevered equity risk premium, and RF_t is the yield-to-maturity on a 10-year Treasury security. In the second-stage, we estimate the following short-run error correction model for each of the nine property types:

$$\Delta R_t = \alpha_0 + \alpha_1 NOIGRW_t + \alpha_2 \Delta RP_t + \alpha_3 \Delta RF_t + \gamma \hat{\upsilon}_{t-1} \qquad (7)$$

Equation 6 postulates that equilibrium cap rate levels are driven by two sets of influences: (1) discount rate influences that reflect the risk-free opportunity cost of equity capital and the equity risk premium and (2) factors that influence the NOI growth expectations of investors (Wheaton 1999). Cap rate changes (Eq. 7) are a function of changes in NOI, risk premiums, risk-free interest rates, and the degree to which cap rates deviated from their equilibrium level in the previous time period.

Equation 6 reserves no explicit role for investor sentiment in the determination of observed cap rates. To address this potential effect, we augment the specification in Eq. 7 with several measures of investor sentiment. We also estimate variants of the second stage regression as additional robustness checks, including specifications that allow us to test whether sentiment is embedded in market participants' forecasts of income growth and expected returns.

DATA

Our primary data source is the Real Estate Research Corporation (RERC). Founded in 1931 in Chicago, RERC is nationally known for its research, analysis, and investment criteria. Published quarterly in the Real Estate Report, the RERC Real Estate Investment Survey summarizes information on current investment criteria such as going-in (acquisition) cap rates, terminal cap rates, unlevered required rates of return on equity, expected rental growth rates, and investment conditions provided by a sample of institutional investors and managers throughout the USA.[9] According to RERC, the survey results are used by investors, developers, appraisers, and financial institutions to "monitor changing market conditions and to forecast fi-

---

[9] Several stock market studies find institutions to be informed investors; i.e., "smart money. See, for example, Chakravarty (2001), Jones and Lipson (2004), and Sias et al. (2006). However, this evidence is tempered by studies that suggest institutions do not outperform individual investors (e.g. Nofsinger and Sias 1999, and Kaniel et al. 2005).

nancial performance."[10] As a robustness check, we also employ survey data from Korpacz PriceWaterhouse Coopers.

Ideally, our cap rate data would be based on a large number of constant-quality (including location) properties with identical lease terms. Such data do not exist. The RERC data, however, represent the cap rates respondents are currently observing in the market for notional investment grade properties of constant quality. Thus, these data are well-suited to our task, except they are not based on actual transactions.

Recall from Eq. 3 that equilibrium going-in cap rates (R_t^e) are a function of unlevered discount rates (r_t) and expected growth rates in net rental income (g_t). However, r_t and g_t cannot be directly observed. Thus, in prior cap rate studies, proxies for these variables, or their component parts, were estimated. One attraction of the RERC data is that expected rental growth rates and required equity returns are two of the survey questions. In addition, survey respondents are asked to rank the "investment conditions" of various property types and markets. These ranking of investment conditions directly measure investor sentiment.

We focus first on the going-in capitalization rates reported by RERC for nine property types: apartment, hotel, industrial research and development, industrial warehouse, central business district (CBD) office, suburban office, neighborhood retail, power shopping centers, and regional malls. Survey cap rates for the nine property types are displayed in Fig. 1. During the first half of the 1996:Q1–2007:Q2 sample period, cap rates remained relatively stable. However, beginning in 2002, cap rates on all property types began to decline. For example, apartment cap rates stood at 8.7% in 2002:Q1; by 2007:Q2 they had declined 300 basis points to 5.7%.

To address potential concerns about the survey-based nature of our cap rate data, we compare RERC cap rates, by property type, to cap rates obtained from two other sources, the National Council of Real Estate Investment Fiduciaries (NCREIF) and Real Capital Analytics (RCA). NCREIF cap rates represent averages derived from valuations of institutional class properties held by firms that are contributing members to the NCREIF Property Index (NPI). RCA cap rates are averages derived from a much larger, but more heterogeneous, population, coming from the sales of all properties of $5 million or more. NCREIF cap rates are appraisal-based, and hence potentially backward looking. RCA cap rates are transaction-based but potentially noisy because they are not constant quality. NCREIF

---

[10] Real Estate Report, Summer 2002.

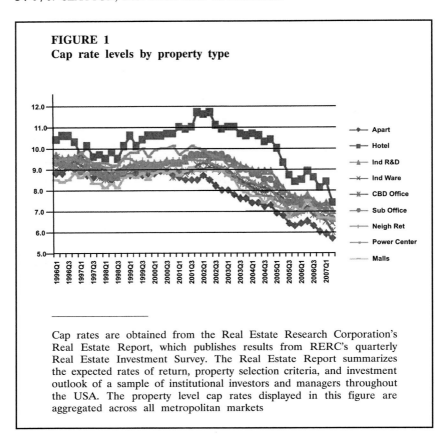

FIGURE 1
Cap rate levels by property type

Cap rates are obtained from the Real Estate Research Corporation's Real Estate Report, which publishes results from RERC's quarterly Real Estate Investment Survey. The Real Estate Report summarizes the expected rates of return, property selection criteria, and investment outlook of a sample of institutional investors and managers throughout the USA. The property level cap rates displayed in this figure are aggregated across all metropolitan markets

data extend back to 1990, whereas RCA data begin in 2001. Correlations between RERC and NCREIF cap rate levels over the 1996:1 to 2007:2 period, and RERC and RCA cap rates over the 2001:1 to 2007:2 period, exceed 90% for all nine property types. Moreover, regressions of RERC cap rates on NCREIF (RCA) cap rates yield highly significant slope coefficients of 0.80 (0.90) and above and R^2s of 85% (90%) and above. In fact, regressions of RERC cap rates on both NCREIF and RCA cap rates together result in adjusted R^2s above 95% in almost all nine cases. The tight connection between RERC cap rates and these two alternative series indicates that our survey based cap rates are tracking pricing dynamics in commercial real estate markets very well.

Table 1 contains summary statistics, by property type, for our key RERC regression variables. The top panel contains means, standard deviations, minimums, maximums, and serial correlations of levels and changes for capitalization rates, expected rental growth rates, required equity returns, and investment conditions. Mean expected rent growth ranges from 2.3% (annually) for power centers to 2.9% for apartments. The levels of expected rent growth display substantial positive serial correlation across quarters. However, changes in expected rental growth rates display significant negative serial correlation, with the exception of apartments and hotels.

These data, coupled with our prior discussion of the cap rate determinates, provide a foundation for the analysis of the widely discussed decline in US cap rates that occurred from 2002 to 2007. Most real estate practitioners largely attribute the unprecedented decline in cap rates over this recent period to the "wall of capital" and related liquidity that has permeated many markets, although market observers do not discount the role declining interest rate levels have also played. However, inspection of the RERC data suggests a more traditional explanation. In panels A–C of Fig. 2, we plot RERC cap rates for apartments, CBD office buildings, and regional malls. Also plotted are the corresponding RERC expected rental growth rates. Theory tells us these two series should be negatively correlated, and this negative correlation is observed over the 1996:Q1 to 2007:Q2 sample period.[11] Similar correlations are observed for the remaining six property types. Thus, it appears that the large cap rate declines since 2002 have been driven, at least in part, by increases in expected rental growth.

Note also that the observed increases in RERC expected rent growth are not consistent with increased capital flows and rising prices. In fact, once market values exceed all-in construction costs, rising prices (lower cap rates) produce increased construction that, in the longer run, leads to lower real rents. Said differently, if increased capital flows and liquidity since 2002 were pushing asset values above fundamental values, then rational market participants should have been reducing their rent growth expectations, all else equal.

With the exception of hotel properties, average unlevered discount rates vary little across property types, ranging from 10.2% for apartment properties to 10.9% for industrial R&D and suburban office properties. This inability of survey respondents to detect cross property variation in ex ante risk premiums is somewhat surprising given the significant variation in ex post returns earned by the vari-

---

[11] Note that, in theory, cap rate movements are driven by variations in expected net rental income (NOI). We assume that such expectations are highly correlated with expected changes in market rental rates.

TABLE 1
Descriptive statistics — selective RERC variables (1996:1–2007:2)

	Mean	SD	Min	Max	Serial correlation Levels	Serial correlation Changes
Cap rates Apartment	8.0	2.0	5.7	9.1	0.99	0.03
Hotel	10.1	2.0	7.4	11.7	0.93	−0.08
Industrial R&D	9.0	1.5	7.0	9.7	0.98	0.21
Industrial Warehouse	8.4	1.6	6.4	9.2	0.98	0.19
CBD office	8.4	1.8	6.0	9.6	0.98	0.34
Suburban office	8.7	1.6	6.6	9.7	0.98	0.29
Neighborhood retail	8.6	2.1	6.5	9.5	0.99	0.12
Power center	8.9	2.3	6.5	10.1	0.98	0.10
Regional malls	8.2	1.5	6.6	9.1	0.94	−0.32
Rental growth rates						
Apartment	2.9	1.2	1.5	3.6	0.92	0.00
Hotel	2.6	2.2	0.3	4.4	0.87	−0.05
Industrial R&D	2.4	1.8	0.1	3.7	0.86	−0.41
Industrial warehouse	2.6	1.4	0.9	3.7	0.92	−0.24
CBD office	2.8	1.8	0.9	4.2	0.89	−0.28
Suburban office	2.6	2.2	0.4	4.1	0.93	−0.35
Neighborhood retail	2.7	1.0	1.5	3.5	0.80	−0.47
Power center	2.3	1.2	0.7	3.5	0.69	−0.58
Regional malls	2.6	1.2	1.3	3.6	0.78	−0.44
Required unlevered IRR						
Apartment	10.2	2.3	7.6	11.3	0.99	0.18
Hotel	12.5	2.4	9.4	14.5	0.95	0.03
Industrial R&D	10.9	2.1	8.3	11.9	0.99	0.31
Industrial warehouse	10.3	2.2	7.8	11.4	0.99	0.12
CBD office	10.6	2.5	7.6	11.9	0.99	0.14
Suburban office	10.9	2.2	8.2	12.0	0.98	0.09
Neighborhood retail	10.5	2.4	7.9	11.7	0.99	0.23
Power center	10.8	2.7	7.9	12.6	0.98	0.02
Regional malls	10.5	2.4	8.1	12.0	0.97	0.04
Investment conditions						
Apartment	6.3	1.4	3.9	7.4	0.67	−0.45
Hotel	5.2	2.4	2.7	7.8	0.84	−0.26
Industrial R&D	5.3	1.5	3.9	6.7	0.81	−0.52
Industrial warehouse	6.2	1.0	5.3	7.7	0.59	−0.50
CBD office	6.0	1.5	4.6	7.3	0.81	−0.34
Suburban office	5.5	2.1	3.8	7.3	0.92	−0.45
Neighborhood retail	6.1	1.0	4.6	6.9	0.23	−0.46
Power center	4.8	2.1	3.3	6.8	0.81	−0.49
Regional malls	5.4	1.3	4.2	6.6	0.26	−0.48

Data are obtained from the RERCs *Real Estate Report,* which publishes results from RERCs quarterly Real Estate Investment Survey. *The Real Estate Report* summarizes the expected rates of return, property selection criteria, and investment outlook of a sample of institutional investors and managers throughout the USA.

FIGURE 2
Selective Rerc Cap Rates and Expected Rent Growth

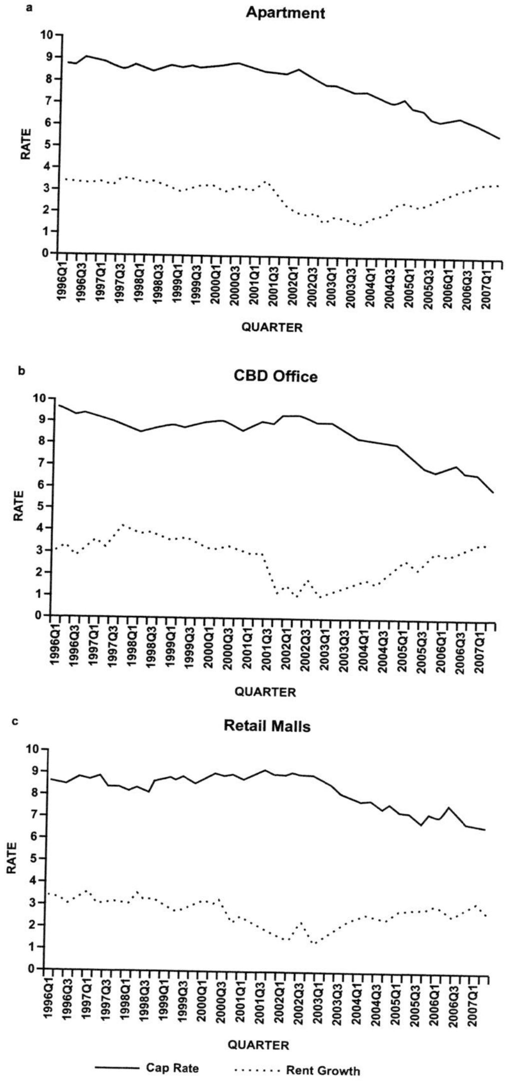

The cap rates and expected rental growth rates are from the Real Estate Research Corporation's Real Estate Report, which publishes results from RERC's quarterly Real Estate Investment Survey.t

ous property types over different historical time horizons. Shilling (2003) and Geltner et al. (2007) report a similar finding in ex ante required returns derived from real estate investor surveys and also report that survey-based IRRs are "too sticky" and overstated, at least historically. In contrast to cap rates, IRRs are difficult to observe empirically. This raises the possibility that the RERC required IRRs may be measured with error and not capturing true variation in risk premiums over time and across properties. We recognize this and account for it in our empirical methodology.

Because OLS regressions with nonstationary variables produce spurious regression results, we test for the stationarity of our regression variables using augmented Dickey–Fuller, Phillips–Perron, and Weighted Symmetric unit root tests.[12] Each of the tests includes intercept terms, time trends, and lags of the dependent variables. Although not reported, each of the tests show that cap rates, rental growth rates, risk premiums, and T-bond yields are each non-stationary (i.e., contain a unit root), but stationary in first differences at the 5% significance level. However, Engle–Granger and Johansen–Juselius cointegration tests reveal that cap rates, rental growth rates, risk premiums, and interest rates are cointegrated, containing one cointegrating vector among the variables at the 5% level. This suggests that a long-run equilibrium cap rate relation (i.e., a cointegrating regression) can be specified in levels.

Measuring Real Estate Investor Sentiment

RERC survey respondents are asked to rank current investment conditions for each of the nine property types on a scale of 1 to 10, with 1 indicating "poor" investment conditions and 10 indicating "excellent" conditions for investing. The bottom panel in Table 1 contains summary statistics for our RERC investor sentiment variable. Note that the consensus opinion of survey respondents over the sample period was that apartment properties, with an average rank of 6.3, were considered to be the most desirable investments, followed by industrial warehouse and neighborhood retail properties. In contrast, retail power centers, with a mean ranking of 4.8, were deemed the least desirable of the nine property types over the study period. Inspection of Table 1 also reveals that RERC's investment condition rankings display a significant amount of variation over the

---

[12] The Weighted Symmetric test is often recommended over the Dickey–Fuller test because it is more likely to reject the unit root null hypothesis when it is in fact false. That is, the weighted symmetric test has higher power. We also obtain similar results using the Phillips–Perron test. The Phillips–Perron test is a variant of the Dickey–Fuller test that addresses the problem of additional serial correlation in the residuals.

sample period. For example, the investment desirability of hotels ranged from a low of 2.7 to a high of 7.8. RERC sentiment levels display positive serial correlation across quarters. However, changes in sentiment display significant negative serial correlation.

In addition to our RERC sentiment variable, we construct a measure of aggregate real estate investor sentiment based on observable market level variables. More specifically, following Brown et al. (2002), Brown and Cliff (2004) and Baker and Wurgler (2006), we construct an index of investor sentiment towards commercial real estate investment based on the common variation in a number of proxies for sentiment. More specifically, we extract an overall market sentiment measure from the following five sentiment-related proxies: (1) commercial mortgage flows as a percentage of GDP; (2) the percentage of properties sold from the NCREIF Property Index (NPI); (3) the ratio of the transaction based (TBI) and "constant liquidity" versions of the NPI value index; (4) the NPI total return over the past four quarters, and (5) the most recent quarterly TBI total return.[13]

Mortgage flows are widely viewed by industry participants as a barometer of market investment sentiment, in part because of the association between past real estate cycles and "excessive" mortgage flows in periods of underpricing of default risk.[14] The percentage of properties sold from the NPI and the ratio of the TBI and constant liquidity versions of the NPI index are related to transaction activity or market turnover and can also be viewed as market liquidity prox-

---

[13] The NCREIF property index is comprised of the same class of properties and investors as the RERC survey. The quarterly "constant liquidity" version of the NPI is developed in Fisher, Geltner and Pollakowski (2007). The authors recognize that private, relatively illiquid asset markets adjust through both changes in prices and liquidity; observed transaction prices are conditional on overall market liquidity at the time of sale (i.e., price and liquidity are jointly determined). A "constant liquidity value " of a property is the value assuming no change in the level of market transaction activity; all adjustment takes place through price. The difference between the constant liquidity and hedonic value index, based on observed transaction prices that implicitly reflect time variation in liquidity, provides a calibration of commercial property liquidity. The TBI, including its constant liquidity version, are available at the MIT Center for Real Estate website.

[14] Dokko et al. (1999) provide an overview of alternative explanations for real estate cycles that includes the potential role of mortgage flows. Pavlov and Wachter (2006) suggest that the underpricing of the borrowers — put option in non-recourse commercial mortgage loans is at the root of the link between mortgage flows and property values. Riddiough (2008) argues that the securitization boom of the past 5 years has been accompanied by mispricing mortgage default risk that once again resulted in excessive mortgage flows and a bubble in commercial property prices.

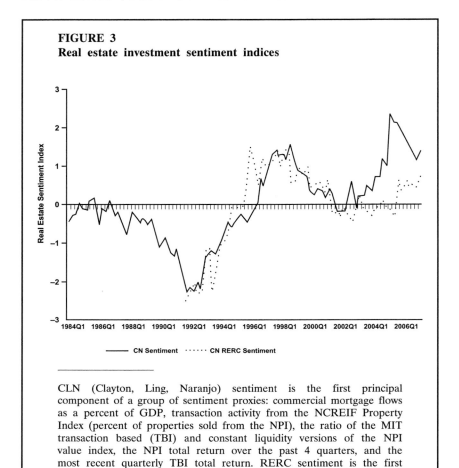

FIGURE 3
Real estate investment sentiment indices

CLN (Clayton, Ling, Naranjo) sentiment is the first principal component of a group of sentiment proxies: commercial mortgage flows as a percent of GDP, transaction activity from the NCREIF Property Index (percent of properties sold from the NPI), the ratio of the MIT transaction based (TBI) and constant liquidity versions of the NPI value index, the NPI total return over the past 4 quarters, and the most recent quarterly TBI total return. RERC sentiment is the first principal component extracted from RERC investment condition question survey responses for nine property types.

ies.[15] Our final two sentiment proxies are current property returns derived from appraisal-based and transaction-based indices used by institutional investors to track investment performance. We are not

---

[15] Baker and Stein (2004) develop a theoretical model in which aggregate liquidity acts as an indicator of the relative presence of sentiment-based traders in the market place and therefore the divergence of asset price from fundamental value. Abnormally high aggregate liquidity (high turnover and/or low bid-ask spreads) is evidence of over-valuation and in fact forecasts a downturn in stock prices.

claiming that each of these time series represents investor sentiment, but rather that if sentiment does exist it is likely to be reflected to some degree in each and it therefore can be extracted as the common component.

To ensure our real estate sentiment measure is not an index of common business cycle risk factors, we first regress each of the five sentiment proxies on the 3-month Treasury yield, a term structure variable (10-year less 3-month Treasury yield), and a measure of economy-wide default risk (the Baa corporate bond yield less the AAA bond yield). We then construct our real estate sentiment index as the first principal component of the five residual series using quarterly observations over the 1984 to 2007:Q2 period. We label this variable CLN (Clayton, Ling, and Naranjo) sentiment and include it in augmented versions of our cap rate error correction model. This additional sentiment factor allows us to examine the extent to which broader measures of real estate sentiment influence capitalization rates. Figure 3 displays the CLN sentiment index and, as a check of consistency with the RERC survey data, compares it to an index constructed as the first principal component of the RERC sentiment variable for the nine property types (RERC Sentiment). Overall, our two sentiment proxies display substantial co-movement; in fact, the correlation between them is 0.76 over the 1996:Q1 to 2007:Q2 period.

RESULTS

Table 2 contains parameter estimates and p values (in parentheses) for our long-run model (Eq. 6) for each of the nine property types over the 1996:Q1 to 2007:Q2 period. Consistent with established cap rate theory, we include rent growth expectations, the risk premium embedded in required discount rates, and the yield to maturity on 10-year Treasury bonds as our explanatory variables.

The estimated coefficient on the contemporaneous equity risk premium and T-bond yield are positive and highly significant for all nine property types. The estimated coefficient on the risk premium ranges from 0.613 to 0.866 and averages 0.755 across the nine property types. The corresponding coefficient estimate on the T-bond yield ranges from 0.579 to 0.871. The coefficient on expected rent growth is negative and highly significant in all but the apartment, hotel, and neighborhood retail specifications. The adjusted R^2 for our nine long-run levels model averages 0.974.

Figure 4, panels A–C, contain plots of the actual and predicted cap rate values from the long-run equation for apartments, CBD office buildings, and regional malls, respectively. As can be seen, the

TABLE 2
Long-run cap rate level models: 1996:1 f2007:2

	Apartment	Hotel	Industrial R&D	Industrial warehouse	CBD office	Suburban office	Neighborhood retail	Power center	Mall
Constant	-0.864 (0.000)	0.986 (0.120)	1.512 (0.000)	0.905 (0.000)	1.565 (0.000)	1.652 (0.000)	-0.350 (0.057)	-0.381 (0.073)	2.334 (0.000)
Rent growth	0.021 (0.657)	-0.077 (0.198)	-0.099 (0.003)	-0.110 (0.003)	-0.221 (0.000)	-0.143 (0.000)	0.033 (0.519)	0.033 (0.449)	-0.172 (0.002)
Risk premium	0.854 (0.000)	0.765 (0.000)	0.711 (0.000)	0.757 (0.000)	0.685 (0.000)	0.705 (0.000)	0.866 (0.000)	0.837 (0.000)	0.613 (0.000)
10-Year T-bond yield	0.871 (0.000)	0.722 (0.000)	0.692 (0.000)	0.752 (0.000)	0.726 (0.000)	0.668 (0.000)	0.819 (0.000)	0.868 (0.000)	0.579 (0.000)
Adjusted R^2	0.986	0.925	0.975	0.987	0.974	0.981	0.987	0.988	0.968

P values are in parentheses. The parameter estimates are from the estimation of Eq. 6 using quarterly data over the 1996:1 to 2007:2 time period. The dependent variable is the quarterly cap rate. Rent growth is the expected change in market rental rates over the next year, risk premium in the required unlevered return on equity minus the yield to maturity on a 10-year Treasury Bond. The remaining independent variable is the 10-year Treasury Bond yield

FIGURE 4
Selective long-run cap rate models

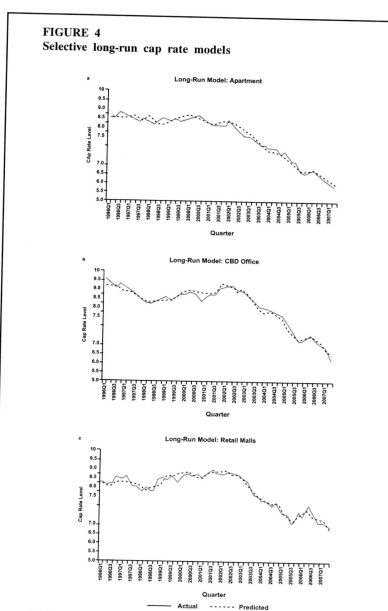

The actual cap rates are from the Real Estate Research Corporation's Real Estate Report, which publishes results from RERC's quarterly Real Estate Investment Survey. The predicted cap rates are obtained from estimation of Eq. 6.

TABLE 3
Short-run cap rate change models without sentiment: 1996:2–2007:2

	Apartment	Hotel	Industrial R&D	Industrial warehouse	CBD office	Suburban office	Neighborhood retail	Power center	Mall
Constant	−0.012 (0.536)	−0.001 (0.987)	−0.020 (0.200)	−0.009 (0.515)	−0.023 (0.240)	−0.016 (0.318)	−0.008 (0.638)	−0.011 (0.554)	−0.003 (0.893)
Rent growth change	0.055 (0.458)	0.006 (0.923)	−0.047 (0.110)	−0.068 (0.150)	−0.093 (0.033)	−0.081 (0.038)	−0.050 (0.262)	0.023 (0.546)	−0.174 (0.003)
Risk premium change	0.723 (0.000)	0.690 (0.000)	0.542 (0.000)	0.641 (0.000)	0.533 (0.000)	0.561 (0.000)	0.794 (0.000)	0.682 (0.000)	0.595 (0.000)
Treasury yield change	0.722 (0.000)	0.833 (0.000)	0.492 (0.000)	0.633 (0.000)	0.597 (0.000)	0.541 (0.000)	0.706 (0.000)	0.692 (0.000)	0.528 (0.000)
Error correction term	−0.576 (0.000)	−0.659 (0.000)	−0.589 (0.000)	−0.692 (0.000)	−0.706 (0.000)	−0.710 (0.000)	−0.466 (0.000)	−0.700 (0.000)	−1.019 (0.000)
Adjusted R2	0.507	0.564	0.669	0.711	0.625	0.694	0.608	0.686	0.712

P values are in parentheses. The parameter estimates are from the estimation of Eq. 7 using quarterly data over the 1996:1 to 2007:2 time period. The dependent variable is the quarterly change in the cap rate. Rent growth change is the change in expected rental growth from quarter t-1 to quarter t. Risk premium change is the change in the required unlevered equity risk premium from quarter t-1 to quarter t. Treasury yield change is the change in the yield to maturity on a 10-year Treasury Bond from quarter t-1 to quarter t. The error correction term is the residual (actual minus predicted) from the long-run levels model (Eq. 6, Table 2), lagged one quarter

estimated equations capture the broad movements in property specific cap rates, although errors do occur, suggesting the appropriate-
ness of our error correction framework.

We next estimate our cap rate change model (Eq. 7). Quarterly
changes in all variables in the long-run model are included in the error correction specifications, as well as the error correction term.[16]
Table 3 reports parameter estimates and p values. As expected, the
estimated coefficient on the change in expected rent growth is negative and significant (at the 5% level) in the CBD office, suburban
office, and regional mall equations. However, the coefficient on expected rent growth is not significant in the remaining six property
type regressions.

Given the theoretical importance of expected rent growth in cap
rate determination, the lack of consistent significance of the RERC
rent growth variable in our second-stage regressions, and the concern
that our RERC rent variable may be "sentiment-laden," we experimented with several alternative proxies for income growth expectations. More specifically, we obtained historical time series of effective
rents from Torto–Wheaton Research for the four main property
types: office, industrial, retail, and apartments. Following Sivitanides
et al. (2001), we split expectations of nominal rent growth into
growth due to expected economy-wide inflation and expected real
rent growth. We experimented with alternative proxies for expected
economy-wide inflation, including simple extrapolations of past
changes in the Consumer Price Index. We also investigated alternative proxies for real rent growth, including simple extrapolations and
more rational mean-reverting expectations. In short, these alternative
specifications did not improve the explanatory power of our rent
growth variable; moreover, their use consumed several more degrees
of freedom. Thus, we report only those results obtained using the
RERC rent growth variable.

The remaining explanatory variables enter the short-run cap rate
regressions with the expected sign and are highly significant. For example, the coefficient on the change in equity risk premium ranges
from 0.533 to 0.794, all with p values of 0.000. The estimated coefficients on changes in the 10-year T-bond yield are of similar magnitude and significance. Thus, RERC cap rates strongly respond to
changes in both the equity risk premium and T-bond yield, as theory
suggests. These results are consistent with previous studies that find

---

[16] The lagged cap rate change was initially included to expand the dynamic adjustment process. However, it was dropped from the analysis because in no specification
was its estimated coefficient statistically significant.

that cap rate changes are primarily driven by changing discount rates (i.e. Treasury yields and risk premiums) rather than changes in rent growth expectations (Geltner and Mei 1995; Plazzi et al. 2004).

As previously discussed, several rationales warrant the application of an error correction model to cap rates, including the lagged and smoothed nature of appraisal-based prices and cap rates. Thus, the difference between actual and predicted cap rates could reflect the aggregate effect of these underlying forces working to return the market to equilibrium (Hendershott and MacGregor 2005a). Examination of Table 3 reveals that the error correction term carries the expected negative sign and is highly significant in all nine property type regressions.

Finally, the adjusted averages 0.642 across the nine cap rate change specifications, with a range of 0.507 to 0.712. The actual and fitted value for our apartment, CBD office, and regional mall data are displayed in panels A–C of Fig. 5. Clearly, the error correction model picks up broad movements in cap rates.

Sentiment Effects

As previously discussed, we employ two proxies for investor sentiment. The first is the RERC "investment conditions" variable; the second is our constructed CLN sentiment index. Table 4 contains cap rate change parameter estimates and p values with the specification altered to include the change in RERC sentiment from time $t - 1$ to t. Although negative and statistically significant in the hotel regression (p value = 0.064) and marginally significant in the industrial R&D and neighborhood retail equations, RERC sentiment is not significant in the remaining six property type regressions. When the change in CLN sentiment is substituted for the change RERC sentiment, the estimated coefficient is positive and significant in the industrial warehouse and neighborhood retail equations only (see panel B at the bottom of Table 4). We also experimented with contemporaneous and lagged values of RERC and CLN sentiment, as well as one, two, three, and four-quarter changes in both variables. Although several of these sentiment variables are statistically significant in one or two of the nine cap rate regressions, the lack of a consistent sentiment effect is noteworthy. These inconsistent sentiment effects are also robust over non-overlapping subsample estimates (1996–2001 and 2002–2007).

A potential concern is that some of the explanatory variables in our reduced form error-correction model are endogenous. For example, if a survey respondent is irrationally optimistic about the investment potential of a particular property type, this non fundamentals-based optimism may bias downward the respondent's required risk

FIGURE 5
Selective short-run cap rate models

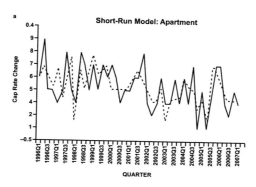

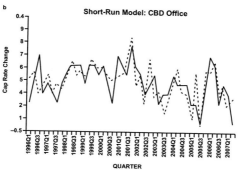

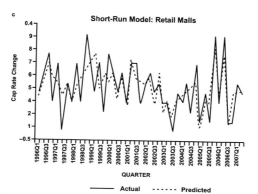

The actual changes in cap rates are from the Real Estate Research Corporation's Real Estate Report, which publishes results from RERC's quarterly Real Estate Investment Survey. The predicted cap rates are obtained from estimation of Eq. 7.

TABLE 4
Short run cap rate change models with sentiment: 1996:2–2007:2

	Apartment	Hotel	Industrial R&D	Industrial warehouse	CBD office	Suburban office	Neighborhood retail	Power center	Mall
Panel A									
Constant	-0.012 (0.549)	-0.009 (0.815)	-0.020 (0.189)	-0.009 (0.541)	-0.022 (0.254)	-0.016 (0.297)	-0.008 (0.613)	-0.011 (0.547)	-0.002 (0.920)
Rent growth change	0.055 (0.463)	0.008 (0.896)	-0.045 (0.125)	-0.069 (0.149)	-0.098 (0.035)	-0.079 (0.044)	-0.042 (0.342)	0.040 (0.352)	-0.181 (0.003)
Risk premium change	0.725 (0.000)	0.659 (0.000)	0.549 (0.000)	0.644 (0.000)	0.535 (0.000)	0.559 (0.000)	0.788 (0.000)	0.674 (0.000)	0.604 (0.000)
Treasury yield change	0.723 (0.000)	0.797 (0.000)	0.501 (0.000)	0.632 (0.000)	0.599 (0.000)	0.547 (0.000)	0.706 (0.000)	0.687 (0.000)	0.540 (0.000)
RERC sentiment change	0.007 (0.832)	-0.101 (0.064)	-0.045 (0.159)	0.013 (0.661)	0.014 (0.721)	-0.030 (0.429)	-0.039 (0.113)	-0.030 (0.354)	0.014 (0.635)
Error correction term	-0.585 (0.000)	-0.613 (0.000)	-0.519 (0.000)	-0.683 (0.000)	-0.708 (0.000)	-0.692 (0.000)	-0.413 (0.004)	-0.678 (0.000)	-1.027 (0.000)
Adjusted R^2	0.495	0.678	0.617	0.623	0.706	0.705	0.628	0.690	0.712
Panel B									
CLN sentiment change substituted for REC	0.073 (0.148)	0.014 (0.905)	0.050 (0.271)	0.067 (0.080)	-0.010 (0.857)	0.045 (0.298)	0.078 (0.062)	0.052 (0.327)	0.064 (0.291)
Adjusted R^2	0.517	0.568	0.671	0.732	0.621	0.705	0.628	0.690	0.712

P values are in parentheses. The parameter estimates are from the estimation of Eq. 7 using quarterly data over the 1996:1 to 2007:2 time period. The dependent variable is the quarterly change in the cap rate. Rent growth change is the change in expected rental growth from quarter t-1 to quarter t. Risk premium change is the change in the required unlevered equity risk premium from quarter t-1 to quarter t. Treasury yield change is the change in the yield to maturity on a 10-year Treasury Bond from quarter t-1 to quarter t. The error correction term is the residual (actual minus predicted) from the long-run levels model (Eq. 6), lagged one quarter. In Panel B, we report the estimated coefficient on the change in CLN sentiment when it is substituted for RERC sentiment, along with the corresponding adjusted R^2 from the estimate

TABLE 5
Short run cap rate change models with orthogonalization: 1996:2–2007:2

	Apartment	Hotel	Industrial R&D	Industrial warehouse	CBD office	Suburban office	Neighborhood retail	Power center	Mall
Panel A									
Constant	-0.012 (0.545)	-0.007 (0.838)	-0.020 (0.190)	-0.010 (0.478)	-0.020 (0.297)	-0.014 (0.352)	-0.009 (0.560)	-0.012 (0.521)	-0.002 (0.913)
Rent growth change orthog	0.053 (0.480)	0.002 (0.975)	-0.043 (0.138)	-0.075 (0.114)	-0.071 (0.121)	-0.092 (0.019)	-0.022 (0.584)	0.045 (0.281)	-0.184 (0.002)
Risk premium change orthog	0.724 (0.000)	0.671 (0.000)	0.549 (0.000)	0.634 (0.000)	0.554 (0.000)	0.581 (0.000)	0.769 (0.000)	0.662 (0.000)	0.603 (0.000)
Treasury yield change	0.721 (0.000)	0.814 (0.000)	0.501 (0.000)	0.612 (0.000)	0.624 (0.000)	0.559 (0.000)	0.690 (0.000)	0.670 (0.000)	0.542 (0.000)
RERC sentiment change	-0.189 (0.003)	-0.554 (0.000)	-0.528 (0.000)	-0.534 (0.000)	-0.294 (0.000)	-0.516 (0.000)	-0.162 (0.000)	-0.269 (0.000)	-0.006 (0.839)
Error correction term	-0.585 (0.001)	-0.629 (0.000)	-0.517 (0.000)	-0.715 (0.000)	-0.744 (0.000)	-0.741 (0.000)	-0.506 (0.004)	-0.696 (0.000)	-1.029 (0.000)
Adjusted R^2	0.492	0.600	0.679	0.716	0.666	0.698	0.659	0.695	0.706
Panel B									
CLN sentiment change	-0.451 (0.000)	-0.741 (0.000)	-0.409 (0.000)	-0.379 (0.000)	-0.552 (0.000)	-0.545 (0.000)	-0.573 (0.000)	-0.632 (0.000)	-0.502 (0.000)
Adjusted R^2	0.517	0.568	0.671	0.732	0.621	0.705	0.628	0.690	0.712

P values are in parentheses. The parameter estimates are from the estimation of Eq. 7 using quarterly data over the 1996:1 to 2007:2 time period. The dependent variable is the quarterly change in the cap rate. Rent growth change orthog is the change in expected rental growth from quarter t-1 to quarter t orthogonalized with respect to RERC sentiment. Risk premium change is the change in the required unlevered equity risk premium from quarter t-1 to quarter t orthogonalized with respect to RERC sentiment. Treasury yield change is the change in the yield to maturity on a 10-year Treasury Bond from quarter t-1 to quarter t. The error correction term is the residual (actual minus predicted) from the long-run levels model (Eq. 6), lagged one quarter. In Panel B, we report the estimated coefficient on the change in CLN sentiment when it is substituted for RERC sentiment

premium and/or bias upward his or her expectations of future rental growth. Said differently, our RERC required risk premiums and/or rental growth expectations may be sentiment laden. This, in turn, may reduce the explanatory power of our sentiment proxies in the cap rate change regressions.

To address this issue, we orthogonalized our expected rent growth and risk premium variables with respect to our sentiment variables. This orthogonalization is designed to strip these fundamental variables of sentiment and load the explanatory power of investor sentiment onto the estimated RERC and CLN coefficients in our cap rate change regressions. The results with the orthogonalized expected rent growth and risk premium variables and RERC sentiment are reported in panel A of Table 5. First, note that the adjusted R^2s are unchanged from Table 4. This is because the information on the right-hand-side of the cap rate change models is not altered by the orthogonalization of rent growth and risk premiums with respect to sentiment. However, the estimated coefficient on the change in RERC sentiment is negative and highly significant in all but the regional mall equation. Thus, although fundamentals are the primary determinants of cap rates, sentiment also has an impact on cap rate determination.

It is also important to note that the estimated coefficients on our fundamental variables are little changed by the orthogonalization (compare panel A in Tables 4 and 5). This suggests that, although orthogonalization of the rent growth and risk premium variables is necessary to isolate the effect of sentiment on cap rates, this orthogonalization does not alter our conclusions about the effects of fundamental variables on cap rates.

We also orthogonalized rent growth and the risk premium with respect to CLN sentiment and estimated our cap rate change regressions using CLN as our proxy for investor sentiment. The estimated coefficients on CLN sentiment, reported in panel B of Table 5, are negative and highly significant in all nine property type regressions. Thus, our finding of a role for sentiment in cap rate determination is not dependent on our choice of sentiment proxy.

Robustness Results Using Alternative Database

Finally, to further examine the robustness of our results, we repeat our estimations using survey data from Korpacz Pricewaterhouse Coopers (KPC). Similar to the RERC survey, the KPC survey consists of quarterly responses from 100-odd prominent pension plans, foundations, endowments, life insurance companies, investment banks, and REITs that invest in US real estate. The KPC survey has been conducted each quarter since 1988 and contains rich information on the expectations of participants in commercial real estate markets. Survey respondents are asked to report the cap rates they are observing on CBD office buildings, major retail properties, apartment buildings, and industrial warehouses. The survey also asks respondents for their required (unlevered) rates of return and rental growth forecasts for each of these property types. Thus, the KPC survey provides us with cap rates and their fundamental determinants: expected rental growth and required rates of return. However, all retail and industrial property types are aggregated together in the KPC survey. Thus, the results are not directly comparable to our retail and industrial RERC results, which are disaggregated by subproperty type. However, the KPC data for apartments and CBD office properties are directly comparable to our RERC data.

The error correction model results using the KPC data for apartments and CBD office properties are very similar to the corresponding results from the RERC estimations over the 1996:2 to 2007:2 sample period. For example, using RERC data, we report in Table 4 that the estimated coefficients on risk premium change and Treasury yield change in the short-run CBD model (without orthoganalization) are 0.535 and 0.599, respectively, and both are highly significant. The corresponding coefficient estimates using KPC data are 0.581 and 0.476, and both estimates are, again, highly significant. The coefficient on the error correction term using the RERC data and KPC data are −0.708 and −0.439, respectively. The only substantive difference in the results is that the estimated coefficient on rent growth change is negative and significant in the RERC estimation. Although negative, this coefficient estimate is not significant in the KPC estimation.

Our error correction model results for apartments using KPC data are also very similar to the RERC results. In particular, the estimated coefficients on risk premium change and Treasury yield change in the short-run CBD model are positive and highly significant, although the magnitude of the estimates is less than in the RERC estimations. The estimated coefficient on the error correction term is negative and significant but is also smaller in magnitude than the estimate obtained with RERC data.

Overall, the error correction results using KPC data for apartments and CBD office properties indicates that our primary findings are robust to the use of an alternative dataset.

VECTOR ERROR-CORRECTION MODEL

To further examine potential endogeneity effects, we also estimate a vector error-correction model (VECM) in which all of the variables are specified as endogenous variables in a five-equation system. A VECM model is a restricted vector autoregressive (VAR) model designed for use with nonstationary time series that are cointegrated (see, for example, Hamilton 1994). A group of nonstationary time-series is cointegrated if there is a linear combination of them that is stationary. These cointegrating relations (error correction terms) are incorporated into the VECM.[17]

For example, consider the following two-variable VECM:

$$\Delta Y_t = a_1 + b_1 \Delta Y_{t-1} + c_1 \Delta Z_{t-1} + \alpha_1 \left(Y_{t-1} - \beta Z_{t-1} \right) + e_{1t} \qquad (8)$$

$$\Delta Z_t = a_2 + b_2 \Delta Z_{t-1} + c_2 \Delta Y_{t-1} + \alpha_2 \left(Y_{t-1} - \beta Z_{t-1} \right) + e_{2t} \qquad (9)$$

where all terms involving Δ are stationary. This two-variable error correction model is a bivariate VAR in first differences augmented by the error-correction terms α_1 $(Y_{t-1} - \beta Z_{t-1})$ and $\alpha_2(Y_{t-1} - \beta Z_{t-1})$ from the cointegrating relation. The β's contain the cointegrating equation and the a α's the speeds of adjustment. In general, the kth order vector error-correction model can be represented by the following system:

$$\Delta X_t = \mu + \Gamma_1 \Delta X_{t-1} + \Gamma_2 \Pi \Delta X_{t-2} + \ldots + \Gamma_{k-1} \Pi \Delta X_{t-k+1} + \Pi X_{t-k} + e_t \ (10)$$

where

X_t	vector of pI(1) variables,
μ	$p \times 1$ vector of intercepts,
$\Gamma_1, \Gamma_2, \Gamma_k, \Pi$	$p \times p$ matrices of parameters,
e_t	error term $[\sim NID(0,\Omega)]$,
Δ	difference operator, and
$I(1)$	integrated of order one (i.e., first-difference stationary).

In the above system, the coefficient matrix Π provides information about the long-run equilibrium (error correction) relations among the variables, while the I's provide information on short-run relations. If all of the elements of Π equal zero, the system becomes a traditional VAR in differences. Using Johansen's (1988) method, we first obtain the number of cointegrating vectors (rank of Π) and then the parameter estimates using the VECM.

---

[17] An alternative approach would be to estimate a structural equation system. However, this would require identifying restriction assumptions and would also be problematic given the non-stationary and cointegrated nature of our data.

As discussed earlier, augmented Dickey–Fuller and weighted symmetric unit root tests suggest that the variables in the system are non-stationary (i.e., we could not reject the null hypothesis of a unit root at the 5% significance level for the variables in the system). The results of Johansen's (trace) cointegration tests also indicate the existence of one cointegrating vector at the 5% level.

Table 6 reports the VECM estimation results for the cap rate equation using our RERC sentiment variable. Similar to our earlier single-equation error correction model results, we find that cap rate changes are positively related to changing Treasury yields and equity risk premiums, although the statistical significance of these two fundamental variables is reduced relative to their significance in our single equation error correction model. However, we find no consistent role for sentiment in explaining the time series variation of cap rates during the 1996:Q1 to 2007:Q2 sample period. Finally, in contrast to our earlier results, we find that the error correction term (cointegrating equation) is often insignificant in the VECM results. This finding is consistent with McGough and Tsolacos (2001) and may result from a limited degrees of freedom problem whereby numerous parameters are being estimated in the system of equations with a limited number of quarterly observations.

The estimation results for the RERC sentiment equation in the VECM also allows us to formally test whether RERC sentiment is explained by lagged changes in our two fundamental variables: equity risk premiums and expected rental growth rates. The results (not shown) indicate that changes in RERC sentiment are not driven by these two fundamental variables. In fact, the only variable that consistently explains the change in RERC sentiment in the current quarter is the prior quarter's change, although this may again reflect the inability of our sample size to fully support the estimation of the VECM.

As noted above, our inability to uncover a role for sentiment in explaining the time-series variation in cap rates over the 1996:Q1 to 2007:Q2 sample period may be the result of limited degrees of freedom in our VECM estimation using RERC data. However, the KPC data for apartments and CBD office properties extends back to 1991:Q4, providing more degrees of freedom than the RERC data. To examine the robustness of our VECM results to the use of a longer time series, we replicated the RERC VECM results reported in Table 6 using the KPC data. The results are encouraging. The estimated coefficient on risk premium chg(–1) for apartments reported in Table 6 is 0.375 (t statistic = 1.906). The corresponding estimate using the KPC data is 0.243 (t statistic = 2.625). Similarly, the coefficient on Treasury yield chg(–1) using RERC data is 0.340 (t statis-

TABLE 6
Vector error correction model-cap rate determinants: 1996:2–2007:2

	Apartment		Hotel		Industrial R&D		Industrial warehouse		CBD office		Suburban office		Neighborhood retail		Power center		Mall	
Constant	-0.061	(-2.179)	-0.068	(-1.077)	-0.029	(-1.299)	-0.013	(-0.498)	-0.025	(-0.748)	-0.038	(-1.309)	-0.035	(-1.190)	-0.054	(-1.478)	-0.019	(-0.508)
Cap Rate Chg (-1)	-0.264	(-1.371)	-0.249	(-0.962)	-0.063	(-0.296)	-0.367	(-1.514)	0.041	(0.184)	0.074	(0.328)	-0.033	(-0.132)	-0.036	(-0.145)	-0.737	(-3.300)
Cap Rate Chg (-2)	-0.290	(-1.500)	0.026	(0.100)	-0.474	(-1.970)	-0.440	(-1.949)	-0.300	(-1.422)	-0.189	(-0.829)	-0.126	(-0.515)	-0.254	(-1.019)	-0.028	(-0.119)
Rent Growth Chg (-1)	0.001	(0.674)	0.003	(0.629)	0.001	(0.428)	-0.001	(-0.578)	-0.001	(-0.445)	0.001	(0.376)	0.002	(1.171)	0.000	(0.036)	0.000	(0.064)
Rent Growth Chg (-2)	0.004	(2.425)	0.001	(0.300)	0.001	(0.528)	0.001	(0.794)	-0.001	(-0.661)	0.000	(-0.149)	-0.002	(-0.864)	0.000	(0.126)	0.002	(0.835)
Risk Premium Chg (-1)	0.375	(1.906)	0.276	(1.206)	0.413	(2.541)	0.563	(2.476)	0.417	(2.139)	0.052	(0.286)	0.166	(0.687)	0.164	(0.850)	0.593	(3.108)
Risk Premium Chg (-2)	0.407	(2.009)	0.089	(0.392)	0.334	(1.699)	0.738	(3.154)	0.255	(1.288)	0.419	(2.320)	0.365	(1.547)	0.273	(1.443)	0.252	(1.179)
Treasury Yield Chg (-1)	0.340	(1.690)	0.129	(0.391)	0.344	(2.083)	0.545	(2.344)	0.420	(1.832)	0.100	(0.504)	0.159	(0.677)	0.147	(0.720)	0.494	(2.446)
Treasury Yield Chg (-2)	0.373	(1.792)	0.079	(0.247)	0.343	(1.794)	0.704	(2.959)	0.274	(1.357)	0.448	(2.340)	0.328	(1.436)	0.239	(1.153)	0.151	(0.673)
RERC Sentiment Chg (-1)	0.029	(0.580)	0.028	(0.267)	-0.035	(-0.649)	0.030	(0.502)	-0.050	(-0.722)	-0.158	(-1.968)	-0.016	(-0.333)	-0.007	(-0.118)	0.012	(0.185)
RERC Sentiment Chg (-2)	0.034	(0.690)	0.002	(0.014)	-0.219	(-4.210)	-0.001	(-0.019)	-0.034	(-0.487)	-0.150	(-1.739)	-0.063	(-1.326)	-0.113	(-1.748)	-0.023	(-0.383)
Vector error correction term	0.000	(0.022)	0.000	(-0.312)	-0.009	(-3.262)	0.001	(0.174)	0.001	(1.222)	-0.004	(-0.681)	0.002	(0.799)	0.001	(0.328)	-0.008	(-1.411)
Adjusted R^2	0.061		-0.188		0.360		0.167		0.085		0.117		-0.022		-0.065		0.187	

P values are in parentheses. The parameter estimates are from the estimation of the equation system (10) using quarterly data over the 1996:2 to 2007:2 time period. We only report the cap rate equation estimates from each property equation system. The dependent variable in this equation from the system is the quarterly change in the cap rate. Rent growth chg is the change in expected rental growth from quarter t-1 to quarter t. Risk premium chg is the change in the required unlevered equity risk premium from quarter t-1 to quarter t. Treasury yield chg is the change in the yield to maturity on a 10-year Treasury Bond from quarter t-1 to quarter t. The vector error correction term is from the estimated cointegrating equation.

tic = 1.690). The corresponding estimate using the KPC data is 0.239 (*t* statistic = 2.474). Overall, the significance of the fundamental variables increases somewhat using a longer time series. Interestingly, unlike the RERC VECM estimations, the coefficient on Sentiment chg(–1) is negative and significant and the coefficient on Sentiment chg(–2) is positive and significant, suggesting a role for sentiment in the determination of apartment cap rates.

The use of the KPC data with a longer time series in the estimation of the CBD office VECM provides similar results. That is, coefficients on the fundamental variables carry the expected sign and significance (with the exception of expected rent growth). In addition, however, the estimated coefficient on RERC sentiment chg(–1) is –0.257 (*t* statistic = –2.220). In summary, the use of the VECM, which allows all variables in the system to be estimated endogenously, also suggests a statistically significant role for sentiment when the longer KPC time series is used.

TIME VARIATION IN THE DISPERSION OF CAP RATES, RENT GROWTH AND DISCOUNT RATES

Our earlier single-equation error correction results suggest that sentiment plays a role in commercial property cap rate determination, once we account for the sentiment embedded in the expected rent growth and risk premiums. In addition to endogeneity issues, another potential concern is that our testing approach implicitly assumes that if sentiment impacts prices it does so at all times. That is, sentiment is essentially another variable in the property pricing equation. However, sentiment may only play a pricing role in "up" or "hot" markets.[18] Short-sale constraints inhibit the ability of rational investors to eliminate overpricing and may imply that irrational investors are only active in the market when they are overly optimistic. Hence, in up markets, asset values reflect the sentiment of these irrational traders. Our tests of a role for sentiment, therefore, may have relatively low power because sentiment is not important in all periods in the sample.

To address this concern, we provide an additional test for the role of sentiment in property pricing dynamics. More specifically, we examine the time series of the coefficient of variation of RERC cap rates, rent growth, discount rates and sentiment, calculated across the nine property types each quarter and test whether variation over

---

[18] See, for example, Baker and Stein (2004). Yu and Yuan (2007) also find that irrationality is more prevalent in rising markets.

FIGURE 6
Time series of dispersion of RERC variables across nine property types

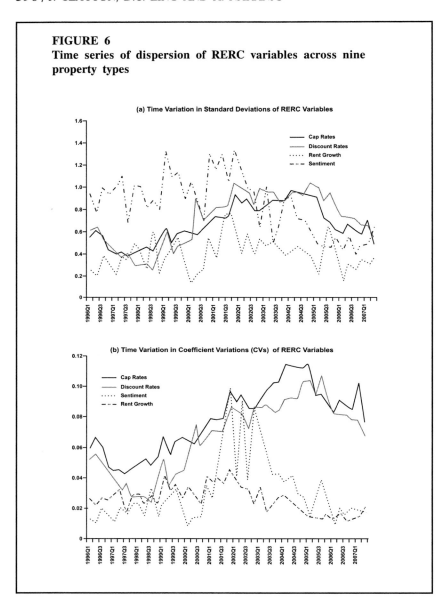

time in these cross-sectional dispersion series is related to investor sentiment, after controlling for macroeconomic fundamentals. If sentiment does impact pricing, then we expect that in periods of high sentiment there will be less cross-sectional dispersion in cap rates and discount rates because all assets in a given "bucket" experience the upswing. That is, cross-property dispersion in pricing will decrease as co-movement in returns tightens and is delinked from co-movement in cash flow and risk fundamentals due to coordinated sentiment-based trading (Barberis et al. 2002). In contrast, cross-sectional variation is likely to increase during economic downturns (Plazzi et al. 2008).

Figure 6 presents the time series of cross-property standard deviations (top graph) and coefficients of variation (bottom graph) of the RERC regression variables. Note that, starting in 2000, the dispersion of RERC sentiment across the nine property types declines, with the dispersion of cap rates and discount rates following soon thereafter. Interestingly, there does not appear to be any systematic change in the variation of rent growth expectations over this time period, except for the much higher coefficient of variation during the recession of 2002, suggesting that the decrease in discount rate and cap rate dispersion is either a sentiment or a capital market (i.e., denominator) phenomenon.

To investigate whether the lower volatility resulting from convergence across property types represent rational repricing based on economic fundamentals or, instead, derives from investor sentiment, we regress the time series of cross property standard deviations on our CLN sentiment measure and three economic factors that have been found to be related to business cycle risks in previous studies; the 3–month Treasury yield, the Treasury term structure, and a corporate default premium variable.[19] All explanatory variables are lagged to avoid simultaneity bias, and lagged dependent variables are included as regressors to account for slow adjustment over time. Table 7 reports the estimation results. Cross-property dispersion in cap rates is strongly persistent and the coefficients on both the 3-month Treasury yield and CLN sentiment are statistically significant and negative. Hence, high investor sentiment predicts a decrease in the cross-property dispersion of cap rates, consistent with our hypothesis about a convergence in pricing during a hot market. We obtain similar results with the IRR dispersion equation, although the statistical significance is not quite as high as in the cap rate equation. Finally, sentiment does not appear to affect the variation in rental growth rates. Overall, these findings suggest that the decrease in cap rates

---

[19] The version of the CLN sentiment index used here is the principal component of the sentiment proxies after first orthogonalizing each proxy by regressing it on the three economic fundamental variables.

and required returns over the past 5 to 6 years is a capital market phenomenon that may, in part, reflect investor sentiment.

CONCLUSION

Classical finance price theory posits no role for investor sentiment, capital flows, or trading activity. Rather, assets are assumed to trade in frictionless markets where unemotional investors force prices to equal the rational present value of expected future cash flows. However, the inability of the standard present value model to explain several dramatic run-ups and subsequent crashes in asset prices has led to a burgeoning "behavioral" finance literature. This behavioral paradigm allows for the existence of both irrational investors and limits to arbitrage. In these models, investor sentiment, capital flows, and trading volume can have a role in the determination of asset prices — independent of market fundamentals.

Private commercial real estate markets differ substantially from public stock markets. First, real estate assets are decidedly heterogeneous. Therefore, unlike the listed shares of a firm for which close substitutes exist either directly of indirectly, the unique location and other attributes of commercial real estate assets severely restrict an investor's set of acceptable substitutes. Moreover, these heterogeneous assets trade in illiquid, highly segmented and informationally inefficient local markets. As a result the search costs associated with matching buyers and sellers are significant. The inability to short sell private real estate also restricts the ability of sophisticated traders to enter the market and eliminate mispricing, especially if they believe property is overvalued. Limits to arbitrage could therefore be expected to lead to deviations of prices from fundamental values in the presence of sentiment investors.

These characteristics of private real estate markets would seem to render them highly susceptible to sentiment-induced mispricing and, indeed, there is a widespread belief among many real estate market participants that real estate markets are subject to fads (i.e., swings in sentiment). Many real estate practitioners devote considerable effort to understanding market sentiment (i.e., what other investors might do), rather than focusing solely on cash flow and discount rate considerations. In fact, the significant reduction in capitalization rates that occurred in most commercial real estate markets from 2002 to 2007 is largely, if not entirely, attributed to the surge in sentiment-driven capital flows that occurred during this period (Downs 2004; House 2004).

Despite the potential importance of fundamentals and investor sentiment in private real estate pricing dynamics, no research exists

TABLE 7

Significance of economic factors versus sentiment in explaining the time series behavior of cross-property type dispersions in cap rates, discounts rates and rent growth expectations

	Dependent variable					
	Cross property type standard deviation of					
	Cap rate		IRR		Rent growth	
Intercept	0.5766	(0.01)	0.5185	(0.01)	0.2780	(0.34)
Dependent variable (−1)	0.5441	(0.00)	0.7215	(0.01)	0.2545	(0.13)
3 Mth Tsy (−1)	−0.0604	(0.02)	−0.0577	(0.01)	−0.0076	(0.84)
Term spread (−1)	−0.0310	(0.25)	−0.0370	(0.01)	0.0085	(0.87)
Credit spread (−1)	−0.0137	(0.85)	−0.0779	(0.01)	−0.0458	(0.75)
CLN sentiment (−1)	−0.0312	(0.03)	−0.0326	(0.01)	−0.0148	(0.54)
Adjusted R^2	84.3%		80.9%		4.4%	

P values are in parentheses. The parameter estimates are from regressions of the standard deviation of the cap rate, rent growth and discount rate, calculated each quarter across nine property types, on economic conditions and sentiment, using quarterly data over the 1996:2 to 2007:2 time period. Cap rate, rent growth and discount rate data were obtained from the Real Estate Research Corporation's *Real Estate Report*, which publishes results from RERC's quarterly Real Estate Investment Survey. The *Real Estate Report* summarizes the expected rates of return, property selection criteria, and investment outlook of a sample of institutional investors and managers throughout the USA. Business cycle conditions are measured by the 3-month Treasury yield, a term structure variable (10-year less 3-month Treasury yield) and a default premium variable (Baa corporate bond yield less AAA bond yield). CLN sentiment is the first principal component from a group of potential real estate investment sentiment proxies including commercial mortgage flows as a percentage of GDP, institutional property transaction activity and liquidity measures as well as property returns in the most recent quarter and over the past year.

that directly examines the relative influence of fundamentals and investor sentiment in commercial real estate pricing. This paper examines the extent to which fundamentals and investor sentiment explain the time-series variation in property-specific national cap rates.

In our analysis, we apply a new dataset to the study of cap rate determinants that includes direct fundamentals and both survey (direct) measures of investor sentiment and composite (indirect) measures of investor sentiment constructed from a set of potential sentiment proxies. Direct survey measures of investor sentiment, along with cap rates, unlevered equity discount rates, and expected rent growth for nine property types at both the national and MSA-level are taken from the Real Estate Report, published quarterly by the Real Estate Research Corporation (RERC). The nature of the RERC data set also allows us to utilize an innovative modeling and econometric approach to the analysis of the relation between sentiment and property pricing. More specifically, we derive an equilibrium model of cap rates specified as a function of real estate space and capital market fundamentals that is estimated using error-correction techniques, thereby capturing both short and long-run dynamics.

Our results show that fundamentals are the key driver of cap rates. However, sentiment also plays a pricing role over our 1996–2007 study period.

ACKNOWLEDGEMENT

We thank David Barker, Bob Edelstein, David Geltner, Norm Miller, Tobias Muhlhofer, Larry Souza, Alan Ziobrowski and participants in the Cambridge-Maastricht-MIT Symposium in Boston (2007), the ASSA/AREUEA session in New Orleans (2008), the UC-Irvine Center for Real Estate Winter Symposium on Urban Research (2008), the USC Lusk Center for Real Estate Annual Research Symposium (2008), the Homer Hoyt session in North Palm Beach (2008), and the Georgia State Department of Real Estate research seminar (2008) for helpful comments and suggestions. We also thank the Real Estate Research Institute for providing partial funding for this project and Ben Scheick for excellent research assistance.

REFERENCES

Archer, W. A., & Ling, D. C. (1997). The three dimensions of real estate markets: Linking space, capital, and property markets. Real Estate Finance Fall, 7–14.

Baker, M., & Stein, J. (2004). Market liquidity as a sentiment indicator. Journal of Financial Markets 7, 271–299.

Baker, & M., Wurgler, J. (2006). Investor sentiment and the cross-section of stock returns. Journal of Finance 61(4), 1645–1680.

Baker, M., & Wurgler, J. (2007). Investor sentiment in the stock market. The Journal of Economic Perspectives 21, 129–151.

Barberis, N., Shleifer, A., & Wurgler, J. (2005). Comovement. Journal of Financial Economics 75, 283–317.

Barberis, N., & Thaler, R. (2003). Chapter 18: A survey of behavioral finance. In: Constantinides G. M., Harris M., Stulz R. (eds) Handbook of the Economics of Finance, pp 1053–1128. vol. 1. Elsevier, Amsterdam.

Brown, G., & Cliff, M. (2004). Investor sentiment and the near term stock market. Journal of Empirical Finance 11, 1–27.

Brown, G., & Cliff, M. (2005). Investor sentiment and asset valuation. Journal of Business 78(2), 405–440.

Brown, S., Goetzmann, W., Hiraki, T., Shiraishi, N., & Watanabe, M. (2002). Investor sentiment in Japanese and U.S. Daily Mutual Fund Flows. Yale Working Paper.

Campbell, J., Shiller, R. (1998). The dividend-price ratio and expectations of future dividends and discount factors. Review of Financial Studies 1, 195–228.

Chakravarty, S. (2001). Stealth-trading: Which trader's trades move stock prices? Journal of Financial Economics 61, 289–307.

Chen, J., Hudson-Wilson, S., & Nordby, H. (2004). Real estate pricing: Spreads and sensibilities: Why real estate pricing is rational. Journal of Real Estate Portfolio Management 10, 1–21.

Chichernea, D., Miller, N., Fisher, J., Sklarz, M., & White, R. (2008). A cross sectional analysis of cap rates by MSA. Journal of Real Estate Research 30(3) (forthcoming).

Clayton, J. (2003). Capital flows and asset values: A review of the literature and exploratory investigation in a real estate context. Homer Hoyt/University of Cincinnati Working Paper.

Clayton, J., MacKinnon, G., & Peng, L. (2008). Time variation of liquidity in the private real estate market: An empirical investigation. Journal of Real Estate Research 30(2) (forthcoming).

De Long, J. B., Shleifer, A., Summers, L. H., & Waldmann, R. J. (1990). Noise trader risk in financial markets. Journal of Political Economy 98(4), 703–738.

Dokko, Y., Edelstein, R., Lacayo, A., & Lee, D. (1999). Real estate income and value cycles: A model of market dynamics. Journal of Real Estate Research 18(1), 69–96.

Downs, A. (2004). Some aspects of the real estate outlook. Retrieved from http://www.anthonydowns.com.

Edelen, R. M., & Warner, J. B. (2001). Aggregate price effects of institutional trading: A study of mutual fund flow data and market returns. Journal of Financial Economics 59(2), 195–220.

Engle, R., & Granger, C. W. J. (1987). Cointegration and error correction: Representation estimation and testing. Econometrica 55, 251–276.

Fama, E., & French R. (2007). Disagreement, tastes, and asset prices. Journal of Financial Economics 83(3), 667–689.

Fisher, J., Ling, D. C., & Naranjo, A. (2007). Commercial real estate return cycles: Do capital flows matter? University of Florida/RERI Working 1aper.

Fisher, J., Geltner, D., & Pollakowski H. (2007) A Quarterly Transactions-based Index of Institutional Real Estate Investment Performance and Movements in Supply, and Demand. Journal of Real Estate Finance and Economics 34(1), 5–33.

Froot, K. A., O'Connell, P. G. J., & Seasholes, M. S. (2001). The portfolio flows of international investors. Journal of Financial Economics 59(2), 151–194.

Geltner, D. M., Miller, N. G., Clayton, J., & Eicholtz P. (2007). Commercial Real Estate Analysis and Investments, 2nd edn. South-Western Publishing, Cincinnati, OH.

Geltner, D., & Mei J. (1995). The present value model with time-varying discount rates: Implications for commercial property valuation and investment decisions. The Journal of Real Estate Finance and Economics 11(2), 119–135.

Gompers, P., & Lerner, J. (2000). Money chasing deals? The impact of fund inflows on private equity valuations. Journal of Financial Economics 5, 281–325.

Greene, W. (1993). Econometric analysis, 2nd edn. Prentice Hall, Englewood Cliffs.

Griffin, J., Nardari, F., & Stulz, R., (2007). Do investors trade more when stocks have performed well? Evidence from 46 countries. The Review of Financial Studies 20(3), 905–951.

Hamilton, J. D. (1994). Time series analysis. Princeton University Press, Princeton.

Hendershott, P. H., & MacGregor, B. (2005a). Investor rationality: Evidence from U.K. Property Capitalization Rates. Real Estate Economics 26, 299–322.

Hendershott, P. H., & MacGregor, B. (2005b). Investor rationality: An analysis of NCREIF commercial property data. Journal of Real Estate Research 26, 445–475.

Hirshleifer, D. (2001). Investor psychology and asset pricing. Journal of Finance 56, 1533–1597.

House, G. C. (2004). Demand for Real Estate: Capital Flows, Motivations, and the Impact of Rising Rates. Institute for Fiduciary Education.

Jones, C. M., & Lipson, M. (2004). Are retail orders different? Working Paper, Columbia University.

Johansen, S. (1988). Statistical Analysis of Cointegrating Vectors. Journal of Economic Dynamics and Control 12, (2–3), 231–254.

Kaniel, R., Saar, G., Titman, S. (2005). Individual investor sentiment and stock returns. Working Paper, Duke University.

Ling, D. C. (2005). A random walk down main street: Can experts predict returns on commercial real estate. Journal of Real Estate Research 27(2), 137–154.

Ling, D. C., & Naranjo A. (2003). The dynamics of REIT capital flows and returns. Real Estate Economics 31, 405–434.

Ling, D. C., & Naranjo, A. (2006). Dedicated REIT mutual fund flows and REIT performance. Journal of Real Estate Finance and Economics 32(4), 409–433.

McGough, T., & Tsolacos, S. (2001). Do yields reflect property market fundamentals? Working Paper, City University Business School.

Nofsinger, J. R., & Sias, R. W. (1999). Herding and feedback trading by institutional and individual investors. Journal of Finance 59, 2263–2295.

Pavlov, A. D., & Wachter, S. M. (2006). Underpriced lending and real estate markets. Retrieved at SSRN from http://ssrn.com/abstract=980298

Plazzi, A., Torous, W. N., & Valkanov, R. (2004). Expected returns and the expected growth in rents of commercial property. Working Paper, The Anderson School at UCLA.

Plazzi, A., Torous, W. N., & Valkanov, R. (2008). The cross-sectional dispersion of commercial real estate returns and rent growth: time variation and economic fluctuations. Real Estate Economics (in press).

Riddiough, T. (2008). On the addictive properties of cheap and easy debt capital. PREA Quarterly, Winter issue, 30–37.

Shilling, J. D. (2003). Is there a risk premium puzzle in real estate? Real Estate Economics 31(4), 501–525.

Shilling, J. D., Sing, T. F. (2007). Do institutional real estate investors have rational expectations? Working Paper.

Sias, R., Starks, L. T., & Titman, S. (2006). Changes in institutional ownership and stock returns: Assessment and methodology. Journal of Business 79, 2869–2910.

Sivitanidou, R., & Sivitanides, P. (1999). Office capitalization rates: Real estate and capital market influences. Journal of Real Estate Finance and Economics 18(3), 297–322.

Sivitanides, P., Southard, J., Torto, R., & Wheaton, W. (2001). The determinants of appraisal-based capitalization rates. MIT Working Paper.

Warther, V. A. (1995). Aggregate mutual fund flows and security returns. Journal of Financial Economics 39, 209–235.

Wheaton, W. (1999). Real estate cycles: Some fundamentals. Real Estate Economics 27, 209–230.

Yu, J., & Yuan, Y. (2007). Investor sentiment and the mean-variance relation. Working Paper, Wharton School, University of Pennsylvania.

Effect of Environmental Factors on Real Estate Value

——————————————————————— JOHN T. GLEN

A. VALUING REAL ESTATE WITH ENVIRONMENTAL PROBLEMS

Just a few short years ago appraisers had very little experience at valuing real estate with environmental problems. Increasing public concern about environmental issues and changes in legislation have created new potential for significant exposure to liability. As a result, a small but expanding body of methodology has been developed to deal with the practical aspects of the question: how does one value real estate with environmental problems? The following, therefore, is an attempt to summarize briefly the current body of concepts in this area.

B. VALUE UNIMPAIRED — VALUE IMPAIRED

The appraisal of properties with environmental problems involves first the valuation of the property as if unimpaired, and then an analysis of the loss in value caused by the environmental impairment. Because environmental problems represent a loss in value, it is a form of depreciation, which must be viewed as a reduction from the value as if unimpaired.[1]

Unfortunately, there is virtually no reliable market data because properties generally cannot be sold in an environmentally impaired condition, as it is unlikely that a knowledgeable buyer would be will-

———————

This article is an update of John T. Glen, "The Effect of Environmental Factors on Real Estate Values" in Henry Bartel and Gavin Arbuckle, *Readings in Canadian Real Estate*, 3rd edition (Toronto: Captus Press, 1997).

ing to take on the burden of contamination problems. The degree of environmental problems can be so specific to a particular property that it is difficult to make meaningful comparisons among impaired property sales.

Any meaningful discussion of properties with environmental problems should involve **both** impaired value and unimpaired values.

C. CAUSE OF REDUCED VALUE

The causes of loss of market value for property with environmental problems fall into three broad categories:

1. Cost to correct or remediate;
2. Liability to the public; and
3. Stigma after cleanup.

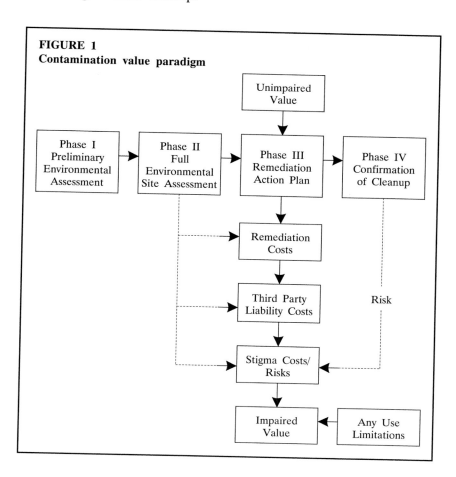

FIGURE 1
Contamination value paradigm

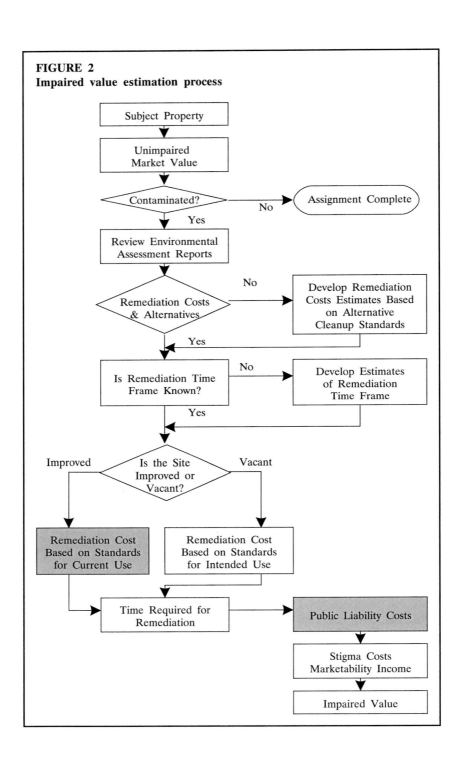

FIGURE 2
Impaired value estimation process

Subject Property

Unimpaired
Market Value

Contaminated? — No → Assignment Complete

Yes

Review Environmental
Assessment Reports

Remediation Costs
& Alternatives — No → Develop Remediation
Costs Estimates Based
on Alternative
Cleanup Standards

Yes

Is Remediation Time
Frame Known? — No → Develop Estimates
of Remediation
Time Frame

Yes

Improved ← Is the Site
Improved or
Vacant? → Vacant

Remediation Cost
Based on Standards
for Current Use

Remediation Cost
Based on Standards
for Intended Use

Time Required for
Remediation → Public Liability Costs

Stigma Costs
Marketability Income

Impaired Value

FIGURE 3
Quantifying the effects of environmental impairment

1. **Estimate Remediation Costs**
   (a) Develop Environmental Cost Estimates
       (i) Environmental Consulting Costs
       (ii) Estimate Capital and Engineering Costs
       (iii) Annual Monitoring Costs
   (b) Total Remediation Cost

2. **Estimate Public Liability Costs**
   (a) Potential Off-site Costs
   (b) Liability to On-Site Tenants

3. **Estimate Stigma Costs**
   (a) Stigma Related Costs
       (i) Costs of Managing Cleanup
       (ii) Costs of Financing Cleanup
       (iii) Cost Amortization Rate
       (iv) Cost Amortization
   (b) Stigma Affecting Marketability
       (i) Lack of Mortgageability
       (ii) Insurability
       (iii) Marketing Time
       (iv) Vend Warranties
   (b) Stigma Affecting Income
       (i) Rents
       (ii) Occupancy
       (iii) Expenses
       (iv) Net Income
       (v) Capitalization and/or Discount Rates

(1) Cost to Correct or Remediate

Until relatively recently, this was called the "cost to cure". Then it became evident that there probably is no such thing as a "cure" for most environmental problems, at least as far as environmental regulatory agencies are concerned. The most that can be done is to "correct" the environmental problems, using the best methods and procedures available at the time.

There are **six** options for remediation.

(i) **Repair**, by restoration or repair of the system that controls the risk or hazard;

(ii) **Isolation**, by separating the risk from the environment and human beings;

(iii) **Encapsulation**, by use of an impermeable membrane to isolate the risk;

(iv) **Enclosure** is like encapsulation, but the enclosure is structurally sound and able to resist shifts in the building or the hazard;

(v) **Removal and disposal**, which require the safe removal of the risk by conversion of the substance to a non-hazardous form, or transfer of the hazardous substance to another approved site.

(vi) **Bioremediation/biogradation** is the use of biological methods, including oxygen or microorganisms, to break down contaminants.

It should be noted that identifying the appropriate methods or procedures to correct environmental problems is a task for trained technical specialists. Both remediation procedure regulations and technology are continually changing. In order to determine which cleanup option is the most desirable, engineering studies are undertaken, and the AEP may require environmental studies to support the recommended procedure.

The cost estimates should be analyzed in terms of whether they are adequate for the job. Care should be taken to ensure that all costs associated with the proposed remediation are included.

Immediate Costs

The most obvious costs relate to *removal of any undesirable substance* and *restoration* of the property to a usable condition. The cost to clean up would also include: *disruption* of the property's normal uses; *increases in operating costs* during the period of environmental problems; and *lack of utility*, in that the property cannot be used for its normal use during the period of environmental problems.

Ongoing Costs

In addition, there is a *contingent liability for future costs* of cleanups. Monitoring the site after remediation has occurred may be required for decades. As a corollary to the monitoring program, restrictions on use of the land may continue and may be registered against title. For instance, hazardous soil may be easily removed in a period of days; however, the treatment of mercury and other heavy metals in a water shed may require decades of monitoring and attention.

These costs can reduce market value as can an estimate of the immediate costs to be expended for removal of environmental problems.

(2) Liability to the Public

Environmental problems of real estate can lead to substantial liability to the public and resultant decline in property values. The market value of a property affected by contamination problems may be affected because of *third party claims* by the public relating to health risks or cleanup costs *resulting from spill over onto adjacent or nearby property*. There can be remediation claims by third parties in the neighbourhood in respect of their own property. Health based claims, such as illness from solvents leaking into ground water, are more difficult to quantify because potential liability exists to a broad range of people: tenants, neighbours, employees and the general public. The potential of such legal exposure is usually sufficient to have a detrimental effect on market value.

(3) Stigma After Cleanup

The term "stigma" is a market imposed penalty that can affect a property that is known or suspected to have environmental problems or property that was once environmentally impaired but is now considered clean, or a never affected property located in proximity to an impaired property. The property may have been cleaned up to the extent that present-day technology allows, and a well-financed indemnity for the benefit of future owners may have been offered to pay for any future site remediation costs. Yet the property may still not sell. Here we see the principle of substitution coming into play, as buyers seek an equally desirable substitute property that does not have the environmental problems.

In a rational market place, once the property has been cleaned up, the value of the property should return to its normal "pre-impaired" market value. Some experience suggests that, despite clean up to the satisfaction of the regulatory authorities, potential buyers remain reluctant to purchase properties with previous environmental problems. It is extremely difficult to place a value on the stigma associated with the property.

In the context of commercial office leasing, some corporate tenants have adopted policies that preclude leasing of premises previously insulated with asbestos, even where the asbestos has been completely removed.

This stigma involved in contaminated properties may be thought of as a negative intangible, as suggested by Peter Patchin in his article, "Contaminated Properties — Stigma Revisited."[2] The subject property's stigma is caused by the following factors:

- The Trouble Factor (Cost of Managing the Cleanup)
- Lack of Mortgageability
- Lack of Marketability
- Purchasers and Vendors
- We have added Lack of Insurability to the above items.

(i) Cost of Managing the Cleanup

This factor is essentially the *cost of managing the environmental cleanup*. The rationale for this deduction is that although buyers are aware of the costs to correct, they should also be compensated monetarily for the trouble of making the necessary improvement. The various considerations concerning managing the cleanup include:

- Costs of Managing the cleanup
- Costs of Financing the cleanup
- Procedures for Amortizing Costs that are high relative to the property's market value.

(ii) Lack of Mortgageability

The *inability to obtain mortgage financing*, either for the sale of a property or its future development, is one of the most frequent causes of stigma-related value loss. Generally speaking, lending institutions avoid properties with or even suspected of environmental problems, altogether. Institutional lenders are extremely reluctant to make conventional loans for real estate with an existing environmental problem. The vast majority of lenders will not even consider a property until it has been cleaned up and tests within required standards have been performed. This reluctance to lend applies not only to hazardous sites, but to sites with comparatively low levels of environmental problems. The net result of the loss of mortgageability is that the property is held off the market until the cure has been accomplished. Time thus becomes an important factor in the measurement of value loss.

In Canada a Task Group on Contaminated Site Liability presented their recommendations to the Canadian Council of Ministers on the Environment (CCME). Both the Appraisal Institute of Canada and the Appraisal Institute (of the United States), under pressure by lending institutions, have now accepted the need for a **Preliminary Environmental Checklist** to be part of an appraisal site inspection.

In Canada, lenders have formed an organization called the Environmental Bankers Association, and have started to develop risk assessment and control practices that may change lenders' aversion to lending for environmentally impaired properties.

(iii) Insurability

Insurance policies do not automatically provide for coverage in the following areas:

- Third party liability coverage relating to pollution or environmental contamination.
- Cost of cleanup should contamination occur after the policy is in effect.
- Cost of cleanup of pre-existing environmental problems.
- Damage exacerbated by the pre-existing environmental condition in the event of fire.

While it is possible to purchase insurance coverage for third party liability related to environmental incidents, such coverage does not cover cost of cleanup of the subject site. The requirements for qualification are rigorous and involve a clean environmental bill of health from the insurer's environmental engineers. Therefore, any site with pre-existing contamination is not eligible for such insurance coverage. The owner may have to self-insure at an indeterminate cost. Recently insurance companies have developed new insurance products that may offset environmental risk.

In addition, a pre-existing condition such as that affecting the subject property might well void certain policies related to replacement of the buildings in the event of fire, since the condition could exacerbate the situation.

(iv) Lack of Marketability

This factor reflects both the additional *time required to market properties with environmental problems* because of the costs of managing the cleanup and the lack of mortgageability, and also either a decrease in demand or downward shift in the entire demand curve. It is indicated by a reduced number or range of buyers making offers, reduced offering prices and longer marketing period. It is ultimately reflected in reduced numbers of sales of similarly affected properties.

(v) Purchaser, Vendors and Warranties[3]

Real estate *purchasers are reluctant to assume the potential liabilities* and duties associated with a property that has environmental problems. For practical as well as legal situations, it is not always possible to recover the cost of these liabilities from previous owners, tenants or polluters. To protect themselves, sophisticated property purchasers, in particular, have adopted liability avoidance steps,[4] such as:

• Commissioning a risk assessment as part of the "due diligence" prior to purchase.
• Obtaining representations and warranties in writing from the vendor as part of the purchase:
  • No outstanding governmental orders or requests for information.
  • No existing, pending or threatened actions of an environmental nature.
  • Compliance with all applicable environmental laws, regulations and bylaws.
  • All applicable permits or licences have been obtained regarding emissions to the air or water.
  • The air, soil and groundwater of the property contain no environmental problems.
  • The vendor has never been convicted of an offence for non-compliance, and is not in default of reporting requirements of environmental protection laws or regulations.
  • There are no waste disposal sites on the property, nor has the property ever been used as a landfill or waste disposal site, or for temporary storage of special wastes on an interim basis pending treatment or fill.

Obviously, in many cases the vendor will resist giving such blanket assurances, and a number of modifications might be made to reflect, "to the best of the vendor's knowledge," liability for specific substances only, and other situations.[5]

D. Quantifying Stigma

In a perfect world, stigma would be quantified on a direct basis. With a good quality set of market data, stigma might be expected to have an influence on market behaviour as measured through the income approach. Bill Mundy suggests the following criteria:[6]

(i) **Rent** — For a stigmatized property rent could be less than for the same property unstigmatized. This is a simple market demand phenomenon.

(ii) **Occupancy** — Occupancy levels would also be expected to be less as a result of such stigma. This could be reflected in a higher pro forma vacancy allowance. Alternatively, it might result in longer lag vacancy between lease expiries and re-leasing.

(iii) **Expenses** — For such a property, higher operating expenses could be expected for such items as marketing to maintain rents and occupancy levels, and professional services to determine whether environmental problems persist. *Insurance coverage* is simply one aspect.

(iv) **Net Income** — Lower rents, higher vacancies and higher expenses, individually or collectively, all lead to lower net incomes.

(v) **Rate** — The capitalization, amortization or discount rate could be influenced by lending institutions' desire to alter the loan-to-value ratio, interest rate, or term of the loan to offset perceived risk. With its mortgage-equity measurement techniques, the capitalization rate offers a more objective means to value properties with environmental problems. A discount rate is dependent on equity-yield requirements, mortgage terms available and anticipated future appreciation or depreciation. For properties with reduced marketability, the three components of the discount rate remain intact, but each is altered because of changing risk *as perceived by the lender and the investor.*

William Kinnard, in his address given at the Appraisal Institute's (of the United States) October 1991 symposium listed similar criteria for the measurement of decreased market value of properties with environmental problems.[7]

E. Environmental Impairment Valuation Model

From the preceding analysis we conclude that the impairment of market value by environmental problems can be established by an **Environmental Impairment Valuation Model**. The model, summarized in Figure 3, reflects *three* kinds of impairment to value: (1) remediation costs, (2) public liability costs and (3) stigma.

F. Recent Developments

(1) Brownfield Legislation

In 2001, the Province of Ontario introduced new legislation designed to encourage owners to clean up Brownfield sites, which were subject to environmental contamination. The legislation had the following underlying aims:

- Reduce the risk of future liability against landowners who restore contaminated property to meet current environmental standards.
- Streamline the planning process for land restoration and giving greater autonomy to municipalities to approve cleanup work.
- Allow municipalities to suspend payment of property taxes while property is being restored.

- Strengthen existing cleanup guidelines by including them in legislation as law.

(2) Lender Risk Management

Environment Risk Stages for Financial Institutions	
1 Risk Identification	Is there a credit or financial effect due to environmental conditions?
2 Risk Appraisal/ Evaluation	Impact on financial transaction. Due diligence.
3 Risk Control	Global agreements and checks and balance to minimize risk.
4 Risk Transfer/Financing	Insurance viable, indemnifications, holdbacks.
5 Risk Monitoring	Effective performance indicators.

RISK IDENTIFICATION

Is there a credit or financial effect due to environmental conditions based on the following criteria:

- Conditions: What is the current condition of the property?
- Character: What is the character of the contamination?
- Collateral: Borrower musty commit more collateral.
- Cash flow: What is the property's cash flow?
- Capacity: Does the owner have the capacity to pay for the remediation?
- Compliance: Is the property in compliance with environmental regulations, or moving towards compliance?

RISK APPRAISAL/EVALUATION
Characterize impact on financial institution

- How much due diligence is required?
- Due diligence. Should include review of the Phase 1, 2 and 3 Environmental Assessments.

RISK CONTROL

What are the checks and balances available to minimize lender risk:

- Legal
- Technical
- Business

Are there affirmative and negative covenants?

RISK TRANSFER/FINANCING
When is it best to use:

- Indemnification
- Global agreements
- Letters of credit
- Escrows
- Is insurance a viable risk alternative?

RISK MONITORING
Can risk be monitored using effective performance indicators?

(3) New Insurance Products Re Environmental Contamination

- Five to six insurance companies (i.e., AIG Environmental) provide cost cap and liability protection
- Fills the gap in government protection
- Helps buyers and sellers minimize or transfer risk
- Allows parties to assess, control and quantify costs
- Provide protection from escalating costs
- Assurance against unknown legal liability through cleanup can be completed quickly and economically.
- Premiums begin at $45,000 to $1 million

New insurance products related to environmental impairment include:

- Pollution legal liability insurance
- Remediation legal liability insurance
- Contractor's pollution coverage
- Contingent contractors coverage
- Project specific environmental impairment liability wrap-up
- Remediation stop loss coverage
- Remediation warranty insurance
- Remediation re-opener insurance
- Pollution errors and omission
- Lender liability environmental insurance
- Real estate environmental liability
- Secured creditor products
- Property transfer insurance

G. Measuring Real Estate Damages Due to Contamination

Randell Bell[8] has suggested a framework for measuring damages due to environmental contamination.

(1) Issues

The three issues to be evaluated for environmental impairment to property are:

- Costs
- Use
- Risk

(2) Stages

The detrimental condition stages are:

- Assessment
- Repair
- Ongoing

Bell's model is summarized in his Detrimental Condition Matrix and his Summary of Time and Impact on Value, shown in Figures 4 and 5.

FIGURE 4
Randell Bell Detrimental Conditions Matrix

| | | *Detrimental Condition Stages* | | |
		Assessment	*Repair*	*Ongoing*
Detrimental Condition Issues	Cost	Cost to assess and responsibility Engineering Phase I, II, III Studies	Repair costs and responsibility Repairs Remediation Contingencies	Ongoing costs and responsibility Operations and maintenance (O&M) monitoring
	Use	All loss of utility while assessed Disruptions Safety concerns Use restrictions	All loss of utility while repaired Income loss Expense increase Use restrictions	Ongoing use disruptions Alterations to highest and best use
	Risk	Uncertainty factor Discount, if any, where extent of damage is unknown	Project incentive Financial incentive, if any, to complete repairs	Market resistance Residual resistance, if any, due to situation

Source: *Bell's Guide: The Real Estate Encyclopedia*

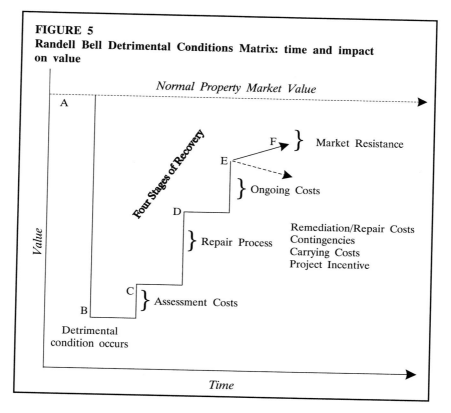

FIGURE 5
Randell Bell Detrimental Conditions Matrix: time and impact on value

H. Conclusions

Appraisers traditionally rely on three approaches when valuing property. The three approaches are:

1. Cost Approach
2. Market Sales Approach
3. Income Approach

We have suggested methods benchmarks for adjusting the valuation approaches to reflect environmental impairment.

(1) Cost Approach for Contaminated Properties

DEPRECIATION

Generally the effect of environmental impairment is measured by increased depreciation. For example, additional physical depreciation arises from changes in economic life due to contamination. Increased functional obsolescence may arise from excess operating

FIGURE 6
Cost approach flowchart for contaminated property

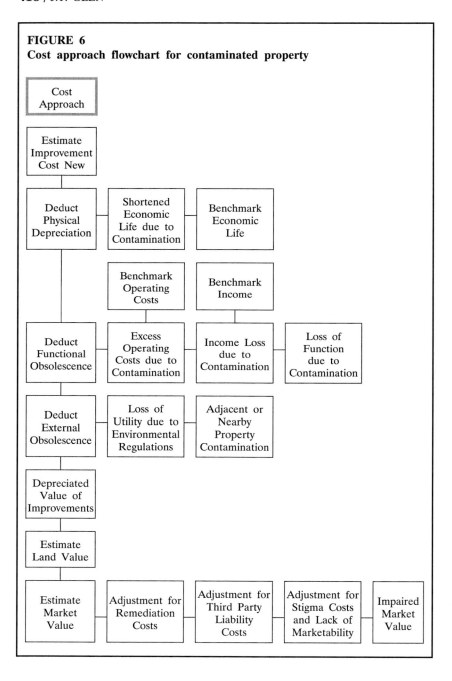

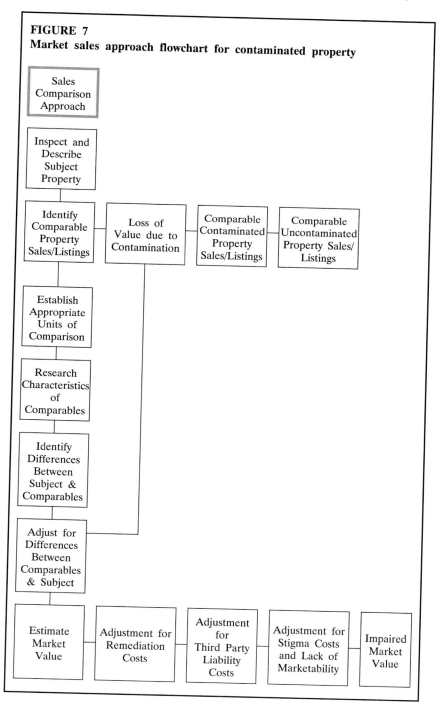

FIGURE 7
Market sales approach flowchart for contaminated property

FIGURE 8
Income approach flowchart for contaminated property

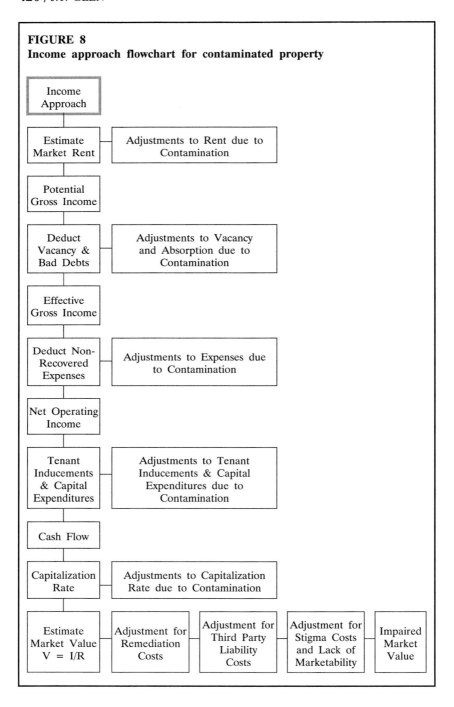

Figure 9
Valuation Benchmarking

Approach	Unimpaired	Impaired	Benchmark Test
Use Affects	Physically Possible	Physically Possible impaired	Benchmark Physically Possible
	Legally Permissible	Legally Permissible impaired	Benchmark Legally Permissible
	Financially Feasible	Financially Feasible impaired	Benchmark Financially Feasible
	Maximally Productive	Maximally Productive impaired	Benchmark Maximally Productive
	Highest and Best Use	Highest and Best Use impaired	Benchmark Highest and Best Use
Cost Approach	Physical Depreciation	Economic Life may be affected	Benchmark Economic Life
	Functional Obsolescence	Income Loss	Income Benchmark
		Excess Operating Costs	Operating Cost Benchmark
		Loss of Function	Function Benchmark
	External Obsolescence	Loss of Utility Environmental Regulations	Former Utility vs Restricted Utility
		Effect of Adjacent Contamination	Stigma Effects
Income Approach	Market Rent	Impairment may affect rent	Benchmark Rents
	Vacancy, Absorption	Contamination may affect Vacancy, Absorption	Benchmark Vacancy
	Operating Expense	Impairment may affect Operating Expense	Benchmark Expenses
	Net Income	Contamination may affect Net Income	Benchmark Net Income
	Tenant Inducements, CapEx	Impairment may affect Tenant Inducements, CapEx	Benchmark Tenant Inducements
	Cash Flow	Contamination may affect Cash Flow	Benchmark Cash Flow
	Capitalization Rate	Impairment may affect Capitalization Rate	Benchmark Capitalization Rates
Sales Approach	Unimpaired Comparables	Impaired Comparables	Adjustment for Impairment

costs, loss of income and decrease in function due to contamination. Additional external obsolescence can arise from changes in environmental regulations.

ADDITIONAL COSTS
In addition to increased depreciation, additional costs will arise due to remediation costs, third party costs and stigma costs.

LAND VALUE
The land value may need to be adjusted for impairment.

(2) Income Approach for Contaminated Properties
INCOME PARAMETERS
Adjustments may be required to the following income parameters due to contamination:

- Rent losses
- Higher vacancy and longer absorption periods
- Additional operating expenses
- Higher tenant inducement and cap expenditures
- Higher capitalization rate due to greater investment risk due to contamination

ADDITIONAL COSTS
Additional costs will arise due to remediation costs, third party costs and stigma costs.

(3) Market Sales Approach for Contaminated Properties
Paired sales from contaminated versus uncontaminated comparables may be the basis for adjustments due to contamination. Paired sales from contaminated versus uncontaminated income property comparables may be the basis for capitalization rate adjustments due to contamination.

ADDITIONAL COSTS
Additional costs will arise due to remediation costs, third party costs and stigma costs.

NOTES
1. Anthony J. Rinaldi, "Contaminated Properties — Valuation Solutions", *The Appraisal Journal* (July 1991): 377–381.
2. Peter J. Patchin, "Contaminated Properties — Stigma Revisited", *The Appraisal Journal*, (April 1991): 168.
3. L.O. Dybvig, AACI *Contaminated Real Estate — Implications for Real Estate Appraisers* (Winnipeg, MB: The Research and Development Fund, Appraisal Institute of Canada, 1992), p. 55.
4. Paul C. Wilson, "Environmental Liability in Real Estate Transactions: The Vendors Perspective", and Lynne B. Hustis, "Avoiding Environmental Liability in

Real Estate Transactions: The Purchaser's Perspective". Presentation Notes, Continuing Legal Education Society of British Columbia, September 1990.

5. J.C. Ruderman, "Negotiating the Agreement of Purchase and Sale to Reduce Environmental Risks". Paper presented at the Environmental Real Estate Transaction Conference, Toronto, 19 September 1988.

6. Bill Mundy, "Stigma and Value", *The Appraisal Journal* (January, 1992): p. 12.

7. William N. Kinnard, "Measuring the Effects of Contamination and Pollution on Property Values: The Focus of the 1991 Symposium in the Context of the Current State of Knowledge". Paper presented at the 1991 Appraisal Institute Symposium, Philadelphia, Pennsylvania.

8. Randell Bell, MAI, *Real Estate Damages; An Analysis of Detrimental Conditions* (Chicago, IL: Appraisal Institute, 1999).

The Development or Land Residual Approach

INTRODUCTION

This approach requires an estimate of the proposed project revenues and all aspects of the development costs. As such, the approach combines aspects of the market data, income and cost approaches to value. After estimating project revenues from sales and capitalizing any income from rentals, a total projected value is developed. From this development costs including hard and soft costs, leasing expenses and financing are subtracted.

If the price of a development site is being estimated the next step is an allowance is made for developer profit. The net project revenue after profit is then discounted to a present value based on the total time required for project development including absorption. The present value thus developed is the residual land value.

If the development return is being estimated the site value is a cost input.

There are three main purposes for which the residual approach is appropriate:

1. To estimate the most probable price of a development site land value) based on the highest and best use of the site.
2. To calculate the likely level of profit from a development scheme given a known site purchase price and a known cost of development.
3. To establish the construction cost ceiling given a known land cost and the minimum acceptable level of profit.

This article is an update of a case study found in Gavin Arbuckle and Henry Bartel, *Readings in Canadian Real Estate*, 2nd edition (Toronto: Captus Press, 1992).

DEVELOPMENT ALTERNATIVES

In this review we have examined the task of estimation of the first two parameters:

Level of Profit or Return
Land Value
Development Approach Process

THE DEVELOPMENT APPROACH PROCESS IS EXPLAINED IN CHART FORM IN THE FOLLOWING PAGES.

A. DEVELOPMENT APPROACH

This approach allows the *Development Return* to be estimated by deducting from the *Project Value* of the development upon completion, the *Development Costs*, including construction costs (either site servicing or building costs), marketing costs, financing, consulting fees, and other costs, to derive the relationship between *Development Profit* and *Costs*.

B. DEVELOPMENT APPROACH STEPS

1. Estimate Project Value
2. Estimate Development Costs
3. Estimate Net Project Receipts (Profit)
4. Present Value of Net Receipts (Profit)
5. Development Return

Determining Development Approach Return

(Project Value – Project Cost) = Project Profit
(Project Profit × Discount Rate) = PV Project Profit
(PV Project Profit ÷ Project Cost) = Development Return

Determining Development Approach Land Value

(Project Value – Project Cost Before Land) = Project Profit before Land
Development Return × Costs = Developers Profit
(Project Profit before Land – Developers Profit) = Land Residual on Project Completion
(PV Factor × Land Residual on Project Completion) = PV Land

C. PROCESS FOR ESTIMATION OF PROJECT VALUE

Estimate Development Project Revenue/Value

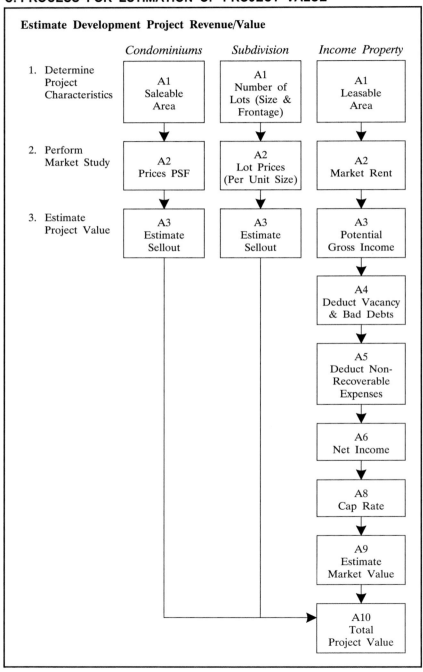

D. PROCESS FOR ESTIMATION OF DEVELOPMENT COSTS

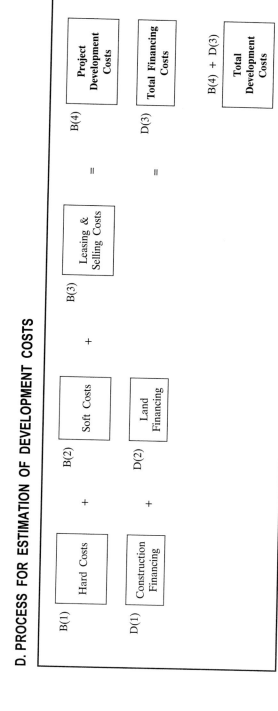

B(1) Hard Costs + B(2) Soft Costs + B(3) Leasing & Selling Costs = B(4) Project Development Costs

D(1) Construction Financing + D(2) Land Financing = D(3) Total Financing Costs

B(4) + D(3) Total Development Costs

E. DETERMINATION NET DEVELOPMENT RECEIPTS, PV PROFIT AND DEVELOPMENT RETURN

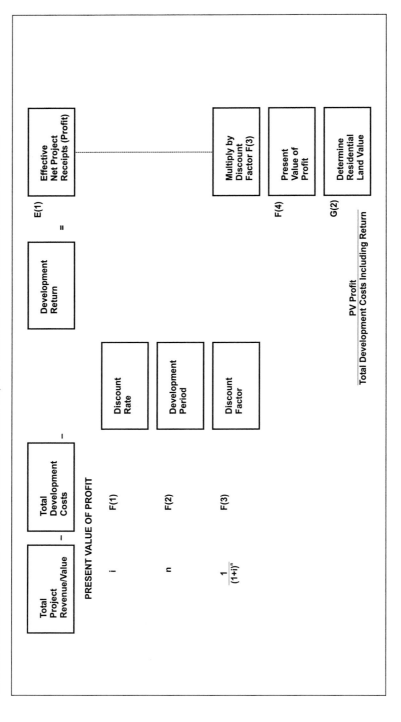

F. DETERMINE NET DEVELOPMENT RECEIPTS, PV PROFIT AND RESIDUAL LAND VALUE

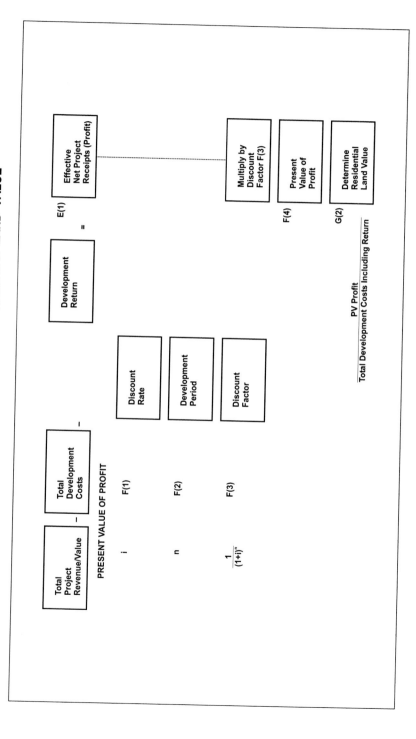

CASE STUDY 1
BUSINESS PARK, GREATER VANCOUVER
BUILD TO SUIT

Project Summary

- 61.94 acres total development
- 4.65 acres sold @ $528,000 per acre
- 8.27 acres already developed with 4 build-to-suit prestige occupants Nissan, Sanyo, Minolta, Toshiba
- To date 4 buildings total 170,796 sq. ft.

Land Costs

Land Acquisition Costs	$168,776 per acre
Land Servicing Costs	$199,422 per acre
Total Land Costs	$368,198 per acre

Build to Suit Costs
Costs vary with the amount of area finished for office as opposed to warehouse

Nissan	74% office	building costs $90.17 psf
Minolta	51% office	building costs $66.96 psf
Toshiba	23% office	building costs $46.90 psf
Sanyo	10% office	building costs $39.73 psf
Average Services Land Rate:		$460,230 per acre

Build to Suit Rents
Rents vary with the amount of area finished for office as opposed to warehouse

Nissan	74% office	Yr.	1–10	$12.00		11–20	$16.00 psf
Minolta	51% office	Yr.	1–5	$ 7.50	6–10 $9.75	11–15	$12.00 psf
Toshiba	23% office	Yr.	1–5	$ 8.00	6–10 $8.00 psf		
Sanyo	10% office	Yr.	1–5	$ 5.20	6–10 $5.70 psf		

Build to Suit Project Revenues

Project Revenues

Occupant Name		Minolta	Nissan	Toshiba	Sanyo	Totals
Lease Commencement		Dec-94	Oct-95	Apr-96	Aug-96	
Building Area	sf	20,165	14,847	40,394	95,390	170,796
Office	sf	10,365	11,000	9,394	9,740	40,499
Warehouse	sf	9,800	3,847	31,000	85,650	130,297
Office %		51%	74%	23%	10%	24%

Lease Details		Flex	Office	Flex	Warehouse	Averages
Year 1–5	$psf	$ 7.50	$12.00	$8.00	$5.20	$8.18
Year 6–10	$psf	$ 9.75	$12.00	$8.00	$5.70	$8.86
Year 11–15	$psf	$12.00	$16.00			
Year 16–20	$psf		$16.00			
Inducements						
Leased Area	sf	20,165	14,847	40,394	95,390	170,796
Gross Income		$ 151,238	$ 178,164	$ 323,152	$ 496,028	$ 1,148,582
Vacancy	3%	$ 4,537	$ 5,345	$ 9,695	$ 14,881	$ 34,457
Effective Gross		$ 146,700	$ 172,819	$ 313,457	$ 481,147	$ 1,114,124
Non-Recoverable Operating	1%	$ 1,512	$ 1,782	$ 3,232	$ 4,960	$ 11,486
Net Income		$ 145,188	$ 171,037	$ 310,226	$ 476,187	$ 1,102,638
Cap Rate		8.25%	8.25%	8.25%	8.25%	8.25%
Development Value		$1,760,000	$2,070,000	$3,760,000	$5,770,000	$13,360,000

Build to Suit Costs and Returns

Project Costs

Description		1	2	3	4	Total
Building Name		*Minolta*	*Nissan*	*Toshiba*	*Sanyo*	*Summary*
Lot(s)		17	18	1	14,15	1,14,15,17,18
Lot Area (acres)	Acres	1.20	1.02	1.80	4.25	8.27
Land Costs (acre of land)		$450,000	$480,000	$480,000	$450,000	$460,230
Coverage		39%	33%	52%	52%	47%
Total Building Area	sf	20,165	14,847	40,394	95,390	170,796
Hard Costs	$psf	$55.00	$69.93	$39.00	$30.40	$38.77
Soft Costs	$psf	$11.96	$20.24	$7.90	$9.33	$10.25
Inducements	$psf	$0.00	$0.00	$0.00	$0.00	$0.00
Total Construction	$psf	$66.96	$90.17	$46.90	$39.73	$49.03
Land Costs (sf of building)	$psf	$26.78	$32.81	$21.39	$20.05	$22.27
Total Development Cost	$psf	$93.74	$122.98	$68.29	$59.78	$71.30
Total Costs		$1,890,267	$1,825,884	$2,758,506	$5,702,414	$12,177,072
Construction Start		1994	1995	1995	1996	
Development Profit						$1,182,928
Return On Costs						10%

CASE STUDY 2
RETAIL POWER CENTRE DEVELOPMENT

Project Summary

- 25,46 acres total development purchased at $98,751 per acre
- 9.59 acres sold @ $344,108 per acre for 139,332 sq ft Real Canadian Superstore
- 15.87 acres developed with a Power Centre
- Centre includes a 107,158 sq ft discount store and 42,112 sq ft of retail.

Land Costs

Land Acquisition Costs	$ 98,751 per acre
Land Servicing Costs	$151,514 per acre
Total Land Costs	$256,286 per acre

Building Costs

Discount store	107,158 sq.ft. building costs	$41.01 psf
Marks Work Warehouse	7,000 sq.ft. building costs	$65.00 psf
EFADS (exec)	5,000 sq.ft. building costs	$65.00 psf
Payless Shoesource	2,258 sq.ft. building costs	$60.19 psf
Penningtons	4,510 sq.ft. building costs	$60.27 psf
Warehouse One	3,517 sq.ft. building costs	$60.13 psf
CRU	12,000 sq.ft. building costs	$60.00 psf
Retail	5,000 sq.ft. building costs	$85.00 psf

Tenant Allowances

Land and Building	$15,032,627

Total Net Costs

Tim Horton's   3,140 sq. ft tenant allowance $85.00 psf
Vary from $10–$20 per sq. ft for stores constructed by developer

Retail Rents

Discount store	107,158 sq.ft. rent at	$ 7.11 psf
Marks Work Warehouse	7,000 sq.ft. rent at	$14.50 psf
EFADS (exec)	5,000 sq.ft. rent at	$18.90 psf
Payless Shoesource	2,258 sq.ft. rent at	$20.00 psf
Penningtons	4,510 sq.ft. rent at	$15.22 psf
Warehouse One	3,517 sq.ft. rent at	$18.00 psf

CRU	12,000	sq.ft. rent at	$14.00 psf
Tim Horton's	3,140	sq.ft. rent at	$22.00 psf
Retail	5,000	sq.ft. rent at	$22.00 psf

Property Sale

Calloway REIT 2004 purchase for	$12,043,419
Adding Land Sale to Real Canadian Superstore	$ 3,300,000
Total Land Costs	**$15,343,286**

Power Centre Development

	Overall Project	Parcel A	Parcel B1	Parcel B2	Parcel C1	Parcel C2	Parcel C3	Parcel D	Parcel E	Parcel F	Parcel H
Tenant		Discount Store	Mark's Work Wearhouse	EFADS (exec)	Payless Shoesource	Penningtons	Warehouse One	CRU	Tim Horton's	RCS (Sale)	Retail
Construction commencement		May-00	03-Oct	03-Oct	01-Jul	01-Jul	01-Jul	03-Oct	01-Aug	03-Apr	03-Oct
Rent commencement/Parcel sale date		Dec-00	04-Apr	04-Apr	02-Jan	01-Nov	01-Nov	04-Apr	02-Jan	03-May	04-Apr
LAND											
Total land area (acres)	25.46	10.52	0.88	0.63	0.3	0.57	0.44	1.51	0.39	9.59	0.63
Total land area (% of development)	100.00%	41.32%	3.46%	2.47%	1.18%	2.24%	1.73%	5.93%	1.53%	37.67%	2.47%
Land purchase price (May-00)	$2,514,070	$1,038,863	$86,944	$62,103	$29,288	$56,016	$43,683	$149,046	$39,000	$947,025	$62,103
BUILDING											
Building area	$2,514,070	107,158	7,000	5,000	2,358	4,510	3,517	12,000	3,140	139,332	5,000
Building Construction Cost	$7,877,000	$4,377,215	$595,000	$415,000	$165,503	$350,722	$246,660	$960,000	$266,900	$870,079	$500,000
Site Costs: site work, utilities, paving, lighting	$4,010,980	$2,082,242	$174,265	$124,475	$58,702	$112,276	$87,556	$298,740	$78,170	$190,879	$124,475
Off-site work	$1,308,391	$740,848	$62,002	$44,287	$20,886	$39,947	$31,152	$106,290	$27,812	$57,600	$44,287
Engineering, Planning, Architect etc.	$635,000	$382,784	$32,036	$22,883	$10,791	$20,640	$16,096	$54,918	$14,370	$278,663	$22,883
Leasing fee (First Professional)	$330,683	$0	$14,000	$4,500	$4,716	$4,059	$3,165	$10,800	$6,280	$0	$4,500
Leasing fee (Outside Agent)	$67,064	$0	$0	$12,500	$0	$13,530	$7,034	$24,000	$0	$43,301	$10,000
Development fee	$468,946	$273,321	$26,401	$18,858	$8,400	$16,065	$12,511	$43,159	$4,571	$0	$22,358
Municipal charges and other levies	$130,000	$86,183	$7,213	$5,152	$2,430	$4,647	$3,624	$12,365	$3,235		$5,152
Rezoning Costs	$172,874	$114,606	$9,591	$6,851	$3,231	$6,180	$4,819	$16,443	$4,302		$6,851
Unrecovered operating during development	$213,793	$25,299	$14,216	$10,154	$2,038	$3,508	$2,735	$24,370	$2,714	$118,605	$10,154
Interest Carry Cost	$603,826	$226,838	$38,994	$27,793	$8,438	$12,620	$9,434	$65,815	$10,669	$173,702	$29,523
Total construction cost	$15,818,557	$8,309,336	$973,718	$692,453	$285,135	$584,194	$424,786	$1,616,900	$419,023	$1,732,829	$780,183
Less: Land Sales	($3,300,000)									($3,300,000)	
Total cost land and building	$15,032,627	$9,348,199	$1,060,662	$754,556	$314,423	$640,210	$468,469	$1,765,946	$458,023	($620,146)	$842,286
ANALYSIS (per square foot)											
Rental rate		$7.11	$14.50	$18.90	$20.00	$15.22	$18.00	$14.00	$22.00	$0.00	$22.00
Hard building cost		$40.85	$65.00	$65.00	$60.19	$60.27	$60.13	$60.00	$0.00	$0.00	$85.00
Tenant allowance		$0.00	$20.00	$18.00	$10.00	$17.50	$10.00	$20.00	$85.00	$0.00	$15.00
Total building cost		$40.85	$85.00	$83.00	$70.19	$77.77	$70.13	$80.00	$85.00	$0.00	$100.00
Total cost land, building and site		$87.24	$151.52	$150.91	$133.34	$141.95	$133.20	$147.16	$145.87	$0.00	$168.46
OPERATING INFORMATION											
Potential Gross Income (PGI)	$1,484,544	$762,356	$101,500	$94,500	$47,160	$68,642	$63,306	$168,000	$69,080	$0	$110,000
Annual Yield (PGI/Total cost)	9.88%	8.16%	9.57%	12.52%	15.00%	10.72%	13.51%	9.51%	15.08%	0.00%	13.06%

CASE STUDY 3
REAL ESTATE REDEVELOPMENT

On the following pages is a case study of an actual property development problem presented to some real estate consultants in 1998. The essentials were as follows:

A large retail discount chain had a large 11-storey warehouse and catalogue shopping facility on Central Toronto's east side on Mutual Street near Church and Dundas Street. Of this facility, 25% had been converted to office space. The firm wished to replace the facility with a more modern facility in a less expensive location, and to that end acquired land in Belleville at $40,000 per acre. This made the property at Mutual Street redundant and available for disposal. Because the property was a legal non-conforming use under current City zoning, demolition would lead to a lower allowable density than the current building coverage. Therefore conversion to residential condominiums (as in the case of the former Queen's Quay Terminal on Harbourfront) or higher class high tech industrial/office uses was determined to be the two most practical possibilities.

Conversion costs for the two alternatives (residential versus office) were prepared by cost experts. At the same time real estate brokers and consultants were estimating the market rates and absorption for residential condominium and office space. Your assignment is to take the material provided and estimate which of the two alternatives is the best one. To do this you must determine the following using the worksheets provided:

1. **The Value of the Proposed Projects When Completed**
   (a) *The Residential Proposal*
   The Value of the proposed residential project will be equivalent to the total selling price of the units. Condominium units values are based on a square foot rate.
   (b) *The Office/Industrial Showroom Proposal*
   The final Value of the project will be based on the capitalized value of the estimated net income.

2. **The Development Costs for the Proposed Projects**
   Development Costs include land acquisition costs, building construction hard costs and soft costs and any marketing or leasing costs. These costs have been summarized for each alternative proposal.

3. **Financing Costs**
   During development the costs of carrying the land and financing constructions must be added to development costs.

4. **Deferral Period**

   The rate of return must take into account the time costs of money at current discount rates because the developer must wait until the proposed project is sold out or leased up in order to realize any profit.

5. **Project Profit**

   The project rate of return is equivalent to the profit that remains after deducting from the "Value of the Project When Completed" the following:

   • Development Costs, Financing Costs

   and then adjusting for the time cost of money by estimating the Present Value of the Residual Profits to the project.

6. **Project Rate of Return**

   The rate of return to the project is equal to the "Present Value of the Project Profits" divided by the "Project Developments Costs Including Financing". The higher the rate the greater the Project Rate of Return.

Note: The land was purchased for $16,700,000 in late 1997.

Assuming Conversion to Residential Condominium

1. **Estimated Project Revenues and Marketing Costs**

   Based on a condominium market survey as of December 1997, we estimate that the average price per square foot of the proposed residential condominium units would average $210 per square foot.

2. **Development Costs**

   On the following page are the conversion costs for a residential condominium conversion project as supplied by the client. Marketing Costs are estimated at 5% of Gross Revenue.

3. **Interest on Construction Financing**

   Interest on Interim Financing for the project over the construction period has been based on an 8.00% interest rate. Because the financing is advanced during the course of development and not at the beginning, interest costs are charged at only 50%. Land Financing is at 8.00% and is charged at 100% of costs because it is advanced at the beginning of the project.

4. **Timing**

   The construction period for the proposed condominium conversion project will be 24 months. Absorption of the condominium units will take 24 months, but we estimate that all units could be sold during the construction period, resulting in a total elapsed time of 24 months.

5. **Discount Rate**
A rate of 12.00% should be used to discount the net project revenues after financing and profit.

6. **Net Project Revenues**
Estimate the net project revenues and rate of return to the developer for the proposed residential condominium conversion using the worksheet provided.

These are the estimated development cost estimates provided by the cost consultants for a potential residential condominium project:

Project Development Costs Residential Condominium Conversion

	Area (sf)	Cost	Rate PSF
Gross Building Size	1,017,815		
Residential GFA (With interior atrium)	650,616		
CONSTRUCTION COSTS			
Hard Construction Costs		$48,955,200	$ 48.10
Demolitions		$ 3,262,000	
Total Hard Costs		$52,217,200	
Site Preparation		$ 325,000	
Total Construction Costs		$52,542,200	
Design & Pricing 10.00%		$ 5,254,000	
Construction Contingency @ 5.00%		$ 2,447,760	$ 3.76
Total Hard Costs		$60,243,960	$ 92.60
Soft Costs on Construction @ 10.00%		$ 5,254,220	$ 8.08
Add Marketing Costs 5.00%		$ 5,806,748	
Total Soft Costs		$11,060,968	
Total Hard Costs and Soft Costs		$71,304,928	$109.60
TOTAL DEVELOPMENT COSTS		$71,304,928	$109.60

Development Profit Analysis

Residential Condominium Conversion				Profit Analysis
A. Estimate Market Value of Development				
Net Area Calculation				
(A1) Gross Floor Area (SF)				650,616
(A2) Net/Gross Ratio (SF)				85.00%
(A3) Net Area (SF)				553,024
Project Revenue Calculation				
(A4) Market Price per sq ft				$210
(A5) Revenue from Condominium Units				$116,134,956
(A6) Other Revenue				$0
(A7) Total Projected Project Revenue (Market Value)				$116,134,956
B. Development Costs				
(B1) Site Acquisition			$16,700,000	
(B2) Total Construction Costs			$71,304,928	
(B3) Total Costs				$88,004,928
C. Determine Effective Net Receipts Before Financing				
(C1) Effective Net Receipts Before Financing				$28,130,028
D. Determine Project Financing Costs				
	Months	Rate	Ratio	
(D1) Construction Period	24	8.00%	50%	$8,556,591
(D2) Land Financing	24	8.00%	100%	$2,672,000
(D3) Total Financing Costs				$11,228,591
E. Determine Effective Net Receipts after Financing (Profit)				
(E1) Effective Net Receipts After Financing (Profit)				$16,901,437
F. Determine Present Value of Profit				
(F1) Deferral Period (Months)		24		
(F2) Discount Rate		12.00%		
(F3) PV Discount Factor		0.78757		
(F4) Present Value Of Net Receipts (Profit)				$13,311,065
G. Determine Development Return				
(G1) Total Development Costs Plus Financing Costs				$99,233,519
(G2) Development Return (Profit / Cost)				13.41%

Note: Round to nearest dollar. Round development return to 2 decimal places.

Assuming Conversion to Office/Industrial Showroom

1. **Estimated Project Revenues and Marketing Costs**
   Based on the office leasing market as in 1998 the market rent per square foot of the space would be $10 per square foot for this type of property.

2. **Gross Project Value**
   The gross project revenues for the project have been estimated by deducting 5% for Vacancy and Bad Debts from the Total Projected Revenues. The resultant net income should be capitalized at a rate of 8.0%.

3. **Development Costs**
   On the following page are the construction cost estimates for conversion to office space as supplied by the client. Tenant inducements of one year's rent would be necessary to lease the space. Tenant commissions would total 16% of the first year's rental income on a grossed-up rent that reflects operating cost recoveries. We also estimate that there will be an operating cost shortfall equivalent to 1 year's operating costs at $6 per square foot during the leaseup period.

4. **Interest on Construction Financing**
   Interest on Interim Financing for the project over the construction period has been based on an 8.00% interest rate. Because the financing is advanced during the course of development and not at the beginning, interest costs are charged at only 50%. Land Financing is at 8.00% and is charged at 100% of costs because it is advanced at the beginning of the project.

5. **Timing**
   The construction and absorption period for the proposed office renovation project will be 24 months.

6. **Discount Rate**
   A rate of 12.00% has been used to discount the net project revenues after financing and profit.

7. **Net Project Revenues**
   Estimate the net project revenues and rate of return to the developer for the proposed office conversion using the worksheet provided.

Project Development Costs Based on Showroom/office Conversion

The cost consultants prepared the following development costs estimates for a potential office showroom conversion:

	Area (SF)		Cost	Rate PSF
Gross Building Area	1,073,715			
Efficiency Ratio	75.00%			
Rentable Area	805,286			
Area Already Renovated	248,000			
Unrenovated Area	557,286			
CONSTRUCTION COSTS				
Hard Construction Costs			$33,437,175	$60.00
Construction Contingency @		5.00%	$ 1,671,859	$ 3.00
Total Hard Costs			$35,109,034	$63.00
Soft Costs on Construction @		10.00%	$ 3,510,903	$ 6.30
Leasing Commissions On Net Rent		16.00%	$ 1,159,612	$ 2.08
$6 Operating Expense Gross-Up		16.00%	$ 773,075	$ 1.39
Tenant Inducements				
1 year's rent for area	100.00%	$9.00	$ 7,247,576	$13.01
Operating Expense Shortfall During Leaseup				
$6 Operating Expense 1 year			$ 4,831,718	$ 8.67
Total Soft Costs			$18,457,016	$33.12
Total Hard Costs and Soft Costs			$53,566,050	$96.12
Total Development Costs			$53,566,050	$96.12

Development Profit Analysis

Showroom Office Conversion				Profit Analysis
A. Estimate Market Value of Development				
Net Leasable Area Calculation				
(A1) Gross Floor Area (sq ft)				1,073,715
(A2) Net/Gross Ratio (sq ft)				75.00%
(A3) Net Leasable Area (sq ft)				805,286
Calculate Project Income				
(A4) Office Market Rent Psf				$10.00
(A5) Potential Income Office Rentals				$8,052,863
(A6) Add Other Income				$0
(A7) Total Potential Gross Income				$8,052,863
(A8) Vacancy & Bad Debt %	5.00%			
(A9) Less Vacancy & Bad Debts				($402,643)
(A10) Effective Gross Income				$7,650,219
(A11) Less Unrecovered Operating Costs				$0
(A12) Net Revenue				$7,650,219
Estimate Project Value				
(A13) Capitalization Rate				8.00%
(A14) Total Projected Project Market Value				$95,627,742
B. Determine Development Costs				
(B1) Site Acquisition		$16,700,000		
(B2) Total Construction Costs		$53,566,050		
(B3) Total Costs				$70,266,050
C. Determine Effective Net Receipts Before Financing				
(C1) Effective Net Receipts Before Financing				$25,361,692
D. Determine Project Financing Costs				
	Months	Rate	Ratio	
(D1) Construction Period	24	8.00%	50%	$6,427,926
(D2) Land Financing	24	8.00%	100%	$2,672,000
(D3) Total Financing Costs				$9,099,926
E. Determine Effective Net Receipts after Financing				
(E1) Effective Net Receipts After Financing				$16,261,766
F. Estimate Present Value of Development Profit				
(F1) Deferral Period (Months)		24		
(F2) Discount Rate		12.00%		
(F3) PV Discount Factor		0.78757		
(F4) Present Value Of Net Receipts (Profit)				$12,807,216
G. Determine Development Return				
(G1) Total Development Costs Plus Financing Costs				$79,365,976
(G2) Development Return (Profit / Cost)				16.14%

Note: Round to nearest dollar. Round Development Return to 2 decimal places.

Sensitivity Approach

Developers, Appraisers and Lenders usually prepare a sensitivity analysis in order to examine the extent to which price or rent affects the expected return from a proposed development.

In the tables below we have prepared Residential and Office Sensitivity Analyses relative to the preceding case study. Complete the missing information and comment on the effect of sales price and/or rent on the projected development project return.

Resodential Sensitivity

How does the residential condominium sale price affect return?

Price per sq. ft.	Price increase	Return
$170		-3.20%
$180	6%	1.00%
$190	6%	5.20%
$200	5%	9.30%
$210	5%	13.41%
$220	5%	17.50%
$230	5%	21.57%
$240	4%	25.60%
$250	4%	29.60%

Office Sensitivity

How does office rent affect return?

Price per sq. ft.	Rent increase	Return
$ 8.00		-2.84%
$ 8.50	6%	1.90%
$ 9.00	6%	6.65%
$ 9.50	5%	11.39%
$10.00	**5%**	**16.14%**
$10.50	5%	20.88%
$11.00	5%	25.63%
$11.50	4%	30.37%
$12.00	4%	35.12%

Residential Condominium Price Sensitivity versus Development Return

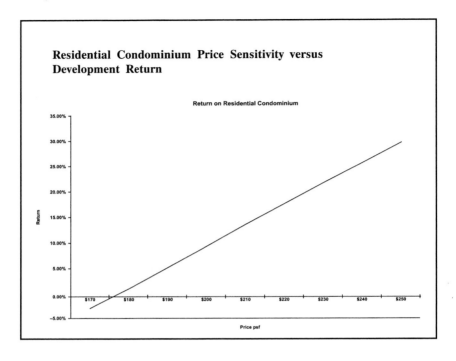

Return on Residential Condominium

Office Rental Sensitivity versus Development Return

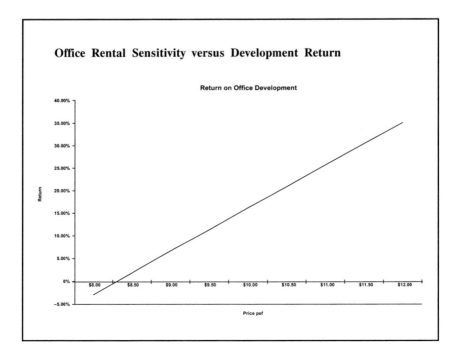

Return on Office Development

The Real Estate Profession

Real Estate Brokerage

———————————————— WALTER H. POSNER

The specialty occupation within the real estate industry that employs more people than any other is brokerage. The number employed in real estate brokerage in Canada varies in tandem with conditions in the real estate market, and has fluctuated between a high of 100,000 plus, in peak activity periods, and a low of about 80,000 in recession periods.

WHAT IS A BROKER?

Persons undertaking transactions are free to arrange their transaction themselves without involving an intermediary. Real estate transactions are no exception, and it is not uncommon for owners to market their real estate personally. It may be a developer of a sub-division or apartment building or commercial building who offers its products for sale, or lease, through its in-house sales group, or an individual whose advertisement specifies "for sale by owner," or any situation in which the objective clearly is to arrange a contract directly, without the help of an intermediary.

However, in real estate transactions, as in others, either party can choose to be represented by an intermediary acting as the party's agent, and if that agent is to receive a commission for its services, then the agent is to act as a broker. A broker is one who is not in the employ of either party, and is contracted by one or the other to bring a buyer and seller together, and is to receive a commission upon performing that mandate. And brokerage is the service a broker renders.

———————————————

Walter Posner, B.Comm., L.L.B., A.L.O., is a specialist in real estate leasing and has developed courses on the subject for The Real Estate Institute of Canada and York University.

BROKERAGE IN REAL ESTATE TRANSACTIONS

Brokerage is particularly suited to transactions in real estate by virtue of the following considerations:

- each estate in real property is unique, by virtue of (i) the rights in the bundle that comprise the estate, and (ii) the physical features and immovable location of the real property; and unique assets are difficult to market without the involvement of a professional who brings to that undertaking prospects and access to prospects, credibility based on training and experience in its market, and access to that market's information base; and

- transactions in real estate involve sums of money large enough that the parties are likely to need financing and/or financial representation, and will find comfort in being represented by a broker who is knowledgeable on the sources of a particular loan at any time and the process of arranging real estate loans; and

- each transaction in real estate has to be progressed through a sequence between decision, offer, acceptance and the closing of the transfer, and a party will welcome the involvement of a person experienced in legal documentation, loan documentation, conveyance and the process of administering real estate trades in general.

There will still be vendors and purchasers who will choose to arrange their real estate trades personally and privately, without involving an intermediary. But any party to a trade in real estate in Ontario who chooses to act through another needs to be alive to the provisions of this province's *Real Estate and Business Brokers Act*, Chapter 431 (and in other provinces, to the provisions of its corresponding statute).

LIMITATIONS DERIVING FROM THE PROVINCIAL STATUTE

The Ontario statute makes it an offence for any person to trade in real estate as a broker or a salesman unless registered, and defines "trade," "broker" and "salesman" in wider terms than most people would anticipate, as the following should illustrate.

A "trade" is defined in the statute as a transaction in real estate, whether by sale, purchase, agreement for sale, exchange, lease or otherwise, both disposition and acquisition; and also any offer or attempt to list real estate; and any act, advertisement, conduct or negotiation in furtherance of a trade.

A "broker" is defined as any person who

- alone or through officials (an undefined and dubious term) or salesmen,
- trades (as that terms is defined above) in real estate (which includes real property and leaseholds),
- for another or others,
- for compensation, gain or reward or hope or promise thereof; or
- holds himself out as such a person.

A "salesman" is defined in the Act as a person who is

- employed, appointed or authorized by a broker,
- to trade in real estate (as those terms are defined in the Act).

The effect of the legislation is to replace, in respect of real estate transactions of every kind, the usual meaning of broker and salesman, and to confer on those registered under that Act the exclusive right to represent for reward any party to a trade in real estate. It is significant, however, that the definitions of broker and salesman have three elements:

- they must be acting as an agent on behalf of someone else; and
- the trade must be in real estate; and
- a reward for performance is arranged or expected.

It follows that the statute does not apply to those owners who personally sell or lease their own property, nor to persons who act for someone else in a trade in real estate, but without any arrangement or hope for a reward, nor to persons the statute exempts from registration, which include the following:

- the full-time salaried employee of a party to a trade in respect of land in Ontario; and
- an auctioneer in a trade made in the course of that function; and
- a bank, trust or insurance company trading in real estate it administers; and
- a practising solicitor of the Supreme Court in respect of a trade made in the course of his/her practice (but note that certified accountants are not similarly exempted); and
- the liquidator, receiver or trustee of a party in bankruptcy; and
- a representative in a trade to create a right of way.

REGISTRATION (COMMONLY REFERRED TO AS LICENSING)

The Act makes provision for the registration of:

- Brokers, who may operate as independents or as associates of another registered Broker; and

- salesmen, who may only be employees of a registered Broker; and
- Broker corporations or partnerships, which may operate through its registered broker partners, officials or salesmen employees.

Registration of salesmen is limited to those who successfully complete a program of instruction, conducted by the Ontario Real Estate Association (OREA) on behalf of the Registrar, and the registration of Brokers is limited to registered salesmen who have been employed as such for a minimum of two years and have successfully completed an advanced program of OREA instruction.

Registration of corporations having share capital is limited to corporations that have registered Brokers holding at least 51% of the voting rights attached to all the corporation's shares. There also are limitations on individual holdings of voting rights (a registered salesman, for example, may not hold in excess of 10% of the voting rights), and an exemption for registered Trust companies.

The effect of this legislation has been to concentrate real estate brokerage among firms that are

- corporations registered under the Act (e.g., the large national and international franchises) that operate through registered broker associates and/or registered salesman employees; or
- registered Brokers (or partnerships registered under the Act), who offer brokerage personally and through registered broker associates and/or registered salesman employees.

Consequences of Licensing

Registered corporations and Brokers are regulated by the statute that requires registration. Ontario's *Real Estate and Business Brokers Act*, for example, imposes a variety of responsibilities on registered Brokers, some administrative (e.g., the records they are to keep with respect to each trade — Section 19, the bank trust account/s they are to maintain — Section 20; notices of change of address they are to submit — Section 21), others regulating trading, including that:

- self-purchase of real estate by a broker or salesman is prohibited unless there has been prior written disclosure; and
- promises to resell, or to procure a mortgage, are not to be made except in writing; and
- the name of the firm, and its advertisements, must not mislead as to who is the broker; and
- the Registrar may order the cessation of advertisements that he considers false or misleading or deceptive; and
- listing agreements must be in writing and state an expiry date.

VOLUNTARY TIES AND COMMITMENTS

There are voluntary associations that Brokers may choose to join, either limited to registered Brokers (the best known being the Canadian Real Estate Association — CREA), or a broader cross-section of real estate professionals (of which the best known is the Real Estate Institute of Canada — REIC).

Membership in CREA is gained by becoming a member of a Local Board of that Association (in Toronto, the local Board is Toronto Real Estate Board — TREB). The Ontario Real Estate Association — OREA is the association of all local Boards within Ontario, and represents the local Boards within CREA in addition to the education function it performs on behalf of Ontario's Registrar.

Real estate brokerage firms, whether Broker corporations, Broker partnerships or Brokers, are likely to join the local Board for the market in which it operates, if only because it is the local Board that operates the Multiple Listing Service — MLS, on which such businesses rely for information regarding the market. The local Boards issue regular lists of the listings on its MLS, and on request can provide extensive information on past trades and other data equally invaluable to those in the industry.

But a condition of joining any of these voluntary associations is that the member must contract with the association to uphold, in its trading, a Code of Ethics that the Association has adopted.

CODE OF ETHICS

Those who register under the *Real Estate and Business Brokers Act* are automatically subject to the Act's regulations, and the complaint procedure and criminal sanctions therein. Registrants who choose to join a voluntary association become bound to uphold its Code of Ethics by virtue of the contract to do that. Accordingly, members are only answerable to the Association for non-compliance, with expulsion the ultimate penalty. The Codes of Ethics of different associations might not be identical, but generally the contents are found to be similar and to aim at fair dealing between members of the Association and between members and the public with whom they have dealings. In some respects the Code will duplicate regulations in the *Real Estate and Business Brokers Act*, but in other respects will go beyond that, for example:

- Secret commissions are forbidden.
- A Broker should make clear to all the parties to the trade which party it is representing, and should not receive commission from

more than one party except with the full knowledge and consent of all the parties.

- All manner of conflicts of interest are to be the subject of full disclosure in writing.
- A property should not be offered without the owner's authorization.
- Disputes with fellow members must be submitted to arbitration according to the Local Board's rules.
- Public criticism of a fellow member is to be avoided.

THE BROKERAGE CONTRACT

Brokerage transactions are contracted in what are termed listings that must conform to the requirements of the *Real Estate and Business Brokers Act*. The listing that is secured by an associate Broker or salesman is given in favour of the Broker firm that is the employer, and not to the employee who is the contact person. The Act does not require that listings be in writing. However, Section 23 precludes an action for payment of a commission on a listing that is not in writing, and that is sufficient inducement to Brokers to insist that their listings are given in writing, and comply with the statute in its requirements that

- a listing contain a provision that it will expire on a date (and no more than one date) that is certain; and
- a listing that is in writing will state the date upon which the *Lister* signed it (being a unilateral instrument, a listing is not signed by the Broker to whom it is granted); and
- the Broker is to immediately deliver a copy of the listing to the Lister.

The listing is the contract between the Lister (the owner) and the Broker firm respecting (i) the marketing of the property, and (ii) the objective to be achieved, and (iii) the reward for performing the mandate. A Lister should detail the marketing initiatives required and ensure the listing addresses all objectives fully before signing it, including:

- when it is to expire; and
- whether the listing is non-exclusive (an Open Listing), or exclusive to that Broker (Exclusive Listing) and, if the latter, then whether the Exclusive Broker is required to co-operate with other Brokers on the MLS (a Co-operative Listing); and

- the Broker's obligations respecting the marketing of the real estate, including signs on the property, advertisements, MLS entries, open-house showings, flyers, and the like; and
- the terms upon which the Lister is willing to transact; and
- what is to constitute performance of the Broker's mandate (which might be as minimal as "introducing a willing and able buyer," or as extreme as "the closing of the transfer"); and
- the commission arrangements, including how much is to be payable, by whom and when.

There is no set form for listing agreements. The large national brokerage firms are likely to have an in-house form; and local Boards sell a standard form to their members. These forms must be expected to have been drafted for the protection of the Listing Broker, and before signing one a Lister needs to exercise an independent judgment to ensure the form also addresses its interests.

The Broker's Objectives

Brokers recognize two objectives as deserving of a share of the commission that derives from the vendor:

1. Soliciting and documenting the listing; and
2. Performing the mandate.

Accordingly, the initial objective of Brokers and salesmen is to solicit a listing that is exclusive and is saleable, and eases performance of the mandate (and generates the commission). The more attractive the listing price, terms and financing on which the Lister is willing to contract, and the longer the period of the listing, the more saleable the listing. But in these respects the interests of the Lister and the Broker conflict. The Lister does not want its listing price to inhibit the price that is attainable, and wants to be free of the Broker as soon as the Lister concludes the Broker is unlikely to produce a trade.

Consequences of a Listing

A listing does not create a contractual relationship between the Lister and the salesman or associate Broker who is the personal contact. The Lister's contract is with the Listing Broker firm, and is the foundation for recourse against the Listing Broker firm only. A listing is an authority to sell, not an offer to sell, and the Lister is not obligated to accept any offer presented to it. But if the Broker's mandate is only to introduce a buyer "willing and able" to purchase, or to present an offer by a qualified purchaser on the terms prescribed in the listing, then commission will be due upon performance of *that* mandate, whether or not the Lister accepts the offer or the sale actually does close.

It is the Listing Broker to whom the commission is payable, because it is the party with whom the Lister has the contract. Should the Listing Broker personally solicit the listing and perform the mandate, then the commission is wholly his (or hers).

The listing may, however, have been solicited by an associate Broker or salesman in the Listing Broker firm's employ. A Broker firm's employment contract with its associate Brokers and salesmen generally recognizes that possibility and confers on the registered employee who solicited the listing a share of any commission the firm receives from that listing (commonly one-quarter).

The listing's trade mandate also may be performed by an associate Broker or salesman in the Listing Broker's employ (whether the same one as solicited the listing or another), and the Listing Broker's employment contract is likely to recognize that possibility too, and confer a share of the commission on the registered employee who introduces the purchaser. The share is a matter for negotiation on the basis of the productivity of the associate Broker or salesman, and commonly is an agreed percentage between one-quarter and one-half. Bigger earners generally command a higher percentage.

Another possibility is that the trade mandate may be performed by another registered Broker firm that arranged a Co-operation agreement with the Listing Broker. The Co-operation agreement will address the reward the Broker firm that performs the mandate (the selling Broker) is to be paid by the Listing Broker, generally one-half of the commission the Listing Broker receives from that listing. And if the trade mandate was performed by an associate Broker or salesman in the selling Broker's employ, then the selling Broker's employment contract with its employee will determine the percentage of the selling Broker's commission that it is to pay the registered employee who performed the trade mandate.

Buyer Brokerage — The Purchaser's Choices

Before showing a listed property to any of its clients, a Broker firm will arrange a Co-operation agreement with the Listing Broker in order to establish its right to a part of the commission paid by the vendor to the Listing Broker in consequence of performance of the listing mandate by one of its clients.

In respect of a listed property, however, every Broker other than the Listing Broker enters the trade process as agent of a client for whom that Broker is surveying available properties, and remains that client's agent through the counselling and persuasion that lead to the client's decision to present an offer to purchase the property. Such agency is not required to be given in writing, and the absence of written authority is not significant.

A time does come when the selling Broker decides whether to invoke its rights under the Co-operation agreement it arranged and receive a part of the commission the vendor is to pay. But from the time it elects to look to the vendor for a reward for its services, the selling Broker will be in an agency relationship with the vendor, as sub-agent of the Listing Broker. It must then place the interests of the vendor above those of its client, and be beholden to the vendor, and no other person, for all the obligations of an agent, including the duty of full disclosure of anything said to it, even by its client in confidence. What is certain is that a Broker cannot serve both principals in a transaction.

For many years Brokers assumed their purchasing clients wanted the selling Broker to be rewarded out of the commission paid by the vendor, but in recent years there has been increasing concern about the dangers inherent in that assumption, including that

1. the purchaser may not realize the selling Broker has changed its ties, and rely on the selling Broker for professional guidance after that Broker is beholden to the vendor and not the client; and

2. the selling Broker's relationship with its client might be too strong to allow that Broker to totally disregard its client's best interests in favour of those of the vendor; and

3. the Listing Broker is responsible for the actions of the selling Broker while acting as sub-agent, and also is exposed to the consequences of the dangers described in (i) and (ii).

It obviously is desirable that each party, and each Broker, know at all times which party's agent each Broker is. (For more detail refer to George C. Shan's text *Let's make an offer!*, published by Elderisle Developments Ltd, 28 Dixon Avenue, Toronto, Ontario M4L 1N3.)

In Ontario the Broker associations have addressed these problems and now recommend that (a) a Listing Broker dealing with persons other than its Lister eliminates the possibility of misunderstanding on the part of a purchaser, by giving such persons a signed Declaration of Representation confirming that the Listing Broker represents the interests of the listing vendor; (b) a Broker, other than the Listing Broker, has each of its clients for a purchase sign a document, termed Purchaser's Exclusive Single Agency Agreement, that retains the Broker as the client's agent and specifies the commission the client agrees to pay the Broker for performance of the mandate, and directs whether the Broker is authorized to negotiate to receive up to that amount of commission from the vendor on the basis that such reward is not to make the Broker the vendor's sub-agent. Such agreement is best obtained before the survey of properties is commenced. Listing Brokers should require it before the Co-operation Agreement is concluded so as to be aware of whether the selling Broker is acting as the Listing Broker's sub-agent, or is not. It is unlikely that an informed purchaser would choose not to sign the Purchaser's Exclusive Single Agency Agreement and require the Broker through whom it is acting to commit to the vendor as sub-agent in order to secure a reward for its services. However, that unlikely outcome has to be addressed.

SUMMARY
(SEE APPENDIX 1: TABLE OF ACCOUNTABILITY)

As many as four players may have claims to a share of the commission payable by the vendor on performance of the mandate, and as many as five separate contracts may regulate the outcome,

- the listing contract between the Lister and the Listing Broker;
- the employment contract between the Listing Broker and its registered employee who either solicited the listing or performed the trade mandate;
- the Purchaser's Exclusive Single Agency Agreement between the purchaser and the selling Broker;
- the Co-operation Agreement between the Listing Broker and the selling Broker who performed the trade mandate;
- the employment contract between the selling Broker and its registered employee who performed the trade mandate.

Each player only has recourse against the other party to his/her contract. The registered employee who canvassed the listing only has a right of recourse against the employer (the Listing Broker), and no recourse against the Lister; and the same is true for the registered employee of the Listing Broker who performed the mandate. The selling Broker under a Co-operation agreement only has a right of recourse against the Listing Broker, and no recourse against the Lister; and the registered employee of the selling Broker who performed the mandate only has a right of recourse against his/her employer, the selling Broker, and no recourse against either the Listing Broker or the Lister or the purchaser.

The Rights and Obligations of
Those Registered under the Act

Although writing is not a statutory requirement, listings can be expected to be formally documented, and to define conditions for the performance of the mandate and entitlement to the commission. The listing will be the primary source of the Listing Broker's rights and obligations, and each listing has to be referred to for its particular terms. For the selling Broker, the same will be true of the Purchaser's Exclusive Single Agency Agreement.

The contract of employment between the Broker employer and the associate Broker or salesman also need not be in writing, but may be formalized in writing and expand the rights and obligations of each party. Co-operation contracts generally are informal and confirmed in a letter, if at all.

Because the relationship between Lister and Listing Broker, and that between the selling Broker and its purchaser client, is one of Agency, each Broker, as agent, is also subject to the rights and obligations of an agent in terms of the Law of Agency. Agency is a fiduciary contract that imposes obligations of good faith and full disclosure on the agent and those for whom the agent is responsible. The Listing Broker is responsible to the Lister for negligence and breaches of good faith committed by the Listing Broker or its employees, or by a sub-agent acting under a Co-operation agreement or its employees. And the selling agent is responsible to its purchaser client for negligence on its or its employees' part.

By virtue of its registration under the *Real Estate and Business Brokers' Act*, each registered Broker and salesman involved in the trade is subject to obligations under that statute, including: Section 23, which limits what is considered performance in actions for commission; Section 29, which precludes employment of unregistered persons to trade in real estate; Section 31, which requires disclosure by a Broker before a purchase is complete; and Section 32, which precludes inducing any party to break a contract.

Registration that is limited to persons who have attended instruction and passed a test of competence conveys to the public at large that those who are registered can be expected to show professional competence (also termed "due diligence") in the execution of a mandate relating to a trade in real estate. A registered Broker employer owes a duty to its principal, and also to all other parties to a trade in real estate, to show due diligence or professional competence, examples of which are that it will not mislead or conceal information, and will provide expertise that is requested or should be expected to be a factor in the person's decision.

The Brokers who have contracted membership in a voluntary association are subject to the obligations implicit in the association's rules of conduct (Code of Ethics) for the performance of each mandate.

APPENDIX I
Table of Accountability

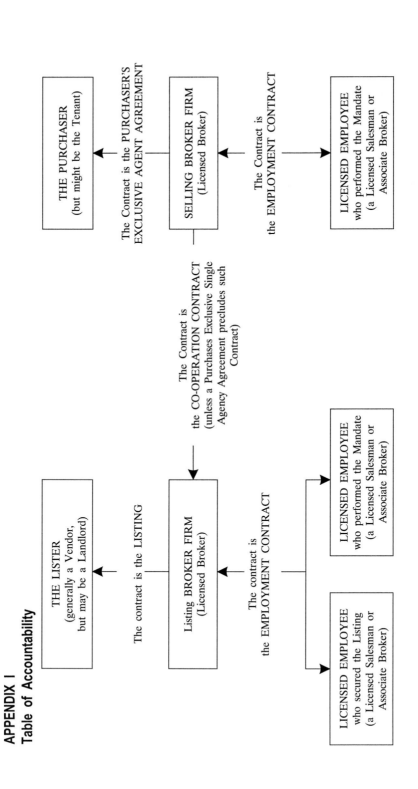

Real Estate Marketing: Concepts and Principles

MICHAEL ROCHON

The process of buying and selling real estate only scratches the surface of real estate marketing. Effective marketing of real estate involves an understanding of marketing concepts, a thorough grasp of marketing techniques and the ability to apply both to dynamic environments. Understanding marketing concepts as they relate to real estate provides an overview of the real estate marketing process. Techniques used to develop a marketing plan provide practical aspects of marketing real estate. The unification of the two will allow for an effective application in the real estate environment.

Marketing has been defined as *a social and managerial process by which individuals and groups obtain what they need and want through creating, offering, and exchanging products of value with others.*[1]

CONCEPTS IN MARKETING

A synopsis of real estate marketing includes understanding what marketing is and the special areas of marketing that relate specifically to real estate. Real estate marketing involves the buying and selling of property, the development of new and existing customer relationships, and the services provided by the real estate representative, to both individual and business clients. These activities draw on marketing concepts in the following areas.

1. Commercial or business to business marketing
2. Consumer marketing

This is a revised and updated version of the article "Real Estate Marketing" by Dr. Kim Snow, which appeared in the 3rd edition of this book. It includes passages from that article which appear with the kind permission of Dr. Snow.

3. Services marketing
4. Relationship marketing

We will look at each of these and how they relate to real estate in the following pages.

Commercial or Business to Business Real Estate Marketing

The effectiveness and value of real estate marketing in the commercial or business to business market can be enhanced with an understanding of the unique characteristics of this market, the participants in the decision making process and the buying decision process. The commercial real estate market has several characteristics:

1. There are fewer buyers in this market in relation to the consumer market. However, a recent survey from Statistics Canada indicates non-residential sectors generate more revenue and spend more money on wages and salaries compared to other sectors.[2] The market for apartment buildings, industrial or retail land and buildings is restricted to those businesses that are large enough to require this type of investment and that have the monetary strength to acquire them.

2. The relationship between the real estate representative and the business purchaser can be complex, quantitatively oriented and political. A smaller number of buyers in the market can mean a closer relationship between a sales representative and the business. Sales representatives are usually expected to customize their offering to particular situations.

3. This market is characterized by associated demand. The demand for industrial or retail property is dependent on the demand for the goods or services produced and sold to the individual consumer.

4. Demand in these markets fluctuates. Fluctuations in demand may be caused by what economists refer to as the multiplier effect.[3] A version of the multiplier effect, a classic Keynesian principle, implies that a small rise in consumer demand can cause a much larger rise in the commercial real estate market. A small fall in consumer demand, on the other hand, can cause a higher decline in demand within commercial markets.

5. The sophistication of the buyers is advanced, as there are several factors influencing their decisions.

The factors influencing buying decisions in the commercial real estate market include environmental, organizational, interpersonal, and individual factors. An important environmental factor in the commercial real estate market is the current and past economic position. Factors such as the level of supply and demand in the market, the rate of inflation, and the cost of money are just a few important economic factors to consider. Other environmental factors include political and legal considerations, the competitive climate, technological adoption and change, and social and cultural elements.

Commercial real estate decisions are influenced by organizational factors. The vision and objectives of the organization, along with the policies and procedures of the company affect the decision making process. More specifically, the decision making process is affected by the structures, processes, and systems within the organization. Organizational liquidity, short and long term financial projections, and internal and external growth strategies also play a role in influencing the commercial real estate decision.

Interpersonal relationships, based somewhat on personal association, authority, and status of those involved in the decision making process, influence the real estate purchase decisions.

Individual characteristics of those involved in the decision making process also affect the purchase of real estate for firms. For example, risk averse individuals will more likely make safer real estate decisions. Conversely, risk takers will take on a higher probability of a greater loss for the chance of a higher return.

There is an established buying process followed in commercial real estate transactions. Its steps are as follows:[4]

Steps in the Process	Example
Problem Recognition	Increased demand, logistics, new markets
Need Identification	New plant, new retail location
Property Specification	Square footage, logistical access, expansion needs
Agent or Company Search	Evaluate several agents and/or companies
Proposal Solicitation	Proposals submitted
Proposal Evaluation	Evaluate proposal(s), needs/specifications considered
Purchase Decision	Reject, accept or modify proposal
Performance Review	Client reviews performance in relation to transaction

Each salesperson deals with different environments and situations; all steps may not be present in every real estate transaction, nor are the steps always followed in the same sequence. For example, the same real estate agent or company may be used for each transaction thereby eliminating the need to do a comprehensive search each time. A positive performance review at the end may allow this step to be excluded. If the results of the review are negative, an agent or company search may again be needed.

Consumer Real Estate Marketing

The consumer real estate market has a distinctive buying process. This market is not as complex as the commercial market, but it still has several environmental factors affecting the purchase decision and marketing initiatives. Environmental factors affecting the consumer real estate market include political/legal, technological, economic, cultural, social, personal and psychological considerations. Cultural factors influencing the real estate decision could include choosing a particular area to purchase because of the proximity to ethnic food stores or cultural venues, such as religious structures and community centres. Social factors that may influence the real estate purchase decision could include the status of having a particular address or being close to parents or friends. Personal influences affecting real estate decisions could include life cycle stages. For example, empty nesters might prefer to have a condominium rather than a single family home because yard work and snow removal are taken care of by others. Psychological factors affecting the real estate decision could include the perception that one area of a city is safer to live in than other areas. Technological factors affecting the real estate decision may include the lack of technological infrastructure available in certain areas. For example, some areas in Canada do not have the infrastructure for specific broadband services. Political and legal factors affecting the real estate decision include factors such as zoning laws and heritage protection rules and regulations. For example, some heritage protected areas in Ontario do not allow satellite dishes to be installed on the front of dwellings in order to preserve the overall "historical feel" of the community. Economic factors affecting the personal real estate decision could include interest rates and banking policies and regulations. The general state of the economy, measured differently by each person, may also affect this decision. A real estate representative who can identify the environmental factors influencing a real estate purchase decision can select properties that satisfy the purchasers' needs, thereby bringing buyers and sellers together more successfully.

The decision making process for the consumer real estate market follows the same steps as the commercial decision making process. The major difference between the two decision making processes involves the number of participants associated with the transaction. There are usually fewer participants in the decision making process for the consumer market, but the transaction itself is very different. While the purchase of real estate may be a monetary investment for companies, for family purchasers, the purchase decision is more personal. The importance of the decision for the consumer market may extend the information search and evaluation of alternatives stages of the buying process. Real estate representatives who can identify the importance of these stages to the individual consumer and adjust the service provided to individuals accordingly may be more successful.

The Service Marketing Characteristic of Real Estate

The real estate industry is a mixture of product and service offerings. The product offering is represented by the physical property under consideration; the service is everything else that takes place within the transaction before, during, and after. Examples of physical product and service mixtures are given in Figure 1.

Service is provided to both commercial and individual buyers and sellers of real estate through real estate representatives. Services include identifying the needs of clients, locating and pricing properties that fit those needs, ensuring the clients are properly represented at the negotiation table, and ensuring that the administrative and legal considerations are completed. For example, when locating and pricing properties, comparisons are made with other properties

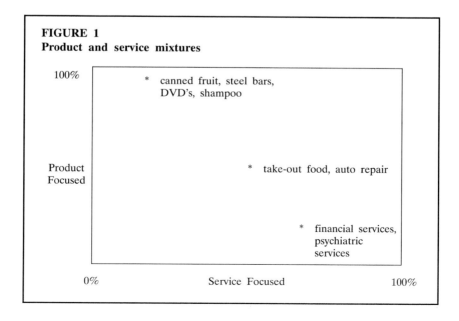

FIGURE 1
Product and service mixtures

100%

* canned fruit, steel bars, DVD's, shampoo

Product Focused

* take-out food, auto repair

* financial services, psychiatric services

0%   Service Focused   100%

recently sold in the area. This provides information for the customer to evaluate alternatives and settle on a price. In the event that prices are not available in the area, similar or comparable areas are identified and researched. Negotiating a deal between the buyer and seller takes a combination of skills, from legal extrapolation to issues management. Understanding the service aspects of real estate transactions and how to successfully provide them will give real estate representatives the advantage of having satisfied customers, whether buyers or sellers.

A customer cannot keep a service: it is experienced, used, or consumed.[5] Services have been defined as intangible activities, benefits, or satisfactions that are offered to customers. Services require more quality conscious suppliers, supplier credibility and adaptability than tangible products. Understanding the characteristics of services assists in marketing them effectively at lower costs. Service characteristics include: intangibility, inseparability, perishability and heterogeneity. Intangibility is the notion that services are an action with little or no physical evidence.[6] Consumers cannot not hear, feel, see, touch, or smell the service before consumption.[7] Inseparability means that services are produced and consumed at the same time. This makes it difficult to hide service inefficiencies and shortcomings. Perishability means that service cannot be stored and sold later. Heterogeneity points out that each service encounter is different. These characteristics of services make marketing of services different than marketing of tangible products.[8] Marketing of services relies on both operational and marketing initiatives. This interfunctional relationship of services has prompted successful service firms to take a holistic approach to marketing. This holistic marketing approach has been referred to as service quality.

Service quality aims at producing satisfied customers. Achieving a quality service requires marketing to people to ensure that all encounters between the customer, buyer or seller, and the service, results in satisfied customers. This requires identifying and prioritizing service attributes and determining their desired levels.[9] For example, making sure that customers are satisfied with each service encounter requires the real estate representative to manage customer expectations. Customers form expectations about what the service encounter with the real estate firm and representatives should be and then compare it to the actual performance they receive.[10] These prior expectations are based on several environmental factors, including information obtained from other customers, media, or friends. Real estate firms and representatives have little or no control over many of the environmental factors affecting the service encounter. Therefore, managing expectations that the firm can control and understanding those that the firm cannot control are important.

Managing customer expectations can be done in a number of ways. It can be managed by delivering what customers expect, by changing expectations to match what will be delivered, by delivering more than what customers expect, or a combination of these techniques. Delivering what customers expect requires the real estate representative to accurately identify what the customer wants. This is not always an easy procedure. The customers may not even be aware of what their expectations are. The real estate representative will need to ask indirect questions, or use observational techniques, to determine expectations. Changing expectations require the real estate representative or firm to educate the customer as to what the role of the real estate representative and firm is and is not. Delivering more than a customer expects seems to be a great approach to customer expectations management. The customers not only get what they want, but they get a little something extra. This, however, can lead to either a well managed relationship or a rise in expectations that cannot be replicated or repeated and, therefore, not satisfied, in future transactions. In most service encounters, a combination of these three approaches to expectation management is used. Managing customer expectations is an ongoing process because expectations are constantly changing, requiring service quality improvements. Effective marketing programs include a constant monitoring procedure to ensure that changing customer expectations are identified and that service quality improvements are implemented. Effective monitoring systems will address several obstacles that may be present in achieving service quality improvements. Service improvements may fall short due to a lack of visibility in relation to service problems, unclear accountability in stages or processes of the service, a lengthy time frame needed for improving service quality, and the delivery unpredictability of people implementing the service.[11] Addressing these obstacles will help ensure that expectation deficiencies, operational deficiencies, and unrealized deficiencies are properly monitored and resolved.

Firms can reap the benefits from this proactive approach to marketing real estate. A proactive marketing program should focus on reducing operating costs and increasing customer satisfaction and perceived value. Accurately identifying what customers want allows the real estate firm to deliver only those parts of the service required by the customer. Those parts of the service offered by the real estate firm that do not increase customer satisfaction need not be delivered and, therefore, operating costs are reduced. Parts of the service that are not required by the majority of customers can be eliminated wholly from the service, further reducing operating costs. Including a part of the service that is not required but that improves value may enhance customer satisfaction to the point where it outweighs the costs. A proactive marketing program should focus the firm on the segment of the market it has identified as its target market. Focusing on a particular target market allows the real estate firm to develop marketing programs to satisfy the needs of that target market through superior service quality. Superior service quality is an effective means of ensuring a competitive advantage.[12]

Relationship Marketing in Real Estate

Relationship marketing is "the understanding, explanation and management of the on-going collaborative business relationship between suppliers and customers".[13]

The real estate representative or firm competes in a dynamic web of interconnected networks and relationships. The development of these networks and relationships is well matched with the interpersonal elements of the services offered.[14] The term relationship marketing, first coined in 1983,[15] was a different way of looking at marketing and how it applied to the modern business world. Today the term fuses with other marketing principles, showing its strengths in our ever evolving marketplace. The nature of relationship marketing is found in the management and marketing of services.[16] Through managing and marketing services, real estate representatives and firms engage in one-to-many and one-to-one relationships. These relationships may be contained in networks, in partnerships, or in communication hubs.

The essence of relationship marketing is found in its primary focus. The focus is to build, maintain, and enhance existing or potential relationships.[17] The transaction is no longer the end goal for real estate representatives and firms. The goal is to meet the expectations of the customers during and after the transaction is complete. This involves the management of relationships during the entire process.

There are many relationships that need to be managed by real estate representatives and firms. Relationships with banks, lawyers, customers, other businesses, and other real estate firms and representatives, are examples of relationships that need to be managed carefully. Primary consumer and business relationships are the focal points of relationship marketing. This, however, does not mean that other secondary business relationships can be ignored. For example, a good relationship with the bank is invaluable for a business owner and could lead to aid in future opportunities. Primary consumer and business relationships are the most critical relationships to be managed.

The real estate representative and firm "should manage its customer base directly through information obtained from the continuous interfaces between customers and employees".[18] This will ensure that the relationship is managed based on what the customer wants or expects from the relationship. This takes great skill and attention to detail for real estate firms and representatives. This is why relationship marketing needs to be integrated in the overall vision and plan of an organization. The overall goal is to improve service quality in an attempt to retain existing customers. Customer loyalty will be achieved if the perceived value is greater in relation to other competitors.[19] It is no surprise that effective relationship marketing can help real estate firms develop a competitive advantage.[20]

THE MARKETING PLAN

A marketing plan is the blueprint for marketing activities.[21] The scope of the marketing plan for a real estate firm depends on what is being marketed. An individual broker selling properties to the consumer market would have a simpler marketing plan than a firm with many representatives. The number of employees, the number of consumers, the type of consumers, and the transaction type all play a role in determining how complex and detailed the marketing plan will be. The contents of the marketing plan are the same in either case and will be used to help increase market awareness. The marketing plan contains an overview of the current environmental situation, marketing activities and initiatives (objectives and strategies), projected profits and costs, implementation directives, and evaluation and control considerations. The process required to develop the marketing plan is ongoing; that is why one of the elements in a marketing plan is its own evaluation. It may not be necessary to constantly adjust the marketing plan, but frequent reviews are necessary to ensure the plan is working as intended. Adjustment to the marketing plan may be caused by changes in the composition of the external environment (economic, political, and legal) and/or changes in the internal environment (vision, culture, and strategic direction). Effective marketing plans are flexible enough to allow for minor adjustments without having to rework the entire plan. This flexibility will result in a more responsive strategy to changing marketplaces.

Current Market Situation

The market planning process begins with an analysis of the current market situation and the identification of opportunities and threats. An analysis of the current market situation is usually determined through market research. Market research is the collection of data relating to the market environment, market characteristics, and consumer behaviour. Information relating to the market environment includes economic, technological, political/legal, and social and cultural data. Information relating to market characteristics includes market size, geographical density, competition, and segmentation data. Consumer behaviour information may include who does the buying, what they buy, and why they buy.[22] This data will be used to guide certain elements of the marketing plan and allow for informed decisions to be made regarding strategic development and deployment. Market research must be carefully planned and implemented to reduce the associated costs and time involved in the process.

Market research falls into two groups: primary research and secondary research. Primary research collects data for a specific purpose: that is, to address a specific research objective or question.[23] Primary research can make use of a questionnaire designed to collect information for quantitative analysis or group discussions (focus groups) used to collect qualitative information. Primary research includes steps such as research design, data collection, error extrapolation, data analysis, and report creation. This is why it is the most time consuming and expensive type of research. Secondary research involves utilizing data collected for another purpose other then the current research objective.[24] This data may include census statistics or studies conducted for other reasons. Secondary research is less expensive and faster to attain. Advancements in computer technology provide access to relevant information using personal computers that are found in even the smallest real estate firms. These advancements, however, have also created problems with the reliability and validity of the information collected. With the advent of Internet technologies, almost anyone can become a writer of research related material and, for that matter, a publisher of any type of information. Careful attention must be paid when using information from an unreliable source. Secondary data can be found in many different places. Government publications, trade associations, industry journals, and research organizations are a few examples that provide secondary data on diverse subject matters.[25] Reviewing secondary data is usually the preliminary step in developing your marketing plan. This review of secondary data provides the necessary information and direction to begin your marketing plan, or provides exploratory information for designing further primary research.

The current market situation is determined by analyzing the information collected through research. Two common forms of analysis are market studies and feasibility studies. A market study analyzes the general market demand for a particular type of real estate, such as single-family homes, apartment buildings, office spaces, or retail spaces. A feasibility study looks at a specific project to determine if the project can be successfully completed from a financial or investment standpoint. Successful completion depends on factors such as potential revenue, market share,[26] costs, and time restrictions. The results of this analysis are often passed on to the customers to provide information for their decision making. Research and analysis can identify opportunities and threats that exist in the current real estate market. The identification of opportunities and threats provides a key ingredient in the foundation of a marketing plan.

Marketing Activities

Focused marketing activities are directed by the objectives and strategy of the real estate representative, real estate firm or individual project. Objectives and strategies in turn are based on the research undertaken to determine current market trends. Marketing objectives state the goals the marketing plan is intended to achieve. Objectives can be stated in sales volume, market share, profit or customer satisfaction measures. Objectives should be clear, precise and, most important, measurable. The time frame for the marketing plan and when objectives should be reached must be stated. When more than one objective is stated in the marketing plan, these objectives should be consistent. Inconsistent objectives may result in objectives not being attained, causing lower profits and higher costs. Objectives should be attainable but challenging. Objectives that are too easily reached may not motivate people to work harder to reach higher levels. Objectives that are unattainable may frustrate people and cause a potential reduction in morale and motivation.

A marketing strategy provides the broad principles (the game plan) that will be used to attain the plan's objectives. Marketing strategy can be determined for each objective or for the plan as a whole. Successful strategy development incorporates the views of all people who will be implementing the plan. Good strategies fail because the people who are implementing the strategies have not supported them. A marketing strategy cannot be developed in isolation from other aspects of the business. To do so will create inconsistencies and integration problems. Real estate, as a service, requires a cohesive strategy incorporating all aspects of the business. The strategic component of the marketing plan should include the target market, positioning statement and action plans.

Target Market

A target market is a homogeneous or like group of customers to whom the real estate company wants to appeal. Which target market the company identifies depends on current market conditions

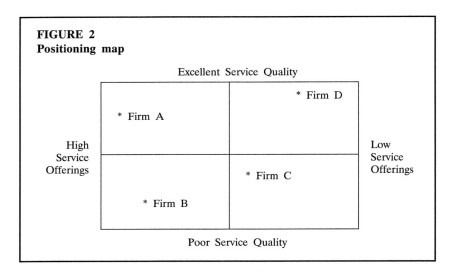

FIGURE 2
Positioning map

Excellent Service Quality

* Firm D

* Firm A

High
Service
Offerings

Low
Service
Offerings

* Firm C

* Firm B

Poor Service Quality

and the position of competitors in the market. The action plans and marketing mix (price, product, place, and promotion) are designed to attract the identified target market. Market research may need to be completed to determine the best action plans and marketing mix to attract the identified target market.

Positioning shows how the customers in a particular market see representatives or real estate firms. For example, one real estate firm may be seen as a specialist in the condominium market while another firm is seen as a specialist in the commercial retail market. These two companies are positioned differently in the market. These companies would need to develop action plans to change the perception of the customers if they want to be positioned differently. A marketing tool often used to show positioning is a positioning map. A positioning map shows how the market views different products, services or competitors along two dimensions. An example of a positioning map is shown in Figure 2.

Action plans can be developed to achieve the stated objectives for targeting efforts. Action plans are specific activities and initiatives relating to sales, advertising, the sales force, public relations and any other activities that have achievable objectives. Action plans answer the *what, who, when* and *how* much will it cost type of questions. The action plan(s) need to be consistent with other marketing activities, strategies, target market(s) and objectives. This relationship is show in Figure 3.

Action plans may include: property signage, classified ads, digital ads, billboards, printed brochures, radio or television advertisements,

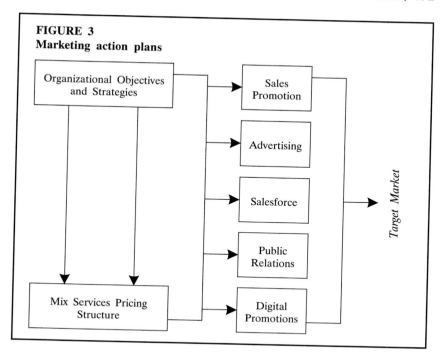

FIGURE 3
Marketing action plans

direct mail or cold canvassing. Action plans will vary, depending on the type of real estate being sold, the area where it is situated, and the cost associated with the action. Residential properties, income properties, and special properties are types of real estate that require different marketing plans.

Types of Real Estate

Residential properties represent the largest number of real estate transactions and include, but are not limited to, new single-family homes, resale of single-family homes, condominiums or apartment rentals. These transactions involve real estate representatives working directly with the buyers and sellers.

New single-family homes are generally part of a new subdivision. The real estate representatives or firm consider: the site, home size, lot size, home design, home builder and advertising as part of the marketing activities. Usually a site evaluation is done to assess site desirability. The proximity to schools, churches, shopping and public transportation would be considered when evaluating a site. The size and shape of the lot, and proximity to environmental concerns (busy streets, hydro poles) might also be part of the site evaluation. Special lot features such as park and ravine backings will also be a consideration. The results of the evaluation criteria used to evaluate the home will focus the marketing efforts on specific target markets. For example, larger homes are generally more expensive, limiting the customer base to higher income earners. The advertising plan for new single-family homes may include printed material, special events, Web publications, radio and television. The number of homes in the subdivision will determine the type of advertising. Television advertising is very expensive and may only be used if a large number of homes are being sold or if a moderate number of expensive homes are being sold. Television advertising is expensive because of the cost of air time and the cost of production. The return on advertising should be carefully monitored to justify its high cost. Another important marketing activity that may be essential for larger developments is the planning of the sales force. Large subdivisions may require a dedicated sales force, requiring specific training to meet customer needs. It may be more cost-effective to list the homes with independent representatives or brokers for smaller subdivisions.

Resales of single-family homes are the bread and butter of the independent representatives and brokers. Resales require a close relationship between the representatives or broker, and the buyers and sellers. The ability of the sales representative or broker to accurately identify the expectations and needs of the customers is critical in determining the success of these individuals. Identifying customer expectations can not only lead to a successful marketing campaign, but also a more satisfied customer. Advertising plans for resales need to be more modest in nature. Classified ads in newspapers, Web listings, local real estate papers and local cable stations advertising homes are the main communication strategies for resale. Condominiums have grown in popularity with consumers as restrictions on rental properties increase. Condominiums offer the purchaser the advantages of ownership with fewer obligations.

Condominium marketing plans are similar to new single-family homes for new buildings and to resale after the initial sales. An added focus in the sale of condominiums is the legal aspect of ownership. The purchaser buys a unit, and all owners have joint obligations for other areas of the property. Obligations include paying condo fees for work such as snow removal and lawn care. Condominiums may also take different forms, with townhouses, row housing and apartment units being the most popular.

Apartment rentals include the leasing of residential units. Apartment rentals may be completed by property managers, representatives or brokers. New apartment rentals may require more advertising once the majority of the units are let. Rental units have a different set of laws governing them; therefore, clients may seek advice regarding these laws and the special restrictions of each building.

Income properties involve the sale or lease of office buildings, shopping centres or apartment buildings. There are two separate transactions involved with income properties: the property is sold to an investor or group of investors, and the units are leased or sold to the businesses or individuals who are, ultimately, going to use the space. Income property sales fall into the business to business or commercial marketing category. The sales of investment properties usually involve more sophisticated buyers, requiring sales people with knowledge of special tax and investment considerations. Purchasers of income properties might be individuals, small businesses, institutional investors, individuals or syndicates. Sales to individuals or small businesses are similar to single-family home purchases, with the exception of the unique requirements of the property. For example, a small family run store would require a different type of facility than would a small manufacturing firm. Institutional purchasers hold portfolios of properties. The investment decisions for institutional purchasers are based on risk and return. The representative or broker in this case requires knowledge of the purchaser's investment needs, and tax considerations, and would require a more polished sales presentation. Individuals and syndicates purchasing investment properties fall into a wide range of sophistication, requiring marketing activities to match their level of sophistication. Marketing activities to rent space in income properties depends on the type of property and the prospective tenants. Marketing activities that may be used to attract prospective tenants include: door-to-door canvassing, telephone solicitation, direct contact or direct mail.

Special properties include vacation homes, building lots, farms, time sharing, and distressed properties. These types of properties require special knowledge and skills from the real estate agent or broker. Sale of special properties may require extra time, effort and expense. Vacation homes are often sold in the same manner as single-family homes. A characteristic of these sales that makes them different is that the buyers may be some distance from the property. Allowing the buyer to get a feel for a property, although far away, has been addressed with new communication technologies supported by broadband technologies. This characteristic of vacation properties means the market is larger and may, therefore, require advertising in national and regional mediums. Selling farm properties requires a specialized knowledge of the agricultural aspects in real estate. The representative or broker might require knowledge of different types of agricultural practices, government restrictions governing land use and unique tax considerations. Rural properties also have unique tax considerations. Marketing rural properties requires more time to show each property because of geographical distance. The location of rural properties may affect the use of the land. Rural properties that are close to major urban centres may be marketed in the same way as single-family homes, with the current "back to nature" trend. When the economy is in a down cycle, the number of distressed properties on the market increases. A property is classified as distressed if there is a negative cash flow or if the property has been foreclosed on by an unpaid lender. Marketing techniques for distressed properties should aim at either a quick sale or an activity plan to get the property back to a profit. Marketing techniques that have been applied to special properties include wide distribution through brokers, auctions, sealed bids, direct offering to principals or limited distribution to brokers.

Sales Skills

The skill of the agent or broker in any real estate transaction is critical to the success of the deal. These representatives or brokers must be appropriately compensated for their selling skills (i.e., incentives, premium commissions). There are two approaches to sales: a sales-oriented approach and a customer-oriented approach. The sales-oriented approach uses hard sell techniques, while the customer-oriented approach uses customer problem solving techniques. The customer-oriented approach is usually the more successful approach, because the agent or broker is addressing problems or concerns that the customer may have, providing solutions that fit them individually. This allows for expectations to be managed, and a closer relationship to be formed. There are several steps involved in the selling process, shown in Figure 4.

Prospect identification is the first step in the sales process. Because prospects come from many different places, it is important to monitor and scan several different channels. Referrals from other customers are one of the most successful channels. Other channels include leads from advertising, Internet campaigning, and switchboard referrals from real estate firms. Although the identification of prospects is critical, screening the prospects is just as important. The pursuit of non-qualified clients can cost time and money for all involved in the transaction. It is important to note that clients who do not qualify for one transaction may qualify for another, so careful identification of a customer's situation is important. Preapproach involves information searches through active information channels. Preapproach includes finding out as much as possible about all parties involved in the transaction, and planning a strategy to approach

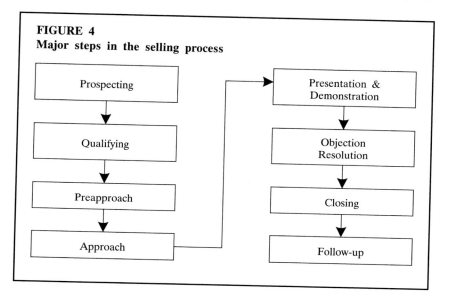

FIGURE 4
Major steps in the selling process

them. The goal is to make the process as smooth as possible during
the approach stage. The approach stage includes meeting the parties
associated with the transaction. Sales people who consider selling
themselves during this phase may be more successful. Presentation
and demonstration is the stage when the facts about the transaction
are presented. The AIDA formula is often used during this stage;
AIDA stands for attention, interest, desire and action. The representative or broker should be evaluating and re-evaluating the customer's expectations during this stage in order to match, meet, or
change these expectations. This stage of the sales process begins the
negotiation of the transaction. The salesperson who handles negotiation effectively has a certain set of skills. The skills required for
negotiation include preparation and planning skills, knowledge of the
deal, ability to think clearly and quickly under pressure, and verbal
and listening skills. Many sales are lost when the salesperson fails to
close the deal due to poor negotiating skills. Follow-up after the sale
is important if the salesperson wants to ensure the customer is satisfied. Satisfied customers will recommend the salesperson to others,
and will come back to the representative or broker the next time
they need real estate assistance. Some of these sales stages will be
more or less important, depending on the type of sale. Sales strategy
is one of the most important parts of the marketing plan for the
real estate industry.

SUMMARY

Real estate marketing is an important factor in the real estate process. Businesses to business marketing and consumer marketing techniques are utilized in both commercial and consumer real estate transactions. Elements of services marketing can be found in every real estate transaction. Effective real estate marketing begins with a marketing plan. The marketing plan includes an analysis of the current market and identification of opportunities and threats. The current market analysis will allow us to identify the target market and help set objectives. Based on the identified needs and expectations of the target market, marketing activities can be planned. Once the marketing plan has been devised, some control measures need to be put in place to monitor the effectiveness of the plan and identify when changes need to be made. The changes that are made will address the ever changing marketplace in today's real estate industry and the complexities of dealing with a diverse consumer base.

NOTES

1. P. Kotler and R.E. Turner, *Marketing Management: Analysis, Planning, Implementation, and Control*, Canadian Seventh Edition (Scarborough, ON: Prentice Hall, 1993).
2. A. Druckman, "Real Estate Institute of Canada Update", *Journal of Property Management* 67(5): 72(1).
3. P.A. Samuelson, *Economics: An Introductory Analysis* (New York: McGraw-Hill, 1948).
4. Material extended and adapted from W. Pride, O. Ferrell, H. Mackenzie and K. Snow, *Marketing. Concepts and Strategies* (Toronto, ON: ITP Nelson, 2000).
5. S. Shapiro, W. Perreault et al. *Basic Marketing — A Global Management Approach* (Toronto: Times Mirror Professional Publishing Ltd., 1996).
6. W. Pride, O. Ferrell, H. Mackenzie, and K. Snow, *Marketing. Concepts and Strategies* (Toronto: ON: ITP Nelson, 2000).
7. A. Ghobadian, S. Speller et al. "Service Quality — Concepts and Models" *International Journal of Quality & Reliability Management* 11(9): 43–66.
8. W. Pride, O. Ferrell, H. Mackenzie, and K. Snow, *Marketing. Concepts and Strategies* (Toronto: ON: ITP Nelson, 2000).
9. Y. Li, K. Tan et al. "Managing service quality: applying utility theory in the prioritization of service attributes" *International Journal of Quality & Reliability Management* 20(4): 417–435.
10. V. Zeithaml, L. Berry et al., "Communication and control process in the delivery of service quality." *Journal of Marketing* 52: 35–48.
11. A. Ghobadian, S. Speller et al. "Service Quality — Concepts and Models" *International Journal of Quality & Reliability Management* 11(9): 43–66.
12. J. Kandampully, "Service quality to service loyalty: A relationship which goes beyond customer services" *Total Quality Management* (August 1998).
13. J. Sheth and A. Parvatiyar, *Relationship Marketing: Theory, Methods, and Applications*. Center for Relationship Marketing, Emory University, Atlanta, GA, Research Conference Proceedings (June 1994).

14. V. Liljander and I. Roos "Customer-relationship levels — from spurious to true relationships." *Journal of Service Marketing* 16(7): 593–614.
15. C. Grönroos, "Relationship Marketing: Challenges for the Organization" *Journal of Business Research* 46: 327–335.
16. Ibid.
17. C. Grönroos, "Keynote paper from marketing mix to relationship marketing — towards a paradigm shift in marketing." *Management Decision* 35(4): 322–339.
18. C. Grönroos, "Relationship Marketing: Challenges for the Organization" *Journal of Business Research* 46: 327–335.
19. J. Kandampully, "Service quality to service loyalty: A relationship which goes beyond customer services" *Total Quality Management* (August 1998) .
20. R. Priluck, "Relationship marketing can mitigate product and service failures" *Journal of Services Marketing* 17(1): 37–52.
21. W. Airich, "The marketing plan — fact or fiction?" *Journal of Property Management* 54(6).
22. D. Aaker, V. Kumar et al. *Marketing Research* 7th ed. (Toronto: John Wiley & Sons, 2001).
23. Ibid.
24. Ibid.
25. J. Grossnickle and O. Raskin, *Online Marketing Research* (New York: McGraw-Hill Inc., 2001).
26. W. Balderson, *Canadian Entrepreneurship and Small Business Management* (New York: McGraw-Hill Ryerson Limited, 1998).
27. W. Pride, O. Ferrell, H. Mackenzie, and K. Snow, *Marketing. Concepts and Strategies* (Toronto, ON: ITP Nelson, 2000).

Real Estate 2.0

MICHAEL ROCHON

TECHNOLOGY

Technology has had far reaching effects on all aspects of the modern business environment. Whether it is the production of a good, or the facilitation of a service, technology plays a role. The real estate industry is no exception. Like other industries, it evolves by embracing technological change. One such technology that has drastically impacted the real estate industry is that of the Internet and its various communication mediums and applications.

A LOOK AT INTERNET TECHNOLOGIES AND CONCEPTS

Internet technologies are built on a historical collection of innovations. From communication technologies, such as the telegraph, to historical computing components, such as the vacuum tube, each has played a role in moulding Internet technologies of today. The primary function of Internet technologies is communication. This communication can lead to the transfer of information from one computing device to another in the form of messaging (text/voice), set or sets of data (file), rich media content (audio/video) or other forms of communication.

The function of computer communication is supported by standards that make this transfer of information possible. Within the Internet, the Internet Protocol (IP) allows for the organization of this transfer, regardless of the type of information. Without the IP standard the transfer of information would not be possible. The Internet Protocol is what lays the foundation. In addition to this foundation you can find other protocols that make a distinction between the forms of communication. For example, the World Wide

Web (WWW) uses the Hyper-Text Transfer Protocol (HTTP) which allows browsers to correctly display information coded in Hyper-Text Markup Language (HTML). Most of the pages you view on the Web use this protocol, or a form of this protocol, to accurately display information on your computer or mobile device. Other protocols enhance our ability to communicate by opening our options to varying information types. File Transfer Protocol (FTP) allows for a direct transfer of files between computing devices, communication through email is supported by POP (incoming mail) and SMTP and IMAP (outgoing mail) protocols, the transport of real-time data such as video and audio on the Web may use the Real-Time Transport Protocol (RTP). New web enabled mobile platforms are becoming standardized for viewing content on mobile devices such as smart phones. Many technological components must work together to allow for communication and information transfers to occur through the Internet.

The Internet itself is a network infrastructure that is built on primary standards (mentioned above), followed by users who want to connect with each other. The key to this technology is that it has the capability of eliminating or targeting geographical segments and opens the door to a global or local communication system that is efficient, effective and ever-evolving. Its efficiency lies in the potential audience reach relative to time and money. The effectiveness lies in the functionality of the technology, which is to communicate and collaborate amongst a diverse online population set. Evolution occurs through new and innovative ways that the communication is delivered and measured. The key is how it is used and what it is used for. The real estate industry, and the professionals who operate within it, have embraced this technology on a number of different levels.

THE WEB AND THE REAL ESTATE INDUSTRY — REAL ESTATE PROFESSIONAL AND CONSUMERS

When considering the real estate industry and the Internet, both the real estate professional and the consumer must be considered separately. The primary function of the Internet for real estate professionals is the World Wide Web and other Internet based technologies such as email. Focus will be placed on the Web and selective revolving Internet technologies for the remainder of this article.

The Web and the Real Estate Professional

Like many other industries, the real estate industry has embraced technological innovations such as the Web. It is no surprise that over 9% of all websites have some sort of association with real estate.[1] The Web allows real estate professionals to stay competitive in the ever changing real estate environment.[2] Competitiveness is achieved by using the Internet to tweak internal operations, to enhance marketing reach and deployment, to reduce operational costs,[3] to generate leads and build relationships, and to improve communication between employees and between employees and clients. The Web not only allows a professional to stay competitive, it may also create a competitive advantage, depending on the Web strategy employed.[4] Real estate professionals who are proactive will be leaders in developing new technologies, or developing new ways to use old technologies, to better improve operations through technological applications.[5]

The Web is built up of many different websites, all with their own Uniform Resource Locator (URL). The URL allows consumers to locate specific information relating to real estate professionals on the Web. The URL is similar to your postal code and address; it is unique to your home. One could now say that there are two real estate environments, the physical and the virtual. Much like physical properties, domain names are commonly sold, but on the Web (i.e. www.afternic.com). Some domain names can command a heavy price. This, however, is another topic in itself.

The most common function of the Web for real estate professionals is to enhance communications.[6] Whether it is the communication of a message, educational material, a price, or other sales information, some sort of information is being relayed to the visitor. Websites are now being used by a very large portion of the real estate industry for this exact reason.[7] Conversely, a large portion of consumers are also using the Web to seek out information. Other

---

[1] Henderson, K., and Cowart, L. "Bucking e-commerce trends: A content analysis comparing commercial real estate brokerage and residential real estate brokerage websites." *Journal of Corporate Real Estate.* London, Sep 2002.

[2] Ibid.

[3] Rothenberg, P., Puentes King, J. "Strategize to maximize: consider both hard and soft factors when evaluating technology investments." *Journal of Property Management.* March–April 2003, v68, i2, p28(8).

[4] McMahan, J. "Preface: case studies on the interface of technology and the real estate industry." *Real Estate Issues.* Summer 2002, v27, i2, p13(7).

[5] Pekala, N. "A 2001 Forecast: Talent, Technology to be Top Trends." *Journal of Property Management.* Jan 2001, v66, i1, p22.

[6] Ibid.

[7] TSE, R., Webb, J. "The effectiveness of a Web strategy for real estate brokerage." *Journal of Real Estate Literature.* Cleveland, 2002.

communication functions of the Web include exchanging information with industry partners such as banks and inspectors, extracting information from consumer segments, and customizing the communication experience for individual users through the use of Cookies, Action Script, Java, ASP (Active Server Pages) and .NET applications.

There is no doubt that the Web has created an environment where communication is enhanced. Enhancements include visual and audio stimulation. Visual stimulation appears in the form of static graphics (JPG, GIF, or PNG), 2D and 3D animations (Flash or Java), video (Mp4, FLV or AVI) or a combination of the three (HTML 5). Further visual stimulation occurs through the structure and layout of the actual website. A discussion on website structure and layout will take place later. Audio stimulation can be experienced on many websites and can take the form of background music, voice guidance, virtual agents, and special effects. Real estate professionals must select the right combination of these stimulants to best fit their target audience(s). Too much stimulation may cloud the message and too little may reflect badly on the brand or real estate professional's image.

How Internet Technologies Change Real Estate

Besides the ability to enhance communication, the Internet directly impacts various stages in the real estate selling and buying process. A brief look at these can be found in Figure 1.

Traditionally, listing a home was done by the real estate professional through the use of the Multiple Listing Service (MLS), a restricted database for professional real estate employees which is delivered through a web portal. While this restriction is still in place, consumers have the option to list with other sites that are commission free or have a reduced cost (i.e. *www.homesales.ca* or *www.ebay.ca).* Some tech savvy sellers may also develop their own website, social networking platforms, and personal online marketplaces to list their properties. In essence, it is now possible for the buyer and seller to find each other more efficiently through the Internet.[8] As a drawback, listing with these secondary sites does not provide inclusion into the primary MLS database, which is the main database searched by agents finding homes for potential purchasers, thus a great segment of the market may be excluded. Conversely, proactive real estate professionals may search these secondary sites if no sufficient match was found using their available resources.

---

[8] TSE, R, and Webb, J. "The effectiveness of a Web strategy for real estate brokerage." *Journal of Real Estate Literature.* Cleveland, 2002.

FIGURE 1
Impacted Real Estate Functions Due to Internet

Basic Real Estate Function	*Basic Internet Technology Aid*
Prospecting	Email Solicitation, Opt-In Lists, Localized and International Websites, Search Engine Listings, Search Engine Optimization (SEO), Banner Ads, Pop-ups, Web 2.0 and Social Networking, Web Retail Listings, Web Directory Listings
Listing Home	MLS Database, Private Databases, Public Databases, Partner or Association Websites, Personal Websites, Online Marketplace, Web 2.0 and Social Networking, Email Notifications, Banners, Pop-ups
Finding a Home	Listing/Broker/Agent Websites, Search Engines, Database Searches (MLS and Others), Online Marketplace, Web 2.0 and Social Networking
Customer Servicing	Virtual Tours, Email, Websites, Digital Marketing Campaigns, Banners, Pop-ups, Web 2.0 and Social Networking, Google Analytics and Web Statistics
Customer Relationship Management	Forms, Websites, Email Marketing, Email Client Lists, Web 2.0 and Social Networking, Web Integrated CRM Software, Google Analytics and Web Statistics

In addition to listing a property, consumers also have the ability to locate their own property of interest.[9] No longer are mass amounts of restricted information only accessible to the real estate professional. For example, access to the MLS database, historically,

---

[9] Littlefield, J., Bao, Y., and Cook, D. "Internet real estate information: are home purchasers paying attention to it?" *The Journal of Consumer Marketing.* Santa Barbra, 2000.

was for real estate professionals only.[10] Now finding a property is easier as these databases are widely available online (i.e. *www.mls.ca*) and will become more technologically driven as time goes on. New mapping and street level view features are being utilized to enhance the MLS platform for agents and consumers. Mobile enabled MLS tools and integration, MLS compatibility for new browsing environments, cross access and integration to separate MLS databases through one dedicated portal, and MLS integration into social networking applications are just a few advancements that will improve usage. Additionally, home buyers can look to other websites that are not driven by the MLS database. The consumer can enter the appropriate search criteria (location, price, size) and available homes will be displayed for them to review. With a swift click of the mouse the specifications and pictures of the property, along with other multimedia options, can be viewed. What this means to real estate professionals is that the market is now much broader than before,[11] with more privately listed homes and enhanced market visibility from various available mediums. Private sales of homes accounted for 13% of home sales in 2008. Fifty-one percent of those private sales used the Internet to market their homes.[12] Real estate agents are dealing with a more educated and informed consumer and must adjust their approach accordingly.

Traditionally, one of the main duties of the real estate professional has been to physically show the home. Today the technological equivalent to the walkthrough is called a virtual tour (See Figure 2 for screenshot). Virtual tours employ 3d and 2d technologies to visually present the home to the consumer. These tours can be viewed on the Web (i.e. *www.virtualproperties.ca*), on mobile devices and/or on physical digital formats (CD, DVD, USB, etc.). The virtual tour still has a long way to go as it does not provide effective interaction with the consumer and does not allow for the "touch and feel" of the walkthrough experience. It does, however, allow the consumer to view the property, virtually, at their convenience and gives the consumer more control while viewing the property remotely. Accompanying sound conveying sales information (virtual agent) is also

---

[10] Muhanna, W., James, R. "The impact of e-commerce on the real estate industry: Baen and Guttery revisited." *Journal of Real Estate Portfolio Management.* Boston, May–Aug 2002.

[11] McMahan, J. "Preface: case studies on the interface of technology and the real estate industry." *Real Estate Issues.* Summer 2002, v27, i2, p13(7).

[12] 2009 National Association of REALTORS® Profile of Home Buyers and Sellers. Website reference: http://www.realtor.org/library/library/fg006. Accessed December, 2010.

FIGURE 2
Virtual Tour

*Screenshot taken from www.virtualproperties.com

common and becoming more popular as part of the digital viewing experience. In the future, virtual tours may also allow for interior design capabilities through floor level measurements, virtual furniture uploads, and colour selection (i.e. paint and cabinet colour). Another common web application employed by consumers to view a home is Google Maps with Street View.[13] Entering an address gives the potential buyer access to a frontal view of the home and the capability to roam the neighbourhood at street level.

Giving advice and demonstrating expertise is another area that is changing for the real estate industry due to the Web. Information is readily available for consumers to download on all elements of the real estate buying process. A discussion of this will take place later when looking at how technology has changed the consumer in the real estate industry. In addition to consumers gaining access to a

---

[13] http://maps.google.com. Accessed December, 2010.

vast repository of information, the real estate professional also has improved access. Real estate professionals have the ability to download and review current information affecting their industry. This implies that they have the capability of gaining knowledge and enhancing their ability to provide services by simply pushing a button. New social networking applications allow the real estate professional to position themselves as an expert and knowledge provider to the masses. This helps in creating an online professional identity which fuels lead generation and the building of relationships.

Finding and attracting a new client, whether it be a buyer or seller, has changed dramatically due to the Web. Real estate professionals are looking to the Web to enhance their ability to gain potential customers and generate leads. The traditional website is used to convey information about the professional and in many cases the affiliated brokerage firm. A website is required to put the real estate professional on a level playing field in today's market. Some potential customers will not even consider a real estate professional who does not appear current when it comes to technology. Consumers may view this as a weakness when considering a potential agent. Thus, the expectations in terms of service have risen.[14] Web platforms, such as a website, demonstrate enhanced visibility and reach to the consumers, thus driving the real estate selling and buying process. In essence, the Web has changed the way real estate professionals market and track their services and products. The Web has created a 24/7 marketing platform for real estate content. These content delivery websites are now becoming the new channel for marketing related functions. Search engines also aid in this dynamic marketing environment by delivering potential clients to a website through Search Engine Optimization (SEO) initiatives.[15] In addition, web analytics are used to customize and strategically alter web content and structure, to fit the user's technological demographics. Most website hosting packages come with the option to monitor and record web related data for a nominal fee. Google Analytics is one of the more popular tools for collecting, analyzing, and reporting on web-based data.[16] Browser type, page views, content usage, geographical location, time spent on website, browsing patterns, search crite-

---

[14] Choi, R, and Graham, J. "Answering the call of the wild Web." *Journal of Property Management.* Chicago, Mar-Apr 2001.
[15] Henderson, K., Cowart, L. "Bucking e-commerce trends: A content analysis comparing commercial real estate brokerage and residential real estate brokerage websites." *Journal of Corporate Real Estate.* London, Sep 2002.
[16] http://www.google.com/analytics/. Accessed December, 2010.

rion and referring URLS are just a few statistics that can be utilized to tailor websites to users. Clearly, websites, analytical tools and search engine technologies have enhanced the real estate professional's ability to find, attract and retain new clients.

Websites are a natural starting point for real estate professionals to gain a quick presence on the Internet. Real estate professionals must now escalate their online presence by engaging in Web 2.0 (Social Networking) applications and services. Web 2.0 is the next generation to the traditional World Wide Web. It is the evolution of generic Websites into interactive content providing social networking and media capabilities. Many Web 2.0 applications are currently available and highly utilized within the industry. They include: social-networking sites and tools, blogspheres, wikis, video-sharing sites, local and hosted web applications, mashups and collaborative tagging. In 2008, 67% of realtors indicated that they *did not use* social networking; when the same study was conducted in 2009, 84% of realtors indicated *they did use* social networking sites.[17] Of those who used social networking sites, 78% had a Facebook account and 58% had a LinkedIn account dedicated for real estate purposes.[18] Other utilized social networking sites include: Twitter, Flickr, YouTube, Active Rain, MySpace, Zillow, Trulia, Ning, Real Town, Zoocasa and StreetAdvisor. With the advent of social networking and other Web 2.0 technologies, the environment on the web has changed considerably from the static web pages driving "canned" content. With this change comes the need to change the approach by the real estate professional. New social networking tools allow for a richer communication in a somewhat natural setting. They allow the real estate professional the opportunity to build his or her brand as an agent, and as a person and expert. With real-time communication facilitated through many of these social applications, the real estate professional gains the ability to be more responsive, to become an educator, and to deliver rich content on many different levels. In addition, one of the largest uses of these types of social mediums is the ability to gain insight and research on potential customers, geographical areas, and industry trends. Although not clearly defined in today's technological sphere, the future, Web 3.0 applications and platforms, are already creating a buzz amongst web enthusiasts.

---

[17]   2009 REALTOR® Technology Survey. Website Reference: http://www.realtor.org/library/library/fg006. Accessed December, 2010.

[18]   2009 REALTOR® Technology Survey. Website Reference: http://www.realtor.org/library/library/fg006. Accessed December, 2010.

The real estate professional of today has to demonstrate they have the technological knowledge to benefit the client during both the buying and selling process. Web savvy real estate professionals will be more likely to search all available digital channels, including social networking sites, to locate the appropriate property for home buyers and utilize all the appropriate digital channels to sell the property for home sellers. In addition, a technologically savvy real estate professional will have the ability to strategically plan and execute digital strategies within conventional strategic plans. This may involve understanding which are the right search engines to use and what types of search criteria are appropriate. For example, not all search engines are the same. Some search engines are "Meta" search engines, others use keywords, while more advanced search engines use a combination of technologies to match search criteria to the relevant websites. Meta search engines historically used words found in the code of websites (Meta Tags) to match search criteria. Today, Meta search engines typically hit other central engines to return results for each search query (i.e. www.webcrawler.com). Not only do real estate professionals have to know which search engines to search, but also how to use the search engines appropriately to ensure maximum searchability of their own listings and information. Often the search engine provider will supply instructions on how to search effectively using their engine and how to configure web related content to better position sites organically on their search results. By understanding how the technology works, real estate professionals can better guide web developers or themselves, when developing websites and search engine optimization strategies. This will allow a better hit ratio (the site appears more often in a search result) when others use the search engine to locate real estate specific information. It is no surprise that training employees is even more critical in today's environment as allocating time and money to educate becomes pivotal for real estate firms.[19]

Another technology that may help in prospecting a new client is email technology. The email of choice amongst real estate professionals is Outlook or Outlook Express as 49% utilize this email platform.[20] Mass email campaigns, from legal opt-in lists, can also aid real estate professionals in finding prospective buyers and sellers. A list is generated, and an email is sent to potential clients with the

[19] Pekala, N. "A 2001 Forecast: Talent, Technology to be Top Trends." *Journal of Property Management.* Jan 2001, v66, i1, p22.

[20] 2009 REALTOR® Technology Survey. Website Reference: http://www.realtor.org/library/library/fg006. Accessed December, 2010.

FIGURE 3
Client Email Mail Out

Dear Carole and Alan,

I just wanted to send a quick email to wish you a Happy Home Birthday. It has been 1 year since your purchase and I hope you are enjoying your home and its community. If I can assist you in any way please do not hesitate to contact me.

All the best,
Nick

---

key messages of the real estate professional or firm. Once contact has been established, some consumers prefer to begin a relationship with email communication rather than a phone or personal meeting. Email allows the consumer to "feel out" the real estate professional before they commit to a business relationship. It is no surprise that email has become the preferred communication amongst both real estate professionals and their customers.[21] Although emails are a great way to quickly and efficiently communicate with prospective buyers and sellers, picking up the phone and making a call may strengthen the communication between the parties.

Customer relationship management (CRM) has also changed with the advent of Internet technologies. Real estate professionals need to ensure an ongoing relationship with their clients. The goal is to be considered for future real estate business with the clients as well as his or her network of friends and family. Internet based platforms such as email, social networking, and Web based forms, have allowed real estate professionals to better manage their relationships with customers. If a real estate professional is diligent, they will keep contact lists of all their clients with their preferred method of communication. Email accounts can be used to maintain existing relationships. For example, sending season's greetings or celebrating the

---

[21] 2009 REALTOR® Technology Survey. Website Reference: http://www.realtor.org/library/library/fg006. Accessed December, 2010.

FIGURE 4
Online Poll

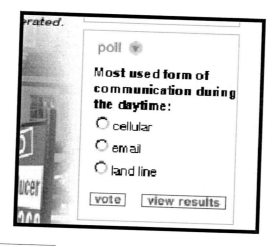

*Screenshot taken from www.remax.ca

anniversary of the purchase of a new home (Figure 3) are excellent ways to maintain the relationship.

Another way a real estate professional can improve existing relationships and harness potential relationships with new prospects, is through digital forms.[22] Forms can be simple or complex surveys that allow the real estate firm and/or professional to collect primary information on their client base. The form is commonly used at the beginning and/or the end of a relationship, however, it can be used at any time during a relationship. The goal of the form is to either gain an understanding of the current or potential customer (See Figure 4 for a Web poll example) or to gain an understanding of the experience the customer has had with the real estate firm and/or professional. By understanding what the customer wants and expects, the real estate professional and firm can better service the cus-

---

[22] Choi, R., and Graham, J. "Answering the call of the wild Web." *Journal of Property Management.* Chicago, Mar–Apr 2001.

tomer's expectations and needs, addressing any deficiencies that may have occurred.

This information can be easily extracted and managed through Internet based languages such as HTML and XML (Extensible Markup Language) and more easily analyzed through readily available statistical software that is automated internally or hosted. Ultimately, the real estate professional has the ability to better manage the relationship from start to finish through convenient forms placed on standard websites, sent through email messages, or delivered to mobile devices.

The Web and Real Estate Consumers

The real estate industry must not only consider the Internet in terms of its own business and sales representatives, it must also consider the Internet in terms of what is available to its consumers. Consumer use of Internet technologies has contributed to and continues to drive the real estate industry's adoption of Internet technologies.[23]

Consumers look to the Internet to collect and transfer information concerning real estate transactions. This in turn makes them more knowledgeable and aware buyers, sellers, and renters. For example, it is not uncommon for consumers to search websites to gain information about what to ask of your broker or sales representative when selling, buying, or renting. This means that consumers are engaging in the real estate process before contacting the real estate professional.[24] Furthermore, it is not uncommon for consumers to do their own background research on a given property, area, builder or even previous owners.[25]

In addition to educating themselves about the real estate transaction, real estate consumers are also finding that many services traditionally provided by the real estate professional are now available on the Web. For example, real estate consumers no longer have to wonder if they can afford a certain price for a home. Many mortgage calculators are available at banking websites (i.e., www.cibc.ca) and personal sales representatives' websites (i.e., www.ellidavis.com).

---

[23] Dermisi, S. "Impact of the Internet on International Real Estate Office Markets." *Journal of Real Estate Portfolio Management.* V8, 4, 2002.

[24] Henderson, K., and Cowart, L. "Bucking e-commerce trends: A content analysis comparing commercial real estate brokerage and residential real estate brokerage websites." *Journal of Corporate Real Estate.* London, Sep 2002.

[25] Bond, M., Seiler, M., Seiler, V., and Blake, B. "Uses of websites of effective real estate marketing." *Journal of Real Estate Portfolio Management.* Boston, Apr–Jun, 2000.

In addition, buyers and sellers can easily choose their own appraisers, financial lenders and lawyers.[26]

This produces a more educated consumer who is more informed about the real estate process and the services that are available to them. Dependency on the sales representative has diminished for many consumers, due to the range and depth of industry related information available. This means that real estate firms and professionals must stay competitive by keeping up with technological changes and their impacts on the overall industry, and with consumer expectations. Real estate firms and professionals should not only be on the Web, but they should also know what is available on the Web to prepare for more knowledgeable consumers. This also means that real estate firms and professionals need to be proactive in delivering content on the Web to demonstrate their expertise and position themselves as the best source for services and information.

The Pros and Cons of Internet Technologies

Thus far we have discussed how the Internet has impacted the real estate industry overall, the elements of the real estate selling process, and the real estate consumer. Caution must be taken as technological innovations can seem very appealing, but without proper research and application, can be costly and ineffective. Understanding some of the negative and positive aspects of these technologies will help the real estate professional make strategic decisions about how best to employ them.

Email Communication

Advantages include: the overall reach capacity, the low cost of emailing, the flexibility of the technology (text, forms, pictures, audio and video), and the ability to effectively maintain customer relationships. Some of the challenges surrounding the use of email include: a poor response rate (lower then most traditional mail outs), legality issues revolving around use (spamming is a major concern), incompatibility issues (some email systems do not accept HTML mail), the non-personal nature of the communication medium, and the popularity of using this medium to deliver information (information overload), which leads to consumers ignoring or deleting unsolicited communications.

---

[26] Alberts, R., and Townsend, A. "Real estate transactions, the Internet and personal jurisdiction." *Journal of Real Estate Literature.* Cleveland, 2002.

Websites

Some advantages include: a very high overall reach capacity, an inexpensive method of marketing, an economical initiative to maintain and monitor, flexibility in terms of content (i.e. Flash, Java, HTML, etc.), delivery of content which is rich and specific, and the ability to segment and, therefore, target specific groups of consumers. In addition, websites allow cost savings in terms of marketing initiatives. The shortening of ad lengths (classified, flyers, television) can also be achieved with the help of the Web.[27] Short details are given with the URL where the consumer can gain additional information about a home or service. Some of the disadvantages include the difficulty of targeting viable users online, the cost of developing the site (depends on complexity and depth), incompatibility issues with user technologies (i.e. browser type, screen type, plug-ins available), the cost of search engine optimization (SEO), and the task of updating and maintaining the website to stay current and connected with consumers.

Online Forms

Advantages include the ability to extract important consumer information, to collect information in a timely and cost effective manner, and to transfer the information to other programs for analysis purposes in real-time. Some of the disadvantages include the autonomy of the person filling out the form, controlling the privacy of information transfer over the Web, and technical problems that impede the transfer of the data causing the data to be unknowingly lost.

Search Engine Technologies

The positive aspects of search engine technologies are that they provide a directory of websites that can be searched using keywords or Meta phrases, they give an option for marketing websites via the Web, and they allow consumers a single location to research given topics. Some of the negative aspects of utilizing search engine technologies are the overall high cost of listing to gain respectable organic results or positioning (top 20 can be very costly to obtain), the inability to control other advertising on the search page (you may work for top position organically, yet other firms may have paid for banner space), the difficulty in designing a site to hit the critical keywords for consumer search criteria, and the time it takes to get listed on some of the engines (i.e., six weeks).

---

[27] Giovannotto, V. "Real Estate Efficiencies Soar as Technology Takes Off." *Journal of Property Management.* March 2001, v66, i2, p42.

Social Networking and Web 2.0 Applications

On the positive side, social networking sites and applications provide a quick and efficient medium to communicate to one or many consumers. This communication is generally more user-friendly and interactive then other forms of communication on the web, allowing for a more genuine rapport to be established via the Internet. These mediums provide the capability of positioning within niche markets or communities, delivering rich content to help facilitate prospecting and relationship management, and they provide real-time gratification to consumers seeking instant communication within the real estate industry. The negative aspects associated with these types of communication platforms include: expectation of instant, real-time communications; the need to update social networking platforms on an hourly, daily, weekly basis; the inability to control postings and responses on some platforms; and the ease of entrance by competitive real estate firms and professionals into the medium.

It is important to be as educated as possible about all of the pros and cons associated with employing each technology in order to provide added value to the consumer, to enhance the strategic direction of the firm, and to ensure operational efficiency companywide.

THE WEBSITE

Website Design 101 — A Real Estate Perspective

The real estate industry has embraced "the website" like no other Web technology. Websites are now used in the real estate industry for corporate and personal purposes. This means that both real estate firms and professionals have a need for a website. Does this mean that a firm or professional must understand all there is to know about developing a website? No, however, it is important for real estate firms and professionals to understand what a properly designed website entails. This will aid in developing a site, hiring someone to develop it, or revamping an existing site. Some design considerations are found in the table below.

SUMMARY

Many options are available to real estate firms, professionals, and their consumers, with respect to Internet technologies.

Consumers of today are more knowledgeable and expect more from the real estate service industry as online technologies bring relevant and current information to their doorstep. Real estate firms and professionals must be aware of available information and be strategic when dealing with consumers who may have enhanced market intelligence.

Most real estate professionals today use some sort of email system to communicate internally or externally and use the Web to communicate their message to a potential buyer or seller. Others engage in real-time media through live virtual tours and/or streaming media through video and audio. Social networking is highly utilized today allowing for a more real-time, personal interaction with consumers and other professionals. Regardless of the technology, the purpose is clear, to effectively communicate and enhance internal operations in an attempt to remain competitive or build a competitive advantage through improved efficiencies and improved market reach. The proper implementation of Internet and evolving technologies can do exactly that.

Basic Website Design Element	Basic Design Considerations
Navigation	Users should be able to navigate through the site in a timely manner. In addition, users must be able to go where they want to go. A cluttered site will lead to poor navigation and frustrated users. It is good to make all primary links (such as "contact") available on every page. This will avoid users getting lost. Pay close attention to links that are internal to your site and those that link to external resources. Flow charts (i.e., site maps) are helpful when designing a website as they allow a pictorial representation of the navigational flow your user will experience.
Graphics	Graphics can give a website visual appeal and a distinctive look. Too many graphics may clutter the site and add to the overall load time. Load time is the time it takes to load the actual website not contained in a computer's cache memory. Real estate sites tend to be graphic heavy due to the pictures of the homes that are for sale. This will make a difference when picking an Internet Service Provider (ISP) to host the site. Hosting packages range depending on how many megabytes (MB) your site will be. Standard Web graphics can take the form of a JPG, GIF and/or PNG. Each has different properties in terms of size, color space, and usability. Ensure proper description tags (i.e., alternative text) are designated to linked or important graphics. These will help visitors with a disability, and improve SEO initiatives.

	Continued.
Basic Website Design Element	*Basic Design Considerations*
Animations	Animations make for a dynamic and rich looking site. Some Web enabled animations include animated Gif's, Javascript, Java Applets, and Macromedia flash. Flash technology is one of the most widely used animation formats on the Web today. If a website has an introduction, it is probably done using some sort of flash media. The virtual spokesperson or virtual agent is also usually streamed using Flash Video which adds a person and scripted sound to home pages. Extensive animation, however, can take away from the message of the site and also cause increased load times. Incompatibility issues also exist depending on the animation format.
Sound	Sound is a great way to personalize a site. Sound is commonly used in "loop" format so that it continues to play the same sound clip over and over. When thinking about sound, close attention must be paid to the overall feel of the site. If the sound does not match the look of the site, it will not provide any value. Sound can be static (embedded in the website) or more dynamic (included in animation formats such as Flash). The size and length of the sound must be considered due to load times. Some common Web enabled sound formats include WAV (wave), WMA (windows media audio), RA (real audio), MP3 (MPEG-1, layer 3), and QT (quick time).
Content	The Content of a website can also add to the overall appeal and functionality of the site. Too much content may overwhelm the user. Not enough content may send the user to another site. Generally, it is good to include relevant information that is direct, written concisely, current, and if possible customizable. Real estate sites often include, but are not limited to, content about the property listings (price, square footage, location), the services they provide, the company or the professional (or both), general information concerning buying and selling homes, financial information (tax, insurance, mortgage), and contact information. It is important to keep in mind that a consumer's response to a personal or corporate website plays a vital role in their choice of a business partner. Strategic content development can also help in SEO initiatives, allowing for better organic search presence.

	Continued.
Basic Website Design Element	*Basic Design Considerations*
Structure	The structure of the website will add to its usability. Most real estate sites will discuss the firm or professional, how to contact them, which houses are listed, links to real estate related information, open house dates, testimonials, information on services, and financial tools (mortgage and tax calculators).
Load Time	Load time depends on the amount, size and type of graphics used, the amount, size and type of animations used, and the amount, size and format of the audio used. It can also depend on database driven data content and style sheets. In addition, load times also depend on embedded content, such as PDF documents, Javascripts and database applications (database used to update website using current information). Content can also play a factor if extensive. The key is to have a small load time. Several Internet tools are available to test this criterion. The load time will also be dependent on the connection speed of your users (i.e. phone line, cable, satellite). This is another reason it is good to collect information on your users, to better tailor the website to their existing needs.
Font Type	Many people overlook this when developing a site. They simply choose a font type they find aesthetically pleasing. Compatibility issues are a concern when choosing font types. Depending on the browser used, specific font types may not be available. The browser then chooses the default font setting, which may not complement the website's visual appeal. Choosing a standard font type will avoid incompatibility issues for different users.
Cross-Linking	Cross-linking websites is an important design consideration that can strategically position your site with consumers. Cross-linking can occur with real estate associations, tools, research and educational material, and other micro sites designed to deliver relevant content. It can also be used to connect your social networking environments to your main website. Cross-linking relevant content is also an important consideration when planning your SEO strategy. Cross-links to websites that deliver complementary content can enhance your ranking points on various search engines.

BIBLIOGRAPHY

2009 REALTOR® Technology Survey. Website Reference: <http://www.realtor.org/library/library/fg006>.

Aalberts, Robert, Townsend, Anthony. "Real estate transactions, the Internet and personal jurisdiction." *Journal of Real Estate Literature.*

Bond, Michael, Seiler, Michael, Seiler, Vicky, Blake, Ben. "Uses of websites of effective real estate marketing." *Journal of Real Estate Portfolio Management.*

Choi, Robert, Graham, John. "Answering the call of the wild Web." *Journal of Property Management.*

Dermisi, Sofia. "Impact of the Internet on International Real Estate Office Markets." *Journal of Real Estate Portfolio Management.*

Google Maps. <http://maps.google.com>

Giovannotto, Vince. "Real Estate Efficiencies Soar as Technology Takes Off." *Journal of Property Management.*

Henderson, Kenneth, Cowart, Lary. "Bucking e-commerce trends: A content analysis comparing commercial real estate brokerage and residential real estate brokerage websites." *Journal of Corporate Real Estate.*

Littlefield, James, Bao, Yeqing, Cook, Don. "Internet real estate information: are home purchasers paying attention to it?" *The Journal of Consumer Marketing.*

McMahan, John. "Preface: case studies on the interface of technology and the real estate industry." *Real Estate Issues.*

Muhanna, Waled, R, James. "The impact of e-commerce on the real estate industry: Baen and Guttery revisited." *Journal of Real Estate Portfolio Management.*

Pekala, Nancy. "A 2001 Forecast: Talent, Technology to be Top Trends." *Journal of Property Management.*

Rothenberg, Pamela, Puentes King, Jacqueline. "Strategize to maximize: consider both hard and soft factors when evaluating technology investments." *Journal of Property Management.*

TSE, Raymond, Webb, James. "The effectiveness of a Web strategy for real estate brokerage." *Journal of Real Estate Literature.*

2009 National Association of REALTORS® Profile of Home Buyers and Sellers. Website reference: <http://www.realtor.org/library/library/fg006>.

Website reference: <http://www.google.com/analytics/>.

Ethics

A Brief Introduction to Business and Professional Ethics

Here is an excerpt from an actual conversation.[1]
"What are you doing?"
"Working on a paper on business ethics."
"That won't take long."

This conversation depicts a popular belief about business and professional life. Happily, the belief is wrong. Most business professionals, as most members of Canadian society, lead moral lives at home and at work. Indeed, if they did not do so our society could not be considered to have one of the best qualities of life of any in the world. Much of the reason for the belief about the immorality of business is the fact that it is only immoral actions that tend to register in the public consciousness. A hundred socially responsible decisions by corporations not to pollute the environment, even if it means a lower profit, will go unnoticed, while the corporation that pollutes will make the headlines.[2]

Perhaps it would be a different perception if business were to talk about the massive body of morally correct decisions made daily. But in business and professional life, as in the rest of life, most people operate on an intuitive level in making their moral decisions, and often make them without reflecting upon the fact that they are making them. They do not have well thought out reasons and justifications for their moral stances. If they did so, and if those articulations were regularly discussed and deepened in the workplace, then people would have to

---

[1] Dr. H.A. Bassford is President Emeritus of the University of the Fraser Valley. This article was written especially for this book.

[2] This is not only the fault of our news gatherers, but also a fact about what pricks the public's interest.

500

revise the opinion with which this paragraph started, for the many circumstances of morally proper decisions would be better known.

One major task of the ethicist is to help people move from the intuitive to the reflective level of ethical discourse. It is the goal of this paper to begin this process with respect to ethics in the profession of real estate. Before addressing that profession, however, it is necessary to make a number of more general remarks. The paper starts with consideration of some general principles of ethics, proceeds to business ethics, and then addresses some specifics of ethics in real estate.

FUNDAMENTAL ETHICAL PRINCIPLES

Throughout history innumerable scholars have considered the theoretical basis of morality, and many highly sophisticated ethical theories have been developed. Virtually every textbook on ethics or business ethics works through the most important theories. Studying them is to be recommended, but it is inappropriate to try to review the many different and often conflicting theoretical viewpoints in a short paper. What I shall do instead is note some of the basic principles upon which most theorists agree, and that can form a useful basis for resolving many of the ethical dilemmas that arise in practical professional settings.

WHY BE MORAL?

I shall start by asking what role morality plays in our society. Why, that is, is it important to have ethical practices in our social institutions? The reason can be found by conducting a small thought experiment, and asking what a society would be like that did not have a moral order. The philosopher Thomas Hobbes asked this question in the seventeenth century. His description of a society without law and morality is as striking now as it was then.

> In such condition there is no place for industry, because the fruit thereof is uncertain: and consequently no culture of the earth; no navigation nor use of the commodities that may be imported by sea; no commodious building; ... no knowledge of the face of the earth; no account of time; no arts; no letters; no society; and, which is worst of all, continual fear and danger of violent death; and the life of man solitary, poor, nasty, brutish, and short.[3]

---

[3] Thomas Hobbes, Leviathan (Library of Liberal Arts, 1958), p. 107. The Leviathan is a classic of political philosophy. It was written at a time when modern commercial communities were developing, and represents the first attempt to state the moral and social bounds within which successful commerce must operate.

Morality is the bond that cements a civilized society. If we did not respect the life or property of others, did not keep our word, told the truth only when we felt like it, etc., our society would rapidly become all too much like that described by Hobbes. Our lives would be the polar opposite of that for which we strive. Rather than living a comfortable life, with friends, family and a decent community, we would lead a life of fear. Rather than being able to develop our human potential, we would struggle to survive at all. Aristotle said that the unexamined life is not worth living. An ethicist's parallel would be to say that an unethical society is not worth living in — a conclusion with which most refugees to Canada would agree.

HUMAN DIGNITY

Morality, then, is an essential ingredient in a society's being able to support a decent quality of life for its members. This fact is a key to understanding the foundation principle of our ethical system. Canada is a liberal-democratic society. That is to say, our citizens are considered to be of equal moral worth and valued as individuals. It is a society that values freedom, and as such believes that people will be happy and have self-respect only when they have control over their own lives. It believes that people must be allowed to have their own life goals, and to achieve them as they want, subject only to their not interfering with others in their own development. In short, the basic moral stance of our society is that people must be treated with dignity and respect.

This basic tenet of a liberal-democratic society was well expressed by the great philosopher Immanuel Kant in the eighteenth century, when he stated his "categorical imperative" as a basic moral norm: "Act so that you treat humanity, whether in your own person or in that of another, always as an end, and never as a means only."[4] The point is that people have inherent or intrinsic value and, as such, have dignity. We violate their human dignity when we treat them only as means to our own ends: when we, that is, treat them as things rather than as persons.

The paradigm case of treating someone only as a means, and thus according them no dignity whatsoever, is slavery. The slave is thought of as a living machine, an implement, a thing that has value only for what it can produce for the slave-owner. And it is because of this complete objectification of the slave and complete

---

[4] Immanuel Kant, Founations of the Metaphysics of Morals, trans. Lewis White Beck (New York, The Liberal Arts Press, 1959), p. 39.

denial of the slave's personhood that slavery has come to be so universally condemned.

The principle of human dignity is equally applicable in less extreme situations. Think of the mine owner who ignores the safety of mine workers. They are being treated merely as means, and their humanity is not being valued. Think of the husband who thinks only of his own pleasure in his sexual relations with his wife. Think of the salesperson who thinks of customers as "marks" or "pigeons." Or think of the customer who couldn't care less about the obvious illness of the salesperson. In all of these cases the moral fabric of society is being undermined because of inattention to or lack of care about basic human dignity.

AUTONOMY

Respect for others entails allowing them to choose how they wish to live. Liberal-democratic societies, such as Canada, tend to value the individual, and to think that the individual is the one who should be most responsible for the conduct of his or her life. The individual, that is, should have free choice, should be autonomous. Autonomy is important not only because according it to others is required if we are to treat them with dignity, but also because it is a crucial part of an individual having self-respect. If one is not allowed to construct one's own life plan, to articulate one's own goals and wants and to work towards them, one will have little self-respect, and will be a lesser being because of it.

Autonomy is not simply a matter of being allowed to choose. It is also a matter of having an informed choice, which means genuinely knowing what the alternatives are. A good example of informed choice is found in the medical doctrine of informed consent. Physicians are required to tell patients enough about the possible treatments so that they will know what the benefits and risks of each will be before deciding whether to undergo the recommended treatment or not. If patients agree to a procedure without having been offered the information, then they are not considered to have given an informed consent, and the physician is legally liable. As shall be seen later in this paper, the doctrine of informed choice becomes an important one for considering the ethical principles of the real estate professional.

HARM

Autonomy is, of course, not without ethical limits. Just as the principle of respect for others demands that we allow others autonomy, so too it limits autonomy. If I choose to act in a way that limits your freedom to act in the same way, then I am treating you as a means rather than an end, and so violating the limits of my legitimate claim to autonomy. As is often said, freedom carries with it responsibility. Much of the work of applied ethics, and indeed of legal and social policy, involves exploring the limits on personal autonomy that are entailed by the ethical foundations of the principle of autonomy.

For purposes of this paper, there is one clear principle that stands on its own, and does serve to limit our choice of action with respect to others. This is the historically basic principle of medical ethics, non nocere, Do not harm. To a large extent understanding and applying this principle is simple. Our physical integrity is a necessity for our being in the world. If someone kills or maims us, or threatens us with physical harm, then we cannot lead a civilized life. Much of the criminal law has been developed to provide a social enforcement of this moral principle.

It is important to realize that the principle enjoins us from more than bodily harm. If you and I enter into a contract for services, and I do not deliver the promised service, then you will suffer a degree of harm. Financial loss, loss to reputation, psychological pain are all forms of harm, and are all to be considered when applying this basic ethical principle. Breaking promises and lying are often wrong because of the harm they do to others. Because of these aspects of the concept, the harm principle can become very relevant in ordinary commercial situations.

JUSTICE AND UTILITY

Two other general principles of social interaction should be articulated: justice and utility. Our society is based upon the notion that every individual is of equal moral worth, and so we strive for a fair and just society. The principle of justice requires that people be treated equally in the absence of morally relevant differences. Much of the political agitation of modern society has been to convince citizens that the differences that had previously been thought relevant for different treatment are not relevant, and that differential treatment in those cases is discrimination. In order to achieve social justice, much discriminatory activity has now been made the subject of law, and specific grounds of discrimination are ruled out. For example, the Ontario Human Rights Code states in part: Every person has a right to equal treatment with respect to services, goods and facilities, without discrimination because of race, ancestry, place of origin, colour, ethnic origin, citizenship, creed, sex, sexual orientation, age, marital status, family status, or handicap.[5]

This statute does not, of course, exhaust the grounds of immoral discrimination against certain of our customers or clients. Refusing service because of clients' eye or hair colour is clearly wrong, but it, like much else, is not often enough used as an actual ground of discrimination to take the large step of making it an illegal ground of discrimination. The principle of equality should always be an active part of our moral consciousness.

So should the principle of utility, which comes into play when we have to decide among several moral actions, each of which seems acceptable when considered by itself. This principle, which is the basic notion of the ethical theory called Utilitarianism, can be stated as: So act as to produce the greatest good for the greatest number.[6] Basically, this is a cost/benefit principle for moral decision making, and it is one that all of us use regularly, both in private and public life. The following sort of reasoning should be familiar: "If I stay home and watch the ball-game, I'll really enjoy it, but the kids will be miserable. But if I take the kids skating they will all have a great time, and I won't have that bad a time. So I had better take them skating." We add up the benefits and costs in happiness (and other goods) for two courses of action, and take the one with the most benefits and least costs.

In using the utility principle, one must be mindful of its limits, just as is the case for the autonomy principle. Sometimes one can do considerable good, but only at the expense of causing harm to or violating the basic dignity of some people. In such cases the principle of utility comes into conflict with those of dignity or harm, and should therefore not be applied. Happily, our most general moral principles do not usually come into conflict, so in deciding how to act we need only check to see whether and how each applies. But since they sometimes do, it is worthwhile considering each of them before we jump to the wrong conclusion.

---

[5] Human Rights Code, R.S.O. 1990, c.H.19, as amended (Ministry of the Attorney General, Government of Ontario, 1990).

[6] The Utilitarians were a group of English intellectuals and social reformers in the eighteenth and nineteenth centuries. Their most prominent members were Jeremy Bentham and John Stuart Mill. Many improvements in social planning come from them.

BUSINESS ETHICS

Let us now move one step closer to the profession of real estate and consider briefly the concept of business and professional ethics. The question is which ethical norms are appropriate in any given business or professional setting. Note that I do not ask whether any ethical norms are appropriate. I have two reasons for not doing so.

First, contemporary business does not exist in and for itself. Private enterprise is the means that our society has chosen for organizing the manufacture and distribution of material commodities. Other societies throughout history have chosen differently. We have chosen capitalism partly because it seems to be the economic organization that best reflects our belief in the individual and partly because we believe it is the economic organization that can best meet our citizenry's material needs. If the enterprise as a whole, or a part of it, comes to act in ways that do not reflect its social purposes, then it will be negatively evaluated and changed.

Second, most of us spend a large part of our lives working in the business or professional setting. That setting is full of personal interactions that must follow some social norms, lest that setting be reduced to a barbarous and inhumane one. As well, the mere fact that we spend so much time in the work setting means that that setting influences our character, that it has an effect on how we live the rest of our lives. Consideration of the norms of business practice, accordingly, must involve how those norms relate to, reflect, and support our basic ethical norms.

ROLE NORMS

The appropriate question is whether there are any special norms that arise because of the social role of business. Are there any general moral considerations that do not apply, or any special ones particularly appropriate for the business setting? Two examples will explain my questions. On the one side, killing, except in self-defence, is the most odious of moral offences. But the soldier and the hangman are excused from the duty not to kill, at least with respect to certain circumstances, because of their particular social role. On the other side, doctors are required, because of their special skills and social role, to offer help to the ill, whether or not they want to do so. They have obligations: that is, that go beyond those of the ordinary citizen. My question is whether either analysis applies to business.

The well-known economist Milton Friedman once wrote a controversial essay entitled, "The Social Responsibility of Business Is to

Increase Its Profits."[7] The title itself provides a suggestion for a special norm for business: Seek profit. The view goes back to Adam Smith, who in the eighteenth century proposed in *The Wealth of Nations* that if everyone in business followed their own self-interest and sought profit first and foremost, the ensuing competition in the marketplace would lead to the lowest price and, thus, the most value for society as a whole. Without questioning the value of competition, and the importance of the profit principle for our social system, the question I wish to ask is whether this principle can be substituted for attending to and following general moral principles in the business world.

The clear answer is that it cannot. The reason is that there are too many situations in which profit could be increased by immoral activity. The murder of a competitor or threats to the well-being of the competitor's family can lead to making profitable acquisitions or contracts. The dumping of industrial waste into a river system can save processing dollars and increase profit, even though it leads to severe health problems for those living down-river. If these sorts of cases became the rule, then commercial life would resemble the world of gang-land movies, and our society would begin to look like Hobbes' state of nature, wherein there is the war of all with all. The pursuit of profit independent of our basic ethical principles does not lead to the sort of world those principles seek to secure. Accordingly, while the social role of business is to provide goods and services while seeking profit, that profit must be sought with due regard for general ethical principles.

This does not make the pursuit of profit amoral. The profit motive is the means by which our society's economic engine is made to work, and so it is the means by which our economic system provides crucial human needs. By seeking to make profits, business people fulfill their particular social role. Within the business setting, profit seeking is a morally good activity, and does provide a special role norm for business. It is, however, a subsidiary principle to the general moral principles previously discussed. Perhaps it would better be expressed as: Seek profit, but only so long as it does not interfere with higher moral principles.

---

[7] Milton Friedman, "The Social Responsibility of Business Is to Increase Its Profits," The New York Times Magazine, September 13, 1970.

LAW AND MORALITY

It could be argued, however, that I have ignored a simpler, but still sufficient, principle: Seek profit, within legal parameters. I argued above that if the business enterprise stops reflecting its social purpose it will be changed. What is wrong with saying that when the search for profit comes, in certain situations, to contravene more basic moral principles, society will enact legislation to bring business practices back into line with ethical practices? Then the businessperson can get on with business and not waste time thinking about morality all the time.

This view would make business lives more difficult, not simpler. Consider what would happen if the moral interactions of our private lives were regulated only by reference to the law. In a word, they would become unbearable. The big brother of the state would be constantly looking over our shoulders. And we would need even more lawyers! We normally want to minimize, not maximize, state interference in our life, so we legislate only with respect to the grossest and most intolerable immorality. For the great majority of moral standards we rely upon social pressures, education, good upbringing, and dialogue with family, friends, and community members. Self-regulation makes for a much happier and more satisfying private life. The same should be the case for our business and professional lives.

In addition, it should be noted that the law is a crude instrument. Laws must be written for general situations. Any fine discriminations can be made only when the whole weight of its enforcement mechanism is brought to bear: police, regulatory agencies, the judicial system. This is very costly, to the society and to the person, or business, that is the object of enforcement. On the other hand, moral dialogue allows for consideration of particular cases, and allows individuals to work out problems as they arise. Nor is it so difficult to know one's way around ethical decision making. We all do so in our private lives. We can do so as well in our business lives, so long as we keep the avenues open to always have the moral point of view considered.

Further, it takes much time and debate to legislate, and this will not be done until matters are very serious indeed. If business always waits to evaluate its activity until legislation is drafted, it will not be seen as socially responsible, and public confidence in it will be undermined. For all these reasons, the "profit + law" norm should be rejected as the way of proceeding in business, and attention to ethical principle should be an everyday part of the business of doing business.

REAL ESTATE ETHICS

The specific application of ethical principles will, however, differ from profession to profession. Every profession plays a unique social role, which will be significant in how ethical considerations will come into play in the life of the profession, and which will determine any special moral obligations or aspirations that profession has. When approaching any profession, one should ask why the profession exists, how it should further society's welfare, how its practice actually works. From this investigation comes a statement of the ideals, role norms and particular standards of practice that should govern the moral life of the profession.

In modern society most professional bodies have spent considerable time with these sorts of reflections, and have embodied them in codes of ethics, or standards of practice. As an ethicist I have found that it helps my understanding of a profession to read these codes carefully and reflectively, to consider which general moral rules each standard embodies, and to decide why it is morally important for the profession to have that particular standard.[8] In the following I shall look at a few of the principles that have been considered important by the North American real estate profession. I shall look at the Code of Ethics and Standards of Practice that have been developed in the United States by the National Association of Realtors, and *The REALTOR Code,* developed by the Canadian Real Estate Association. Within the space limitations of this paper, I cannot look at all the provisions of the codes, so shall concentrate upon those that give a general moral perspective. But I would urge the reader to think through and analyze each of the principles articulated.

STEWARDSHIP

The preambles to both *Codes* start with the same two sentences.

Under all is the land. Upon its wise utilization and widely allocated ownership depend the survival and growth of free institutions and of our civilization.

---

[8] This study should be critical as well as investigative. It is important to examine codes of ethics to see how they can be improved: in clarity, in completeness, and in ease of application. It is a process that time does not allow here. A good start on a critical analysis for the Code of Ethics of the National Association of Realtors in the United States can be found in Chapter 10 or Jerry Cederblom and Charles J. Dougherty, Ethics at Work (Wadsworth Publishing Company, Belmont, California, 1990).

They both go on to state what this means for the Realtor's obligations. I shall quote from the Canadian *Code.*

> Through the REALTOR, the land resource of the nation reaches its highest
> use and private land ownership its widest distribution. The REALTOR is in-
> strumental in moulding the form of his or her community and the living and
> working conditions of its people.
>
> Such functions impose grave social responsibilities which REALTORS can
> meet only by diligent preparation, and considering it a civic duty to dedicate
> themselves to the fulfillment of a REALTOR'S obligations to society.

Now, this may be taken cynically as high sounding puffery used to
promote the image of the profession. Or, as I would prefer, it may
be taken as an attempt to state the basically important social role of
the real estate profession. The distribution and use of land, and the
buildings upon it in which we live and work, are of crucial importance to the quality of our lives. We have turned a significant part
of the development and exchange of land and building over to the
real estate profession. We have made them stewards of our domin-
ions.

In their stewardship, real estate professionals have obligations to
society in general with respect to their work, and not merely to their
clients or to themselves.[9] They should consider the public interest
in their business decisions, which makes their stewardship of the land
a limiting principle in those decisions. They also should participate
in public discussion about development, and should use their special
knowledge to help inform public thinking about these matters. These
public concerns, it should be noted, are not usually inconsistent with self interest, for either the individual Realtor or the profession. An active and informed participation in public life and a
demonstrated concern for the public interest can only raise the public's evaluation of the profession and confidence in the individual
professional.

FIDUCIARY OBLIGATIONS

The greatest percentage of the codes, as is appropriate, deals with
the moral relations of Realtors and their clients. Both codes empha-
size the primary duty of the Realtor to the client (though both recognize that the general ethical principle of fairness must be applied
with respect to other parties): In accepting employment as an agent,
the REALTOR pledges himself to protect and promote the interests

---

[9] The same point is made in the REALTOR CODE OF ETHICS: "As REAL-
TORS, we accept a personal obligation to the public and to our profession."

of the client. This obligation of absolute fidelity to the client's interests is primary, but it does not relieve the REALTOR of the obligation to treat fairly all parties to the transaction (US Code, Article 7). A REALTOR shall protect and promote the interest of his or her Client (Canadian *Code,* Article 3. Primary Duty to Client).

What these articles represent is the fact that Realtors, as is the case with lawyers and physicians, have a fiduciary obligation to their clients. Realtors have special knowledge and skills, which come from their professional training and experience. For the most part clients come to Realtors to take advantage of this professional knowledge.

In accepting the service of Realtors, clients put themselves into the hands of the Realtors, and entrust themselves to the good will of the Realtors. In accepting the clients, the Realtors accept this trust relationship, which creates an obligation to use their skills on behalf of their clients. The Realtor/client relationship is thus morally very different from the ordinary buying and selling relationships of commerce.

The difference is a direct result of real estate having become a profession. Three duties are immediately derivable from the basic fiduciary duty: the duties to maintain professional competence, not to have conflicts of interest, and to tell the truth. The first duty is put as follows.

A REALTOR shall render a skilled and conscientious service, in comformaty with standards of competence which are reasonably expected in the specific real estate disciplines in which the REALTOR engages. (Canadian Code, Article 12).

In justice to those who place their interests in his care, the REALTOR should endeavour always to be informed regarding laws, proposed legislation, governmental regulations, public policies, and current market conditions in order to be in a position to advise his clients properly (American Code, Article 2).

A REALTOR is expected to provide a level of competent service in keeping with the standards of practice in those fields in which the REALTOR customarily engages (American Code, Article 11).

The reason for this professional duty is clear. The client contracts because of the professional knowledge of the Realtor. But if the Realtor does not have that knowledge, because of improper training or a failure in continuing study and education, then the very basis for the fiduciary obligation will not exist. One's obligation to education does not cease when one's training in real estate comes to an end.

The requirement not to have conflicts of interest is stated in several different articles of both codes.[10] For example the Canadian Code states (Article 8) that Realtors shall "disclose to their Clients any financial or other benefit the REALTOR ... may receive as a result of recommending real estate products or services to that party." And Article 11 makes it clear that realtors must disclose any financial interest they or any of their family members have in a property being bought or sold.

What is being recognized here is the human fact that a fiduciary obligation is more difficult to discharge if one has other interests conflicting with it. If my interest, my family's interest or my partner's interest is involved, then it is more difficult to attend exclusively to my client's interest.

Of course, the difficulties caused by potential conflicts of interest do not excuse Realtors from discharging their fiduciary duty when they occur. Some professional and organizational codes enjoin their members against ever being in a conflict of interest situation, and to withdraw from any situations where conflicts may appear, so that they do not have to face the moral struggle that can occur. The real estate profession does not do this. But, to ensure that clients make informed decisions, Realtors are required to disclose possible conflicts.[11] The moral standard thus becomes double barrelled, and quite a high one: to disclose possible conflicts of interest, and not to allow them to interfere with client interest when they do occur.

The idea of informed choice also underlies the duties of truthtelling or full disclosure within the codes of ethics. The duties are stated as follows.

> A REALTOR shall fully disclose to his or her Client at the earliest opportunity any information that relates to the transaction (Canadian Code, Article 3.1)

The REALTOR shall avoid exaggeration, misrepresentation, or concealment of pertinent facts relating to the property or the transaction (American Code, Article 9).

It is of course obvious that a relationship of trust requires truthtelling, but there is something more to the principle. While the Realtor is obligated to the interests of the client, and must make decisions in the client's best interest, the ultimate decision to buy or

---

[10] See also articles 8, 12, and 13 of the American Code.

[11] In effect, the general ethical principle of respect for personal autonomy is being applied within the fiduciary relationship.

build will be made by the client. This decision will not be an informed one, and thus not an autonomous one, unless the Realtor's knowledge is made available to the client. What we see here is how the general ethical principle of autonomy, as part of the basic duty of respecting human dignity, is to be given a particular application in the practice of the profession of real estate.

LOYALTY

In looking at ethical practice in real estate, I have looked briefly at the relationship of the Realtor to society (stewardship), and of the Realtor to clients (fiduciary obligation). One other ethical dimension should be mentioned: the relationship of the real estate professional to other real estate professionals. The basic moral relationship is one of loyalty and fairness, both to the profession and to other professionals.

These relationships are stated in several articles of the codes.[12] Two quotes will give sufficient information for general comment:

> In the best interests of society, of his associates, and his own business, the REALTOR should willingly share with other REALTORS the lessons of his experience and study for the benefit of the public, and should be loyal to the Board of REALTORS of his community and active in its work (US Code, Article 5).

> The REALTOR should not comment in a derogatory manner as to the capacity, integrity, and competence of any other Registrant (Canadian Code, Article 19.1)

A cynical reading of the Code's emphasis upon professional loyalty would suggest that its function is to maintain a higher market share for members of the associations. I think there are deeper and ethically important reasons. Professional relationships among Realtors are varieties of normal human relationships, and they need to be conducted within the same bounds of respect for the dignity of others as do other human relationships. Competition among real estate professionals for clients is a part of our economic system, but it should not be the competition of warring armies, or of street gangs. That sort of dog eat dog competition smacks too much of the Hobbesian state of war quote with which this paper started. The relevant sections of the codes serve to remind us that general ethical considerations must be part of day to day professional life. Further,

---

[12] See articles 3, 5, 6, 14, 21 of the US Code, and articles 19, 20 and 25 of the Canadian Code.

the personal standards demanded for the fiduciary relationship with clients should not be in sharp contrast to those of professional interaction.

Moral character is difficult enough to maintain, even if we are to act with the same principles in the various aspects of our lives. It becomes even more difficult when the different aspects have very conflicting behavioural standards.

The role of the professional association is also important. The first professional association was that of the Hippocratic school of physicians. The Hippocratic oath, which in revised form is still taken by most graduating physicians, promises potential patients that the physician is competently trained and will look after patients' health interests. The physician's professional body, which is today the College of Physicians and Surgeons, licenses physicians and supervises their practice to be sure it remains competent and ethical. An important part of the regulation is that physicians have been trained to identify with the profession and are loyal to it: that they follow the profession's dictates because they value being a member of the profession, and not merely because they fear its sanctions.

The self-regulatory function has become an integral part of most professions. When it succeeds good service is provided to the public, and it is provided without the heavy hand of state authority. The calls to loyalty to and participation in a professional association are part of the process by which self-regulation can succeed. They play an important part in having any profession fulfill its social role. As in any professional code, such principles are properly part of the codes of ethics of the real estate profession.

Having the relevant principles in a code of ethics is, of course, not enough. Professional groups must understand the relation of their codes to general social morality, and must have a critical approach to their codes, so they can revise and develop them as necessary. They must see to it that their members use them, by providing education and, when necessary, enforcement mechanisms. And they must show the public that they and their members are behaving in ethically responsible ways. In short, theoretical and practical ethical dialogue must become a part of the day-to-day life of the real estate association, and of the real estate professional. This is a major, but worthwhile, task.

APPENDIX

Making Ethical Decisions

The present essay has been mainly a theoretical one, listing principles of general ethics, business ethics, and real estate ethics, and explaining their basis. In this appendix, I wish to present a schema that individuals can use when faced with moral uncertainty, and that will help to put the theoretical considerations to more practical work.

The process can be time consuming, but one gets faster with practice, and using the schema does give one a well articulated and non-arbitrary position. I propose a five step process, which can be used by an individual or by a group.

1. State the Case

When one encounters a moral problem, it is usually embedded in a more general situation. It is worthwhile stepping back from the problem and becoming clear about the parameters. A distinction should be made between the factual considerations and the ethical considerations. Try first stating the relevant facts of the case, including those about which there may be disagreement. It is surprising how often apparent moral disagreement turns out to be disagreement over how to describe the case. And often this disagreement can be resolved by discussing the differing descriptions. Then state as clearly as you can what the ethical problem or disagreement is. Finally, consider what possible decisions are available to you. If you have time, write this down. Many cases are complex, and it is easy to lose track of relevant considerations. At this point you will have a clear understanding of the problem, and can proceed to making the best decision.

2. Check Your Intuitions

Most of our day-to-day ethical decisions are unreflective, and are based upon our moral feelings. They are based upon our training and moral character, and upon our general experience. Professional experience is a necessary part of a successful professional life, and should not be ignored. Accordingly, you should ask what your "gut" feeling is in the present case.

Once the intuition is stated, ask yourself why you feel this way. What other situations have you experienced that were similar? What ethical decisions were taken in them, and how did they work out? What parts of those cases (which are the experiences that form your intuitions) apply to the present case?

3. Consider Ethical Principles

Check through the general ethical principles, and see how they apply to the present case. This check should include considering the relevant professional codes of ethics. Sometimes the check of principles can give an immediate answer; sometimes it gives useful directions for more detailed reasoning.

4. Engage in Dialogue

The first three steps will usually incline you towards one or two resolutions. Before making a firm decision, talk your way through its pros and cons. It is always useful to talk to others, for doing so can give you perspectives you may miss on your own. And if it is a dialogue with others actually involved in the particular case, the discussion can help to produce a meeting of the minds — or an understanding that there may have to be an agreement to disagree.

But even if you are deciding by yourself, have a dialogue with yourself. Put down your proposed solution, then state the reasons you have for supporting it. Ask what might be said against it. Look at other possible solutions, and state their pros and cons.

At the end of this process, you will usually be able to take a decision and to act on it. Often, this will be with moral certainty. Sometimes it will be with uncertainty, and be based on probabilities. This is not always bad. In our complex, changing world, and with the time deadlines often faced, probabilities are the most we can expect. In either case, the decision will be an informed one. It will be based upon a careful consideration of principle and experience, and it will allow one to act with a rationally justified confidence.

5. Reflect on Policies and Practices

This last step is not necessary before acting, but it is useful later on. Moral dilemmas are difficult. Often, although the decision we take is the morally best one in the circumstances, we would like not to have had to decide between the alternatives in the first place. If one later reflects upon a situation, and asks what could have been done differently to keep the problem from arising, one can come up with practices that can succeed in doing this.

The solution of moral dilemmas is also time consuming. Reflecting back upon a solution to a particular case, one can sometimes state a principle or policy that can apply to many similar cases when they occur, and that can be used to make timely and proper decisions. This sort of reflection is particularly appropriate for setting policies in an organizational setting. It also is why regular case reviews are important for professional bodies.

The Ethical Obligations of Real Estate Practitioners

MARK S. SCHWARTZ

Are there any ethical concerns with the real estate industry? What sorts of ethical obligations do real estate practitioners have? Should real estate agents ever have to behave in a manner that goes beyond the law and the expectations as set out in their professional codes of ethics? In order to initially reflect on such questions, consider the following two possible scenarios. First, imagine you are trying to purchase a home, and the first home you like is being sold by a 'dual agent'. This means that the agent is representing both the purchaser and the vendor at the same time, and both you and the vendor are aware of this fact. The house looks great, and you instruct the agent to put in an offer on a Wednesday. You are then told by the dual agent that the vendor is not going to look at any offers at that point in time, and that you will have to wait until Monday for your offer to be presented. When Monday finally arrives, you are informed by your dual agent that unfortunately two other potential purchasers have also put in bids, so that you are now effectively in a bidding war, and you will have to substantially increase the offer to have any chance of success. Not being in a financial position to do so, you lose the opportunity to purchase the house. Did the agent fulfill her ethical obligations?

Or how about the following scenario? The very next time you try to purchase a home, you hire your own exclusive agent, hoping that this time things will work out better. After finding another suitable house, you enter into an agreement of purchase and sale on condition with the vendor that the house will pass a home inspection, which will need to take place within three days of signing the purchase and sale agreement. You clearly have the right in the agreement to select your own home inspector. The next day you receive a phone call directly from the vendor's agent, indicating that he will make things easier for you by arranging for a very affordable and experienced inspector to look over the home for you. You are somewhat surprised by this, and when you indicate that you would prefer to make arrangements for your own inspector, the other agent begins to put pressure on you. He says: "Look, I've been selling homes for years, you can trust me." When you ask your own agent about this, you are told that you really should just accept what the other agent has proposed, since all home inspectors are essentially the same. Knowing that this was the most significant purchase in your life on behalf of your family, you indicate that you will nevertheless find your own suitable inspector. In the end, your inspector discovers many significant problems, including serious electrical issues that could have led eventually to a home fire, along with a massive crack in the foundation of the house that was conveniently hidden behind a large couch in the basement. In the end, the vendor refuses to drop the purchase price to reflect the cost of repairing these defects, and you don't buy the house. While all works out for the best, you do remain concerned for the next potential purchaser, and wonder if the vendor's agent and even your own agent acted appropriately.

While the above two situations are fictional, they nonetheless raise important potential ethical concerns for those involved in purchasing and selling real estate property. In order to examine these sorts of issues, the following chapter will briefly explore the ethical obligations of real estate practitioners as follows. First, a brief overview of some of the major ethical issues facing the real estate industry will be identified. Second, the question whether real estate agents should be considered professionals will be considered. Third, an ethical framework for potentially resolving ethical dilemmas will be provided, followed by a series of ethical real estate dilemmas that one might face. The chapter will conclude with a discussion of the importance of maintaining the ethical reputation of the entire real estate industry.

ETHICAL ISSUES IN THE REAL ESTATE INDUSTRY

When it comes to the real estate industry, it does not take too long to unearth a wide variety of ethical issues. From the moment one decides to buy a home or condominium, or rent an apartment, or try to change the zoning of land, or to obtain a mortgage, many ethical issues can arise. Unfortunately, it seems that academic discussions regarding real estate ethics have been minimal.[1] Most of the ethical is-

---

[1] As some examples of academic discussion regarding real estate ethics, however, see Brinkmann, 2000, 2009; Clarke, 1995; Clarke et al., 1994; Izzo, 2000; Izzo et al., 2006; Larsen et al., 2007; Long 1998; Miller, 1999; Okoruwa and Thompson, 1999; and Roulac, 1999.

sues might be placed into three categories. The first category relates to real estate transactions involving the real estate lawyers or agents. These issues tend to revolve around conflict of interest situations, sometimes leading to the misuse of funds. The second category relates to land development and related environmental concerns. For example, this might involve the use of bribery, kickbacks, or gifts and entertainment, leading to zoning approvals for developers. The third category relates to real estate financing (e.g., mortgages). For example, mortgage fraud is a serious problem for many banks, while mortgage lenders themselves can be engaged in irresponsible lending through sub-prime mortgages. While much can be written about each of these issues, the rest of the chapter will instead focus on the ethical obligations of real estate agents, which anyone who eventually purchases or rents property will no doubt experience.

ARE REAL ESTATE AGENTS PROFESSIONALS?

When it comes to deciding who is a professional, there are several potential criteria. For example, professionals should have a self-regulating body, which is involved in the accreditation of their professionals. There should be specialized training and an exam process that leads to certification as part of the process of accreditation and/or licensing. The self-regulatory body should possess the ability to discipline their members if necessary, and discharge them from the profession. All of these factors determine when a group can be distinguished as a 'profession'. But of all the potential criteria, there is one that stands out: Professionals must abide by a professional code of ethics, which goes beyond legal requirements. So should real estate agents be considered to be professionals?

Based on the above criteria, the answer appears to be yes. In terms of professional obligations, real estate agents are required to be licenced, and abide by several pieces of legislation, as well as professional codes of conduct.[2] Provincial bodies, such as the Real Estate Council of Ontario (RECO), are responsible as non-profit organizations to promote ongoing education, and to address concerns and complaints about the conduct of brokers or agents, as well as take "appropriate action to protect the public interest."[3] In the case of RECO, the complaint process can lead to several possible conse-

---

[2] For example, the "Realtor Code of Ethics and Standards of Business Practices," from The Canadian Real Estate Association; as well as the "Code of Ethics," Ontario Regulation 580/05, *Real Estate and Business Brokers Act,* 2002.
[3] See RECO "What We Do: Protecting the Public Interest" at: http://www.reco.on.ca/PubResources.aspx?section=MediaRoomWhoWhat [accessed 18 March 2011].

quences for agents including mediation, a written warning, a requirement to take further educational courses, a fine of up to $25,000,
temporary or immediate suspension of a registration, the freezing of
trust accounts, or further prosecution in the Ontario Court of Justice
system leading to fines of up to $50,000 and/or prison terms of up
to two years. The general requirements of the CREA Code of Ethics
can be found in Appendix A. (In the U.S., real estate agents are required to abide by the "Code of Ethics and Standards of Practice of
the National Association of Realtors".)

A FRAMEWORK FOR ETHICAL DECISION-MAKING[4]

When it comes to a real estate agent's potential ethical responsibilities, one can draw from a vast literature on moral theory, in some
cases thousands of years old, to establish or determine appropriate
ethical or moral standards. In my opinion, when it comes to professionals, and in particular real estate professionals, the following are
the key moral standards to take into account: (1) Trustworthiness
(i.e., Honesty; Integrity; Promise-Keeping; Loyalty); (2) Responsibility; (3) Caring; (4) Citizenship; (5) Kantianism (i.e., Respect); and
(6) Justice/Fairness.[5]

These initial moral standards are really a collection of core ethical values. These values have been determined to be universal in nature as they exist in one form or another throughout the world
among different nationalities, religions, and even corporate codes of
ethics.[6] Some have referred to this moral standard as "common morality" whereby basic ethical values are understood and accepted to
be applicable to everyone.[7] On this basis alone they are considered
to be important to abide by. One could also argue that in some respects, this moral standard is closest to Aristotle's virtue ethics, al-

---

[4] This part of the paper is based on the chapter "The Nuts and Bolts of Ethical Responsibility" in M.S. Schwartz, Corporate Social Responsibility: An Ethical Approach
Peterborough, Ont., Broadview Press (2011), pp. 29–49.

[5] Several of these moral standards are specifically referred to by the Real Estate
Council of Ontario (RECO) when it states: "The Real Estate Council of Ontario is
dedicated to organizational behavior characterized by: Integrity (Be truthful and trustworthy); Accountability (Administer the Act competently in accordance with the law);
Fairness (Act impartially and equitably); Respect (Treat all with courtesy)." See: http://
www.reco.on.ca/AboutReco.aspx?section=Values [accessed on 18 March 2011].

[6] See Schwartz, M.S. 2005. "Universal Codes of Ethics," *Journal of Business Ethics*,
59(1): 27–44 as well as Josephson, M. 1996. Making Ethical Decisions (4th ed.) (Ma-
rina del Rey, CA, Josephson Institute of Ethics).

[7] See: Beauchamp, T.L., Bowie, N.E., and Arnold, D.G. 2009, *Ethical Theory and
Business* (8th ed.), Upper Saddle River, N.J.: Pearson-Prentice Hall, at pp. 35–38.

though the virtues that he suggests are somewhat different than those proposed below (e.g., goodness, excellence, reasoning, and intelligence).[8]

The moral standards that are sometimes used to (unfortunately) rationalize unethical behaviour by professionals (along with business firms) tend to include: (7) Relativism; (8) Ethical Egoism; and (9) Utilitarianism. The following will now discuss each of these moral standards.

(1) *Trustworthiness*: The initial core value is trustworthiness. There are a number of other values that must be exhibited before a real estate professional or a firm would be considered trustworthy: honesty; integrity; promise-keeping; loyalty; and transparency.

The first component of trustworthiness is honesty; real estate professionals must be honest with their stakeholders. For example, when an agent suggests the proper home sale price for the vendors, and the vendors are not in a rush to sell their home, the sale price should be reasonable and not set below the market rate just in order to get a quick sale.

The second component of trustworthiness is integrity. While some have equated integrity with ethics (i.e., you act with integrity therefore you are ethical), this would not be accurate. The definition of integrity literally means 'wholeness' or 'being complete', which is achieved by acting consistently according to one's (or the firm's) stated values or principles. In other words, one sticks to their principles, or walks the talk, even when there are pressures (such as financial pressures) to do otherwise. When firms have a mission, credo, or code of ethics, do they act accordingly and thus with integrity? When real estate agents try to set themselves apart as being more 'ethical' than the others, they must live up to such claims. On this basis, integrity is a key component of trustworthiness.

A third component is promise-keeping, which includes abiding by contractual obligations even when one might be better off financially to break the contract. Promise-keeping also doesn't just mean keep your promises, but don't make promises you may not be able to keep. For example, when it comes to confidentiality in business, when someone says, "I want to tell you something confidentially, can

---

[8] Aristotle also suggested that through training, the virtuous activity (i.e., activity based on the virtues or values) can become habitual, and eventually one will be considered to have moral character (Aristotle believed that the moral character of the agent is more important than the morality of the act itself). See: Bragues, G. 2006. "Seek the Good Life, Not Money: The Aristotelian Approach to Business Ethics," *Journal of Business Ethics* 67 341–357.

you keep it a secret?", the response really should be, "It depends". For example, what if the information could lead to the direct harm of others if not disclosed? Confidentiality is a cornerstone within the realm of the professional-client relationship, not only for lawyers, doctors, and accountants, but real estate agents as well. If the vendor has told the real estate agent what the actual lowest sale price is, can this be disclosed to prospective purchasers in order to secure the sale? Clearly not, if trustworthiness is to be maintained.

Loyalty is also part of trustworthiness, in other words, one must act in the best interests of one's client and the real estate agent profession, rather than one's firm, managers or even one's family. Some might argue that loyalty to one's client (e.g., fiduciary duty to one's principal) is the ethical cornerstone of being considered a professional. The main difficulty with loyalty, however, is when there is a conflict. For example if one must decide between the interests of one's firm and one's family, which should take precedence? If one knows that making a sale and earning the commission is critical to remaining with one's firm or putting food on the table, will this potentially lead to ethical corners being cut? Finally, transparency is also important. In order for a firm to be considered transparent, sufficient relevant information must be disclosed on a timely basis for interested stakeholders to properly judge the actions of the real estate agent or one's firm.

(2) *Responsibility*: The second core value is responsibility, or what is often referred to as accountability. This is not just a question of an individual doing what they are supposed to do, but being accountable for one's actions. Responsibility is about acknowledging when one has made a mistake, or has been at fault. Often, as individuals we tend not to admit fault, even when we clearly realize that we are at fault. For business firms, this can often be the case due to pressures from the firm's legal department to act defensively, i.e., once the firm admits fault, the lawsuits commence. This can also happen on an individual professional basis, as any acknowledgment of mistakes can lead to a lawsuit for professional negligence. While this may be true, there may also be cases whereby firms or professionals ultimately benefit financially more by immediately admitting fault and by sincerely apologizing to those who were harmed. For many legal plaintiffs (i.e., the injured client), all they may want to hear from firms, their executives, or their professional real estate agent is that they were wrong, and that they are sorry for the harm caused. The last thing many plaintiffs want to hear is that someone else (e.g., the other agent, the other party, or the client himself or herself) is at fault. Responsibility also means that once you admit fault, you take

reasonable steps to correct the mistake so that it will not happen again in the future.

(3) *Caring*: The third core value is caring. This ethical value is about taking necessary precautions to prevent unnecessary harm in order to be considered a caring firm or professional.[9] The reason for indicating 'unnecessary' harm is that in the production of goods and services or in the sale of real estate property, there can always be some harm. For example, the production of cars means that people will be killed in car accidents, but on this basis alone we would not prohibit cars. The sale of property means that each side (vendor and purchaser) may not get exactly what they want in terms of price or other desired items. Firms and professionals can be expected however to take reasonable steps however to prevent harm from occurring, and certainly can disclose to others (e.g., through warnings) of potential risks and dangers. The last component of caring is being sensitive to others' feelings, for example avoiding making harmful comments to one's clients.

(4) *Citizenship*: The fourth core value is citizenship. As an individual citizen, one has expected obligations, including obeying the law, assisting the community, and protecting the environment. One can argue that not only firms should also have these same obligations, as citizens of society, but professionals as well. Not only are all real estate professionals obviously obligated to follow the laws of whichever jurisdiction they are operating within, but the value of 'citizenship' may also push real estate professionals to consider the impacts of their actions (e.g., real estate development) on communities and the surrounding natural environment.

(5) *Respect* (i.e., Kantianism): The next moral standard, respect, is based on one particular philosopher, and is significant enough to deserve its own representation as a distinct standard. The standard, known as 'Kantianism', is based on the work of 18th century German philosopher Immanuel Kant. For Kant, the moral worth of an action is based on the reasons or motive for acting (i.e., one's 'good will'). The motive to act should be based on one's moral duty, as opposed to inclination or self-interest. As a duty-based principle, this moral standard is referred to as a form of deontology (or non-consequentialism). The question then becomes, how does one determine one's moral duty? Kant developed a particular principle to determine moral duty, which he called the 'categorical imperative'.

---

[9] This could also be considered as a duty of 'non-maleficence'. See: Ross, W. D. 1930. *The Right and the Good.* Oxford: Clarendon Press.

While there have been numerous explanations of Kant's categorical imperative, I would suggest the following three different formulations: (i) universalizability; (ii) reversibility; and (iii) respect.

Universalizability. Kant's first formulation is that one should act only according to that maxim (i.e., rule) by which you can universalize it. He states: "Act only according to that maxim whereby you can at the same time will that it should become a universal law without contradiction."[10] The basic idea is that if the rule applied universally is self-defeating, then the act is immoral. Upon first reading however, it's not very clear what Kant means by this, or how it could ever be applied. In fact, this formulation of the categorical imperative may be one of the more difficult moral principles to understand or to apply to cases. The following will provide a more simplistic example in an attempt to demonstrate how universalizability might apply.

Consider the following: You are very late for a real estate closing with a very important client. Should you drive on the shoulder of a busy highway to get there on time? As discussed further below, an egoist approach would focus on the long-term perceived self-interest. Utilitarianism would determine the net benefits to all those affected, taking into account your own needs (e.g., not to miss an important meeting) versus the possible harm caused to others as a result. To answer this question according to universality, however, one does not consider the consequences of the action. Instead, one first needs to determine the intended purpose of the shoulder of the highway, i.e., that the shoulder exists for emergency vehicles (e.g., police, fire, ambulance) or for car breakdowns. If everyone were to drive on the shoulder, would the purpose of the shoulder become self-defeating? The answer is yes, therefore according to Kant's universalizability principle, one should not drive on the shoulder. In other words, one cannot 'will' driving on the shoulder of a highway into a universal law.

Other possible examples where Kant's universalizability can be applied include: Should I cheat on a real estate agent examination? (Ask: if every potential agent cheated on tests, would the purpose of tests, presumably to test one's knowledge relative to other potential real estate agents, become self-defeating?). Should I break my promise to my client? (Ask: if all promises were broken, would the purpose of making promises becomes self-defeating?) Can I violate my real estate profession's code of ethics? (Ask: if all codes of ethics

---

[10] Kant, I. 1964. *Groundwork of the Metaphysics of Morals*, H.J. Patron, trans. New York: Harper & Row, Publishers Inc. at p. 70.

were violated, would the purpose of the code provisions become self-defeating?) If the answer is 'yes' to any of these questions (i.e., the act cannot be universalized), then according to Kant's universalizability, one cannot engage in the action. One should try to be careful whenever applying universalizability, however, it can be quite easy to slip into considering the consequences of the action instead of the motive for the action (e.g., and end up applying egoism or utilitarianism).

Reversibility: This formulation has been referred to as directly related to universalizability. As part of universalizing the reasons for one's decision, one must also consider whether one would be willing to have others act towards them based on similar reasons. In other words, the basic question one needs to ask is, "How would I feel if I were in the other person's shoes? (e.g., discriminate, withhold information, break a promise, etc.). How would I feel if they did the same thing to me? Would I still act the same way?" Some suggest that the 'golden rule' — "Do unto others as you would have them do unto you" — is derived from this formulation of Kant's categorical imperative (although Kant clearly indicates that they are not one and the same).[11] The difficulty of applying reversibility, however, is that it is not clear whose shoes you ought to put yourself into when it comes to case analysis. Generally, the answer should be the party most directly affected. For example, if the question is, "Should I cheat my client?", you go into the client's shoes, as opposed to the employees or shareholders who may benefit from the action but are only indirectly affected.

Respect: This formulation is based on Kant believing that one should treat people as "ends" in themselves (i.e., having intrinsic worth as a free rational human being) rather than merely as a "means" to an end. In other words, one should not treat others only as a means to advance one's own or the firm's self-interest (e.g., profits), or be able to exploit, manipulate, or take advantage of others, even for the greater good. The concept of treating others with respect, i.e., one's clients, can be considered crucial to being considered a professional, and in particular, a real estate agent. Kant states: "Act in such a way that you treat humanity, whether in your own person or in the person of any other, always at the same time as an end and never

---

[11] For example, see: M.G. Velasquez, *Business Ethics: Concepts and Cases* (6th ed)., Upper Saddle River, N.J.: Pearson/Prentice Hall, at p.79. While Kant makes it clear that the golden rule is not equivalent to his categorical imperative in his *Groundwork for the Metaphysics of Morals,* some debate remains over their similarity, with some suggesting that they are one and the same.

merely as a means to an end."[12] In business, this typically refers to the prohibition against taking advantage of clients or exploiting one's employees, even if this improves one's bottom line or even the overall good of society.

Criticisms: Several criticisms have been raised against Kant, and the application of his categorical imperative. For example, there can be difficulties in trying to determine whether or not someone is being used merely as a means to an end. Second, a landlord who is a racist might come to a different conclusion regarding the universalizability of discrimination than a non-racist. Third, Kant is inflexible when it comes to certain actions like lying, stealing, or breaking promises: they can never be justified even to save a life according to Kant. In addition, one might argue that the categorical imperative is ultimately consequentialist. In other words, in determining whether or not the maxim can be applied universally, one must ultimately make reference to consequential considerations.[13]

(6) *Justice (or Fairness)*. When it comes to ethical responsibilities, another major ethical concern is whether a professional or their firm's actions can be considered just or fair. When individuals use the term 'fairness', however, they often use it in different ways, each with its own meaning and criteria. The different types of justice or fairness include: distributive justice; compensatory justice; retributive justice; procedural justice; and societal justice. For the purposes of real estate professionals, the focus will be on justice following wrongdoing: (i) compensatory justice; and (ii) retributive justice. These two types will now be briefly reviewed.

Compensatory justice is concerned with appropriately compensating people for a past harm or injustice (e.g., restitution). Of course, one should not be obligated to compensate others unless the person's action was the cause of injury and the injury was intentional (as opposed to being an accident). Quite often this involves real estate or practitioners which have caused injury or harm despite awareness of hidden dangers to their clients (e.g., defects) or communities (e.g., pollution).

Retributive justice is concerned with serving punishment to someone (e.g., through a fine or imprisonment) or to a firm (e.g., through a fine of the professional or even requiring dissolution of

---

[12] Kant, I. 1964. *Groundwork of the Metaphysics of Morals*, H.J. Patron, trans. New York: Harper & Row, Publishers Inc. at p. 96.

[13] Whether or not this highly contentious interpretation of Kant is correct, the risk remains for those attempting to apply Kant to slip into a discussion of the consequences of universalizing a particular action.

THE ETHICAL OBLICATIONS OF REAL ESTATE PRACTITIONERS / **527**

the firm) who has inflicted harm on others. Retributive justice focuses then on punishing the agent or firm committing the harm, as
opposed to compensatory justice which focuses on providing compensation to the one who has been injured. Before enacting punishment
however, it should be established that the person was responsible for
the harm, and that the punishment is consistent with and
proportionate to the harm inflicted on others.

As opposed to the above moral standards, the following three
moral standards tend to be used to ethically justify improper behaviour on the part of real estate agents or their firms: Relativism; Ethical Egoism; and Utilitarianism.

(7) *Relativism*: This conventionalist approach is based on the moral
theory of ethical relativism. In fact, it might be one of the more
dominant approaches used around the world by firms and individual
professionals to establish right versus wrong. In other words, one
asks the question: Does the majority of a particular reference point
believe that the action in question is morally acceptable? Many refer
to this position as 'When in Rome, do as the Romans do'. Relativism rejects the view that there are single, universal standards or
rules to determine the morality of an act. In order to ask this question however, one needs to identify the particular reference point. In
terms of analyzing professional responsibility cases, the following are
the typical reference points: the real estate firm (e.g., brokerage) itself (which could include the employees, managers, and/or board of
directors), the profession, industry/competitors, clients, or the community. One can turn to levels of activity, polls or surveys, legislation, or code of ethics as evidence of what the majority of a
particular reference believes is morally acceptable.

For example, should you use pressure tactics on the other agent,
when you know that a new inexperienced agent they will most likely
comply to your request? Using relativism, one could refer to the majority of agents, would most act this way under similar circumstances? According to relativism however, the views of a single
person should not constitute sufficient justification for determining
what is ethical (this is known as 'naive relativism'), there must be a
group reference point that is referred to (known as 'cultural relativism'), otherwise the standard (in my opinion) collapses completely.

Criticisms: There are many potential deficiencies to using relativism
as a moral standard. First, if one relies on relativism, moral judgments can easily change based on time, circumstance, or culture. It
almost becomes too easy to justify one's action. As long as the majority of the firm, industry, profession, or any other reference point
believes the action is morally acceptable, then the argument ends.

Even if the majority position on a particular matter changes from one day to the next, it would still be considered morally legitimate under relativism. Second, an application of relativism can lead to certain results that might be considered problematic. For example, consequences or individual moral rights can be ignored: if the majority of a particular group accepts an action as being appropriate, then such practices are ethically justified and must be respected (e.g., discrimination against selling property to a particular ethnic group).

(8) *Ethical Egoism*: Egoism indicates that what is perceived to maximize the long-term best self-interest of the individual is the morally appropriate action. For the purposes of business decisions, egoism would also include the best interests of the firm, typically based on either perceived long-term profits or share value. For the individual professional, the extent of the 'guilt' they might feel upon making a particular decision, should also be taken into account in the calculation of perceived best self-interest. One can argue that egoism (i.e., self-interest) is the basis of laissez-faire capitalism, and is often referred to in connection with 18th century economist and moral philosopher Adam Smith (but only as 'conditional egoism', in other words self-interest is acceptable but only when it leads to the betterment of society). Others typically connected with egoism as a moral standard include economist Milton Friedman[14] and philosopher Ayn Rand in her various novels such as *The Fountainhead* and *Atlas Shrugged*. It may be that egoism has been the most dominant moral standard driving firm and individual professional behaviour in the marketplace since the beginning of commerce.

Criticisms: Many criticize egoism as leading to significant socially irresponsible or unethical actions of individuals or firms. Some of the more significant scandals might include Enron, WorldCom, and Bernie Madoff's massive Ponzi scheme. In terms of the real estate industry, many have suggested that the 2008 U.S. financial crisis, primarily involving sub-prime mortgages, was caused by unrestricted egoism or self-interest on the part of mortgage lenders and investment banks.[15] Typically, such criticism of egoism is contingent on regarding egoism as equivalent with the notion of 'greedy' individuals or firms, often leading to highly problematic consequences for others

---

[14] See M. Friedman. 1970, "The Social Responsibility of Business is to Increase its Profits," *New York Times Magazine.*

[15] For example, 'greedy' mortgage lenders were lending even to those who had no incomes, while investment banks created complex investment vehicles based on such highly speculative mortgages. See: Barry Rithholtz. *Bailout Nation,* (2009), Hoboken, N.J.: John Wiley and Sons.

who are taken advantage of. This comparison, however, is not accurate. Greed, should only be considered as representing one extreme end of the entire spectrum of egoism. Greed has been defined as acting to gain something, typically money, wealth, power, or status, in an insatiable (i.e., never satisfied) and excessive manner. In addition, one is willing to cut ethical corners, harm others, or even break the law (if they don't think they will get caught) in order to fulfill their insatiable desires.[16] Greed should be contrasted with other expressions of egoism, such as selfishness (i.e., concern excessively or exclusively with oneself; love of oneself; or inability to share with others), self-interest (i.e., own's own perceived interest or material well-being); or acting out of enlightened self-interest (i.e., initially focusing on the interests of others based on the belief that by doing so one's own best self-interest will be served). In other words, one can argue on behalf of egoism, while still rejecting the notion of greed as ethically unacceptable.

(9) *Utilitarianism*: This moral theory focuses on the consequences of a given action, and in this respect is a teleological or consequentialist theory. It is often expressed by the classic phrase from 19th century philosopher Jeremy Bentham: "The greatest good for the greatest number of people." His other important statement is that: "The greatest happiness of the greatest number is the foundation of morals and legislation." Unlike egoism, which focuses only on the consequences of an action upon a particular individual or firm, utilitarianism focuses on the impact of a decision on all those affected. The typical process for applying utilitarianism is to first identify all the alternatives, determine the costs and benefits for each stakeholder (e.g., shareholders, employees and their families, clients, suppliers, competitors, community, etc.) under each alternative, and then select the alternative that produces (or tends to augment) the great-

---

[16] The famous quote of corporate raider Gordon Gekko (played by Michael Douglas) in the movie *Wall Street* (1987) that "Greed, for lack of a better word, is good," might have more appropriately been "Enlightened self-interest, for lack of a better expression, is good." The quote in the movie was apparently taken from an actual statement made by Ivan Boesky during a University of California commencement speech when he said: "Greed is all right, by the way...I want you to know that. I think greed is healthy. You can be greedy and still feel good about yourself." Boesky later went to jail for three years and paid a $100 million fine for insider trading. See: J.B. Stewart. 1992. *Den of Thieves*. New York: Simon and Schuster Paperbacks. Later, in *Wall Street: Money Never Sleeps* (2010), the same character, Gordon Gekko (played again by Michael Douglas), after leaving jail decades later and promoting his new book, *Greed is Good*, makes the following statement during a university guest lecture: "Someone once reminded me I once said 'Greed is good.' Now it seems greed is legal."

est net good (i.e., also referred to as utility, happiness, benefit, pleasure, or absence of pain). As one classic example, there is a runaway
train which is about to crash into another train with 100 passengers.
You have the ability to switch the train tracks so that the runaway
train will crash into a train with 50 people. If you have no other
information about the passengers, and you must make an immediate
decision, do you switch the tracks so that only 50 people are killed?
If the answer was yes, then you appear to be deciding on the
basis of utilitarianism, i.e., the greatest net good for all those affected. When it comes to real estate development, many will use
utilitarianism to justify long-term harm to the natural environment
and local communities, due to the arguably more significant benefits
enjoyed by new home dwellers, industry, shareholders, employees,
and shareholders.

Criticisms: One major criticism of utilitarianism is with respect to the
difficulties in measuring utility. For example, how does one put a
value on life or health? To what extent can the natural environment
be valued? Such determinations are often subject to individual, sub-
jective assessments. As well, it is very difficult to reliably predict the
future, and it is not always so clear whether something is a benefit
or a cost. While this remains an important criticism, utilitarians
might respond by suggesting that despite the difficulties, society does
place economic value on things like life (e.g., life insurance policies,
lawsuits, etc.). In addition, one can still attempt to make reasonable
predictions about the future. Others, known as 'preference utilitarians', have their own response to any concerns raised over measurement of utility. They would suggest that what is determined as 'good'
or as a 'benefit' should simply be based on whatever action leads to
the greatest satisfaction of the preferences and desires for all those
involved (which can be unique for each individual).[17]

   Table 1 below summarizes the seven key moral standards, along
with possible criticisms and examples related to each.

RESOLVING CONFLICTS AMONG THE MORAL STANDARDS

One of the major difficulties in terms of establishing a real estate
professional's ethical responsibility is that often the various moral
standards can come into conflict. The major conflict typically relates
to egoism and relativism versus the other moral standards. No un-

---

[17] For example, economists use this approach when they establish people's preferences based on the choices they make in the marketplace.

controversial solution to reconciling conflicts has ever been established. On this basis, the best one can do is to at least attempt to apply the various moral standards to identify on what basis a given action may be ethically justified. This is basically taking a pluralistic approach to establishing ethical responsibility. Regardless of whether one adopts a morally pluralistic approach, at the end of the day,

TABLE 1
Brief Summary of the Moral Standards

Moral Standard	Brief Definition	Potential Criticisms	Examples
1. Trustworthiness	One is acting in a trustworthy manner if they are honest, act with integrity (consistent with their stated values/ principles), transparent, loyal, and keep their promises.	Difficult to resolve conflicting loyalties (e.g., to firm versus to one's family).	Dishonesty: Lack of full disclosure of conflicts of interest.
2. Caring	One is acting in a caring manner if they avoid unnecessary harm, do good when of little cost to themselves or the firm, and are sensitive to others' feelings.	Difficult to establish what constitutes unnecessary harm.	Not avoiding harm: Failure to disclose defects in home.
3. Responsibility	One is responsible if they do what they're supposed to do, accountable for actions, accept fault, apologize, don't blame others.	Taking full responsibility can lead to potential lawsuits.	Not accepting fault: Blaming the owner or the other agent for failing to secure purchase of property.
4. Citizenship	One is a good corporate citizen if they obey the law, protect the natural environment, and assist the community.	Could lead to abiding by even unethical laws.	Good corporate citizen: Engaging in community service as a real estate professional.
5. Respect (i.e., Kantianism)	Action ethical if motive based on one's moral duty. Duty must be based on categorical imperative (i.e., universalizability; reversibility; respect).	One can never lie for any reason. Consequences are potentially ignored.	Lack of universalizability: Aggressive accounting of the financial statement of the real estate firm which defeats the purpose of financial statements.

Continued.

6. Justice/Fairness	Action ethical if outcomes are determined to be fair (e.g., Compensatory/ Retributive/ Distributive/ Procedural/Societal).	Not clear which punishment suits the inappropriate activity.	Lack of retributive justice: Executives of mortgage lenders are not prosecuted despite reckless lending.
7. Relativism	Action ethical if the majority of the reference point (e.g., firm, industry, society) believes the act in question is morally acceptable.	Moral judgment constantly changes depending on the circumstances.	Justified due to accepted behaviour of majority: Accept gifts from other party's real estate agent in order to convince client to reduce sales price since everyone's doing it.
8. Egoism	Act according to one's (or the firm's) own perceived long-term best self-interest.	Focus on profit maximization can lead to harming others (i.e., danger of greed). Altruism or self-sacrifice is unacceptable.	Best for bottom line: Long-term perceived self-interest leading to actions that put others at greater risk (placing funds in firm's general account instead of client's trust account).

each individual will have to decide which moral standard or standards are the ones that make the most sense to them to apply in determining what is ethically right or wrong in real estate. At the very least, attempting to apply or reflect upon all of the moral standards discussed above (other than ethical egoism and relativism) will provide several potentially differing ethical views or perspectives that can lead one to better justify their own decision-making, or better critique the decision-making of others including the actions of other real estate professionals or their firms.

EXAMPLES OF REAL ESTATE ETHICAL DILEMMAS

The following will now suggest a few examples of ethical dilemmas one might face in the real estate world. One might reflect on how each of the moral standards (and in particular the core ethical values of trustworthiness, caring, responsibility, and citizenship) would apply to resolving the ethical dilemma.

Bonus Payment? Imagine the following. You work for a commercial tenant that has been told with sufficient notice that they must relocate to a different location on the premises. The landlord has indicated that according to their reading of the terms of the contract, the tenant is entitled to an additional payment in the tens of thousands of dollars beyond the standard moving expenses due to the relocation request. You carefully read over all contractual documents, and you are certain that your client, the tenant, is not entitled to the additional payment. Are you obligated to disclose this to the other side? While loyalty might suggest not disclosing, based on trustworthiness, this should be disclosed.

Delayed Move In? You have sold a commercial unit. Just before closing, there is a flood, and the carpet is destroyed and will need replacing. This will delay the move-in date of the new tenant by at least one month. You know that the tenant has insurance that will cover all the expenses, including the delay of one month. There is a slight risk that as a result, the closing will be delayed, which will have a financial impact on your client who is counting on the funds coming on the closing date. Do you request that your client disclose the flood damage to the new owner? Again, based on trustworthiness, disclosure is required.

Exclusive Agreements? You are a real estate agent, and your friend is selling their house. They have engaged another agent through an exclusive agent agreement, that is set to expire in one week. You have another friend who you know would love the house. Your friend has already indicated that if the current agent is not successful over the next week, that he would like to sign a new exclusive agent agreement with you. Do you let either friend know about the house at this point, or do you wait until your friend signs the exclusive agreement with you? While ethical egoism might push one to wait, loyalty to one's professional colleagues indicates that this would be unacceptable.

Illicit Purposes? You have a client that wants to purchase a large home. The client does not have a family, yet wants to buy a home much larger than he apparently currently needs. Based on the sorts of questions that are asked, the focus on the requirements of an appropriate basement, the apparent intoxicated state of the client, and some conversations that are overheard, you begin to strongly suspect that the home will eventually be used for illicit purposes, i.e., growing marijuana. Do you have any obligations to do anything? While loyalty to one's client might suggest you say nothing, citizenship suggests otherwise.

Racist Client? Someone says they do not want you to sell their house to a particular racial or ethnic group. They say that the neighbourhood has been changing over the years, and they do not wish to be contributing to the trend. A potential purchaser who belongs to the particular ethnic group contacts you about buying the property, and offers above the asking price. The purchaser says he is not interested, despite the substantial offer for the property. What do you do? While one might try to use utilitarianism or loyalty to one's client to justify not accepting the offer, respect (i.e., Kant) and justice/fairness would suggest otherwise.

CONCLUSION

Like all professional groups, real estate agents need to recognize that any ethical lapses affect the ethical reputation of the entire real estate profession. Clearly, there is room for improvement in terms of the public's perception of real estate agents, for example in a U.S. Gallup poll conducted in 2008, only 17 percent of those surveyed felt that real estate agents should be rated "high" or "very high" on honesty and ethical standards.[18] With increasing pressures to move away from competition reducing features such as the multiple-listing-service (MLS), and with even greater competition through the use of on-line virtual realtors, real estate agents are under even greater pressure to establish that they provide a valuable service to their clients. There is no question that with further technological developments, along with new privacy concerns, additional ethical issues will continue to arise for real estate practitioners. Hopefully real estate professionals will understand that they must strive to be ethical under all circumstances, even when it is not in their own best self-interest to do so, and even when no one else is watching or will ever discover their ethical wrongdoing.

APPENDIX A

As part of its "Mission Statement", The Canadian Real Estate Association (CREA, with close to 100,000 real estate brokers and agents) states as one of its "Key Objectives": "To formulate, promote and foster consistent professional standards of business practice, integrity and ethical conduct." As part of this objective, CREA has promulgated a "Code of Ethics" (effective January 1st, 2008) for all real estate practitioners who are members of a real estate Board or a Provincial Association. The following is a summary of its "Code of Ethics" (effective January 1st, 2008) at: http://www.crea.ca/public/realtor_codes/code_of_ethics.htm [accessed 18 March 2011]:

---

[18] See Gallup Poll at: http://www.gallup.com/poll/1654/honesty-ethics-professions.aspx [accessed 18 March 2011].

CREA's Code of Ethics and Standards of Business Practice has been the measure of professionalism in organized real estate for over 40 years. The first code was approved in 1913 at the convention of the National Association of Real Estate Boards held in Winnipeg. The first Code of Ethics specifically prepared for members of The Canadian Real Estate Association was approved by members in 1959.

The Code establishes a standard of conduct, which in many respects exceeds basic legal requirements. This standard ensures that that the rights and interests of consumers of real estate services are protected. As a condition of membership, all REALTORS® agree to abide by the Code.

Some of the requirements of the Code include:

REALTORS® must disclose in writing whom they are representing as an agent in the transaction. Parties to a transaction must be told what their agency relationship is to the REALTOR®.

Definitions, terminology and presumed agency relationships vary from province to province. Most jurisdictions have their own forms for complying with disclosure requirements, which have been drafted to accommodate agency relationships as they exist in your province or territory.

All financial arrangements between REALTORS® and others (e.g. referral fees, compensation from more than one party, rebates or profits on expenditures) must be fully disclosed to clients;

REALTORS® cannot acquire an interest in property (either directly or indirectly) without disclosing the fact that they are real estate professionals;

REALTORS® cannot use the terms of an agreement of purchase and sale to negotiate commission.

While the Code of Ethics establishes obligations that may be higher than those mandated by law, in any instance where the Code of Ethics and the law conflict, the obligations of the law must take precedence.

A REALTOR®'s ethical obligations are based on moral integrity, competent service to clients and customers, and dedication to the interest and welfare of the public. The Code has been amended many times to reflect changes in the real estate marketplace, the needs of property owners and the perceptions and values of society. For more than forty years, through a variety of updates, the CREA Code of Ethics is unchanged in demanding high standards of professional conduct to protect the interests of clients and customers and safeguard the rights of consumers of real estate services.

REFERENCES

Brinkmann, J.: 2009, 'Putting Ethics on the Agenda for Real Estate Agents'. *Journal of Business Ethics* 88, 65-82.

Brinkmann, J.: 2000, 'Real Estate Agent Ethics. Selected Findings from Two Norwegian Studies', *Business Ethics: A European Review* 9, 163–173.

Clarke, M. J.: 1995, 'Ethical Dilemmas for Estate Agents', *Business Ethics: A European Review* 4, 70–75.

Clarke, M. J., D. Smith and M. McConville: 1994, *Slippery Customers* (Blackstone, London).

536 / M.S. SCHWARTZ

Izzo, G.: 2000, 'Compulsory Ethics Education and the Cognitive Moral Development of Salespeople: A Quasi-Experimental Assessment', *Journal of Business Ethics* 28, 223–241.
Izzo, G. M., B. E. Langford and S. Vitell: 2006, 'Investigating the Efficacy of Interactive Ethics Education: A Difference in Pedagogical Emphasis', *Journal of Marketing Theory and Practice* 14, 239–248.
Larsen, J. E., J. W. Coleman and J. A. Petrick: 2007, 'The Ethics of Real Estate Agents: A Comparison of Realtor and Public Perceptions', *Journal of Real Estate Practice and Education* 10, 41–60.
Long, D. H.: 1998, *Doing The Right Thing: A Real Estate Practitioner's Guide to Ethical Decision-Making* (Prentice Hall, Upper Saddle River, NJ).
Miller, N. G.: 1999, 'Ethics as Economically Influenced: A Preliminary Test', in S. E. Roulac (ed.), *Ethics in Real Estate* (Kluwer, Boston), 153–161.
Okoruwa, A. A. and A. F. Thompson: 1999, 'An Empirical Analysis of Real Estate Brokerage Ethics', in S. E. Roulac (ed.), *Ethics in Real Estate* (Kluwer, Boston).
Roulac, S. E. (ed.): 1999, *Ethics in Real Estate* (Kluwer, Boston).